Hong Kong

timeout.com/hongkong

Published by Time Out Guides Ltd, a wholly owned subsidiary of Time Out Group Ltd.
Time Out and the Time Out logo are trademarks of Time Out Group Ltd.

© Time Out Group Ltd 2007
Previous editions 2001, 2004.

10 9 8 7 6 5 4 3 2 1

This edition first published in Great Britain in 2007 by Ebury Publishing
Ebury Publishing is a division of The Random House Group Ltd,
20 Vauxhall Bridge Road, London SW1V 2SA

Random House Australia Pty Limited 20 Alfred Street, Milsons Point, Sydney, New South Wales 2061, Australia
Random House New Zealand Limited 18 Poland Road, Glenfield, Auckland 10, New Zealand
Random House South Africa (Pty) Limited Isle of Houghton, Corner Boundary
Road & Carse O'Gowrie, Houghton 2198, South Africa

Random House UK Limited Reg. No. 954009

Distributed in USA by Publishers Group West
1700 Fourth Street, Berkeley, California 94710

Distributed in Canada by Publishers Group Canada
250A Carlton Street, Toronto, Ontario M5A 2L1

For further distribution details, see www.timeout.com

ISBN 10: 1-84670-013-2
ISBN 13: 978184670 0132

A CIP catalogue record for this book is available from the British Library

Printed and bound by Firmengruppe APPL, aprinta druck, Wemding, Germany

The Random House Group Limited makes every effort to ensure that the papers used in our books are made from trees
that have been legally sourced from well-managed and credibly certified forests. Our paper procurement policy can be
found on www.randomhouse.co.uk.

Time Out Guides Limited
Universal House
251 Tottenham Court Road
London W1T 7AB
Tel + 44 (0)20 7813 3000
Fax + 44 (0)20 7813 6001
Email guides@timeout.com
www.timeout.com

Editorial

Editor Andrew Dembina
Deputy Editor John Shandy Watson
Commissioning Editor Lesley McCave
Listings Editor Rehana Sheikh
Proofreader Patrick Mulkern
Indexer Jonathan Cox

Managing Director Peter Fiennes
Financial Director Gareth Garner
Editorial Director Ruth Jarvis
Deputy Series Editor Dominic Earle
Editorial Manager Holly Pick

Design

Art Director Scott Moore
Art Editor Pinelope Kourmouzoglou
Senior Designer Josephine Spencer
Graphic Designer Henry Elphick
Junior Graphic Designer Kei Ishimaru
Digital Imaging Simon Foster
Ad Make-up Jenni Prichard

Picture Desk

Picture Editor Jael Marschner
Deputy Picture Editor Tracey Kerrigan
Picture Researcher Helen McFarland

Advertising

Sales Director Mark Phillips
International Sales Manager Fred Durman
International Sales Executive Simon Davies
International Sales Consultant Ross Canadé
Advertising Assistant Kate Staddon

Marketing

Group Marketing Director John Luck
Marketing Manager Yvonne Poon
Marketing & Publicity Manager, US Rosella Albanese

Production

Group Production Director Mark Lamond
Production Manager Brendan McKeown
Production Coordinator Caroline Bradford

Time Out Group

Chairman Tony Elliott
Financial Director Richard Waterlow
Time Out Magazine Ltd MD David Pepper
Group General Manager/Director Nichola Coulthard
Time Out Communications Ltd MD David Pepper
Time Out International MD Cathy Runciman
Group Art Director John Oakey
Group IT Director Simon Chappell

Contributors

Introduction Andrew Dembina. **History** Jason Wordie. **Hong Kong Today** Andrew Dembina (*Smog gets in your eyes, When the in-laws drop in* Jason Wordie). **Modern Architecture** Andrew Dembina. **Culture & Customs** Andrew Dembina. **Identity Crisis?** Jason Wordie. **Where to Stay** Andrew Dembina. **Sightseeing** Jason Wordie (*Introduction, Lamma, Rural road hogs* Andrew Dembina). **Restaurants** Andrew Dembina. **Pubs & Bars** Andrew Dembina. **Shops & Services** Jade Lee-Duffy (*Savings made in China* Ellen McNally; *A good day's rest* Lesley McCave). **Festivals & Events** Chris Baker. **Children** Vikki Weston (*Variations on a theme* Jason Wordie). **Film** Vikki Weston. **Galleries** Vikki Weston. **Gay & Lesbian** Chris Baker. **Nightlife** Andrew Dembina. **Performing Arts** Chris Baker. **Sport & Fitness** Ruth Williams. **Macau** Jason Wordie. **Directory** Rehana Sheikh.

Maps john@jsgraphics.co.uk.

Photography by Andrew Moore except: page 13 Bettmann/ Corbis; page 14 MEPL; page 19 Images of Empire; page 23 Getty Images; page 26 TopFoto/Empics; page 27 Michael Setbourn/Sygma/Corbis; pages 72, 73, 86, 88, 105, 110, 203, 206, 245 Hong Kong Tourism Board; pages 219, 220 Rex Features; pages 278, 283, 287, 288, Jonathan Perugia.

The following images were provided by the featured establishments/artists: pages 144, 145, 148, 212, 213, 231, 234, 247.

The Editors would like to thank Nicola Chilton and Prima Wong at Four Seasons Hong Kong, Tarcisio Costa and Winny Mui at Langham Hotel, Cecilia Wong, Sherona Shng and Shelley Tso at Langham Place Hotel, Lamey Chang, Sian Griffiths and Emma Salvadori at the Peninsula, Ilona Yim at Island Shangri-La, Jenny Chan at LKF Hotel, Kiri Sinclair at Grebstad Hicks Communications, Ada Ho, and all contributors to previous editions of *Time Out Hong Kong*, whose work forms the basis for parts of this book.

Contents

Introduction

'Asia's World City', the clumsy slogan dreamed up by the Hong Kong Tourism Board, shoots wide of the mark in attempting to describe this self-governing Special Administrative Region (SAR), a mere dot on the map on China's southernmost tip. Likewise, do not be misled by the gleaming glass and steel skyscrapers into thinking that Hong Kong is a slice of the first-world West transported to Asia. In the shadows of these towers thrive temples thick with incense smoke, cacophonous dim sum restaurants and noodle shops, and lively and colourful street markets – all doused in Southern Chinese character.

In fact, 96 per cent of the population is ethnic Chinese, and many of these are recent immigrants from Mainland China. Unlike in other parts of the former British Empire, English is not as widely spoken as is commonly assumed. Though you'll have few problems conversing in basic English in tourist zones, you will need a phrase book once you start exploring the city's nooks and crannies or heading out into the countryside. But at least you shouldn't get too lost. All street signs, public transportation information and other official documentation is written in both English and Chinese – a remnant of more than 150 years of British colonial rule.

The interconnecting urban sprawl that makes up much of Kowloon and Hong Kong Island is what most visitors come for – the shops, restaurants and bars thrumming with energy until the early hours. Taking in all the activity from Victoria Peak's new panoramic viewing platform never ceases to blow the mind of residents, let alone visitors, as the cityscape spread out below is in perpetual change.

So what do you do if you're feeling zapped by the pace of some of the most densely populated streets on the planet? Jump on a ferry and visit one of the Outlying Islands, where the pace is much slower and the buildings are low-rise. Or catch a train or bus into the New Territories, also home to rural villages, country parks and quiet sandy shores. Beach culture is a lesser-known aspect of the SAR – even city beaches offer a good dose of downtime, though popular ones such as Repulse Bay can get as crowded on peak summer weekends as downtown Causeway Bay at rush hour.

Back in the urban mayhem, Hong Kong's image as a shopping mecca is still, to an extent, deserved – it may not be the bargain basement it was for electronics decades ago but high-tech gadgetry still arrives here before many Western countries. And while home-grown casual clothing brands – such as Giordano and Bossini – have bargain price tags, international designer labels do not. For dining, there are few places like Hong Kong: choices span well beyond regional Chinese fare, taking in almost every national cuisine thinkable, from peasant fare to gastronomic wonders. In 2006 alone, three of the world's top chefs – Pierre Gagnaire, Nobu Matsuhisa and Joël Robuchon – opened restaurants here.

Even with such swishness, Hong Kong as a whole is not as sanitised as, say, Singapore or Tokyo – it still has plenty of grittiness. But for a far more earthy experience take the two-hour express train ride to Guangzhou, Southern China's frenetic industrial boomtown. Meanwhile, the ex-Portuguese colony of Macau – an hour's jetfoil ride from Hong Kong – is seeing a different kind of boom, as Vegas-style casinos attempt to cash in on the newly affluent Chinese market.

ABOUT TIME OUT CITY GUIDES

This is the third edition of *Time Out Hong Kong*, one of an expanding series of Time Out guides produced by the people behind the successful listings magazines in London, New York and Chicago. Our guides are all written by resident experts who have striven to provide you with all the most up-to-date information you'll need to explore the city or read up on its background, whether you're a local or a first-time visitor.

THE LIE OF THE LAND

Hong Kong falls fairly neatly into four basic areas: Hong Kong Island, the Kowloon Peninsula (across Victoria Harbour), the New Territories (the vast swathe of land ballooning out from the north of Kowloon up to the border with Guangdong province and the rest of China) and the Outlying Islands. Each of these areas has its own chapter within the Sightseeing section, and each is further subdivided into districts. In this guide, in chapters not already

divided by area, these districts are included within the addresses. Wherever possible, a map reference is provided for places listed.

ESSENTIAL INFORMATION
For all the practical information you might need for visiting the area – including visa and customs information, details of local transport, a listing of emergency numbers, information on local weather and a selection of useful websites – turn to the Directory at the back of this guide. It begins on page 294.

THE LOWDOWN ON THE LISTINGS
We have tried to make this book as easy to use as possible. Addresses, phone numbers, transport information, opening times and admission prices are all included in the listings. Specific locations of hotels (❶), restaurants (❶) and bars (❶) are pinpointed on the maps.

Businesses can change their arrangements at any time. Before you go out of your way, we'd strongly advise you to phone ahead to check opening times and other particulars. While every effort and care has been made to ensure the accuracy of the information contained in this guide, the publishers cannot accept responsibility for any errors it may contain.

Advertisers

PRICES AND PAYMENT
We have noted where venues such as shops, hotels, restaurants and bars accept the following credit cards: American Express (AmEx), Diners Club (DC), MasterCard (MC) and Visa (V). Many businesses will also accept travellers' cheques and/or other cards.

The prices we've listed in this guide should be treated as guidelines, not gospel. If prices vary wildly from those we've quoted, ask whether there's a good reason. If not, go elsewhere. Then please let us know. We aim to give the best and most up-to-date advice, so we want to know if you've been badly treated or overcharged.

TELEPHONE NUMBERS
The international code for Hong Kong is 852; there is no area code. All phone numbers (including mobile numbers) are eight digits. For more on telephones and codes, *see p309*.

MAPS
The map section at the back of this book includes overview and neighbourhood maps of Hong Kong and the public transport system, as well as street maps of the city with a useful street index. The maps start on page 324.

LET US KNOW WHAT YOU THINK
We hope you enjoy the *Time Out Hong Kong Guide*, and we'd like to know what you think of it. We welcome tips for places that you consider we should include in future editions and take note of your criticism of our choices. You can email us at guides@timeout.com.

There is an online version of this book, along with guides to over 100 international cities, at **www.timeout.com**.

Time Out
Travel Guides

Worldwide

All our guides are written by a team of local experts with a unique and stylish insider perspective. We offer essential tips, trusted advice and honest reviews for everything you need to know in the city.

Over 50 destinations available at all good bookshops and at timeout.com/shop

Time Out
Guides

In Context

Bank of China Tower, Cheung Kong Centre and **HSBC Building**. *See p33.*

History

First Britain, now China: colonialism has defined Hong Kong.

The Portuguese mariner Jorge Alvares was the first European to visit the area surrounding Hong Kong. In 1513 he landed on the island of Lintin, which lies west of the New Territories in the middle of the Pearl River Delta.

THE PORTUGUESE ARRIVE

Alvares' mission had started in Malacca, now in Malaysia, which the Portuguese had captured in 1511. He was intent on establishing a sea route to China, so that greater profit could be made on goods purchased direct from their source, rather than through Chinese traders. Chinese porcelain, for example, fetched extremely high prices in Europe, with good-quality ceramics commanding twice their own weight in silver when resold in Goa.

When Alvares arrived on Lintin, the local mandarinate received him in a friendly manner and trade commenced. As a result, Alvares spent most of the next ten months on the island, before returning to Malacca when the south-west monsoon winds permitted his little flotilla to sail. Although they were not given much freedom of movement, the traders visiting Lintin were not as closely confined by the Chinese

authorities as in later centuries, and, while it is not recorded, it is highly likely that Alvares and his men visited the nearby mainland.

While on Lintin, they erected a *padrão* (or stone) carved with the Portuguese cross and crest, though nothing of it survives today. These stones functioned more as markers of passage for later seafarers than as territorial claims, and were erected wherever Portuguese mariners sailed, from Mombasa and Ormuz to western India and the Moluccas. Alvares' young son died at Lintin and was buried at the base of the *padrão*. Alvares himself made two more voyages to China, in 1519 and in 1521. During the latter, he died and was also buried beneath the *padrão*.

Other navigators followed in his wake, of course. Periodic trade developed between the Portuguese and Chinese at various locations up and down the coast. These changed from season to season, but one of the most regularly used was the island of Lampacao. It was here that the Catholic missionary St Francis Xavier died and was buried, later being exhumed and reburied in Malacca and then Goa.

At this time, the prevalence of pirates on the islands around the mouth of the Pearl River Delta led to them being dubbed the *Ilhas Ladrones* or 'Islands of Robbers'. In fact, piracy remained a major problem in these waters up to the mid-20th century. But that did not stop trading ships from all over Asia anchoring in the triangle between Lintin, the northern side of Deep Bay and present-day Tuen Mun, in the hope of trading with south China. The Siamese, in particular, had a large seasonal presence, mooring further out by Lantau's northern coast.

MACAU'S GOLDEN AGE

However, when the Portuguese established Macau as a permanent trading settlement with the permission of the local Chinese mandarinate in about 1557, the face of South China trade changed. The tiny port rapidly developed as a centre of entrepôt trade between China and

Japan, using Portuguese vessels and mariners as carriers. Repeated pirate raids by the Japanese had led to their prohibition from Chinese ports. This, together with Ming Dynasty restrictions on the movement of Chinese abroad, meant that the Portuguese were in the perfect position to act as middlemen, bringing raw Chinese silk to Japan, and returning with silver and copper. Thus, the Portuguese all but monopolised the carrying trade, ushering in a period of wealth and prosperity that Macau has not seen since; 1560 to 1640 is often referred to as the Golden Age of Macau.

In addition to trade, the Portuguese played a major role in exporting Catholic missionaries to Japan, an unwelcome activity that eventually led to the complete closing down of Japan to Portuguese trade in 1639.

The first British navigator to reach the China coast, Captain Weddell, had by now landed at

Hong Kong's streets were as full of activity in 1910 as they are today.

Macau (he arrived in 1637), and, in spite of orders by the Chinese not to approach, tried to enter the city of Canton (now Guangzhou) in Guangdong province. He was driven away, and no further British vessels visited these waters for several decades.

The closure of Japan to Portuguese trade was an important factor both in Macau's period of slow decline (which continued until the late 18th century) and the subsequent rise of British and Dutch colonial power in Asia. Throughout this period, Hong Kong remained unnoticed on the other side of the Pearl River Delta, just one more island among hundreds up and down the Guangdong coast, inhabited by only a few fishermen, farmers and pirates.

DODGY DEALINGS IN CANTON

For centuries after the establishment of Macau, European traders were not permitted any permanent trading station in China other than Macau itself. Seasonal trade at the port of Canton was permitted, but merchants had to leave the city at the end of the trading season and return to Macau. While in Canton, they were prohibited from bringing their wives and families with them, forbidden to learn Chinese and had their movements around town restricted. Few were allowed to venture beyond their trading compounds, or 'factories', as they were known. These restrictions became increasingly irksome, accompanied as they were by bribery, corruption and constantly changing standards and expectations.

'The key to unlocking the Chinese treasure chest was opium.'

The mid 18th century witnessed a growing passion in Europe for tea, silk and other luxury goods, thanks to a long period of steadily rising prosperity. Tea, especially, was in enormous demand and, at this time, China enjoyed a world monopoly on supply. The Chinese insisted that everything be paid for in silver specie (China remained on the silver standard until the early 1930s), which, in due course, led to serious balance of trade deficits in favour of China, as it had little use for European trade goods at the time, other than a few clocks, trinkets and curios. The key to unlocking the Chinese treasure chest was opium.

GETTING CHINA HOOKED

The British East India Company grew opium under government monopoly in India and sold it at public auction in Calcutta every year. Merchants associated with the company bought

opium at the Calcutta auctions and smuggled it to China aboard specially built vessels. Numerous trading houses that later became big names on the China Coast – such as Jardine Matheson, Dent's and Russell's – were heavily involved in the opium trade. Still, while it is the British who are usually vilified for introducing opium to China, it is worth remembering that numerous Scandinavian and American firms were heavily involved as well. The major opium-smuggling depot was located on Lintin, where Alvares had made his China landfall back in 1513. Although numerous opium bans were introduced by the Chinese government, they were largely ineffectual due to local corruption and the active involvement of Chinese officials in the illicit trade. What's more, a couple of attempts by British East India Company officials to formalise diplomatic relations between Britain and China were rebuffed by the Chinese.

The increasing volume of foreign merchant shipping in the region alarmed the Chinese authorities, and they constructed coastal defences, including forts at Fan Lau and Tung Chung on Lantau island, at the Bocca Tigris (Bogue), some of which still stand today.

THE FIRST OPIUM WAR

From 1830 there was a gradual increase in tension between the British merchants and the Chinese authorities in Canton over opium. As a result, in 1834, Lord William John Napier was appointed Commissioner of Trade, with the directive to regularise trade and establish diplomatic relations between the two empires. Napier's name, unpromisingly, transliterated into Chinese as 'laboriously vile'.

When Napier died while on official duty, he was succeeded by Captain Charles Elliot. Elliot was in the unenviable position of having to support a trade of which (subsequent correspondence has shown) he did not personally approve, and negotiate with the Chinese, who – at this time – had no experience of dealing with other nations.

In 1839 Commissioner Lin Tse-hsü was appointed to suppress the opium trade. Lin's campaign resulted in the surrender and destruction of over 20,000 chests of (mostly British-owned) opium at Canton. This action provided the *causus belli* for military action for which many merchants had long been agitating in the British Parliament, and a British fleet dispatched from India attacked the Bogue forts on the Pearl River approaches to Canton.

Various attempts at conciliation failed, but eventually the Convention of Chuen Pi (which was signed in 1841) ended hostilities. The subsequent Treaty of Nanking, signed

Foreign devils in a 'world city'

One of the more unappealing and obvious aspects of life in Hong Kong for many local residents – but effectively invisible to the average visitor – is racial discrimination. Being openly looked down upon by the Hong Kong Chinese is an insidious and all-too-frequent part of daily life for thousands of ethnic Hong Kong residents. The problem is made worse by its obvious nature and the official denial that it ever occurs at all.

One doesn't have to live in Hong Kong long to realise that it is obsessed with fairness of skin; the darker you are, the lower on the social hierarchy you are perceived to be. Japanese manners, fashions and concepts of beauty are admired, at least partly due to their fair complexions. (There is thus a tremendous market in Hong Kong for skin-whitening products from Japan and Korea.)

Probably Hong Kong's hottest topic is the perceived rights and privileges enjoyed by recent mainland migrants to Hong Kong. Almost anything concerning *sun yee mun* (new immigrants) stimulates impassioned debate. More than 150 new entrants come legally into Hong Kong from the mainland every day; a total of 50,000 per year. But one salient fact that most members of the public conveniently forget is that, until relatively recently, almost everyone living in Hong Kong was either a *sun yee mun* or the child of one.

Mainland women are routinely referred to in the Chinese-language tabloid press – especially if they are young, single and pretty – as '*paak kwu*' – a slang term meaning 'northern aunties'. These women are openly dismissed as being on the make and out to snare a husband. The grasping, scheming *paak kwu*, speaking broken, Mandarin-accented Cantonese, is a stock character of Hong Kong soap operas and films.

Pakistani guards are a common sight outside pawn shops, banks and jewellery stores all over the island. Among the Chinese population, the Sikh and Punjabi policemen are known as '*dai tau luk yee*', or 'big heads and green jackets', a reference to the turbans and the colour of their uniforms. Punjabis, Sikhs and other minorities from the Indian subcontinent face considerable discrimination from the Chinese majority, with Cantonese epithets such as '*dai tau gwai*' ('big head devils') and '*chau cha*' ('stinking Indians') commonly used. Ironically, most local Indians

were born and raised in Hong Kong and are fluent Cantonese speakers who understand fully what is being said about them. There are numerous families of Indian and Pakistani heritage who have lived in Hong Kong for well over a century, and who have as legitimate a claim to being truly 'Hong Kong people' as most Hong Kong Chinese, many of whose parents arrived in the 1950s.

Filipinos, Indonesians and Thais form the majority of Hong Kong's community of domestic workers, which accounts for almost two per cent of the population. These groups are discriminated against, routinely underpaid and overworked. They have few legal rights, and taking a case to the Labour Tribunal is usually more trouble than it is worth. Discouraged from using many shops and facilities – and contemptuously referred to as '*ah bun*' (for Filipinas) or '*nai mui*' (for Indonesians) – they receive little sympathy from the wider community.

Black people fare no better than the rest. They are referred to by the Cantonese as '*haak gwai*', meaning 'black devils', and it is by no means unusual for those in this group to be refused job interviews or given poor service in shops or restaurants solely because of their race. Many people of African heritage living in Hong Kong report that on buses and the MTR, Chinese will pointedly get up and walk away if black people sit down near them. Some Hong Kong Chinese openly refer to blacks as dirty and primitive; such slurs even appear now and again in the popular press.

Europeans and those of anglo heritage are generally referred to as '*gweilo*', literally 'devil men' (or 'ghost men'), or as '*faan gwai*' ('foreign devils'). Despite being openly derogatory, the use of *gweilo* is ubiquitous in Hong Kong, and many Europeans openly refer to themselves as *gweilo*. The term '*sai yan*' ('Western person'), is much more polite, though, unfortunately, few Chinese use it.

So far the local government has refused to enact any anti-discrimination legislation at all, though a decade-long consultation process is now almost complete. One senior official went so far as to claim, astonishingly, that 'as Hong Kong has so few black people, there is almost no racism'. Thus, the daily, officially denied racism routinely endured by many Hong Kong residents remains one of the most shameful open secrets in 'Asia's World City'.

in 1842, arranged for the opening of five Chinese ports to foreign trade, and for the cession of Hong Kong Island 'in perpetuity' to the British Crown, as a place of permanent, stable, safe British trade.

LOCATION, LOCATION, LOCATION

Hong Kong Island was chosen over other larger and more prosperous locations (such as the island of Chusan at the entrance to the Yangtze in eastern China) because it was well known to mariners and possessed an excellent natural harbour. Ships travelling to Canton or further up and down the coast would usually call at Waterfall Bay (near where you'll now find Wah Fu Estate on the western side of Hong Kong Island) for fresh drinking water; they also took shelter from stormy weather and typhoons at Shek Pai Wan (modern Aberdeen). The name Hong Kong is a corruption of Heung Gong, meaning 'fragrant harbour', a reference to the sandalwood incense mills then found at Aberdeen that could be smelled from the sea.

Hong Kong Island was formally occupied on 26 January 1841, and developed rapidly as merchants and traders previously based in Canton and Macau moved to the island.

COLONIAL BEGINNINGS

Central district was the first area of planned urban development in Hong Kong. At land sales held in June 1841 (five months after the British flag was raised at Possession Point), 51 lots of land were sold to 23 merchant houses for the purpose of building offices and 'godowns' (as warehouses are known in Asia). These firms included Jardine Matheson, which is still prominent today, and its then-rival Dent's (which would later be wiped out in the slump of 1867). Office buildings were constructed between the waterfront and Queen's Road.

In November 1841 the ridge of land between Albany Nullah (now Garden Road) and Glenealy Nullah (now Glenealy) was set aside for Crown use, and subsequently became known as Government Hill. The Colonial Secretariat, Government House, Albany Government Quarters and St John's Cathedral were all built on this slope. The area extending between Government Hill and Wan Chai was designated for military use. Victoria and Wellington Barracks were built, and the area remained on the defence estate until the late 1970s. This officially created division between the districts of Central and Wan Chai meant that additional residential and commercial areas could only be developed to the east of the military cantonment.

In 1843, after Hong Kong had officially become a Crown Colony – and thus a permanent settlement – the rapidly developing city was named Victoria; it extended over what is now Sheung Wan, Central and Wan Chai. Central became the principal business district and centre of administration. In addition to the military cantonments to the east of Government Hill, a military camp was built at Stanley soon after the British arrival.

From the 1840s the area around Lyndhurst Terrace, Hollywood Road and Aberdeen Street was a European residential area. From the 1870s onwards, however, increasing numbers of Chinese merchants bought properties in this area, converting the buildings into tenements. So the Europeans moved up the hill to the area around Caine Road and Robinson Road.

> ## 'The colony's early days were characterised by an attitude of "make it quick, get out fast".'

The Crown Colony's first two decades were buccaneering in spirit, characterised by corruption, lawlessness, brutality and an attitude of 'make it quick, get out fast' that some would say has persisted ever since.

A key problem in the beginning was the lack of an efficient civil service, as almost no Government officers for the first 20 or so years of the colony's existence were able to speak or read Chinese. The legal system was hopelessly inadequate, with many government posts filled by almost anyone who happened to be in Hong Kong when a job was going.

There was little interaction between the Chinese and European communities, leading to fear, bigotry and misunderstanding on both sides. An attempted poisoning of the main European bread supply in 1857 caused widespread panic and alienation between the two communities.

The first specially recruited Hong Kong Government administrative cadets to be taught Cantonese were appointed in 1862, and this led to the gradual improvement in government standards and relations between the Europeans and the Chinese in the city.

THE SECOND OPIUM WAR AND EXPANSION INTO KOWLOON

A Chinese-led raid on a British registered vessel – the *Arrow* – led to what became known as the Second Opium (or Arrow) War (1857-60). During this conflict, the Summer Palace in Beijing was burned, and afterwards an Anglo-French force governed Canton from 1858 to 1860.

Locally, the conflict led to the cession of the Kowloon peninsula and Stonecutter's Island to Britain in 1860. The new extent of the territory stretched northwards to Boundary Street, and included Tsim Sha Tsui in the south.

The first European settlers in Kowloon were the local Portuguese community, who moved across the harbour from the late 19th century. By the 1920s Tsim Sha Tsui was almost a Portuguese district, and, until the 1950s, the Portuguese represented the largest non-British, non-Chinese section of the population.

From the 1860s onwards commercial and residential opportunities in Kowloon became apparent, leading to the gradual expansion of the new area. At around the same time, Hong Kong experienced a prolonged economic boom.

The original (pre-1860) land area of Tsim Sha Tsui and the Kowloon peninsula has been greatly enlarged by numerous phases of reclamation over the years; much of which involved removing the tops of the hills that once dominated the area. The result is that the topography has changed completely. The names of some Kowloon streets today, such as Reclamation Street in Yau Ma Tei, provide some clues to the peninsula's former coastlines and hills. *See also p103* **Walking on water**.

The early settlement comprised a British military encampment at Tsim Sha Tsui and a few scattered Chinese hamlets, the most significant being Tai Hang, located near the present-day Granville Road. The military presence continued for many years, with permanent barracks at Gun Club Hill on Austin Road and Whitfield Barracks (now Kowloon Park) on Nathan Road.

Hung Hom, further to the east, and Sham Shui Po, to the north, were both early industrial areas, and were established long before the post-war boom in industry that led to Hong Kong's phenomenal growth and resounding international success. The industry that developed here was light manufacturing and included the production of plimsolls, torches and low-technology goods.

On Hong Kong Island, the Peak district gradually became more popular as a retreat from hot weather, and the first houses were built there in the 1860s. The hillside funicular Peak Tram commenced operations in 1888, and has been popular with both visitors and residents ever since.

Reclamation work aimed at extending the business district started in 1890 and finished in 1904, adding a large new area. Industry started its initially tentative development at this time with the construction of commercial dockyards at Aberdeen, Hung Hom and Taikoo. These catered to the annually increasing volume of shipping that frequented the colony's harbour. All major and many minor shipping lines called at Hong Kong.

Communications with the world's markets were swift and efficient, as the island became a telecommunications hub; telegraph cables linking Britain and Hong Kong's southern coast (the cable house can still be seen today at Deep Water Bay) were laid in 1870.

THE ROLE OF TUNG WAH HOSPITAL

For its first 30 years as a British colony, Hong Kong lacked a general hospital. The Government Civil Hospital was established in 1850, and at first catered mainly to the police force and the destitutes they picked up; around 1864 it became accessible to private paying patients as well. The then-expensive fees of HK$1 were a discouragement for most, and very few Chinese wished to use it anyway. Part of this reluctance was due to a general distrust of foreigners, and a deeply held belief that their intentions – however noble they might seem on the surface – were ultimately evil. Western medicine, in particular, emphasised surgery and post-mortem examinations at a time when most Chinese devoutly believed that after death one should return to one's ancestors with an unmutilated body. To an extent they had a point, since 19th-century Western medical science, with its dirty, badly administered hospitals, poorly trained nurses and few specific cures for diseases did little to inspire public confidence – even among those familiar with its practices.

The closest thing that the Chinese had to a hospital was the I Ts'z, where the terminally ill were sent to die because death at home was reckoned to render the house unclean. In 1869, however, the then Governor Sir Richard MacDonnell closed the I Ts'z on account of the appalling conditions, and the idea of a hospital funded and administered by Chinese was proposed. Consequently, the Tung Wah Hospital was established as 'a Chinese hospital for the care and treatment of the indigent sick, to be supported by voluntary contributions', which is how it has largely remained to this day. Sir Richard MacDonnell laid the foundation stone in 1870 on Po Yan Street in Western district, and it is still there today.

The hospital was run by a committee, the members of which were drawn from the comprador (mercantile middle-man) class. Compradors at this time were at the height of their wealth and influence in Hong Kong and the Treaty Ports, but in time their influence declined as Chinese independently engaged in business, medicine or the law took their place. Later still, the compradors were further pushed aside by bankers, department store owners, rich overseas Chinese and émigrés from the 1911 Revolution. This last group formed a

Travel by sedan chair.

more diversified Chinese elite than existed in the 19th century, and eventually replaced the compradors as arbiters of power and influence within the Tung Wah.

> **'The committee wielded so much influence that it became a sort of 'shadow' Legislative Council.'**

Another important component of the Tung Wah Hospital Committee was the representatives of the various merchant guilds, such as the Nam Pak Hong (dealing mainly with the import of rice and South-east Asian products), the California Merchants Guild (which dealt with the lucrative West Coast trade) and the Chinese Medicine Guild. The guilds elected representative members to the Tung Wah Hospital Committee from among their own number – a forerunner of today's functional constituencies.

Kaifongs (street committees), which were to be found all over Hong Kong, also elected members to the Tung Wah Hospital Committee. *Kaifong* members were simply groups of civic-minded, status-seeking citizens who voted themselves in as a public body. They were accepted – or at least tolerated – by the general public because they were either affluent or 'fixers'; none of their 'constituents' ever actually

voted for them. They chose themselves. Elections to the Tung Wah Hospital Committee were conducted from among these closed ranks.

The committee wielded so much influence among the Chinese community that in time it became a sort of 'shadow' Legislative Council, and was often resented and criticised by the Hong Kong government for its wide-ranging power over the Chinese community. However, much later, the more senior members of the committee would be appointed as unofficial Chinese members of the Legislative Council, with the result that their influence was regularised and channelled into political development for the Chinese community.

LOCAL REPRESENTATION

The first tentative steps at involving representatives of the Chinese community more actively in government affairs in Hong Kong started in the late 1870s. The experiment, which did not prove to be a great success, involved the forward-thinking governor Sir John Pope Hennessy and Ng Choy, also known as Wu Ting Fang.

When Pope Hennessy arrived in Hong Kong in 1877, one of his first thoughts was that the time had come to accord more representation to the Chinese community. The Chinese community had already begun to demand representation, and, in January 1879, sent a memorandum to London arguing that as there were ten times more Chinese than foreigners in Hong Kong, 'it would be but fair to allow the Chinese community a share in the management of the affairs of the colony'. Regional precedents for such a move existed – Singapore had appointed a Chinese member to the Legislative Council in 1869, and Pope Hennessy had made a similar appointment when he was Governor on Labuan, an island off the Borneo coast.

Pope Hennessy's sympathetic attitude to Asians was partially coloured by his marriage to Kitty, the vivacious and attractive Eurasian daughter of the early Malayan administrator Sir Hugh Low. He certainly had no problem with appointing Ng Choy (a British subject born in Singapore into the famous Canton merchant family of Howqua) to the Legislative Council. Educated from an early age in England, Ng Choy trained as a barrister, becoming the first Chinese person called to the English bar, although he subsequently practised in Hong Kong.

The appointment was criticised by European merchants who felt that the move was too conciliatory to the Chinese, and would only encourage further demands for participation in public life. They also questioned how it was possible for a Chinese to be loyal to Britain, as questions of race and nationality were so closely intertwined. Ng Choy finally resigned from the Legislative Council in 1883, but, using the name Wu Ting Fang, he later became a national figure on the mainland, serving over the years as Chinese Ambassador to the United States, Peru, Mexico and Cuba, and as China's Foreign Minister.

As a British subject, Ng Choy (who became more nationalistic as he grew older) represented the dilemma of the 'overseas' Chinese. Where did their ultimate loyalties lie? With China or with the countries in which they were born and raised? This question is still faced by overseas Chinese communities in places such as Indonesia today.

EXPANDING THE COLONY

Towards the end of the 19th century, tensions increased between the various European powers with interests in China. The Germans were heavily involved in Shandong province in northern China, where the city of Tsingtao – still world famous for its brewery today – remained a Teutonic enclave until the Germans

Wartime remembrances

Memorials and tombstones abound in Hong Kong commemorating those who died defending the former British colony against the Japanese during World War II. Harder to find are a number of long-disused concrete pill box gun emplacements, which were scattered across the territory in a vain attempt to spot and repel Japanese troops. One of the most accessible examples is found on a small ridge off the picnic and playground area on the circular walking track on **Victoria Peak** (see p88).

Small networks of bomb-shelter tunnels were cut into hillsides around this time and used in both Japanese air raids and then the ensuing American bombing campaigns when Hong Kong was officially under Japanese occupation. Again, all are now sealed up and many are inaccessible, but one of the easiest to find is in the car park of **St Andrew's Church** in Tsim Sha Tsui, where two bricked up entrances are clearly visible under Observatory Hill.

Few visitors or residents, though, know that the grand colonial **Peninsula** hotel (see p62) played host to a major historic event that occurred during this period. Room 336 was the place where Hong Kong officially

surrendered to invading Japanese troops. When the territory's six defending battalions became overwhelmed on Christmas Day 1941 and retreated to Hong Kong Island, British territorial Commander-in-Chief General CM Maltby informed Governor Mark Young that resistance was no longer possible. The pair was escorted across Victoria Harbour, littered with burned-out vessels, into the Peninsula. There, on behalf of the British Government, they formally surrendered the British colony to Lieutenant-General Sakai. Governor Young remained under guard in this room for two months of interrogation, before he was transferred to a prisoner-of-war camp on the outskirts of Shanghai.

In **Stanley** (see p92), on the south side of Hong Kong Island, a Commonwealth War Graves Commission cemetery holds the remains of the scores who died fighting the invaders, while part of today's maximum-security prison at Stanley was used by the temporary occupiers as a prisoner of war camp. And **Stanley Main Beach** (see p93) was the site of a particularly gruesome episode – the beheading of 33 Hong Kong residents of various ethnic origin by the Japanese – all charged with espionage.

were expelled by the Japanese in 1915. The French leased the port of Kwangchowwan between Hong Kong and Haiphong on the Guangdong coast, in 1898 (at the same time as the British leased the New Territories), and remained there until 1943.

It was also in 1898 that the British leased the tiny port of Wei Hai Wei in Shandong, where they remained until 1930. Used as a cool-weather station for the Royal Navy, Wei Hai Wei later played a role in recruiting Shandong men into the Hong Kong Police force.

The principal reason behind the lease of the New Territories was the British belief that it would be impossible to defend Hong Kong Island and Kowloon against attack without having possession of the hills north of the Kowloon peninsula. Unlike the two previous cessions of land from China to Britain (which were essentially the spoils of war and 'unequal treaty'), the New Territories (and around 230 islands) were obtained on a 99-year lease through the 1898 Convention of Peking, sparking off the entire 1997 issue. Without this additional expansion, Hong Kong and Kowloon might still be British today.

Another key element of Hong Kong's relationship with the New Territories has always been fresh water. From the earliest days of British settlement, demand has continually outstripped supply, due to the steady increase in population that the colony's politically stable environment encouraged. Tank streams were quickly over-utilised, and wells in urban areas became contaminated and unsafe.

In the 19th century a number of reservoirs were built on Hong Kong Island. For a while they were adequate for the needs of the growing city. By the late 1920s, however, the growth of urban Hong Kong made the need for a new reservoir extremely urgent. The only viable location was in the Kowloon hills, at the head of the Shing Mun valley. The project was opposed by the Colonial Office on the grounds that the reservoir would be built in the New Territories, which were leased and would, therefore, revert to China in around 70 years. Building a capital-intensive scheme on someone else's land, as it were, was, they felt, a great waste of money.

This was a view strongly countered by Sir Cecil Clementi, one of Hong Kong's most able and visionary colonial administrators. A possible solution to the problem of the Shing Mun reservoirs, in Clementi's view, lay over a thousand miles to the north of Hong Kong.

Clementi's proposal involved offering to return Wei Hai Wei to Chinese control – as it was a disposable backwater that had never really prospered – in return for outright cession by China of the New Territories, which were

vital to Hong Kong's continued growth. His proposal was rejected by the Foreign Office as unnecessary and unworkable, and likely to stir up demands from the Nanking Government for further abandonment of British concessions and privileges elsewhere in China. Yet, in 1930, as a gesture of goodwill, Wei Hai Wei was returned to Chinese rule.

The Shing Mun reservoirs were eventually built anyway, as the growing demand for reliable water supplies overrode all else. Extensive reforestation was undertaken to safeguard the water catchments. Photographs of the Shing Mun area taken in the late 1930s show large areas of thriving new forestry, in stark contrast to the treeless grassy hills in much of the rest of the New Territories. The villages in the valley were removed and their inhabitants were resettled in the north-west New Territories. The village built for them at Kam Tin was named Shing Mun San Tsuen, or Shing Mun New Village. Located between Tai Hong Wai and Wing Lung Wai, the resettlement village still maintains a distinct and separate identity from the rest of the community. There are numerous old people who remember the move from the old village (which has been under water for decades now). Even after more than 60 years the Shing Mun people are still outsiders at Kam Tin.

CHINESE NATIONALISM TAKES HOLD

In 1900, two years after the New Territories lease was ratified, the Boxer Rebellion broke out in China. Overspill into the Hong Kong region was limited, with the areas most affected being in north China. Support for radical change in China during this period was generated in southern China by Dr Sun Yat-sen and the earlier reformer Kang Yu-hwei (both of whom were Cantonese). Sun Yat-sen attended school in Hong Kong and was a graduate of the Hong Kong College of Medicine. Giving a lecture at Hong Kong University in 1923, he said that it was the peace, prosperity and good government that he had experienced in the British colony, which – contrasted with the chaos and corruption in China itself – had turned him into a revolutionary.

Escalating periods of Chinese nationalist agitation during the years following the fall of the Qing (or Manchu) Dynasty and beginning of the Republican period spilled over into Hong Kong with a tramways strike and boycott in 1912-13, a seamen's strike in 1922 and a General Strike in 1925. The Nationalist (or Kuomintang) Government was based at Canton, and China was divided into numerous feuding warlord fiefdoms. The country was unified under the Nationalists after Chiang Kai-Shek led the Northern Expedition in 1927-28, and subsequently removed the capital to Nanking.

THE RISING SUN IN SOUTH CHINA

Around 1853-54 Japan emerged from a period of self-imposed isolation, during which time it was known as *sakoku*, or 'the locked-in country'. Rapidly opening itself up to the West, it modernised every aspect of government, industrialised rapidly and started encroaching on foreign borders.

Japan went to war with – and defeated – the Chinese in 1894-95. Then, while fighting on the Allied side during World War I, it occupied German ports, mines, railway concessions and other enterprises in China, most of which were granted to Japan in the 1919 Versailles Peace Conference.

Throughout the 1920s there was continued Japanese expansion throughout the north-east of China. The rise of Chang Hsueh-liang (known as the Young Marshal) – who only came to power after the Japanese assassinated his father, Manchurian warlord Chang Tso-lin (known as the Old Marshal), at Mukden in 1928 – stemmed the Japanese advance for a time.

However, in 1934, Pu Yi, the last Manchu Emperor of China, was made the puppet Emperor of Manchukuo by the Japanese, formalising their annexation of China's north-eastern provinces. All-out war between Japan and China began in July 1937. The Japanese quickly captured Chinese coastal cities (surrounding Shanghai's International Settlement in the process) and advanced up the Yangtze valley, where they perpetrated the notorious Rape of Nanking. In October 1938 the city of Canton fell to the Japanese, who advanced to the Shum Chun River (forming the border between the Chinese mainland and Hong Kong) a week or so later.

The Japanese push led to a massive influx of refugees into Hong Kong, which would eventually lead to a post-war housing crisis. Gradually forested from the 1860s to the 1930s, Hong Kong's hills were now being deforested by refugees searching for fuel and somewhere they could build huts.

'The Japanese territorial incursions included strafing a packed refugee train.'

The late 1930s marked the start of Hong Kong's small-scale industrialisation in northern Kowloon and elsewhere in the colony, a process that continued into the 1950s. In spite of – or perhaps because of – the unsettled conditions on the Chinese mainland, Hong Kong itself experienced a prolonged period of economic boom. Japanese territorial incursions, which on one occasion included flying over Hong Kong territory and strafing a packed refugee train near Fanling, led to a steady strengthening of defensive measures and an increase in the size of the garrison.

HOSTILE OCCUPATION

In December 1941, at the same time as they launched attacks on Pearl Harbor, north Malaya and the Philippines, the Japanese crossed the border into the New Territories and bombed the airport at Kai Tak. Hong Kong's garrison, while prepared for war, was small and hopelessly outnumbered by the Japanese.

In the late 1930s a string of defensive tunnels, bunkers and machine-gun emplacements had been built in the Kowloon hills as Hong Kong's answer to the Maginot Line. Known then as the Inner Line, post-war it was referred to as the 'gin drinker's line', due to its location between Gin Drinker's Bay (now part of modern Kwai Chung) and Port Shelter. Unfortunately, it did not stand for long. After three days of fighting the line fell and Kowloon was evacuated, crowding Hong Kong Island with refugees. This further added to existing accommodation shortages and caused a water supply crisis that eventually played a large part in forcing the British to surrender.

After waiting almost a week, during which time they sent across two peace missions, the Japanese landed on Hong Kong Island on 18 December 1941. There followed a period of heavy fighting on the eastern side of Hong Kong Island, in the centre of the island at and around Wong Nai Chung Gap, and at Stanley. After 18 days of hostilities, the British finally surrendered on Christmas afternoon 1941, becoming in the process the first British colony to surrender to Japan during the Pacific War.

Partly as a measure of controlling Hong Kong's housing, food and fuel problems, the Japanese immediately initiated a policy of depopulation by forcing the local Chinese to evacuate to their mainland homes. Given the difficult conditions in Hong Kong, many Chinese residents in the urban areas decided to voluntarily return to their ancestral villages in the hinterland, where, although conditions may have been difficult, they would at least have enough to eat.

Following the British surrender, there was widespread co-operation between the erstwhile local elite and the new Japanese occupation authorities; these events later prompted a post-war enquiry into collaboration, the findings of which were, perhaps not surprisingly, never released.

Kai Tak Airport.

Almost the entire Allied civilian population – men, women and children – were interned in a concentration camp at Stanley. Male military prisoners of war were imprisoned in their former barracks in Kowloon; many were later transported to Japan to work as slaves in the mines and on the docks.

One of the most aesthetically pleasing legacies of Japanese rule in Hong Kong is Government House. The original, built in the mid 19th century in tropical Georgian style, was in desperate need of repair when it was renovated by the Japanese. It still stands on Upper Albert Road in Central. The gardens can be visited by the general public once a year when the azaleas are in stunning full bloom.

Throughout their occupation, Chinese guerrillas operating from Kwangtung's East River district harried the Japanese and mounted a number of operations within Hong Kong, including a daring raid on the railway bridge in central Kowloon, but otherwise there was little resistance and the city was remarkably peaceful.

Following the Hiroshima and Nagasaki atomic bombs, the Japanese surrendered on 15 August 1945, much earlier than the Allies had anticipated. This left a brief power vacuum, which was filled by British officials coming out from internment and assuming control from the Japanese. A British fleet was dispatched from Sydney (where it had been undergoing a refit) when the surrender came through; it arrived in Hong Kong on 30 August 1945.

A period of British Military Administration followed, but civilian government was restored in May 1946 under Sir Mark Young, the pre-war governor, who returned to the role after his release as a prisoner of war.

BACK TO BUSINESS

As business – and more especially the entrepôt trade – had always been Hong Kong's lifeblood, the port was back in full operation very soon after the British returned. The fact that Hong Kong used the dollar rather than sterling, and was able to buy supplies direct from the USA, without having to wait for quotas to be approved from London, meant that the local economy was back on an even footing very swiftly.

Sir Mark Young left Hong Kong in 1947, and was succeeded as governor by Sir Alexander Grantham, a former cadet who had started his administrative career in Hong Kong. For the next ten years Grantham oversaw a prolonged period of uncertainty. In 1949 civil war and the communist takeover tore apart the mainland. A year later the Korean War broke out and the subsequent American embargo on trade with China – which as far as they were concerned included Hong Kong – stifled the colony's traditional reliance on the entrepôt trade.

Yet much was achieved during the decade, including the extension of Kai Tak airport. Rapid and efficient industrialisation, mainly fuelled by Shanghainese entrepreneurs who had fled the communists, was in full swing by the mid-1950s. It took advantage of the large pool of refugee labour willing to work for low wages.

It was around this time that marginal areas, such as Kwun Tong and Tsuen Wan on the outskirts of Kowloon, rapidly developed into industrial towns, full of spinning, dyeing and weaving mills, toy and plastics factories, and other labour-intensive light industries. Industry of this kind remained a mainstay of the Hong Kong economy until the late 1980s, when the re-opening of China to foreign and overseas investment made manufacturing on the mainland, with its low wages and lax controls, much more economical than in Hong Kong.

In the post-war period it was thought that many of the refugees who had fled to Hong Kong following the end of the civil war and the communist takeover would return to the mainland as the dust settled, much as waves of refugees had done in the past. Gradually, it became apparent that this latest influx had no intention of returning, and provision had to be made for their integration into Hong Kong.

Housing policy (which hitherto had been to tolerate the theoretically temporary squatter settlements that had grown up in various parts of the city) changed dramatically following a massive fire in one of the largest squatter settlements in Kowloon, which made 53,000 people homeless on Christmas Day 1953. The government's response was to develop a public housing programme that is probably post-war Hong Kong's most notable success. The largest single commercial landlord in the world, Hong Kong's Housing Authority, provides subsidised housing to over half the population.

'Ironically, the communist-fomented Star Ferry Riots were over the increase in price of first-class tickets.'

There were other problems around this time. The aftermath of civil war on the mainland often spilled over into Hong Kong, and low-level nationalist/communist confrontations continued throughout the 1950s. Kowloon had serious nationalist-inspired riots in 1956, while the Star Ferry Riots in 1966 were communist-fomented (ironically, considering they were over the increase in price of first-class ferry tickets). Finally, in the summer of 1967, the Cultural Revolution spilled over into Hong Kong and Macau – bombs were thrown and a number of people were killed, but, in the end, the people of Hong Kong came out firmly in favour of the local government.

In addition, rapid industrialisation, massive population movements and a get-rich-quick refugee mentality all led to a spectacular growth of official corruption, especially within the Hong Kong Police. Eventually, the situation became so bad that a special Independent Commission Against Corruption with wide-ranging powers was introduced in 1974. The commission was remarkably effective – by the 1980s Hong Kong, formerly known as one of the most corrupt places in Asia, was one of the straightest and most transparent.

BOOM-TIME AND END-OF-ERA PLANS
Under Governor Sir Murray MacLehose, who was in Hong Kong from 1971 to 1981, Hong Kong expanded into a regional financial centre. This resulted in a gradual move away from its traditional entrepôt role and the industrial reliance it had developed since the early 1950s.

After the domestic turmoil of the Cultural Revolution (1966-76), China re-emerged as a major consideration, especially as the time for the expiry of the New Territories lease drew closer. By the late 1970s big businesses were beginning to press for a closer examination of the future of Hong Kong, as the issue of major developmental loans that would still be operational after 1997 needed to be addressed.

In 1979 MacLehose visited Beijing, where he was told by Deng Xiaoping to tell Hong Kong investors to 'put their hearts at ease'. Confidence in the future of Hong Kong soared, as many took this statement to be tacit approval for Hong Kong remaining under British rule beyond 1997. Behind the scenes, however, diplomatic moves were made to determine exactly what the situation was, and, following Margaret Thatcher's visit to Beijing in 1982, both governments moved towards what eventually became the Joint Declaration, signed in 1984.

The Joint Declaration guaranteed that in 1997 Hong Kong would revert to full Chinese administration (China had, after all, never admitted any British sovereignty), with legal guarantees and safeguards for the future 'stability and prosperity' of Hong Kong.

Confidence, badly eroded in the early 1980s, was restored and Hong Kong continued to prosper. The professional classes, many of whom – or whose families – had fled China in the aftermath of the communist takeover, had no desire to become Chinese subjects, and the 1980s and '90s saw over 50,000 a year emigrate to Australia, Canada, New Zealand and the United States. Many have since returned, having acquired a foreign passport or permanent residence, creating a returnee backwash with mixed loyalties, with interesting implications for the future of Hong Kong. See also p48 **Return of the astronauts**.

RUN-UP TO THE HANDOVER
June 1989 saw the violent suppression of student-led protests in Beijing's Tiananmen Square and, for a while, a deteriorated confidence in Hong Kong. Government policy at the time was not to further antagonise the Chinese Government in any way, but this attitude radically changed with the appointment of Chris Patten as the last British governor in 1992.

Iconic or ironic?

With every passing year, it seems, the search for an 'authentic' Hong Kong experience becomes more and more elusive as the city, its sights, culture and lifestyle become ever more internationalised and homogenised. In a sense the arrogant self-designation 'Asia's World City' rings true; in every fundamental respect, Hong Kong is more and more like anywhere else. Whether this trend is positive or otherwise remains a matter for personal judgement – the fact remains that to discover something uniquely 'Hong Kong' requires homework, persistence and a bit of good luck.

In the past certain fairly common local sights became internationally recognised symbols of Hong Kong. Two in particular were elevated to the status of local icons – the rickshaw and the bat-wing rigged sailing junk.

Both sights have long-since disappeared from the local scene. The last remaining rickshaw-pullers, who operated outside the Star Ferry concourse on Hong Kong Island gradually vanished in the years after the Handover. And now the Star Ferry terminal itself has moved, to an inconvenient location way out on the reclamation (*see also p103* **Walking on water**).

Sailing junks have been on the way out ever since co-operative fisheries and motorised deep-sea fleets were introduced in the post-war years. By the late 1960s sailing junks were in annually decreasing numbers in Hong Kong waters, and by the early 1980s they were almost extinct. There haven't been any in operation – at all – for two decades now. This inconvenient fact does not stop the local tourism authorities using scenes of a Chinese sailing junk, backed by Hong Kong Island's glittering skyline, as some sort of East-meets-West, traditional versus modern image.

The problem with continuing to use these outmoded images to give tourists a flavour of 'authentic' local life is that, while residents may smile a little wearily at the endlessly repeated clichés, visitors travel to Hong Kong genuinely expecting to see junks and rickshaws as part of the territory's everyday experience – and often leave more than a little disappointed that there were none of these icons to be seen at all.

Likewise the famous backstreet life – the bustling, vibrant markets that are meant to epitomise the Hong Kong experience. These days, shopping-mall culture has taken over in a very big way, all over Hong Kong, and with every passing year the street markets have less and less to offer either residents or visitors. Declining popularity is particularly true of one-time tourist draws such as Kowloon's legendary Temple Street Night Market (*see p191*); it's still fun for a wander, but locals have given the place a wide berth for many years now. Other traditional markets are still to be found – and some are as vibrant as ever – but you'd best see them while you still can.

Hong Kong has yet to define its iconic sights for the new millennium, and what series of images it wishes to project to the world. As things stand, ever-taller skyscrapers, endless air-conditioned shopping malls and year-round, smog-filled skies pretty much sum up modern Hong Kong. But one thing is for certain. It's about time that – once and for all – the junks and rickshaw images were permanently retired. All that they epitomise today are stale images from a long-ago past that – like so much else in ever-changing Hong Kong – has well and truly passed into the history books.

Patten launched a series of wide-reaching electoral reforms without the backing of the Chinese Government, and a long period ensued when very little constructive was achieved. The small flurry of popular interest in democracy kicked up at the time subsided back into general political apathy within a few years. Urgently needed environmental and education reforms were sidelined due to politics, and are only now being introduced.

June 1997 saw the long-awaited Handover, a media feeding frenzy for the world press, which nevertheless turned into something of a non-event. The riots and unrest that the film crews

were not-so-secretly hoping for didn't happen, the People's Liberation Army didn't have any opportunity for an immediate crackdown on the streets of Central, it rained continually for weeks and, finally, on the night of 30 June, the last governor boarded the *Britannia* and sailed away in a flood of his own tears.

POST-HANDOVER HONG KONG

Much of the gloom and disaster somewhat gleefully forecast for Hong Kong by the world's media in the lead-up to the Handover has failed to materialise, although the new Special Administrative Region (SAR) has had more

The Prince of Wales and Governor Chris Patten wave goodbye on 30 June 1997...

than its fair share of problems over the last six years. The Asian economic crisis in 1997-98, which decimated the so-called 'tiger economies', hit Hong Kong quite badly, and its effects still linger. But the political fallout that rocked other regional economies, such as Indonesia, was cushioned here by massive government intervention in the stock market. Similarly, the Hong Kong dollar remained stable due to considerable intervention on the part of the administration. One lasting casualty was Hong Kong's international reputation as a laissez-faire economy – no bad thing as far as many people were concerned.

> **'The property collapse here had nothing to do with the Handover, and everything to do with ridiculous prices.'**

Hong Kong's hyper-inflated property sector, which had been in overdrive throughout the 1990s, finally started to lose steam in late 1997, trapping many local property owners in negative equity. The collapse here had nothing to do with the Handover, and everything to do with prices rising to absolutely ridiculous levels. The luxury end of the market was particularly badly hit, with some developments losing between 50 and 70 per cent of their boomtime value. But the decline in property asset value affected the entire housing market, and the incidence of associated problems, including

bankruptcies, have soared in recent years and, although there are signs of improvement and general economic recovery, there will be no major improvements any time soon.

A massive avian flu outbreak in 1997, when a deadly virus crossed the species barrier from poultry to people, was partially averted by the slaughter of millions of chickens. Scientists repeatedly warned that the only way to prevent further outbreaks in Hong Kong was to ban live poultry shops from wet markets and centralise slaughtering facilities. Reluctant to antagonise the grass-roots population, which insists that poultry be bought while still alive (it apparently tastes much better that way), the government backed down from this measure and as a result periodic avian flu outbreaks have continued to occur, with resultant mass culls.

An avian flu-like analogy can be made – at least in part – to the 2003 SARS outbreak. This has been conclusively linked in many cases to the generally low levels of civic cleanliness and a lack of awareness of the importance of environmental hygiene. While this is a societal problem that has been obvious to many for years now, without effective leadership little can be achieved in changing public attitudes. Although clean-up attempts were made after SARS, now that the threat has passed civic hygiene standards are returning to pre-SARS levels. Most tellingly, to the despair of veterinarians, live poultry is still on sale in wet markets.

...as residents celebrate Hong Kong's final hours as a British colony before the Handover.

RUMBLINGS OF DISCONTENT

Dissatisfaction with the way Hong Kong is run is currently at an all-time high. Barely a week passes without rowdy demonstrations in one form or another taking place through the streets of the city. While some would say that this practice signals continued governmental tolerance towards vocal dissent – undoubtedly a good sign – there are two major downsides to it all. The first is that an awful lot of ordinary people are fed up – the most vocal demonstrations are about everyday livelihood issues such as negative equity and rising unemployment, not the big issues of greater representative government or other political freedoms. Secondly, and perhaps most telling, street protests are not a regular weekly feature of life in London, New York or Sydney – but they are in Hong Kong. Many ordinary residents feel deeply frustrated that their voices are not heard, and that the issues and concerns of the average person are not given enough attention by those in positions of authority. Some critics, though, also point to the regular protests and plethora of small political parties as evidence of Hong Kong's general level of political immaturity. It seems that there are elements of truth in both assertions.

To its credit, the mainland government has taken an admirably hands-off approach to Hong Kong affairs since the Handover, and without doubt many of the territory's ongoing problems have been exacerbated by a vacillating, indecisive leadership that constantly kowtows to powerful vested interests, especially in the property sectors, at the expense of the rest of the population.

In July 2002 Chief Executive Tung Chee-hwa was appointed to a second term in office, to the surprise of no one and the chagrin of many. Sparked by public discontent at the years of bumbling, high-handed arrogance of various key officials, and by the handling of the SARS crisis, a massive public demonstration on 1 July 2003 changed matters. It was clear to most observers after this resounding vote of no-confidence that Tung had to go. He resigned early in 2004, citing ill-health as the reason, and was replaced by his chief secretary, Sir Donald Tsang, a long-serving career civil servant who had been Patten's financial secretary and was knighted the day of the Handover. According to the Basic Law – Hong Kong's mini-constitution published in 1988 – full direct elections to the legislative council were to have been permitted from 2007, but this has now been ruled out. The earliest anyone expects a semblance of genuine elections to take place in Hong Kong is now 2012.

Another noticeable and steadily growing trend is a broad sense of wounded national pride and festering disappointment on the part of many local people that – so far, anyway – the much-vaunted pre-Handover concept of Hong Kong people ruling Hong Kong has been a conspicuous flop. The people of Hong Kong don't feel like they are ruling anything.

Key events

1513 Portuguese explorer Alvares lands on Lintin in the Pearl River Delta.
c1557 Macau settled by the Portuguese as a base to trade between China and Japan.
1637 First British ship to reach China is driven back from Canton (Guangzhou).
1639 Japan closed to the Portuguese.
1685 Limited trade to Canton permitted; the British East India Company starts trading.
1799 The spread of opium addiction causes Beijing to ban it, driving the trade underground.
1834 British East India Company loses its opium trade monopoly; Lord Napier aims to regularise Sino-British trade and diplomatic relations.
1839 Lin Tse-hsü tries to stamp out the opium trade; he confiscates 20,000 chests of opium in Canton, sparking the First Opium (or Anglo-Chinese) War.
1841 The British attack Canton and occupy its forts. The dispute is settled by the Convention of Chuen Pi, which cedes the island of Hong Kong to Britain, although neither side ratifies the treaty.
1842 The Treaty of Nanking ends the war, confirming British sovereignty over Hong Kong and opening up five Chinese cities to trade.
1860 Kowloon and Stonecutter's Island are ceded by China to Britain during the Second Opium (or Arrow) War.
1862 China signs over Macau to Portugal.
1870 Founding of the Tung Wah Hospital.
1898 The British lease the New Territories from China for 99 years.
1911 Sun Yat-sen overthrows the Qing Dynasty and establishes the Republic of China.
1925 General strike in Hong Kong.
1941-45 Japanese troops occupy Hong Kong.
1945 China's civil war between the communists and the nationalists continues as World War II ends.
1949 The communists triumph, founding the People's Republic of China; the nationalists flee to Taiwan.
1956 Riots between nationalists and communists leave dozens dead, with triad involvement on the nationalist side.
1966 Rioting in Hong Kong over the increase of the price of first-class tickets on the Star Ferry; the start of the Cultural Revolution.
1971 Taiwan is replaced in the UN General Assembly by the People's Republic of China; Sir Murray MacLehose appointed as governor.

1974 Independent Commission Against Corruption (ICAC) formed.
1979 Opening of Mass Transit Railway (MTR).
1982 British Prime Minister Margaret Thatcher visits Hong Kong and Beijing, beginning talks on the future of Hong Kong. China starts to develop Shenzhen as a Special Economic Zone.
1983 China announces that Hong Kong will become a Special Administrative Region (SAR) after the 1997 Handover, retaining capitalism, its police and judiciary.
1984 A Sino-British 'Draft Agreement on the Future of Hong Kong' (aka the 'Joint Declaration') is announced.
1988 Publication of the Basic Law, Hong Kong's post-Handover constitution.
1989 The Tiananmen Square massacre provokes a huge demonstration in Hong Kong.
1992 Arrival of Chris Patten, Hong Kong's 28th and last governor. His proposed reforms of the political system are criticised by Beijing.
1994 Legislative Council passes Patten's proposed electoral reforms; arguments with Beijing continue for three more years.
1997 Handover of sovereignty from Britain to China at midnight on 30 June. Swearing in of new government; the Beijing-appointed provisional legislature supplants the Legislative Council; Tung Chee-hwa is appointed Chief Executive.
1997-98 Asian economic crisis damages regional economies; Hong Kong emerges relatively unscathed but with troubling deflation problems.
1999 Handover of Macau after 442 years of Portuguese rule.
2001 China joins World Trade Organisation.
2002 Official celebrations mark the fifth anniversary of the Handover, but meet with lukewarm public response as the economic downturn continues.
2003 SARS causes worldwide panic; the WHO warns against travel to Hong Kong, and the local economy experiences a severe setback. Over 500,000 people take to the streets on 1 July, protesting unpopular 'national security' legislation, which is scrapped a few days later.
2004 Resignation of Tung Chee-hwa; Sir Donald Tsang appointed as his replacement.
2005 Opening of Hong Kong Disneyland, accompanied by mixed fanfare and criticism.
2006 Relocation of Central Star Ferry Pier.

Hong Kong Today

The morphing face of a city in overdrive again.

Hong Kong might as well be a byword for flux. Reclamation of land from the sea in this Special Administrative Region (SAR) of China goes on relentlessly. The economy was on a prominent upswing as this third edition of the guide went to press, reflected in a surge of new hotels, restaurants and bars. And tourists who have been here before can expect fresh sights as well: there is a new cable-car attraction on Lantau (*see p125*), Victoria Peak's viewing amenities have been upgraded (*see p89*) and, appealing to those with kids or a vintage cartoon fetish, Hong Kong Disneyland has opened. In response to the last of these, the territory's much-loved marine-themed attraction, Ocean Park, which had got rather ragged around the edges, has upped its game (*see p212* **Variations on a theme**).

The rollercoaster of changes over the past few years has kept the ride a white-knuckle one for this small dot in the South China Sea. In the decade leading up to the late 1990s, property prices, salaries and inflation – along with associated hedonism and a sense of superiority over less-well-off mainland China and Asia in general – had spiralled. The bubble was ripe for bursting, and burst it did spectacularly. First came the Asian financial meltdown – it was felt more significantly in South-east Asia from around 2001 but the faltering of these nations, in which much Hong Kong money was invested, had a knock-on effect too. Then came the SARS

outbreak in the first half of 2003; the number of visitors plummeted for the whole year and many residents stayed locked up in their own homes, donning surgical masks to venture out to work or buy essential groceries.

From early 2004, however, signs of an upturn began to appear, kick-started by the collaboraton between the local and mainland governments to allow more independent visitors to travel here freely than were ever allowed before, thus tapping into the wallets of the world's largest nouveau riche tourism segment (*see p32* **When the in-laws drop in**). Total tourist figures for 2005 were 23.6 million – up seven per cent on 2004.

Talk of foreign companies relocating from Hong Kong on account of the air pollution here (*see p30* **Smog gets in your eyes**) has not amounted to a significant pull-out thus far and the SAR appears to have kept its position as a regional base for overseas operations and multinationals. Mainland China may offer cheaper overheads but Hong Kong still offers strict adherence to the rule of law and, generally speaking, transparency within business practices. The government-funded Independent Commission Against Corruption (ICAC), established in 1974, is also a strong deterrent to the smoothing of deals with backhanders. In December 2006 this terrier of an organisation announced an 89 per cent conviction rate of its cases – despite an increase in challenges.

Smog gets in your eyes

There's just no getting away from it: for most of the year, air pollution is a serious problem in Hong Kong. The thick pall of air-borne gunk that clouds the skies and catches the throat and lungs is all too obvious – except perhaps to those at the top levels of government and big business whose actions might translate into some lasting change and improvement.

Air pollution has been an annually increasing problem for many years but has really reached a crisis point in the last few years. As ever in Hong Kong, the unholy alliance of deeply entrenched business interests and dilatory government means that serious anti-pollution initiatives remain only so much hot air. Despite top-level noises expressing concern, the Hong Kong Government has consistently refused to implement revised World Health Organisation guidelines on air quality and instead announced an 18-month 'consultation period' in 2006 to study the matter further – a tacit admission that it has been impossible to meet earlier, less stringent pollution targets. Meanwhile, the region – and its hapless residents – continues to choke.

On some days it is almost impossible to see from Hong Kong Island to the Kowloon peninsula through the thick smog that blankets Victoria Harbour – greatly narrowed as it is by massive reclamation projects. And forget about taking in the majestic views from the Peak across to the Kowloon hills and the islands beyond; for months of the year – in cumulative terms – these scenic vistas might just as well not be there. Airline pilots mention that the air quality visibly declines a couple of hundred kilometres out of Hong Kong, and on a bad day visibility at the airport can be almost nil.

Anecdotal evidence suggests that top-level executives, and some companies, have made decisions not to come to Hong Kong because of the foul air quality. Most people, though, have no choice but to live in it – and suffer the health consequences. The cooler months are the worst, as the winds from China bring pollution from the rapidly industrialising mainland; in the summer, during the southerly monsoons, air quality can be quite good.

A recent report undertaken by medical researchers at Hong Kong University indicated that steadily worsening air pollution was directly responsible for over 3,000 deaths a year – far more than occurred during both the SARS and avian flu outbreaks combined.

In fairness, much has been done within Hong Kong in recent years to combat the problem. And much – though by no means all – of the region's pollution is a cross-border phenomenon, one exacerbated by China's unreliable electricity grid. Factories around the Pearl River Delta – mostly owned, ironically, by Hong Kong business interests – maintain their own heavily polluting, bunker-fuelled generators to deal with frequent power shortages. Until the mainland's electricity supply is sorted out and some serious remedial action is implemented, Hong Kong, sadly, will continue to deserve its unfortunate reputation – both for choking layers of smog and a population and administration largely unprepared to deal with it on any level.

There are some things being done, though nowhere near enough. Since a fair share of the pollution is from bus and car emissions (27 per cent), a pressure group, Clear the Air (www.cleartheair.org.hk), has developed an idling engine scheme that encourages people

While the local population has never been overly concerned with politics, it certainly voices its opinion from time to time. From 2003, the public at large, whipped up by the Chinese-language popular press, showed its dissatisfaction for the current election of legislators from within – mass rallies formed every 1 July to shout and march for a democratically elected government. Hong Kong's government is completely autonomous, though, not directed by Beijing, and despite earlier indifference it has begun to show itself concerned with public opinion. In early December 2006, for instance, it withdrew its own proposal for a government sales tax

(essentially a value-added tax), which Chief Executive Sir Donald Tsang – successor to the unpopular Tung Chee-hwa, the inaugural leader following the 1997 Handover of government from Britain back to China (*see p25*) – and his cabinet were insisting was a certainty only two months earlier. The December about-face included a request to Hong Kong residents to come forward with alternative suggestions for ways to bolster their government's coffers. Hong Kongers know they have a comparatively privileged rate of income tax – most workers pay around 17 per cent – so time will tell whether they willingly offer up any further contributions.

factor, where wealth was flaunted at every opportunity, through designer products and private club memberships. With the recent upward surge in the economy, however, people are showing signs of a readiness to spend and be showy once more. In November 2006 an antique bowl from China sold at a local Christie's auction for HK$151 million – setting a record both for any work of art in Asia and also for any Qing dynasty ceramic piece.

'One prominent tycoon spent HK$1.4 million for a "1 LOVE U" number plate.'

Rather more egocentric auctioneering took place in September 2006, in which the issuing of previously unreleased 'auspicious' vehicle number plates fetched astronomical sums. One prominent tycoon spent HK$40 million on various plates, paying HK$1.4 million for one reading '1 LOVE U'. Members-only clubs are also a big hit with moneyed types. A branch of the London-founded M1NT club opened in late 2006 and was almost instantly deemed a success, with those that want to be seen on the scene clambering for membership.

An improved economy doesn't necessarily mean a healthier society, and smoggy Hong Kong still – unbelievably – tops the world's longest human lifespan statistics. But with 20 per cent of primary school children in the territory being reported as clinically obese in late 2006, it may be less developed nations, where fast-food chains have made slower inroads, that take this honour in the future. Parents in Hong Kong seem to give in too readily to the 'collectable' toys and other promotions that target kids and lure them in for a platter of fat. Recent media concerns over diet may help turn this trend around.

It's somewhat ironic that the fast-food joints have made such inroads: as a visitor, you'll find few places on earth that serve such a diverse selection of wholesome food. Indeed, it's the cuisine – once you've recovered from Hong Kong's visual wow factor – that will stick in your mind. In-your-face architecture rules supreme in this city that seems never to have time for nostalgia – as it recently proved yet again by bulldozing a landmark 1950s clock tower and terminal building in Central, when the Star Ferry relocated in 2006 to make way for the development of more harbourfront land. And though Hong Kong is mostly about the buzz of high-rise urban renewal – punctuated by ever glitzier shopping malls – be sure to contrast this with one or two of its rural pockets to get the full picture.

to report smoky vehicles and idling engines. Taxis are switching to low-emission liquid petroleum gas (LPG) and minibuses are expected to convert to electric or LPG as well. With figures showing that nearly half the pollution comes from energy plants, the Environmental Protection Department has set up a TV and print media advertising campaign to advise residents how to use less energy – practical suggestions like setting air-conditioning units to 25.5°C, or using fans where possible.

Actions have also been taken to improve indoor air quality: legislators implemented a smoking ban covering most public places, which went into effect on 1 January 2007.

Meanwhile, the smog remains.

The relative prosperity of the SAR manifests itself in a number of ways. Domestic helpers are the norm for the majority of families – even for childless couples – and have been for decades, as a live-in helper is much more affordable here than in the West. Today some 230,000 such workers – mostly from the Philippines and Indonesia – are relied upon. Before the 1970s it would have been unthinkable that the elderly would not live with and be supported by their children, simultaneously looking after their grandchildren. The custom of three generations living under one roof, though, is dying out.

The dive in Hong Kong's economy a few years ago erased a very self-conscious bling

When the in-laws drop in

For many years it was almost impossible for visitors from mainland China to visit Hong Kong. Then, in the 1990s, as the Handover approached, regulations were relaxed and mainland tour groups started arriving in Hong Kong (and travelling to other parts of the world) in annually increasing numbers. After the CEPA (Closer Economic Partnership Agreement) was concluded between China and Hong Kong in 2003, individual travellers from a number of locations in China could apply to come to Hong Kong.

Visitor numbers swiftly surged and now tourists from mainland China, whether independent travellers or those on group tours, make up half of all tourist entries to Hong Kong (a statistic assisted by the drop in foreign visitors following the SARS crisis). Hong Kong has become increasingly geared towards tourists from the PRC, to the extent that, since 2003, banks officially exchange Chinese currency (RMB) and it can also be withdrawn from some ATMs.

Few mainland visitors come to Hong Kong for more than token sight-seeing – a whistle-stop bus tour around a few scenic lookout points, such as the Peak (*see p88*) and Repulse Bay beach (*see p92*), major temples such as the massive Wong Tai Sin complex (*see p104*) or Hollywood Road's venerable Man Mo Temple (*see p80*), followed by a prolonged shopping binge.

But what exactly do they come to Hong Kong to buy? Ironically, while Hong Kong residents go to Shenzhen for made-in-China rip-off handbags, garments and other items, mainland visitors come down to Hong Kong for the genuine article. And not only for designer-label luxury goods: gold, precious stones and other jewellery items, cosmetics, pharmaceuticals, Chinese herbal medicines, exotic food items such as shark's fin and bird's nests – all are very popular purchases.

While retail scams and rip-offs are far from unknown, mainland tourists know that if items are bought in Hong Kong or Macau there is a far better chance that they are the genuine item. Modern Chinese society has very little place for trust these days, alas, and mainlanders know the sorry moral state of their own society only too well.

Mainland tourists are much in evidence in the less 'international' parts of the city. Large numbers stay – and shop – in Hung Hom,

Tsuen Wan and around North Point on Hong Kong Island. Chung On Street, in the heart of gritty post-industrial Tsuen Wan, is a good place to see mainland tourists in action; the streets around King's Road in North Point is another. Inevitably, along with the legitimate tourists, a variety of illegal, undocumented workers, particularly in the sex trade, come down to Hong Kong for extended periods.

Unfortunately, many mainland Chinese tourists epitomise the absolute worst aspects of modern China. Pushy, crass, rude, loud-voiced and dirty – there are, sadly, plenty of walking stereotypes. Even the Chinese government has come to recognise that the manners, deportment and general behaviour of many of its tourists is a national disgrace, and guidelines were issued late in 2006 to would-be travellers telling them how to behave.

Spitting, still a problem among Hong Kong Chinese residents despite generations of public education campaigns, reaches epic proportions in areas popular with mainland tourists. The floors of hotels, shopping arcades and restaurants are as liable to get a full-throated, creamy gob as a pavement or the gutter. Smoking in designated non-smoking areas is also a major issue; mainland tourists light up with impunity, ignore all references to signage, and loudly insult and abuse anyone who attempts to remonstrate with them.

For just how much longer the mainlander influx will continue to set Hong Kong's tills ringing is anyone's guess. Anecdotal evidence – brushed aside by Hong Kong's tourism authorities – indicates that visitor numbers are not what they once were, especially when compared with visits to Macau. High prices for food and accommodation, generally poor value and service, notoriously mercenary Hong Kong tour guides and very little Mandarin being spoken are frequently voiced complaints that have been widely reported in China in recent years.

Another issue is that, while most Hong Kong Chinese are only too happy to take the mainland tourists' money, they regard their northern cousins as gross-mannered bumpkins – and tend not to conceal their views. Factor in that sort of attitude and the boom in mainland tourists – Hong Kong's perceived cash cow for years to come – may not last as long as many wish to think.

Modern Architecture

Upward and onward.

As Hong Kong's population exploded and useable land diminished from the mid 20th century onwards, almost no care at all was given to the preservation of historic buildings – thus the majority of the territory's most impressive structures have been built in the past few decades. And while it is still the case that the tightly packed towers of Hong Kong Island make for the most striking architectural spectacle in the city, this could change in the coming decades. The closure of the old Kai Tak airport led to the lifting of height restrictions in Kowloon in 1998 and already a number of new skyscrapers have appeared, and construction cranes continue to swing between the gaps. These new edifices are likely to obliterate the view of the hills beyond – after which Kowloon is named – in a way similar to how Victoria

Peak is slowly disappearing behind glass, steel and concrete on Hong Kong Island. But the array of gleaming towers on both sides of the harbour could make for one of the world's most impressive ensembles of modern high-rise architecture – if handled sensitively.

HONG KONG ISLAND

Arguably Hong Kong's best-known modern architectural symbol is IM Pei's asymmetrical **Bank of China Tower** (*see p76*; **photo** *p36 far left*), built on the original site of Murray House, a 19th-century British Officers' mess (which was subsequently re-erected out at Stanley; *see p93*). The Bank of China Tower attracted heated controversy almost from the moment that its design was first made public, and this continued for years after its completion

Poles apart

One of the few sights in Hong Kong that has barely changed in recent decades is bamboo scaffolding, seen all over building sites. Towering skyscrapers clad in bamboo frameworks are one of those emblematic sights that immediately grab visitors' attention, but are so commonplace that local residents often fail to notice.

Flimsy though it looks, once the bamboo framework reaches above a few storeys it becomes immensely strong. Indeed, each 'square' of bamboo – typically a little over a metre in diameter – can support up to a thousand pounds without buckling or breaking. What's even more amazing is that no nails, staples or screws are used in the construction; the bamboo is held together by thousands of thin plastic strips. Workers shinny upwards along the poles lashing it all together.

High-quality bamboo is expensive and, unlike rainforest timber used elsewhere in the local building industry (and invariably thrown away), bamboo is continuously recycled. Its use in construction in China dates back hundreds of years, and it is still preferred to steel because of its excellent tensile qualities and resistance to wind – an important consideration on high-rise buildings.

Erecting bamboo scaffolding is a highly skilled occupation, but these days it's a trade that few young men wish to enter. The work is arduous, and hours and wages are erratic. It's also dangerous. Very few workers use protective equipment, partly because the macho image of the trade discourages

it, and partly because of perennially slack Hong Kong legislation. As a result, many bamboo scaffolding workers are injured – and several killed – every year.

in 1990. In feng shui-obsessed, rumour-crazy Hong Kong, the 70-storey building's sharp angles were immediately said – and therefore popularly believed – to be a symbolic mainland dagger aimed at the heart of Hong Kong, its negative vibes radiating towards Government House to foil and distort any administrative decisions made there. Then there were the two white antennae on top of the building – they were deemed inauspicious as, according to Chinese custom, two sticks of incense are burned only for the dead. Artificial ponds and waterfalls inside the building help soften the stark exterior effect and – apparently – help mitigate some of the worst feng shui effects. But whatever your cosmic feelings about the tower, it remains one of the city's most striking modern buildings.

A favourite with many an architect in town, and predating the Bank of China Tower by four years, is the **Hongkong & Shanghai Banking Corporation Headquarters** (also known as the HSBC Building; *see p76*), completed in 1985. The third HSBC incarnation to occupy the site, Lord Foster's Meccano-like, steel-and-glass masterpiece immediately became a recognisable symbol of the Central business district, and it features prominently on most of the territory's banknotes. This building replaced Hong Kong's first true skyscraper – a graceful granite building that opened in 1935, which had centralised air-conditioning, lifts and – best of all in the memories of many – magnificent mosaic ceilings. All that remains of that earlier incarnation are the two large bronze lions at the base of the present one; the lion on the Chater Garden side still bears the scars of Pacific War shrapnel on its flanks. The ground floor of 'The Bank' – as it is popularly, even somewhat reverentially, known in Hong Kong – is a completely open space, and is actually a thronging pedestrian thoroughfare during the week. It's also a popular gathering spot for legions of off-duty Filipina maids on weekends and public holidays.

A short distance away from HSBC, across Statue Square, is the **Hong Kong Club**, which first opened in 1985. This tower block replaced a beautiful Italianate structure dating from 1897, which was demolished in 1980. This building was the subject of a bitterly fought heritage conservation battle in the late 1970s, but like most such campaigns in those years – and likely those in years to come – it failed, mainly due to the confluence of powerful vested interests and general public apathy. The new structure is graceful and stylish (the club section is closed to the public), and you can't help but wonder how much of a landmark the original building would have been now, marooned among the packed expressways and soaring office towers.

> **'Jardine House has one of the most enduring of sobriquets – "The House of a Thousand Arseholes".'**

Situated opposite the General Post Office is **Jardine House** (see p75), Hong Kong's oldest modern office tower, built in 1973. The sleek aluminium-clad structure rises more than 50 storeys above Hong Kong Island's newest section of reclaimed waterfront (where the Star Ferry Terminal stood until 2006; see also p103 **Walking on water**). Now surrounded – dwarfed, in fact – by numerous other buildings like it, Jardine House was the first of its kind in Hong Kong and remains a popular local landmark. Nevertheless, with hundreds of porthole-shaped windows, the building has attracted one of the rudest and most enduring of Hong Kong sobriquets – 'The House of a Thousand Arseholes', directed at both the building and the type of person believed to work within it.

Out on the waterfront reclamation, rising above the Hong Kong terminus of the Airport Express, is **Two International Finance Centre** (officially called Two ifc but commonly referred to as IFC2 or 2IFC; see p74; **photo p37** far right). While architecturally stunning, this 88-storey tower (completed in 2003) was, like many buildings in Hong Kong, built without any reference to the surrounding landscape. Seen from the Tsim Sha Tsui waterfront promenade, the IFC2 tower completely obscures the view of soaring Victoria Peak behind it, and offers no public viewing area as compensation.

Known irreverently to some as the 'disco building' because of its luridly coloured, constantly changing evening illumination, **The Center** (99 Queen's Road, Central; built 1998) is one of Hong Kong's most emblematic buildings, immediately visible from all directions; you might even see it flashing at you when you fly into the city. Glassy, gleaming, 73 storeys high, but nevertheless unattractively hemmed in by many other grubby old office buildings, the Center is one of the five tallest structures in Hong Kong – at least for now. A series of horizontal light bars are built into the structure, undetectable during daylight hours and unobtrusive to those inside. These produce 175 different colour sequences and patterns in shades ranging from electric blue and lime green to flame red and bright purple. While many people love it, and it's certainly eye-catching, the Center is, in some respects, an unintended architectural metaphor for urban Hong Kong: stunning and hypnotic at a distance, but gradually less than amazing (and frankly, somewhat tacky and OTT) the closer you get to it.

One of Hong Kong's best-known and most striking buildings is the **Peak Tower** (built by British architect Terry Farrell in 1996; see p89), at the upper terminus of the Peak Tram, and visible for miles around. To some people it's a bird with outstretched wings, to others it's a pair of open hands, and to others still it's a gigantic wok straddled across Victoria Gap. However you choose to look at it, the tower is unmistakable and a year-long renovation, completed in November 2006, has converted its rooftop into a viewing platform. The cable-operated funicular Peak Tram has connected Hong Kong Island's relatively uncrowded hilltop district with the teeming city since 1888. While for many years nothing more remarkable than a station platform and sedan-chair depot stood here, progressively larger and more expansive terminal buildings – incorporating cafés, souvenir shops and look-out points – were built, culminating in this latest one, which opened in 1995. The Peak complex neatly illustrates the split personality of the Peak itself: part exclusive residential area, part tacky tourist trap. But with stunning views in every direction on an ever rarer clear day, it has to be seen – indeed, experienced – at least once.

Amid the city's air-conditioned steel-and-glass boxes, the notion of sustainable development is reflected in the **Kadoorie Biological Sciences**

Building (Pok Fu Lam Road; built 2000) at the University of Hong Kong in the New Territories, which has won numerous awards for its energy-efficient design. Parabolic aluminium shades shield the building from the sun and enhance its 'green' design and energy efficiency. It's well worth making a trip to this somewhat out-of-the-way location to see it.

Built on a small man-made island of reclaimed land off the Wan Chai foreshore, and to some people vaguely reminiscent of Sydney's Opera House, the **Hong Kong Convention & Exhibition Centre** (*see p83*) was begun in 1994 and completed just in time for the 1997 Handover ceremonies to be held inside. Depending on your point of view, the building looks like automotive airfoils, the wings of a bird, lotus petals or a series of semi-open clam shells. A massive, gold-leafed, stylised bauhinia flower on a pedestal situated on the waterfront provides a focal point for package-tour groups from the mainland. Few locals bother.

Nothing written about modern architecture in Hong Kong can possibly exclude or ignore the massive, government-planned, hideous-beyond-all-imagination **Hong Kong Central Library** (Moreton Terrace, Causeway Bay). With an exterior caked in pale, honey-coloured stone cladding and almost-hilarious Greco-Roman pretensions – including a Parthenon-style pediment – the building was designed by a committee of the now-defunct Urban Council, and the bureaucratic approach certainly shows.

Step inside and the lashings of blond wood fittings and escalators to everywhere bring to mind a four-star(ish) hotel anywhere on the mainland, rather than emulating the sober dignity of a world-class library. That said, research facilities within the Central Library are excellent and stand up to comparisons with the best in the world, but no one – except its designers – has found a good word to say for the structure itself. It must be seen to be believed.

Potentially one of Hong Kong's architectural success stories, but in reality probably its most resounding failure, is the Hong Kong Jockey Club-funded **Hong Kong Stadium** (55 Eastern Hospital Road, Causeway Bay). Unveiled in 1994, the enormous scalloped structure quickly became enmeshed in controversy. Situated in a bowl-like valley surrounded by housing blocks, the stadium works like an enormous loudspeaker, amplifying the volume of what is taking place there to excruciating levels. In consequence it can only really be used for sporting activities, and is best appreciated during the annual Hong Kong Sevens, the internationally famed rugby event. (It remains a mystery why they haven't enclosed the roof to allow the city a more useful downtown venue.)

Love it or hate it, one thing that's immediately visible from the bend in Repulse Bay Road as you travel along Hong Kong Island's southern coast is the sinuously curving pastel-blue tower between the mountains and the beach. **The Repulse Bay** apartment

The **Bank of China Tower** (*see p33*) and **Two International Finance Centre** (*see p35*) bracket the Central skyline.

building (109 Repulse Bay Road) was built to replace the venerable Repulse Bay Hotel, dating from 1920, which was demolished despite strenuous public opposition in 1982. A new version of its famed sea-view veranda restaurant (*see p146*), using many of the original fittings, was incorporated in the structure. This has proved very successful with a new generation who are charmed by its 'historic' ambience, but many of them are completely unaware that the building they are admiring is a very well-made fake. A large space was left vacant in the new apartment building, which frames the rocky green mountainside behind, rather like a picture window. But, this being Hong Kong, a popular urban legend quickly grew up concerning the alleged feng shui of the building, which had it that the hole was left there so the dragon who lived on the hillside could get down to the sea to bathe. A delightful tale to be sure, and the tourists love it, but the reality behind the decision was much more prosaic: the owner once saw something similar in Florida, and wanted to incorporate the feature back home in Hong Kong.

KOWLOON AND BEYOND

Over on the Kowloon side, one of the rare examples of a magnificent old building with a sympathetic new addition, the tower extension of the **Peninsula** hotel (*see p62*), has been consistently praised since it was unveiled in 1994. The Peninsula proves that a modern

addition can actually enhance and improve the original, which retains all the gracious features that have made it such a favourite for both overseas visitors and local residents for the past eight decades. Die-hard avant-garde design fiends go into raptures over the Philippe Starck-designed restaurant Felix (and its dramatically lit private lift access), with the harbour and city spread out below it.

Around the corner on Peking Road, **One Peking**, looking something like a slender curving yacht sail, brings unusual softness to the local skyscraper collective. Its triple-glazed façade incorporates aluminum sunshades and motorised blinds that use computerised sensors to adjust them to the position of the sun. On the top floors are bars and restaurants – Aqua and Hutong (*see p147 and p149*) – which have superb Hong Kong Island views.

'It was the most extensive single civil engineering project ever undertaken in history.'

The massive **Hong Kong International Airport** (*see p294*) at Chek Lap Kok on Lantau, with associated highway, railway and bridging works, was the most extensive single civil engineering project ever undertaken in history; now *that* really is a rare superlative. Designed by Lord Foster, who was also responsible for the HSBC building in Central (*see p34*), the terminal's immense curves of glass and canvas-like material give you the impression that you're in the clouds when you're still on the ground.

Even on the journey to and from the airport there's more to see – three soaring bridges link Lantau and the international airport with the rest of the urban area: the massive **Tsing Ma Suspension Bridge** (built 1997), which connects the islands of Tsing Yi and Ma Wan, is vaguely reminiscent of San Francisco's Golden Gate Bridge; the smaller **Kap Shui Mun Bridge** (1997), which joins up Ma Wan and Lantau; and the **Ting Kau Bridge** (1998), linking Tsing Yi and the mainland New Territories. All are spectacularly illuminated at night.

For those who want to explore further other iconic modern buildings in Hong Kong – as well as a few incongruous survivors from earlier times – *Skylines Hong Kong* by Peter Moss (FormAsia, 2000) is a great read. For an overview with a more modern focus, check out *Hong Kong Architecture and Design* by Anna Koor (Te Neues, 2006).

Paper money to be burnt as an offering.

Culture & Customs

Old traditions suffuse every aspect of life in Hong Kong, from business to pleasure, and from spiritual to physical well-being.

The image that Hong Kong tends to project to the world is one of a place where East meets West, in both appearance and mindset – after all, it was governed by Britain for a century and a half. This perception, however, is way off the mark: despite an abundance of Western architecture and a love of European and US fashion labels, the territory's psyche is firmly rooted in Chinese tradition.

AN ETHNIC MIX

Hong Kong is usually regarded as being a multi-cultural, cosmopolitan city, yet 96 per cent of its population is Chinese. Most of this comprises **Punti**, or **Cantonese**, who built their power base through land ownership. In the 19th century, for example, the five great

Cantonese clans (Tang, Hau, Pang, Liu and Man) had their own areas over which they ruled. However, there are still pockets of three other Chinese races – **Hakkas**, **Hoklos** and **Tankas**. The Hakkas are the largest of these minority groups, living together in villages throughout the New Territories.

The very first inhabitants of the region, however, were **Yao** and **Maio** peoples (racially similar to Taiwan's aboriginals and Filipinos); although clusters still survive in Guangdong (Canton) and Guangxi provinces, no trace of them remains in Hong Kong.

These days there is an even greater mix, with immigrants, both legal and illegal, having flooded into the territory from mainland China

– many as political and economic refugees after 1949, when the country became communist, and intellectuals and the wealthy felt threatened. More recently Hong Kong has seen waves of economic chancers, who believe that its streets are paved with golden job opportunities (which was all but true until 1997). Most of them come from neighbouring provinces like Guangdong, Fujian and Shanghai.

The remaining four per cent of the population is composed of non-Chinese, who – despite their small numbers – form highly visible groups as they tend to work and hang out in central areas. Despite Hong Kong's former British colonial status, not many **British** citizens remain – of some 30,000 Brits registered living here, many are Chinese with UK passports. Prior to 1997 British citizens did not need a work visa to get a job in the territory, so many young Brit backpackers would stop off in Hong Kong for a few months and earn some quick cash working in a bar, before continuing the trail around Asia or on to Australia. **Americans** have had a strong presence for several decades, mainly thanks to the large number of businesses with regional head offices in Hong Kong. In fact, American residents outnumber Brits by more than three to one. There's also a smaller mix of other Europeans, including French and Italians. White foreigners are dubbed '*gweilo*' (meaning 'ghost men' or, sometimes, 'devil men') or '*gweipor*' ('ghost women') by the Cantonese, a term that some Caucasians find offensive – but most *gweilo* old hands happily accept the tag and even use it themselves.

Over the last couple of decades the largest immigrant group in Hong Kong has been from the Philippines. There are currently over 120,000 **Filipinas** (they're nearly all female) based here working as maids (or *amahs*) for Chinese or Western employers. Indonesia and Thailand also provide thousands more domestic helpers. They are poorly paid as it is (earning an average of HK$3,670 per month), and often work 14 hours a day, but the situation recently became worse when a ten per cent income tax was introduced (the maids were previously exempt from this). Some people claim this is an attempt by the government to deter them from coming to work here and a ploy to make such work more appealing to locals during the current period of high unemployment. Maids' pay has always been more than they could earn in their native countries (and this will no doubt continue to be the case, despite the new levy), but in Hong Kong they must also deal with the fact that they are generally relegated to second-class status. Still, every Sunday and on public holidays, thousands of *amahs* gather in the

squares and streets of Central to sit on the pavement, eat, chat, sing, worship and relax.

There is a small, but important, **Indian** population – which includes some of Hong Kong's wealthiest families – as well as a number of **Nepalese**, most of whom are the children of Gurkhas who served in the British army. More than 15,000 **Vietnamese** refugees also call Hong Kong home. They are part of the 225,000-plus 'boat people' who escaped their war-torn country in the late 1970s. While 67,000 were repatriated and 143,000 resettled overseas, the remainder have been allowed to stay in Hong Kong. The majority survive on casual manual jobs.

RELIGIOUS BELIEFS

While it may appear that the Hong Kong dollar is the object of worship for most residents, religion does plays an important role in many people's lives. Most of Hong Kong's population is either Buddhist or Taoist, but there are also about half-a-million Christians, up to 100,000 Muslims and a smattering of Hindus, Sikhs and Jews. Religion is evident throughout the city, from ornate monasteries, temples and cathedrals to tiny shrines outside residents' homes and even inside staff quarters of nightclubs. Indeed, unlike the mainland, the territory enjoys total freedom of religious practice. There are some fears, though, that intimidation from Beijing may interfere with this in future, particularly in light of the crackdown on the Falun Gong, a quasi-religious group.

> **'Tin Hau, the protector of seafarers, was honoured with temples that, due to land reclamation, now lie mostly inland.'**

The earliest religious beliefs are tied to the region's first needs – those of the fishing community. The protector of seafarers, **Tin Hau**, was honoured with temples that used to overlook the South China Sea but, due to land reclamation, they now lie mostly inland. The 40 or more Tin Hau temples here overflow when the **Birthday of Tin Hau** (*see p203*) is celebrated in spring. Like many local deities, Tin Hau is of Taoist origin. But as the faiths of Taoism and Buddhism frequently blur into one integrated belief system, both tend to be honoured in the same temple.

Taoism, based on the writings of Lao Tse, aims to put mankind in context with nature. Its esoteric philosophies are in perpetual debate and defy simple explanations: the word Tao itself is usually translated as 'the way'. The most widely recognised Taoist symbol in the world is the yin-yang pictogram, in which all existence struggles infinitely to find harmony.

Buddhism, originally from India, is based on principles of dharma; these spiritual and moral codes are strictly adhered to within Hong Kong's monk and nun communities, which are found in monasteries in the New Territories and on Lantau (the Po Lin Monastery being the best known; see p125). Buddha's birthday is celebrated on the eighth day of the fourth moon (he is currently believed to be more than 2,500 years old, though figures vary) – and is a public holiday in Hong Kong.

Taoist deities **Wong Tai Sin** (see p104) and **Che Kung** (see p107), found in temples named after them, are approached for general matters of health, while **Kam Fa** – a saint from Guangdong – is said to protect pregnant women. Two of Hong Kong's most popular deities are polar opposites: Buddhist **Kwun Yum**, goddess of mercy, and Taoist **Kwan Kung**, god of war. The former is regarded as a compassionate protector of all, while the fearsome-looking latter is the god of choice for both police officers and triads. Porcelain representations of the two deities adorn many homes, often on altars.

The average Hong Konger goes to Taoist or Buddhist temples to appease the deities and, usually, to ask for compassion or good fortune. Gifts of food (in particular fruit) are presented, and incense and paper offerings are burned in respect. Donations are given for the upkeep of the temple. Unlike many other religions, individuals visit temples independently, rather than attend services held by priests; the exception to this rule is when special ceremonies, such as weddings and funerals,

The animal in you

Before the Brits arrived, Hong Kong, like the rest of China, relied on the Chinese lunar calendar, the longest chronological record in history, dating from 2637 BC. An entire cycle takes 60 years to complete and is made up of five mini cycles of 12 years. We are currently in the 78th cycle, which began in February 1984 and ends in February 2044. From this calendar came the Chinese zodiac, represented by an animal for each lunar year, with 12 in total.

According to legend, it all started when the Buddha summoned all the animals in the world to him to say goodbye before he departed from earth. As only 12 animals appeared to bid him farewell, he named a year after each one in the order that they came to see him. The first one to arrive was the rat (or mouse), then the ox, tiger, rabbit, dragon, snake, horse, sheep (or ram), monkey, rooster (or chicken), dog and boar (or pig). Thus the 12 signs that are still recognised today came into being.

Today the belief in the Chinese zodiac remains strong in Hong Kong. In general, Hong Kongers pay much more attention to their Chinese zodiac sign and associated astrological readings than their Western ones. The animal ruling the year in which you were born is said to have a profound influence on your life and your character; in the lunar year straddling 2000-2001, pregnancies increased because parents wanted their children to be born in the Year of the Dragon, which is believed to be the most powerful of all animals.

During the complete 60-year cycle, each of the animal signs (sometimes also referred to as the 12 earth branches) is combined with the five elements of wood, fire, earth, metal and water. The element of your lunar sign will also exercise its influence on your life. No element is called the strongest or weakest – they are dependent on one another.

The lunar year is divided into 12 months of 29 days. Every two-and-a-half years an intercalary month is added to adjust the calendar. The addition of this month every third year produces the lunar leap year. For easy reference, the beginning of each lunar month is the date of the new moon marked on the Western calendar.

The importance of the lunar calendar remains significant in Hong Kong to this day, and particular care is taken to ensure certain events such as marriages, business openings and ancestral worship take place on the most auspicious days.

The following are some of the characteristics associated with each animal and year. Funnily enough, many seem to echo the nature of the beast in question, so whether or not you believe them is another matter. Note that if you were born before the Chinese New Year (late January/early February) you take the animal from the previous year.

take place. Temples often have one or more fortune-tellers in residence who, for a fee, will interpret a visitor's palm, face, foot or the symbol written on a *chim* (bamboo stick), which is selected by gently shaking a bamboo beaker full of *chim* in front of a temple altar until one rises up above the rest of the pack.

Besides idols, domestic altars often carry a memorial plaque to departed relatives, which is regarded as one way of maintaining a spiritual link between ancestors and the living; some families who own space in rural parts of the territory also have ancestral temples in memory of several generations. During the **Ching Ming** and **Chung Yuen** festivals, families flock to these temples (or, alternatively, to cemeteries and crematoria) to clean the memorials of their loved ones and present offerings that are to be enjoyed symbolically in the afterlife. Popular paper offerings to be burned these days include

meticulously crafted mobile phones, home entertainment systems and cars, which join the old staples of money, silver and gold ingots, and smart clothes. Somewhat creepily, even papier-mâché models of favoured domestic helpers are known to be burned.

Western missionaries did an efficient job of promoting **Christianity** from the 19th century onwards. There is a pretty even split between Catholic and Anglican (as well as Protestant) congregations, with the highest proliferation of churches being in Kowloon Tong, Tsim Sha Tsui (look out for the Rosary Church on Chatham Road South) and the Anglican St John's Cathedral in Central (*see p77*).

The **Muslim** community is 50 per cent Chinese, while faiths with smaller numbers have predominantly non-Chinese congregations. The mosque on Shelley Street, Mid-Levels, is older and more charming than the main one

Rat (or mouse)
Characteristics: Dynamic, protective, open-minded, thrifty and compassionate.
Years: 1924, 1936, 1948, 1960, 1972, 1984, 1996, 2008.

Ox
Characteristics: Patient, self-reliant, industrious and sure of foot.
Years: 1925, 1937, 1949, 1961, 1973, 1985, 1997, 2009.

Tiger
Characteristics: Honourable, hard-working and warm-hearted.
Years: 1926, 1938, 1950, 1962, 1974, 1986, 1998, 2010.

Rabbit
Characteristics: Popular, artistic, stylish, romantic and calm.
Years: 1927, 1939, 1951, 1963, 1975, 1987, 1999, 2011.

Dragon
Characteristics: Charismatic, principled, discriminating and self-sufficient.
Years: 1928, 1940, 1952, 1964, 1976, 1988, 2000, 2012.

Snake
Characteristics: Amusing, discreet, intuitive and philosophical.
Years: 1929, 1941, 1953, 1965, 1977, 1989, 2001, 2013.

Horse
Characteristics: Warm-hearted, strong-minded and sociable yet independent.
Years: 1930, 1942, 1954, 1966, 1978, 1990, 2002, 2014.

Sheep (or ram)
Characteristics: Intuitive, creative, generous, modest and sensitive.
Years: 1931, 1943, 1955, 1967, 1979, 1991, 2003, 2015.

Monkey
Characteristics: Faithful, loving, intelligent, entertaining and candid.
Years: 1932, 1944, 1956, 1968, 1980, 1992, 2004, 2016.

Rooster (or chicken)
Characteristics: Brave, loyal, hard-working, communicative and witty.
Years: 1933, 1945, 1957, 1969, 1981, 1993, 2005, 2017.

Dog
Characteristics: Sincere, loyal, affectionate, fair-minded and helpful.
Years: 1934, 1946, 1958, 1970, 1982, 1994, 2006, 2018.

Boar (or pig)
Characteristics: Sensible, sensual, frank, charitable and amusing.
Years: 1935, 1947, 1959, 1971, 1983, 1995, 2007, 2019.

Paying respects at the **Wong Tai Sin Temple**. *See p40.*

next to Kowloon Park; not far away from it is the Ohel Leah Synagogue, in the shadow of the Jewish Community Centre, which also has old-world appeal. An impressive **Hindu** temple in Happy Valley caters to a mostly Indian congregation. Smaller places of worship for Methodists, Mormons, Quakers, Scientologists and Sikhs are scattered around the territory.

SAVING FACE

You've just enjoyed a feast in a restaurant with your local host and the time has come to pay. Your host reaches for his credit card. 'No,' you say, 'I'll pay.' A 'No, I'll get it' to-and-froing then ensues. To end the discussion, you grab the bill and take it to the cashier's desk, where you pay, believing your generosity will be appreciated. Wrong. You've just committed a serious faux pas. Your host has lost 'face' and that's just about the cardinal sin in Hong Kong. If you were hoping to close a business deal, you can forget it.

Face is a peculiar Chinese value and its importance in Hong Kong can never be underestimated. It can lead to arguments, broken friendships and even fights, so a little care is needed to avoid stepping on people's toes. The concept is like pride in other countries (and everyone has that to a degree), but in Hong

Kong face is accorded the utmost seriousness and people are judged by it. Some folk go to great lengths to acquire it by displays of wealth or generosity. It confirms social status. The big shot in the restaurant wearing the chunky Rolex and handing around expensive brandy may look and talk like a billionaire, but he could be a small-time entrepreneur blowing more money than he can really afford just to gain face in front of potential clients.

But issues of face are not always so obvious. Subtlety and sensitivity are needed, since the concept of giving face is easier to explain than the potential for losing it. Complimenting someone on their clothes, hairstyle and business acumen – especially in front of their pals or colleagues – is a sure-fire winner. Confrontation and criticism are guaranteed face-destroyers. In general, in both China and Hong Kong, Western-style bluntness is not appreciated or expected: a polite and gentle approach is more likely to endear guests to their hosts. That might seem at odds with Hong Kong's very visible boldness and brashness, but behind closed doors, or with friends and acquaintances, manners matter. Common sense, as ever, goes a long way in dealing with the issue. When in doubt, lavish those compliments.

FENG SHUI

This ancient Chinese belief may be seen in the West as little more than a trendy, almost past-it fad, but here it's serious business. Although Hong Kong is a commercial, modern city, it still pays great heed to this time-honoured art. Feng shui is more than another quirk of a superstitious culture – many of its principal tenets are the basics of good and effective design. The main aim – of aligning oneself and one's home or workplace within an environment – has been followed by successive generations of Chinese in Hong Kong. There is a general belief that businesses and personal health will flourish if this age-old practice is employed under the direction of an experienced master. Even the biggest multinationals follow it when laying out an office or constructing a building, partly out of deference to their staff and partly out of honouring Chinese custom.

The term feng shui is Mandarin (it is known as *fung shui* in Cantonese) for 'wind water', but this philosophy of how to live in harmony with nature taps into more than just these two elements. Experts in the field claim that the interplay of wood, fire, earth and even gold also have to be taken into account and balanced to obtain the optimum result, which is harmony in all areas of one's life. Believers are convinced good fortune is not determined by chance, but by correct feng shui.

> **'Villagers' feng shui issues often seem to disappear when compensation terms are raised.'**

The basic tools of the feng shui practitioner's trade are a multi-ringed compass, astronomical charts and ancient texts on the processes of divination. The master will note the natural and man-made features in the building's environs, and will then decide the direction certain rooms and furniture should face, and the items that should be introduced to enhance positivity. These will usually be mirrors, engraved coins and bamboo flutes, hung on walls, from beams or in the corner of rooms. Water features such as small babbling electric mini fountains or fish aquariums are also often used. Even the number and colour of fish has to be right – if they die over time, this is said to be a sign that they have absorbed bad luck that would otherwise have wreaked havoc on human occupants. Dead fish therefore need to be replaced, to maintain the fortuitous number in the tank.

Typically, feng shui has been more strongly adhered to in Hong Kong's rural areas. When tunnelling for the Kowloon–Canton Railway began early last century, for example, no Chinese labourers could be persuaded to work on the project for fear of disturbing the earth spirits. Even in 2001 the Kowloon-Canton Railway Corporation (KCRC) called in a feng shui expert for input in a feasibility study for a proposed new rail link in the New Territories. (Strangely enough, villagers' feng shui problems often seem to disappear when compensation terms are raised.)

Some buildings, although built in accordance with a geomancer's instructions, are believed to give off bad feng shui. The angular **Bank of China Tower** (*see p33* and *p76*), for instance, with its prominent criss-cross cladding, is said to shoot out poison arrows from the apex of these exterior panels, some say targeting the former Government House (which was one of the reasons why Chief Executive Tung Chee-hwa declined to live there). A weeping willow is said to have been planted in the grounds of Government House to deflect the negative influence. Other buildings include a large hole in their structure or are built on stilts, in order to prevent energy flows being blocked.

Like partially blocked Chinese temple doorways, which are believed to bar the entry of bad spirits, it is quite common for building entrances to be constructed at an angle – the Mandarin Oriental hotel on Hong Kong Island has one of many angled entrances around town. Some home-owners opt for a staggered entrance into their flat for the same reason.

With space at such a premium in Hong Kong, these days murals are sometimes used as a substitute for natural environments. They will often feature components such as rivers and waterfalls emptying into a lake, surrounded by ripe rice fields and fruit-bearing trees, against a backdrop of hills populated by birds and butterflies. These elements read logically: water stands for money and the full lake ensures it stays plentiful; the rice and fruit symbolise full dinner tables; the hills offer protection; and the fauna represents harmony.

Whether or not feng shui actually works is a matter for debate. But enough people opt for it to make it a real business, as well as a preoccupation for many. And scoff if you like, but who wouldn't want to live in a home next to a waterfall, a lake and green fields?

THE BIG FESTIVALS

There are five major Chinese festivals that are celebrated in the calendar – the **Lunar New Year**, the **Dragon Boat Festival**, the **Hungry Ghost Festival**, the **Mid Autumn Festival** and **Ching Ming**. For these and more, *see pp202-206*. Most are used as time off work, rather than for lengthy religious ceremony; as with Christmas in the West, these festivals provide families with an opportunity to come together to eat well and exchange gifts. Christian festivals such as Easter and Christmas are still acknowledged public holidays, even in these post-colonial times.

TRADITIONAL ARTS

Although Hong Kong is one of the most modern cities in the world, it is still possible to see traditional Chinese arts here. You'll find ancient tea paraphernalia at the **Flagstaff House Museum of Tea Ware** (see p78), calligraphy at the **Hong Kong Museum of Art** (see p98) and (basic) Chinese opera at **Temple Street Night Market** (see p190). But the local arts scene is also in touch with contemporary global trends, so don't be surprised if a West End theatre production is enjoying a run while you're here. For more on traditional music, opera and dance, see p246 **Chinese performing arts**.

LEISURE PURSUITS

Besides eating, Hong Kongers traditionally spend their leisure time playing games (from the computer to the finger-guessing variety), singing karaoke, gambling on horses, games or at the casinos in Macau, and keeping fit through martial arts and breathing exercises.

Wherever you are in Hong Kong, chances are you'll hear a furious clatter accompanied by lots of shouting and raucous behaviour emanating from flats and village homes, especially during holidays. The cause of this racket? **Mah-jong** – Hong Kong's favourite game. Tracing its origins as far back as 2350 BC, it is played with 144 tiles made up of three suits (bamboo, Chinese characters and circles), numbered from one to nine, of which there are four of each kind, meaning that there are 36 tiles per suit – and 108 suit tiles in total. The remaining 36 tiles are composed of three groups (flowers, winds and dragons), which have different functions depending on the house rules. It's as complex as bridge in terms of explaining the rules, but there are two certainties – the game will last a long time (with many rounds over several hours) and as much noise as possible will be made clattering the tiles on the table.

Chinese chess, or *xiangqi*, is more sedate. The game is one of the four Chinese arts along with *qin* (music), *hua* (brush painting) and *shu* (calligraphy). It involves two players, each of whom is assigned 16 pieces: one king, two chariots, two horses, two elephants, two guards, two cannons and five soldiers. The object, as in Western chess, is to capture the king. Games can be seen being played by elderly men in public areas across Hong Kong – usually surrounded by crowds placing bets.

More active is the martial art of **t'ai chi**. As dawn breaks, people (mostly elderly) head for the city's hills, parks and beaches to bend, stretch and meditate in silence. It's an amazing sight. Because t'ai chi emphasises correct form and feeling in each movement – to improve the flow of internal energy within the body – it is undertaken in a very slow and gentle manner.

> ## 'As dawn breaks, people head for the city's hills, parks and beaches to bend, stretch and meditate.'

People who practise it regularly claim it promotes strength, stamina and flexibility, cultivating the link between mind and body, and enhancing balance and co-ordination. If you would like to give it a go, the Hong Kong Tourism Board conducts free t'ai chi classes for tourists (see p253).

ANCIENT REMEDIES

Every district you visit in Hong Kong has old-fashioned shops dispensing Chinese remedies and herbal treatments from shelves stacked with oversized jars and medicine chests with tiny drawers. The largest concentration of these shops is in **Sheung Wan**, where you can see all manner of powders, pills, plants and animal parts, each of which is purported to play a distinctive role in the health of human beings.

Non-Chinese may scoff at their healing powers, and animal rights activists regularly protest at the use of bear gall-bladders, tiger penises and sea horses to boost such functions as sexual virility and hair growth, but there's more to Chinese medicine than age-old myths. An extremely high percentage of Hong Kong people turn to Chinese medics before, or along with, Western doctors when illness strikes.

The origin of Chinese medicine dates back some 5,000 years to the genesis of Chinese civilisation, but the first recorded case of diagnosing and treating disease can be traced back to about 1500 BC. The concept is holistic – both in treating and preventing illness – and is as relevant today as it ever was. As well as being credited with remedying ailments and altering states of mind, Chinese medicine is also said to enhance recuperative power and immunity, as well as the capacity for pleasure, work and creativity.

The herbal medicine practice is linked to Chinese cosmology, in the belief that creation is born from the marriage of two polar principles, yin and yang: earth and heaven, winter and

Moniker mayhem

Fruit Chan, Fanny Sit, Bentley Wong: these are all names of real people in Hong Kong. Surely this can't be true, you might think. Well, it is true in the sense that this is how they introduce themselves to others, print their names on their business cards and are known by their friends and family.

Initially, most ethnic Chinese Hong Kongers are given a double-barrelled Cantonese first name, which follows the family name. Usually these names are chosen for their positive connotations, and modesty dictates that the meaning is not over-done. So the word *siu* ('small') is often used. For example, Bruce Lee's Cantonese first name is Siu-long, which translates as 'small dragon', and thus his full Chinese name would be written as Lee Siu-long.

At primary school, if not at kindergarten, Hong Kong kids pick their own first name, though some wait till they are older – and this is when their imagination can run riot. Lee, however, chose the non-silly name of Bruce, so on official documents he likely would have been identified as Bruce Lee Siu-long. But when signing off or introducing themselves in the English language, ethnic Chinese Hong Kongers are more likely to use their chosen English name followed only by their family name – hence the Bruce Lee that Western audiences are familiar with.

Hong Kongers who are now in their late 40s or above generally chose something easy to pronounce and remember – often a name of few letters and only one or two syllables. It's for this reason that there are so many old-fashioned names about that might remind Westerners of an elderly relative – you are likely to meet several Adas, Evas, Alexes and Rickys in Hong Kong, as well as a few, more ambitiously named Adriennes and Anitas (guys don't generally go for three syllables).

Girls often have a penchant for what they consider cute-sounding; so try not to laugh when you're introduced to a Pinky or a Winky.

Boys, meanwhile, are most likely to pick a celeb they admire for their chosen English name: Bowie, Elton and Sting are all out there, prefixing Chinese surnames. Less explainable, perhaps, are the few business-suited types that now have to somehow live with either Adolf or Hitler.

The more recent generation of children and young adults has tended to select not only names that are related to people that they admire but also those of people or things they think project something about themselves (or who they aspire to be). Many a twenty-something female introduces herself by her designer-label-inspired self-selected moniker; there are a number of Chanels and Guccis walking about the city. The sickly-sweet mouthless Japanese cat Hello Kitty has inspired a legion of teenage Kittys and at least one young student uses the full two words for her first name. More bizarrely, a sister and brother at one primary school chose Dinosaur and Caveman as their names. And though there was at least one Walkman in Hong Kong in the 1990s, we're still waiting to hear of an iPod or MP3 from the current generation.

Some chosen English names simply do not sit well with Chinese surnames in the eye of the native English-speaker. School teacher Fanny Pong is one such memorable example. Even unluckier was (unrelated) Ivan Pong, a local pastor. When he emigrated to Britain, he got so much stick for the fact that his handle could be abbreviated to 'I Pong' that he soon felt compelled to change his name.

It's not only English-speakers who find some of these translations humorous: Cantonese speakers also have fun with the way English names sound in their native tongue. George is a homonym for 'stop me' (Georgio Armani sounds like 'stop your mother'); and Ada has a similar sound to 'I hit'. So it's chuckles all round then.

---

summer, night and day, cold and hot, wet and dry, inner and outer, body and mind. Harmony of this union means good health, good weather and good fortune, while disharmony leads to disease, disaster and bad luck.

The main strategy of Chinese medicine is to restore harmony. Each human is seen as a world in miniature, with a unique ecology to be maintained. Practitioners assess a person's

health by feeling the pulse and observing the colour and form of the face, tongue and body. This information is interpreted in the context of a patient's present and past complaints, working and living habits, environment, family health history and emotional life. Treatments include acupuncture, acupressure, exercise, massage and diet (tonic soups are drunk by everyone, as you'll notice as you explore the city).

Identity Crisis?

Life in Hong Kong a decade after the Handover.

'So, what's changed since the Handover?' Over the past decade this must be the single most-asked question put to any long-term Hong Kong resident. For the first few years after 1997 the best and most accurate answer was, 'Not a great deal.' But with the passage of the first decade under Chinese sovereignty, there have been numerous changes to Hong Kong society, some positive, many less so; indeed, a few have been quite negative.

Whisper it very softly, but one thing has not changed since 1997. Hong Kong is still ruled, to all practical purposes, as a colony – with China, of course, rather than Great Britain, as the sovereign power. All major external decisions, and the majority of top-level internal ones, are all made with reference to Beijing, just as in the past they were made after consultation with London. This is not to say that Hong Kong is in any way micro-managed from Beijing, any more than it was from London in colonial times; the central government has been remarkably – and at times admirably – hands-off in its handling of Hong Kong affairs. But make no mistake; Beijing is the real and final political reference point for any major political decision. And everyone in Hong Kong – from street hawkers to the chief executive – knows it.

Meaningful representative government – as distinct from the current toothless legislature – is still as far away as ever it was. The year 2012 is the most tentative of dates generally mentioned, and most local residents, with the exception of a number of die-hard political activists, have resigned themselves to this fact.

While the 'high degree of autonomy' promised by the Joint Declaration still holds firm, Hong Kong people still do not control their own political destiny to any significant extent. A great many of the city's problems, from rising pollution levels to the dysfunctional local education system, are at least partly connected to the lack of ultimate political accountability. No one in real power in Hong Kong is forced to resign by popular pressure, or as a last resort faces getting booted out of office at the next election. And so without this threat, officials need not pay too much attention to what the population really wants.

Part of the problem is the way government in Hong Kong is structured. The legislature – partly appointed, partly elected – now has financial power and is in effect the elected component, and at the same time the permanent opposition to the bureaucracy. Put that way, it should surprise no one that at a higher level the administration seems permanently on the defensive – even when policies are obviously good and effective ones.

Administrators, academics, business community figures and even some centrist politicians regularly state that Hong Kong's citizens are simply not yet ready for truly representative government, or even meaningful elections. And when one observes the generally appalling levels of civic consciousness in Hong Kong – the people's approach to littering and general public hygiene are the most obvious examples – it is hard not to concede the critics a few points in this direction. Hong Kong's vapid, celebrity-focused Chinese-language press gives an entire new dimension to 'gutter' reporting (London's tabloids are distinctly highbrow by comparison) and does nothing to encourage higher standards in public life.

> **'Democratic evolution in Hong Kong is completely dependent on how fast the Mainland wants to go.'**

A timeline for developing a form of government that approximates a democratic administration has been repeatedly called for; 2012 – the end of term for the next chief executive – is now seen by everyone in Hong Kong as the earliest possible date. Democratic evolution in the Special Administrative Region is, of course, completely dependent on how fast the Mainland wants to go; too quickly, and they risk offering a potentially challenging model to the rest of the country, but too slowly, and the people of Hong Kong become even more alienated. For now, that is by far the lesser of two evils. The major problem in contemporary Hong Kong is neither political nor economic – it is environmental.

DIRTY POLITICS
Pollution levels have become a critical threat to public health (*see also p30* **Smog gets in your eyes**), but as yet there is no concerted public voice calling for immediate remedial action. Every year Hong Kong's air quality visibly declines, and still, officially at least, this problem is downplayed, and unconvincingly denied. The current governmental response to pollution, in a way, resembles the response to official and police corruption in the 1960s; the problem then was of such seemingly insuperable magnitude that the best way to deal with it was largely to ignore and deny it, while catching a few 'small fish' to show that the government was at least trying to do something about the problem.

And so the pollution issue is handled in much the same way as corruption was in the 1960s; legislate a few mostly cosmetic changes, but refuse to tackle seriously the major polluters. Part of the problem is that the vested interests of the local power companies and road transport sectors in the local economy make them politically too powerful. As well,

these groups comprise major voting blocs on the Election Committee – read 'Selection' Committee – that 'elects' Hong Kong's chief executive.

'Discussion with decision – decision without action,' was former Chinese Premier Zhu Rongji's widely reported criticism of the Hong Kong government some years ago; the denunciation pithily, and sadly, summed up all that wasn't working with the Hong Kong administration, and the situation still remains the same. Since the beginnings of colonial rule, government policy has been to consult as widely as possible on any matters of potential controversy, and at the same time leave ordinary people to their own devices as much as possible, and not interfere in matters that directly concern family and livelihood. So it remains today.

MONEY MATTERS
On an economic level Hong Kong has not greatly changed. The place was established for commercial reasons, and business interests remain paramount. But only the most blinkered members of the public are taken in by regular announcements that Hong Kong is the world's freest economy; at an SME (Small and Medium Enterprises) level, it must be admitted, Hong Kong is a very good place to operate, with a simple, straightforward tax regime, low start-up costs, general high levels of infrastructure

People's Liberation Army headquarters.

Return of the astronauts

From the time the Joint Declaration was signed in 1984, the pace of emigration from Hong Kong accelerated. For tens of thousands of educated, financially mobile Hong Kong Chinese, the agreement simply gave them 13 years' notice to jump a ship that they felt was destined to founder without Britain at the helm.

Over the next decade or so, Canada, Australia, New Zealand, the United States and other countries accepted hundreds of thousands of Hong Kong Chinese immigrants. But while the families established legal domicile and started school in these destination countries, all too often the principal breadwinner stayed behind in Hong Kong and regularly commuted through the stratosphere – thus becoming known locally as 'astronauts' – between their homes on different continents.

Contrary to gloomy press predictions, Hong Kong's world did not come to a crashing end in 1997. Yes, the local economy faltered – largely as a result of fallout from the regional financial crisis in 1997-98 – the property market cooled considerably, pollution steadily worsened, the bird flu and SARS crises struck, and Tung Chee-hwa's government fumbled and stumbled.

But as for the media-fuelled fears of a dire erosion of human rights, PLA tanks brutally suppressing demonstrations in downtown Central in finest Tiananmen Square style, and a frenzied mass exodus of all who could escape the Communist hordes – none of these apocalyptic scenarios came to pass.

Because most migrants left Hong Kong to obtain the security of a Western passport against an imagined future contingency that might well never happen – rather than positively embrace a new life in a Western country – almost as soon as their passports had been issued many came straight back home again.

Many returnees had been given a taste of life in Western countries and decided that, in many respects, it simply wasn't for them. High crime rates, punitive taxation, the stresses and expectations of life as an ethnic minority (however much the host

efficiency and – unusual for most of Asia – an almost complete lack of petty corruption.

Above this point, however, Hong Kong remains one of the most heavily cartelised places on the planet, and the level of official denial that this is so is simply breathtaking. Companies that operate with worldwide success, such as Europe-based supermarket giant Carrefour, tried and failed to enter the Hong Kong market. Monopolies, duopolies, and very small circles, whether for supermarkets, bus companies, electricity generation or property development, are the name of the game in the local economy. Part of the issue, of course, is Hong Kong's small size. Major decisions are made by a few key players, without any real need to involve the wider public in the decision-making process. Cronyism thrives in these circumstances, and in the last decade has reached new heights – or plumbed new depths – in Hong Kong.

Since the Handover, and in particular during the recession-plagued early years of the Tung administration, more-or-less open crony-capitalism helped fuel steadily growing public discontent – particularly among Hong Kong's tax-paying middle classes, who were most affected by the post-Asian economic crisis and collapse of the 1990s property bubble.

One highly controversial low point was the acquisition of a valuable tract of waterfront land on the Pok Fu Lam coast of Hong Kong Island by a telecommunications company owned by Richard Li, the younger son of Li Ka-shing – Hong Kong's wealthiest man. Pacific Century Cyber Works (PCCW) planned to build a technological hub – known as Cyberport – that would provide a home for the thousands of high-tech companies that would make their bases in Hong Kong. Criticism of the tendering procedures led to accusations that Cyberport was a sweetheart deal for the Li family companies, and simply a property development – it also comprises a hotel, retail outlets and posh residences – by another name.

In spite of the public furore at the time, Cyberport was duly built, with the Hong Kong government paying for additional roads and other infrastructure in the area. With the burst of the dot-com bubble, Cyberport has become – surprise, surprise – just what its critics suggested it would be; a cluster of high-end residential developments, an under-used luxury hotel complex, and – oh, yes – some office blocks where a few tech-related companies have their operations. This was the most flagrant example of unthought-out cronyism – there have been many others.

countries officially accommodated that status), lack of economic opportunity and straight-up alienated boredom with suburbia – all impelled people homewards. By the late 1990s the reverse migration trend was very marked, and a decade on from the Handover the effects are striking.

Places in international schools, originally established to cater for genuinely foreign-born students, all now have overwhelmingly Hong Kong Chinese-filled classes – whichever country's name may be embossed on their passport. This, in turn, has created another raft of politically delicate issues. Many astronaut families lived in expat Hong Kong Chinese enclaves in destination cities such as Vancouver and Melbourne, with little interest or incentive to participate in the wider society. As a result, poor English standards among overseas returnee students at international schools is endemic, and a frequently voiced problem among educators.

Recent years have witnessed an overall rise in civic consciousness on the part of Hong Kong's notoriously apathetic middle classes, which has been manifested in previously marginal areas such as heritage preservation, nature conservation and environmental issues.

This growth in civic attitudes has been at least partly driven by a rediscovered commitment to Hong Kong as a place and a society on the part of these re-grounded astronauts. In the past most residents simply regarded Hong Kong as a place to make money and then leave. There was no real thought of the city's future; Hong Kong was broadly assumed not to have one, or if it did, they and their families would not be a part of it.

This transient mindset has changed greatly over the last decade – at least on the part of the middle classes – and offers numerous broad-ranging implications for future developments in many aspects of Hong Kong life. Unless, of course, quality of life issues – in particular the region's annually worsening air quality – impel Hong Kong's astronaut immigrants back 'home' again to Canada or Australia.

CONFLICTING LOYALTIES

An absence of connected thinking – on the part of both the public sector and the general public – also shows through in the post-Handover era. Hong Kong is all too frequently – and, in many ways, erroneously – described as an international, cosmopolitan 'world city'. Yet post-1997, Hong Kong is also a city in China, and that factor sits uneasily with many residents, especially non-Chinese ones.

'Patriotism' towards China, and the perceived need to cultivate its outward signs, such as recognition of the national anthem, remains a priority in post-Handover Hong Kong. This particular issue has always been a difficult one to manage, as Chinese patriotism, all too often, spills over into unproductive displays of Chinese racial and cultural chauvinism, which, while unattractive and alienating, are almost never physically violent.

The first manned Chinese space launch was an illustrative example. The 2003 orbit of the Earth used obsolete, 40-year-old technology, yet was widely hailed in the local press – and in numerous private conversations by members of the public who should have known better – as some tremendous groundbreaking achievement for the Chinese people. Anyone – especially foreigners – who suggested that nothing new was achieved by the launch, except massive additional expense that a Third World country with China's widespread poverty issues could have spent on other forms of development, was automatically labelled a naysayer – or worse.

Occasional loud trumpeting of Chinese 'patriotism', especially the not-so-secret official orchestration of anti-Japanese sentiment on the mainland, opposition to any rational discussion of the Taiwan independence issue, and National Day-style flag-waving exercises rapidly become mindlessly jingoistic. These displays often leave non-Chinese Hong Kong people, of which there are a considerable number, wondering just where they fit into the overall matrix – or whether indeed they do at all.

> ## 'Around half of Hong Kong Chinese either have an overseas passport or have a family member with one.'

The challenge is, paradoxically, most acute for some Hong Kong Chinese. By some surveys, around 50 per cent of Hong Kong Chinese either have an overseas passport – usually Canadian or Australian – acquired in the lead-up to the

Decision makers wanted: submit applications to the **Legislative Council Building**.

Handover, or a spouse, child or parent with one. Take-up for Chinese-issued SAR passports has been high since the Handover; but those who acquired Australian, Canadian or other passports in the lead-up to 1997 quietly retain them, along with, in many cases, a steadily rising degree of Chinese nationalist feelings. The challenge for Hong Kong society – and for the nations that accepted for immigration people who left again almost as soon as they obtained citizenship – is to successfully manage such aspirations. Dual, and at times, conflicting loyalties, have yet to be a major problem in Hong Kong, but could become one at any time.

PERFECT HARMONY?

Nevertheless, in today's world, if you are going to be an ethnic minority, Hong Kong is one of the better places to undergo that experience. Overt hostility towards minorities, whether Europeans, Indians or South-east Asians, is very minimal, though discrimination does exist. Generally speaking, the browner or blacker you are, the more likely you are to face some level of racism. Hong Kong lags well behind most other developed societies in that there is still no race-discrimination legislation, and in spite of repeated calls for review, the government continues to drag its heels on the issue. Cynics might suggest that as Chinese racism in Hong Kong is certainly alive and well, there would be too many embarrassing challenges and complaints. (*See also p16* **Foreign devils in a 'world city'**.)

This becomes a potentially serious issue when one considers that more foreigners than ever before have bought property in Hong Kong and made it their official residence.

One aspect of post-Handover life that bears some discussion in the light of today's world is just why so many foreigners choose to make their homes in Hong Kong. For a long time, the prevailing belief held that, with the exception of a few Sinologues, foreigners were only in Hong Kong for the money, lifestyle and other comforts that fantastic expat packages afforded. But back in the days when poverty was widespread, disease common and discomforts more manifest, this was a convenient, if not always very accurate means of dismissing foreign residents as so many essentially transient carpetbaggers with little vested interest in Hong Kong as a place and a society.

No longer. Luxurious expat packages are a thing of the past, and many long-term foreign residents, especially those originally from Europe, North America and Australia, now cite the high levels of personal safety they enjoy in Hong Kong as a major advantage. Policing is effective, and there is almost no fear of being mugged, burgled or otherwise randomly assaulted, even late at night in out-of-the-way places. The general absence of a 'booze culture' means that the alcohol-fuelled weekend violence sadly so common in many Western cities is not a factor to consider in Hong Kong life. Terrorism is not an obvious threat, and the worst thing most people complain about is the pollution.

Probably the key aspect you might want to consider when visiting today is that Hong Kong in the post-Handover era has become a fundamentally different place to how it was pre-1997. In some respects it is a better place, in others less so. The transfer of sovereignty has brought about fundamental changes. Anyone visiting for the first time would be unaware of such differences. However, to a repeat visitor – especially someone who was familiar with Hong Kong even 15 years ago – the alterations have been profound.

Where to Stay

Hotel LKF. *See p55*.

Where to Stay

The choice of rooms gets better and better in Hong Kong – and not only in the swanky top-tier categories.

Hong Kong hotels' notoriously high room rates have morphed into a wider range of late. Top-end hotels are still certainly no bargain but, whether it's a post-SARS phenomenon, a necessity for the increasing number of independent mainland Chinese visitors or a reflection of a worldwide trend in well-designed comfortable accommodation in the lower and moderate price categories, the territory offers a better class of bedroom for your buck than ever before. But fans of opulence, fear not: some seriously swanky new hotels have recently opened and the best of the old five-stars are regularly renovated to keep up with the luxury hospitality game.

Hong Kong has finally signed up to the boutique hotel trend with a number of smallish independent establishments – such as the Philippe Starck-designed **Jia Boutique Hotel** and **Hotel LKF** (for both, see p66 **Designer digs**) – though with rooms numbering a fair few more (a little under a hundred) than you might find in this category in other parts of the world. Their individuality is both welcome and surprising in what has previously been a fairly conservative hospitality scene.

Nonetheless, by Chinese or Asian standards the city remains very costly, and five-star luxury still comes at a price tag that will make anyone but the all-expenses-paid business traveller tremble.

Most major hotels are located in Central, Wan Chai, Causeway Bay and Tsim Sha Tsui. Any of these districts will place you right at the heart of the urban action. Clusters of luxury hotels can be found facing Admiralty's Supreme Court Road (including the **Island Shangri-La**; see p55) and Central's Chater Road (the **Ritz-Carlton** and the flagship **Mandarin Oriental**; for both, see p56), and along the Tsim Sha Tsui and Wan Chai harboursides (among them opulent and impressive five-star institutions such as the **Peninsula** (see p62) and the **Grand Hyatt** (see p57), which are rightly considered among the best hotels in the world).

After being virtually non-existent for years (other than a number of drab properties), the mid-range sector is finally growing. Hotels outside the main districts – in areas such as Western, North Point and the more northerly parts of Kowloon – offer similar standards to the more central hotels for less money. Hong Kong is a small city with excellent and cheap public transport (or free or bargain-rate shuttle buses), so the minor inconvenience of being further out is easily balanced by the savings. A few good examples are **Ibis North Point** (see p61), beyond Causeway Bay, the **Novotel Century Harbourview Hotel** (see p57), towards the western end of the island, and **BP International House** (see p63) in Jordan, north of Tsim Sha Tsui. But downtown mid-rangers have also started cropping up – notably in Causeway Bay and Wan Chai.

Next down the scale are the guesthouses. These are mainly concentrated in Causeway Bay and Tsim Sha Tsui. The latter is famous for its guesthouses, which nestle virtually cheek-by-jowl with some of the city's flashiest hotels. Many backpackers end up in **Chungking Mansions** (see p64) on Nathan Road. The rabbit-warren buildings house scores of guesthouses; some are good, some are gritty, but all offer a prime location for a fraction of the price charged by the more upmarket hotels – naturally, for good reason. The worst guesthouses offer a grim combination of poor facilities or, worse, poor security, so always check out a place before you stay and try to haggle over the price (normally, the longer you commit to staying, the cheaper the daily rate). More guesthouses can be found further north along Nathan Road towards Jordan and Yau Ma Tei. If you're walking around with a backpack, touts often come and hand you business cards urging you to stay in one of them.

A good alternative to guesthouses are **youth hostels**. These do not enjoy such prime locations but often have beautiful settings amid the extensive country parks near the city. You'll usually need to be a YHA member to stay at a hostel; membership cards can be bought from YHA offices in your home country, or from the Hong Kong head office (Room 225-226, Block

> ❶ Green numbers given in this chapter correspond to the location of each hotel as marked on the street maps. *See pp328-333.*

19, Shek Kip Mei Estate, Sham Shui Po, Kowloon, 2788 1638, fax 2788 3105, info@yha.org.hk). An email booking form is available on the Hong Kong Youth Hostels Association website (www.yha.org.hk).

THE LOWDOWN ON PRICES
The period from late September through to Christmas and around Chinese New Year usually denotes the high season. The best deals are to be found in the spring and during the humid summer months, and can be around 50 per cent of the official rates. In this chapter, we use the following categories, based on the lowest double room price: **Deluxe** (HK$3,000 or above), **Expensive** (HK$2,000-$2,999); **Moderate** (HK$1,000-$1,999) and **Cheap** (under HK$1,000); **hostels** have their own category. Check whether hotel prices are inclusive or exclusive of taxes – the current

The best Hotels

For afternoon tea
The **Peninsula** (*see p62*) is a classic for atmosphere but the new **Four Seasons** (*see p55*) is better for selection and value.

For the best deal in town
The clean and compact **Harbour View International House** is set back just off the urban buzz and well connected by public transport. *See p61.*

For business travellers on a budget
The **Fleming** combines no-nonsense minimalism and work facilities at reasonable prices. *See p58.*

For foodies
The restaurants at the **InterContinental** (*see p62*), **Island Shangri-La** (*see p55*), **Jia Boutique Hotel** (*see p66* **Designer digs**) and the **Peninsula** (*see p62*) top the tables.

For getting away from it all
Award-winning **Pak Sha O Hostel** in the wilds of Sai Kung Country Park. *See p68.*

For shopping on your doorstep
Four Seasons (*see p55*), **Island Shangri-La** (*see p55*), **Landmark Mandarin Oriental** (*see p55*) – all built within malls – or the **Excelsior** (*see p58*), a short walk from malls and independent boutiques.

For spa treatments
Four Seasons (*see p55*), the **InterContinental** (*see p62*), **Island Shangri-La** (*see p55*), **Landmark Mandarin Oriental** (*see p55*) and the **Peninsula** (*see p62*).

For tickling the underbelly of Hong Kong
Chungking House. *See p64.*

For cheap but decent digs
Alisan Guest House. *See p61.*

The Landmark Mandarin Oriental. *See p55*.

Hip is happening. Here. Now, in Hong Kong

Lan Kwai Fong Hotel @ Kau U Fong

Be Hip, be Stylish, in a location that is perfect for trendy dining, nightlife & entertainment area of Lan Kwai Fong and SoHo.

Central Park Hotel @ Hollywood Road

For reservation, call us at 852 3650 0299   www.centralparkhotel.com.hk
Email: rsvn@lankwaifonghotel.com.hk   www.lankwaifonghotel.com.hk

hotel service charge and government surcharge often add up to an additional 13 per cent. Unless otherwise indicated, rates listed here are official rates, exclusive of taxes and of breakfast. When TV is indicated (and it always is), presume that any hostelry above guesthouse level will be hooked up to a multitude of cable and satellite channels. Rates for internet access vary by hotel, but you can expect to pay around HK$50-$60 per hour or HK$120-$150 for 24 hours, if it's not included in the room cost.

Hong Kong Island

Central

As Central is the business heart of the city, it's no surprise that its few hotels are geared towards business travellers. A 'six-star' **Four Seasons** (Hong Kong's first; *see below*) opened in 2005, as did the boutique **Landmark Mandarin Oriental** hotel (*see below*) in the rebuilt Landmark mall complex. Admiralty has a cluster of fantastically luxurious hotels – among them the **Island Shangri-La** (*see below*) – which jut skywards from the vast Pacific Place shopping mall.

Deluxe

Four Seasons

8 Finance Street (3196 8888/fax 3196 8899/www. fourseasons.com/hongkong). Central MTR (exit A, E)/Airport Express Station. **Rates** HK$3,000-$4,000 double; HK$5,500-$6,500 suite. **Rooms** 399. **Credit** AmEx, DC, MC, V. **Map** p329 D2 ❶
One of two new big-impact hotels in the top tier category, the Four Seasons boasts some of Hong Kong's largest rooms. Deeming every one of the 399 rooms and suites worthy of 'executive' category, the hotel allows guests who pay a premium of HK$700 to use the executive lounge, with its complimentary food and beverage privileges (a perk that's already factored into the cost of all the suite accommodation). Off the lounge, a dedicated CNN screen runs permanently in a viewing room, allowing guests to catch the headlines (or battle insomnia) without disturbing their partner. Rooms all contain multiple-function printers, fitted next to large desks, as well as 42-inch plasma TV sets and a quality audio-visual system. **Photo** *p56*.
Bar. Business services. Concierge. Disabled-adapted rooms. Gym. Internet (wireless). Limousine service. No-smoking floors. Parking (HK$60/hr). Restaurants (3). Spa. Swimming pool (outdoor). TV (pay movies).

Hotel LKF

33 Wyndham Street (3518 9688/fax 3518 9699/ www.hotel-LKF.com.hk). Central MTR (exit D1, G)/buses along Queen's Road Central. **Rates** HK$3,000-$3,800 double; HK$4,500-$6,500 suite.

Rooms 95. **Credit** AmEx, DC, MC, V.
Map p328 C4 ❷
See p66 **Designer digs** for review. **Photo** *p59*.
Business services. Concierge. Disabled-adapted rooms. Internet (wireless). Restaurant. TV (pay movies, DVD).

Island Shangri-La

Pacific Place, 88 Queensway, Admiralty (2877 3838/ fax 2521 8742/www.shangri-la.com/hongkong/ island/en). Admiralty MTR (exit C1)/free shuttle bus from Central Airport Express Station/buses along Queensway. **Rates** HK$3,700-$5,500 single; HK$4,000-$5,800 double; HK$8,400-$35,000 suite. **Rooms** 565. **Credit** AmEx, DC, MC, V. **Map** p329 F5 ❸
At one of the most luxurious hotels, no expense has been spared, from the artworks and chandeliers in the lavish lobby, to the 565 rooms (including 34 suites), which are among the largest on Hong Kong Island and have views of either the Peak or the harbour. In the atrium hangs the 16-storey-high *Great Motherland of China*, thought to be the largest Chinese silk painting in the world. Business travellers are well catered for, with wireless connectivity in all public areas, and three IDD phone lines in all rooms. But shopaholics will also enjoy it here – the hotel is within the upmarket Pacific Place mall. Dining options, which are among the best in the city, include the casual Café TOO and the award-winning Petrus (*see p137*), with its jaw-dropping views over the harbour. Perks for guests paying rack rates include free airport transfer, local phone calls, Broadband internet access, laundry and dry-cleaning, late (6pm) checkout and phone calls and faxes at cost.
Bars (2). Business services. Concierge. Disabled-adapted rooms. Gym. Internet (wireless). Limousine service. No-smoking rooms. Parking (HK$120 1st 2hrs; then HK$80/hr) Restaurants (3). Spa. Swimming pool (outdoor). TV (pay movies, DVD).

Landmark Mandarin Oriental

15 Queen's Road Central (2132 0188/fax 2132 0199/www.mandarinoriental.com/landmark). Central MTR (exit G)/buses along Queen's Road Central. **Rates** HK$4,300-$5,700 double; HK$8,800-$42,000 suite. **Rooms** 113. **Credit** AmEx, DC, MC, V. **Map** p329 D4 ❹
This is the second big deluxe newcomer in recent years. So what can you expect from an establishment that names itself after the pioneer of Hong Kong's glitzy designer-label fashion malls? Lots of lush style, of course – but without being so painfully hip that it would be laughably passé next season. It also offers some of the city's largest guest rooms, starting at 50 square metres (540 square feet). The circular room configurations are an interesting twist, with a bathroom and freestanding tub at the centre. High-tech entertainment systems and other gizmos are prominent in all 113 rooms. **Photo** *p53*.
Bar. Business services. Concierge. Disabled-adapted facilities. Internet (wireless). Limousine service. No-smoking floors. Restaurants (2). Spa. Swimming pool (indoor). TV (pay movies, DVD).

Big is beautiful: the **Four Seasons** has some of the largest rooms in HK. *See p55.*

Ritz-Carlton

3 Connaught Road (2877 6666/fax 2877 6778/
www.ritzcarlton.com/hotels/hong_kong). Central
MTR (exit J3)/buses through Central/Central Ferry
Pier. **Rates** HK$3,600-$4,800 single/double;
HK$7,500-$25,000 suite. **Rooms** 216. **Credit** AmEx,
DC, MC, V. **Map** p329 E4 ⑤

The Ritz-Carlton attracts a mix of business and
leisure travellers. Although it has 216 rooms (many
with harbour views), it has an intimate feel, which
extends to its restaurants and the wonderfully discreet Chater Lounge. The rooms are elegantly furnished, with marble bathrooms and luxuries like the
24-hour 'technology butler' on hand to fix any computer, fax or internet problems you might face. The
food is equally impressive: Toscana (*see p139*), the
hotel's signature restaurant, is a gem.

Bar. Beauty salon. Business services. Concierge.
Disabled-adapted rooms. Gym. Internet (wireless).
Limousine service. No-smoking floors. Restaurants
(6). Swimming pool (outdoor). TV (pay movies, DVD).

Expensive

Mandarin Oriental

5 Connaught Road (2522 0111/fax 2810 6190/
www.mandarinoriental.com). Central MTR (exit F,
H)/buses to Central Ferry Pier/Central Ferry Pier.
Rates HK$2,000-$2,950 single/double; HK$5,500
suite. **Rooms** 502. **Credit** AmEx, DC, MC, V.
Map p329 E3 ⑥

The multi-award-winning Mandarin Oriental chain
now has hotels around the world, but the original
one – freshly renovated and reopened in October
2006 – stands in the heart of Central's financial district, with stunning views of Victoria Harbour. What
were tiny, underused balconies have been converted
into either more room space or 'terrace' chill-out
areas. Probably the best-located hotel in Hong Kong,
the Mandarin is a local (expense-account) institution,
The Mandarin Grill, the setting for many a deal
between *tai pans* (the tycoons who ran the *hongs*

in colonial times), has undergone a Terence Conran transformation, but the wood panelling of the Chinnery Bar – an old favourite of the social elite that served men only up until as recently as 1990 – remains untouched.

A towering landmark when it was built in 1963, the hotel is now dwarfed by modern towers. The guest rooms and suites are more modest than some newer luxury hotels, but the renovation has introduced plenty of low-key high-techery, such as a bathroom central mirror and TV panel that pivots. Leisure facilities are first class, and impeccable service remains a signature.

Bars (2). Beauty salon. Business services. Concierge. Gym. Internet (wireless). Limousine service. No-smoking rooms. Restaurants (5). Swimming pool (indoor). TV (pay movies, DVD).

Sheung Wan, Mid-Levels & Western

Moderate

Novotel Century Harbourview Hotel

508 Queen's Road West, Kennedy Town (2974 1234/fax 2974 0333/www.novotel.com/asia). Buses 5, 10, 18, 104, M47. **Rates** HK$1,100 single/ double; HK$2,700 suite. **Rooms** 274. **Credit** AmEx, DC, MC, V.

As you might guess from its name, the Novotel offers great sea views from many of its rooms. The 274 rooms are tastefully furnished, and facilities are modern, if only because the hotel is quite young. The area is a bit of a tourist backwater, but the price is good, and if it's real Hong Kong street life you want then this is your place (and if you really must go to Central it's only a short bus or taxi ride away).

Bar. Business services. Concierge. Disabled-adapted rooms. Gym. Internet (wireless). Limousine service. No-smoking rooms. Parking (HK$50 1st 2hrs; then HK$30/hr). Restaurants (2). Swimming pool (indoor). TV (pay movies).

Other locations: Novotel Century, 238 Jaffe Road, Wan Chai, HK Island (2598 8888).

Cheap

Garden View International House

1 MacDonnell Road, Mid-Levels (2877 3737/fax 2845 6263/http://hotel.ywca.org.hk). Central Airport Express Station then taxi/green minibus 1A from Central Ferry Pier. **Rates** HK$1,350-$1,750 single/double; HK$2,500-$2,950 suite. **Rooms** 130. **Credit** AmEx, MC, V. **Map** p328 C5 ⑦

For such a prime location – in the upmarket Mid-Levels residential area, close to SoHo, Hong Kong Park and the Botanical Gardens – this place is a bargain. Another bonus is the outdoor swimming pool, a godsend during the summer heat. The 130 rooms are fairly small and basic (though they do at least have a mini fridge), but if you're using it as a base

for exploring then this probably won't bother you. If your budget will allow, pay the extra for a harbour-view room or a suite (which includes kitchenette). The food options aren't great, but there are plenty of excellent restaurants just a short walk away. Hotel shuttle buses make the run down to Central every few minutes.

Bar. Disabled-adapted rooms. Gym. No-smoking rooms. Restaurant. Swimming pool (outdoor). TV.

Hostels

Jockey Club Mount Davis Youth Hostel

Mount Davis Path, Mount Davis, Kennedy Town (2788 1638/2817 5715/fax 2788 3105/www.yha. org.hk). Sheung Wan MTR (exit D to Shun Tak Centre) then taxi or free shuttle bus (9.30am-10.30pm)/M4, 5, 5B, 971 bus then 35mins walk. **Rates** HK$50-$80 dorm bed; HK$260-$600 private room. Non-YHA members HK$30 extra. **Beds** 169. **No credit cards**.

Formerly known as Ma Wui Hall, this hostel enjoys a magnificent setting on top of Mount Davis at the west end of Hong Kong Island. The views of Tsing Ma Bridge and Victoria Harbour are breathtaking, and have made the place so popular that it expanded from 111 beds to 169 a few years ago. The hostel is just a short bus hop into the main areas of Hong Kong, but be warned: if you miss the hostel's free shuttle bus, which runs only four times a day, there's a 35-minute walk uphill from the nearest bus stop.

Kitchen.

Wan Chai & Causeway Bay

If you want to experience the hustle and bustle of Hong Kong, Wan Chai and Causeway Bay, just east of Central, give you just that. With a 24/7 culture and strip after strip of bars, clubs and shops, these districts never sleep.

Deluxe

Grand Hyatt

1 Harbour Road, Wan Chai (2588 1234/fax 2802 0677/www.hongkong.grand.hyatt.com). Wan Chai MTR (exit A1, C)/A12, 18, 88 bus/Wan Chai Star Ferry Pier. **Rates** from $5,200 single/double; $7,500-$50,000 suite. **Rooms** 549. **Credit** AmEx, DC, MC, V. **Map** p330 B2 ⑧

Hyatt International's flagship hotel has a lavish art deco lobby that gives way to surprisingly minimalist yet ultra-luxe rooms, most of them with harbour views. Business travellers are well catered for – each room has a self-contained work station, broadband internet access and fax machine with personal number; booking an executive floor room gains access to the Grand Club, with private lounge and complimentary breakfast; and the adjoining convention centre makes it an ideal hotel for delegates. Leisure facilities are equally impressive, and include Hong

Where to Stay

Kong's largest freeform swimming pool, and two of the city's best restaurants, One Harbour Road (see p142), which showcases excellent Cantonese cooking, and Grissini (see p143), serving outstanding Italian cuisine; afternoon tea and the evening dessert buffet in the Tiffin Lounge are also memorable experiences (for afternoon tea in the latter, see p153 **A fancy cuppa**). Celebs also get a look-in – there are 13 speciality suites, including two presidential suites, plus a luxury junk for hire.

Bar. Beauty salon. Business services. Concierge. Disabled-adapted rooms. Gym. Internet (wireless). Limousine service. No-smoking floors. Parking (HK$50 1st hr; then HK$60/hr). Restaurants (4). Swimming pool (outdoor). TV (pay movies, DVD).

Expensive

Excelsior

281 Gloucester Road, Causeway Bay (2894 8888/fax 2895 6459/www.excelsiorhongkong.com). Causeway Bay MTR (exit D1)/buses along Gloucester Road. **Rates** from HK$2,400 single/double; HK$6,000-$16,000 suite. **Rooms** 883. **Credit** AmEx, DC, MC, V. **Map** p331 E2 ❾

With nearly 900 rooms and suites, the Excelsior is the largest hotel on Hong Kong Island. It's run by the Mandarin Oriental group, so the service here is better than you might expect for such a big operation. It's located right on the harbour – with great views of the Royal Hong Kong Yacht Club – and near the Noon Day Gun, which is fired every day, should you ever oversleep. The hotel is always busy with business travellers, tourists and airline personnel drawn by its location in the heart of vibrant Causeway Bay. The rooms are a bit '70s in style, but comfy and spacious nonetheless. Dickens Bar is a lively sports pub, and ToTT's Asian Grill & Bar is great for a snack.

Bar. Beauty salon. Business services. Concierge. Disabled-adapted rooms. Gym. Internet (broadband). Limousine service. No-smoking floors. Restaurants (4). TV (pay movies).

Moderate

Fleming

41 Fleming Road, Wan Chai (3607 2288/fax 3607 2299/www.thefleming.com.hk). Wan Chai MTR (exit A1, C)/buses along Gloucester Road & Hennessy Road. **Rates** HK$1,200-$2,060 single/double; HK$2,300-$2,460 executive. **Rooms** 66. **Credit** AmEx, MC, V. **Map** p330 C3 ❿

Finally, someone has had the sense to provide a reasonably priced business-oriented hotel with a warm contemporary interior. The Fleming is a one-off. It's small size (66 rooms) would qualify it as a boutique hotel, should the Fleming want to be thus pigeonholed. While clean lines, bright bathrooms with fun amenity packs and large flat-screen TVs all feature, it is basically a no-nonsense inn at heart. Its *raison d'être* is to make its guests comfortable, without

unnecessary bells and whistles; for instance, plans are afoot to open a female-only floor soon. Exec rooms have a three-in-one scanner/printer/fax, DVD player and kitchenette as standard. **Photo** *p61.*

Concierge. Disabled-adapted rooms. Internet (broadband). No-smoking rooms. Restaurant. TV.

Jia Boutique Hotel

1-5 Irving Street, Causeway Bay (3196 9000/fax 3196 9001/www.jiahongkong.com). Causeway Bay MTR (exit F)/buses along Causeway Road. **Rates** HK$1,800 studio; HK$2,600-$6,000 suite. **Rooms** 54. **Credit** AmEx, DC, MC, V. **Map** p331 E3 ⓫

See p66 Designer digs for review.

Business services. Disabled-adapted rooms. Internet (broadband). Limousine service. No-smoking rooms. Restaurants (2). TV (DVD).

Lanson Place

133 Leighton Road, Causeway Bay (3477 6888/fax 3477 6999/www.lansonplace.com.hk). Causeway Bay MTR (exit F)/free shuttle bus from Central Airport Express Station. **Rates** HK$1,190-$3,200 double; HK$2,880-$9,800 suite. **Rooms** 194. **Credit** AmEx, DC, MC, V. **Map** p331 E3 ⓬

See p66 Designer digs for review.

Business services. Concierge. Disabled-adapted rooms. Gym. Internet (wireless). Limousine service. No-smoking rooms. TV (DVD).

Luk Kwok

72 Gloucester Road, Wan Chai (2866 2166/fax 2866 2622/www.lukkwokhotel.com). Wan Chai MTR (exit A1, C). **Rates** HK$1,600-$2,100 single/double; HK$2,300-$2,600 executive; HK$3,800-$5,800 suite. **Rooms** 195. **Credit** AmEx, DC, MC, V. **Map** p330 B3 ⓭

Built on the site of the hotel where Suzie Wong and her hussy entourage used to hang out, the Luk Kwok is now a respectable hotel with 195 rooms catering to a largely business customer base. The facilities are impressive given the decent prices.

Bar. Business services. Concierge. Disabled-adapted rooms. Gym. Internet (wireless). Limousine service. No-smoking floor. Restaurants (2). TV (pay movies).

Rosedale on the Park

8 Shelter Street, Causeway Bay (2127 8888/fax 2127 3333/www.rosedale.com.hk). Causeway Bay MTR (exit E)/buses along Gloucester Road. **Rates** HK$1,580 single/double; HK$2,380-$2,880 suite. **Rooms** 274. **Credit** AmEx, DC, MC, V. **Map** p331 E3 ⓮

This good-value hotel across the road from Victoria Park in bustling Causeway Bay opened in 2001. The 274 rooms are on the small side but they have above-average bathrooms and are equipped with an impressive array of facilities for these prices. OK, it's not the height of luxury, but if you're a business traveller and/or staying a while you could do a lot worse. The friendly young staff is a further bonus.

Bar. Business services. Concierge. Disabled-adapted rooms. Gym. Internet (broadband). No-smoking rooms. Restaurants (2). TV.

Hotel **LKF**. *See p55.*

timeout.com

The hippest online guide to over 50
of the world's greatest cities

Wesley

22 Hennessy Road, Wan Chai (2866 6688/fax 2866 6633/www.hanglung.com). Admiralty MTR (exit F)/ Wan Chai MTR (exit B1)/free shuttle bus from Central Airport Express Station/buses along Hennessy Road. **Rates** HK$1,050-$2,400 single/ double. **Rooms** 251. **Credit** AmEx, DC, MC, V. **Map** p330 A3 ⑮

If you're planning on spending two weeks or longer in Hong Kong and money is an object, you might think about the Wesley. With 251 well-furnished rooms and good facilities it offers bargain long-term accommodation (from HK$8,000 per month) and is popular with temporary residents. It's very convenient for entertainment, shops and public transport. *Business services. Concierge. Disabled-adapted rooms. Internet (broadband). Limousine service. No-smoking rooms. Restaurant. TV.*

Cheap

Alisan Guest House

Flat A, 5/F, Hoito Court, 275 Gloucester Road, Causeway Bay (2838 0762/fax 2838 4351/ http://home.hkstar.com/~alisangh/). Causeway Bay MTR (exit D1)/buses along Yee Wo Street. **Rates** HK$280 single; HK$320 double; HK$390 treble. **Rooms** 21. **Credit** MC, V. **Map** p331 D2 ⑯

Cleanliness and friendliness are the bywords that have led to a solid reputation for these downtown digs since it opened in 1987. Guests don't slum it here. All 21 rooms have ensuite shower and loo, and there are free local calls from the in-room phones. There are also communal refrigerators and dining areas and CCTV coverage in all public spaces. *TV.*

Harbour View International House

4 Harbour Road, Wan Chai (2802 0111/fax 2802 9063/www.harbour.ymca.org.hk). Wan Chai MTR (exit A4, A5)/free shuttle bus from Central Airport Express Station to Convention Centre. **Rates** HK$700-$1,950 single/double. **Rooms** 320. **Credit** AmEx, MC, V. **Map** p330 B3 ⑰

Location and cost are the paramount reasons for staying here, as it's close to the throbbing heart of Wan Chai but just enough removed from the madness. It's also next door to the Arts Centre and a few metres from the Academy for Performing Arts, which means it's often packed with touring dancers and musicians. Many of the 320 rooms in the tower block hotel – officially a hostel – offer great views. Most of the rooms are quite small and simply decorated, but have reasonable facilities. *Concierge. Disabled-adapted rooms. Internet (wireless). No-smoking rooms. Restaurant. TV.*

Hwa Seng Guesthouse

Block B1, 5/F, Great George Building, 27 Paterson Street, Causeway Bay (2895 6859/fax 2838 7052/ www.guesthouse.com.hk). Causeway Bay MTR (exit E)/buses along Yee Wo Street. **Rates** from HK$400 single/double. **Rooms** 4. **No credit cards.** **Map** p331 E3 ⑱

The Fleming. *See p58.*

This family-run guesthouse offers small but decent rooms for a reasonable price but little English is spoken here. It's close to Causeway Bay MTR station. Some rooms have private baths. *TV.*

Hostels

Noble Hostel

Flat A3, 17/F, Great George Building, 27 Paterson Street, Causeway Bay (2576 6148/fax 2577 0847/ www.noblehostel.com.hk). Causeway Bay MTR (exit E)/buses along Yee Wo Street. **Rates** HK$280-$340 single; HK$360-$450 double. **Rooms** 45. **No credit cards. Map** p331 E3 ⑲

In the same building as Hwa Seng (*see above*), Noble Hostel is another excellent guesthouse, especially for those who want assurance that slumming it doesn't mean dirty rooms. There are 45 air-conditioned and spotlessly clean rooms, newly renovated for 2007. *TV.*

East Hong Kong Island

Cheap

Ibis North Point

136-142 Java Road, North Point (2588 1111/fax 2588 1123/www.accorhotels.com). North Point MTR (exit A1, A2)/free shuttle bus from Central Airport Express Station/10 bus. **Rates** HK$800-$930 single/double; HK$2,859 suite. **Rooms** 275. **Credit** AmEx, DC, MC, V.

Staying out of the main commercial areas means you get more for your dollar. But in this case, because North Point is accessible by MTR, tram and bus, inconvenience isn't really an issue. Also on the plus side, the hotel is well equipped, and of the 275 rooms, many have harbour views and all have satellite television. As if that weren't enough, the business centre offers net facilities, computer hire and mobile phone rental.
Business services. Disabled-adapted rooms. Internet (wireless). No-smoking rooms. Restaurant. TV.

Kowloon

Tsim Sha Tsui

The southern tip of the Kowloon peninsula is where most people stay when they come to Hong Kong, either at one of the flash five-star hotels or in a cheap guesthouse. It's a great area to wander around, with the recently improved promenade offering a jaw-dropping night-time view of the Hong Kong Island skyline. There are also plenty of museums and shops and good transport links to anywhere in the city.

Deluxe

InterContinental
18 Salisbury Road (2721 1211/fax 2739 4546/ www.hongkong-ic.intercontinental.com). Tsim Sha Tsui MTR (exit F)/buses along Salisbury Road/Tsim Sha Tsui Star Ferry Pier. **Rates** HK$2,590-$3,500 single/double; HK$5,500-$87,000 suite. **Rooms** 495. **Credit** AmEx, DC, MC, V. **Map** p333 C6 ⑳
The InterContinental (formerly the Regent) underwent a luxurious modern revamp a few years back. Situated right on the waterfront at Tsim Sha Tsui, the hotel has some of the best views of Victoria Harbour. The open-plan Lobby Lounge (*see p166* **A higher crawling**), most of the restaurants, all 92 suites and two-thirds of the rooms share these views (the rest overlook the lovely pool and sun deck). The InterContinental has among the best business services in Hong Kong, and for an extra HK$700 a day, guests get access to the impressive business lounge, with perks such as free local calls, and complimentary breakfast, afternoon tea and extensive evening drinks (including champagne) and substantial nibbles. Leisure travellers will also feel thoroughly spoiled with the facilities, which include the excellent I-Spa (*see p196* **A good day's rest**), a swimming pool and three spa pools overlooking the harbour. And the rooms? Spacious and luxurious, with home-entertainment systems (including iPod docking stations) and huge bathrooms featuring oversized sunken tubs and luxury showers. Plus there's 24-hour butler service. Dining options are also among Hong Kong's best, with two

endorsed by international celeb chefs: Nobu (*see p150*), which opened at the end of 2006, and a branch of Alain Ducasse's upmarket international chain, Spoon (*see p149*). A real gem.
Bars (2). Beauty salon. Business services. Concierge. Disabled-adapted rooms. Gym. Internet (wireless). Limousine service. No-smoking floors. Parking (free). Restaurants (5). Swimming pool (outdoor). TV (CD/DVD).

Peninsula
Salisbury Road (2920 2888/fax 2722 4170/www. hongkong.peninsula.com). Tsim Sha Tsui MTR (exit E)/free shuttle bus from Kowloon Airport Express Station/buses to Tsim Sha Tsui Ferry Pier & along Salisbury Road/Tsim Sha Tsui Star Ferry Pier. **Rates** HK$3,200-$4,600 double; HK$5,600-$42,000 suite. **Rooms** 300. **Credit** AmEx, DC, MC, V. **Map** p333 B6/C6 ㉑
There may be newer and trendier hotels in town these days, but the grande dame of them all, which celebrates her 80th birthday in 2008, still reigns supreme. Anyone who's anyone has stayed here, from rock stars to royalty, and it was in Room 336 that the surrender of Hong Kong to the Japanese was signed on Christmas Day 1941. The hotel goes to great lengths to keep up with the times while maintaining its prized sense of tradition, all without a hint of pretension or stuffiness: a 30-storey extension in 1994, which almost doubled the number of rooms to 300 (including 54 suites), carefully harmonises with the original building.
The luxurious guest rooms blend Eastern and Western decor, and traditional and modern touches (the latter includes flat-screen TVs, computerised controls for air-conditioning and lighting, free broadband, and custom-made Molton Brown products in the lavish marble bathrooms). Rooms with views of the harbour are the best, but if you're lucky enough to be staying in a corner suite, sink into the jacuzzi and admire the panoramic vistas that also take in Kowloon. Indeed, it's worth going for the priciest room you can afford (let's face it: if you're staying at the Pen, you're presumably not on a tight budget) but if sleeping here is out of your league, try dinner or a drink at one of the hotel's highly rated eating and drinking spots – among the best are opulent French restaurant Gaddi's (*see p149*), Cantonese restaurant Spring Moon (*see p147*), and the Philippe Starck-designed restaurant and bar, Felix (*see p146*). Alternatively, an affordable way to enjoy the opulence is to come for afternoon tea in the sweeping lobby (*see p153* **A fancy cuppa**), or at the award-winning Espa spa (*see p196* **A good day's rest**). You can even slip off on a 'flightseeing' tour of the city in the hotel's own helicopter, or make use of the Peninsula's own fleet of Rolls-Royces – bolstered by new Phantoms in December 2006. This place is sheer class.
Bars (3). Beauty salon. Business services. Concierge. Disabled-adapted rooms, facilities. Gym. Internet (wireless). Limousine service. No-smoking floors. Restaurants (6). Swimming pool (indoor). TV (DVD).

Royal Garden Hong Kong

*69 Mody Road (2721 5215/fax 2369 9976/www.
theroyalgardenhotel.com.hk). Tsim Sha Tsui MTR
(exit C1)/free shuttle bus from Kowloon Airport
Express Station/203, 973 bus/buses along Chatham
Road South & Salisbury Road.* **Rates** HK$2,900-
$3,900 single; HK$3,100-$4,100 double; HK$4,800-
$15,800 suite. **Rooms** 422. **Credit** AmEx, DC,
MC, V. **Map** p333 C5 ㉒

Step inside the Royal Garden and for a moment you
forget you're in the heart of Tsim Sha Tsui. The central atrium, with its lush greenery, is a haven from
the streets outside. This hotel is unbeatable for the
price; and although the 422 rooms aren't as lavish
as in higher-end outfits, they are still on the right
side of luxurious, and the bathrooms have powerful
showers and deep tubs. Check out the new executive
floors for an upgraded experience. All the necessary
facilities are present and correct and there is a gorgeous rooftop pool (covered in winter) with stunning
views over the harbour. Like many other Hong Kong
hotels, the Royal Garden has excellent dining and
drinking facilities – in this case the Japanese restaurant Inagiku (*see p150*), Sabatini, with its upmarket
northern Italian food, and the sleek Martini Bar.
*Bar. Business services. Concierge. Gym. Internet
(wireless). No-smoking floors. Parking (HK$80 1st
2hrs; then HK$50/hr). Restaurant. Swimming pool
(outdoor). TV.*

Moderate

BP International House

*8 Austin Road (2376 1111/fax 2376 1333/www.
megahotels.com.hk/www.bpih.com.hk). Jordan MTR
(exit C1, D)/free shuttle bus from Kowloon Airport
Express Station/A21 bus from the airport/buses
along Nathan Road.* **Rates** HK$1,100
single/double; HK$3,100 suite. **Rooms** 529.
Credit AmEx, DC, MC, V. **Map** p333 B5 ㉓

Despite its name, this hotel has nothing to do with
the oil multinational. It is handily located between
the consumer mecca of Tsim Sha Tsui and the busy
nightlife of Jordan, and offers value for money for
those on a budget who don't want to go quite as
downmarket as a guesthouse. The 529 rooms are
satisfactory and clean, and if you're lucky you might
get one with a view over Victoria Harbour.
*Bar. Business services. Disabled-adapted rooms. Gym.
Internet (wireless). Limousine service. No-smoking
rooms. Parking (HK$22/hr). TV (pay movies).*

Holiday Inn Golden Mile

*50 Nathan Road (2369 3111/fax 2369 8016/www.
goldenmile-hk.holiday-inn.com). Tsim Sha Tsui MTR
(exit C1, C2)/free shuttle bus from Kowloon Airport
Express Station/buses along Nathan Road.* **Rates**
from HK$1,500 single; HK$1,700-$2,500 double;
HK$5,800 suite. **Rooms** 600. **Credit** AmEx, DC,
MC, V. **Map** p333 C6 ㉔

This old stalwart of the 'Golden Mile' has plenty to
offer. A web of escalators and elevators take you
between its thriving bars (*see also p166* **A higher**

crawling) and restaurants, of which Loong Yuen
is the best, offering decent dim sum and award-
winning fried rice (yes, really). The hotel's 600 rooms
are on the small side but are comfy and feature
marble bathrooms.
*Bar. Beauty salon. Business services. Concierge.
Disabled-adapted rooms. Gym. Internet (wireless).
Limousine service. No-smoking floors. Parking
(HK$130 1st 2 hrs; then HK$80/hr). Restaurants (4).
Swimming pool (outdoor). TV.*

Kowloon Hotel

*19 Nathan Road (2929 2888/fax 2739 9811/www.
kowloon.peninsula.com). Tsim Sha Tsui MTR (exit
E)/free shuttle bus from Kowloon Airport Express
Station/buses along Nathan Road & Salisbury Road/
Tsim Sha Tsui Star Ferry Pier.* **Rates** HK$1,600-
$4,000 single/double; HK$3,900-$4,600 suite. **Rooms**
736. **Credit** AmEx, DC, MC, V. **Map** 313 B6/C6 ㉕

If convenience and communication are your watch-
words, this high-tech hotel should be top of your list.
The Kowloon has a combined TV/computer moni-
tor in each room, offering high-speed internet access.
You'll even get an email address and fax number
under the hotel's network. The 736 rooms (including 17 suites) are fairly small but comfortable
enough, and some have a harbour view. Sitting in
the heart of Tsim Sha Tsui's entertainment and
shopping district behind the famed Peninsula hotel,
the Kowloon is part of the same group, meaning
service here is exemplary. Guests also enjoy signing
privileges at the Pen, although the Kowloon's Wan
Loong Court (Cantonese) and Pizzeria (Italian) are
excellent dining options.
*Bar. Beauty salon. Business services. Concierge.
Internet (wireless). No-smoking rooms. Restaurants
(3). TV (pay movies).*

Ramada

*73-75 Chatham Road South (2311 1100/fax 2311
6000/www.ramadahongkong.com). Tsim Sha Tsui
MTR (exit B1)/973 bus.* **Rates** HK$1,500 single/
double; HK$2,800-$4,200 suite. **Rooms** 107. **Credit**
AmEx, DC, MC, V. **Map** p333 C5 ㉖

Chinese businessmen tend to fill up the Ramada, if
only because it is near the KCR train terminus, with
a direct service to China. This might explain why
this 107-room hotel has all the necessary business
amenities – from internet connections to conference
facilities. Leisure travellers headed to China might
also find this a convenient place to stay, especially
if they're only in Hong Kong for one or two nights.
*Bar. Business services. Concierge. Disabled-adapted
rooms. Internet (wireless). No-smoking rooms.
Restaurant. TV (pay movies).*

Stanford Hillview

*13-17 Observatory Road, Knutsford Terrace (2722
7822/fax 2723 3718/www.stanfordhillview.com).
Tsim Sha Tsui MTR (exit B2)/free shuttle bus from
Kowloon Airport Express Station/buses along
Nathan Road.* **Rates** HK$1,130-$1,898 single/double;
HK$2,480 suite. **Rooms** 170. **Credit** AmEx, DC,
MC, V. **Map** p333 C5 ㉗

Luxury comes as standard at the 42-storey **Langham Place Hotel**. *See p65*.

This place isn't much to look at from the outside, but inside it has a certain charm, albeit with a retro feel. The 170 rooms are standard but have all the necessary facilities, and there's a café, bar and lounge to relax in, plus a fitness facility and two driving nets for golfers. The view of the observatory isn't bad from here, and it's close to Knutsford Terrace, Tsim Sha Tsui's leading bar and restaurant district.
Bar. Business services. Concierge. Disabled-adapted facilities. Gym. Internet (wireless). Limousine service. No-smoking rooms. Restaurant. TV (pay movies).

Cheap

Chungking House

Block A, 4-5/F, Chungking Mansions, 40 Nathan Road, Tsim Sha Tsui, Kowloon (2366 5362/fax 2721 3570). Tsim Sha Tsui MTR (exit E)/buses along Nathan Road/Tsim Sha Tsui Star Ferry Pier. **Rates** HK$250-$400 single; HK$300-$450 double. **Rooms** 80. **No credit cards. Map** p333 C6 ㉙
This is the best guesthouse in Chungking. The rooms are clean and have the luxury of air-con, televisions and phones (some even have private baths). You pay up to 50 per cent more than at smaller guesthouses, but it's money well spent. *TV.*

Salisbury YMCA

41 Salisbury Road (2369 2211/fax 2739 9315/www.ymcahk.org.hk). Tsim Sha Tsui MTR (exit E)/free shuttle bus from Kowloon Airport Express Station/buses to Tsim Sha Tsui Ferry Pier & along Salisbury Road/Tsim Sha Tsui Ferry Pier. **Rates** HK$230 dorm bed; HK$760-$860 single/double; HK$1,450 suite. **Rooms** 28 dorm beds; 356 private rooms. **Credit** MC, V. **Map** p333 B6 ㉙
You might find the price a bit steep for a YMCA, but this Y is no hostel. Instead it's a hotel in every sense – and an excellent one at that. From the well-equipped, well-designed rooms to the quality service and facilities, the Salisbury offers outstanding value

for money. But what makes this place a real steal is its location next to the city's premier hotel, the Peninsula. Here you can enjoy the same panorama of the harbour for a fraction of the price (it's certainly worth paying a little extra for a high-floor harbour-view room). There's also a well-equipped gym (extra cost) and an indoor swimming pool.
Beauty salon. Business services. Concierge. Disabled-adapted facilities. Gym. Internet (wireless). No-smoking rooms. Restaurants (2). Swimming pool (indoor). TV.

Hung Hom

Cheap

Holy Carpenter Guesthouse

1 Dyer Avenue (2362 0301/fax 2362 2193). Kowloon KCR/buses along Hung Hom South Road/Hung Hom Ferry Pier. **Rates** HK$450 single/double. **Rooms** 14. **Credit** MC, V. **Map** p333 E4 ㉚
Bigger and brighter than the guesthouses down the road at Chungking Mansions, the Holy Carpenter, with its 14 rooms, is a pleasant budget option, and even has conference facilities (though admittedly not the plushest).
Business services. TV.

Yau Ma Tei, Mong Kok & around

Expensive

Langham Place Hotel

555 Shanghai Street, Mong Kok (3552 3552/3552 3558/http://hongkong.langhamplacehotels.com). Mong Kok MTR (exit C3). **Rates** HK$2,600-$3,400 single; HK$2,600-$3,550 double; HK$3,500-$15,000 suite. **Rooms** 666. **Credit** AmEx, DC, MC, V. **Map** p332 B2 ㉛

The newer, trendier, more luxurious sister to Tsim Sha Tsui's Langham Hotel, the 42-storey Langham Place opened in 2005. Much has been made of its incongruous location, slap-bang in the middle of down-at-heel Mong Kok, but somehow the combination seems to work. The decor of the 666 rooms is just the right side of corporate, and the comfort factor is high: beds are luxurious, huge flat-screen TVs hang on the wall, and the glassed-in bathroom areas boast raindrop showers and deep tubs. The (more expensive) rooms on the top six floors come with access to the executive lounge, which provides complimentary extras such as a buffet breakfast and evening cocktails. But despite the corporate facilities, the hotel attracts a good proportion of leisure travellers too – the emphasis is as much on play as work. The Chuan Spa has garnered good reviews (*see p196* **A good day's rest**), and chilled-out, spa-floor guest rooms were recently launched. The open-air rooftop pool has fantastic views over the city. For shopping and dining, you can either hole up inside – the hotel has several bars and restaurants – or head down to the Langham Place mall. But it's much more fun to slip outside and lose yourself in the nearby attractions (the Night Market, Ladies' Market and Flower Market). **Photo** *p64*.
Bar. Business services. Concierge. Disabled-adapted rooms, facilities. Gym. Internet (wireless). Limousine service. No-smoking floors. Restaurants (3). Spa. Swimming pool (outdoor). TV (DVD).
Other locations: Langham Hotel, 8 Peking Road, Tsim Sha Tsui, Kowloon (2375 1133).

Moderate

Eaton Hotel

380 Nathan Road, Jordan (2782 1818/fax 2782 5563/www.eaton-hotel.com). Jordan MTR (exit A, B1)/A21 bus from the airport/buses along Nathan Road. **Rates** from HK$1,950 single/double; from HK$2,650 suite. **Rooms** 461. **Credit** AmEx, DC, MC, V. **Map** p333 B4 ㉜
What makes this place stand out from the crowd is its friendly and helpful service. Its 461 rooms aren't very big, but they do have all the necessities (as well as some luxuries, like broadband internet access). The Eaton's restaurants and bars are pleasant, and there's plenty of life in the neighbourhood.
Bars (2). Business services. Disabled-adapted rooms. Gym. Internet (broadband). Limousine service. No-smoking rooms. Restaurants (2). Swimming pool (outdoor). TV (pay movies).

Cheap

Anne Black Guest House (YWCA)

5 Man Fuk Road, Ho Man Tin (2713 9211/fax 2761 1269/http://hotel.ywca.org.hk). Yau Ma Tei/Mong Kok MTR then taxi or 20min walk/shuttle bus (Vigor; HK$100) from the airport/3, 7, 103, 111, 170 bus. **Rates** HK$480 single/double. **Rooms** 169. **Credit** AmEx, DC, MC, V. **Map** p332 C2 ㉝
If you don't mind being a little out of the action, the Anne Black is a great, affordable choice. The 169 rooms (with en suite facilities) are clean and safe, and service is friendly. And if you're on your own but would like to meet fellow travellers, there's a restaurant, reading room and common room for guests' use. Shopping and dining are also available in Ho Man Tin and nearby Mong Kok.
No-smoking rooms. Restaurant. TV.

Booth Lodge

11 Wing Sing Lane, Yau Ma Tei (2771 9266/ fax 2385 1140/http://boothlodge.salvation.org.hk). Yau Ma Tei MTR (exit C) then 10min walk/A21 bus from the airport. **Rates** HK$620-$1,500 single/double. **Rooms** 60. **Credit** AmEx, MC, V. **Map** p332 B3 ㉞
This hotel run by the Salvation Army is a reasonable deal. With the 60 rooms more suited to a hotel chain, plus a decent restaurant and alfresco dining in its coffee shop, Booth Lodge is more than just a place to crash out. Its distinctive (read: ugly), sloping front makes it a landmark in Yau Ma Tei. It's pretty far removed from the action, but if you like your night-time decibels low, that's a bonus.
Concierge. No-smoking rooms. Restaurant. TV.

Caritas Bianchi Lodge

4 Cliff Road, Yau Ma Tei (2388 1111/fax 2770 6669/www.caritas-chs.org.hk). Yau Ma Tei MTR (exit C)/A21 bus from the airport/buses along Nathan Road. **Rates** HK$450-$1,000 single/ double/triple. **Rooms** 90. **Credit** AmEx, DC, MC, V. **Map** p332 C3 ㉟
A true bargain. Run by Caritas, the official social welfare bureau of the Roman Catholic Church in Hong Kong, Bianchi Lodge has a welcoming atmosphere. The 90 rooms are clean with good-sized beds and en suite bathrooms, and triple rooms are available for families or groups. Facing Nathan Road, the location is convenient for shopping.
TV.

Dorsett Seaview

268 Shanghai Street, Yau Ma Tei (2782 0882/ fax 2781 8800/www.dorsettseaview.com.hk). Yau Ma Tei MTR (exit C)/buses along Nathan Road. **Rates** HK$880-$1,280 single/double; HK$2,400-$3,000 suite. **Rooms** 268. **Credit** AmEx, DC, MC, V. **Map** p332 B3 ㊱
This tower block may have a partial sea view from the top-floor lounge, but don't expect a panorama of the harbour from your room. The best thing about Dorsett Seaview's location is that it's next to the thriving Temple Street Night Market, which is spilling over with curios and kitsch. The 268 rooms are reasonably decorated and have decent facilities.
Bar. Business services. Concierge. Disabled-adapted rooms. Internet (wireless). Limousine service. No-smoking floor. TV (pay movies).

Nathan Hotel

378 Nathan Road, Jordan (2388 5141/fax 2780 1643/www.nathanhotel.com). Jordan MTR (exit B1)/A21 bus from the airport/buses along Nathan

Designer digs

In Hong Kong the astronomical price of land has, for decades, seemingly dictated that hotels should be either large and glitzy or large and drab. Thankfully, a few bright sparks spotted a niche in recent times – the draw of small-scale accommodation with an eye towards both comfort and design: yes, the 'boutique hotel' has arrived. Here we review three of the best, all on Hong Kong Island.

Jia Boutique Hotel (*see p58*) trumpets itself as such, and was arguably the pioneer boutique hotel in the territory. Opened in 2004, Philippe Starck's first foray into Asia – barring the Felix restaurant at the Peninsula (*see p62*) – comes in the form of this sleek hotel-cum-serviced-apartment in Causeway Bay. The blink-and-you-miss-it entrance, not to mention the cooler-than-thou lobby manned by beautiful staff in Shanghai Tang uniforms, might hint at style over substance but these are fully working abodes that equally suit a short or long stay. The 54 rooms and suites vary in size (tip: it's worth spending the extra for a suite, which has a separate living, working and dining area) and each is fully kitted out – from state-of-the-art TV and DVD units, free broadband and proper desks to irons and ironing boards, they've thought of everything. Kitchens come with fridge, Smeg microwave, hob, toaster and kettle, plus decent tableware, while the small but stylish marble shower rooms feature upmarket toiletries. The overall style is trademark

Starck – all white and floaty, with hints of humour (stools in the shape of gnomes in the lounge, and a panel saying 'Dream' above the beds, for instance).

Though there are decent dining and entertainment options in the area, you needn't step outside the door: either soak up the swank at one of Jia's two award-winning restaurants or be even lazier and dial room service (for the record, it's pretty good). Further bonuses include complimentary continental breakfast, afternoon cakes and evening cocktails in the lobby, free local gym membership and access to the private members' Kee Club in Central. And the name? Pronounced 'jiar', it means 'home' in Mandarin.

Launched in late November 2005, **Lanson Place** (*see p58*) has 194 sleek contemporary rooms in a converted office block. It's located in a relatively quiet street in otherwise bustling Causeway Bay – turn a corner and you are suddenly strolling past luxury-brand boutiques and stylish restaurants of the Lee Gardens I and II malls. Lanson Place has no reception area; instead, there's a very small desk inside the entrance. The overall ambience is quite homely, though – thanks to lots of warmth from wood panelling and cosy lighting – and there's a general feel of spaciousness. The top four categories are referred to as 'residences', each containing kitchenette with cooking utensils;

Road. **Rates** HK$600-$800 single; HK$700-$1,280 double; HK$1,400-$2,000 suite. **Rooms** 188. **Credit** AmEx, DC, MC, V. **Map** p333 B4 **⬤**

Another cheap-ish alternative on the 'Golden Mile', the Nathan makes a useful exploration base. The 188 rooms are a bit poky, but the facilities are pretty good and you'll find plenty of 24-hour entertainment right outside.

Bar. Business services. Restaurant. TV.

Rent-a-Room

Flat A, 2/F, Knight Garden, 7-8 Tak Hing Street, Jordan (2366 3011/fax 2366 3588/www.renta roomhk.com). Jordan MTR (exit E)/buses along Nathan Road. **Rates** HK$155 dorm bed; HK$360 single; HK$460 double. **Rooms** 10 dorm beds; 60 private rooms. **No credit cards.** **Map** p333 C4 **⬤**

At the Jordan end of the 'Golden Mile', this pragmatically named place is experienced in catering to the needs of budget travellers. Their 60 rooms are a very good value too, considering each has en suite

shower, TV, phone and air-con, and some have kitchen facilities. Service is very efficient, and there's even a patio if you fancy a spot of sunbathing. What's more, Tsim Sha Tsui's many attractions are just a short stroll away.

Internet (dataport). TV.

Stanford Hotel

118 Soy Street, Mong Kok (2781 1881/fax 2388 3733/www.stanfordhongkong.com). Mong Kok MTR (exit E2)/buses along Nathan Road. **Rates** HK$900-$1,180 single/double. **Rooms** 194. **Credit** AmEx, DC, MC, V. **Map** p332 C2 **⬤**

The poor relation to Stanford Hillview (*see p63*), the Stanford offers the same facilities but in a less attractive environment. This area of Hong Kong isn't for everybody – Mong Kok is pretty dirty and crowded, with drug dealers, illegal hawkers and brothels dotted in among the bars and shops – but it's certainly action-packed, and with the Ladies' Market nearby is actually a reasonably safe place to stroll around.

Bar. Gym. Internet (broadband, wireless). No-smoking rooms. Restaurant. Swimming pool (indoor). TV.

other room categories have compact kitchen areas and microwave ovens. Wireless broadband operates throughout the hotel, and limousine service is another optional extra.

It may be lodged in the hub of Hong Kong's drinking and dining mecca, Lan Kwai Fong – after which **Hotel LKF** (*see p55*) is named – but the guest rooms occupy the 12th to 28th floors of a new tower, so you'll be well above the hubbub. Launched in spring 2006, this 95-room establishment bills itself as an entirely executive-floor hotel. Rooms are spacious, ranging from 47 to 88 square metres (500 to 950 square feet) and have an earthy masculine decor – fitting, as 90 per cent of guests are of the corporate variety – in which chocolate brown and ochre are dominant.

In-room espresso machine, broadband connection, Herman Miller desk chair and large-screen TV (rooms: 42-inch plasma; suites: 37-inch LCD) are standard, as are Bulgari bath products. To make life easier, a butler is available at the touch of a phone button. Suite numbers 2707 and 2708 have the best views in the house – of Victoria Harbour and the greenery of Government House's gardens, respectively. A satisfying buffet breakfast, as well as cocktails and canapés, is included in the rates.

Bar. Business services. Concierge. Internet (wireless). Limousine service. No-smoking rooms. Restaurant. TV (pay movies).

YMCA International House

23 Waterloo Road, Yau Ma Tei (2771 9111/fax 2771 5238/www.intlhouse.ymca.org.hk). Yau Ma Tei MTR (exit A2, D)/A21 bus from the airport/buses along Nathan Road. **Rates** HK$880 single/double; HK$2,080 suite. **Rooms** 409. **Credit** AmEx, DC, MC, V. **Map** p332 B3 ⑩

There are 380 comfortable rooms and 29 suites in this 25-storey tower with all the amenities of a top hotel, for a third of the price. The YMCA International House offers healthy extras such as tennis and squash courts, a health centre and sauna, though the best feature is the swimming pool – a great attraction on a muggy summer's day. Along with a bar, coffee shop and banqueting facilities, there's also a Chinese restaurant, a relaxing lounge and even a chapel. Rooms have simple and comfortable furnishings.

The New Territories

Central New Territories

Hostels

Sze Lok Yuen Hostel

Tai Mo Shan, Tsuen Wan (2788 1638/2488 8188/ fax 2788 3105/www.yha.org.hk). Tsuen Wan MTR then 51 bus to junction of Tai Mo Shan Road and Route Twisk then red taxi or 45mins walk. **Rates** HK$65 dorm bed; HK$35 tent pitch. **Credit** MC, V. Hikers love this place. It's perched on top of Tai Mo Shan (Hong Kong's tallest mountain), so the only way to get here is on foot or by taxi. By the time you arrive you'll settle for a bed anywhere, which is just as well as there is no air-conditioning – not even an electric fan – so summer nights can be practically unbearable. The hostel has a kitchen and barbecue pits, but you'll have to bring your own food. Open on Saturday, Sunday and public holidays only.

East New Territories

Hostels

Bradbury Hall Hostel

Chek Keng, Sai Kung (2788 1638/2328 2458/fax 2788 3105/www.yha.org.hk). Choi Hung MTR (exit C) then 1A minibus to Sai Kung then 94 bus or taxi to Wong Shek Pier then ferry (2272 2022/2272 2000). **Rates** HK$65 dorm bed; HK$35 tent pitch. **Beds** 100. **Credit** MC, V.
This 100-bed hostel mainly takes in hikers mid-hike; thus, the facilities and decoration are rather basic. It does, however, have barbecue pits, use of a kitchen, and a nice view of the neighbouring hillside.

Bradbury Jockey Club Hostel

66 Tai Mei Tuk Road, Tai Mei Tuk, Tai Po (2788 1638/2662 5123/fax 2788 3105/www.yha.org.hk). Tai Po Market KCR then 75K bus or 20C minibus. **Rates** HK$80 dorm bed; HK$270 double; HK$310 four-bed; HK$450 six-bed; HK$590 eight-bed; HK$60 tent pitch. **Beds** 94. **Credit** MC, V.
The facilities in this 94-bed lodge are better than in most hostels. It offers more than a brief stop on your hiking route as it is located near the waterfront and has a water-sports centre nearby. Air-conditioning is included in the cost of the two- and four-bed rooms, but costs extra per night in the dorms. The campsite has a wonderful bay view.

Pak Sha O Hostel

Pak Sha O, Hoi Ha Road, Sai Kung (2788 1638/ 2328 2327/fax 2788 3105/www.yha.org.hk). Choi Hung MTR (exit C) then bus 92 or green minibus 1A

Hollywood Hotel.

to Sai Kung then green minibus 7. **Rates** HK$50 (HK$80 non-YHA members) dorm bed; HK$35 tent pitch. **Beds** 112. **No credit cards**.

Built inside an abandoned village school, this beautiful development has won awards for design. It holds up to 112 people and has a campsite too. Located in Sai Kung Country Park, it's hard to reach, but is worth it for the spectacular views. There is also a huge barbecue area and a basketball court.

The Outlying Islands

Lantau

Moderate

Hollywood Hotel

Hong Kong Disneyland, Penny's Bay (3510 6000/fax 3510 6333/www.hongkongdisneyland.com). Hong Kong Disneyland MTR. **Rates** HK$1,600-$2,100 single/double; HK$2,300-$2,800 Fantasia/Kingdom Club rooms; HK$5,600 suite. **Rooms** 600. **Credit** AmEx, DC, MC, V.

This newish addition to the territory's mid-range bracket has an unusual location: it's at Hong Kong Disneyland on Lantau Island. The funkier of the theme park's two on-site accommodation options, it pays tribute both in name and decor to the golden age of movies – from the 1930s to '50s – and is designed in an art deco style, albeit with obligatory Mickey Mouse-inspired motifs. Some 600 guestrooms gather around a grand piano-shaped pool. *Bars (2). Business services. Concierge. Internet (broadband). Limousine service. No-smoking rooms. Restaurants (3). TV (pay movies).*

Hostels

Hongkong Bank Foundation SG Davis Hostel

Ngong Ping (2788 1638/2985 5610/fax 2788 3105/ www.yha.org.hk). Tung Chung MTR (exit B) then 23

bus/bus 2 from Mui Wo Ferry Pier. **Rates** HK$70 dorm bed; HK$180 double room; HK$35 tent pitch. **Beds** 52. **No credit cards**.

Formerly known more pithily as the SG Davis Hostel, this place is located near the Big Buddha, high in Lantau's beautiful mountains. The quaint fishing village of Tai O is just about within walking distance. The hostel has only 52 beds and offers plenty of facilities, including a kitchen, barbecue pits and badminton court, so get in quick.

Jockey Club Mong Tung Wan Hostel

Mong Tung Wan (2788 1638/2984 1389/fax 2788 3105/www.yha.org.hk). Taxi from Mui Wo Ferry Pier/sampan to Mong Tung Wan Pier/ferry from Cheung Chau. **Rates** HK$65 dorm bed; HK$35 tent pitch. **Beds** 88. **No credit cards**.

This is the newest of Hong Kong's seven hostels and consequently offers a selection of clean rooms and modern facilities. It can hold up to 88 people, mostly hikers exploring Lantau's verdant trails or nearby beaches. Bonuses include the lovely view of the sea from the hostel and a communal kitchen. Camping is permitted.

Cheung Chau

Cheap

Cheung Chau Warwick

East Bay (2981 0081/fax 2981 9673/www.warwick hotel.com.hk). Cheung Chau Ferry Pier then 15min walk. **Rates** HK$840 single/double. **Rooms** 71. **Credit** AmEx, MC, V.

The Cheung Chau Warwick is dated and fairly run-down, but it is close to a nice beach and is pretty cheap. The design certainly won't win any awards – it's a dark concrete blot on Cheung Chau's traditional Chinese landscape – but the views from the balcony of the 71 seafront rooms make it worth staying a night, especially for water-sports fans, who can go windsurfing or sea kayaking from the beach below. *Restaurant. TV.*

Sightseeing

Star Ferry and the **IFC2** tower. *See p74.*

Introduction

There's never a dull moment in Hong Kong, whether in the shadows of its high-rises or out in its surprisingly quiet rural pockets.

The Tsim Sha Tsui promenade offers a grand view of Hong Kong Island's skyline.

Sure, Hong Kong is best known for its array of skyscrapers, rising ever higher above – and into – Victoria Harbour. But walk just a few paces from these glitzy towers and you're likely to encounter steaming noodle shops, street stalls and tiny stores full of curiosities that spill almost underfoot on to the pavement. A half-hour's train, bus or ferry ride out of the city, though, brings the biggest surprise: a much greener and more laid-back face of the territory, with plenty of character and points of interest for visitors.

Depending on where you are staying, the first areas you are likely to explore are those that line Hong Kong harbour. **Central**, on the northern coast of **Hong Kong Island**, is a natural starting point, being home to the seat of government and the all-important financial district. Its highlights include glamorous shopping, some striking modern architecture, a lovely park and a thriving nightlife.

Sheung Wan may only be minutes to the west of Central, but it is worlds apart in terms of atmosphere. This is where you'll get a feel for

an older, and distinctly more Chinese, Hong Kong, packed with antiques, Chinese medicine, dried food and funeral shops.

To the east of Central, **Wan Chai** and **Causeway Bay** are primarily dedicated to nightlife and shopping, respectively. Heavily built up, the urban crush is relieved by the large open space of Victoria Park and Happy Valley Racecourse, just to the south.

Towering above Central is the **Peak**, best reached via the old Peak Tram; the fantastic panoramas from up here should not be missed (but save it for a day when you can see the Peak from below – otherwise you'll only view mist or smog). There are fine walks up here too.

Most visitors also enjoy a trip to the comparatively rural parts in the centre of the island and along the **south and east coasts**. Here you can hike, relax on a beach, potter around a market or have fun in a theme park.

Across the harbour from Central, **Kowloon** – particularly the district of **Tsim Sha Tsui** on the peninsula's tip – contains the greatest concentration of museums. It's also a terrific place from which to admire Hong Kong Island's stunning skyline. Shop-lined Nathan Road, forming the spine of Kowloon, starts here and extends north through the districts of **Yau Ma Tei** and **Mong Kok**, which are home to a number of specialist markets.

Once you've spent a couple of days exploring the more built-up areas of the city, travel out into the **New Territories** to discover a side of Hong Kong that few visitors experience. There's a fair amount of unsightly industrial and urban sprawl in places, but also interesting

museums and walled villages, plus – and this is the most surprising attraction – great swathes of unspoiled countryside criss-crossed by hiking trails, and some remote, pristine beaches.

An alternative is to head to the **Outlying Islands**. Depending on your interests, you can explore the peaceful monasteries of huge, hilly Lantau, the laid-back charm and seafood restaurants of Lamma or villagey Cheung Chau.

And if you have the time, a visit to the former Portuguese colony of **Macau** or the dynamic city of **Guangzhou** is well worthwhile.

Must-see Hong Kong

... in a day

● Take a tram to **Western Market**, mooch around **Sheung Wan** (for both, *see p79*), then browse the antiques shops strung along **Hollywood Road** (*see p80*).

● Head to **Hong Kong Park** (*see p78*) for an alfresco lunch.

● Take the Peak Tram up to **Victoria Peak** (*see p88*).

● Stroll around Lugard and Harlech roads (*see p88* **Peak around**), and up to the Peak itself, taking in the stunning panoramas.

● Return to Central by the Peak Tram and walk down to the Central Ferry Pier, crossing over to Tsim Sha Tsui to admire the Hong Kong Island skyline (**photo p70**).

● Enjoy afternoon tea in the **Peninsula** hotel (*see p151* **A fancy cuppa**) or early evening drinks in its sky-high **Felix** bar (*see p168*).

● Either ride the MTR to **Temple Street Night Market** (*see p100*) and chance your luck at a street-side *dai pai dong* food stall, or return via the Star Ferry for dinner and drinking in **Lan Kwai Fong** (*see p77*) or **SoHo** (*see p82*).

... in two days

● Spend the morning walking the **Dragon's Back** (*see p90* **Taming the dragon**) or, if you have kids, take them to **Ocean Park** (*see p210* **Variations on a theme**).

● If you do the walk, lunch in **Shek O** (*see p93*), then relax on the beach for a couple of hours; if you take the Ocean Park option, then, afterwards, catch the bus into **Stanley** to eat and peruse the market (*see p92*).

● Take the bus and MTR to **Causeway Bay** (*see p85*) for a bit of late-afternoon shopping.

● End the day by exploring **Wan Chai**'s nightlife (*see p231*) or, if the day and season are right, go to **Happy Valley** for a night at the races (*see p86*).

... in three days

● Rise early to practise **t'ai chi** on the Tsim Sha Tsui waterfront (*see p253*).

● Spend the morning visiting a museum in Tsim Sha Tsui that interests you, be it **Art** or **Space** (for both, *see p97*), **Science** or **History** (for both, *see p98*).

● Take the ferry across the harbour for dim sum at **City Hall Maxim's Palace** (*see p133*).

● Walk to the nearby Outlying Islands Ferry Piers and catch a ferry to **Yung Shue Wan** on Lamma (*see p120*).

● Walk across the island to **Sok Kwu Wan** (*see p122*), stopping off at a beach along the way; eat an early seafood dinner (*see p156*) and catch the ferry back to Central.

... in four days

● Early in the morning, take the KCR north into the New Territories to Sha Tin and visit the **Hong Kong Heritage Museum** (*see p109*) and the colourful **Ten Thousand Buddhas Monastery** (*see p107*).

● Grab a bite to eat in **Sha Tin** (*see p107*), before taking a taxi to the **Sai Kung Peninsula** (*see p118*).

● Hire a sampan from Sai Kung's main ferry pier if you wish to spend the afternoon on a secluded beach (*see p119*) or, if you're feeling more energetic, hike through the countryside near **Pak Tam Chung** (*see p118*).

● Dine in one of Sai Kung's good restaurants (*see p153*) before heading back to the city.

... in five days or more

● Venture further afield, with a day or two in the intriguing ex-Portuguese colony of **Macau** (*see p261*) or the chaotic, buzzing city of **Guangzhou** (*see p278*).

● Alternatively, if you have kids in tow, keep them occupied for the day at **Hong Kong Disneyland** (*see p212* **Variations on a theme**).

Hong Kong Island

There's more behind Hong Kong's majestic skyline than just the Peak.

Sightseeing

The image many visitors have when they think of Hong Kong is the glittering forest of skyscrapers ranged along Victoria Harbour. But as you step back from the (ever extending) shoreline, you'll discover pockets of Chinese tradition down ramshackle lanes and inside exotic markets, scattered colonial structures, a vibrant array of shops in glitzy mega malls and a surprising amount of greenery. Well away from the pulsing business district are the Ocean Park theme park, some good beaches and several very beautiful, easily accessible country parks. And afterwards it's only a short journey back to sample a thriving nightlife that rivals the best in the world.

One of the most enduring curiosities about Hong Kong is that, despite being less than a kilometre across the water from each other, those who live on Hong Kong Island rarely visit Kowloon, and vice versa. The residents of the island, however, definitely consider themselves superior to their counterparts on the north side of the harbour – and have done since the 19th century.

Much of this perceived superiority has to do with the fact that Victoria, as the administrative centre and official capital was once known, was on Hong Kong Island. It is also partly because the smartest shopping centres, social clubs and residential areas are all found on the island, but this geographical and psychological division very accurately reflects just how truly insular and small town this big city can be at times.

Hong Kong Island certainly seems to have it all: a plethora of business opportunities, shops galore, trendy bars and restaurants, its fair share of sights, plenty of sandy beaches, and a varied landscape – much of it protected and laced through with invigorating walking trails (*see also p115* **Walks on the wild side**).

Central

Vertiginous skyscrapers, impatient crowds, streaming traffic, disorientating tangles of raised pedestrian walkways: Hong Kong's political, financial and commercial centre is an undeniably exciting, occasionally overwhelming and often rather ugly place. Squeezed into a narrow coastal strip between

harbour and hillside, along the western end of Hong Kong Island's northern side, **Central** is where it all happens – or starts happening.

In many respects Central is a glittering temple to high-end conspicuous consumption, and fashion victims will have no problem finding every possible designer boutique in which to part company with their money. In broader cultural terms, however, offerings are far more meagre compared with almost any other city of its size – and certainly those of the West. Constantly re-inventing itself, and without the slightest vestige of sentimentality (or sense of history, its critics would argue), Central epitomises here-and-now Hong Kong – the few remnants of its built heritage that survive are little more than fragments, which half a century's inexorable development and land reclamation (*see p103* **Walking on water**) have left marooned like waifs from another time among the towers of steel and glass.

Despite these caveats, there is still plenty to see and do in Central. Some of its most impressive modern buildings can be examined up close; Lan Kwai Fong is, along with nearby

SoHo, the main partying enclave and a lively lunch- and night-time destination for eating; and there are even a couple of green spaces, such as Hong Kong Park and the Zoological & Botanical Gardens, in which to take a breather.

Star Ferry & the waterfront

By far the most breathtaking way to approach Central is to take the eight-minute **Star Ferry** ride across Victoria Harbour from Kowloon (costing a mere HK$2.20 for a seat on the first-class, upper deck). These double-ended, green-and-cream ferries have been ploughing across the waters here since 1874, and it's no exaggeration to say (and it has been said many, many times before) that this short crossing remains one of the world's great ferry journeys.

Comparisons with the Manhattan skyline aren't entirely fanciful, the north side of Hong Kong Island having the added element of a backdrop of deep green, thickly wooded mountains, rearing majestic and indifferent above the bustle and the clamour. Although undeniably the most romantic approach to

Sightseeing

The view from **the Peak**. *See p88.*

IFC Mall.

Central, the Star Ferry is just one spoke in the district's transport hub, and unless you're travelling directly from somewhere close to the pier in Tsim Sha Tsui to a similar destination in Central, it is probably not the fastest or most convenient transport option.

In November 2006 the iconic Star Ferry pier on the Central waterfront was replaced by a new, faux-Edwardian style terminal, built 200 metres (650 feet) further into the harbour on reclaimed land adjacent to the Outlying Districts piers (where you can catch ferries to Lantau, Lamma, Cheung Chau and other islands). There have been numerous complaints about the new pier's inconvenient location and the new terminal's execrable design.

The Airport Express line from Chek Lap Kok terminates at Hong Kong Station (also referred to as Central Airport Express Station), just south-west of Central Ferry Pier. The station is connected by underground walkway to the busy Central MTR (metro) station, a key transport node. Most bus routes along the north side of the island pass along one of three parallel roads accessible from Central MTR: Connaught Road/Harcourt Road, Des Voeux Road/Chater Road and Queen's Road Central/Queensway.

RECENT DEVELOPMENTS

For most visitors, Central's most interesting 'sights' are architectural. The district has changed beyond all recognition since the 1970s, and the profusion of modern towers that have sprung up in the last couple of decades – some

markedly more aesthetically appealing than others – all define modern Hong Kong.

Just east of Hong Kong Station is the **General Post Office** and, to the south and accessible by elevated walkway, stands the **Exchange Square** complex (1985), where Hong Kong's Stock Exchange has operated since the merger of its four exchanges in 1986. Swiss architect Remo Riva's strategy of 'architecture as sculpture' is best appreciated from mid-harbour on the Star Ferry. Close up, the scale and layout of its three interlinked buildings don't really work and can be quite confusing to get around. More pleasing is its open piazza, with its fountains and Henry Moore's *Single Oval* sculpture, Dame Elizabeth Frink's *Water Buffalo* bronzes and Taiwanese artist Chu Ming's stylised human figure in t'ai chi pose. It's an agreeable spot to sit out with a snack or a drink – there are plenty of bars, cafés and restaurants nearby – and watch the stockbroker types scurrying by.

Out on the waterfront reclamation, rising above the Airport Express terminus, are the two modern towers of the **International Finance Centre**, better known locally as IFC. While architecturally stunning, the 88-storey **IFC2** tower (also known as Two IFC; *see also p35*) was nevertheless – like many buildings in Hong Kong – built without any reference to the surrounding landscape and was likened by some critics to a gigantic nose-hair clipper. Less happily, the IFC development was also built in complete contravention of existing planning guidelines, which state that new buildings should not block the view of Victoria Peak from the Tsim Sha Tsui waterfront promenade, one of urban Hong Kong's most magnificent viewing points. Despite this 'safeguard', the IFC2 building almost completely obscures the Peak – yet another example of Hong Kong's vested interests getting their own way regardless. Next door, the high-end **Four Seasons** hotel (*see p55*) recently opened.

Just east of Exchange Square, opposite the General Post Office, stands **Jardine House** (1973; *see also p35*), known locally as the 'House of a Thousand Arseholes' (partly due to its 1,700-plus porthole-style windows, partly as a comment on those who work behind them). This 52-storey structure, once the tallest in Asia, is the Hong Kong headquarters of Jardine Matheson, one of the major trading houses that virtually founded commerce in Hong Kong (it moved its official domicile to Bermuda in 1984). Another Henry Moore piece, *Double Oval*, can be seen to the east of the building.

On a prime waterfront site just to the east of the former Star Ferry Pier stands Hong Kong's **City Hall** (*see p242*). Its two blocks, with their 1960s civic architecture, reflect the general disregard for aesthetics, especially when you compare them with (a picture of) the original – a rather grand mid-19th-century French classical incarnation. The Low Block contains a theatre and a concert hall, as well as a pleasant enclosed garden, which was built by public subscription in memory of the Hong Kong Volunteer Defence Corps who died during World War II. The High Block, to the rear, houses a succession of libraries, a recital hall and various committee rooms. The Chinese restaurant on the second floor – **City Hall Maxim's Place** (*see p133*) – with views out over Kowloon, is rightly famed for its dim sum.

A little further to the east is the **Chinese People's Liberation Army Forces Hong Kong Building**, formerly known as the Prince of Wales Building (and sometimes likened to an upturned gin bottle – look at it closely and you'll immediately understand why). Also previously known as HMS Tamar (named after the naval vessel that was moored offshore and used as a floating naval base until it was scuttled in World War II), this former British naval headquarters is now occupied, in a very low-key way, by the PLA.

Heading south

The old colonial area of Hong Kong centres around **Statue Square**, which was once flanked by granite colonial buildings with columned verandas. The square was originally named after a bronze statue of Queen Victoria; in Chinese the area is still referred to as the 'Empress' Statue Square'. Along with other statues in the area she was removed by the Japanese during World War II, but was recovered and later resituated in Causeway Bay, where she can still be seen to this day. Nowadays Statue Square has just one statue; the former HSBC Chief Manager Sir Thomas Jackson. The square is best known – at least on weekends – for the hundreds of Filipina maids who gather here (and in many other open spaces on the Island) on Sundays to make the most of their day off.

On the eastern edge of the square stands one of the few remaining colonial buildings, the neo-classical, granite **Legislative Council Building**. Originally built as the Supreme Court – the scales of justice can still be seen on the outside – it now houses the Hong Kong Legislative Council, the closest thing the SAR has to a representative government. The eastern side of the Legislative Council Building faces **Chater Garden**, which was the site of the Hong Kong Cricket Club until the mid 1970s. A pleasant Fenough public park, it has been a popular gathering place for political activists and pressure groups to vent loudly their disapproval of various official policies.

The **IFC2 Tower** scrapes the sky. *See p74.*

Along Des Voeux Road, on Statue Square's southern side, Hong Kong's clattering old trams have trundled between Kennedy Town and Shau Kei Wan since 1904. With a HK$2 flat fare, these wood-panelled relics are a cheap and enjoyable way to travel along the northern side of the island. But they are definitely not recommended for anyone in a hurry.

Dominating the south side of Statue Square is Norman Foster's phenomenally expensive (HK$5.2 billion) **HSBC Building** (*see also p34*). The world's costliest building when it was completed in 1985, this colossal structure made of steel and glass rests on four tall pillars, creating an airy, open-air forum that remains a public space. It is worth taking the escalator up to the quiet, business-like first floor for a sense of the scale of the place, and to feel for a moment like nothing more than one of the stick people in an architectural concept drawing.

According to those 'in the know', the building has some of the best feng shui in Hong Kong. Its views of the harbour and the hills behind it are favourable, but, more significantly, it sits at the only local junction of five dragon lines (magnetic fields thought to follow the direction of underground water flows, which carry powerful channels of positive *chi*, or life-force energy). This energy is said to be sucked inside the huge atrium of the bank by the angled escalators and the undulating floor. The two huge lions (known as Stitt and Stephens, after pre-war bank officials) guarding the entrance – war-damaged remnants of the earlier building – help block negative energy (according to feng shui beliefs) and are also supposed to confer good luck on passers-by who rub their paws.

Corporate competition between HSBC and the Bank of China extended to a feng shui war. When the Bank of China outgrew its former home alongside the HSBC (the old building still stands, and the top floor houses the China Club), Chinese-American architect IM Pei was commissioned to build the new headquarters. The result is probably the city's most striking modern building. Completed in 1990, the **Bank of China Tower's** (*see also p33*) elegant, dynamic, asymmetrical geometry, resembling black, triangular building blocks, presents an unmistakable aspect from every angle. But its knife-like structure, inauspicious chopstick-shaped antennae and dominant position undid much of the HSBC's allegedly good feng shui. If your luck holds and it happens to be a clear day, it's well worth going up to the 47th-floor viewing gallery for a panoramic view.

The Bank of China Tower also encroached on the feng shui of the old Government House and was one of the reasons that former Chief Executive Tung Chee-hwa gave for preferring not to move into the traditional seat of power. Local tycoon Lee Ka-shing built the **Cheung Kong Center** between the Bank of China Tower and HSBC Building, thus restoring much of the harmony and energy flow and resultant prosperity – or so the urban legend relates.

COLONIAL FRAGMENTS

South of the HSBC Building, up the hill, lie a few lingering reminders of Hong Kong's colonial heritage. Climb the steps up to Battery Path and the cathedral precinct and you'll find the whitewashed, cool and quiet **St John's Cathedral** (*see p77*), which was completed in 1849. Its entrance doors are made from the wood salvaged from HMS *Tamar*, the Royal Navy's floating HQ that was scuttled during World War II, and numerous moving memorials and historical relics are hidden away inside.

Across from the cathedral you'll find Hong Kong's **Court of Final Appeal**, housed in the green-shuttered, neo-classical **French Mission**

Flagstaff House Museum of Tea Ware. See p78.

第六屆國際名茶評比總決賽

Building, which dates in part from the 1860s. French Catholic missionaries added a chapel to the original when they took it over in 1917.

On the other side of Lower Albert Road and further up the hill stands **Government House**, residence of Hong Kong's British governors since 1855. Originally constructed in a tropical Georgian style, the structure was completely rebuilt by the occupying Japanese, who added its distinctive central tower. The building, which is closed to the public, is still used for official functions and, after eight years of lying idle, is the new home to the new chief executive, Sir Donald Tsang. The pretty gardens are opened to the public once a year when the azaleas are in bloom (call the HKTB for details; see p310). While it used to enjoy a prime location, with uninterrupted views of the harbour, the building is now hemmed in from all sides by corporate towers – neatly illustrating how quickly Hong Kong turns its back on its past.

Nearby, at the junction of Ice House Street and Lower Albert Road, stands the early 20th-century, brown-and-cream brick old **Dairy Farm Building**, which houses the **Fringe Club** (see p243), the superb **M at the Fringe** restaurant (see p138) and the Foreign Correspondents' Club. Ice House Street gained its name from an ice storage facility that stood at the bottom of the road in the days when ice was imported from North America. Opposite is the gracious old **Bishop's House**, with its tower; dating from 1848, it's one of Hong Kong's oldest extant European buildings.

St John's Cathedral

4-8 Garden Road (2523 4157/www.stjohns cathedral.org.hk). Central MTR (exit K)/buses along Garden Road. **Open** 9am-5pm Mon-Fri; 9am-noon Sat, Sun. **Admission** free. **Map** p329 E4.

Now marooned by ultra-modern towers, St John's is one of the oldest Anglican churches in Asia (it was completed in 1849 – and later extended in 1873). Within, the cathedral is pleasingly airy and light, but there is little evidence of its former parishioners – the memorial brasses that marked the deaths of prominent local residents were removed during World War II by occupying Japanese forces (who used the church as a social club). In a side chapel are some old flags and standards belonging to the Hong Kong Volunteer Defence Corps, which were buried to avoid their capture by the Japanese in 1941 and only unearthed in the late 1950s.

Lan Kwai Fong & around

The backstreets to the west of the old Dairy Farm Building are largely devoted to shops, restaurants and bars. The best concentration of drinking and eating joints is on and around

Lan Kwai Fong, off D'Aguilar Street. During the day the place is not much to look at – and is actually rather grubby – but after work hours, particularly Fridays, the neon shines brightly above a raucous procession of diners, drinkers, demob-happy suits and pre-clubbers. For a quintessential Hong Kong experience, be sure to grab a plastic stool, a bottle of Singha and a fine curry outside **Good Luck Thai Café** (see p141) on Wing Wah Lane and enjoy the street life. These days, however, more discerning expats tend to favour the burgeoning drinking and dining scene of the area (west of here) informally known as SoHo (see p82).

Close by, north of Queen's Road Central, stands one of Central's biggest upmarket shopping complexes: **The Landmark** (see p179), containing most of the area's swankiest boutiques (with prices to match). If it's relative bargains you're after, head for Pedder Street and explore the **Pedder Building** – one of the last old office buildings in the area – which houses a series of small shops selling a mixture of genuine, cut-price and fake labels, beautiful embroidered shawls and a fair helping of tat (see p186 **Second-hand luxury**). Also on the first floor of the Pedder Building, looking down on the throng of Pedder Street, is the China Tee Club, a quiet restaurant and café with a faux colonial air, with old ceiling fans, dark woods and trilling songbirds in ornate cages. On the ground floor is **Shanghai Tang** (see p185), a stylishly retro, tongue-in-cheek kitsch boutique, selling Chinese-style clothes, ornaments and chic, fun gifts. It's not cheap, though, and numerous imitations have sprung up, selling virtually the same items for much less.

Running between Des Voeux Road Central and Queen's Road Central, a few minutes' walk north-west, are Li Yuen Street East and Li Yuen Street West (known as '**The Lanes**'; see p171), which are crowded with cheap clothing, beads, handbag stalls and shoppers. It's a place to come as much for the spectacle as for the bargain-hunting; similar fare is also on offer in nearby Pottinger Street. A little further beyond, at the foot of the Mid-Levels Escalator (see p80), stands **Central Market**. For many years this wet market has provided a lively contrast to Central's homogeneous shopping malls, but it is under threat of redevelopment.

Nearby green spaces

When the swirling maelstrom of Central becomes too much, it's worth remembering that there are a few green havens in among the concrete and the crowds. The extensive **Hong Kong Zoological & Botanical Gardens** (see p78) overlooks Government

Sightseeing

House across Upper Albert Road. Featuring dozens of animal (mainly primates) and bird species, and more than a thousand types of flora, the gardens are small but full of interest, as well as being peaceful and well shaded – a very important feature on a sweltering Hong Kong summer's day.

To the east of the gardens, beyond the Peak Tram Lower Terminal, is **Hong Kong Park** (*see below*), located on the old Victoria Cantonment. Spreading across one square kilometre (0.4 square miles) of prime real estate, the park is proof positive that Hong Kong doesn't always put money over quality of life. Spectacularly bordered by some of Central's most striking tower blocks, the park contains landscaped gardens, an artificial lake (complete with multicoloured fish and sunbathing terrapins), a children's playground, a t'ai chi garden, an amphitheatre, a restaurant and bar, and the architecturally stunning **Edward Youde Aviary** (*see below*) This elegant expanse of undulating mesh, stretched over a series of arches, manages to be both spectacular and discreet, and provides a perfect setting in which to wander along the raised wooden walkway, trying to spot the 150 species of South-east Asian birdlife therein.

Also in the park is the **Flagstaff House Museum of Tea Ware** (*see below*), which occupies an elegant colonial building that was constructed between 1844 and 1846; it served as official residence of the Commander British Forces (CBF) in Hong Kong until 1978. Now devoted to displays of Chinese tea and tea ware, the building itself is a well-preserved gem, and worth a visit in its own right.

As well as being a marvellous expanse of open space within the city, Hong Kong Park is one of the best places to see Hong Kong's identikit wedding couples, dressed in flouncy wedding dresses and completely unfeasible tuxedos. Photo shoots in the park after a quick trip to the Registry Office within the park's boundaries are a near-obligatory part of getting married in Hong Kong. (The Cultural Centre environs in Tsim Sha Tsui offers a Kowloon version of the same cheesy experience.)

Edward Youde Aviary

Hong Kong Park, Cotton Tree Drive (2521 5041/ 2521 5092/www.lcsd.gov.hk). Admiralty MTR (exit B)/buses & trams along Queensway/buses along Cotton Tree Drive. **Open** 9am-5pm daily. **Admission** free. **Map** p329 E5.

For many the highlight of a visit to Hong Kong Park, this imaginative aviary contains a whole other world below its spectacular expanse of steel netting. An aerial walkway passes through the aviary, offering excellent branch-high vantage points. All of the birds here are from South-east Asia, and more than

a few are increasingly endangered in their natural habitats, especially in Indonesia. Almost every variety of parrot found in the region can be seen here, including vivid purple and green eclectus parrots from Papua, lively white-and-yellow lesser sulphur-crested cockatoos from the eastern Moluccas, fire-red Ambon parrots, and massive hornbills from Borneo. You don't have to be an amateur naturalist to enjoy this well-designed complex, which really is stunning. Unfortunately, since the avian flu outbreaks in recent years, this aviary – along with all others in Hong Kong – has been closed to the public as a safety measure. This situation may well change, so call ahead to see if it has re-opened before you visit.

Flagstaff House Museum of Tea Ware

Hong Kong Park, 10 Cotton Tree Drive (2869 0690/ 2869 6690/www.hk.art.museum). Admiralty MTR (exit B)/buses & trams along Queensway/buses along Cotton Tree Drive. **Open** 10am-5pm Mon, Wed-Sun. **Admission** free. **Map** p329 F5.

This small museum offers a comprehensive, if not too exciting, display of tea ware and the different types of tea and tea preparation, but there are some beautiful and extraordinarily well-crafted antique and modern pieces. A couple of dozen different teas are for sale in the museum shop – some are rare and rather expensive, while others are much more reasonably priced. There are also plenty of teapots for sale; among the most popular are the Yixing teapots made from a special variety of clay. While quality here is high, prices are too, and similar items can often be obtained in Shenzhen (*see p194* **Savings made in China**) for substantially less money. The best reason to visit the museum, though, is for the marvellous old colonial building itself. **Photo** *p76*.

Hong Kong Park

19 Cotton Tree Drive (2521 5041/2521 5092/ www.lcsd.gov.hk). Admiralty MTR (exit B, C1)/buses & trams along Queensway/buses along Cotton Tree Drive. **Open** 6.30am-11pm daily. **Admission** free. **Map** p329 E5.

Opened in 1991 on the site of the sprawling old Victoria Barracks complex, this delightful, unusual park, dwarfed by surrounding corporate towers and endlessly busy flyovers, centres around a large artificial lake, replete with multi-hued fish, mostly koi and goerami. Among its numerous attractions are a bar/café, a conservatory (open 9am-5pm daily), a pleasant t'ai chi garden, a children's playground and the very impressive walk-through Edward Youde Aviary (*see above*).

Hong Kong Zoological & Botanical Gardens

Albany Road (2530 0154/www.lcsd.gov.hk). Buses along Upper Albert Road. **Open** 6am-7pm daily. **Admission** free. **Map** p328 C5/p329 D5.

The western side of the gardens (founded in 1864), is where you'll find most of the animal enclosures. There's an impressive collection of primates, which includes macaques, tamarins and a family of rather bored-looking orang-utans, including an immense, pot-bellied and impressively grumpy male named Datu. Other exotic residents are a tree kangaroo and a family of improbably cute ring-tailed lemurs. It's not a place for those who object to seeing caged animals as the enclosures are not huge, though most of the creatures look fairly content. In the eastern half of the gardens, on the other side of Albany Road, there are several bird enclosures, housing dozens of pink, stick-legged African flamingos and a flock of vivid scarlet ibis. You'll also find a large fountain, lawns, well-tended flowerbeds and a bronze statue of King George VI presiding over it all.

Admiralty

If all this open space and massed greenery proves overwhelming, shopping junkies can cross Supreme Court Road and immerse themselves in **Pacific Place**, an immense multi-storey mall (*see p180*). A food court and restaurants provide plenty of decent eating and drinking choices, although most are a little on the pricey side. This area, which links Central and Wan Chai, is known as **Admiralty**, due to the long-vanished Royal Naval Dockyard that stood across the road here until the late 1950s. Its most interesting buildings are the two glittering silver towers of the **Lippo Centre** (made all the more startling by their proximity to the golden **Far East Finance Centre**), overlooking Hong Kong Park. Designed by American architect Paul Rudolph in 1988, the Lippo Centre has something of an aura of bad luck, having seen three large corporate occupants go bankrupt in the past two decades, including the Australian entrepreneur Alan Bond, after whom the building was originally named.

Sheung Wan & Mid-Levels

Blending into Central on its western side, Sheung Wan (also known as Western) is the Chinese heart of old Hong Kong. It's a vibrant, colourful area that's best explored on foot. Although development has obliterated most of the formerly distinct streetscapes, there's still a real old-fashioned Chinese character to the Sheung Wan area, and few of the bland mega-malls that dominate so much of the north side of the island. As you climb the hill – or ride the world's longest escalator – you'll cross over Hollywood Road (the main centre for Hong Kong's important antiques and curio trade, and the location of the atmospheric Man Mo Temple) and reach the trendy bar and restaurant enclave of SoHo, prior to the upmarket residential district of Mid-Levels.

Sheung Wan

In **Sheung Wan**, the area around the MTR makes for some of the most colourful and interesting sightseeing in Hong Kong. Many of the streets around here specialise in specific trades. For instance, head to **Man Wa Lane** for name chop stalls. Chops are made from pieces of wood, bamboo or bone, on to which Chinese names are carved. You can watch them being carved and have one made with a Chinese translation of your name for about HK$100.

Wing Lok Street, **Queen's Road West** and many neighbouring streets are filled with shops piled high with sacks of dried seafood and other ingredients used both for Chinese medicine and in soups and other dishes. If you know what to look for, you can uncover entire desiccated deer foetuses, dog's penises, dried seahorses and horse bezoars (hard balls of hair or vegetable fibre that collect in their stomachs; said to make an excellent antidote to poison).

This is also the centre of the completely out-of-control shark's fin trade, which is sharply reducing shark populations around the world. Most of the fins collected here are resold to emerging markets on the mainland. Good-quality shark's fin soup sells for about HK$300 a bowl, and the import trade was estimated to have been worth HK$3.5 billion in 2002. A number of shops in the area seem to base their businesses entirely on the sale of ginseng roots or swifts' nests, the latter gathered at great risk from the frighteningly high sides of caves in Borneo, Vietnam and southern Thailand. Constructed of swifts' spittle, they are used in a number of Chinese dishes, but most commonly for bird's nest soup, which is often served as a dessert at formal dinners. If you want to sample some, check out one of the numerous shops around Queen's Road West, Wing Lok Street and Bonham Strand; prices for a bowl start at about HK$240 and increase sharply depending on the other ingredients. Despite its alleged health-giving properties, bird's nest tastes much like ordinary egg albumen.

Another popular ingredient in both Chinese medicine and cuisine can be found sleeping in a rather dingy shop at 13 Hillier Street: snakes. Their blood, flesh and, particularly, their bile are favoured as a warming food, and are very popular during the winter months. Snake is not available in summer – the Chinese consider their flesh too 'heaty' to consume at that time.

A good place to browse for knick-knacks is the red-brick and granite, Edwardian-style **Western Market** (www.westernmarket. com.hk), just west of Sheung Wan MTR. It's a light, airy three-storey building, built in 1906 and renovated in the 1990s (after 80 or so years

Sightseeing

as a food market). On the ground floor are stalls selling jade trinkets, Hong Kong memorabilia of varying grades of authenticity, faux opium pipes, and antique cameras and clocks. The second floor is dedicated to the sale of fabrics and the third floor is home to the Grand Stage Ballroom (2815 2311), a Chinese restaurant for weddings, banquets and ballroom dancing, and a popular lunch venue.

Continuing westwards from Sheung Wan, the tram line terminates at **Kennedy Town** (named after 19th-century governor Sir Arthur Kennedy). Few visitors make it this far, as there is little to see other than an authentic working district of Hong Kong. **Mount Davis** rises 269 metres (883 feet) behind Kennedy Town and is well worth a climb. Along the summit are several disused gun batteries and a popular youth hostel (*see p57*).

The Mid-Levels Escalator

In 1993, in a (not all that successful) attempt to ease traffic congestion, a 792-metre-long (2,600-foot) escalator opened between Central Market and the residential area of Mid-Levels. It is actually a series of 20 escalators and three travelators, with exits to all of the streets across which it cuts. It's a good way to reach the hip bars and restaurants of SoHo (*see p82*), and to get to the concrete canyons of the Mid-Levels, but otherwise not of much use. The Escalator heads downwards from 6am to 10.20am (taking commuters to work in Central), but after that changes direction and remains running uphill until midnight. Worth trying at least once.

Hollywood Road & Tai Ping Shan

Hollywood Road, along with many of its neighbouring side streets, is almost entirely taken up by shops selling real and replica antique furniture, ornaments, statues, trinkets and curios. The more upmarket stores tend to congregate at its eastern end, where you'll also find a couple of surviving colonial structures: **Central Police Station** and the adjacent **Victoria Prison**.

Running parallel to Hollywood Road, but further west, is **Upper Lascar Row**, also known as Cat Street, which is well known as a hunting ground for cheap antiques, bric-a-brac and plain junk. Although its days as the place to find bargain antiques have, like most shopping experiences in Hong Kong, long since passed, there's still plenty to look at. You'll find items such as jade, jewellery, old photos of Hong Kong and plenty of kitsch memorabilia, like Chairman Mao ashtrays, ornaments and badges. Something may well take your fancy along here but be prepared to bargain hard.

Close by, at the corner of Hollywood Road and Ladder Street, stands **Man Mo Temple** (*see p81*), one of the most atmospheric places on Hong Kong Island. Dating from the late 1840s, and still a popular place of worship, its

Movin' on up: the **Mid-Levels Escalator** spirits the crowds up the hill from Central.

Sightseeing

incense-blackened interior is dimly lit by red lanterns. Sandalwood smoke hangs thick in the air from suspended coils of incense, the largest of which take a couple of weeks to burn through. To propitiate the spirits of the dead, Chinese burn paper offerings in two huge iron urns. There's quite a choice of spirit world combustibles available in nearby specialist shops. The most popular are 'Bank of Hell' banknotes, but you can also send up in flames complete mini-sets of kitchenware, cars, and gold and silver ingots, as well as computers and portable CD-players. The temple became a cultural and political focal point for the Chinese community soon after it opened. Meetings were held, grievances aired and a customary tribunal established by and for Chinese residents. If you've seen the film of Richard Mason's Hong Kong novel *The World of Suzie Wong*, then this part of town may look at least superficially familiar, as several scenes were filmed around here. Although visiting the temple is free, any donations made go towards local charities.

More temples can be found a little further west at the junction of Tai Ping Shan Street with Pound Lane (which lies just south of Hollywood Road). The district of **Tai Ping Shan** (meaning 'peaceful mountain') was one of the first areas to be settled by the Chinese after the colony was founded. It was anything but peaceful, being notorious for its overcrowded housing and periodic outbreaks of plague, and as an early haunt of the Hong Kong triad societies. Above street level, the temples are easily missed, resembling parts of homes rather than places of worship, an impression that persists until you see the incense sticks.

The **Kuan Yin Temple** is dedicated to the Buddhist goddess of Mercy (very popular with prostitutes and homosexuals as this deity embodies compassion and does not morally judge those who worship her), while the **Sui Tsing Pak Temple** next door holds a statue of the god Sui Tsing Pak, known as the 'pacifying general' and revered for his ability to cure illnesses (the statue was brought here in 1894 during a particularly virulent outbreak of plague). One of the rooms is used by fortune tellers, and there are rows of *tai sui* – statues of 60 different gods, each relating to a specific year in the 60-year cycle of the Chinese calendar (*see p40* **The animal in you**). In times of strife, or to avert trouble, people make offerings to the god of their year of birth.

Of the shrines nearby, the most interesting is the **Pak Sing** ('hundred surnames') **Ancestral Hall**. First created in the mid 19th century, it was rebuilt in 1895, when most of the buildings in the area were razed due to the plague. Used to store the bodies of those awaiting burial back

in China, it still houses ancestral tablets (little wooden boards bearing the name and date of birth of the deceased, and often a photograph). Some of these tablets are hardly recognisable, they have been so completely blackened by years of incense and smoke. The incinerator in the courtyard behind the altar is for burning paper offerings to the dead.

Nearby, the **Hong Kong Museum of Medical Sciences** (*see below*) gives an interesting overview of the history of public health and medical services in Hong Kong, and the building itself (built in 1906) is an attractive reminder of how the Mid-Levels looked before the tower blocks.

Across Hollywood Road from Pound Lane is **Possession Street**. It was here, above the one-time shoreline, that the British planted the Union Jack and officially took possession of Hong Kong Island in 1841. No memorial marks the occasion or the location – one stood here till the mid 1970s but is now in the Hong Kong Museum of History. The considerable distance from here to today's harbourfront illustrates the extent of land reclamation in Hong Kong (*see p103* **Walking on water**).

At the far western end of Hollywood Road is **Hollywood Road Park**, a small but charming place with pagoda-style tiled walls and roofs, running water, goldfish ponds and plenty of shade under venerable old trees. Opposite are several coffin-makers, with some massive Chinese-style caskets on display, even the cheapest of which are very expensive.

Hong Kong Museum of Medical Sciences

2 Caine Lane, off Caine Road (2549 5123/www. hkmms.org.hk). Bus 23, 40, 26/minibus 8, 22. **Open** 10am-5pm Tue-Sat; 1-5pm Sun. **Admission** HK$10; HK$5 concessions. **No credit cards. Map** p328 A3. Located in the Old Bacteriological Institute, which was established in 1906 (and later known as the Pathological Institute), the three floors of this small museum have displays of old medical equipment and some basic information on public health and the treatment of disease in Hong Kong. A handful of exhibits make it worth a quick visit, though; most notably, the story of the 1894 outbreak and treatment of the bubonic plague in Hong Kong. A potentially interesting section on Chinese medicine is, alas, only labelled in Chinese. Outside the main building there is a very interesting and well-labelled medicinal herb garden that's worth a wander.

Man Mo Temple

126 Hollywood Road (2540 0350). Sheung Wan MTR (exit A2)/26 bus. **Open** 8am-6pm daily. **Admission** free; donations appreciated. **Map** p328 B3. Sandalwood incense adds to the experience of this already atmospheric (and popular) temple, which is dedicated to Man, the god of literature and civil servants, and Mo, the god of war. They are reputed to have been real men, who were deified by later emperors. Zhang Yazi (Man) was a celebrated administrator from the third century, while Guan Yu (Mo) was a successful military leader from the second century. The statues of Man and Mo sit at the far end of the temple. Against the eastern wall rest the elaborately carved, gold-plated sedan chairs on which the statues are taken out during processions.

SoHo

The Mid-Levels Escalator (*see p80*) may have done little to decrease traffic congestion, but it has opened up a previously overlooked tangle of streets between Hollywood Road and the swanky Mid-Levels residential blocks. This area, informally known as **SoHo** (**So**uth of **Ho**llywood Road), has become the hippest – and according to some critics one of the priciest and most pretentious – places to hang out in Hong Kong over the past few years. On Staunton, Elgin, Shelley and surrounding streets, a cool new bar or restaurant seems to be opening up (or closing down) almost every week. Whereas once Hong Kong's main nightlife options were a cheap bowl of noodles, a pretentious Italian or French meal or a pie and a pint in a beery expat boozer, you can now eat and drink in fashionable bars and cosmopolitan eateries that wouldn't look out of place in London, Sydney or New York – and with prices in excess of those places. And – for the moment at least – SoHo remains one of Hong Kong's most mixed and characterful areas, with traditional Chinese businesses that have been there for decades operating beside the latest DJ bars, cutting-edge restaurants and chic shops (*see p193* **SoHo shopping**). Take it for what it offers.

A red sign on Staunton Street marks the former headquarters of Xing Zhong Hui (Revive China Society), the revolutionary organisation established by Dr Sun Yat-sen in 1895 and dedicated to overthrowing the Qing Dynasty in China. It marks the start of the **Sun Yat-sen Historical Trail**, an easy-to-follow walk around 13 sites bearing marker plaques (none of the buildings survive, however) related to the revolutionary's life, all in and around Hollywood Road, where he lived briefly during the 1890s. Just south of the trail, the **Dr Sun Yat-sen Museum** (7 Castle Road, www.hk.history.museum, 10am-6pm Mon-Wed, Fri, Sat, 10am-7pm Sun, HK$10, HK$5 concessions, free on Wed), an extension of the Hong Kong Museum of History, opened in December 2006 in the grand Edwardian residence of **Kom Tong Hall** after painstaking restoration work.

University of Hong Kong

Much further west is the entrance to the main campus of the **University of Hong Kong** (founded in 1912) on Bonham Road (Sun Yat-sen was a student of the Hong Kong College of Medicine that preceded it). If you have any interest in Chinese art and archaeology, it's worth visiting the **University Museum & Art Gallery** (*see below*) – its collection of antique bronzes, ceramics and paintings is exquisite, and the attractive old buildings are a lovely reminder of times past.

University Museum & Art Gallery

University of Hong Kong, 94 Bonham Road, Pok Fu Lam (2241 5500/www.hku.hk/hkumag). Bus 3B, 23, 40, 40M, 103. **Open** 9.30am-6pm Mon-Sat; 1.30-5.30pm Sun. **Admission** free.
This collection of Chinese pottery, paintings and artefacts spanning 5,000 years is small, but contains some beautiful exhibits from the Han Dynasty, including terracotta horses and blue and white Ming porcelain. It also features the world's largest collection of bronze crosses belonging to the Christian Nestorian church. In addition, the museum hosts art exhibitions, which change every couple of months.

Wan Chai & Causeway Bay

Wan Chai and Causeway Bay hug the northern edge of the island to the east of Central. Wan Chai's colourful 1950s and '60s past, evoked in Richard Mason's novel *The World of Suzie Wong*, has faded as it has become more of an extension of Central. The seedy streets of a once-considerable red light district have given way to ongoing new development – but the sleaze continues in some areas, especially along Lockhart Road and the neighbouring side streets. Two of Wan Chai's least attractive aspects are its heavy pollution and an almost total lack of open space. There have been various proposals mooted to make more of the area's features and create some green spaces and alfresco dining and drinking areas, but so far these have come to nothing.

For relief, a stiff climb up towards Wan Chai Gap to traffic-free Bowen Road affords pleasant walking and some fine views out through the crowded towers and over the harbour.

At first sight, Causeway Bay's huge – and numerous – department stores make it just another sprawling shopping district. However, the area has various points of interest that many people manage to overlook. Victoria Park, Hong Kong's largest (and one of its best) public parks, lies at the far end of Causeway Bay. And there are a few relics from its colonial past, most notably the Noon Day Gun, fired daily from the edge of the Typhoon Shelter, and a bronze statue of Queen Victoria herself, which once stood in Central's Statue Square (that's where the name comes from).

South of these two districts you'll find the island's celebrated racecourse at Happy Valley. It is a terrifically atmospheric place during midweek race nights.

Wan Chai

Just to the east of Central, **Wan Chai** is easily accessible by foot, tram, bus, MTR or taxi; the Wan Chai MTR is a good starting point for a walking tour. Wan Chai can be divided into the area of land reclamation north of Hennessy Road, crowned by the grandiose Hong Kong Convention & Exhibition Centre, and the warren of narrow streets of 'old' Wan Chai between Johnston Road and Queen's Road East, where you'll still find a few interesting corners.

NORTH OF HENNESSY ROAD

A walk along **Lockhart Road**, which runs east to west parallel to the waterfront, reveals the area's few remaining ties with *The World of Suzie Wong*. Along a 100-metre (328-foot) strip, you'll find a handful of sorry-looking topless bars rejoicing in classy names, such as Club Lady and Club Romance; this is where the mostly Thai and Filipina successors of Mason's 1950s muses ply their trade. These seedy places are notorious for their extortionate, sometimes invisible, extra charges just for entering and ordering a drink; but then having a drink is not the point of going. A better place to sample

some of the area's character without being ripped off is the **Old China Hand** (G/F, Lily Mansion, 104 Lockhart Road, 2865 4378), a rakish but friendly pub in the midst of all the seedier joints (though a refurbishment has left it far less dingy than previously). Local denizens, sometimes with working girls in tow, frequent the pub. Happy hour here lasts all afternoon.

A five-minute walk north of the MTR exit on Lockhart Road is **Central Plaza**, the tallest skyscraper in Hong Kong at the time of its construction in 1992 (374 metres/1,227 feet). Apart from its height, Central Plaza is fairly undistinguished, but it does at least allow visitors to enjoy its views. Walk through the lofty, marble-clad foyer and take the escalator up to the lift lobby. The vantage point on the 46th floor has tall plate-glass windows, offering spectacular views of the city's streets and harbour.

Facing Central Plaza across Harbour Road is the **Hong Kong Convention & Exhibition Centre** (*see p36 and p242*). Its HK$4.8 billion extension, which juts out into the harbour and marks the most northerly section of the extensive land reclamation in Wan Chai, is one of the city's most striking buildings, its sweeping lines creating the impression of a bird taking flight. This was the appropriately impressive venue for the 1997 Handover ceremony. Although most of the building is given up to exhibition space, it's definitely worth a wander round. Gaze at the harbour through high glass windows, take

Hong Kong Convention & Exhibition Centre.

Sightseeing

a break at one of several cafés and restaurants, or surf the internet for free at a couple of access points. Outside, there's a large promenade around the edge of the building and a sitting area that's perfect for making the most of the breeze. There's also a black obelisk marking the Handover, which is inscribed with a rhetorical celebration of the SAR's return to Chinese rule. Flag-raising ceremonies are held here with police bands – these parades are very popular photo-opportunities for mainland Chinese tour groups, and largely ignored by the rest of the population.

The **Hong Kong Arts Centre** (see p242), as well as the **Hong Kong Academy for Performing Arts** (see p241), are a couple of minutes' walk west of here. The Arts Centre, on Harbour Road, hosts regular exhibitions of art and photography (Artslink, its monthly magazine, contains full listings for, and reviews of, the local arts scene). It also has a café serving reasonable food.

SOUTH OF HENNESSY ROAD

The narrow streets and older tenement buildings between Johnston Road and Queen's Road East offer a flavour of older Wan Chai. Wander along any one of these streets and you're sure to stumble across something a little out of the ordinary – be it a market stall, shop or small factory turning out anything from printed matter to metalwork and furniture. Queen's Road East has been the high-end furniture centre of Hong Kong for over a

century; a selection of shops along here specialise in rattan, mahogany and rosewood; most will readily take orders or commissions.

Dating from the 1860s, the small and rather smoke-caked **Hung Shing Temple** stands at 129 Queen's Road East. It is dedicated to a government official from the Tang dynasty who became a patron saint of seafarers due to his excellent weather-forecasting skills. It used to be right next to the sea, before land reclamation marooned it far inland.

The **Revolving 66** restaurant (2862 6166) on the top (62nd) floor of the tall, tubular **Hopewell Centre** on Queen's Road East makes a scenic lunch stop, with particularly good views over the harbour and east towards Happy Valley. Even if you don't want to eat, the ride up the glass lifts on the outside of the building is a very good way to get a glimpse of the surrounding area; definitely not for those afflicted with vertigo.

Further east along Queen's Road East, under a venerable mango tree, you'll find the **Old Wan Chai Post Office**, built in 1912-13. This small, one-storey building ceased service in 1992, and now houses an Environmental Resources Centre. It also marks the start of the steep one-and-a-half-kilometre (one-mile) Green Trail. The trail's early stage consists of a rather pitiful selection of marker plaques pointing out a variety of unremarkable (but in Wan Chai, rare) trees. The second section is rather better as it winds up Wan Chai Gap Road into the woods. It ends close to **Wan Chai Gap**, near

Causeway Bay Typhoon Shelter. See p86.

one of the entrances to Aberdeen Country Park and the small **Police Museum** (*see below*) located on Coombe Road.

Further along Queen's Road East, close to Happy Valley, is **Wan Chai Park**, a small, unremarkable but precious speck of green space in among the tower blocks, which is very popular with students from nearby schools.

Police Museum

27 Coombe Road, Wan Chai Gap (2849 7019/www. info.gov.hk/police). Bus 15, 15B. **Open** 2-5pm Tue; 9am-5pm Wed-Sun. **Admission** free.
This small museum at the top of Wan Chai Gap Road is worth dropping by on the way to or from the Peak. The mostly static displays include a motor bike and field gun, and the exhibits themselves tell an interesting and coherent story of the Hong Kong Police. There is also a small section containing some interesting ritual items from the triads.

Causeway Bay

At the beginning of **Causeway Bay**, by the busy Canal Road flyover, **Bowrington Road Market** has separate floors for fruit and vegetables, fish and meat. Walk along the side streets nearby and you'll find similar items, at slightly lower prices. The colourful produce on offer here, and the steaming, white bean curd being scooped from massive wooden tubs, makes for great photos.

All manner of seafood, including writhing eels and fidgeting crustaceans, is picked live from its tub and dismembered before your eyes,

while frogs and turtles blink nonchalantly in baskets nearby. Hanging from hooks overhead, meanwhile, is every imaginable cut of cow and pig, including whole heads, tails, lungs and brains. For sensitive souls, it's probably not a good idea to linger too long around the poultry stalls, where live birds are dispatched with a casual flick of a blade and stuffed still twitching into a vat of hot water, after which they are tossed into a plucking machine. Perhaps the most absorbing and grisly sight, though, is the spectacle of live fish being deftly sliced lengthways and expertly gutted, while the exposed heart keeps beating.

Across Canal Road in Causeway Bay, the gargantuan **Times Square** shopping mall (*see p180*) marks the start of Hong Kong's busiest shopping district. It's packed with stores of every description, from less expensive chains to upmarket boutiques. There are also a number of department stores, including the Japanese giant **Sogo** (*see p177*), which sells everyday household goods. These days, this is one of the most popular hangouts for young Hong Kongers to see and be seen.

East of Times Square, close to Causeway Bay MTR station, are two small streets, **Jardine's Bazaar** and **Jardine's Crescent**, which are crammed with market stalls selling food and bargain-priced clothes.

From here it's a couple of minutes' walk east to sprawling **Victoria Park** (*see p86*), Hong Kong's largest public park. Beyond the park, on Tin Hau Temple Road, is a small and fairly

Victoria Park.

typical **temple to Tin Hau**, the goddess of
the sea. As one of Hong Kong's most popular
Taoist gods, there are at least 40 temples in
the SAR dedicated to her (*see also p39*).

A major road separates the northern side
of Victoria Park from the **Causeway Bay
Typhoon Shelter** (photos *pp84-85*). By
the side of the shelter, roughly in front of the
Excelsior Hotel, stands the **Noon Day Gun**,
fired daily since the 19th century and celebrated
in the song *Mad Dogs and Englishmen* by Noël
Coward. A small plaque details the (completely
apocryphal) story of the gun. According to its
own legend, Jardine Matheson, one of Hong
Kong's largest and oldest trading houses, often
fired the gun to salute the arrival of its senior
managers in port, which so incensed one naval
officer's sense of protocol that he ordered
Jardine's to fire the gun daily as a punishment
for its presumption. The firing of the gun is
now something of a charity fund-raising event,
with Jardine's distributing the money that
people pay to fire it to local charities. The small
enclosure housing the gun is open for half-an-
hour after noon. From Victoria Park, the gun is
best reached via the walkway crossing Victoria
Park Road, or from Causeway Bay via a badly
signposted underpass, the entrance to which
is in the multi-storey car park beneath the
World Trade Centre Mall.

In the Typhoon Shelter there are about a
dozen tiny houseboats, which are essentially
sampans converted into floating residences,
neatly kept with flower boxes on their 'porches'.

On a promontory at the western end of the
typhoon shelter stands the **Royal Hong
Kong Yacht Club** (*see p255*). Keen or
aspiring sailors should leave their details on
a noticeboard outside the club's bar if they
wish to join the crew of any yacht sailing out
of Hong Kong. There's more chance of those
with experience being signed on, but it's not
unheard of for an inexperienced but willing
deckhand to hitch a ride.

Victoria Park

*Between Gloucester Road, Victoria Park Road,
Causeway Road & Hing Fat Street.* **Open** 24hrs
daily. **Map** p331 E/F2.
Aside from plenty of open space, the park contains
a running track, a 50-metre (164-foot) swimming
pool, basketball and tennis courts, and a model boating lake. This deservedly popular park is the venue
for large gatherings, such as at Chinese New Year,
when a popular flower fair is held here, and the Hong
Kong Flower Show (in March), featuring plants as
varied as bonsai, cacti and orchids.

Happy Valley

Just to the south of Causeway Bay lies one of
Hong Kong's most powerful institutions, the
Happy Valley Racecourse (closed July and
August; *see p258*). The easiest way to get to
the racecourse is to hop on a tram to Happy
Valley. Although smaller than its sister site
at Sha Tin in the New Territories, the Happy
Valley Racecourse, in use since 1846, is the
traditional home of horse racing in the city.

An evening's racing here, with the stands packed out with more than 55,000 enthusiastic spectators, is still one of the quintessential Hong Kong experiences.

Ironically named Happy Valley when still a mosquito and malaria-ridden marsh, the site was chosen because it was the only piece of flat ground on the island large enough for a race track. Wednesday evenings are the best time to visit the brightly floodlit track. With the lights of apartments twinkling in the high-rises beyond, the excitement is palpable. It seems that every second person is a chain smoker and, if you stand at the bottom of the huge racing stand you will see, caught in the glare, a thick smoke plume rising from the cigarettes of thousands of nervous punters.

The small but well laid-out **Hong Kong Racing Museum** (*see below*), on the second floor of the stand, records the history of racing in Hong Kong. You can stop off for a bite to eat at **Moon Koon** (2966 7111) next door, a reasonably priced Chinese restaurant with good food and terrific views on to the racetrack through large plate-glass windows.

The old cemeteries at Happy Valley provide an interesting glimpse into Hong Kong's cosmopolitan past and are well worth a wander if you're in the area. In particular, the well-kept **Hong Kong Cemetery**, more commonly known as the Colonial Cemetery, merits exploration, with magnificent trees and views out across the racecourse from the upper levels.

Hong Kong Racing Museum

2/F, Happy Valley Stand, Happy Valley (2966 8065/ www.hongkongjockeyclub.org.hk). Trams to Happy Valley. **Open** 10am-5pm Tue-Sun. **Admission** free. **Map** p331 D5.

Hong Kong's racing history and Chinese depictions of the horse in art are the focus of these eight galleries. The museum tells the story of horse racing in Hong Kong from the early days of Happy Valley in the 1840s, and of horse breeding and trading in northern China and Mongolia, where the tough, highly prized 'China ponies' were raised. The skeleton of Hong Kong's legendary champion racehorse Silver Lining is mounted in pride of place.

Further east

Beyond Causeway Bay, the monotonous residential and commercial towers continue to stretch eastwards through North Point and Quarry Bay to Shau Kei Wan, where the **Hong Kong Museum of Coastal Defence** (*see below*) is the main attraction.

Hong Kong Museum of Coastal Defence

175 Tung Hei Road, Shau Kei Wan (2569 1500/ www.hk.coastaldefence.museum). Shau Kei Wan MTR (exit B2)/84, 85 bus. **Open** 10am-5pm Mon-Wed, Fri-Sun. **Admission** HK$10; HK$5 concessions. Free to all Wed. **No credit cards.**

This HK$300 million branch of the Hong Kong Museum of History in Kowloon opened in 2000 within the 120-year-old Lei Yue Mun Fort. The core

The **Peak Tram** has been responsible for mass uprisings since 1888. *See p89.*

of the museum is the Redoubt, which features an exhibition covering '600 Years of Hong Kong's Coastal Defence', which is supplemented by a range of artefacts and multimedia displays. Follow the Historical Trail that links the various parts of the fort together to see other restored military structures, such as the gun batteries and the Brennan Torpedo. The museum is a 15-minute walk from Shau Kei Wan MTR; there is also a free shuttle bus to the museum from Heng Fa Chuen MTR on Saturdays and Sundays.

The Peak

Towering above the commercial heart of Hong Kong Island, **Victoria Peak** – otherwise simply known as 'the Peak' – offers the most spectacular views in Hong Kong. On a rare clear day the 552-metre (1,810-foot) summit overlooks not just the improbable towers of the north side of Hong Kong Island, but also Victoria Harbour, Kowloon and the hills of the New Territories

Sightseeing

Peak around

Once you've visited the **Peak Tower** (pictured; see p89), one of the best ways to enjoy the Peak area is to meander along the paved, pushchair-friendly three-kilometre (two-mile) circular path that follows the base of the Peak, along Lugard Road and back along Harlech Road. It's a pretty, tree-shaded route affording spectacular views of land and sea, and some tantalising glimpses of the Peak's most expensive properties. At night it is fully lit and the views are particularly impressive.

Another easy five-kilometre (three-mile) walk starts from outside the Peak Galleria and heads down Pok Fu Lam Reservoir Road, through the wooded **Pok Fu Lam Country Park**, to the reservoir and back. If you can't face the trudge back up the hill, you can always walk down to Pok Fu Lam Road, from

where there are plenty of buses back into Central. More adventurous ramblers can also walk to **Aberdeen** (see p91), turning left halfway down Reservoir Road, and along the side of Mount Kellett.

Victoria Gap is also the starting point for the 50-kilometre (31-mile) **Hong Kong Trail** (see p115 **Walks on the wild side**), which passes through the island's four country parks, ending at **Shek O** (see p93).

A short circular tour of **Mount Gough**, along Findlay Road, east from the Peak Tower, will take you past some more of the area's swankiest properties and more superb views. Be aware, though, that you'll have to walk along the road itself for much of its length, and some of the corners are very tight. Traffic is busiest at the weekends.

beyond. To the south, the lush vegetation of Hong Kong Island's quieter side leads down towards Lamma island (with the chimneys of its power station very prominent); while to the west lie the islands of Cheung Chau, Peng Chau and massive, rugged Lantau. The vistas are just as spectacular by night. But don't bother coming up if the weather is foggy or heavily polluted – because you won't see a thing.

The Peak is also the best starting point for a number of fine walks, ranging from the gentle to the arduous (*see left* **Peak around**).

Its milder temperatures (an average 5°C/9°F lower than at sea level) and its extraordinary vantage points have long made the Peak the most sought-after address in Hong Kong. Governor Sir Richard MacDonnell built a summer house here around 1868, when the trip from Central, by horse, sedan chair or on foot, took around an hour. The commencement of the **Peak Tram** services in 1888 cut the arduous journey down to just under ten minutes, making it an increasingly popular journey. Remarkably, the tram (actually a funicular railway) has never suffered any fatal accidents – its most serious setback occurred during a severe typhoon in the 1960s, when much of the track was washed away. The arrival of the tram also opened the Peak up to substantial development (it was intended as a commuter service, not a tourist ride). Today the Peak is among the most expensive places in the world to buy property, and many of Hong Kong's movers and shakers live here.

At their height in 1997, Hong Kong's property prices were briefly the highest in the world – up to HK$20,000 per square foot at one point. Houses on the Peak regularly went for more than HK$100 million, and at the time their purchase was thought to have been a popular way for triads to launder large amounts of money. A subsequent property slump led to prices dropping by up to half. Property has long been the base on which tycoons, triads and middle-class folk in Hong Kong have built their wealth and long-term prosperity. The severe

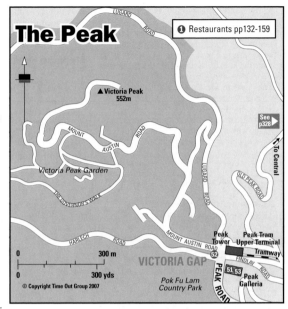

drop in the market has, therefore, plunged many citizens into negative equity, a legacy that is likely to linger; it remains a major source of discontent in the territory.

Peak Tram

Lower Terminal *Garden Road, Central.*
Upper Terminal *Lugard Road, The Peak (2849 7654/www.thepeak.com.hk).* **Open** 7am-midnight daily (every 15mins). **Tickets** *Single* HK$20; HK$6 concessions. *Return* HK$30; HK$9 concessions. **Credit** (over HK$350) MC, V. **Map** p89. **Photo** p87.

Victoria Gap

Although bus 15 (from Exchange Square) and minibus 1 (from the IFC mall) both run up to the Peak, the classic ascent is to take the Peak Tram from its Lower Terminal on Garden Road (reached by taking the 15C shuttle bus from Central Ferry Pier 7). Victoria Gap – not the Peak itself – is the final stop on the 373-metre (1,224-foot) steep (up to 27°) tram ride up from Mid-Levels – make sure you sit on the right-hand side going up for the best views.

The tram empties into Terry Farrell's **Peak Tower** (*see also p35*), which has recently undergone massive renovations, resulting in improved shops and eating places. The viewing terrace on the roof of the tower affords some excellent views (Hong Kong's fickle weather and increasingly bad air pollution permitting).

The tower's new eateries range from coffee shops and burger bars to high-end restaurants: for Japanese sushi there's **Kyo Hachi**; **Tien Yi** serves fine wines alongside contemporary Chinese cuisine; **Pearl on the Peak** (*see p145*) is helmed by top Melbourne chef Geoff Lindsay; and Southern US-style seafood features at **Bubba Gump**. There's also a branch of **Madame Tussaud's** here (*see below*).

Next to the Peak Tower is the **Peak Galleria**, with a plethora of tacky tourist shops, more cafés and restaurants, and a supermarket. For westward views towards the Outlying Islands, head across the road to the **Peak Lookout** (*see p145*), a comfortable, well-appointed but pricier place for lunch, dinner or refreshments.

Madame Tussaud's

Shop P101, Peak Tower, 128 Peak Road (2849 6966/Ticketek advance booking 3128 8288). Peak Tram/15 bus/1 minibus. **Open** noon-8pm daily. **Admission** HK$115 Mon-Fri; HK$120 Sat, Sun. **Credit** AmEx, MC, V. **Map** p89.
Madame Tussaud's first Asian venture opened in summer 2000, with more than a hundred waxy celebs to bump into. As in London, the credulous can hang

Taming the dragon

The **Dragon's Back** is one of Hong Kong Island's easiest and most popular hiking routes. Although the very beginning of the walk is at Big Wave Bay (*see p94*), this shorter version is a perfect beginner's hike – and one that you can take kids on too.

Starting near **Mount Collinson** (named after the maker of the first detailed topographical map of Hong Kong Island), this walk ends in the former fishing village of **Shek O** on the island's east coast. The eight-kilometre (five-mile) trek rarely takes more than two hours, even at a leisurely pace, and is easy to reach via public transport.

Walking along the gentle ridge reveals unrivalled views of the South China Sea, the outlying islands, Tai Tam Country Park's reservoirs, the peaks of Mount Parker, Mount Butler and Violet Hill, as well as clear views of Stanley, the Red Hill Peninsula and parts of Kowloon. On most weekend afternoons you can spot paragliders leaping off the Dragon's Back, enjoying some of Asia's finest thermals and then floating down to land on one of Shek O's smaller beaches. The reward at the end of the hike is the laid-back village of Shek O, which has a great beach, several restaurants and a small headland to explore (*see p93*).

GETTING THERE

Catch the MTR to Shau Kei Wan station (exit A3) and take the number 9 bus to Shek O from the bus station outside. Stay on the bus for about five kilometres (three miles) and ring the bell as soon as you see a mini roundabout (the only one along this road), so that you can get off at the next stop.

THE HIKE

Remain on the same side of the road as the bus stop. Walk straight ahead and you will see a set of steps. Climb the steps and turn right at the top by the women's prison. Walk past the prison and up a concrete water-catchment road. At the top, the road forks. A sign indicates a path to the left that leads to the surfer hangout of Big Wave Bay, but for Shek O continue ahead along a muddy, worn path lined by trees and bushes. (Don't worry about getting lost; there are no turn-offs along this route.)

After about 30-40 minutes, look for a knee-high wooden post (No.90). Shortly after that you'll see another post next to a right-hand turning. Take this right turn, and walk uphill for about five minutes (off path). When you reach the top you are officially at the start of the Dragon's Back. Turn right at the top (the sea is on your left) and walk along the whole of the Dragon's Back. Looking down the hill, you will see the village of Shek O on your left side and Tai Tam Harbour on your right. The path runs out after about 30-40 minutes of ridge walking (a seat marks the end of the trail) and you'll see a path and steps leading downhill. Follow them for about 15 minutes and you'll reach the main road (Shek O Road) next to a bus stop. Rather than walk on the main road (there is no path and traffic is fast), hop back on to the number 9 bus – it is a five-minute journey into Shek O, where the bus terminates.

THE AFTER-HIKE REWARDS

There are a couple of inexpensive, casual restaurants in Shek O. A good hiker hangout is the **Shek O Chinese-Thai Seafood Restaurant** (*see p146*). There are plenty of others with similar food, prices and standards nearby, although reservations are recommended, especially at weekends, when things can get pretty busy.

out with Sly, Arnie, Jacko and friends, see replicas of David Beckham and his pop-star missus, shoot hoop with Yao Ming, or be snapped posing next to local heroes like actor Jackie Chan, Olympic gold-winning windsurfer Lee Lai-shan and (only in Hong Kong) top business supremo Li Ka-shing.

Victoria Peak

Victoria Peak itself, immediately to the west of Victoria Gap, is a steep, signposted 20-minute walk up Mount Austin Road. For a gentler and longer stroll, head along Harlech Road (until its junction with Lugard Road on the south-west side of the Peak) and head up the Governor's Walk, which threads a gently rising path up to the small, but well-tended **Victoria Peak Garden**. Located on the site of the old Governor's lodge, which was demolished after World War II, it offers viewing areas looking west, south and east. The very summit of the Peak is occupied by telephone masts and surrounded by a large fenced-off area.

South & east coasts

When the hustle and hassle of the northern coast of Hong Kong Island becomes too much, jump on a bus and head over to the more relaxed south and east coasts, where the pace of life is slower and a variety of man-made and natural attractions awaits. Aberdeen is a vibrant – if rather smelly – mixed commercial/industrial fishing town with a busy harbour. Close to it is Ocean Park, a sprawling, varied and spectacularly situated amusement park. Further south are the beaches of Repulse Bay and Deep Water Bay, and the pretty seaside town of Stanley. To really get away from it all, head to the sleepy village of Shek O at the far south-eastern end of the island for a striking coastline and great beaches. And don't neglect the hilly interior of the island, which features great hiking and superb views.

Aberdeen

Drab high-rise blocks edge **Aberdeen** harbour. Ignore the ugly town centre and head to the typhoon shelter, which is always jammed with dozens of fishing boats – most of them the old-fashioned, high-prowed wooden type. Sampans festooned with tyres dodge deftly among them and at the harbour edge small-scale shipyards refit ageing vessels. Towards the western end of the harbour is the large, and often frantically busy, wholesale fish and seafood market. During the day it's crowded with merchants and restaurateurs buying all kinds of seafood and loading up their trucks.

Sampan tours of the harbour are available from pushy elderly women lying in wait for meandering tourists, or from the **Aberdeen Sampan Company**, prominently signposted east of the wholesale market. HK$60 (less if there's more than one passenger – be prepared to haggle a bit) will buy a 15-minute tour of the harbour. You won't get much out of your 'guide' – unless you speak Cantonese – but she will point out the few remaining family junks, which used to be a common sight here. Most of the folk who once lived on their fishing boats have moved into the new developments around Aberdeen over the last 30 years, completely transforming an age-old way of life.

The ferry constantly shuttling diners from the quayside to the three giant floating seafood restaurants moored out towards the southern end of the typhoon shelter will provide you with a slightly less extensive, but free, tour of the harbour. These floating restaurants are what put Aberdeen on the map for many tourists.

The most famous, and by far the most garish and elaborate, is the red and gold hulk of the **Jumbo Floating Restaurant**, resembling something between a technicolour pagoda and a Mississippi paddle steamer turned casino. There's a production line approach to business at the Jumbo, with the result that an estimated 30 million people have dined here since it opened in the 1970s. The impersonal approach extends to the assigning of tables (for which you are issued with a ticket at busy times), the service and the food itself, which does not have a particularly great reputation and is by no means cheap. None of this seems to deter diners – tourists and locals alike pack it out at weekends. The Jumbo also organises a number of tours that usually involve a cruise and meal – details are available at any HKTB info centre.

If the Jumbo experience does not appeal, and time permits, you can always catch a ferry from Aberdeen to the much better seafood places on Lamma. Go either to Yung Shue Wan, the main settlement (see p121), or the quieter (and closer) Sok Kwu Wan (see p122) on the east side of the island for a seafood dinner which – while not that cheap either – will not have you taking out a second mortgage.

Incidentally, Aberdeen has no connection with the Scottish city of the same name. It's named after Lord Aberdeen – Secretary of State for the Colonies in the mid 19th century.

Deep Water Bay & Repulse Bay

Travelling east along the south coast from Aberdeen towards Stanley takes you past **Ocean Park** (see p212 **Variations on a theme**) and a number of decent beaches.

Deep Water Bay is a pretty spot, long favoured by the wealthy – as the number of plush houses in the area attests. The long stretch of beach, lined by trees, has an almost Riviera-like air. As with most major beaches in Hong Kong, there are barbecue areas, but be warned that on Sundays legions of Filipina and Indonesian domestic workers on their day off are likely to have staked their claim to every barbecue pit very early in the morning.

Just around a headland to the south, huge, upmarket apartment blocks, populated by well-paid executives, surround the long, well-tended beach at **Repulse Bay**. The beach is a popular destination in the summer and gets very crowded. Above it, **The Verandah** restaurant (*see p146*) is a lovely, if expensive, place for a drink or afternoon tea. Behind The Verandah, there's a supermarket and a couple of cafés.

Located at the southern end of the beach, the Hong Kong Life Guards' Club resembles a Chinese temple. Among the canoes and lifesaving equipment you'll find scores of statues of gods, animals and fabulous beasts dotted around its grounds. There are huge statues of Kwun Yam, the goddess of mercy, and Tin Hau, plus several bronze Buddhas, their bald heads and ample bellies polished bright by hundreds of human hands.

Middle Bay, just around the coast between Repulse Bay and South Bay, is Hong Kong's popular gay beach (for Middle Bay and South Bay, *see p230*) and is always thronged with cruising males, whatever the weather.

Stanley

The pretty town and sandy beaches of **Stanley** are a 25-minute bus ride from the high-energy bustle of Central (take bus 6, 6A, 6X or 260) or ten minutes by minibus 52 from Aberdeen. Stanley – known as Chek Chue – was a Chinese settlement long before the British arrival. Until the 1960s it was a thriving fishing village, but that industry has declined over the past decades and today it feels more like an English seaside town, complete with pubs and red-faced Europeans roasting in the sun. But despite extensive – and at times unsympathetic – development, Stanley still retains considerable charm and it's possible to spend a leisurely half-day wandering around the town.

The extensive sprawl of **Stanley Market**'s 'stalls' (many of them now actual shops; *see also p190* **To market, to market**) is one of the main reasons for Stanley's continued popularity with visitors. There are perhaps a couple of hundred outlets selling export-order clothes, beachwear, silk, accessories, jewellery, jade, trinkets, paintings, DVDs and furniture, usually cheaper than in central Hong Kong or Kowloon (though the days of real bargains – as in Hong Kong generally – have long-since gone). The market is open from around 11am to 6pm daily.

A pleasant promenade links the market area with the quiet seafront, populated by several restaurants serving Italian, Thai, Spanish, Vietnamese and Chinese food, as well as the friendly **Smugglers Inn** on Stanley Main

The beach at **Deep Water Bay**.

Road. This is also where you'll find the Old Police Station, a historical landmark and the oldest surviving police station building in Hong Kong (built 1859), which has been converted into – believe it or not – a supermarket. The **Stanley Plaza** shopping development at the western end of the promenade was recently introduced with, by Hong Kong standards at least, some sensitivity. Five storeys high, it is tucked unobtrusively away and includes a supermarket, car park and attractive sea-facing square with canopy-covered seating for outdoor public events.

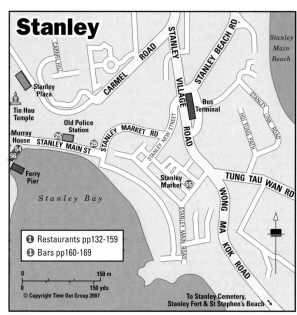

The large neo-classical building beside the square is **Murray House**. It contains some smart but reasonably priced restaurants with views over the bay. The original building stood for a century and a half in Central (at the spot now occupied by the Bank of China Tower) until 1982, when it was dismantled, the granite blocks numbered (still visible if you look closely) and put into storage. It was only recently that it was reassembled here. One of the earliest colonial structures in Hong Kong, it dates to 1843, when it was used as a mess for British army officers.

Nearby is Stanley's **Tin Hau Temple**, which can trace its origins back to 1767, thus making it one of the oldest – and, inside at least, most evocative – temples on the island. Incense coils fill it with scented smoke, while the altar is populated by elaborate statuary depicting Tin Hau (*see p39*) along with a bodyguard of grimacing warriors.

On the other side of town is **Stanley War Cemetery**, a beautifully kept place in which you can trace the earliest colonial days through the gravestones of military personnel and their families. The toll once taken by disease (particularly on young children and babies) is shocking, but perhaps most moving is the profusion of stones marking the deaths of British and Commonwealth servicemen, who perished during the fall of Hong Kong in 1941

and, subsequently, as Japan's prisoners of war. A memorial at the entrance to the cemetery details the desperate defence of the New Territories and the island by British and Commonwealth forces, who finally surrendered on Christmas Day 1941.

Below the cemetery is the relatively clean **St Stephen's Beach**, with views towards Stanley and across to Lamma Island. South of the beach lies **Stanley Peninsula**, home to **Stanley Fort**, which was previously occupied by the British Army and is now used by the People's Liberation Army. It is not accessible without a permit.

On the other side of the peninsula, a short distance from the bus terminus in the centre of town, is **Stanley Main Beach**, a good long stretch of sand and the venue for the local dragon boat race in June (*see p204*).

Shek O

The tiny, sleepy village of **Shek O**, clustered on a small headland at the far south-eastern corner of Hong Kong Island, has so far escaped any unsightly development. This is the place to go for a day of sea breezes, great beaches and peace (especially on weekdays). It's a thoroughly relaxing spot with some dramatic shoreline and great South China Sea views.

Shek O is also one of the finishing points for the **Dragon's Back Trail** (*see p90* **Taming the dragon**) and the **Hong Kong Trail** (*see p115* **Walks on the wild side**). It is most easily reached by taking bus 9, which runs every 15 minutes from the bus terminus just outside Shau Kei Wan MTR. At the end of the long, winding and scenic route, the bus drops you in the centre of the village. From the bus stop, turn right at the mini roundabout for the main beach, an immaculately kept stretch of golden sand with changing facilities and lifeguards. It's also worth taking a walk to the small rocky islet at the tip of the headland (straight ahead across the roundabout from the bus stop). The five-minute walk will take you past Shek O's mix of small, pretty, weather-beaten dwellings and the larger mansions on the edges of the headland. On the shoreline there's usually a strong, fresh breeze blowing and large waves crashing against the strikingly pitted and fissured rocks.

From the headland there's a footbridge to a small island called **Tai Tau Chau**, from where there are great views across to the New Territories. Eating and drinking choices are limited in Shek O to the restaurants that circle the mini-roundabout. The largest is the **Shek O Chinese-Thai Seafood Restaurant** (*see p90 and p146*), which offers average prices and quality but an extensive menu, including the theatrical 'Chicken on Fire', which is flambéed in brandy at your table.

Close to the roundabout, and tucked down a narrow alley off Headland Road, is a small but immaculately kept **Tin Hau Temple** (*see also p39*). The flowers decked outside and the smiles on the faces of the statues make it one of the most cheerful on the island.

Big Wave Bay, a couple of kilometres to the north, has a good sandy beach set between ruggedly beautiful cliffs and rocks. It's virtually the only place – with the exception of a few remote spots in the New Territories – where Hong Kong's small surfing community can go to catch a wave. It's an easy walk, but not particularly pleasant (there's no pavement so watch out for passing traffic), from Shek O along the road to Big Wave Bay. The road cuts through the Shek O golf course and passes several large mansions set in extensive grounds, homes to some of Hong Kong's wealthiest residents.

If surfing is the idea, there are two hire shops by the beach, although they are closed at quiet times of year. Long and short boards can be hired starting at about HK$60 a day (HK$100 deposit) on weekdays, jumping in price on weekends and holidays.

At the far north-eastern end of the bay, close to the furthest lifeguard's station, is one of Hong Kong's ancient rock carvings, thought to date back to the Bronze Age (between 2,500 and 3,000 BC). Faint geometric designs and stylised animal figures can just be made out on a small area of rock inside the small protective shelter.

Don't be a fish out of water – join the locals in Repulse Bay. *See p92.*

Kowloon

A feast for the senses: the visual splendour across to the harbour skyline of Hong Kong Island, exotic market scents and a lot of noise.

Gritty rather than glitzy, Kowloon feels a million miles away from its flashier cross-harbour neighbour. But Hong Kong Island's glittering array of towers are only a kilometre or so away (less than a mile) – and getting closer with each new stage of land reclamation – providing one of the world's most striking cityscape views from the waterfront promenade at the tip of the Kowloon peninsula. Here, you'll also find the city's best museums and flashest hotels, but delve inland and you'll discover a more 'authentic' Chinese atmosphere as shopping malls give way to jostling markets and crowded neighbourhoods.

There is no more memorable experience in Hong Kong than standing at the southern tip of the Kowloon peninsula and gazing out over Victoria Harbour at the jostling ranks of gleaming towers crowding the northern shore of Hong Kong Island, with richly wooded hills and the Peak beyond (admittedly now half obscured by the IFC2 tower). But Kowloon offers much more than just a vantage point. Though it certainly lacks the polish of its island neighbour, it has a far more tangible Chinese feel to it, superb shopping opportunities and the territory's major concentration of museums and galleries.

The peninsula's 12 square kilometres (4.5 square miles) are densely packed with shops, bars, hotels and housing in a vibrant, untidy jumble of new skyscrapers and old,

low-rise tenements. Within this relatively small area lie quite a number of temples and museums, the Cultural Centre and, hidden away on the side streets, atmospheric old Chinese neighbourhoods and extensive street markets waiting to be explored.

Kowloon's name derives from the Cantonese phrase *gau lung*, or 'nine dragons'. According to local legend, the peninsula was named eight centuries ago when the boy emperor Zhao Bing, the last emperor of the Southern Song Dynasty, arrived in the area while fleeing invading Mongols. It is said that he pointed to the eight hills above the peninsula and announced that eight dragons must dwell there – one for each hill. He was then reminded that, as emperors were also considered dragons, his own presence meant that there were nine dragons in the area. No giant lizards saved the little emperor, though, as he met his end to the west of present-day Macau, throwing himself into the sea to escape the approaching Mongols. Today the dragons of the Kowloon hills look down upon serried ranks of public housing blocks, one of Hong Kong's most unsung post-war success stories.

When the British claimed Hong Kong Island in 1841, Kowloon was not included in the settlement (the Treaty of Nanking, signed the following year). It was soon realised that the proximity of potentially hostile territory represented an emergent threat to the fledgling colony. Following the Second Opium War in 1860, the peninsula was ceded 'in perpetuity' to Great Britain. Around three kilometres (two miles) inland, Boundary Street, which runs west to east in a ruler-straight line, once defined the frontier between British Hong Kong and China but Kowloon has long since spilled into the lands beyond (part of the New Territories leased by Britain in 1898).

The roads criss-crossing Kowloon may be as jammed as those in Central, but they encroach less on pedestrian space than those over the water, so getting about on foot is a realistic option. And when you tire, just hop on the MTR or one of the numerous buses patrolling Nathan Road, which forms the spine of Kowloon from Tsim Sha Tsui in the south through the districts of Yau Ma Tei and Mong Kok.

Tsim Sha Tsui

Tsim Sha Tsui (pronounced 'Chim Sa Choy'), at the very southern tip of Kowloon, is the grubbier cousin of Central, which it faces across the harbour. Its major thoroughfare, shop-lined **Nathan Road**, is a wide, straight highway that has attempted to adopt the nickname 'the Golden Mile'. In truth, the epithet is overly flattering – as a rule, shops here are far less glitzy than those of Central – and inaccurate, as it's considerably longer than a mile. Hundreds of electronics stores, clothing shops, a handful of topless bars and, every few yards it seems, Indian tailors or their touts, line Nathan Road and its side streets.

Tsim Sha Tsui isn't entirely devoted to commercial activities, however: it also contains most of Hong Kong's museums and the excellent, though very ugly, Cultural Centre. This area of the city is also a major tourist accommodation area, with hotels available from the cheapest backpacker doss-house (nevertheless very expensive by Indian or South-east Asian standards) to some of the world's finest five-star hotels.

When setting out to explore Kowloon, a natural starting point is the **Tsim Sha Tsui Star Ferry Pier** – where cross-harbour ferries arrive from Central and Wan Chai. Within the Star Ferry Pier building, there is a branch of the **Hong Kong Tourism Board**; it's worth stopping by to pick up free maps and information on local tours and upcoming events.

Next to the Star Ferry Pier is the old **Kowloon–Canton Railway Station clock tower**. Overlooking the tip of the peninsula, the 44-metre (144-foot) tower is all that remains of the southern terminus of the Kowloon–Canton Railway, which stood here from 1915 until it was demolished in 1978. However, a subterranean KCR extension, which re-links the main station at Hung Hom with Tsim Sha Tsui, has recently been completed at enormous cost. (So much for long-term civic planning.) The new station, East Tsim Sha Tsui, won't remain a terminus for long: work is already underway to continue the line so it links up with the West Rail line, giving direct access to the north-west New Territories.

Near the Star Ferry Pier are two sprawling shopping arcades. The nearer (and smaller) one, **Star House**, is known for its extensive offerings of Asian arts and crafts, and holds the massive **Chinese Arts & Crafts** store (*see p192*), selling an impressive array of jewellery, ornaments, furniture, embroidered tablecloths, clothing and jade. Larger – and somewhat more upmarket – **Harbour City** (incorporating Ocean Terminal and Ocean Centre; *see p178*) features an enormous number of high-end shops (including all of the major international brand names), as well as a handy first-floor café with free internet access.

From the pier, sweeping past the clock and beyond, there is a long waterfront promenade, a section of which has been ambitiously renamed the **Avenue of Stars**. As in Hollywood, well-known Chinese actors and celebrities have left their handprints in the pavement. This promenade gives fabulous views by day and night over the water towards Hong Kong Island. Such a prime site would seem made in heaven for outdoor cafés and waterfront bars– but there are none, mainly because of arcane licensing laws and other seemingly insurmountable bureaucratic difficulties.

Just to the east of the Star Ferry Pier (along the waterfront promenade) is the **Hong Kong Cultural Centre** (**photo** *p101*), one of the territory's wasted architectural opportunities. When the Kowloon–Canton Railway station

was demolished in 1978 it freed up one of Hong Kong's – and indeed the world's – most spectacular sites. Facing the incomparable city-and-mountains vista on the northern side of Hong Kong Island, what was built to replace it? A soulless structure without any windows, clad in insipid pink-beige lavatory-style tiles, the whole thing resembling an outsize public toilet cross-bred with a ski-jump. Its only saving grace is that it at least provides a wide-ranging cultural programme within its excellent concert hall and two theatres (*see p243*).

On the waterfront next door to the Cultural Centre, the **Hong Kong Museum of Art** (*see p99*) hosts excellent permanent exhibitions of Asian ceramics, jade and gold ornaments, and a pictorial history of Chinese artworks, with an emphasis on classic, as well as contemporary, Hong Kong art.

Sandwiched between the art museum and the Peninsula hotel, the **Hong Kong Space Museum** (*see p99*) has a few interesting interactive displays. Inside a tiled hemisphere within the museum's lobby is the Space Theatre, where so-called 'sky shows' – half-hour documentaries on various animals, countries, oceans and, indeed, space itself – are projected at regular intervals on to the domed ceiling. Not surprisingly, these presentations are very popular with rowdy local school groups. Sensational surround-sound Omnimax films are regularly screened here too.

At the opposite end of the architectural universe, and directly across Salisbury Road, is the handsome, neo-classical exterior of **The Peninsula** hotel (*see p62*), with its sympathetic tower extension. Arguably the grandest hotel in Hong Kong, this effortlessly classy place is a must-see. Even if you can't stretch to staying the night, don't miss the chance to take afternoon tea in the elegant, high-ceilinged and pillar-bedecked lobby (served between 2pm and 7pm every day, but most popular on Sundays; *see p151* **A fancy**

Avenue of Stars. *See p96.*

cuppa). If you mistakenly think that the Pen is stuck in the past, go to the top floor and visit the Philippe Starck-designed Felix restaurant and bar (*see p146*). Floor-to-ceiling windows deliver astonishing views (on a clear day) out over the harbour to Hong Kong Island on one side and back over Kowloon towards the New Territories on the other. Gents shouldn't miss going to the loos – the urinals are placed in front of vast windows, giving the user the somewhat god-like feeling that he is relieving himself over all of Kowloon.

A couple of minutes' walk east of the Peninsula along Salisbury Road is the tiny, somewhat secluded **Signal Hill Garden**. This under-appreciated green corner contains a steep hill topped by a tower (open 9-11am, 4-6pm daily) offering a good vantage point. The tower was originally built in 1904 to send time signals to ships in the harbour, thus enabling seafarers to verify the accuracy of their chronographs. Over time, though, more advanced technology rendered it redundant.

An inescapable feature of the southern tip of Tsim Sha Tsui is construction noise. Even though the KCR extension has been completed there is considerable urban renewal underway, roads are partially blocked off, and the noise level from pile-drivers and other equipment can be excruciating. In short, it all makes the area not very pleasant to wander around these days. So if all the uproar is making you crave more expansive greenery, walk up Nathan Road to Kowloon Park (*see p99*), one of the urban area's larger and most precious open spaces.

Just past the south-eastern edge of the park, the minarets of the **Jamia Masjid Islamic Centre** rise near the intersection of Nathan and Cameron roads. Hong Kong's largest mosque, it was built in the early 1980s to replace a 19th-century mosque that had been constructed for the use of British Indian troops. Tourists are not allowed inside, though.

For a choice of places to eat and drink, head down Kimberley Road opposite the park. Tucked away off the street is a short strip of restaurants and bars, on **Knutsford Terrace**. It may not rival Lan Kwai Fong in Central, but it is one of the few areas in Kowloon to offer some version of alfresco dining. To the east of here, a massive new area is being created off Mody Road, to be imitatively known as KLKF – Kowloon Lan Kwai Fong – but it remains to be seen whether it develops into more than just a wannabe version of the popular nightlife zone across the harbour.

Along Chatham Road South are two major museums: the **Hong Kong Museum of History** (*see p99*) and the popular, hands-on **Hong Kong Science Museum** (*see p99*). There is also the delightful old **Rosary Church**, one of Kowloon's oldest surviving places of worship, which was paid for at the end of the 19th century by a prominent local Portuguese medical doctor.

A stellar attraction for kids of all ages: the **Hong Kong Space Museum**. *See p99*.

Sightseeing

Hong Kong Museum of Art

10 Salisbury Road (2721 0116/www.hk.art.museum).
Tsim Sha Tsui MTR (exit E)/buses to Tsim Sha Tsui
Star Ferry Pier & along Salisbury Road/Tsim Sha
Tsui Star Ferry Pier. **Open** 10am-8pm Mon-Wed,
Fri-Sun. **Admission** HK$10; HK$5 concessions.
Free to all Wed. **No credit cards. Map** p333 C6.

Despite its relatively small size, this waterfront
museum has enough to keep visitors occupied for at
least a couple of hours. Works are arranged in six
galleries, five of which house permanent displays.
The sixth accommodates visiting exhibits from
China and further afield, of frankly variable quality. Among the permanent displays are a collection
of crafts from southern China and elsewhere in Asia
dating from neolithic times to the present day,
including jade and gold ornaments and artefacts
from various Chinese dynasties.

While the exhibitions are wide-ranging, porcelain
and other ceramic items form the museum's core display, with an extensive collection of extraordinarily
fine pieces, and a useful explanation of the manufacturing process and development of porcelain-making
techniques. There is also a permanent exhibition of
historical paintings and lithographs of Hong Kong,
Macau and Canton (now Guangzhou) in colonial and
pre-colonial days, and a collection of contemporary
art from the region.

Audio guides (available for HK$10) help explain
some of the exhibits, but for the most part the information is heavy on facts and thin on context, which
can be frustrating for those without much prior
knowledge. On the ground floor, the well-stocked
shop is well worth a look. It sells a range of art
books, prints and postcards, many at very reasonable prices. *See also p224.*

Hong Kong Museum of History

100 Chatham Road South (2724 9042/www.hk.
history.museum). *Tsim Sha Tsui MTR (exit B2)/*
buses along Chatham Road South. **Open** 10am-6pm
Mon, Wed-Sat; 10am-7pm Sun. **Admission** HK$10;
HK$5 concessions. Free to all Wed. **No credit
cards. Map** p333 C5.

Opened in 2001, this long-awaited museum gives a
magisterial overview of Hong Kong's history from
palaeolithic times to the present day. Well-curated
displays and sensitive captions mean there's something of interest for nearly everyone here. Political
correctness has not been allowed to rear its sancti-
monious head, and even a few unlikely candidates
have been included among the displays – there are
pictures of the Tiananmen Square incident in 1989,
for instance. Not to be missed for those who want
to know more about how and why Hong Kong
came about. (A new satellite of the museum, with
a focus on Dr Sun Yat-sen, opened in Mid-Levels in
December 2006; *see p82.*)

Hong Kong Science Museum

2 Science Museum Road, Tsim Sha Tsui East
(2732 3232/www.hk.science.museum). *Buses along*
Chatham Road South. **Open** 1-9pm Mon-Wed, Fri;
10am-9pm Sat, Sun. **Admission** HK$25; HK$12.50
concessions. Free to all Wed (except special
exhibitions). **No credit cards. Map** p333 C5.

The four floors of this museum are almost entirely
filled with excellent interactive displays that neatly
demonstrate the basic principles of physics, electricity, chemistry and everyday technology. A popular
destination for both parents and children, it's a fun,
boisterous place, often filled with excitable local
school parties. Most adults – especially visitors with
limited time – can live without a visit here, though.

Hong Kong Space Museum

10 Salisbury Road (2721 0226/Omnimax bookings
2734 9009/www.hk.space.museum). *Tsim Sha Tsui*
MTR (exit E)/buses to Kowloon Star Ferry Pier
& along Salisbury Road/Kowloon Star Ferry Pier.
Open 1-9pm Mon, Wed-Fri; 10am-9pm Sat, Sun.
Admission *Museum* free. *Omnimax Theatre*
HK$24-$32; HK$12-$16 concessions. **No credit
cards. Map** p333 C6.

This is not the most thrilling museum in Hong Kong,
but children will like the four or five good interactive exhibits, including rides simulating the gravity
on the moon and the landing of the lunar module, a
centrifuge and a gyroscope. Displays explaining the
workings of rockets, the solar system and the stars
are reasonably well put together but, like the Science
Museum, are more for kids than adults. In addition,
some of the displays are starting to show their age,
and many are poorly explained. The same goes for
the Sculpture Garden outside; some of its dozen or
so pieces are labelled, but otherwise there's little
information available about either the works or their
creators. Documentaries in Cantonese, Mandarin
and Japanese (in English via headphones) are shown
every day in the Omnimax Theatre. **Photo** *p98.*

Kowloon Park

Between Kowloon Park Drive & Nathan Road. *Tsim*
Sha Tsui MTR (exit A1). **Open** 6am-midnight daily.
Map p333 B5.

One of the city's best-loved green spaces, Kowloon
Park was previously the site of Whitfield Barracks,
which was used for British (in practice, though,
mostly Indian) soldiers. The park is well designed,
so there's lots to see, plus plenty of space in which
to stroll or just sit and relax. An attractive open-
plan swimming area (open daily, April-October)
takes up the northern section of the park – be
warned: it gets very busy. (There's also an
Olympic-sized indoor heated pool). Just south of the
pools are an aviary alive with birdlife and a pond
crowded with flamingos and waterfowl alongside
a secluded Chinese garden. On the park's eastern
edge are a small, waist-high maze, a lovely sculpture garden and a number of fountains and other
water features. Near the south-west corner, the barracks building itself has been restored and recently
reopened as the Hong Kong Heritage Discovery
Centre, showcasing aspects of Chinese and
European architecture in Hong Kong (2208 4400,
www.amo.gov.hk, open 10am-6pm). **Photo** *p100.*

Sightseeing

Get up early to watch locals practise t'ai chi in **Kowloon Park**. *See p99*.

Hung Hom

East of the museums, beyond Tsim Sha Tsui East, lies **Hung Hom**. At its southern end stands the 12,500-seater **Hong Kong Coliseum** (*see p238*), an inverted pyramid that plays host to major sporting events and music concerts. Next door is Hung Hom Station, the terminus of the Kowloon–Canton Railway (KCR). Trains depart from here to the New Territories, Guangzhou, Shanghai, Beijing and other places in China. The reclaimed land on the eastern edge of Hung Hom – formerly the site of the Hong Kong and Whampoa Dock Company, better known as the Kowloon Docks – has been developed into a largely utilitarian area of housing, shops and office blocks known as **Whampoa Gardens**. A mirage rises up from the thicket of retail outlets on Hung Hom Road – you can't miss the massive hull of the **Whampoa** (visible from the path to Tsim Sha Tsui; on Shung King Street at Tak Fung Street), a ship-shaped hunk of concrete that will never set sail, as it is, in fact, a shopping mall. With four levels (or 'decks'), the 100-metre-long (328-foot) ship houses Japanese department store Jusco, a Chinese restaurant, a playground and a cinema.

Aside from the Whampoa, there are only a few other parts of Hung Hom worth visiting. Close by, on the waterfront near the bus terminus, is the impressive five-star **Harbour Plaza**. The Patio bar/restaurant outside is a relaxed, if somewhat expensive, place for snacks in an al fresco setting with easterly views of the harbour.

A hidden gem worth seeking out in the area is **Sung Kit Street**, a pedestrian alley off Bailey Street that is crowded with – unusually

for Hong Kong – cheap and unpretentious (though not entirely authentic) Japanese restaurants; elsewhere in the city such places are often both pricey and posey. Be warned, though – Sung Kit Street is a *very* long walk from the ferry pier.

Conveniently, the Star Ferry sails frequently from the Hung Hom Ferry Pier (just in front of the bus terminus) to Wan Chai and Central.

Yau Ma Tei & Mong Kok

North of Kowloon Park, Tsim Sha Tsui melds almost imperceptibly into the district of **Yau Ma Tei** (the southern portion of which is often referred to as **Jordan**, after Jordan Road, a main thoroughfare that crosses Nathan Road beyond Austin Road. Along with **Mong Kok** further north, Yau Ma Tei is a gritty but very interesting district whose name means 'hemp oil ground' in Cantonese, although the only examples to be found in this completely urbanised area today are in shops. But what the area does have to offer are street markets, temples and masses of authentic backstreet atmosphere. Both Yau Ma Tei and Mong Kok are crammed with markets, including the perennially popular Jade Market in Yau Ma Tei and the bustling, fragrant Mong Kok Flower Market on – you guessed it – Flower Market Road.

Yau Ma Tei

Jordan MTR is a good starting point from which to explore Yau Ma Tei. To find the heart of the district, take exit A out of the MTR station and head west along Jordan Road to Temple Street and walk north. This is where you'll find the heart of the **Temple Street**

Night Market (*see p190* **To market, to market**; **photo** *p102*), which, as its name implies, is at its best after dark. There is a good deal of junk on sale here, but you can usually find a few decent buys – particularly cheap designer fakes – if you look hard enough. On the corner of Temple and Pak Hoi Streets, half a dozen or so inexpensive canteen-style restaurants operate out of a small covered area, serving food until late. The prudish may want to avoid it, however, as it's considered entirely acceptable table etiquette here (as in most basic Chinese establishments) to spit gristle and bone fragments on to the plastic table tops.

If you haven't already seen a Chinese food and produce market, **Reclamation Street**, which runs parallel with Temple Street (two blocks to the west), hosts a large **food market** during the day. Virtually the entire area around the street, stretching between Argyle Street to the north, Ferry Street to the west and Nathan Road to the east, is full of interesting Chinese shops and businesses, including funeral parlours, herbalists and health tea shops. **Ning Po Street** is particularly impressive: check out the shop at No.21, which specialises in snake products; its walls are lined with jars and jars of pickled reptiles. You'll also find a number of paper shops here selling items destined to be burnt at funerals, such as paper clothes, cars, paper money, mah-jong sets and fragile paper houses.

At the end of Temple Street (on Kansu Street under the flyover just west of the top end of Temple Street) is the famous **Jade Market** (*see p190* **To market, to market**). Inside the small covered market, around 50 stalls sell jade ornaments and jewellery, as well as carved bone trinkets. Be prepared for some heavy-duty bargaining, and know how much the items cost elsewhere before you buy. Unless you're a jade expert (or have one handily in tow), don't part with any significant sums – it's all too easy for novices to be ripped off. The market officially stays open till 6pm but it's best to go early as some vendors close up shop around lunchtime.

A minute's walk north-east of the Jade Market is Yau Ma Tei's sizeable **Tin Hau Temple** (open 8am-6pm daily), divided into three separate areas for the worship of Hong Kong's favourite deities: Tin Hau (the sea goddess), Shing Wong, the city god, and To Tei, the earth god. It costs nothing to enter and look around, but it is considered polite to make a small contribution. Photography is frowned upon, though not expressly forbidden. In the evenings, numerous fortune-tellers gather outside the temple to offer their services. There is a choice of face and palm readers, as well as 'birds of fortune' (small birds that supposedly tell your fortune by picking out tarot-style cards when they're released from their cages). A couple more fortune-tellers, one of them advertising fortunes told in English, also operate from the annexe at the far end of the temple building during the day.

Mong Kok

Most of the sights and shopping in Mong Kok are located to the east of Mong Kok MTR, although the new **Langham Place** complex of shopping malls and restaurants (*see p179*)

Hong Kong Cultural Centre. See p96.

opened on Shanghai Street, to the west. One of Mong Kok's busiest markets is known as the **Ladies' Market** (running the length of Tung Choi Street), even though it sells a huge range of goods not necessarily restricted to female tastes. Clothes, CDs, luggage, sandals, feather boas and wigs are all here in abundance, along with other essentials like clothes-fluff removers and eyelash curlers.

Running parallel to the market is **Fa Yuen Street**, where dozens of shops sell trainers and other sports goods, while at the northern end of the market, along Tung Choi Street, is the **Goldfish Market**, which is more a cluster of well-stocked goldfish shops than an actual market. Goldfish are extremely popular among the Chinese (they are believed to bring good luck and to help absorb bad vibes – and are good quiet pets for small noisy flats), and there is a fascinating variety of breeds on offer. While most are reasonably priced, some are mind-bogglingly expensive.

A short walk north of here along Prince Edward Road West brings you to the **Flower Market**. This delightful place consists of a long line of shops and stalls selling a huge array of exotic flowers and budding branches, often at very reasonable prices. This vivid street teems with customers year round, but is particularly crowded around Chinese New Year.

A stretch of garden running alongside Yuen Po Street at the far end of Flower Market Road is a gathering place for local bird lovers. **The Bird Market** (*see also p190* **To market,**

to market) is alive with the twitter and chirp of many species of songbird and parrot (many illegally smuggled). Many enthusiasts take their own birds along, usually in delicately wrought (and often wretchedly tiny) cages. A dozen or so stalls sell birds, bird food and accessories, including bags of grasshoppers, which are fed to the birds using chopsticks. The ornate cages make fine souvenirs themselves and are reasonably priced. The bird flu outbreaks of recent years have ironically led to beneficial effects for both visitors – the market is no longer as thronged as it was before – and for the birds, as they are now kept in more sanitary conditions.

At the top end of the garden runs **Boundary Street**, the old Kowloon–China border. After Britain forced China to cede the Kowloon Peninsula to them in 1860, they then became worried that it wasn't enough. As fears about the growing influence of other Western powers over China grew (particularly considering new gunnery technology that increased the range of artillery) and concerns about the lack of a fresh water supply for the colony were raised, the British persuaded the Chinese government into leasing the New Territories to them for 99 years in 1898. The decision to ask for only a temporary lease on the land made for tremendous administrative and diplomatic problems in subsequent decades. Hong Kong Island and Kowloon had been permanently ceded, but the necessity of returning the New Territories to China in

Temple Street Market. *See p100.*

Walking on water

If you take one of the earliest maps of the city from the 1840s and lay it over a present-day version, the difference is astonishing. Today's Hong Kong is, unsurprisingly, vastly bigger, but it's the pattern of growth that's unusual. Rather than creep outwards across the land, Hong Kong takes earth from the quarries and uses it to fill in the sea. Jagged coastlines have been steadily transformed into straight lines, and entire bays have disappeared. Even Victoria Harbour is smaller than it used to be. Including the airport expansion, the territory has now reclaimed 7,000 hectares (27 square miles) of land from the sea, two-thirds of which was in the past three decades.

One of the main reasons why land reclamation has such a long history here is to do with Hong Kong's system of land tenure and the various means that have been employed to generate revenue. Land holdings are all ultimately vested in the government, and supply has always been kept restricted to maintain an artificially high price. To this day, land sales provide the government with a sizeable chunk of its annual income.

In the 19th century the government raised revenue from the sale of monopolies on retail alcohol and opium sales and – bizarrely – nightsoil collection for fertiliser, as well as land sales. There were no customs duties, limited excise, no VAT and no income taxes until after World War II; even now, over 70 per cent of the population pays little or no tax.

So the money for roads, waterworks and hospitals has had to come from elsewhere, and land sales have traditionally filled the gap. In areas such as Central, where land for building has been exhausted, filling in the adjacent sea bed becomes an attractive option, made even more tempting by the fact that land created by reclamation is cheap to make and can be sold for a premium.

To get some perspective on the full extent of land reclamation, consider two examples. The electric tramlines running along the northern side of Hong Kong Island, from Kennedy Town to Shau Kei Wan, roughly follow the original 1841 shoreline; anything to the north – including most of the business district – is built on landfill. On the Kowloon side, Yau Ma Tei's Tin Hau Temple was once on the shoreline, as befits a shrine to the goddess of the sea. It is now marooned almost three kilometres (two miles) inland. The road in front of the temple, Reclamation Street, is named after the first phase of harbour fill undertaken here in the late 19th century.

Reclamation continues to be a source of major political controversy in Hong Kong. Few agree on the ultimate uses of the new land, but most pressure groups feel that simply building more roads on stretches of former harbour provides no long-term answer to Hong Kong's worsening traffic congestion and pollution problems.

The closure and relocation of Central's iconic Star Ferry piers to make way for – you guessed it – more landfill for yet more roads – sparked heated public protests. But as is usual in Hong Kong, the die had been cast long before, and demonstrations were to no avail. Further extensive reclamation work is planned around the former Kai Tak Airport runway site, as part of a proposed cruise liner terminus.

The financial rationale for land reclamations in Hong Kong is so closely tied to the government's fiscal base that until some serious rethink of the tax structure is undertaken – politically a near-impossibility – reclamation projects, and the resultant cash from land sales at a premium, will be a feature of Hong Kong life for some time to come.

1997, and the overspill of development from the 1910s onwards, along with water-supply problems, made the retention of the rest of the colony untenable.

Eastern Kowloon

Although the area just to the north of Boundary Street is officially part of the New Territories (see also p17), it became locally known as 'New Kowloon' in the early 20th century; that designation has long-since lapsed, and today the sprawling conurbation goes by the name of **Eastern Kowloon**.

While much of it is of little interest to tourists, there are a handful of places worth visiting. To the east along the Quarry Bay MTR line is the large, busy Wong Tai Sin Temple and the beautiful and strange Kowloon Walled City Park (where a museum describes the walled neighbourhood, a law unto itself until 1992), while to the west along the Tsuen Wan MTR line is the cheap clothes and goods market of Sham Shui Po.

East along the Quarry Bay line

When you arrive in Eastern Kowloon, you are likely to feel that you've wandered into a massive building site – much of it is continually being torn down and replaced by newer, taller tower blocks, shopping centres and office blocks. (The height restrictions in Kowloon, necessary while the old Kai Tak airport was in use, have now been lifted.) The construction noise is easily avoided, however, and a good starting point for exploring the area on foot is the Lok Fu MTR station. When you come out of the station, walk down Wang Tau Hom East Road and turn left at the T-junction along Junction Road. On the left-hand side of the road you'll see the **Chinese Christian Cemetery**, with its graves stacked up and squeezed into every available piece of ground. Nearby is the tiny and very lovely **Hau Wong Temple** (open 8am-5pm daily), built in 1737 and shaded by tall feathery bamboo. The temple is dedicated to one of the exiled boy-emperor Zhao Bing's most loyal generals.

Close to the temple is an oasis of fountains, elaborate topiary, sculptures and meandering walkways in the **Kowloon Walled City Park** (open 6.30am-11pm daily). Inside the old almshouse, facing the main entrance on Tung Tsing Road, is a display about the intriguing history of the Walled City, which once stood where the garden is today. Built by the Chinese in the mid 19th century as part of the empire's southern coastal defences, the fortress was inexplicably left out of the lease of the New Territories by the British in 1898. After World War II much of the fort was levelled by Japanese forces to provide stone for the Kai Tak Airport extension, and ramshackle high-rise apartments sprang up. Squatters and, later, triads moved in, creating a lawless underworld that thrived until 1992, when the buildings were pulled down.

Also worth a visit is **Wong Tai Sin Temple** (*see p105*). Located close to the Wong Tai Sin MTR station (one stop from Lok Fu), the temple is one of Hong Kong's largest, busiest and most interesting places of worship. The complex contains altars and shrines to several Buddhist, Confucian and Taoist deities, and is regularly filled with thronging worshippers, an almost unbelievable level of noise and – inevitably – swirling incense. Near the main temple is a large covered area containing more than a hundred fortune-teller stalls. Several of these soothsayers can reveal your fortune in English, mostly through palm and face reading. You're likely to be quoted about HK$300 for a five-minute consultation, but it should be possible to haggle them down to HK$100 or even less. Kneeling in front of the main temple's altar, many Chinese can be seen and heard solemnly shaking small canisters of bamboo sticks – known as *chim* – until one finally emerges from the container. Each stick is marked with a numeral and a corresponding meaning. Many users immediately head to the fortune-tellers to have their stick interpreted.

An alternative method of divination known as *sing pei*, or 'Buddha's lips', uses *bui*, two pieces of wood shaped like orange segments. A question is asked, the *bui* are thrown and the 'lips' answer 'yes' or 'no', depending on which way they land.

The next stop on the MTR line is Diamond Hill, from where it is a short and well-signposted walk to the austerely beautiful **Chi Lin Buddhist Nunnery** (*see below*), larger but more serene than the Wong Tai Sin Temple. Its yellow cedar timbers and elegantly tiled roof are new (although built in the ancient Tang style of architecture), while the carefully contrived layout of the large courtyard, temple and gardens all contribute to a sense of order and calm. The temples hold large and finely sculpted golden statues representing various incarnations of the Buddha.

The small, charming village of **Lei Yue Mun**, which has long been a favourite for seafood lovers, lies at the very southern tip of Kowloon in the eastern part of Victoria harbour. (To get there, take the MTR to Kwun Tong station, and then the number 14C bus to its terminus at Sam Ka Tsuen typhoon shelter.) Once you arrive in the village, walk east from the edge of the small harbour (past the large modern library) and turn right around the edge of the harbour to find the heart of the village. Here, there are dark and narrow alleyways, hemmed in by hundreds of tanks filled with marine life, and, further into the village, several seafood restaurants. Prices aren't cheap – most people are attracted more by the experience of eating in the village's bucolic environs than the food itself. But there's the advantage of being able to buy your dinner from one of the seafood vendors; the restaurants will then cook it for a fee. Make sure you agree on a price first, as tourist rip-offs do occur here.

Aside from the seafood restaurants, Lei Yue Mun is still a thriving coastal village. If you make it out here on a weekday, wander further into the village and along the shore towards the small Tin Hau Temple on the shoreline, where you can see dozens of rod fishermen crouching on the rocks.

Chi Lin Buddhist Nunnery

5 Chi Lin Drive, Diamond Hill (2354 1730). Diamond Hill MTR (exit C2). **Open** 9am-4.30pm daily. **Admission** free.

This elegant complex was first constructed in the 1930s and rebuilt in the 1990s in the style of the Tang Dynasty (AD 618-907). The attached nunnery has some fine statues of the Sakyamuni Buddha, and the water lily ponds in the courtyards are beautiful.

Wong Tai Sin Temple.

Wong Tai Sin Temple

2 Chuk Yuen, Wong Tai Sin (2328 0270/2327 8141/www.siksikyuen.org.hk). Wong Tai Sin MTR (exit B2). **Open** 7am-5.30pm daily. **Admission** free. **Map** p325.

This sprawling temple complex is mainly dedicated to the god Wong Tai Sin. Before he was deified, Wong Tai Sin was a shepherd from Zhejiang Province who was taught how to make a healing potion by a *xian* ('fairy immortal'). He then went on to perform many miracles among the sick, and was deified. Religious devotion in the temple is not strictly limited to Wong Tai Sin, however, as it also takes in a broad sweep of Taoist, Confucian and Buddhist deities. One of the best-known temples in Hong Kong, it is thronged with visitors, many of whom are tourists from the mainland, Taiwan and South-east Asia. The excellent website has useful background information.

West along the Tsuen Wan line

As you travel west through New Kowloon, one of the first worthwhile stops is the open-air market and surrounding shops of **Sham Shui Po**, near the MTR station of the same name. Although not unique, they do sell a diverse range of goods and the prices are very low. Outside the **Apliu Street** exit of the MTR, the extensive street market stretches away in all directions. Here, luggage and clothes are probably as cheap as they get this side of the Chinese border, although the choice is not as great as in Shenzhen (*see p194* **Savings made in China**).

To the north-west of the MTR station, on Yen Chow Street, there's a large computer market in the upstairs section of the Golden Shopping Centre; prices are marginally better than in Kowloon (*see p178* **Tech savvy**). A few metres away, at 100 Yen Chow Street, a good VCD and DVD shop has an extremely comprehensive selection of US and UK TV series, as well as hundreds of (mostly Cantonese-language) films. For more on Apliu Street, *see p190* **To market, to market**.

After perusing the wares on offer at the centre, get back on to the MTR and head one stop north-west to Cheung Sha Wan, home of the **Lei Cheng Uk Han Tomb Museum** (*see below*), located an easy walk from the station. Turn left up Tonkin Street and the museum is just over Po On Road, past the public garden.

Lei Cheng Uk Han Tomb Museum

41 Tonkin Street, Sham Shui Po (2386 2863/www.hk.history.museum). Cheung Sha Wan MTR (exit A2, A3)/bus 2 from Kowloon Star Ferry Pier. **Open** 10am-1pm, 2-6pm Mon-Wed, Fri, Sat; 1-6pm Sun. **Admission** free.

This Han-era burial chamber dates from the Eastern Han Dynasty (AD 24-220). Uncovered by workmen in 1955 while building a public housing estate, it's worth a quick look if you're in the area as there's a small display of the finds excavated from the tomb. The tomb itself, visible through a Perspex sheet and resembling a small brick kiln, is outside in the courtyard. Alas, there's very little information about who built the complex and for whom it was constructed.

The New Territories

A dramatically beautiful region of lowland valleys, jagged mountain ranges, deeply incised coastline and hundreds of islands.

Sightseeing

The New Territories – which extend from Boundary Street in the middle of downtown Kowloon northwards to the border along the Shum Chun River – were leased from China in 1898 for 99 years under the Convention of Peking – hence the beginning of the entire '1997' issue. Largely ignored by tourists, this lesser-known side of Hong Kong is home to stunning landscapes and wide open spaces, while its sprawling New Towns are home to a large portion of Hong Kong's residents. Today more than three million people (over 40 per cent of the SAR's total population) live in this extensive region.

Despite some unsightly, badly planned urban, commercial and industrial developments (particularly in the west), large tracts of unspoiled countryside still remain, and hundreds of square kilometres are given over to country parks. More than 40 per cent of Hong Kong's total land mass comprises country parks, and wonderful hiking and wildlife-watching are to be had along the New Territories' many mountainous trails (*see* p115 **Walks on the wild side**). In addition, many of Hong Kong's finest beaches are in the remote and difficult to access north-east New Territories.

Significant rural settlements have existed here for hundreds of years, and as a result there is a considerable amount of authentic Chinese village heritage in the New Territories. Dozens

of temples, ancestral halls and walled villages – some dating back several centuries – are dotted around the countryside. Just don't expect to find the Forbidden City, the Great Wall or other impressive Imperial Chinese treasures here; the New Territories' heritage is overwhelmingly small-scale and rural. As a result, the real attractions are the mountains and countryside.

Happily, despite the region's lingering rural feel and considerable size, travel is very easy here. The branches of the Kowloon–Canton Railway (KCR), the Light Rail Transit (LRT), the Mass Transit Railway (MTR) en route to Lantau's northern coast, excellent bus and minibus services and ferries all make even quite remote areas fairly accessible for the day-tripper. Recent expansions to the KCR system are making the region even more accessible to visitors: the West Rail extension has opened a route which extends from Nam Cheong (on the Tung Chung MTR line) to Yuen Long and Tuen Mun in the western New Territories. A branch of East Rail – the Man On Shan Line – carries travellers to Wu Kai Sha in the eastern New Territories, from where superb hiking possibilities open up in the Sai Kung region. Further works will bring an East Rail spur to the border town of Lok Ma Chau in 2007, and enable visitors to hop on the West Rail at East Tsim Sha Tsui from 2009.

Before exploring the mainland New Territories or the outlying islands, pay a visit to the Government Publications Centre (*see* p175) for one of the Countryside series of maps. These are an inexpensive way to help you get your bearings, plan your journey and make the most of what the region has to offer. Various small local outfits can help you organise guided walks and visits to the New Territories. While most trips can be done fairly easily on your own, for those with limited time who still want to experience something of this 'other Hong Kong', Walk Hong Kong (9187 8641, www.walkhongkong.com) may be of help.

Central New Territories

A day trip along the Kowloon–Canton Railway's East Rail line from Sha Tin to Sheung Shui is a convenient way to experience something of life beyond the Kowloon hills, especially if you're only in Hong Kong for a short time. Along here you'll find hillside temples, two sprawling New Towns (Sha Tin and Tai Po) that are the 'real Hong Kong' for millions of local residents these days, Sha Tin's excellent **Hong Kong Heritage Museum** (*see p109*), and, glimpsed through the choking smog on a clear day, Shenzhen, Hong Kong's neighbouring Special Economic Zone.

Tai Wai

The first stop on the KCR after passing through the Kowloon hills is **Tai Wai** (which today virtually merges into Sha Tin; *see below*). **Amah Rock**, said to resemble a woman who was turned to stone by the gods after her husband failed to return from a fishing expedition (though it's actually a pre-Chinese phallic symbol), is the most prominent sight in the area. The stone can be reached from the station via Hung Miu Kuk Road and a subsequent path that leads steeply uphill.

Closer to the station on Che Kung Miu Road is the popular **Che Kung Temple** (*see below*), while another ten minutes' walk up the road is the impressive walled village known as **Tsang Tai Uk**. Translated as 'Tsang's big house', this mid 19th-century structure was built for members of the Tsang clan and is very well preserved, unlike other New Territories walled villages, most of which are squalid, rubbish-strewn and badly decayed.

Che Kung Temple

7 Che Kung Miu Road (no phone). Tai Wai KCR. Follow exit sign to the temple; take the pedestrian subway. **Open** 7am-6pm daily. **Admission** free.

Dedicated to Che Kung, a legendary general who reputedly rid part of Guangdong province of plague, this is one of Hong Kong's most popular local temples and is especially thronged around the Lunar New Year period.

Sha Tin

Hong Kong's first 'New Town', **Sha Tin** is large, well planned and extensive – and for many people a surprisingly attractive and interesting place, with generous expanses of parkland running along its riverfront.

The Sha Tin KCR station empties into the sprawling **New Town Plaza**, a popular shopping destination that, like many in other New Towns, represents the new face of the 'real Hong Kong'.

A 15-minute walk from the northern exit of the KCR is the **Ten Thousand Buddhas Monastery** (*see p109*). Cross the road in front of the station and follow the signposts to the temple at the top of a wooded hill. You'll know you're on the right path when, after about five minutes or so, you begin to see the large,

Back yourself a winner at the impressive **Sha Tin Racecourse**. *See p109.*

Strike a pose: **Ten Thousand Buddhas Monastery**. *See p109.*

golden, scarlet-lipped Buddhas lining the steep route. Over 400 steps must be climbed to reach the temple, but it's worth the effort – there are more than 10,000 Buddha statues inside.

Within walking distance of Sha Tin KCR station (and situated next to the Shing Mun riverside park) is the **Hong Kong Heritage Museum** (*see below*). This superb facility offers a fascinating and comprehensive social and anthropological history of Hong Kong – dating back to the region's geological formation. Its extensive static displays, audio-visual exhibits and interactive terminals cover more than 6,000 years of human existence in the region; it's well worth a visit.

Sha Tin's other main attraction – especially for legions of locals – is the **racecourse** (*see below*). Opened in 1980, this huge, high-tech stadium is strikingly juxtaposed against the backdrop of nearby hills. Tens of millions of dollars are wagered here every race-night.

Hong Kong Heritage Museum

1 Man Lam Road (2180 8188/www.heritage museum.gov.hk). Sha Tin or Tai Wai KCR then 15min walk/A41, E42, 72A, 80M, 86, 89, N271, 282 bus. **Open** 10am-6pm Mon, Wed-Sat; 10am-7pm Sun. **Admission** HK$10; HK$5 concessions. Free to all Wed. **No credit cards**.

The Hong Kong Heritage Museum, along with the Hong Kong Museum of History in Kowloon (*see p98*), is one of Hong Kong's best museums. There are six excellent permanent collections, plus plenty of space for temporary displays. The best, and largest, of the permanent exhibitions is the New Territories Heritage Hall. It explains how the landscape was formed, and illustrates the arrival of animal and prehistoric human life, the rise of the traditional village society, eventual colonial rule and the large-scale development of the New Territories towns. While you could spend all day in this one gallery, there's much more to see. Beautiful calligraphy and renderings of plants and animals by the acclaimed Lingnan artist Zhao Shao'ang hang from scrolls on the first floor, while the TT Tsui Gallery holds a wide range of ceramics dating back to neolithic times. There's also a colourful, educational exhibition on Cantonese Opera that explains some of the elaborate ritual involved.

Sha Tin Racecourse

Sha Tin (2966 8111/www.shatinracetrack.com). Racecourse KCR. **Admission** prices vary. **No credit cards**.

While it does not quite have the atmosphere of the night races at Happy Valley, the vast scale of Sha Tin Racecourse is nonetheless impressive. Its backdrop of wide-open spaces and rugged hills is perhaps its greatest appeal. During the racing season (September-June), visitors can either pay the regular admission fee of HK$20 or stump up HK$50 to enter the Members' Enclosure, which guarantees entry to busy race meetings (you must be over 18, have been in Hong Kong for less than 21 days and bring your passport with you for inspection). Alternatively, you can join one of the excursions organised by the Hong Kong Tourism Board, which include a decent buffet meal. **Photo** *p107*.

Ten Thousand Buddhas Monastery

Sha Tin (2691 1067/www.10kbuddhas.org). Sha Tin KCR (exit B) then 20min walk (via pedestrian bridge towards Grand Central Plaza). **Open** 9am-5pm daily. **Admission** free.

After a rather arduous climb up to the monastery's main building (especially taxing in the summer heat), you are rewarded at the top by the delightful sight of thousands of tiny golden Buddhas in hundreds of poses lining shelves that reach to the ceiling. More Buddha images can be found outside – there's a Buddha astride a giant white elephant and another atop a huge dog. Nearby, Buddha statues peer down from a bright red nine-storey pagoda. In a small annexe above the main temple lies the body of the temple's founding monk, who died in 1965. This annexe was recently closed to the public for repairs, but should it be open when you're here; you can see him lying inside a glass case, covered in gold leaf. If the climb has made you peckish, the vegetarian canteen next to the main temple is cheap and tasty (a meal costs about HK$50). **Photo** *p108*.

University

Two stops north of Sha Tin on the KCR is University station, serving the **Chinese University of Hong Kong**. Constantly changing exhibitions at the **Chinese University Art Museum** (*see below*) make the otherwise fairly ugly, 1960s-style campus worth a visit. The museum has a good – and extensive – collection that includes gold jewellery and jade ornaments.

The area around the University KCR station is an ideal location to launch a boat trip to the islands of **Tap Mun Chau** ('Grassy Island') and **Ping Chau** near the mainland coast, as well as to the remoter parts of the Sai Kung Peninsula at the mouth of Tolo Harbour. Ferries to the islands can be caught at Ma Liu Shui, a 15-minute walk from the station. Tap Mun Chau is noted for its rugged peacefulness, beautiful beaches, the caves along its shores, its fishing village and a small **Tin Hau Temple** that dates back to the Qing dynasty. Also worth seeing is much smaller Ping Chau for its soft coral formations and excellent white sand beaches – beware of sharks here, though.

Chinese University Art Museum

Chinese University of Hong Kong, Tai Po Road (2609 7416/www.cuhk.edu.hk/ics/amm). University KCR then bus/coach. **Open** 10am-4.45pm Mon-Sat; 12.30-5.30pm Sun. **Admission** free.

Tang clan members gather at 500-year-old **Tang Chung Ling Ancestral Hall**. *See p111.*

The Hong Kong Museum of Art in Kowloon (*see p98*) and the Hong Kong Heritage Museum in Sha Tin (*see p109*) both have more interesting traditional Chinese paintings than the permanent collection on display here, but the museum is worth a visit for its large, impressive collection of decorative arts, including fine ceramics, sculptures and jade. Some of the more than 7,000 items displayed date back to neolithic times. These, and other special collections, are shown on rotation, so if you want to see something specific, it's advisable to check what's on display before setting out.

To reach the museum, exit the KCR on the campus (west) side, turn right and board the free campus shuttle bus. Get off at the second stop – the museum is close to the library and the administration building. The buildings are on the south side of the road, but are not immediately obvious and are badly signposted, so you may have to ask one of the students to point it out if you're in doubt.

Tai Po

While at first glance **Tai Po** is just another of the newly created towns that dot the New Territories countryside, it is in fact centred around one of the area's oldest market towns and there are plenty of sites of interest here, including numerous buildings from the early British period.

One feature that's been the victim of its own popularity in recent years is the **Wishing Tree**. This large Chinese banyan lies a 20-minute bus ride from Tai Po Market station (take the number 64K bus to the Fong Ma Po stop). For a few dollars, the stallholders around the tree will sell you an orange with a vividly coloured streamer attached to it. Write your wish on the streamer and hurl the orange at the tree. If the fruit lodges among the branches, supposedly your wish will come true. The tree itself wasn't so lucky – the weight of the fruit caused part of it to collapse in 2005, and it's no longer quite the attraction it once was.

You can wander around **Tai Po Market** for an hour or so, and the old district office and police station on the hillside can also be visited. Both are popular nesting places for egrets: hundreds of the bony creatures can be seen perched on the trees surrounding the buildings.

The **Hong Kong Railway Museum** (*see p111*) near the market also warrants a peek if you are a train lover. The Chinese-style station is a reminder of what all the original KCR stations looked like. Nearby on Fu Shin Street is the 19th-century **Man Mo Temple**.

From Tai Po you can board a bus for the wild country and walking trails around the man-made **Plover Cove reservoir**. This inlet on the Tolo harbour was dammed in the 1960s; it's a popular spot for weekend strollers.

Nature lovers should also make the effort to visit the lovely **Kadoorie Farm & Botanic Garden** (*see p113*), which is a pioneering education and conservation project outside Tai Po.

Hong Kong Railway Museum

13 Shung Tak Street, Tai Po Market (2653 3455/ www.heritagemuseum.gov.hk/english/branch.htm). Tai Po Market KCR then 25K minibus. **Open** 9am-5pm Mon, Wed-Sun. **Admission** free.

It's hardly a must-see sight, but rail enthusiasts and those with time to kill can peruse exhibits that include an old narrow-gauge engine, a few railway carriages and some models. Photos of the old waterfront Tsim Sha Tsui KCR railway station provide interesting glimpses of Kowloon in earlier times.

Fanling & Lo Wai

Continuing north along the KCR, the biggest attraction for most visitors to the small town of **Fanling** is the Lung Yuek Tau Heritage Trail.

Before setting off on the hike, pop into the **Fung Ying Sin Koon Temple** (open 9am-5pm daily), located a three-minute walk from the west exit of the station. A large, modern Taoist temple, it includes a section dedicated to the deities of particular years (past, current and future) and their corresponding Chinese birth signs.

A ten-minute ride on the number 54K bus from the eastern side of the KCR will bring you to the **Tang Chung Ling Ancestral Hall** (*see below*), one of the largest of its kind in the New Territories. The hall lies along the **Lung Yuek Tau Heritage Trail**, which passes five *wai tsuen* (walled villages) and six *uk tsuen* (unwalled villages), within a couple of kilometres of one another. The Ancestral Hall is the best starting point for hitting the trail – it is on a bus route and there's a detailed map posted outside. Walking the trail is easily accomplished in a morning or afternoon, but be aware that the signposting is patchy along the way, and there are numerous stretches of unsightly village developments, salvage yards and the like.

Probably the best-preserved walled village on the trail is **Lo Wai**. The village gate and watchtower, along with the old walls, are all still intact. Tourists are welcome to visit, but don't prowl around too close to private houses. Nearby **Ma Wat Wai** still has its well-preserved main entrance, first built in the 1700s, along with its iron chain-link gate.

Tang Chung Ling Ancestral Hall

Ping Che Road, Lo Wai (Antiquities & Monuments Office 2721 2326/www.lcsd.gov.hk/CE/Museum/ Monument). Fanling KCR then 54K minibus. **Open** 9am-1pm, 2-5pm Mon, Wed-Sun. **Admission** free.

Dating back more than 500 years, this large ancestral hall was founded by the Tang clan, one of the five great New Territories clans. You'll find some ancient and ornate ancestral tablets at the end of the temple, including those of the Wong Kwu (Emperor's Aunt), a 12th-century princess of the southern Song Dynasty who married into the Tang clan after escaping the invading Mongol hordes. Despite its popularity with tourists and visitors, Tang Ching Ling is still an active meeting hall where clan members pay respects to their ancestors, and hold meetings and celebrations, much as their families have done for centuries. **Photo** *p110.*

Sheung Shui & beyond

Sheung Shui is the last stop on the KCR before it reaches the border at Lo Wu. Sheung Shui is the most convenient stop for bird-watching trips to the world-famous **Mai Po Marshes**, seasonal home to numerous species of migratory birds. The marshes lie within the Closed Border Area, but the World Wildlife Fund runs tours (book well in advance; 2526 1011, www.wwf.org.hk/eng/maipo).

Not far from Sheung Shui, near the village of Wing Ping Tsuen, is **Tai Fu Tai** (*see below*), a mansion known locally – and somewhat erroneously – as the 'Mandarin's House'. This attractive Chinese home incorporates various European decorative elements. It was first built in 1865 by a senior member of the Man clan from nearby San Tin.

Two kilometres (one-and-a-quarter miles) to the north-east of Tai Fu Tai is the old border lookout of **Lok Ma Chau** (while it's possible to walk the route from Tai Fu Tai, it's certainly simpler and much faster to take a taxi). The lookout is just a few hundred metres from the Shum Chun River, the border between the Hong Kong Special Administrative Region and the neighbouring city of **Shenzhen** (*see p194* **Savings made in China**). Shenzhen has grown rapidly over the past two decades, changing from a quiet country village into the bustling modern city it is today.

Tai Fu Tai

Antiquities & Monuments Office 2721 2326/www. lcsd.gov.hk/CE/Museum/Monument. Sheung Shui KCR then 76K bus/17 minibus towards Yuen Long; alight at Wing Ping Tsuen. **Open** 9am-1pm, 2-5pm Mon, Wed-Sun. **Admission** free.

This large, ornate house, built in about 1865, is one of the New Territories' better restored heritage sites. It was once the home of Man Chung-luen, a senior Qing Dynasty civil servant, or *dai fu*. To get here, take the number 76K bus from outside Sheung Shui KCR station, or the No.17 minibus – alight when you see San Tin post office. Signposts mark the way to Tai Fu Tai, a few minutes' walk north.

West New Territories

Large, modern satellite towns dominate much of the southern coast and low-lying valleys of the western New Territories. Beyond them are vast expanses of wilderness, much of it contained within the borders of country parks at Lam Tsuen, Tai Lam and Tai Mo Shan. The **Mai Po Marshes**, one of Hong Kong's most pristine wilderness areas, is also nearby, along the southern shores of Deep Bay.

Tsuen Wan & Tai Mo Shan

An industrial/residential/commercial agglomeration at the end of the MTR line, **Tsuen Wan** gradually developed in the immediate post-war era from a small market settlement into a major industrial area. While at first glance it is rather ugly, crowded and traffic-congested, Tsuen Wan and places like it are nevertheless the 'real Hong Kong' and merit a visit for a flavour of that authenticity, if for nothing else.

A five-minute walk east of the MTR (take exit B3 to Sai Lau Kok Road) is the **Sam Tung Uk Museum** (*see p114*). Actually an 18th-century walled village, it was only recently made into a museum, because until then it was an active residential site – home to members of the Chan clan, Hakka people who originally migrated to the Hong Kong region from Fujian province. In 1980, when the last residents finally moved out as part of clearances for the Tsuen Wan MTR line construction, it was turned into a museum. Many people feel that its authenticity was damaged when it was

subjected to a restoration programme, and while worth a look, like many village museums, it has a curiously dead air about it.

Another thing to be enjoyed near Tsuen Wan is a walk in the hills nearby. Up above the city is one of the area's best temple complexes – **Chuk Lam Shim Yuen Monastery** ('Bamboo Forest Monastery'; *see p114*), a working Buddhist retreat, founded in 1927. Unfortunately, it's not a particularly pleasant stroll to reach the monastery from the town – as much of it is along and under busy highways – so it is more sensible to treat yourself to a taxi (about HK$30).

A short distance away is another temple facility, the **Yuen Yuen Institute** (*see p114*), which is the one sight that most visitors to Tsuen Wan want to see. It's a large, active facility housing Buddhist, Taoist and Confucianist temples.

On the hillside just above the institute are footpaths leading up to **Tai Mo Shan**, Hong Kong's highest peak (its name means 'Big Hat Mountain', a reference to its shape as seen from a distance). It's a serious climb to the top, and you'll need to be well prepared: equip yourself with a decent map, plenty of water and suitable attire. You'll need to allow about six hours for a round trip from Tsuen Wan. There are no facilities or shops on the way or at the summit (except a small kiosk at the visitors' centre on Route Twisk open only on weekends and public

The wonderfully tranquil, atmospheric **Chuk Lam Shim Yuen Monastery**. *See p114*.

Kadoorie Farm & Botanic Garden

For a wonderful antidote to the city's forest of concrete and glass, head out to the **Kadoorie Farm & Botanic Garden** (KFBG), which nestles below Kwun Yum Shan (Goddess of Mercy Mountain) in the central New Territories. It can be a bit of an expedition to get to, but a half-day trip to these lush pastures passes low-rise villages on the way – and you'd be hard-pressed to find a better way to squeeze in this much flora and fauna.

For several decades after British rule was extended in 1898, the New Territories remained, for the most part, an underprivileged, under-serviced, under-policed rural backwater. Contrary to popular belief, the massive post-war population influx that greatly transformed Hong Kong did not only settle in the urban areas. Many New Territories villagers, especially in the northern areas, had relatives on the other side of what until 1950 was a porous, largely theoretical land border. Communist campaigns against rich peasants and rural landlords in the early 1950s saw many villagers moving across to the British side of the Shum Chun River, thus putting further population pressure on existing villages and farmland.

In response to this situation, in 1951 prominent Sephardic Jewish businessmen (Lord) Lawrence and (Sir) Horace Kadoorie set up a rural improvement project, the Kadoorie Agricultural Aid Association (KAAA), to help alleviate the situation. Priority was given to providing much-needed facilities that would have long-term benefits, thus producing self-reliance rather than ongoing welfare dependency. Many rural pathways and bridges over small streams in more remote parts of the New Territories, now mostly used by weekend ramblers, were originally paid for by the KAAA to help improve village access. Far-flung outlying islands were given piers to enable farmers to take produce to market and bring back fertilisers and supplies; the association also made gifts of sampans and outboard motors where necessary. Small dams, wells and irrigation sumps were built; sumps – small concrete tanks set below ground level with steps leading in and out – were especially welcome as they are a great time- and labour-saver for farmers who would otherwise have to water their vegetable fields with watering cans.

With the decline in commercial farming in Hong Kong over the past two decades the organisation now focuses more on education and conservation, based at the magnificent Kadoorie Farm & Botanic Garden (KFBG). More than a half of all the diverse plant species found within Hong Kong are now growing at the KFBG, but its activities don't stop with the study and preservation of flora. Many of Hong Kong's larger mammals, as well as amphibians, reptiles and insects, can also be seen here, and there is an organic farm.

One of the KFBG's particular concerns is the protection of native orchids and other rare flora, and the rehabilitation of raptors (birds of prey) originally destined for restaurant tables. Other features include a waterfowl enclosure, a butterfly house, a deer haven and an animal rescue centre.

Except for Sunday, when no cars are allowed, people can hike up or drive up to all of the exhibits. Guided tours for groups of 20 are offered but advance booking is required. Indeed, phoning before a visit is the normal procedure (parking space can also be reserved). It's worth asking about special activities, which include tree planting, Earth Day celebrations and an organic festival.

Kadoorie Farm & Botanic Garden

Lam Kam Road, Tai Po (2488 1317/ www.kfbg.org.hk). Tai Po Market or Tai Wo KCR then 64K bus. **Open** (by prior appointment only) 9.30am-5pm daily. **Admission** free.

holidays), and there's no fast ride down on a funicular if you get tired or bored. The route is pretty, although more spectacular trails to the top lie along the **MacLehose Trail** (*see also p115* **Walks on the wild side**), which runs roughly east to west on either side of Tai Mo Shan's summit. The peak is dominated by a telecommunications complex, which is off-limits to the public, but there are still good views of the countryside, and you should be able to take photos that aren't filled with aluminium scaffolding and cables.

Nevertheless, despite the direct line of sight across to Hong Kong Island, it is likely to be almost totally obscured, even on a cloudless day, by smog. But if you're lucky and hit the trail on a really clear day, the views are absolutely stunning. The best way back to the city is to walk down the road to the edge of **Tai Mo Shan Country Park** and then catch the number 51 bus back to Tsuen Wan MTR station.

Chuk Lam Shim Yuen Monastery

Fu Yung Shan, Tsuen Wan (2490 3392). Tsuen Wan MTR (exit B1) then 85 minibus/taxi from Shiu Wo Street to Fu Yung Shan. **Open** 9am-5pm daily. **Admission** free.

This hillside facility houses several large and precious statues of the Buddha. On most days monks clad in mustard-coloured robes can be seen chanting and offering prayers in the temple at the far end of the complex. With its large grounds and tranquil setting, the monastery is atmospheric and often free of tourists – it's almost worth visiting for that reason alone. **Photo** *p112*.

Sam Tung Uk Museum

2 Kwu Uk Lane, Tsuen Wan (2411 2001/www.lcsd. gov.hk/stum). Tsuen Wan MTR (exit E) then 10mins walk/40, 43X, 905 bus. **Open** 9am-5pm Mon, Wed-Sun. **Admission** free.

Those looking for bustling village authenticity may be a little disappointed, as this walled village was largely rebuilt when the last residents were resettled in nearby high-rise estates more than 20 years ago. In addition, many of the materials used in the reconstruction were sourced from southern China. However, it's an interesting and creditable (if somewhat sanitised) attempt to paint a picture of life in a New Territories walled village a century or so ago.

Yuen Yuen Institute

Sam Dip Tam, Tsuen Wan (2492 2220/www. yuenyuen.org.hk). Tsuen Wan MTR (exit B1) then 81 minibus from Shiu Wo Street. **Open** 8.30am-5pm daily. **Admission** free.

This highly popular Buddhist, Confucianist and Taoist complex is on the agenda of most New Territories tourists, as well as worshipping locals making offerings. It includes a temple dedicated to the deities in charge of certain years and birth signs (similar to the Fung Ying Sin Koon temple in Fanling; *see p111*). The statues within are all finely carved, while a sign outside updates believers as to which birth signs might have trouble with the earth god of the current year and suggests making offerings to the relevant deity at the beginning and end of the year to help balance out the potential ill effects. The on-site vegetarian restaurant is also popular with both local worshippers and tourists – the former including mostly elderly or retired people.

Along the LRT line from Tuen Mun towards Yuen Long

Tuen Mun was the site of the first known landfall in China by European mariners; Portuguese sailor Jorge Alvares landed there in 1513 and returned again in 1524. The district is now a large New Town close to the far western edge of the New Territories, and dominated by the steep, dramatically beautiful **Castle Peak**.

Although unpromising at first sight, the Tuen Mun district contains a couple of interesting and accessible temples, as well as the Ping Shan Heritage Trail, close to Yuen Long. Getting to Tuen Mun is easy – take the number 960 or 962 bus from Central and around an hour later you'll arrive. Once you're here, it shouldn't take long to get the hang of the excellent Light Rail Transit (LRT), a very simple, efficient and cheap tram network. The LRT links Tuen Mun with Yuen Long further east via the sprawling conurbation between them. (Octopus cards are accepted on the LRT and must be validated at the correct terminal before boarding and again when alighting.)

As soon as you arrive, your first stop should be the **Ching Chung Koon Temple** (*see p116*), a Taoist temple set in lovely, carefully cultivated grounds. Climbing back on to the LRT and travelling two stops further north to Lam Tei LRT station will bring you to the modern and elaborately endowed **Miu Fat Buddhist Monastery** (*see p116*).

Perhaps the most rewarding place to spend an hour or so in the western New Territories is a few stops further up the line, where the short **Ping Shan Heritage Trail** starts just south of Yuen Long. Like the Lung Yuek Tau Heritage Trail outside Fanling (*see p111*), the Ping Shan trail features several historic buildings dating back hundreds of years. To reach the trail, take the LRT to Ping Shan station and walk five from the tram/road crossing for about five minutes. Look on the right side of the road for the map detailing the route of the trail, which begins at the Hung Shing Temple. It's best to be armed with a map from the start, as the signposting from the LRT to the trail is not clear. Villagers at Ping Shan take a mixed view of visitors – you may be welcomed, and then again you may not be; best to take a chance and see how it feels on the day.

The first two buildings you'll come across en route are the 18th-century **Hung Shing Temple** and the beautifully painted, high-ceilinged **Kun Ting Study Hall**, which was built in the 19th century as a place where members of the Tang clan could study for their imperial civil service examinations. (Unfortunately, the study hall has been closed to the public for over a decade due to a long-running dispute between local villagers and the government.) Also on the trail you'll find the recently restored, 700-year-old **Tang Ancestral Hall** – one of the finest in Hong Kong – and the 16th-century **Yu Kiu Ancestral Hall**.

Walks on the wild side

If hiking along mountain ridges with spectacular views, swimming on remote beaches or simply getting away from everything (and everyone) appeals to you, then turn your back on the territory's monolithic skyscrapers and discover its extraordinary natural beauty. There are few major cities in the world that have such dramatic proximity of mountains, sea and teeming humanity.

Some 40 per cent of Hong Kong's land area falls within 22 country parks, and the wide open spaces of the New Territories and 235 outlying islands offer considerable opportunities for getting away from it all, generally very easily.

Trails through woodland and open countryside range from gentle family walks near barbecue sites suitable for children and the elderly to adventurous, full-on hiking routes that pass remote sandy beaches, hidden valleys, deserted villages, waterfalls and streams. Most trails are well mapped, and while you can do sections of the 'Big Four', the longest extends for 100 kilometres (62 miles). But what they all offer is generous amounts of that rarest of Hong Kong commodities – solitude.

THE 'BIG FOUR' TRAILS

The 100-kilometre (62-mile) **MacLehose Trail** in the New Territories, named after the hill-loving former governor Sir Murray MacLehose, is divided into ten stages, taking in around 20 mountains and stretching east to west across almost the breadth of the New Territories, starting from Sai Kung Country Park and ending at Perowne Barracks in Tuen Mun. This is one of Hong Kong's most diverse and beautiful trails, and each November several thousand hikers compete in a charity event to finish the trail in less than 48 hours. The fastest times on record are around 13 hours.

The 70-kilometre (44-mile) **Wilson Trail** (named after another ex-governor, Sir David Wilson) is also split into several different sections. It starts near Stanley on Hong Kong Island and heads across Tai Tam Country Park, before hopping over the harbour (on the MTR, no less) to the New Territories. The Wilson Trail crosses the MacLehose Trail at several points and finally ends at the rugged Pat Sin Leng mountain range, not far from Tai Po.

The 50-kilometre (31-mile) **Hong Kong Trail** is the most 'gentle' of the four, with fewer mountains and inclines, considerably more shade, and easier and more accessible starting and finishing points right across the length of Hong Kong Island. An annual hiking competition, the Green Power Hike, takes place along the trail (usually during February or March).

The 70-kilometre (44-mile) **Lantau Trail** curls around the whole of Lantau island. Considerably larger than Hong Kong Island, Lantau offers some of the city's highest and most scenic mountains, along with magnificent remote bathing beaches. The two most popular mountain hikes within the trail are Lantau Peak and Sunset Peak, which are both very challenging. Despite its obviously mountainous nature, Lantau is much more than just hills. There are numerous beach hikes at Cheung Sha, and to the hidden waterfalls just outside Tai O. There are also beautiful reservoirs, and island views at Shek Pik and around the coast to Fan Lau. The Lantau Trail is another annual hiking challenge that attracts many competitors.

BE PREPARED

Probably the most important piece of advice you'll ever receive about hiking in Hong Kong is to take a decent map and as much water as you can carry. Excellent maps can be found in book shops around town, as well as the Government Publications Centre (see p175), but water is another matter. Each year, several people die from dehydration when hiking in Hong Kong; most of them are local residents who go out unprepared. By the time you feel flushed and thirsty, it's already serious – you're in the early stages of dehydration. Along with lots of water, it's a sensible idea to pick up some iodine or chlorine tablets from a local pharmacy so you can purify stream/reservoir water if your own supply runs out. It's also a good idea to carry a small first aid kit.

Many people underestimate just how remote the out-of-the-way parts of Hong Kong are – you can easily be six to eight hours' walk from the nearest main road in some locations. It is also advisable to take a mobile phone with you, just in case. The general accident and emergency number in Hong Kong is 999.

Keep an eye out for the narrow alleyways and tiny houses of **Sheung Cheung Wai**, a walled village that is still inhabited today. Also at Ping Shan is the **Tsui Shing Lau**, a small pagoda built several hundred years ago for geomantic reasons. Though hemmed in by developments and surrounded by general village squalor, it is nevertheless worth a visit and is an integral part of the Ping Shan Heritage Trail.

Another sight worth visiting in the Tuen Mun area is the Buddhist **Ching Shan Monastery** (*see below*), perched halfway up a steep hillside south-west of town.

Ching Chung Koon Temple

Tsing Chung Path, Tsing Chung Koon Road, Tuen Mun (2393 7495/www.daoist.org/ccta/ccta.htm). Kwai Fong MTR then 58M bus/Mong Kok MTR then 58X bus/Admiralty MTR then 960 bus/Ching Chung LRT then short walk. **Open** 9am-6pm daily. **Admission** free.

This Taoist complex is a peaceful oasis, complete with ponds, sculptures, fountains and hundreds of venerable bonsai trees. In addition, if you happen to be in the area during the third or seventh lunar months, you might stumble upon one of the large religious ceremonies that are held in its ancestral memorial halls.

Ching Shan Monastery

Ching Shan Tsuen, near Tuen Mun (no phone). Bus 962 to Sham Shing LRT station then taxi or 20mins walk. **Open** 9am-5pm daily. **Admission** free.

This Buddhist monastery is a rare quiet corner in generally noisy Hong Kong, with cool breezes blowing in from the sea. Muted, chanted prayers seem to come from nowhere (but are actually broadcast by a concealed modern sound system). The nearest LRT stop is Ching Shan Tsuen, but it's a hard, steep trudge of about one-and-a-half kilometres (one mile) to the monastery from the station. An easier means of access is to take a taxi up the hill to the monastery (about HK$30 from the town centre) and then walk back down to the LRT station.

Miu Fat Buddhist Monastery

18 Castle Peak Road, Lam Tei (2461 8567/ miufat@hongkong.com). Tsing Yi MTR then 263M bus to Lam Tei LRT/Kwai Hing MTR then 68A bus to Lam Tei LRT. **Open** 9am-5pm daily. **Admission** free.

Flanked by two temple lions, two large dragons coil up the pillars by the front door of this lavish, active and modern monastery. Inside is plenty of gold and marble, huge chandeliers, and the obligatory surfeit of large and small golden Buddha statues. There's a popular vegetarian canteen on the second floor serving reasonable Chinese vegetarian food. The monastery is located just a five-minute walk north of the LRT station, on the eastern side of a busy highway – you can see it from the pedestrian bridge at the station.

East New Territories

The eastern New Territories are the most sparsely inhabited and least developed part of the SAR. To the north is the jagged peninsula containing the remote and very lovely Pat Sing Leng and Plover Cove Country Parks. To the south is the extensive Sai Kung Peninsula, with its long hiking trails, spectacular scenery and rock formations, and numerous beautiful, isolated beaches.

Plover Cove & the north-east

Prior to the development of the New Territories, the few incursions by humans into the wilderness of the north-east amounted to little more than small pearl fisheries and tiny Hakka settlements (the Hakka people migrated from north to southern China centuries ago, and first settled in the Hong Kong region in the late 17th century; most were originally farmers and quarrymen, and you will still see the women working as labourers, wearing distinctive flat bamboo hats with black cloth fringes).

Even today the area remains a haven for adventurous hikers and wildlife enthusiasts. The **Wilson Trail** (*see p115* **Walks on the wild side**) winds north of **Plover Cove**, the huge reservoir that was created when a natural seawater bay was sealed with a massive dam. Larger fauna, such as barking deer and wild boar, still thrive in the area, although sightings from the trails are increasingly rare.

The best way to get here is to catch the number 75K bus from Tai Po Market KCR station – it'll take about 40 minutes to reach **Tai Mei Tuk**. Here you will find a youth hostel and a watersports centre (which unfortunately does not allow the casual hire of boats or windsurfing equipment).

There are numerous walking opportunities in this district, ranging from ambitious hikes to easy walks. Probably the easiest is the path around **Bride's Pool** – a naturally formed pool with a waterfall at the end of Bride's Pool Road, just under five kilometres (three miles) from Tai Mei Tuk. You can even make a picnic out of it, as there are barbecue areas close to the pool and at various points along the road.

For stronger walkers, Bride's Pool lies at the end of another walk – the well-marked six-kilometre (four-mile) **Pat Sing Leng Nature Trail**, which begins just above the Plover Cove Park Visitor Centre (a ten-minute walk east along Ting Kok Road from the Tai Mei Tuk bus stop). The route offers wonderful views of Plover Cove Reservoir and Tolo Harbour. A taxi ride from the bus stop back to Tai Po Market KCR station should cost around HK$40.

Urban escape: the town of **Sai Kung** is the gateway to some great beaches. *See p118.*

Pak Tam Chung.

Sai Kung & the south-east

This more easily accessible area of the New
Territories takes in fine parkland, golden
beaches, rolling surf and – in Sai Kung and
Clearwater Bay – numerous waterfront cafés,
bars and seafood restaurants. You can hire a
sampan to see the islands offshore from Sai
Kung, or just wander to the gorgeous beaches
near Wong Shek.

Note that getting into, out of and around the
wilderness on the Sai Kung Peninsula does
nonetheless take time – it would be best to
allow at least a very full day out to explore the
area. Careful planning and quite an early start
will be necessary for all but the shortest walks.
The 92 bus to Sai Kung leaves frequently from
Diamond Hill MTR.

Sai Kung (photo *p117*) town is a quiet place
– at least during the week – with a small boat
harbour that has become a popular refuge for
expats, who enjoy the area's beaches and open
spaces. But while it's surrounded by a fairly
wild mountainous area, Sai Kung itself offers a
pleasant haven of civilisation, with a reasonable
selection of restaurants, cafés, pubs and bars.

If heading out on to the water is your goal,
your best bet is to start near the main ferry pier,
where middle-aged women offer sampan rides
around the harbour. Sampan hire costs about
HK$50 per half-hour, although it's always
worthwhile trying to haggle the price down.
The sampans are the only way to get to the

small, secluded beaches on the islands close to
Sai Kung (although the best beaches lie on the
south-eastern tip of the peninsula). If you do
hire a sampan, the tiny island of **Yim Tin
Tsai** is worth a stop. Most of its devout
Christian residents have departed, and many
of the buildings are dilapidated – including
St Joseph's Chapel at the top of the hill –
but the remaining community is of interest.

Visiting the beaches at the south-eastern
edge of Sai Kung is much more difficult, but it
is feasible in a day if you set off early. Bus 94
runs from Sai Kung to the coast at **Wong
Shek Pier** every half-hour (every hour at
weekends); this is a strategic spot from which to
head for the beaches, and from which to begin
walks to the north and east of the peninsula.
One particularly dramatic day-long hike hugs
the southern edge of the High Island Reservoir,
ending at the lovely beach of **Long Ke Wan**.
If you want to spend more than a day in the
area, you can either camp or stay at the youth
hostels in Wong Shek.

If time and/or energy are in short supply,
there are walks closer to Sai Kung at **Pak Tam
Chung**. For instance, if you take the 94 bus to
the Pak Tam Chung Visitor Centre from Sai
Kung, a short stroll along the nearby nature
trail will take you past the well-preserved, but
otherwise underwhelming, **Sheung Yiu Folk
Museum** (*see p119*). This partially rebuilt
19th-century Hakka village is a branch of
the Hong Kong Heritage Museum (*see p109*).

It's also worth popping in to the visitor centre, which has some good displays on the wildlife and geology of the area.

The scenery and wilderness of **Clearwater Bay**, ten or so kilometres (six miles) south of Sai Kung, may be less spectacular than in Sai Kung or Plover Cove, but the area has some good, easily accessible beaches. (Take the 91 bus, which departs regularly from Diamond Hill MTR station.) The best two are those with the not particularly descriptive names of **Beach One** and **Beach Two**, where the water is clear and the golden sand is clean. They also have lifeguards and good facilities. Perhaps not surprisingly, these beaches are popular and tend to be very busy at weekends. Under no circumstances should you be tempted to stop at Silverstrand Beach, which – despite its nicer name – is fairly unappealing; its dingy shores are lapped by dirty water awash with detritus. And there have been numerous shark attacks here in recent years – some of them fatal.

Aside from sunbathing and swimming, there's not much to do at Clearwater Bay, which isn't necessarily a bad thing. However, if you can tear yourself away from the surf there are a few short excursions worth making. Two kilometres (one and a half miles) from Beach Two is the oldest (by descent) Tin Hau Temple

in Hong Kong, which dates back to 1274. Although it has been rebuilt and renovated numerous times since then, it's still one of the most impressive and atmospheric of Hong Kong's many Tin Hau temples. The walk to the temple is fairly flat, and follows the road from the Clearwater Bay bus stop south to Clearwater Bay Country Club. The path from the Club to the temple is not clearly marked, but lies to the right of the Club's guardhouse.

When your day in the sun is over, you can either take the number 91 bus all the way back to Diamond Hill MTR station or as far as the Pik Uk prison on Clearwater Bay Road, where you can change to the number 101 bus, which continues on to Sai Kung town.

Sheung Yiu Folk Museum

Pak Tam Chung Nature Trail, Sai Kung (2792 6365/ www.heritagemuseum.gov.hk/english/branch.htm). Choi Hung MTR (exit C) then 94 bus to Sai Kung Town then 1A minibus. **Open** 9am-4pm Mon, Wed-Sun. **Admission** free.

This museum was once a fortified village. Built in the late 19th century, it includes dwellings, animal sheds and a watchtower. The displays feature farm implements, household goods and everyday belongings of the Hakka people. In many ways, it is a smaller version of the Sam Tung Uk Museum in Tsuen Wan (*see p114*).

Sightseeing

Explore the history of the Hakka people at **Sheung Yiu Folk Museum**.

The Outlying Islands

Set sail to a world well away from the concrete canyons.

Ngong Ping 360 cable-car. *See p125.*

When you've had your fill of the frenetic urban buzz of Central and Tsim Sha Tsui and crave greenery and solitude, make for the ferry piers in Central and head to one of the 230-odd unspoiled islands scattered to the west and south of Hong Kong Island. Secluded bays, isolated swimming beaches, stunning hiking and plenty of seafood restaurants are all just a short journey away.

For energetic hikes through dramatic mountainous landscapes or relaxing on quiet beaches, head for Lantau. For gentler walking and superb seafood restaurants or just sitting in a bar and watching the world go by, try Lamma. Or spend a day enjoying the varied attractions of the smaller outlying islands such as Cheung Chau and Peng Chau.

While Central's Outlying Ferry Piers may imply that the term 'outlying islands' applies to only the few it serves – namely Lamma, Lantau, Cheung Chau and Peng Chau – there are less-populated islands fringing the New Territories and comprising the Hong Kong archipelago, which we have also detailed in this chapter. These are accessible by ferry from other ports and feel like some of the most remote places in the territory.

Lamma

You would never guess that **Lamma** is the third largest island in Hong Kong. Its 13 square kilometres (five square miles) is only sparsely developed with buildings of maximum three storeys. This verdant isle is renowned for its excellent open-air seafood restaurants, its often colourful collection of international residents, an almost complete lack of motorised transport (but *see p129* **Rural road hogs**) and abundant hillside trails. You could easily while away a day walking across the island, taking in the sun on one of the decent beaches or just lounging about in the bars, pubs and cafés.

Most ferry departures from Central and Aberdeen head to the main settlement of Yung Shue Wan on the island's north-west coast, but it is also worth taking the boat to Sok Kwu Wan on the south-east coast for its stretch of waterside seafood restaurants, and the secluded walks and beaches nearby. A popular and not too strenuous day trip is to head out to one destination, then walk the four kilometres (two and a half miles) across the island and depart from the other. The most usual route is to start at Yung Shue Wan, take in some of the cafés and complete the hike to Sok Kwu Wan's seafood restaurants, in time for supper.

As it's one of the most easily reached bits of greenery in Hong Kong, many urban residents head to Lamma at weekends, so weekdays offer the best chances to enjoy the sea air without having to share it with thousands of others on packed ferries buzzing with boisterous activity. If you just can't tear yourself away from Lamma, there are a few modest guesthouses and a youth hostel on the island.

Yung Shue Wan

At first sight, haphazard-looking **Yung Shue Wan**, which straggles around a small inlet that can be a bit whiffy when the tide goes out, seems – and, indeed, is – full of unexpected curiosities and charm, especially if you've come straight from the urban frenzy of Central.

This was an isolated fishing settlement until after World War II, and thereafter grew only slowly, with much of its income earned from factories that churned out plastic goods in the 1970s. Today it's a low-key place with plenty of expats, attracted by lower rents, relatively cleaner air, and a friendlier and more relaxed atmosphere than on Hong Kong Island. From the 1980s, it drew in an alternative foreign crowd of hippies; the '90s brought New Agers and Eurotrash partiers, but since the Handover their numbers – and something of the frenetic, end-of-an-era party spirit – have diminished. However, an influence remains in the form of veggie cafés and the occasional full-moon party (or other rave-type event) held on the beach next to the power station.

As you leave the ferry at Yung Shue Wan, look to the left and you'll see a smaller harbour with fishing boats and stilt houses overhanging the rocks and water. To the right is the narrow main street with most of Lamma's shops, bars and restaurants. While the island's seafood restaurants are not particularly cheap – most of them source their seafood from outside Hong Kong's over-fished, heavily polluted waters – there are a couple of good ones worth trying. But if fish isn't really your thing there are other culinary options. The Sampan serves good, cheap dim sum until about noon, while the Green Cottage next door has some outdoor seating and offers health food. For a drink with a waterside view, head to the superbly named **Deli-Lamma** (*see p169*). Otherwise, the cheerfully alternative **Bookworm Café** (*see p158*), towards the far end of the main street, is a peaceful place to have a drink, eat excellent veggie food and read a book (from its library-cum-bookshop).

Beaches

There are two beaches close to Yung Shue Wan, both within a 15-minute walk of the village. The first, **Tai Wan To** (*photo p122*), is overlooked by Lamma's huge power station, which supplies most of Hong Kong Island's electricity requirements. Despite the industrial-era view, it's not a bad stretch of sand: its waters are shallow and calm, and it is also conveniently close to Yung Shue Wan. It's known by many residents – perhaps not too surprisingly – as 'Power Station Beach'.

A few minutes' walk further south, past the island's small police station, there's an excellent and popular beach at **Hung Shing Ye** – unlike Tai Wan To, there are changing rooms, showers and lifeguards here. The Concerto Inn, overlooking the beach, is a cheap, cheerful café with holiday accommodation.

Sightseeing

Don't miss — Island experiences

Lamma
A Bohemian air hangs over this once-hippie hangout, full of walking trails with views, beaches... and a power station. *See p120.*

Cheung Chau
For a food and culture fix – there's cheap, decent seafood year-round, and, in May, a bizarre bun festival. *See p127.*

Po Toi
Steep walking trails and glorious views are reasons to visit this rocky island. *See p128.*

Lantau
Famous for its Big Buddha, this huge island is also home to expats and the new Ngong Ping 360 sightseeing cable-car. *See p123.*

Peng Chau
Small but perfectly formed, with an alluring laid-back atmosphere that can be enjoyed in a few hours. *See p128.*

Tap Mun Chau
Excellent, clean beaches are tiny Tap Mun Chau's main draw. *See p129.*

Sok Kwu Wan & southern Lamma

Hung Shing Ye beach is just off the main concrete path to Sok Kwu Wan, which is about an hour's steady walk from Yung Shue Wan. The more rugged dirt trail running over the hills, with fantastic views over the harbour and Hong Kong Island, offers a dramatically scenic route to the south of the island via Mount Stenhouse (*see p123*), but you'll need a decent map, soles that can cope with gravel and plenty of time in case you lose your way; the path along here is not always obvious.

In the geographical centre of Lamma, at its narrowest point, is **Lo So Shing**, an excellent, secluded beach that is also an archaeological site. Whether you've decided to take the path or the trail, you should see signs to the **Kamikaze Caves** on your right as you hit the eastern shore, very close to Sok Kwu Wan. Created by Japanese occupying forces during World War II, the caves were designed to hide small speedboats packed with explosives intended for suicide attacks on Allied shipping, but the war ended before they were ever employed.

Sok Kwu Wan has about a dozen seafood restaurants, none of which are that cheap. All have views over the harbour, and while there's not much to differentiate them, the Lamma Hilton is consistently good, the Lamma Mandarin Seafood Restaurant is well known for its pigeon dishes, and **Rainbow Seafood** (*see p157*), which has its own ferry to and from

Central, is always popular. The disused quarry that faces the restaurants is gradually being filled and landscaped.

If you're not ready to eat, there's a fairly flat, circular five-kilometre (three-mile) walk to the southern tip of the island that offers good shoreline views. You'll also come across the sleepy hamlet of **Shek Pai Wan**; this isolated place is about as far from Hong Kong's built-up areas as it's possible to imagine. The lovely south-facing beach, like many stretches of coastline elsewhere in Hong Kong, is somewhat marred by broken glass and other jetsam, so take care if you go paddling. There's also a small temple to the sea god Hung Shing (who was a Tang Dynasty official credited with developing a basic form of meteorology), sacred to fishermen. **Tung O**, the small and all-but-deserted village nearby, is where Chow Yun-fat, star of *Crouching Tiger, Hidden Dragon*, was born and raised.

Perhaps the best and most secluded beach on Lamma is just on the other side of the headland at **Sham Wan** – it is only accessible via a very narrow, overgrown track. This is the only beach in Hong Kong where green turtles still lay their eggs (it's closed during the June to October nesting season). It's also an archaeological site, where finds dating back 6,000 years have been discovered. The oldest known settlement in Hong Kong, it was inhabited by the Yueh, a little-known pre-Chinese people.

Locals refer to **Tai Wan To** as 'Power Station Beach', for obvious reasons. *See p121.*

A steep climb away to the west, on the circular path back to Sok Kwu Wan, is **Mount Stenhouse**. The 353-metre-high (1,150-feet) summit is a spectacular vantage point, offering an almost complete view of Lamma, fine vistas of Hong Kong Island to the north and Lantau to the west, and vertiginous views down to the wave-battered rocks below. The route up is a tough scramble along a rocky, overgrown path, but well worth the effort if you're reasonably fit. On a clear day the island and sea views from here are amazing.

Lantau

Although twice the size of Hong Kong Island, **Lantau** remains largely unspoiled, except for the massive development around Chek Lap Kok – the site of the international airport on the northern coast. Many parts of the island look much as they did when the island was acquired along with the mainland New Territories in 1898. Two huge country parks contain the peaks that form the backbone of the island and numerous hiking trails. On a misty day the steep wooded hillsides are reminiscent of the Scottish Highlands, a comparison that has been made by travelling writers since the late 19th century.

The development of the new airport on Chek Lap Kok and the Tsing Ma Bridge linking the northern coast of Lantau with the mainland have not had a hugely noticeable impact on the rest of the island – so far. However, the opening in 2005 of **Hong Kong Disneyland** (*see p212* **Variations on a theme**) at Penny's Bay, which is expected eventually to attract 18 million (mostly mainland Chinese) visitors annually, looks likely to change all that.

Today the main settlements are limited to the mostly expat enclave of Discovery Bay (a California-style toy-town settlement where transport is by golf-cart – honestly), the town of Tung Chung across from the new airport, the area around the ferry terminal at Mui Wo – with its many restaurants and bars – and the nearby valley. Plenty of open space can be found all over the island, particularly at the south-western end, making the place a terrific retreat from the noise and crowds so prevalent elsewhere in Hong Kong. The seclusion offered on Lantau has made it a popular retreat for (mainly Buddhist) religious orders. Probably the most striking sacred site is the Po Lin Monastery, high in the hills near Lantau Peak, which is home to one of the world's largest outdoor Buddha statues and is accessible by cable-car (with fine views on smog-free days).

There are some good beaches along the southern coast of Lantau, as well as some very wild and inaccessible areas inland. One of the few remaining (and probably the most interesting) traditional fishing settlements in Hong Kong clings to the western coast of Lantau at Tai O. Here you will still find a large cluster of traditional stilt houses on the muddy banks of the small estuary. Tai O has terrific character and a wander around this sleepy town is highly recommended. It's also a good place to stock up on dried fish and seafood items.

Discovery Bay & around

Discovery Bay lies a few kilometres north-east of the ferry port of Mui Wo (*see p124*), from where you can catch a bus. The most direct route to Discovery Bay, though, is the fast, smart catamaran, which takes about 25 minutes from Central, costs HK$27 and empties on to the neat piazza next to the pier.

The settlement here is like nowhere else in Hong Kong. For some of its residents, that's the whole point of the bay's existence, while for other Hong Kong citizens, nothing would induce them to live there. Love it or hate it, Discovery Bay is a fascinating glimpse into the way at least some Hong Kong people choose to live. Apartment blocks here have names like Brilliance Court, Bijou Hamlet and Neo Horizon. With no cars allowed, golf buggies are the norm; parked all over the place, some have baby seats while others sport football stickers in their windscreens. Other than people-watching, probably the main reasons for coming here are the long sandy beaches, the short scenic walk to the Trappist Monastery (*see below*) and the *kaido* (small ferry) to Peng Chau (*see p128*). With a numerically significant, mostly well-heeled resident population, there are some good, although not outstanding, restaurants here, and a few coffee shops. The clean, man-made beach just north of the ferry pier is pleasant enough and the water looks relatively clean, but if the wind is blowing from behind the beach it whips up a stinging sandstorm.

Kaidos to Peng Chau run hourly from the quayside at the southern edge of the headland that divides Discovery Bay from the small harbour and beach of **Nim Shue Wan**. From the plaza by the Discovery Bay ferry terminal, walk to the far end of the bus station, turn left and then walk along the small quayside, looking out for a very small timetable and steps, from where the *kaidos* depart.

If you fancy a short hike, there's a well signposted two-kilometre (one-mile) or so shoreline path starting at the top of Nim Shue Wan beach, which leads south to the **Trappist Monastery**. Originally established by Roman Catholic priests who fled China after the Communist takeover, by the 1960s the monastery had established an unusual means of support – as one of Hong Kong's best dairies. For the next three decades it supplied the city's top hotels and restaurants with high-quality milk.

If you want to skip the hike, there are also a few *kaidos* each day that go from Nim Shue Wan to the monastery's ferry pier, though it's still a short, steep trudge up to the monastery (the way is lined – appropriately enough – with the Stations of the Cross). These *kaidos* continue on to Peng Chau, although only ten run each day and none operates between 12.20pm and 3pm. Each *kaido* rides cost just a few dollars and takes about ten minutes.

Mui Wo & the southern beaches

Mui Wo, also known as **Silvermine Bay**, is the main jumping-off point for excursions on Lantau and the place to catch buses to most destinations on the island. It's 40 minutes and HK$11.30 (HK$17.80 deluxe, HK$22.20 fast ferry, higher fares on Sunday and public holidays) away on the ferry from Central, and the bus terminus is right outside the Mui Wo ferry terminal. Catch a bus from here to the beaches on Lantau's southern coast, to Ngong Ping for the Big Buddha and Lantau Peak (*see p125*), or to the fishing village of Tai O on the south-western coast (*see p126*).

On its own, Mui Wo is a pleasant enough place to visit, but there are more interesting destinations nearby. If you want to spend some time here, though, Mui Wo's long stretch of beach, complete with shark net, is a five-minute walk north along the edge of the bay. Another pleasant option is a walk through the valley towards the mountains, past clear streams, village houses and deserted farms and fields.

There are a few bars and some restaurants at Mui Wo, mostly around the ferry and bus terminals; one popular spot is China Beach Club (18 Tung Wan Tau Road, 2983 8931). The cooked-food market above the bus station has several eateries with cheap, if not hugely appetising, canteen fare. The Sea View offers dim sum from 6am to 1pm. A number of pricier – but better – places just west of the bus station serve up everything from curry to pizza.

One possible excursion from Mui Wo is the three-kilometre (two-mile) walk to the Trappist Monastery (*see p123*) north-west of town, although the route is steep in parts. Be sure to take a good map with you.

A number of beaches run along the southern coast, and most are deserted during the week. Two of the best, in terms of cleanliness and facilities, are **Pui O Wan** and **Cheung Sha**. All buses leaving Mui Wo (except number 7, which only goes as far as Pui O) pass them.

Cheung Sha (which appropriately enough means Long Sand) is just over two kilometres (one mile) west of Pui O. Look out for the signs marking Cheung Sha and ring the bell for the stop just after the police station, which you should see on your right. The path to the beach is a few metres further west along the road. The beach here is excellent (long, clean and empty,

Po Lin Monastery. *See p125.*

The **Big Buddah** at Po Lin Monastery.

Sightseeing

with changing facilities and a gay section; *see p230*), while the water is as clean as anywhere in Hong Kong, although, excitingly, there's no shark net. There are a couple of places to eat, including **Stoep** (*see p158*), which offers a mix of good value Mediterranean and South African food. The house speciality is the barbecue menu, which includes home-made *boerewors*, a type of South African sausage.

Ngong Ping, Po Lin Monastery & the Big Buddha

From Mui Wo, it's a winding and rather bumpy 16-kilometre (ten-mile) journey on the number 2 bus to **Ngong Ping**. En route, the bus passes along the edge of **Lantau South Country Park** and **Shek Pik Reservoir**. If it's a clear day and you're sitting on the right-hand side of the bus, you will get a good view of the 34-metre-high (110-foot) Buddha statue at Ngong Ping as the bus passes the reservoir. When the bus finally reaches its destination, tourists and devotees (the former usually greatly outnumbering the latter) disgorge and head for the nearby **Po Lin Monastery** and the **Big Buddha** (*see p126*) – the largest bronze outdoor seated Buddha in the world.

Buddhist monks from China began arriving on Lantau in the early 20th century, but the monastery really developed in the 1920s when the first abbot was appointed and the great hall built. It further expanded in the 1940s, and from the '60s has experienced constant growth and

development. Its popularity means that it can be very crowded and noisy – not quite what many would expect from a Buddhist retreat.

The monastery is now accessible by cable-car, known as **Ngong Ping 360** (www.np360.com.hk, HK$58-$68 single, HK$28-$35 children; *photo p120*), which travels 5.7 kilometres (3.5 miles) from its 'terminal' next to the Tung Chung MTR station. Be warned – delays and operating glitches have meant that numerous visitors have experienced problems, and as this part of Hong Kong experiences the worst air-pollution readings, visibility is often negligible. (Some local wits deem the name appropriate – 360 metres is about as far as you can see on the average smoggy day.)

Ngong Ping is also a good starting point from which to tackle the steep slopes of **Fung Wong Shan** (or **Lantau Peak**), the second-highest mountain in Hong Kong. The route up begins to the east of the monastery past the **Tea Farm**. Many walkers choose to stay overnight at the **Hongkong Bank Foundation SG Davis Youth Hostel** (*see also p68*) and get up early to make it up the peak in time for sunrise. Call ahead to book a bed and check opening times, as the hostel is often closed during the day.

Other walking options include the relatively gentle trek down from the monastery north to **Tung Chung**, which is about six and a half kilometres (four miles) away. From there, a fast MTR train will take you back to Central (a single ticket costs HK$23). Take care if you decide to tackle the concrete path, as parts are slick with moss and very slippery after rain. On the way down, you'll pass two Buddhist monasteries. The path takes you through the gardens of the first; these are often tended by nuns, and smell of incense and freshly dug earth. It's a place of quiet religious retreat, so visitors are not usually permitted to enter the buildings. At the bottom of the path, where it meets the road, you'll find the more welcoming **Lo Hon Monastery** (2988 1419). It serves a vegetarian lunch every day, costing HK$60.

Po Lin Monastery & Big Buddha

Ngong Ping (2985 5248/polin@plm.org.hk). Mui Wo Ferry Pier then 2 bus/Tung Chung MTR then 23 bus or Ngong Ping 360 cable-car. **Open** 10am-6pm daily. **Admission** free. **Map** p324.

The monastery is grand, although it's somewhat outshone by the towering presence of the nearby Big Buddha. Inside the grounds are bauhinia and orchid gardens. Two canteens inside the grand hall serve decent vegetarian food (11.30am-4.30pm; *see also p159*). The filling, if somewhat stodgy, snack menu (noodles and dim sum) costs HK$28, while the full vegetarian lunch costs HK$60-$100. You buy a meal ticket at the foot of the steps to the Buddha statue – this also grants access to the display rooms underneath the Buddha, which tell the story of Buddha's path to enlightenment. **Photos** *p124 and p125*.

The Fan Lau Trail

An excellent day-long hike, taking in old ruined villages, stunning sea views and beaches, and a Qing Dynasty fort, the trail snakes around the edges of the south-western coast of Lantau to Tai O. There are two possible routes. The first, flatter option follows the path that starts at the south-western tip of **Shek Pik Reservoir** (*see p125*) and hugs the coastline all the way. The second, steeper and more dramatic route starts from the top of a hill on the **Lantau Trail** (*see p115* **Walks on the wild side**), just to the north-west of the reservoir. The distance covered by each trail is around 12 to 14 kilometres (seven to nine miles), depending on the detours taken, and both end up at Tai O (*see below*), a journey of five to six hours. If you take the first option, there are a couple of places to camp along the way.

Fan Lau is home to an old Tin Hau temple, an abandoned school house and a few elderly residents. There's also a ruined Chinese fort built in the early 1800s, which is a good place to gaze out to sea and watch the jetfoils to Macau streak past. The path becomes much easier once you've passed the abandoned village of **Yi O San Tsuen** on the western side of the spur, as it has been concreted pretty much all the way into Tai O. A good map and plenty of water are essential if you want to tackle this trail.

Tai O

A large but quiet village perched on the far south-western coast of Lantau, **Tai O** is one of the last remaining fishing villages with stilt houses, which were first built here by the Tanka people (nomadic boat people who have fished in Hong Kong's waters for centuries) hundreds of years ago. If you're not walking to Tai O, you should take the number 1 bus from Mui Wo – a journey that takes about 40 minutes and costs HK$8. From the bus station, the village spreads out around the mouth of a small estuary. A walk over the short pedestrian bridge will take you into the heart of the settlement. Close to Tai O Market Street, you'll find a temple dedicated to Kwan Tai, the god of loyalty and righteousness, which dates back to the 1530s. The main cluster of stilt houses lies a short walk east along the street. Walk behind them and you'll find that there is a small boat moored at almost every house.

The left-hand fork on Tai O Market Street (in front of the Kwan Tai temple) leads to the western edge of town, past the fire station, complete with tiny fire tenders, and a couple of pungent-smelling *haam-ha* (shrimp paste) manufacturers. You will probably pick up the distinctive smell of the paste before you see the blue plastic tubs in which the stuff ferments in the sun. If it still seems like a good idea to you after seeing how it's made, you can buy jars of shrimp paste and shrimp sauce here for HK$15-$30. These sharp, powerful sauces are similar to Thai fish paste or Indonesian *terasi*, and impart a strong flavour to simple dishes like stir-fried vegetables. It's used to add dimension to squid dishes in many of the seafood restaurants on the outlying islands.

About 200 metres (650 feet) past the shrimp-paste manufacturers, you'll come across the old Tai O police station. Built in 1902, it dominates the edge of the island. The ferries to Sha Lo Wan (further north along the coast) and Tuen Mun (in the New Territories; *see p114*) stop here. There are two sailings each way, one in the morning and one in the afternoon, from Monday to Friday; three sailings on Saturday and five on Sunday. The fare is about HK$15 to Sha Lo Wan and HK$28 to Tuen Mun.

Food in Tai O is very basic Cantonese fare and, needless to say, seafood dishes dominate. The **Fook Moon Lam Restaurant**, next door to the Kwan Tai temple on Tai O Market Street, does good seafood. The **Wing Fat Restaurant** close to the bus stop (before you head over the bridge) has a varied menu of simple Cantonese dishes and Western snacks. Prices are very reasonable.

Lantau's **Tai O** fishing village.

Cheung Chau

West of Hong Kong Island and off the southern coast of Lantau, the tiny former pirate haven of **Cheung Chau** supports a population of around 20,000. It somehow accommodates them all without ever seeming too crowded – except, of course, when visitors from the rest of Hong Kong flock here at weekends. Even when it's packed, though, this is an intriguing place with secluded areas and good beaches. It's perfectly feasible to spend quite some time here, so allow a couple of days to relax and explore. Orienting yourself on the island is simple: the narrow spine where the ferries dock forms the centre of town, while the blocks of land to the south and north (once two separate islands) contain walking trails and smaller beaches to explore.

Ferries from Central or Lantau berth next to a wide road running the length of the harbour that is mostly occupied by seafood restaurants. In terms of going out and eating, Cheung Chau does not have the diversity of Lamma, but on the other hand, the seafood here is somewhat cheaper (*see p159*). Standards and prices are pretty uniform, but one of the most popular places (with Westerners and Chinese alike) is the **Baccarat Seafood Restaurant** (2981 0606) towards the northern end of the harbour.

The small alleys running off Pak She and San Hing streets contain dozens of small shops and businesses, selling incense, paper offerings, Chinese medicine and all manner of daily necessities. A couple of minutes' walk away from the ferry pier is the recently rebuilt **Pak Tai Temple**, at the top of Pak She Street. The god Pak Tai is credited with bringing to an end a virulent outbreak of the plague in 1777, prompting the grateful islanders to build an ornate temple in his honour in 1783.

The temple is the centre of the religious fervour that brings the entire island to a standstill every May during the famous **Cheung Chau Bun Festival** (*see also p203*). This religious festival has evolved into a busy three-day carnival attracting thousands of visitors. It all goes back to about a century ago, when an episode of bad luck and illness beset the island. In response, the islanders started offering lotus-paste buns to the spirits of the dead. Health and prosperity returned, so the locals decided to make the ceremony an annual event – just in case. As part of the event, three 13-metre-high (40-feet) bamboo towers covered in thousands of steamed buns are erected in front of the Pak Tai Temple and left out for three days. Taoist priests hold the requisite ceremonies to encourage the return of all the restless ghosts to the underworld. Before they come back, the spirits consume the 'essence' of the buns, while islanders and visitors eat the remains. Today the focus of the festival is on the procession of floats, lion dancers and the colourful 'floating' children, representing characters from myth and legend, who are strapped to cleverly hidden poles.

Dozens of small temples and shrines dot the island, many of them dedicated to To Tei Kung earth spirits. One of the most important is the banyan tree on Tung Wan Road, close to the end of San Hing Street. The tree and the spirits said to inhabit it are held in such esteem that when the road had to be widened, a restaurant opposite was demolished instead of the tree.

One of the best (and most popular) beaches in this area is **Tung Wan**, at the eastern end of Tung Wan Road. The beach is fairly large by local standards and is well kept. The shark nets are removed and the facilities closed in winter (Nov-April), but you can still swim with due care.

Although there are some pleasant, secluded paths in the northern section of the island, the southern part of Cheung Chau offers the best walks. From Tung Wan beach, head south around the back of the Warwick Hotel and go past the Kwun Yum temple. It's an easy walk to the south-western tip of the island along Peak Road West. When you reach the cemetery, make a detour down to **Pak Tso Wan**, one of the nicer small beaches in southern Cheung Chau. Peak Road West heads into the small village of **Sai Wan**, where you can catch the constantly shuttling HK$2.50 sampan back into the centre of Cheung Chau. Not only handy, this is also a good way to see the harbour.

Turning sharp left opposite the main Cheung Chau pier will take you along the path to the far western tip of the island, where signs point to a tiny cave with dubious claims that it is the place where the 19th-century pirate Cheung Po-tsai hid the plunder from his raids on shipping in the area. There's not much to see, but the rocky outcrop offers good sea views and it's a pleasant walk. The cave itself is really just a small hole; you'll need a torch to see inside it.

Other islands

There are hundreds of small islands scattered about Hong Kong's waters, many of them uninhabited and inaccessible without a boat. Unless you hire a boat for the day or evening, you will be tied to infrequent ferry services to Po Toi and Tap Mun Chau. Access to Peng Chau is much easier as it, like Cheung Chau, is a popular commuter island. Hiring a junk with a crew is not out of the question if you are in a group of five or more. Prices start at about HK$2,000 for a day, although you may be able to haggle the price down on weekdays. The *Yellow Pages* has extensive junk hire listings.

Peng Chau

The tiny island of **Peng Chau** lies just across the water from Discovery Bay on Lantau. Partly owing to its size, there's less to see than on the other populated islands. Peng Chau's charm lies in its very quiet village character, which is in sharp contrast to the Costa del Something-or-Other feel of Discovery Bay (*see p123*).

The main settlement, around the ferry pier, is a compact area of small interlinking alleys, local shops and tiny temples, all echoing to the clatter of mah-jong tiles. As Peng Chau covers less than one square kilometre (half a square mile), the island has few extensive beaches and fairly limited eating and drinking options. An hour or two is all that's needed to stroll around the entire island. A good place to head first is

south down Wing On Street and Shing Ka Road, then east along Nam Shan Road to **Finger Hill**, Peng Chau's highest point. It's about ten minutes' walk from the ferry pier, but the final stretch is steep. The reward is to share the view over the island with the black kites that hover lazily around the summit.

The little township near the pier, thus far largely untouched by development, is the only place to go for food or drink. Although the seafood restaurants here are not especially celebrated, they are relatively cheap, and are popular at weekends. If you crave Western snack food, try the adjacent Typhoon Shelter (2983 8033) or Sea Breeze (2983 8785), at 38-40 Wing Hing Street; Forest (2983 8837) serves Thai food next door. The outside seating at the former looks across to Lantau.

In recent years the construction of a new road and rocky breakwater along the edge of the small harbour at Tung Wan on the other side of Peng Chau has essentially destroyed the beach. It's not a great loss, however, as both water and beach have long since been polluted to the point where few bathers dared to go in.

Peng Chau is easily accessible from the outlying islands ferry pier in Central, with ferries leaving every 45 minutes. A single fare on the slow ferry, which takes 45 minutes, costs HK$10.50 (the slightly faster express is HK$21). There are also less frequent ferry and *kaido* services from Discovery Bay and Mui Wo on Lantau, and from Cheung Chau. Some of the *kaidos* plying their trade between Discovery Bay and Peng Chau also stop at the ferry pier near the Trappist Monastery.

Po Toi

The hills and cliffs of the small rocky island of **Po Toi** shelve steeply into the ocean a few kilometres south of Hong Kong Island. The island has some rugged walking trails, which give terrific views over the South China Sea and across to Hong Kong Island, and a Neolithic rock carving. The tiny, pretty harbour and beach of **Tai Wan** contains one good seafood restaurant, the **Ming Kee**, which is open daily.

Despite its proximity to Hong Kong, Po Toi is remote and sparsely populated. Travelling to the island without chartering a boat is only really practical on Sunday (*see p129*), as there's no return ferry during the week and the island has no accommodation or flat ground on which to camp. However, you can go to Po Toi during the week – and it's especially good for seafood – if you hire a junk for the day.

There are several walking routes around the island, ranging from concrete paths to rocky, semi-overgrown trails. The most dramatic

Rural road hogs

On Lamma island's quiet streets, where cars and motorcycles are strictly forbidden, pedestrians can be lulled into a false sense of ambulatory security. Until, that is, they discover just how the island's wannabe wide boys have got around the anti-car law. One minute you're walking along the footpath, the next a miniature tractor-truck hybrid is bearing down on you at breakneck speed.

And the driver is laughing.

A loophole in Hong Kong's motorised vehicle legislation allows the use of so-called 'village vehicles'. These are legal forms of transport in rural parts of the New Territories and outlying islands where conventional forms of motorised road vehicle are not permitted. Licences were originally granted for farmers and ranchers to operate small tractors and trucks that are no longer than 3.2 metres (ten feet), and no wider than 1.2 metres (four feet), to till the soil and carry harvested produce.

These days Hong Kong's version of wide boys are to be found at the wheel of toytown-like trucks, hired for things like transporting construction supplies to building sites, or for bringing goods to shops. Fun though this looks, passengers are not allowed.

If you're on Lamma long enough, you can be sure to encounter these vehicles, whose would-be triad drivers wear a vest or no top at all, the better to show off their tattoos. They can often be recognised by their peroxided mop, and the way they enjoy playing 'chicken' with pedestrians. They also hurtle themselves at crazy speeds around blind corners on Lamma's network of footpaths.

Day-trippers may be surprised to hear the sound of an emergency vehicle siren from time to time on the island. But what finally comes into view is either a tiny ambulance or a beach-buggy-like fire engine. The resident police force, rather embarrassingly, has to make do with bright yellow push-bikes.

walking is on the eastern side of the island, on the steep (and often slippery) trail above the **Tin Hau temple**. One of Hong Kong's ancient rock carvings, thought to date back to the Bronze Age and similar to the one found at Shek O (*see p94*), is on the western side of the island. It's not far, and in two hours you should have circumnavigated the island.

The *kaido* from the ferry pier at St Stephen's Beach in Stanley takes about 40 minutes and costs HK$40 return; on the way out, you'll need to tell the operator which afternoon boat you intend to return on. The kaido leaves Stanley on Sunday at 10am and 11am, and returns at 3pm and 4.30pm. A ferry also leaves from Aberdeen (right next to the fish market) at 8am on Sunday and returns at 6pm.

Tap Mun Chau

Tap Mun Chau is a tiny island just over two kilometres long (one mile) and about one kilometre wide (half a mile), located off the north-east tip of the Sai Kung Peninsula. It's a real out-of-the-way place with considerable charm, clean water and some small but good beaches on its eastern side. There's a large and pretty **Tin Hau Temple** in the village of **Tap Mun**, whose few inhabitants still largely live off the sea. It's one of the few places in Hong Kong where you can still see seafood – mostly fish and squid – drying in the sun.

The short walk past the police post to the eastern shore goes through Tap Mun Chau's open countryside. A refreshing breeze blows off the South China Sea and big waves break against the striking rock formations. Unfortunately – and typically for Hong Kong – many weekend visitors to the island dump their rubbish along here and so it is strewn all over this side of the island. (In fact, the only rubbish-free places on the island are its rubbish bins.)

Boats for Tap Mun Chau depart from the Ma Liu Shui ferry pier on the outskirts of Sha Tin (*see p107*). To reach the ferry pier, exit the Sha Tin KCR station on the east side and walk north past the station. The path goes over and then under the busy carriageway. As you emerge from the short tunnel, the ferry pier will be visible a couple of hundred metres to the north. As there are only two sailings a day to Tap Mun Chau, it's advisable to plan ahead. You can either go early and spend the whole day there, or you can take the afternoon sailing, which will give you an hour to look around the island. The journey takes about an hour on the slow *kaido*, and costs HK$16 each way during the week and HK$25 each way at the weekend. The *kaido* leaves Ma Liu Shui at 8.30am and 3pm, returning at 11.10am and 5.30pm, Monday to Friday. Weekend departures are at 8.30am, 12.30pm and 3pm, with return journeys at 11.10am, 1.45pm and 5.30pm. Phone the ferry company (2527 2513) to double-check times.

Eat, Drink, Shop

Shanghai Tang. *See p185.*

Restaurants

Welcome to the undisputed culinary capital of Asia.

Eat, Drink, Shop

Even resident food lovers never get the chance to do the rounds of Hong Kong's thousands of places to eat and drink. Some restaurants come and go so fast that the chance to try them is fleeting – you can often miss out on what may have been a great place to eat that just hadn't got its act together in this territory of extraordinarily high rental costs. In this maelstrom of change, the biggest challenge for the visitor is simply where to begin – especially as some menus are in Chinese script only – in a city where windows might display yellow-skinned boiled chickens or a pressed roast goose hanging by its neck.

While adventurous diners might approach such traditional guts-and-all restaurants with glee, some visitors may find them a bit overwhelming. The contrast couldn't be stronger in elegant top-end Chinese and Western-menu joints with English-speaking staff and translated menus. For a local compromise, shopping malls, which usually contain medium and lower-priced places to eat, aren't a bad place to start. Many house a food court, where you can select a meal or a number of items from a row of counters, then eat at communal tables. These dining halls have all but replaced the street stalls that were once such a vibrant part of Hong Kong life, but were removed in the last decade by the government, which cited hygiene and safety concerns as the reason. The New Territories and Outlying Islands, however, still provide laid-back outdoor dining, while trendy establishments in Lan Kwai Fong and SoHo also try to provide a few square feet of terrace where possible – these days expect them to be packed with smokers, who were banished from indoor sections by law on 1 January 2007.

If you do run into language difficulties, looking at what's in the bowls of other diners and pointing if you fancy the same is always possible, although a busy waiter might not be able – or willing – to tell you in English what the ingredients are. In general, courtesies are dispensed with at most busy low to moderately priced restaurants, with rushed staff tending to be abrupt and keen to usher you out before you can say '*mei dan, mgoi*' ('bill, please'). Cultural differences also extend to table manners. In Hong Kong people don't nibble chicken or fish, they pile everything in and spit out the bones on to the table.

While you may not have the stomach to try some of the more exotic foods that are popular with locals – snake, duck tongue, chicken feet and all manner of offal, for instance – there are more familiar alternatives, such as chicken, pork and plenty of vegetables. The seafood restaurants found in the Outlying Islands or on the coast of Sai Kung in the New Territories are also an essential experience. Pick your catch of the day from one of the many crowded aquariums and pay for the crustacean or fish according to its weight. And a trip to Hong Kong without sampling dim sum is unforgivable.

Like everywhere, the attitude to hygiene in Hong Kong restaurants varies. Since the SARS outbreak in spring 2003, many lax restaurants have upped standards, while careful ones went for clinical levels of cleanliness. However, there will always be some places that cut corners. Locals suspicious of hygiene in Chinese restaurants habitually wash their chopsticks with freshly boiled tea in a bowl at the table. As a rule of thumb, if the crockery is clean you're probably OK.

PRICING GUIDELINES

When it comes to Western food, prices tend to jump considerably from the HK$20-$50 you might pay for a modest but satisfying noodle or rice meal, or the HK$100-plus for something a little more fancy. Even in an unremarkable Western restaurant, dinner for two with wine can easily top HK$1,000, while a seriously high-end place will dent your wallet by upwards of HK$2,500. Many of the latter are located in the city's five-star hotels but scores of independent restaurants have opened in the past few years, with several offering truly world-class menus. Because of high rents, many are small and cosy – some might say cramped. Menus in these places tend to feature classic Western dishes or creative contemporary 'fusion' cuisine – combining traditional Western ingredients with Asian spices.

> ❶ Purple numbers given in this chapter correspond to the location of each restaurant as marked on the street maps. *See pp328-333.*

Note that a ten per cent service charge is automatically added to most restaurant bills in Hong Kong (but not to those in noodle bars and cafés). Unfortunately, however, this is rarely passed on to the staff, so a further gratuity is normal; the amount is discretionary (an additional few dollars is appreciated in low-priced places, but note that many top-end restaurants – which still amounts to only a few per cent).

We have given the ranges of main course prices where applicable, but note that many places also offer set lunch and/or dinner menus in addition to (and occasionally instead of) à la carte menus. These can help keep the price of the meal to acceptable levels, especially within the posher hotels.

In addition to the places within this chapter, many of the pubs and bars listed on pp160-169 also offer excellent food (*see also p155* **Superior pub grub**).

OPENING TIMES
Please note that, unless otherwise stated, the later times listed below refer to when last orders are taken, not the closing time. However, in very casual establishments the later time refers to closing time, though these are prone to a certain amount of flexibility.

Hong Kong Island

Central

American

Archie B's
7-9 Staunton Street (2522 1262/www.dining concepts.com.hk). Central MTR (exit D2)/Mid-Levels Escalator/buses along Des Voeux Road. **Open** noon-10.30pm daily. **Main courses** HK$60-$120. **Credit** MC, V. **Map** p328 B3 ❶
This New York deli-style place serves pastrami and Reuben sandwiches, matzo ball soup, chopped liver, pickles, and, to finish, cheesecake and black and white cookies. The high metal stools aren't particularly comfortable, and the walls are plastered with autographed photos of Madonna and various other superstars who have surely never been here, but it's as close to the Big Apple as you're going to get in Hong Kong.

British

The Phoenix
G/F, 29 Shelley Street (2546 2110). Central MTR (exit D1, D2, G)/13, 23, 23A bus. **Open** 4-11pm Mon-Thur; 11am-11pm Fri; 9am-late Sat, Sun. **Main courses** HK$115-$180. **Credit** MC, V. **Map** p328 B4 ❷

The best Restaurants

For alfresco dining
Stoep (*see p158*); Han Lok Yuen (*see p156*).

Dim sum with a buzz and a view
City Hall Maxim's Palace. See p133.

Chinese fine dining with style
Lung King Heen. See p135.

Chinese seafood
Lamcombe (*see p156*); Man Fung (*see p156*).

Western seafood
Oyster & Wine Bar. See p152.

Western fine dining
Gaddi's. See p149.

Quality Italian without pretence
Angelini. See p150.

Mod Oz
Opia. See p144.

Steakhouse
The Steakhouse. See p152.

Vegetarian curry
Branto. See p149.

This gastropub is a short walk up the steps from Man Mo Temple near SoHo. The menu is always changing, and while the bangers and mash or roast may set you back more than usual, the quality is high. Weekend breakfasts are authentic full-English affairs and Brit newspapers are provided to further soothe homesick expats. The blackboard menu of hot or cold bites changes regularly. It's also free BYOB on Mondays and Tuesdays (HK$120 corkage charge on other days).

Chinese

City Hall Maxim's Palace
2/F, Low Block, City Hall, 7 Edinburgh Place (2521 1303). Central MTR (exit J2, J3)/buses along Connaught Road/Central Ferry Pier. **Open** 11am-3pm, 5.30-11.30pm Mon-Sat; 9am-3pm, 5.30-11.30pm Sun. **Main courses** HK$80-$100. *Dim sum* HK$20-$45. **Credit** AmEx, DC, MC, V. **Map** p329 E3 ❸
With its old-fashioned charm, and elderly women pushing around trolleys packed with savoury treats, Maxim's was always being voted the city's best dim sum joint. So what did the owners do? Refurbished it so it looks like any other fancy Chinese restaurant,

Lung King Heen – stunning food in stunning surroundings. *See p135.*

of course. Prices went up and the ambience was lost, but the food is still good and the views of the harbour remain enticing. Reservations required.

Crystal Jade

Shop 2018, Level 2, IFC Mall, 8 Finance Street (2295 3811). Central MTR (exit A)/buses to Central Ferry Pier. **Open** 11am-11pm daily. **Main courses** HK$35-$120. **Credit** DC, MC, V. **Map** p329 D2 ❹

A little tucked away in the mall – perched just above the main entrance to the Airport Express Station – this earthy Northern Chinese restaurant is so popular that queues form every lunchtime and often at dinnertime. *Xiao long bau* – seasoned minced pork dumplings – are a speciality. Several other meat and fish dishes are fried or braised with rich soy-based sauces, made more robust with garlic, spring onion, chilli and ginger – perfect warming fare in the cooler months. The waiting staff's English-language ability is not so hot but they tend to be friendly and most of the menu is translated into English.

Cuisine Cuisine

Shop 3101, Level 3, IFC Mall, 8 Finance Street (2393 3933/www.cuisinecuisine.hk). Central MTR (exit A)/buses to Central Ferry Pier. **Open** noon-10.30pm Mon-Fri; 1-11pm Sat, Sun. **Main courses** HK$98-$780. **Credit** DC, MC, V. **Map** p329 E2 ❺

Elegant Cantonese dining – with a few exquisitely prepared regional Chinese dishes on the menu for good measure – can be enjoyed at well-spaced tables here, set against a Victoria Harbour backdrop. Extravagant dishes include the likes of fresh crab meat and bird's nest, baked in a crab shell. But there is simpler fare – such as noodle soups, and roast goose, duck or pork with vegetables – that need not be that expensive, and the house-made soy and chilli sauces are flavourful. Dim sum is several notches above that served elsewhere; twists include the incorporation of the occasional Western ingredient such as foie gras.

Lung King Heen

4/F, Four Seasons Hong Kong, 8 Finance Street (3196 8880). Central MTR (exit A)/buses to Central Ferry Pier. **Open** noon-2.30pm, 6-10.30pm Mon-Sat; 11.30am-3pm, 6-10.30pm Sun. **Main courses** HK$80-$300. **Credit** AmEx, DC, MC, V. **Map** p329 D2 ❻

There are few restaurants anywhere that really take your breath away – this is one of those rarities. The high quality of the mostly Cantonese cuisine, thoughtful presentation, stylish ambience with harbour view, service, beverage selection… it simply gets everything right. The chef's signature dish – braised goose liver in abalone sauce and fish maw (stomach), with rehydrated mushroom – is a real treat, as is the house dessert platter. This is also perhaps Hong Kong's only quality Chinese restaurant with a properly thought-out children's menu: a choice of eight dishes for either under-eights or nine- to 12-year-olds are served in portions of appropriate size. **Photo** *p134.*

Shui Hu Ju

G/F, 68 Peel Street (2869 6927/www.aqua.com.hk). Central MTR (exit C)/Mid-Levels Escalator/buses along Des Voeux Road. **Open** 6pm-midnight daily. **Main courses** HK$108-$368. **Credit** DC, MC, V. **Map** p328 B3 ❼

A stylish, retro Chinese decor provides a suitable backdrop for contemporary Northern Chinese dining at Shui Hu Ju. Everything from the delicious food to the way the bill is presented (in an antique-looking wooden box) seems well conceived. Expect dishes with heavy flavours and lots of spices. Chilli chicken and boneless deep-fried lamb ribs are specialities, and the dumplings and noodles are of a very high standard.

Tsim Chai Kee Noodle Shop

Shop B, 98-102 Wellington Street (2850 6471). Central MTR (exit D2). **Open** 9am-10pm daily. **Main courses** HK$13-$18. **No credit cards.** **Map** p328 C3 ❽

Tsim Chai Kee Noodle Shop sells its egg and rice noodles topped with only three things: prawn dumplings, fish balls or sliced beef. It's all under HK$20 a bowl, while a small plate of fresh veg is HK$5. Diners sit at communal or small private tables, which are quite comfortable since a recent makeover. Unbelievably low prices for Central, thus the lunchtime queue is long. **Photo** *p137.*

Yung Kee

32-40 Wellington Street (2522 1624/www.yungkee.com.hk). Central MTR (exit D1, D2, G)/12M, 13, 23A, 40M, 43 bus. **Open** 11am-11.30pm daily. **Main courses** HK$80-$360. **Credit** AmEx, DC, MC, V. **Map** p328 C4 ❾

No trip to Hong Kong would be complete without a visit to Yung Kee. It's famous for its classic Cantonese fare, especially roast goose and barbecued pork. The '1,000-year-old' duck eggs (they're not really that old, just preserved) served with fresh ginger are given to every table on arrival, but they can be an acquired taste. Staff are helpful and an English menu is available. You can just drop in, but book if you can – it's a large place but tends to be very busy. While dishes featuring abalone can jump up to HK$1,120, *congee* (rice porridge) varieties are just HK$25 a bowl.

French

Chez Moi

10 Arbuthnot Road (2801 6768). Central MTR (exit G)/12, 13, 40M bus. **Open** noon-3pm, 7-11pm Mon-Sat. **Set menu** *Lunch* HK$190. *Dinner* HK$390-$475. **Credit** AmEx, DC, MC, V. **Map** p328 C4 ❿

Recently renovated, this cosy, romantic room is filled with whimsical knick-knacks. There's a husband-and-wife team (chef and pastry chef) in the kitchen, between them dishing up cuisine with all the Gallic flair you could wish for. The menu always lists a couple of rich game dishes as well as lighter fare. Fresh oysters, oyster shooters, potato gnocchi and lobster tails in garlic and butter are among the highlights. The quality of the food and luxurious setting make it worth the price.

La Bouteille

10/F, Pinocine Building, 80-82 Queen's Road Central (2869 1499). Central MTR (exit D1, D2). **Open** days and times vary (call in advance to reserve). **Main courses** HK$120-$200. **Set menu** *Lunch* HK$80. *Dinner* HK$310. **Credit** MC, V. **Map** p328 C3 **⑪**
See below **Private kitchens** *for review.*

Le Tire Bouchon

45A Graham Street (2523 5459). Mid-Levels Escalator/26 bus. **Open** *Bar* 11am-11pm Mon-Sat. *Restaurant* noon-2.30pm, 6.30-10.30pm Mon-Sat. **Main courses** HK$135-$280. **Credit** AmEx, DC, MC, V. **Map** p328 C3 **⑫**
Central's oldest independent French restaurant – at 20-plus years – is a hidden treasure. The entrance is almost cave-like, but the interior is extensive and homely, and ideal for a romantic meal or group get together. The Gallic staff are knowledgeable about their classic French cuisine – the pièce de résistance

Private kitchens

Beginning in the mid-1990s, a new, partially underground and not always quite legal dining scene emerged in Hong Kong. Dubbed 'private kitchens', these small dining rooms often do not possess proper restaurant or alcohol licences (nor other required restaurant safety features), but have gained loyal patronage.

Why? Because they are mostly run by passionate chefs (specialising in various cuisines) whose concern over food authenticity is unquestioned, while their disregard of, say, fire escapes – as many lodge anonymously in residential, office, and even light industrial buildings – is questionable. Diners often enjoy interesting tasting menus at these joints and the thrill of a somewhat illicit and exclusive meal. Below, we review some of the most interesting – all on Hong Kong Island.

Chow Chung-choi's reputation as one of Hong Kong's most talented chefs dates back to his legendary Cantonese specialties at the now defunct Hyatt Regency in Tsim Sha Tsui. Now Chow cooks at **Chow Chung Restaurant** (*see p141*), with the assistance of his wife, in a dining room in their flat in Sheung Wan.

Each meal is different and depends on what's in season. Given that the likes of lotus-leaf-wrapped, flavoured steamed rice, long-simmered soups, meat, seafood, bean curd and vegetables regularly appear in an eight-course dinner, and that desserts might include bird's nest soup with lotus seed and fresh lily bulb, the HK$800 price tag is worth the splurge. Soft drinks and beer are included, while wine may be brought by diners, with no corkage charged.

Open every Thursday, Friday and Saturday night (pre-booking only), **Magnolia** (*see p141*) dishes up authentic New Orleans-style Cajun and Creole cuisine. The simple but stylish

private dining room that opened in summer 2006 has a reception area where cocktails and canapés can be enjoyed before dinner. For the meal, expect jambalaya, crawfish pie and the like, followed by desserts such as Louisiana honey pecan pie. A surprise menu is always served – so any special dietary requirements should be mentioned in advance. The HK$450 per person must be pre-paid 72 hours in advance by bank transfer. Complimentary soft drinks, coffee and tea are offered but alcohol is unavailable – bring your own; there is no corkage charge.

The second incarnation of **La Bouteille** (*see above*) has a homely atmosphere, reflected in the rustic ingredients – though the level of cooking is definitely gourmet and justifies the HK$310 price tag for a set dinner.

Mains might include beef bourguignon and oxtail braised in red wine with fava beans and vegetables; salmon with asparagus; baby duck breast on pineapple with port sauce; fillet of lamb with courgette; and duck confit. Desserts are light renditions of Continental classics such as crème brûlée and fruit crumble. The daily set lunch goes for a reasonable HK$80. French wine is available or you can bring your own (HK$50 corkage fee). Book ahead for weekend evenings.

Ex-Renaissance Harbourview hotel chef Ricky Cheung launched the intimate 40-seater **Le Mieux Bistro** (*see p145*) as a casual, stylish Gallic oasis in light-industrial Chai Wan. A set lunch of four courses (HK$150) includes canapé-style appetisers with salad and a selection of fish, poultry and meat main courses. Evening meals are available by booking a personalised tasting menu only (HK$500). Signature dishes include roast quail, and barramundi stuffed with seafood mousse. Wine is served or you can bring your own – there is no corkage charge.

It's noodles, noodles or noodles at **Tsim Chai Kee**. *See p135.*

being the *tournedos rossini* (beef fillet in a port and shallot sauce with duck liver). On the lighter side, Marmite Dieppoise – Norman-style stewed seafood – is another speciality worth trying. For dessert, the soufflés are wonderful. Of nearly 200 wines, around 80 per cent are French.

Petrus

56/F, Island Shangri-La Hotel, Pacific Place, 88 Queensway, Admiralty (2877 3838). Admiralty MTR (exit C1)/buses along Queensway. **Open** noon-2.30pm, 6.30-10.30pm daily. **Main courses** HK$250-$400. **Credit** AmEx, DC, MC, V. **Map** p329 F5 ⑬

One of the local kings of French cuisine for years, Petrus has a new sommelier and chef. The former has introduced premium wines by the glass, while the latter changes the menu often and offers (for those who ask) personalised tasting menus using the freshest ingredients in his kitchen. Alongside the likes of faultless matured house foie gras terrine are lighter dishes such as roasted Maine lobster with basil and sautéed vegetable shavings. Gracious, knowledgeable service and sweeping harbour views complete the wonderfully gourmet experience that is priced in the 'very special occasion' bracket for most diners. Note: jacket required for gents.

Pierre

25/F, Mandarin Oriental, 5 Connaught Road Central (2825 4001). Central MTR (exit F)/buses along Connaught Road. **Open** *Lunch* noon-2.30pm daily. *Dinner* from 7pm daily (last reservation 9pm). **Main courses** HK$400-$580. **Credit** AmEx, DC, MC, V. **Map** p329 E3 ⑭

French Michelin-starred celebrity chef Pierre Gagnaire is at the helm of this restaurant, launched in October 2006 and perched atop the renovated Mandarin Oriental. Though the decor is minimalist monochrome (including the adjoining M Bar), the food certainly isn't – expect to be surprised. Whether you choose from the set or à la carte menu, dishes are always intriguing, and one course if often made up of a few separate small dishes, each extraordinary in themselves. Enjoy starters such as this trio: a cucumber mousse with bitter miniature turnip and beaten ricotta; sole terrine with salad leaves; and cuttlefish, thinly sliced veal and sweet-and-sour cherry tomato – a lighter combination than you'd imagine. Dinnertime creations get yet more elaborate, and there are tasting menus for HK$1,200 per person.

Indian

Veda

1/F, 8 Arbuthnot Road (2868 5885/www.veda. com.hk). Central MTR (exit H, K)/12M, 13, 23A, 40M bus. **Open** noon-3pm, 7-11pm daily. **Main courses** HK$158-$298. **Credit** MC, V. **Map** p328 C4 ⑮

Radically changing the image of Indian food, this minimalist, stylish space offers light and even healthy contemporary Indian cuisine. The buffet

Choose from Cantonese, Thai, Japanese or Indian at **Café TOO** at Pacific Place.

lunches (HK$118) now feature a counter with a chef freshly cooking a speciality dish, alongside spiced salads, curries and tandoori meats. Dinners are a lot pricier but the fresh imported ingredients are excellent and vegetarians are well catered for. A popular hangout for *tai tais* (rich housewives who lunch).

International

Café TOO

7/F, Island Shangri-La Hotel, Pacific Place, 88 Queensway, Admiralty (2877 3838). Admiralty MTR (exit C1)/buses along Queensway. **Open** 6.30am-11pm daily. **Set menu** (buffet) *Lunch* HK$268 Mon-Sat; HK$308 Sun. *Dinner* HK$368 Mon-Thur; HK$398 Fri-Sun. **Credit** AmEx, DC, MC, V. **Map** p329 F5 ⑯
Although there is a menu here, it is the open kitchen buffet – with its several 'food stations' where staff theatrically prepare cuisines such as Cantonese, Thai, Japanese and Indian – that most diners opt for. Highlights include the chilled seafood, a noodle bar that offers a cracking Thai tom yum soup with a choice of king prawns, mussels or veggies, and the South-east Asian counter. At the salad bar, a chef tosses your choice of ingredients in one of five infused olive oils. The colourful range of desserts includes crêpes and mini-soufflés made to order.

M at the Fringe

2 Lower Albert Road (2877 4000/m-onthebund.com/ at_the_fringe). Central MTR (exit D1)/23A bus. **Open** noon-2.30pm, 7-10.30pm Mon-Fri; 7-10.30pm Sat, Sun.* **Main courses** HK$208-$286. **Credit** AmEx, DC, MC, V. **Map** p328 C4 ⑰
This whimsical yet cosy dining room is one of Hong Kong's oldest independent Western restaurants – and there are many reasons it has lasted so long. The largely Mediterranean-inspired food is reliably excellent and reflects the international, eclectic tastes of the 'M' behind the name, Michelle Garnaut, who also owns the M on the Bund in Shanghai. The ever-changing menu usually features a Middle Eastern dish or two as well as organ meats that appeal to the adventurous diner. Longstanding signature dishes include lamb baked in a salt crust, and roasted suckling pig served with poached apple. Crab soufflé, which is served in light puff pastry, is a recent winner. The pavlova makes for a wonderfully light finish.

Peak Café Bar

9-13 Shelley Street (2140 6877). Mid-Levels Escalator/buses along Caine Road. **Open** 11am-2am Mon-Fri; 9am-2am Sat, Sun. **Main courses** HK$92-$188. **Credit** AmEx, DC, MC, V. **Map** p328 C3/C4 ⑱
The Peak Café was originally located where you might expect it – up on Victoria Peak with views over Hong Kong Island. But when the restaurant lost its lease (the Peak Lookout replaced it; *see p145*) it packed up its successful formula and moved it down the slope. The menu offers the same eclectic mix of dishes, including pizza, Thai, Indian and Western. And, as it overlooks the Mid-Levels Escalator, the joint makes a good coffee or drinking spot.

Italian

Isola

Shop 3071-3075, Levels 3-4, IFC Mall, 8 Finance Street (2383 8765/www.isolabarandgrill.com). Central MTR (exit A)/buses to Central Ferry Pier. **Open** noon-11.30pm daily. **Main courses** HK$128-$338. **Credit** AmEx, DC, MC, V. **Map** p329 D2 ⑲

Part of the same small restaurant group as Va Bene (*see below*), sprawling Isola, with its light contemporary monochrome interior, fountain terrace with views of Victoria Harbour and hopping in- and outdoor bar, is a favourite yuppie, expense-account and *tai tai* (wealthy housewife) hangout. The menu features some of the highest quality Italian food to be found in the city – and prices are accordingly hefty. The open kitchen produces perfect pizzas featuring black or white truffles when in season.

Nicholini's

8/F, Conrad Hotel, Pacific Place, 88 Queensway, Admiralty (2521 3838). Admiralty MTR (exit C1)/buses along Queensway. **Open** noon-3pm, 6.30-11pm Mon-Sat; 11am-3pm, 6.30-11pm Sun. **Main courses** HK$240-$680. **Credit** AmEx, DC, MC, V. **Map** p329 F5 ⑳

Top-notch Italian food is served in the Conrad's luxurious, somewhat formal surroundings. On the whole it's expensive, but the weekday lunch is a pretty good deal – for HK$318 you get an antipasti buffet and a hot main course cooked to order, plus tea or coffee; select a dessert for an extra HK$50. It's popular for Sunday brunch (HK$468), which is one of the best in town. The floor-to-ceiling windows mean good views of the harbour, so try to bag one of the window seats. Be sure to book.

Pizza Express

21 Lyndhurst Terrace (2850 7898/www.pizza express.com.hk). Mid-Levels Escalator/Central MTR (exit D1)/23A bus. **Main courses** HK$88-$110. **Open** noon-11.30pm daily. **Credit** AmEx, DC, MC, V. **Map** p328 C3 ㉑

Yep, the UK-founded chain known for its fine thin-crust pizzas has a couple of branches in Hong Kong – this is the only downtown joint though. It dishes up numerous and faultless tomato-based pizzas, plus some that use mushroom as a base, as well as a few pastas and salads. The Peking duck pizza exceeds expectations, doused in hoisin (plum) sauce, sprinkled extravagantly with chopped spring onion, pepped up with a little chilli and paired with just a touch of mozzarella. Desserts are a high point: try the sweet pizza-base tarts, cooked à la minute. On Thursday evenings a live jazz trio plays. The only letdown is the sloppy service.
Other locations: 35 Ashley Road, Tsim Sha Tsui, Kowloon (2317 7432); 10 Wing Fung Street, Wan Chai, HK Island (3528 0541).

Toscana

Ritz-Carlton Hotel, 3 Connaught Road (2532 2062). Central MTR (exit J1). **Open** noon-2.30pm, 6-11pm Mon-Sat; 6-11pm Sun. **Main courses** HK$320-$390. **Credit** AmEx, DC, MC, V. **Map** p329 E4 ㉒

Though complete with crystal chandeliers and a drawing-room feel, this, one of Hong Kong's most respected Italian fine-dining restaurants, is comfortable rather than stuffy. Expect some of the best jet-fresh truffles, seafood, meat and vegetables from Europe here, all expertly cooked. Condiments on the table include six-year-matured balsamic vinegar and premium extra virgin olive oil. Simplicity speaks volumes in linguine with sea urchin, prepared with minimal seasoning. Roast rack of lamb with black olives and artichoke compote is a house favourite. The list of Italian wines is phenomenally long.

Va Bene

G/F, 17-22, Lan Kwai Fong (2845 5577/www. vabeneristorante.com). Central MTR (exit D1)/23A bus. **Open** noon-2.30pm, 6.30-11.30pm Mon-Thur; noon-2.30pm, 6.30pm-midnight Fri, Sat. **Main courses** HK$238-$368. **Credit** AmEx, DC, MC, V. **Map** p328 C4 ㉓

Though it recently moved to its current cosily elegant location, this Lan Kwai Fong operation has been rated as one of the city's best Italian kitchens for more than a decade and a half, regularly attracting socialites and local movers and shakers. And for good reason – its quality ingredients are expertly cooked. Antipasti include salted Culatello ham with artichoke salad and parmesan shavings, and baked scallop on spinach with mustard *zabaglione*. The standout home-made pasta is a phenomenal *casoncelli* (small ravioli-like pockets) with mixed meat and sage ragoût, butter bacon and black truffle. Service is a dream and the wine list is predominantly Italian.

Mexican

El Taco Loco

LG/F, 7 Staunton Street (2522 0214/www.dining concepts.com.hk). Central MTR (exit D2)/Mid-Levels Escalator/buses along Lyndhurst Terrace. **Open** noon-midnight daily. **Main courses** HK$15-$68. **No credit cards. Map** p328 B3 ㉔

Here's a place where you can have your fill of Mexican food and walk out with change from HK$100. Tacos come either steamed or fried, while burritos are so stuffed they could feed an army. This is a semi self-service restaurant – you place your order at the front and pick up your food at the back, along with whatever salsa or hot sauce (from mildly spicy to incendiary) your mouth can handle, and it's served on a disposable plate.

Middle Eastern

Assaf Lebanese Cuisine

G/F, Lyndhurst Building, 37 Lyndhurst Terrace (2851 6550). Central MTR (exit D2)/Mid-Levels Escalator/buses along Lyndhurst Terrace. **Open** noon-midnight daily. **Main courses** HK$120-$138. **Credit** AmEx, DC, MC, V. **Map** p328 C3 ㉕

Eat, Drink, Shop

This is the sister restaurant to Beyrouth Café next door (which is more of a takeaway, although it does have a few tall stools to perch on), but since Assaf is a sit-down place, prices are more expensive here. Falafel balls are crisp and delicious, lamb schwarma is well seasoned and set mezedes offer full-on veggie or carnivorous feasts.

Habibi/Habibi Café

G/F, 112-114 Wellington Street (restaurant 2544 9298/café 2544 3886). Central MTR (exit D2)/Mid-Levels Escalator/buses along Wellington Street. **Open** *Restaurant* 11.30am-11.30pm Mon-Sat. *Café* 9am-midnight daily. **Main courses** *Restaurant* HK$120-$200. *Café* HK$45-$130. **Credit** AmEx, DC, MC, V. **Map** p328 C3 🐵

With its low lights, comfortable banquettes and chairs, and a belly dancer who makes an appearance on weekends, Habibi (the restaurant) is the more atmospheric of these two adjacent Egyptian eateries. It's also reasonably pricey compared with the more casual set-up next door, though the food at both places is delicious and authentic. Try out the Habibi Café's 'koshary' – a healthy mix of rice, pasta, grain and vegetables.

Pan-Asian

Good Luck Thai Café

13 Wing Wah Lane, Lan Kwai Fong (2877 2971). Central MTR (exit D2, G)/12M, 13, 23A, 40M, 43 bus. **Open** 11am-1am Mon-Sat. **Main courses** HK$35-$80. **Credit** MC, V. **Map** p328 C4 🐵

Residents may nickname Wing Wah Lane 'Rat Alley' but expats still come here in droves to perch on a rickety stool in this bustling side street and tuck into top Thai tucker. The tom yum soup and roast chicken are especially delicious. The alley is wall-to-wall with rival alfresco restaurants, serving Malaysian and Vietnamese food, but this one remains our pick. It's not for the unadventurous, but it must be doing something right as on most evenings it's hard to find a stool.

Indochine 1929

2/F, California Tower, Lan Kwai Fong (2869 7399). Central MTR (exit D2, G)/12M, 13, 23A, 40M, 43 bus. **Open** noon-2.30pm, 6.30-11pm daily. **Main courses** HK$125-$260. **Credit** AmEx, DC, MC, V. **Map** p328 C4 🐵

One of the best dining experiences in Hong Kong, this place is as much about atmosphere as food – though that's first-class too. The decor harks back to French colonial Indochina, and is ideal for both a romantic dinner and a group gathering. Vietnamese food here is perhaps the most refined in Hong Kong, and the budget-conscious can eat reasonably if they mix and match starters rather than opt for the pricier mains, which include beef tenderloin with tomato and deep-fried eggplant. Vegetarians will enjoy crunchy sautéed lotus root with water chestnuts, snow peas and walnuts, and drinkers will appreciate the good wine list.

Kyoto Joe

LG-G/F, The Plaza, 21 D'Aguilar Street (2804 6800). Central MTR (exit D2). **Open** noon-2.30pm, 6.30-11pm Sun-Thur; noon-2.30pm, 6.30pm-12.30am Fri, Sat. **Main courses** HK$100-$250. **Credit** AmEx, DC, MC, V. **Map** p328 C4 🐵

A younger sister to Tokio Joe around the corner at 16 Lan Kwai Fong, Kyoto Joe is brighter and more modern. The food is excellent at both – from the sushi and sashimi platters (the soft-shell crab roll is sensational) to the *robatayaki* grill and innovative mains. It's not cheap, but then good Japanese restaurants rarely are.

Spanish

Olé

1/F, Shun Ho Tower, 24-30 Ice House Street (2523 8624). Central MTR (exit D2, G)/13, 23A, 26, 43 bus. **Open** noon-3pm, 6.30-11.30pm daily. **Main courses** HK$100-$360. **Credit** AmEx, DC, MC, V. **Map** p329 D4 🐵

Authentic Spanish food is served up with true passion at Olé. The excellent paella is the highlight of the menu, but if you feel like splurging, try the delicate suckling pig. The atmosphere is informal, with musicians serenading diners and the sangría flowing freely.

Sheung Wan

Cajun/Creole

Magnolia

Shop 5, G/F, 17 Po Yan Street, Sheung Wan (2530 9880/www.magnolia.hk). Central MTR then 26 bus to Hollywood Road. **Open** Thur-Sat (times vary; by reservation only). **Set menu** HK$450. **No credit cards.** **Map** p328 A2 🐵

See p136 **Private kitchens** for review.

Chinese

Chow Chung Restaurant

Flat B, 5/F, Kin Tye Lung Building, 27-29 Bonham Strand West (2805 1116). Sheung Wan MTR (exit A2). **Open** 6-9.30pm. **Set menu** HK$800. **No credit cards.** **Map** p328 A1/A2 🐵

See p136 **Private kitchens** for review.

International

Canaan Café

Shop D, G/F, 27 Hillier Street (2850 7668). Sheung Wan MTR (exit A2). **Open** 7.30am-5.30pm Mon-Fri; 8am-2pm Sat. **Set menu** *Lunch* HK$28-$50. **No credit cards.** **Map** p328 B2 🐵

In a network of streets catering mostly to nearby office workers, amid lots of noodle shops where non-Cantonese speakers must use hand signals to order, this friendly café is one of the few places that has an

Eat, Drink, Shop

English menu. Set lunches are made to order, and usually include homemade soup or a tea or coffee. Sandwiches come with a choice of bread and two fillings – focaccia with chicken and egg is great, served with an apple and raisin-laced salad. Several pastas are also listed. The café's four tables and small counter are usually packed, so many customers order takeaways.

Das Gute

Shop 1-3, G/F, Western Market, 323 Des Voeux Road (2851 2872). Sheung Wan MTR (exit B). **Open** noon-2.30pm, 6-9.30pm daily. **Set menu** *Lunch* from HK$52-$62. *Dinner* HK$95-$135. **Credit** MC, V. **Map** p328 B1 **34**

Part of a small bakery chain, this calm cosy interior spills into Western market with an indoor terrace effect. Instead of an à la carte menu, there are eight to ten set meals for both lunch and dinner, each inclusive of a soup starter and tea or coffee, which can be had iced with the meal or hot afterwards (the coffee is good-quality ground stuff). Lunch offerings include pastas, meat and veggies, and salads – the smoked duck breast Caesar is satisfying – starting at a reasonable HK$52. Among the dinner options are garlic prawns and imported US steaks.

Wan Chai, Causeway Bay & Happy Valley

Chinese

American (Peking) Restaurant

20 Lockhart Road, Wan Chai (2527 7277). Wan Chai MTR (exit C)/buses along Hennessy Road. **Open** 11.30am-11.30pm daily. **Main courses** HK$80-$140. **Credit** AmEx, DC, MC, V. **Map** p330 A3 **35**

Expats and tourists love the American, fuelling criticism that it's too westernised. But it's an institution of some five decades and the mainly Beijing dishes are rooted in the capital's rich culinary heritage, from the sinfully delicious Peking duck to the moreish minced pigeon in lettuce leaves and sliced beef in mini-bread pockets. Beware the MSG rush at the meal's end. It's a busy place, so book ahead.

Canton Room

1/F, Lockhart Hotel, 72 Gloucester Road, Wan Chai (2866 2166). Wan Chai MTR (exit C)/buses along Hennessy Road & Gloucester Road. **Open** 11.30am-2.45pm, 6-10.45pm Mon-Fri; 10.30am-2.45pm, 6-10.45pm, Sat, Sun. **Main courses** HK$60-$240. **Credit** AmEx, DC, MC, V. **Map** p330 B3 **36**

This excellent restaurant is cosy and understated: the food does the talking, with a thick menu of Cantonese staples and regularly changing seasonal specials; the latter are listed only in Chinese but friendly waiting staff are (ready and able) to translate into English. A flavoursome winner, when in season, is Chinese spinach boiled in Yunnan ham

broth. From the à la carte menu, classic steamed garoupa is spot-on and excellent value at around HK$130 for two. For presentation, it's hard to beat the edible yin-yang symbol – comprising steamed egg white topped with bird's nest, and steamed yolk topped with fish and crab roe – an imaginative mix of flavour and texture.

FF Hotpot

340-44 Jaffe Road , Wan Chai (2838 9392). Causeway Bay MTR (exit B)/buses along Hennessy Road. **Open** 5am-1am daily. **Main courses** HK$20-$60. **Credit** V. **Map** p330 C3 **37**

'Fay fay', as this place is known to its fans, serves only Sichuanese hotpot, but there's still plenty of choice on offer. You can order your broth in varying degrees of spiciness, or you can opt for a plainer broth (try a split pot of spicy and non-spicy, preferably the one with preserved egg). Then you have to decide which of the myriad meat, seafood, vegetables and noodles (each costing around HK$18-$88) to cook in the broth. It's a tough decision to make. If you don't like offal, there are many alternatives – sliced beef, chicken or pork, or fish, prawns and other seafood. Even vegetarians can come out of here stuffed on gluten puffs, fried bean curd and a vast array of vegetables.

King's Palace Congee & Noodle Bar

G/F, 22 Sing Woo Road, Happy Valley (2838 4444). Bus 1, 19/trams to Happy Valley. **Open** 11.30am-12.30am daily. **Main courses** HK$22-$98. **Credit** DC, MC, V. **Map** off p331 E5 **38**

A top place to come at weekends, especially if you've overdone it on the alcohol the night before. *Congee* (rice porridge) is brilliant for sensitive stomachs as it's light, subtle and comforting. And whereas many other congee places are not conducive to soothing throbbing heads and bleary eyes – they tend to be bright, loud and filled with cigarette fumes – King's Palace has comfortable booths, plays classical music at a low volume and makes outstanding *congee* (especially the one with fresh crab) and noodles.

Lao Shanghai

Basement, Century Hotel, 238 Jaffe Road, Wan Chai (2827 9339). Wan Chai MTR (exit A1)/buses along Gloucester Road. **Open** 11am-11pm daily. **Main courses** HK$56-$300. **Credit** AmEx, MC, V. **Map** p330 C3 **39**

Because of its location, in the basement of a fairly average hotel, this roomy restaurant is often overlooked by those not in the know – but the Shanghainese cuisine here is first-rate. From staple dishes such as tofu noodles to more unusual specialities like braised lion-head meatballs and drunken Shanghai crab, the food is a great introduction to Shanghainese fare.

One Harbour Road

7-8/F, Grand Hyatt Hotel, 1 Harbour Road, Wan Chai (2588 1234, ext 7338). Wan Chai MTR (exit A1, C)/A12, 18, 88 bus/Wan Chai Star Ferry Pier.

Open noon-2.30pm, 6.30-10.30pm daily. **Main courses** HK$160-$500. **Credit** AmEx, DC, MC, V. **Map** p328 B2 ④

The Grand Hyatt's opulent art deco dining room may seem a strange venue for Cantonese cuisine, but it works. And the dishes may sound familiar: dim sum, chicken with shallots and black bean sauce, hot and sour soup, but here they're given such expert treatment, that you'd hardly recognise them. Service is exemplary, and the wide-ranging wine list and great harbour views are further draws. Note that the dress code is smart.

Red Pepper

G/F, 7 Lan Fong Road, Causeway Bay (2577 3811). Causeway Bay MTR (exit B)/buses along Percival Street & Leighton Road. **Open** 11.30am-midnight daily. **Main courses** HK$80-$235. **Credit** AmEx, DC, MC, V. **Map** p331 E3 ④

Red Pepper has been winning awards for many years, but recent diners have given the place some mixed reports. Admittedly, its decor is looking a bit long in the tooth but dishes are more hit than miss – all as spicy and intensely flavoured as Sichuan cuisine demands. Try sizzling chilli prawns, sour and pepper soup or the dry-fried spring beans with minced pork.

Water Margin

Shop 1205, 12/F, Food Forum, Times Square, Causeway Bay (3102 0088/www.aqua.com.hk). Causeway Bay MTR (exit A)/trams to Happy Valley. **Open** noon-3pm, 6-11pm daily. **Main courses** HK$108-$398. **Credit** DC, MC, V. **Map** p331 D3 ④

This Northern Chinese restaurant is a 'wealthy relation' to Shui Hu Ju in Central (*see p135*) – it's a much bigger, more stylish space and the menu is far more extensive (and a little more expensive). Fortunately, the owners haven't toned down the rich, spicy flavours. The cooks here are known for using some unusual ingredients in delicious ways – the fried pig's palate with onions and coriander shouldn't be missed by more adventurous diners.

French

Olala

Upper G/F, Hung Dak Building, 1 Electric Street, Wan Chai (2294 0450). Buses along Queen's Road East. **Open** 11.30am-3pm, 6-10.30pm daily. **Main courses**: HK$180-$600. **Credit** MC, V. **Map** p330 A4 ④

There's no menu at Olala. At lunchtime the owner comes out, tells the customers what ingredients he has and composes a meal around what they like and how hungry they are. At dinner you just sit down and eat what the chefs have decided to cook. French haute cuisine this isn't – the food is served 'family style', on plates in the middle of the table so everybody can help themselves, but it's always plentiful, innovative and delicious. The service is just as casual, and should you call on the manager's day off, expect very poor English on the phone.

Indian

Viceroy

2/F, Sun Hung Kai Centre, 30 Harbour Road, Wan Chai (2827 7777/www.chiram.hk). Wan Chai MTR (exit A1)/buses along Gloucester Road. **Open** noon-3pm, 6-11pm daily. **Main courses** HK$88-$168. **Credit** AmEx, DC, MC, V. **Map** p330 C3 ④

The harbour view from the terrace makes Viceroy a popular venue for parties, and there are regular stand-up comedy nights, but mostly it's a good Indian restaurant, with a smaller line in Middle Eastern dishes. Efficient, friendly staff serve up food that's fit for a rajah, with piquant curries and mouthwateringly tender tandooris. It's swisher than your average curry house, and on the whole worth the extra you have to pay. The buffet lunch is reasonable, though, costing HK$108.

Italian

Grissini

2/F, Grand Hyatt Hotel, 1 Harbour Road, Wan Chai (2588 1234, ext 7313). Wan Chai MTR (exit A1, C)/A12, 18, 88 bus/Wan Chai Star Ferry Pier. **Open** noon-2.30pm, 7-11pm daily. **Main courses** HK$160-$500. **Credit** AmEx, DC, MC, V. **Map** p330 B2 ④

One of the finest Italian restaurants in Hong Kong, Grissini has undergone a menu transformation following the arrival of a new chef from Liguria – meaning a lot more seafood. Baby octopus salad, with a burst of fresh veg and a zesty vinaigrette, and Italian sea bass with potato, red onion, cherry tomato and capers have become immediate hits. With such high-quality crustaceans and fish, as well as veal and home-made pastas, on the menu, it can be difficult to choose what to eat. Seasonal specials – particularly those incorporating white and black truffles – are astounding. The crowd tends firmly towards businessmen on expense accounts at lunchtimes (the restaurant forms part of the Grand Hyatt Hotel), but the clientele broadens to anyone who appreciates good food at dinner. Provided they can afford it, that is.

Milano

2/F, Sun Hung Kai Centre, 30 Harbour Road, Wan Chai (2598 1222). Wan Chai MTR (exit A)/buses along Gloucester Road/Wan Chai Star Ferry Pier. **Open** noon-3pm, 6-11pm daily. **Main courses** HK$108-$198. **Credit** AmEx, DC, MC, V. **Map** p330 C3 ④

Walk in the entrance and turn right for Italian food at Milano (or left for Vietnamese cuisine at sister restaurant Saigon). If you can't decide between the two, the staff will let you order dishes from both menus. Milano's most coveted seats are located out on the small terrace with its view of the harbour and Tsim Sha Tsui. The pasta dishes are pretty dependable, as are the pizzas, with thin, crisp crusts and generous toppings.

Pan-Asian

Chili Club

1/F, 88 Lockhart Road, Wan Chai (2527 2872).
Wan Chai MTR (exit C)/buses along Hennessy Road.
Open noon-3pm, 6-10.30pm daily. **Main courses**
HK$40-$180. **Credit** AmEx, MC, V. **Map** p330 B3 **47**
Don't come here for the service, which can be atro-
cious, but for the sizzling hot food at cool prices. The
steamed fish arrives simmering in a sauce bubbling
with fresh chillis and coriander. The tom yum soup,
and curries are also good. Impressive non-spicy
orders include pad Thai and fried chicken in pan-
dana leaf. All dishes are big enough to share.

Opia

1/F, Jia Boutique Hotel, 1-5 Irving Street, Causeway
Bay (3196 9100/www.jiahongkong.com). Causeway
Bay MTR (exit F)/buses along Yee Woo Street.
Open 7-11pm daily. **Main courses** HK$270-$350.
Credit AmEx, DC, MC, V. **Map** p331 E3 **48**
Teague Ezard – a darling of the Melbourne dining
scene – set up this innovative addition to Hong
Kong's culinary landscape as consultant chef at the
end of 2006, leaving executive chef Dane Clouston
to helm the kitchen. Don't be fooled by Clouston's
youthful looks: this boy wonder knows his greens
from his galangal – which is just as well, as he has
recently transformed the South-east Asian influenced menu to a modern continental fine dining one.
The new degustation menu (HK$695) includes a
Japanese-inspired, wasabi-laced oyster shooter with
mirin (sweet rice wine) as a keynote, followed by five
delectable courses. A la carte items include seared
foie gras, caviar and milk-chocolate mousse, and
pan-roasted line-caught sea bass and vanilla potato
cake with white beans and thyme. Mains are listed
with wine pairings. For afters, creative cheese and
fruit concoctions are a highlight.

Perfume River

G/F, 89 Percival Street, Causeway Bay (2576 2240).
Causeway Bay MTR (exit A). **Open** 11am-11pm
daily. **Credit** AmEx,
DC, MC, V. **Map** p331 D3 **49**
This joint doesn't look anything special, but the
South-east Asian food is always good and the low
bills even better. The huge menu is all over the place,
but you'll soon find some tempting dishes. The
frog's leg curry is a good alternative to the usual
chicken, and the prawn crackers topped with spicy
minced pork make an excellent starter. The decor is
nothing to write home about… and be careful not to
bump your head on the low ceiling upstairs.

WasabiSabi

Food Forum, 13/F, Times Square, 1 Matheson
Street, Causeway Bay (2506 0009/www.aqua.
com.hk). Causeway Bay MTR (exit A). **Open** noon-
midnight Mon-Thur, Sun; noon-2am Fri, Sat. *Food*
served noon-3pm, 6-10.45pm Mon-Thur, Sun; noon-
3pm, 6-11pm Fri, Sat. **Main courses** HK$128-$398.
Credit DC, MC, V. **Map** p331 D3 **50**

WasabiSabi's sleek compartmentalised interior, separated by flowing chain curtains and with plush red
furnishings, is big on visual 'wow' factor. The food
is contemporary Japanese – think traditional dishes
with modern twists. The WasabiSabi *tataki* sushi
platter comes with 12 pieces of sliced and minced
fresh seafood, Wagyu beef and foie gras; the top
sushi rice is rolled in finely hand-sliced cucumber
sheets, rather than dried seaweed. Sea urchin, mushroom and clam soup, served in individual clay
teapots and dainty cups, is outstanding. A DJ spins
tunes until late on Saturday nights for those who
wish to linger.

The Peak

International

Café Deco

1-2/F, Peak Galleria, 118 Peak Road (2849 5111/
www.cafedecogroup.com). Peak Tram/15, 15B bus.
Open 11am-11pm Mon-Thur, Sun; 11am-midnight
Fri, Sat. **Main courses** HK$98-$598. **Credit** AmEx,
DC, MC, V. **Map** p89 **51**
This is a huge space and the setting is impressive,
especially if you're lucky enough to get a window
table. As to be expected from the name, there are

(reproduction) art deco touches everywhere. The menu is eclectic but features lots of fresh seafood, Mediterranean pastas and salads and top-notch burgers and pizza. If you can manage to tear your eyes away from the magnificent views of Hong Kong, you can watch the Café Deco chefs at work in the open kitchen.

Peak Lookout
121 Peak Road (2849 1000/www.thepeaklookout. com.hk). Peak Tram/15 bus. **Open** 10.30am-11.30pm Mon-Thur; 8.30am-1am Fri, Sat; 8.30am-11.30pm Sun. **Main courses** HK$118-$390. **Credit** AmEx, DC, MC, V. **Map** p89 🟦

This restaurant replaced the much-loved Peak Café, which relocated to Central a few years ago (*see p138*). The new owners were smart enough to let the magnificent space speak for itself, and they also kept the same mix of Eastern and Western dishes that proved so popular in the past. If it's a balmy day or evening, try to get a seat outside on the extended terrace, where the aromas from the outdoor barbecue will get your tummy rumbling.

Pearl on the Peak
Shop 2, Level 1, The Peak Tower, 128 Peak Road (2849 5123/www.maxims.com.hk). Peak Tram/15 bus. **Open** 11.30am-midnight (last orders 11pm) Sun-Thur; 11.30am-1am (last orders midnight) Fri, Sat. **Main courses** HK$250-$450. **Credit** AmEx, MC, V. **Map** p89 🟦

Geoff Lindsay, co-owner and hotshot chef of Pearl, one of Melbourne's most highly regarded restaurants, is behind the menu at Pearl on the Peak. The food lives up to the dramatic view over Mid-Levels and Central's landmark towers visible from the plush velvet-upholstered interior and the small terrace. Fresh, mostly imported ingredients include the meat of the pearl-producing oyster – flash fried with shiitake, chive buds, ginger and soy. 'Coddled' (poached) egg toasty with seared scallop, chives and salmon caviar explodes with rich flavours. Seafood, poultry, steak and lamb all get curious treatment, where South-east Asian and Turkish influences are apparent, and the Yabby Lake pinot noir is a winner. Afternoon tea is also served.

South & east coasts

French

Le Mieux Bistro
407-408, Block B, MP Industrial centre, 18 Ka Yip Street, Chai Wan (2558 2877/www.givemefive.hk). Heung Fa Chuen MTR (exit C) then 60, 62 green

minibus. **Open** noon-3pm, 7pm-midnight Mon-Fri; 7pm-midnight Sat. **Set menu** *Lunch* HK$150. *Dinner* HK$500. **Credit** AmEx, MC, V.
See p136 **Private kitchens** for review.

International

Black Sheep
G/F, 452 Shek O Village, near Tin Hau Temple (2809 2021). Shau Kei Wan MTR then 9 bus.
Open 7-10.30pm Mon-Fri; 1-10.30pm Sat, Sun.
Main courses HK$100-$165. **Credit** AmEx, MC, V.
Diners flock to this fussily decorated terrace for mainly French-style European food in a cosy village atmosphere. The menu is pretty varied but the fish and seafood dishes are the things to go for. A reasonable selection of wines and beers too.

The Verandah
1/F, Repulse Bay Hotel, 109 Repulse Bay Road, Repulse Bay (2812 2722/www.therepulsebay.com). Bus 6, 6A, 6X, 61, 66, 260, 262. **Open** noon-11.30pm, Mon-Sat; 11am-11pm Sun. **Main courses** HK$200-$345. **Credit** AmEx, DC, MC, V.
With its superb romantic setting – think lazy over-head fans and stately decor – inside the landmark Repulse Bay Hotel, the Verandah is a blast from the colonial past. The view of the bay is sublime, the food classic (the likes of wild mushroom and truffle soup, crab cakes, foie gras and slow-cooked lamb shank) and the list of aperitif champagne cocktails, wines and digestifs extensive. The Sunday brunch (HK$338, HK$169 children) is legendary, so book weeks in advance.

Wildfire
Murray House, Stanley Plaza, Stanley (2813 6060/ www.igors.com). Bus 6, 6A, 6X, 61, 66, 260, 262. **Open** noon-10.30pm Mon-Fri; 11.30am-10.30pm Sat; 10am-10.30pm Sun. **Main courses** HK$140-$158. **Credit** DC, MC, V. **Map** p93 **54**
The speciality at Wildfire is thin-crust pizzas baked in a wood-fired oven. There's a huge choice, from a simple margharita to the fancier Black Forest (with mushrooms, roasted garlic, spinach, parmesan and pine nuts). Pastas are also popular, as is grilled fish and meat, served on long metal skewers. Not expensive but prices can soon add up; however, the after-noon set tea is a bargain (*see p153* **A fancy cuppa**). This branch has a kids' play area with toys. **Other locations**: 13 Bonham Road, Central, HK Island (2540 6669); 21 Elgin Street, Central, HK Island (2810 0670); 2 Knutsford Terrace, Tsim Sha Tsui, Kowloon (3690 1598).

Mediterranean

Lucy's
G/F, 64 Stanley Main Street, Stanley (2813 9055). Bus 6, 6A, 6X, 61, 66, 260, 262. **Open** noon-3pm, 7-10pm Sun-Thur; noon-4pm, 6.30-10pm Fri, Sat. **Main courses** HK$170-$210. **Credit** MC, V. **Map** p93 **55**

Hidden in the rabbit warren of Stanley Market, Lucy's offers an oasis of calm amid the shopping madness. Its bamboo furniture reflects its unpre-tentious atmosphere, which also extends to the good, simple food, including couscous, salads, pastas and ever-popular beef and lamb filets.

Pan-Asian

Chilli N Spice
Shop 101, Murray House, Stanley Plaza, Stanley (2899 0147/www.kingparrot.com). Bus 6, 6A, 6X, 61, 66, 260, 262. **Open** noon-midnight Mon-Thur; 11am-11.30pm Fri, Sat. **Main courses** HK$80-$150. **Credit** AmEx, DC, MC, V. **Map** p93 **56**
The seafront setting of this handsome colonial-style building makes this place a great choice. The speciality is spicy South-east Asian food – Singaporean, Thai, Vietnamese and Malaysian – but flavours are toned down for the more timid Hong Kong palate; if you can take the heat, be sure to inform your waiter.

Shek O Chinese-Thai Seafood
303 Shek O Village (2809 4426). Shau Kei Wan MTR then 9 bus. **Open** 11am-10pm daily. **Main courses** HK$45-$90. **Credit** AmEx, MC, V.
You can't miss this big open restaurant situated next to the main bus stop and right on the only round-about in Shek O. It dishes up everything from fried rice and steamed fish Cantonese-style to spicier cur-ries and hot chilli dishes typical of Thailand. Brightly lit and sparsely decorated, the restaurant is most popular with hikers looking for a filling meal and a few beers after walking the Dragon's Back (*see p90* **Taming the dragon**).

Kowloon

Tsim Sha Tsui

American

Felix
28/F, Peninsula Hotel, Salisbury Road (2315 3188). Tsim Sha Tsui MTR (exit E)/buses to Tsim Sha Tsui Ferry Pier & along Salisbury Road/Tsim Sha Tsui Star Ferry Pier. **Open** 6-11pm daily. **Main courses** HK$160-$350. **Credit** AmEx, DC, MC, V. **Map** p333 B6/C6 **67**
Jason Oakley took over as the new chef here late in 2006, so his modern American cuisine was only beginning to make its mark on the existing Pacific Rim menu at the time of updating this guide. Examples include seared tuna with garlic mashed potato and wine-braised onion, and grilled lamb medallions, also with mash and 'fondue style' sauce. Premium fresh ingredients continue to be a hallmark and the Philippe Starck interior still vies for atten-tion with the stunning harbour view.

Afternoon tea at **The Peninsula**. *See p151*.

Chinese

Heaven on Earth

G-1/F, 6 Knutsford Terrace (2367 8428/www.king parrot.com). Tsim Sha Tsui MTR (exit B1, B2). **Open** 3.30pm-2.30am Mon-Thur; 4pm-3.30am Fri-Sun. **Main courses** HK$55-$108. **Credit** AmEx, DC, MC, V. **Map** p333 C5 ➎

The busy restaurant area of Knutsford Terrace is hidden from the busy streets of Tsim Sha Tsui, but it's worth searching out. Heaven on Earth has a popular bar on the ground floor and a quieter restaurant upstairs. Staff are friendly and will recommend their favourites from the menu, which lists mostly Beijing and Sichuan specialities. The cold dishes, such as the spicy green bean noodles and the unusual 'jade' vegetable, are particularly good. If you want lunch, you'll need to head to the branch in Central (open noon-midnight daily).

Other locations: in the basement of Century Building, 1-13 D'Aguilar Street, Central, HK Island (2537 8083).

Hutong

28/F, One Peking Road (3428 8342/www.aqua. com.hk). Tsim Sha Tsui MTR (exit C1, E)/Tsim Sha Tsui Star Ferry Pier. **Open** noon-3.30pm, 6pm-11pm daily. **Main courses** HK$100-$200. **Credit** AmEx, DC, MC, V. **Map** p333 B6 ➎

The Northern Chinese food at Hutong is more widely accessible than at sister restaurant Water Margin (*see p143*), with tourists making up many of the numbers at the well-spaced tables replete with jaw-dropping harbour views. Though many of the dishes pack some spice – such as razor clams marinated in rice wine, garlic, chilli and soy; and asparagus shoots dipped in spicy sesame crust – less fiery dishes are also served: the crispy lamb loin and pork spare ribs are both superb. You'll be reminded of the minimum HK$300 charge when you book, which you should – reservations are essential.

Mask of Si Chuen

Shop 33, G/F, East Tsim Sha Tsui KCR Station, Salisbury Road (2311 9233). East Tsim Sha Tsui KCR Station (exit K)/buses along Salisbury Road. **Open** noon-1am Mon-Sat; noon-midnight Sun. **Main courses** HK$60-$108. **Credit** AmEx, DC, MC, V. **Map** p333 C6 ➏

Though food from north-western Sichuan province is traditionally mercilessly loaded with fiery chillis and peppercorns, any dish from this newish kitchen's spicy repertoire can be toned down upon request. The restaurant name echoes the oversized Chinese opera-style decorative masks that hang over the cosy booths and tables here. Peppery fish and turnip soup is one of a few varieties served in individual sized portions. Wonderfully textured deepfried mandarin fish comes with either a thick vinegar or chilli sauce. Fried rice with egg white and plump shrimps is a crowd pleaser. Desserts include an impressive subtly flavoured green tea and lime tiramisu. Later in the evening, when traffic has died down, the outdoor tables at the entrance are a laidback place to dine. (The inconspicuous entrance is opposite the New World Centre.)

Spring Deer

1/F, 42 Mody Road (2366 4012). Tsim Sha Tsui MTR (exit D2)/buses along Nathan Road. **Open** noon-3pm, 6-11pm daily. **Main courses** HK$60-$220. **Credit** AmEx, DC, MC, V. **Map** p333 C6 ➏

There's one reason to come here: Peking duck. Almost every table orders one because it's one of the best versions in town (and reasonably priced too). Waiters scurry around with trolleys and carve the golden brown skin of the basted bird on to a platter ready for you to roll up with cucumber, celery and sweet, tangy hoisin (plum) sauce. There are plenty of other northern Chinese dishes – such as fried freshwater shrimps – but if you skip the duck you'll never forgive yourself.

Spring Moon

1/F, Peninsula Hotel, Salisbury Road (2315 3160). Tsim Sha Tsui MTR (exit E)/buses to Tsim Sha Tsui Ferry Pier & along Salisbury Road/Tsim Sha Tsui

Eat, Drink, Shop

High-calibre French cuisine meets fine wines at Alain Ducasse's **Spoon**. *See p149.*

Star Ferry Pier. **Open** 11.30am-3pm, 6-11pm daily.
Main courses HK$110-$480. **Credit** AmEx, DC,
MC, V. **Map** p333 B6/C6 ⑫
Located inside the Peninsula hotel, Spring Moon
lives up to all expectations. Classic and creative
Cantonese cuisine is served to a cultured crowd who
don't mind working through their wallet for dining
of the highest quality. Whether you plump for the
premium dim sum, roast duck or goose, abalone or
lobster, everything is magnificently done and served
up with a large helping of style.

French

Gaddi's

*1/F, Peninsula Hotel, Salisbury Road (2315 3171).
Tsim Sha Tsui MTR (exit E)/buses to Tsim Sha Tsui
Ferry Pier & along Salisbury Road/Tsim Sha Tsui
Star Ferry Pier.* **Open** noon-3pm, 7-11pm Mon-Sat.
Main courses HK$420-$880. **Credit** AmEx, DC,
MC, V. **Map** p333 B6/C6 ⑬
Note: jacket required for gents.
With more than three decades of experience and
accolades, recently appointed chef David Goodridge
has kept certain dishes – such as the 72-hour marinated foie gras confit and beef tartare – on offer at
this half-century-old fine-dining stalwart. Lighter
Mediterranean influences often appear, applied to
an outstanding quality of seafood. You can reserve
the 'chef's table' in the kitchen for lunch or dinner
and watch the man and his team in action. The dining room has an air of grandeur, but the dress code
has been somewhat relaxed of late, allowing smart-
casual for lunch and jacket (but no tie required) at
dinner. The nightly lounge singer and band are
excellent (pianist only on Mondays). For gourmands
with time, the ten-course tasting menu (HK$2,008)
shouldn't be missed, and seasonal promotional
dishes regularly feature – for example, the white
truffle dishes in October and November are simple
yet spectacular.

Spoon

*InterContinental Hotel, 18 Salisbury Road (2313
2256/www. hongkong-ic.intercontinental.com).
Tsim Sha Tsui MTR (exit E)/buses along Salisbury
Road/Tsim Sha Tsui Star Ferry Pier.* **Open**
6-11.30pm Mon-Sat; noon-2.30pm Sun. **Main
courses** HK$200-$400. **Credit** AmEx, DC, MC, V.
Map p333 C6 ⑭
French super-chef Alain Ducasse's local branch of
Spoon, which enjoys a fantastic harbourfront location, recently simplified its menu. No more complex
sauce decisions; instead, high-calibre modern French
cuisine – such as lamb salad with green apple,
steamed duck foie gras with pear and ginger chut-
ney, and sea bass with asparagus and coconut and
lemongrass sauce – meets fine wines. Sunday lunch
is now offered for HK$518 per person. Given that
this includes a glass of champagne and free flow of
four kinds of wine, alongside three courses containing five choices each, it's a great way to experience
a Ducasse restaurant. **Photo** *p148*.

Indian

Branto

*1/F, 9 Lock Road (2366 8171/www.yp.com.hk/
branto). Tsim Sha Tsui MTR (exit C1, C2)/Tsim
Sha Tsui Star Ferry Pier.* **Open** 11am-3pm, 6-11pm
daily. **Main courses** HK$35-$80. **No credit cards**.
Map p333 B6 ⑮
Vegetarian South Indian food rarely comes much
better. The masala dosa – a large crispy pancake
filled with vegetable curry, served with a selection
of relishes – is a meal in itself. Other dosas are available and so are a few Jain and Punjabi dishes. The
Tuesday lunchtime buffet, at HK$68, is worthy of a
visit. The restaurant overlooks a bustling street,
competing for attention with the Bollywood movies
playing on wall-mounted flat-screen televisions.

Gaylord

*1/F, Ashley Centre, 23-5 Ashley Road (2376 1001).
Tsim Sha Tsui MTR (exit C1, C2)/Tsim Sha Tsui
Star Ferry Pier.* **Open** noon-3pm, 6-11pm daily.
Main courses HK$88-$175. **Credit** AmEx, DC,
MC, V. **Map** p333 B6 ⑯
Rated by many as Hong Kong's best traditional
curry house, Gaylord is always packed to the rafters
with Indian diners, which is a good sign. The restaurant is more upmarket than other Kowloon curry
houses and a live Indian music trio performs every
night. As for the food, the tandoor oven cooks fish,
chicken and lamb to perfection, and the curries are
not too greasy.

Khyber Pass

*Block E, 7/F, Chungking Mansions, 36-44 Nathan
Road (2721 2786). Tsim Sha Tsui MTR (exit C1,
D1).* **Open** noon-3.30pm, 6-11.30pm Mon-Thur, Sat,
Sun; 1.45-3.30pm, 6-11.30pm Fri. **Main courses**
HK$30-$60. **No credit cards**. **Map** p333 C6 ⑰
Chungking Mansions is a labyrinth of shops, South
Asian restaurants, dirt-cheap hostels and vice. More
seedy than scary, its reputation is worse than reality.
You should, however, take all the usual precautions
if venturing inside – leave any jewellery back at the
hotel and don't flash around wads of cash; that said,
muggings are very rare. Khyber Pass is much better than most of the other Indian restaurants in
Chungking Mansions – it's clean, and curries are
dependable though basic, and cheap.

International

Aqua

*29-30/F, One Peking Road (3427 2288/www.aqua.
com.hk). Tsim Sha Tsui MTR (exit C1, E)/Tsim Sha
Tsui Star Ferry Pier.* **Open** noon-11pm Mon-Thur;
noon-1am Fri-Sun. **Main courses** *Aqua Roma*
HK$258-$308. *Aqua Tokyo* HK$188-$558. **Credit**
AmEx, DC, MC, V. **Map** p333 B6 ⑱
The stunning harbour views from almost any angle
are second to none – and the design inside is just as
captivating – at this two-in-one restaurant. The floor
is divided into Aqua Roma (Italian fare) and Aqua

Tokyo (Japanese cuisine), and the former is the clear winner. The Italian menu was revamped in 2006, with highlights including a formidable deep-fried baby artichoke, castelmagno cheese and black truffle crostini, and 'ebony' squid-ink pasta, flavoured with sea urchin, cherry tomato and garlic virgin olive oil. There's a minimum charge of HK$380 per person and reservations are essential.

Main Street Deli

Basement, Langham Hotel Hong Kong, 8 Peking Road (2375 1133/www.langhamhotels.com). Tsim Sha Tsui MTR (exit C1, E)/Tsim Sha Tsui Star Ferry Pier. **Open** 10am-10pm Mon-Thur, Sun; 10am-11pm Fri, Sat. **Main courses** HK$98-$328. **Credit** AmEx, DC, MC, V. **Map** p333 B6 ❻❾

As well as offering great New York Jewish deli-style food, much of which is available nowhere else in Hong Kong, this is also home to possibly the most luxurious speciality burgers in town. The 'gourmet lobster burger' contains a whole 450g (one pound) Canadian lobster, chopped and mixed with aged cheddar, whereas the Wagyu beef and foie gras burger speaks for itself. Both come with coleslaw and either chunky Idaho potato fries or thin sweet-potato fries and cost HK$328. Salt-beef sandwiches, potato latkes and chopped liver are commendable comfort food options.

Italian

Angelini

Mezzanine Level, Kowloon Shangri-la Hotel, 64 Mody Road (2733 8750). Tsim Sha Tsui MTR/East Tsim Sha Tsui KCR (exit P1)/buses along Salisbury Road/Tsim Sha Tsui East Ferry Pier. **Open** noon-2.30pm, 6-11pm daily. **Main courses** HK$240-$380. **Credit** AmEx, DC, MC, V. **Map** p333 C6 ❼❿

Like some of the world's best restaurants, this place sources superb ingredients and cooks them simply to allow premium natural flavour to be the focus. Every splash of olive oil, fresh herb and slice of seafood or meat, treated lightly, is designed to bowl the diner over. Highlights include sea bass and John Dory, served with Mediterranean sauces or baked. The risotto and pasta lists are long, as is the wine selection. The warm, clean-lined interior, great views across the harbour and perfect, unobtrusive service all further contribute to making this one of Hong Kong's best restaurants.

Fat Angelo's

Basement, The Pinnacle, 8 Minden Avenue (2730 4788/www.fatangelos.com). Tsim Sha Tsui MTR (exit G)/East Tsim Sha Tsui KCR (exit M2)/ buses along Nathan Road/Tsim Sha Tsui Star Ferry Pier. **Open** noon-midnight daily. **Main courses** HK$138-$218. **Credit** AmEx, DC, MC, V. **Map** p333 C6 ❼❶

Giant servings of food and a convivial ambience have made this cheap and cheerful Italian mini chain a huge success. As soon as you sit down, there are complimentary salads and hot chunks of bread to tuck in to. Mains include pasta and meat dishes, and while none is spectacular, they're decent enough. An ordinary serving is enough for two to four people, while bigger portions can feed up to eight, so be careful not to over-order. Child-friendly.

Other locations: 49A-C Elgin Street, SoHo, Central, HK Island (2973 6808); 1/F, Elizabeth House, 414 Jaffe Road, Wan Chai, HK Island (2574 6263); G/F, Wu Chung Building, 213 Queen's Road East, Wan Chai, HK Island (2126 7020).

Pan-Asian

Daidaya

2/F, Empire Hotel, 62 Kimberley Road (2367 3666). Tsim Sha Tsui MTR (exit B1, B2)/buses along Nathan Road. **Open** noon-3pm, 6-11pm daily. **Main courses** HK$80-$300. **Credit** AmEx, DC, MC, V. **Map** p333 C5 ❼❷

Daidaya serves what's known as 'fusion Japanese' – but don't let that put you off. The creative chefs are influenced by many other cuisines, including French, Korean and Italian. The 'king of kimchee' is an unusual-sounding dish that works – raw fish and vegetables are wrapped in spicy Korean pickled cabbage. Foie gras is present in several dishes, including *chawan mushi* (steamed egg custard). This is a beautifully designed restaurant, so take a little time to explore the space.

Inagiku

1/F, Royal Garden Hotel, 69 Mody Road (2733 2933/www.rghk.com.hk). Tsim Sha Tsui East MTR (exit C1)/203, 973 bus/buses along Chatham Road South & Salisbury Road. **Open** noon-3pm, 6-11pm daily. **Main courses** HK$220-$680. **Credit** AmEx, DC, MC, V. **Map** p333 C6 ❼❸

At Inagiku, in the Royal Garden Hotel, you get authentic Japanese food in exquisite, work-of-art presentations. Tempura is the speciality, but virtually everything is excellent. Sushi and sashimi come with freshly ground wasabi, which is a revelation if you've only ever had the powdered stuff – it's astonishingly delicate. Each table has a built-in sunken hotplate so that hotpot dishes can be tended to by diners as they simmer away.

Nobu

2/F, InterContinental Hotel, 18 Salisbury Road (2313 2323/www.hongkong-ic.intercontinental.com). Tsim Sha Tsui MTR (exit J2)/buses along Salisbury Road/Tsim Sha Tsui Star Ferry Pier. **Open** 6-11.30pm daily. **Main courses** HK$250-$1,080. **Credit** AmEx, DC, MC, V. **Map** p333 C6 ❼❹

At the end of 2006 big-name chef Nobu Matsuhisa, after much speculation, finally opened his first Hong Kong branch of the global Nobu chain beloved by celebrities at its US and UK incarnations. The stylish interior is notable for its undulating sea urchin ceiling – but can it distract from the superb harbour view? Modern Japanese signature dishes include fresh yellowtail sashimi with jalapeño, broiled black cod with miso, toro (fatty tuna) tartare with caviar

A fancy cuppa

Teatime in Hong Kong is an institution for many residents. The nod to colonial times past may still exist when three-tiered silver platters are served at certain hotels but cheap and cheerful eateries all over town also try to fill their tables between the lunch- and dinnertime rushes by offering reasonably priced set-tea deals.

THREE OF THE TRADITIONAL BEST

The grandmother of English teatime in Hong Kong takes place in **The Peninsula** (2315 3146 – but note that no bookings are taken, 2-7pm daily; *see also p62*), under the whirling fans of the lobby's ornate ceiling. For added class, a string quartet is visible playing up in a gallery – except Monday afternoons. The three-tiered tea tray (HK$238 for one; HK$338 for two) includes plain and raisin scones with clotted cream and house strawberry preserve. The selection of finger sandwiches and other savouries such as mini quiches and a pastry platter changes every month. From the à la carte menu, 'giant' cakes are popular, while iced chocolate and American-style milkshakes are new additions.

The **Tiffin Lounge**, on the mezzanine level at the **Grand Hyatt** (2584 7822, 3.30-6pm Mon-Fri, 1-6pm Sat – 2 sittings, 3.45-6pm Sun; *see also p57*), has a top-notch buffet menu of savouries and sweets that changes regularly. Hot dishes might include crispy lemon sole, braised *e fu* noodles or mini hamburgers. Five varieties of open sandwiches appear daily, as do scones with cream and jam, an unfeasibly wide selection of cakes and pastries, three types of sliced fresh fruit and two flavours of home-made ice-cream. Priced at HK$180 (HK$120 children) on weekdays and HK$198 (HK$138 children) on weekends, it would be easy to treat this tea as a very late lunch or early dinner if timing allows. A la carte tea options are also available. The spread is great but service could be more efficient and

courteous for this price, though the classical trio playing throughout does lift one's mood.

Relative newcomer **The Lounge**, on the lobby level of the **Four Seasons Hong Kong** (3196 8820, 3-5.30pm daily; *see also p55*), has entered the triple-tray foray with gusto. Alongside classic finger sandwiches, savouries include a delectable salmon *confit mille feuille*. Tall scones are paired with house four-berry, apricot and gooseberry jams; and there is a new take on Chinese egg tarts – that instead of egg uses dark chocolate custard. The reasonable set menu (HK$190 for one; HK$320 for two) includes a choice of 12 premium tea blends (five are caffeine-free) and a complimentary pastry refill. A trio of pianist, double bass and trombonist play on Sunday afternoons, while a pianist tinkles for the rest of the week.

CASUAL SET TEAS

One of very few bookstores to take up the US (and now European) phenomenon of an in-house coffee shop, **Commercial Press Café** (3/F, Star House, 3 Salisbury Road, Tsim Sha Tsui, Kowloon, 2904 1988, noon-8pm daily), offers afternoon respite from the mayhem of the Star Ferry and bus terminals below. The set tea on weekdays (2.30-5pm) includes Austrian coffee, or organic Chinese or herbal tea, with a savoury snack or a slice of cake for a mere HK$25.

Out of town, **Wildfire** (*see p146*) in Stanley offers a great-value set tea. For just HK$70 from 3pm to 5pm, you get a small pizza, smoked salmon canapés and a generous handful of other savouries and mini cakes with your tea or coffee.

Almost every large restaurant that serves dim sum from morning through until lunchtime will reduce its prices after 2.30pm or 3pm and continue serving till around 5pm, for those who fancy off-peak Cantonese-style afternoon tea.

and soft-shell crab roll. New creations featuring local ingredients are in constant evolution. There are plans to start serving lunch in the near future; phone ahead for details.

Seafood/fish

Island Seafood & Oyster Bar

G/F, 10 Knutsford Terrace, Kimberly Road (2312 6663/www.kingparrot.com). Tsim Sha Tsui MTR

(exit B1, B2)/buses along Nathan Road. **Open** noon-11pm daily. **Main courses** HK$160-$290. **Credit** AmEx, DC, MC, V. **Map** p333 C5 ⑦⑤
This high-ceilinged, multi-level restaurant is great not just for its food, but also for watching the people wandering by on Knutsford Terrace. The seafood and raw oysters are delicious, but there are also enough dishes to satisfy meat eaters. The oyster varieties change according to the season, but there's always an extensive choice.

Other locations: Shop C, Towning Mansion, 55-6 Paterson Street, Causeway Bay, HK Island (2915 7110).

Oyster & Wine Bar

18/F, Sheraton Hong Kong Hotel & Towers, 20 Nathan Road (2369 1111, ext 3145). Tsim Sha Tsui MTR (exit E)/buses along Nathan Road/Tsim Sha Tsui Star Ferry Pier. **Open** 6.30pm-1am Sun-Thur; 6.30pm-2am Fri, Sat. **Main courses** HK$120-$900. **Credit** AmEx, DC, V. **Map** p333 C6 **76**

The view alone is worth a visit to this place, but the oysters are the main event. Stroll over to the oyster bar and choose from the 20 or more varieties nestled in ice; the oyster captain will explain the differences and suggest in which order they should be eaten. The oysters are then shucked and rushed to your table. There are also plenty of Mediterranean and Continental European mains available, and the wine list is extensive.

Steakhouses

Morton's of Chicago

4/F, Sheraton Hong Kong Hotel & Towers, 20 Nathan Road (2732 2343/www.mortons.com). Tsim Sha Tsui MTR (exit E)/buses along Nathan Road/Tsim Sha Tsui Star Ferry Pier. **Open** 5.30-10.30pm Mon-Sat; 5-11pm Sun. **Main courses** HK$275-$590. **Credit** AmEx, DC, MC, V. **Map** p333 C6 **77**

Don't come to Morton's in search of a light meal – the portions are American-size. Steaks are excellent, whether it's filet mignon, rib-eye or the enormous porterhouse. Starters, side dishes and desserts are also huge, so those with smaller appetites – or who are on a diet – might want to share one steak and a plate of vegetables.

Ruth's Chris Steakhouse

G/F, Empire Centre, 68 Mody Road (2366 6000/ www.ruthchris.com). Tsim Sha Tsui MTR (exit D1, D2)/buses along Chatham Road. **Open** noon-11pm daily. **Main courses** HK$320-$550. **Credit** AmEx, MC, DC, V. **Map** p333 C6 **78**

As with Morton's, this New Orleans-based chain serves steak, and lots of it. The beef is top quality, which is reflected by the prices – don't come here if you're on a budget or a diet. Fortunately, you get what you pay for: the steaks are perfectly cooked, beefy and tender.

Other locations: G/F, Lippo Centre, 89 Queensway, Admiralty, HK Island (2522 9090).

The Steakhouse Wine Bar & Grill

Lower Lobby Level, InterContinental Hotel, 18 Salisbury Road (2721 1211/www. hongkong-ic. intercontinental.com). Tsim Sha Tsui MTR (exit E)/ buses along Salisbury Road/Tsim Sha Tsui Star Ferry Pier. **Open** 6-11pm daily; noon-2.30pm Sun. **Main courses** HK$290-$1,155. **Credit** AmEx, DC, MC, V. **Map** p333 C6 **79**

Prime cuts of the world's finest meat, seared to perfection on Hong Kong's only charcoal-fired grill and served with one of eight home-made sauces (classic barbecue, cabernet and shallot jus, béarnaise and forest mushroom…), make a meal here a winner. There are also a dozen specially blended mustards and if you're not already overwhelmed by too many choices, you can also select from one of the world's top ten steak knives. Char-grilled surf sides include jumbo king prawns and jumbo scallops. The oversized desserts – such as American chocolate fudge cake, New York-style cheesecake, and a stunning baked apple tart tatin with vanilla ice cream – are best shared.

Hung Hom

Pan-Asian

Robotayaki

Harbour Plaza Hotel, 20 Tak Fung Street (2621 3188/www.harbour-plaza.com). Buses to Hung Hom/Hung Hom Ferry Pier. **Open** noon-2pm, 6-10.30pm Mon-Fri daily. **Main courses** HK$80-$900. **Credit** AmEx, DC, MC, V. **Map** off p333 E5 **80**

At a *robatayaki* restaurant, you sit around a communal grill with other customers and watch the chef cook your meal. It's casual, interactive and fun, though perhaps not the ideal place for a private discussion. While this restaurant also serves other types of Japanese food – including sushi, sashimi and tempura – the *robatayaki* chef is the star here. Quite pricey.

Yau Ma Tei

Vegetarian

Light Vegetarian Restaurant

G/F, New Lucky House, 13 Jordan Road (2384 2833). Jordan MTR (exit B1, B2)/buses along Nathan Road. **Open** 11am-11pm daily. **Main courses** HK$28-$180. **Credit** DC, MC, V. **Map** p333 B4 **81**

This restaurant's mock meats are passable, but the best dishes are those that don't pretend to be anything else, like the fried beancurd and mushroom rice, and stir-fried vegetables. OK, it's not great, but while vegetarians risk finding unadvertised bits of meat in dishes in many restaurants in this part of town, at least here they can rest easy.

Kowloon City & Kowloon Tong

Chinese

House of Canton

Shop 40, LG2/F, Festival Walk, 80 Tat Chee Avenue, Kowloon Tong (2265 7888). Kowloon Tong MTR (exit C1, C2). **Open** 11am-11pm daily. **Main courses** HK$45-$160. **Credit** AmEx, DC, MC, V.

One of the most reliable Cantonese restaurants in the area, the repertoire here is predictable but well executed and politely served in a glitzy environment. Dim sum from mid-morning till early afternoon offers a particularly wide selection of steamed dumplings and other small dishes. Seafood listings are long. For a little 'wow' factor, try the flambéed 'drunken' (rice wine marinated) shrimp. Garoupa cutlet with crabmeat is another house special.

Pan-Asian

Cambo Thai Restaurant

14-15 Nga Tsin Long Road, Kowloon City (2716 7318). Bus 101, 104, 110. **Open** 11.30am-1am daily. **Main courses** HK$35-$70. **Credit** MC, V. **Map** off p332 E1 ㉜

Since the old Kai Tak airport closed there has been little reason to head out to Kowloon City, but the area remains a treasure trove of South-east Asian food if you're prepared to make the journey. What you'll find are around a dozen no-nonsense Thai restaurants, which serve the large Thai community resident here. There's not much to choose between many of them, but Cambo is popular. The chilli in the *tom yum kung* will force you to bolt upright, the fish cakes are moreish and the salads will have you reaching for the fire extinguisher.

Wing Chun Vietnamese Restaurant

18 Lion Rock Road, Kowloon City (2382 1051). Bus 101, 104, 110. **Open** 11am-11.30pm daily. **Main courses** HK$25-$65. **No credit cards**. **Map** off p332 E1 ㉝

Fast food doesn't come much speedier than it does here. But the cuisine is good enough to justify popping in, with tasty (and stomach-filling) meat and seafood dishes, often fried with lemongrass, chilli and garlic. The cold glass-noodle dishes and soft-shell crab and sesame chicken are also worth a try.

The New Territories

Central New Territories

Chinese

Royal Park Chinese Restaurant

2/F, Royal Park Hotel, 8 Pak Hok Ting Street, Sha Tin (2601 2111). Kowloon Tong MTR/Sha Tin KCR. **Open** 11am-3pm, 6-11pm Mon-Sat; 9am-3pm, 6-11pm Sun. **Main courses** HK$60-$280. **Credit** AmEx, DC, MC, V.

The nearby New Town Plaza is often overflowing with shoppers, so this hotel restaurant feels like a bit of an oasis. Cantonese standards are up for grabs here, along with some decent dim sum at the weekends. Seafood is a speciality; try the deep fried crab with crab roe.

Pan-Asian

Chung Shing Thai Curry House

G/F, 69 Tai Mei Tuk Village, Ting Kok Road, Tai Po (2664 5218). Tai Po Market KCR then 75K bus. **Open** 9am-midnight daily. **Main courses** HK$20-$138. **No credit cards.**

If you're in the New Territories and it isn't rainy season, you'll probably want to eat alfresco. The strip along this road has many options, but locals always pack this place out first. The curried crab and chilli prawns are delicious, especially when paired with a cool beer. You can't book, but the wait for a table on busy nights is worth it.

West New Territories

Indian

Shaffi's Indian Restaurant

G/F, 7 Fau Tsoi Street (off Main Road), Yuen Long (2476 7885). Tuen Mun Ferry Pier then 610, 614, 615 bus. **Open** 11am-3pm, 5.30-11pm daily. **Main courses** HK$50-$100. **Credit** DC, MC, V.

Shaffi's owner Liaqat Ali cooked for British troops at Shek Kong army barracks (as did his uncle before him); when the soldiers sailed away in 1997 after the Handover he set up on his own restaurant. Now civilians can have a taste of what they were missing: namely creamy, spicy curries that go well with big, fluffy naan breads.

East New Territories

Chinese

Sai Hing Seafood Restaurant

Shops 1 & 2, G/F, Fiu Yat Building, Hoi Pung Square, Sai Kung (2792 1481). Choi Hung MTR (exit C2) then 1A minibus. **Open** 6am-11.30pm daily. **Main courses** HK$48-$120. **Credit** AmEx, DC, MC, V.

This restaurant regularly draws Hong Kong expats for dependable, sometimes spicier, seafood dishes alongside Cantonese preparations. Try the fried king prawn with garlic and chilli or choose from a variety of fish species simmered in lemongrass and chilli and accompanied by stir-fried morning glory enhanced with fish sauce and shrimp paste.

Tung Kee Restaurant

96-102 Man Nin Street, Sai Kung (2792 7453). Choi Hung MTR (exit C2) then 1A minibus. **Open** 11am-11pm daily. **Main courses** HK$50-$120. **Credit** AmEx, DC, MC, V.

Sai Kung's waterfront is typical of South China Sea ports – junks bobbing in the harbour filled with old fishermen hawking the day's catch, tanks (over-) filled with a range of exotic sea creatures, and screeching restaurateurs begging you to dine at one of the hundreds of alfresco tables. Tung Kee can on

Eat, Drink, Shop

occasion be hit or miss with both the quality of food and service but generally serves up a decent meal.

Indian

Dia Indian Restaurant
Shop 2, Sai Kung Building, 42-56 Fuk Man Road, Sai Kung (2791 4466). Choi Hung MTR (exit C2) then 1A minibus. **Open** 11am-3pm Mon-Fri; 11am-11pm Sat, Sun. **Main courses** HK$58-$88. **Credit** AmEx, MC, V.

The Curry Hut was for a long time the only option for lovers of Indian cuisine in Sai Kung. Dia's, with its soothing blue and bamboo decor, is a welcome newcomer to the scene, offering good (if perhaps a little pricey) subcontinental food.

International

Jaspas
G/F, 13 Sha Tsui Path, Sai Kung (2792 6388). Choi Hung MTR (exit C2) then 1A minibus. **Open** 8.30am-10.30pm daily. **Main courses** HK$60-$180. **Credit** AmEx, MC, V.

For Australian-style food in Sai Kung – head to this laid-back spot. Portions are big, the staff friendly and welcoming, and the food flavourful and plentiful. The menu features plenty of seafood, cooked here with light, Asian influences, though the Peking duck pancake rolls are pure Asian. The signature dish of Beijing sits alongside Western salads, goat's cheese in filo pastry and the like.
Other locations: 28 Staunton Street, SoHo, Central, HK Island (2869 0733).

Italian

Pepperoni's
1592 Po Tung Road, Sai Kung (2791 1738/2869 1766/city-wide deliveries 2792 2083/www. pepperonis.com.hk). Choi Hung MTR (exit C2) then 1A minibus. **Open** 10.30am-11pm daily. **Main courses** HK$95-$125. **Credit** AmEx, MC, V.

Now a large chain with outlets across Hong Kong, the Pepperoni's concept began in Sai Kung more than a decade ago. The recipe for its success: big portions of old favourites like nachos, spaghetti carbonara, deep-fried calamari, pork knuckle and an exotic array of pizzas. It's all filling and pretty tasty.
Other locations: throughout the city.

Modern European

Sauce
9 Sha Tsui Path, Sai Kung (2791 2348). Choi Hung MTR (exit C2) then 1A minibus/Hang Hau MTR then 101 minibus. **Open** 11am-10pm Mon-Fri, Sun; 10am-11pm Sat. **Main courses** HK$82-$135. **Credit** AmEx, MC, V.

Sai Kung's Sha Tsui Path is always a great place to watch the world go by, but now this welcome addition has made it even better. The restaurant excels at the basics – serving up top-notch, delicious European fare (including fresh pasta dishes and hearty desserts such as sticky toffee pudding), tasteful decor, outdoor seating, friendly service and a value-for-money wine list. There's live music on Friday nights.

Forget Peking duck, **Bookworm Café** is meat-free and proud of it. *See p157.*

Superior pub grub

There was a time not too long ago when pub and bar menus felt like something of an afterthought in Hong Kong. Drinks were (and still are) where the biggest profits were to be had in watering holes. So why offer more than fish and chips, the local favourite of fried chicken wings, occasionally nachos or, in fact, anything salty, oily and maybe a bit spicy to get the punters guzzling faster?

Fortunately, an increasing number of establishments seem to have asked themselves this question. British-style pubs such as **Bulldogs** (G/F, 17 Lan Kwai Fong, Central, HK Island, 2523 3528, www.lankwaifong.com) and **Bar George** (*see p162*) have raised the bar in terms of 'pub grub'. Yes, fish and chips and bangers and mash are still on the menu but the quality has vastly improved, and Bar George has added excellent salads and stews. The environment, too, in pubs such as these and **The Keg** (52 D'Aguilar Street, Central, HK Island, 2810 0369) is as down to earth as a pub should be but with an eye for a bit of style. The Keg, as its name suggests, is actually shaped like the interior of a wooden beer barrel. Here, the menu draws from recently revamped offerings of its affiliate bar next door, **Stormies** (G/F, 46-50 D'Aguilar Street, Lan Kwai Fong, Central, HK Island, 2549 4467, www.lankwaifong.com), which means that both establishments are now dishing up well-above-average fare with a seafood bent, in addition to top-notch versions of pub grub.

Along with the spate of Irish pubs that arrived since the late '90s came something of an interest in Irish fare. **Delaney's** (*see p165*) does a great beef-and-Guinness pie and 'champ' (mashed and baked) spuds. The recently opened new branch of **Dublin Jack** (*see p163*) does a fancy fried chorizo with spinach as one of its nods to modern Dublin cuisine. **McSorleys** (55 Elgin Street, Central, HK Island, 2522 2646,

www.mcsorleys.com.hk), another newish arrival, has deliberately gone a tad more sophisticated, with its branch in fashionable SoHo offering a smoked salmon starter and seven types of 'gourmet burger'.

George & Co (G/F, The Park Lane Hotel, 310 Gloucester Road, Causeway Bay, HK Island, 2839 3377) ups the ante too. Though not the only hotel pub in town, this one feels more like a casual lounge bar. Its menu includes a sushi starter platter and unbelievably deluxe nachos – covered in grilled cheddar, sour cream and guacamole and served with a supreme chopped-steak chilli con carne. In the same neighbourhood, the evening menu at **Dicken's Bar** (Excelsior Hotel, 281 Gloucester Road, Causeway Bay, HK Island, 2837 6782) is not much to rave about but its weekday lunch curry buffet (noon-2.30pm) and weekend brunch buffet (11.30am-4pm) are above-average spreads. Also in Causeway Bay, **Inn Side Out** (G/F, 10 Hysan Avenue, Causeway Bay, HK Island, 2895 2900) offers possibly the most tender barbecued ribs in Hong Kong, best enjoyed at its alfresco tables. The rest of its menu may be more hit than miss but it's hardly gourmet fare.

The gastropub phenomenon has not really taken off in Hong Kong. The sole exception to this is **The Phoenix** (*see p133*), which has taken up the mantle of quality no-nonsense interpretations of traditional and Mediterranean-inspired Brit cuisine; expect the best in pies and liver and onions here, alongside a premium ale or glass of wine.

The **Chinnery Bar** (*see p162*) offers perhaps the most refined of all pub grub, so much so that it seems bizarre to define it as such. Fish pie, for instance, conceals salmon, haddock and prawn under a potato crust, and beef Stroganoff pairs fine sirloin with mushrooms. The bread pudding with rum sauce puts the streamed puds on other pub menus to shame.

Seafood/fish

Anthony's Catch

G/F, Lot 1826B, Po Tung Road, Sai Kung (2792 8474). Choi Hung MTR (exit C2) then 1A minibus. **Open** 6-10pm Mon-Wed; 6pm-midnight Thur-Sat; 10.30am-3.30pm, 6pm-midnight Sun. **Main courses** HK$130-$250. **Credit** AmEx, MC, V.

So many of the Western restaurants in the Sai Kung area are characterised by friendly service, big portions and comfortable surroundings; and this place is no exception. Try to come here on a Sunday if you can, when Anthony's does a champagne brunch (HK$200). There are far worse ways to while away a lazy Sunday afternoon than with unlimited bubbly to drink (a California sparkler rather than real French champagne) and some delicious food,

Chinese cuisines

Chinese people are renowned for eating practically anything. In practice, this means anything that's not poisonous. This extends to some items most of us wouldn't immediately think of as being edible, such as bird's nests, snakes' blood and turtle shells. China is huge, and producing enough food to feed so many people (1.3 billion at the last count) is difficult. And while some ingredients might once have been used out of necessity, skilled Chinese chefs have turned them into delicacies.

In the West, people would never say, 'Let's go out for European food' – instead, they would specify French, Italian, German or whatever. In the same way, Chinese people in Hong Kong don't say, 'Let's go out for Chinese food' – they pin it down to Cantonese, Shanghainese, Sichuanese and so on. Cuisines from most provinces of China are available in Hong Kong, although some are more popular than others.

CANTONESE AND HONG KONG

Hong Kong is made up mostly of Chinese people from the south (Guangdong province), from the city previously known as Canton (now Guangzhou). It's not surprising, then, that the most popular cuisine in Hong Kong is Cantonese. In this type of cooking, the freshness of ingredients is paramount and cooking techniques (especially steaming) are evolved to highlight this freshness. Because subtlety of flavours is so important, Cantonese cooks use a light, delicate hand with seasonings. To those who prefer more robust flavours, Cantonese food might seem bland.

Many restaurants show exactly how fresh their seafood is by displaying it alive in large tanks. The variety is extensive, not just the expected fish, lobsters, crabs, prawns and scallops, but also more unusual items such as squilla (called 'pissing prawns' because they squirt water), horseshoe crabs and foot-long cuttlefish. The fish and seafood are ordered, scooped from the tank and brought in nets to the table so guests can inspect their order for liveliness. The 'victim' is then taken to the kitchen to be dispatched and cooked, often by steaming. Fish is steamed with soy sauce and shredded ginger; after it's removed from the steamer, it is covered with spring onions and fresh coriander and hot oil is poured over to wilt the vegetables. Scallops in their shells (with the roe still attached) and baby long-necked clams are cooked in a similar method, sometimes with fried garlic, in place of spring onions, while fresh abalone is steamed with black beans.

Another traditional Cantonese cooking technique (although it's used all over China) is stir-frying, which seals in the flavour of

---

such as waffles with maple syrup and fresh fruit. For something different, there's also live folk music every Thursday.

The Outlying Islands

Lamma

Chinese

Han Lok Yuen
16-17 Hung Shing Ye (2982 0680). Yung Shue Wan Ferry Pier then walk. **Open** 11am-9pm daily. **Main courses** HK$46-$96. **Credit** AmEx, MC, V.
The short hike from Lamma's main beach to this hillside eatery is well worth it, even in the summer heat. It's nicknamed the 'pigeon restaurant' after its speciality dish, and the roast pigeon is the best in Hong Kong. Chris Patten, known by the Chinese as Fei Pang ('Fatty Patten'), regularly made the trek. Drunken pigeon (cooked, marinated in Chinese wine

and served chilled) is also recommended. Minced quail eaten in rolled-up lettuce leaves is also delicious, as are the vegetable dishes.

Lamcombe
G/F, 47 Main Street, Yung Shue Wan (2982 0881). Yung Shue Wan Ferry Pier. **Open** 11am-2.30pm, 5-10.15pm Mon-Fri; 11am-10.15pm Sat, Sun. **Main courses** HK$55-$160. **Credit** AmEx, MC, V.
Choose a table inside on one of Lamcombe's cosy two floors or dine on its small stepped terraces, which jut into the lapping tide. Favoured by an international mix of local Lamma residents, Lamcombe dishes up well-cooked Cantonese food – seafood's a speciality – for fair prices. Steamed beancurd with scallop and shrimp, that sets like a pudding, is a house favourite. There is a small wine selection on offer or you can bring your own bottle (HK$40 corkage fee).

Man Fung Seafood Restaurant
5 Main Street, Yung Shue Wan (2982 0719). Yung Shue Wan Ferry Pier. **Open** 10am-10pm daily. **Main courses** HK$42-$180. **Credit** AmEx, MC, V.

foods by cooking it quickly over high heat for no more than a minute. Much prized by the discerning diner is *wok hay*, which translates as the 'breath of a wok' – an elusive aroma and flavour that comes when a skilled chef cooks in a well-seasoned wok.

The most popular meat for most Chinese (except those who belong to the Muslim or Jewish faiths) is pork. Cantonese cooks marinate long strips of slightly fatty pork in a sweet and savoury sauce and then barbecue the meat to make *char siu*, or else they roast whole pigs until the skin becomes blistered and crisp. Both of these are commonly available at roast meat shops that also sell soy sauce chicken and roast duck or goose. Even the best home cooks will rarely make any of these meats, preferring to leave it to the experts.

Because Hong Kong is affluent compared with most of mainland China, and is also more influenced by other Asian countries and the West, many agree that it has developed a cuisine of its own. Hong Kong cuisine takes the form of Cantonese dishes that incorporate less-than-traditional ingredients. Some unusual dishes you'll find here include crab or shrimp and mayonnaise in fried dumplings, and lobster with cheese sauce and noodles. Outside influences are also seen in the so-called Hong Kong-Western restaurants, which combine rather old-fashioned Russian, British, American and 'Continental' cuisine in an unusual way. The menus have borscht and chicken Kiev, steaks covered in brown sauce served on sizzling platters and accompanied by spaghetti in tomato sauce, and for dessert, Black Forest gateau or crème brûlée.

SHANGHAINESE

This is probably the second-most popular cuisine in Hong Kong. Shanghainese people tend to be wealthy, and many government officials, including the former Chief Executive, Tung Chee-hwa, are originally from Shanghai. The cuisine, too, is rich, both in flavour and texture.

Heavy, unctuous brown sauces are used for braising meats such as pork shanks or knuckle, or to simmer fatty pork balls with vegetables. Dumplings are popular, and very different from the lighter Cantonese variety. The most famous Shanghainese dumplings are *xiao long bao*, which are filled with pork and flavourful broth made solid with gelatine. The gelatine melts in the heat of the steamer and fills the interior of the dumpling with liquid. They're then dipped in a sauce made with Shanghainese brown vinegar and shreds of ginger.

This unusual vinegar is an essential flavouring to other dishes – it's an ingredient

▶

Lamma's busiest harbour, Yung Shue Wan is lined with Cantonese seafood restaurants – and its view of fishing boats and junks is more picturesque than Sok Kwu Wan. Man Fung is the first one you reach from the ferry pier and probably the best (and priciest). Here you'll find live crabs, prawns and fish swimming in tanks – just pick out the one you want, and minutes later it'll turn up sizzling hot on a plate. The delicious house speciality is crab sticky rice hotpot.

Rainbow Seafood

16-20 First Street, Sok Kwu Wan (2982 8100/ www.rainbowrest.com.hk). Sok Kwu Wan Ferry Pier/free private ferry from Central or Tsim Sha Tsui (see website for schedule). **Open** 10am-11pm daily. **Main courses** HK$60-$300. **Credit** AmEx, DC, MC, V.

Sok Kwu Wan is the less-populous end of Lamma, with fewer expats and bars. Many daytrippers come here specifically for lunch or dinner at the row of waterfront seafood restaurants lying immediately next to the ferry pier. There are tanks filled with live lobsters, fish of many colours and all manner of sea creatures clambering over one another in a vain attempt to escape the chef's hands.

Italian

Pizza Milano

Flat A, G/F, 2nd Back Street, Yung Shue Wan (2982 4848). Yung Shue Wan Ferry Pier. **Open** 6-11.30pm Mon-Fri; noon-11.30pm Sat, Sun. **Main courses** HK$65-$80. **No credit cards**.

This casual open-air trattoria has been a Lamma favourite for years. Of the thin crust pizzas on offer, the seafood version is excellent; the pasta and salad options are also satisfying. Beers and wine are both reasonably priced.

Vegetarian

Bookworm Café

79 Main Street, Yung Shue Wan (2982 4838/www. bookwormcafe.com.hk). Yung Shue Wan Ferry Pier.

in some braising sauces and stir-fries and is drizzled over seafood, including delicate freshwater shrimp.

While the main starch of Chinese from the South is rice, the Shanghainese prefer bread to accompany their dishes. The poetically named 'silver threads' bread (so called because the interior dough is formed into long, thin strands and then wrapped in a flat sheet of dough) is subtly sweet and comes either steamed or fried; the former is better for sopping up juices.

Shanghainese also specialise in so-called 'cold dishes', which are not actually cold, but room temperature or tepid. They're most often eaten as an appetiser but are so delicious and varied it's easy to make an entire meal of them. They include jellyfish flavoured with sesame oil, mashed soybeans with preserved vegetables, sweet and crispy fried eel, and 'drunken' chicken or pigeon, which has been marinated in rice wine until the flavour permeates the meat.

SICHUANESE

Most people think of Sichuan food as hot and spicy, although this isn't always the case – it's more that it has strong flavours. When chillies (both dried and fresh) are used, they're usually paired with tiny, reddish-brown Sichuan peppercorns, which have a unique, numbing/tingling effect on the tongue. Sichuan food is hearty and rich, with sauces that ideally blend sweet, sour and spicy flavours. Hot and sour soup is probably the Sichuanese dish best known in the West – it combines vinegar, pepper and chillies to make a powerful, sinus-clearing broth. Dumplings and breads are also popular in Sichuanese cuisine. Plain steamed buns are usually served with tea-smoked duck; meat dumplings look similar to Cantonese won ton, but instead of being served in a subtle broth, they're smothered in a sauce of soy, garlic and chillies.

BEIJING

Beijing has been the capital of China since the time of the emperors, and, as such, developed an imperial cuisine. Unfortunately, much of this highly developed, intricate cuisine was lost during Mao's 'Great Leap Forward' in the late 1950s. Some restaurants in Hong Kong serve an abbreviated version of imperial Beijing banquets, but they are hard to come by.

Beijing cuisine is rich and oily. Lamb and mutton are popular, and stir-fried slivers of meat and vegetables are frequently served stuffed into pockets of sesame-coated baked breads. The cuisine's most famous dish is Peking duck. It is always served with great ceremony by a white-gloved waiter carving off

Open 10am-9pm Mon-Wed, Fri; 9am-10pm Sat; 9am-9pm Sun. **Main courses** HK$40-$80. **Credit** MC, V. Bookworm is as right-on as you can get. Everything is vegetarian and organic, although the food is basic – beans on toast and poached eggs both feature on the menu. It can feel a bit like New Age overload, but at least it's downright cheap. **Photo** *p154.*

Lantau

International

Stoep

32 Lower Cheung Sha Beach (2980 2699/9465 9226). Tung Chung MTR then 3M, 13, A35 bus/Mui Wo Ferry Pier then any bus (except 7) towards Lower Cheung Sha Beach. **Open** 10am-10pm Tue-Sun. **Main courses** HK$45-$150. **No credit cards.**
Stoep enjoys the best location in Hong Kong – slap bang on one of the most beautiful stretches of sand. Food is served alfresco, and South African-inspired barbecued meats are the speciality, although there are also plenty of Mediterranean dishes and a reasonably priced wine list. Its homemade breads are legendary. The place to go if you're looking for peace on Lantau, or just generally.

Middle Eastern

Bahce

G/F, 19 Mui Wo Centre, Ngan Wan Road, Mui Wo (2984 0222). Tung Chung MTR then 3, 3M bus/Mui Wo Ferry Pier. **Open** 11.30am-10pm Mon-Fri; 10am-10pm Sat, Sun. **Main courses** HK$62-$284. **No credit cards.**
Billing itself as 'Turkish restaurant café bar', Bahce seems to cover all bases well. Drop in on a Friday evening and the place is abuzz with a mix of local residents of various nationalities, clasping pints or bottles of beer and nibbling on a selection of meze dishes. Fish and lamb kebabs come with salad, a choice of pitta bread or seasoned rice and two dips (from a choice of four). It's also an excellent spot for weekend breakfasts.

the deep, mahogany-coloured skin, wrapping the pieces in a thin pancake with a dab of plum sauce and a sliver of spring onion. When it's good, the skin is the best part of the duck – it should be crisp, flavourful and with just a hint of fat. Traditionally, the meat comes as a separate course – usually stir-fried with vegetables – while the bones are simmered into soup and served at the end of the meal.

CHIU CHOW

The Chiu Chow region of south-east Guangdong province in home to a popular Cantonese splinter cuisine. It's easy to recognise Chiu Chow restaurants – they always have whole cooked goose, crabs and other pre-cooked dishes displayed at the front. These dishes are served at room temperature – never hot. The goose is simmered in a strong broth, chopped to order and served with a sauce of garlicky white vinegar; the same dipping sauce is used for the flower crabs (so called because of the pattern on the shells).

One characteristic of Chiu Chow cuisine is pickled vegetables, which are eaten as a condiment or cooked with other ingredients. The chefs make extensive use of finely ground white pepper, which flavours soups and other dishes. A small shaker of white pepper is always served alongside the typical Chiu Chow dish of *ho jai jook* (rice congee with preserved vegetables and small oysters). These small oysters are also used in oyster omelettes, which again are served with white pepper.

HAKKA

The Hakka are a nomadic group of people, many of whom ultimately settled in Hong Kong (they can be seen mostly in the New Territories farmlands – they're easily recognised by their distinctive triangular straw hats).

There's nothing particularly subtle about Hakka cuisine – it's oily and flavourful. Because Hakka people were traditionally poor, their cuisine makes great use of inexpensive ingredients, especially offal. A popular dish is *jah dai cheung* – lengths of pig's intestine, sometimes stuffed with whole spring onions, and fried so it has a crackling crisp exterior. Fresh pork belly is braised with preserved vegetables or taro. The most famous Hakka dish is salt-baked chicken – a whole chicken is wrapped in paper, buried in salt and baked, which seals in the flavour. It's served with two dipping sauces – one made with thick sesame paste and the other with spring onions, ginger and oil.

Vegetarian

Chinese Vegetarian Restaurant

Po Lin Monastery, Ngong Ping, Po Lin (2985 5248). Tung Chung MTR then 23 bus or Ngong Ping 360 cable-car/Mui Wo Ferry Pier then 2 bus. **Open** 11.30am-4.30pm daily. **Main courses** HK$60-$100. **Credit** MC, V.
No visit to Po Lin Monastery would be complete without a trip to the Chinese Vegetarian Restaurant, where there is a vast buffet of vegetarian delights. For less than HK$100 you can gorge yourself on bean curd, mock-meat dishes and a wide range of vegetables.

Cheung Chau

Chinese

East Lake Restaurant

85 Tung Wan Road (2981 3869). Cheung Chau Ferry Pier then 10mins walk. **Open** 10am-9pm Mon-Fri; 10am-10pm Sat, Sun. **Main courses** HK$40-$180. **No credit cards**.
East Lake is situated in the main village cluster of Cheung Chau. This friendly family restaurant offers an eclectic Cantonese menu alongside a selection of seafood and fish. Stir-fried shrimp or chicken with vegetables is a tasty house favourite, and there are heaps of meat, bean curd and veggie dishes and soups available too.

International

Morocco's/India Curry House

G/F, 71 San Hing Praya Street (2986 9767). Cheung Chau Ferry Pier. **Open** noon-2am daily. **Main courses** HK$52-$100. **No credit cards**.
If you're not quite sure what your tastebuds are after, Morocco's/India Curry House is an odd but useful eatery. 'Jack of all trades' springs to mind when looking at the menu, which covers all the bases from standard British pub grub to decent Indian curries – but it's the reliable Thai food that the regulars wisely go for.

Eat, Drink, Shop

Pubs & Bars

Quaff in the company of refreshingly unpretentious punters,
whether in a swish lounge bar or a no-nonsense pub.

Drinking establishments come and go at a
similar speed to restaurants in this city –
fast. Another similarity, though, is that those
establishments that really fill a niche seem to
endure. Some stalwarts may be freshened up a
tad but there are a few that, thankfully, remain
popular and mostly intact.

Whether in a swanky lounge bar or an earthy
watering hole, you'll usually be drinking
alongside an international crowd of Hong Kong-
based patrons. In many places in Hong Kong,
it's a lot easier to get chatting to strangers than
in urban European and US bars, where the
crowd might be suspicious of chatter or just
plain not interested. Many a dressed-up gal or
guy sipping a cocktail at an über-chic bar here
will crack a smile if greeted with affable
repartee by a friendly stranger.

Whatever time of day or night, there's always
somewhere to drink in Hong Kong. In recent
years the city's bar scene has undergone a not-
so-quiet revolution, with new wine bars, theme
pubs and restaurant bars cropping up all over
the place. Many are stylish, comfortable spaces
with glass- and open-fronted bars, often making
for great people-watching.

A night out on the town, however, comes at
a price. When people first arrive in Hong Kong
and order a round of drinks, the cost often
makes them splutter out their first mouthful.
A long night of drinking can leave you nursing
not only a hangover but an economic depression.
While cocktail prices are comparable to those
in major world cities, beers often cost double
international pub prices. A swanky bar or club
might sting you for upwards of HK$90 for a
fancy martini, but spirits are still around HK$40
to HK$50 in most places, while a pint often costs
HK$55 or more and bottled beer not much less.

An astute drinker, though, can cut the cost
of an evening out by almost half. Happy hours
are very popular in Hong Kong and – contrary
to the name – usually run for a long part of the
day or evening. Each place has a different
happy-hour schedule, so you can find cheap
drinks somewhere at pretty much any time of
day or night. Happy hour in Hong Kong usually
means cut-price drinks – they're often slashed
by about 30 per cent, though in some places it
means two drinks for the price of one – but in a
few bars it only means regular prices but with
complimentary bar snacks. House policies vary,
so check with bar staff before ordering.

NAME YOUR POISON

In terms of beers, San Miguel and Carlsberg are
local favourites, once brewed in Hong Kong but
now fermented north of the border; the former,
whether on tap or in a bottle, has a tendency to
taste overly chemical and to leave your head
pounding in the morning. Tsing Tao (made at a
German-modelled brewery in China) is popular
and easygoing, while Heineken appears to have
won the battle of the imports – it's often priced
the same as local brews in bars and tastes
better. Recently popular tap beers include Stella
Artois and Warsteiner lagers, wheat beers such
as Hoegaarden, and dark beers. Irish bars, of
course, serve Kilkenny and Guinness (minus the
Irish water as it's brewed in Malaysia, but the
taste is still pretty authentic). Although local
microbreweries do exist, they haven't had a big
impact yet. Hong Kong's premier small-scale
operation – Hong Kong Brewing Company –
recently began to produce the new and tasty
Lan Kwai Fong lager and Aldrich Bay pale ale.

Wine is expensive by global standards, as
excessive import duties have been placed on it
by the cash-strapped (and presumably teetotal)
local government. Not all bars have a good
choice of wines, but there are more places
springing up offering a decent range by the
glass. Cocktails tend to be well made and often
give better value than standard spirits and
mixers, since you get two or three shots in a
glass for just a few extra dollars.

DRINKING BY DISTRICT

Although you can find a watering hole in just
about any part of town, there are several
districts with thriving bar and restaurant
subcultures. A bar crawl here can include ten
very different types of joint in just one block.
(For something that requires a bit more effort,
try our swanky alternative bar crawl; see p166
A higher crawling.)

► Pink numbers '❶' given in this chapter
correspond to the location of each pub
and bar as marked on the street maps.
See pp328-333.

Hong Kong's best-known drinking area is **Lan Kwai Fong** (LKF) in Central. Over the past two decades or so it has grown from a cluster of rag-trade go-downs to a world-class entertainment centre. There's a huge variety of bars and eateries here, most under the ownership of tycoon Allan Zeman – often dubbed 'Mr Lan Kwai Fong' – who kick-started the whole thing in the late 1980s. It's a good place to start for first-time visitors, since every taxi driver knows it and everything is clustered together. Although centred on the street called Lan Kwai Fong, the district also includes adjoining **D'Aguilar Street**, **Wo On Lane** and **Wing Wah Lane**. It's busy every night, when no traffic is allowed, so drinkers have ample staggering space. The downside is that it seems to comprise mainly expense-account suits and well-to-do expats, as trendier bar-hoppers venture further afield.

A short lurch from Lan Kwai Fong takes you to **SoHo** (which in Hong Kong is the somewhat forced abbreviation of 'south of Hollywood Road') – centred around **Staunton Street** and **Elgin Street**, which cut across the Mid-Levels Escalator. As LKF became clichéd and somewhat overpriced, SoHo took over as the most vibrant and happening hotspot. Over the past decade, though, SoHo has seen a similar exponential growth to what LKF experienced. Most of the old Chinese ceramic, dried-food and mortician shops have been replaced by bars and restaurants as rents skyrocketed. The area has grown and most surrounding roads are now part of SoHo; indeed, the bit downhill, to the north of Hollywood Road (**NoHo**), is also getting in on the act, especially cobbled **Pottinger Street**. SoHo shuts down earlier than LKF, as restrictive licensing authorities have set midnight – or 2am for some privileged establishments – as the curfew to protect local residents from noise. NoHo, Hollywood Road itself and Wyndham Street above Lan Kwai Fong all stay open till later.

Wan Chai is the other main bar area on Hong Kong Island. A gradual facelift has seen an increase in upmarket bars here – a far cry from the endless girlie-bar strip it once was (a few still remain), but it continues to be one of the liveliest parts of town to drink. If you like to let your hair down or are out on the pull, this is where you should go. Also worth checking out nearby are **Causeway Bay** – particularly around Yiu Wa Street (behind the Times Square mall), frequented mainly by trendy locals – and **Happy Valley**, which offers a range of quieter, more intimate watering holes.

In Kowloon, bustling **Tsim Sha Tsui** used to be the heart of Hong Kong's nightlife. From the 1980s it fell into something of a decline but

recently, a cluster of bars and restaurants on **Knutsford Terrace** and nearby **Knutsford Steps** has added colour. **Ashley Road** has also picked up, although the cul-de-sac is grim looking, with its motorcycle parking area and vans often blocking the road. Local traders have been campaigning to get the street pedestrianised for the past few years.

Hong Kong Island

Central

Some of the posher hotel bars in Central are included in our upscale pub crawl – *see p166* **A higher crawling**.

 Bars

Agave
Kick into action with the best Margaritas in town and – at well over 200 – the biggest range of tequila outside North America. *See p162.*

Bar George
The best take on a British pub in town – earthy in atmosphere, with a decent, unpretentious menu. *See p162.*

China Bear
Steps from the ferry pier, this Lantau pub has a friendly vibe and prices – plus an ocean view. *See p169.*

Chinnery Bar
Sink into a deep armchair and savour one of 200-plus single-malt Scotch whiskies, in a cosy wood-panelled interior. *See p162.*

Delaney's
A Hong Kong Irish institution with top pub grub and Guinness. *See p165.*

Felix
Its Long Table bar may be one of the world's coolest cocktail spots but it's the men's loo – with a Kowloon panorama – that gets everyone talking. *See p168.*

Lotus
Cutting-edge cocktails and Thai food in minimalist but warm surroundings. *See p163.*

1/5
Where the glitterati sip champagne through a straw on weekends. *See p165.*

Eat, Drink, Shop

Agave

33 D'Aguilar Street, Lan Kwai Fong (2521 2010).
Central MTR (exit D1, D2)/12M, 13, 23A, 40M bus.
Open 5pm-2am Mon-Thur, Sun; 5pm-4am Fri, Sat.
Credit AmEx, DC, MC, V. **Map** p328 C4 ❶
Mexican beers, such as Modelo or Dos Equis, which
both come in light or dark brews, make favourable
companions to some of the tastiest chilli-filled tacos
and quesadillas in town. But if it's strictly a
tequila blast you're after, you've definitely come to
the right place. There are 200-plus varieties here,
which accounts for Agave being one of the constant
party hubs in the LKF neighbourhood, on any
night of the week. Margaritas, served in bowl-like
glasses, and other tequila-based cocktails and
slammers account for a smiley and, later at night,
rather raucous patronage.
Other locations: G/F, Beverly House, 93-107
Lockhart Road, Wan Chai (2866 3228).

Baby Buddha

18 Wo On Lane, Lan Kwai Fong (2167 7244).
Central MTR (exit D1, D2)/12M, 13, 23A, 40M bus.
Open 5pm-2.30am Mon-Thur; 5pm-4.30am Fri; 6pm-
4.30am Sat; 8pm-2am Sun. **Credit** AmEx, DC, MC, V.
Map p328 C4 ❷
After the success of Claude Challe's Buddha Bar in
Paris, the god's name has been taken in vain by bars
and clubs worldwide. Baby Buddha, born in early
2003, is as small as the name implies. It's an open-
fronted bar, occupying what was once a tiny alley,
and borders a small, recently redeveloped public
square that leads up to Pottinger Street. It can be a
bit chilly during the winter but the laid-back vibe
more than compensates.

Bar George

*G/F, 46 D'Aguilar Street, Lan Kwai Fong (2521
2202). Central MTR (exit D1, D2)/12M, 13, 23A,
40M bus.* **Open** 3pm-2am Mon-Thur; 3pm-4am Fri,
Sat; 3pm-1am Sun. **Credit** AmEx, DC, MC, V.
Map p328 C4 ❸
Named after George Charles D'Aguilar, the 19th-
century commander-in-chief of the Royal forces and
deputy governor of Hong Kong, this Brit joint
nonetheless has a few contemporary touches,
including a dance floor and DJ booth. Bitters, ciders
and wheat beer make an appearance among the five
draft options and abundance of bottles. Alongside
gastro-pub-like dishes such as smoked salmon
Caesar salad, the lengthy menu has plenty of home-
made dishes, including an authentic northern UK
chippie option of curry sauce with chips. *See also*
p155 **Superior pub grub**.

Blue Bar

*Lobby Level One, Four Seasons Hong Kong, 8
Finance Street (3196 8830). Central MTR (exit A).*
Open 7am-1am Tue-Thur, Sun; 7am-2am Fri, Sat.
Credit AmEx, DC, MC, V. **Map** p329 D2 ❹
Defying workaholic Hong Kong, this joint is
jumping when the 'Blue Hour' kicks off at 5.30pm
and a small spread of Indian and Mediterranean
snacks is laid on. The banker crowd soon disperses,

though, leaving behind a more sedate and relaxed
atmosphere in this minimalist and mildly blue-
tinged bar that overlooks the harbour. Signature
drinks include no fewer than 88 house cocktails that
are all coloured… blue – the Blue Ferrari packs a
sweet punch, loaded with vodka, blue Curaçao and
Amaretto – but the extensive list of mixers includes
other colours too. Award-winning ENA (whose
initials remain a mystery) features fresh pomelo and
strawberry, with lychee liqueur, vodka and soda.
The mocktail list is also impressive.

Boca

65 Peel Street, SoHo (2548 1717/www.boca.com.hk).
Central MTR (exit D1, D2)/Mid-Levels Escalator/
buses along Caine Road. **Open** 5pm-2am daily.
Credit AmEx, DC, MC, V. **Map** p328 B3 ❺
The choice of wines by the glass here is among the
best in Hong Kong, and the tapas (both traditional
and fusion) are pretty good too. But what makes
Boca stand out above everything are its sumptuous
couches and seats, on which you can idle away
many pleasant hours; weekend afternoons are prime
chilling-out times. Tables by its open front make for
good people-watching.

Chinnery Bar

*1/F, Mandarin Oriental, 5 Connaught Road Central
(2825 4001/www.mandarinoriental.com). Central
MTR (exit F)/buses along Connaught Road.* **Open**
11am-11pm daily. **Credit** AmEx, DC, MC, V.
Map p329 E3 ❻
The genteel, wood-panelled and -beamed Chinnery
Bar, with its mahogany tables, deep armchairs and
200-plus premium single-malt Scotch whiskies, is a
rare environment for Hong Kong, and something of
a legend. A variety of beer is served in silver
tankards – regulars, and there are many, hang theirs
above the bar counter. The wine list is impressive
and top-notch renditions of British home-style fare
is served (*see p155* **Superior pub grub**).

Club Feather Boa

*38 Staunton Street, SoHo (2857 2586). Mid-Levels
Escalator/12M, 13, 23A, 26, 40M bus.* **Open** 8pm-
midnight Mon-Thur, Sun; 5pm-midnight Fri, Sat.
Credit AmEx, DC, MC, V. **Map** p328 B3/C3 ❼
The ambience at the Feather Boa is part boudoir,
part bordello – giving its customers a feeling of
intimacy, as if they had been invited into the home
of its genial host, Stella. This former antiques shop
stays true to its roots, elegantly furnished with
heavy drapes, candelabras and paintings, while
drinks come in generous measures served in large,
ornate glasses. If you're feeling daring, try the
moreish Chocolate Martini (trust us: it's impossible
to have just a couple). For guaranteed comfort try to
get here early and nab one of the two sofas.

Club 1911

*27 Staunton Street, SoHo (2810 6681). Mid-Levels
Escalator/12M, 13, 23A, 26, 40M bus.* **Open** 5pm-
1am Mon-Thur, Sun; 5pm-2am Fri, Sat. **Credit**
AmEx, DC, MC, V. **Map** p328 B3/C3 ❽

This small, British-owned place is named in honour of Chinese revolutionary leader Dr Sun Yat-sen, who once lived on this street, before playing a role in China's 1911 revolution. The club underwent a makeover a while back, and is now a relaxed, quiet setting for a pint and a good old-fashioned chinwag. Good complimentary nibbles are served too.

Club 71

Basement, Man Hing Lane, 67 Hollywood Road, SoHo (2858 7071). Central MTR (exit D1, D2)/23A bus. **Open** 4pm-2am Mon-Fri; 4pm-3am Sat; 7pm-1am Sun. **Credit** MC, V. **Map** p328 C3 ⓷

For more than a decade, Club 64 – named in commemoration of the 1989 Tiananmen Square massacre (which occurred on 4 June) – had been a meeting point for artists, intellectuals, media types and would-be revolutionaries. When the landlord doubled the rent, the owners moved from Lan Kwai Fong to nearby SoHo and the regulars duly followed. This new, cosy joint, optimistically named after the first day of Hong Kong's return to China in 1997 (1 July), has tables spilling through its open front.

Dublin Jack

1/F, 17 Lan Kwai Fong (2543 0081/www.delaneys. com.hk). Central MTR (exit D1, D2)/Mid-Levels Escalator/buses along Queen's Road Central. **Open** noon-2am daily. **Credit** AmEx, DC, MC, V. **Map** p328 C4 ⓾

Since recently moving to this prime LKF location, the old Irish theme has been tempered a bit, in favour of art deco-like Celtic. The black stuff and Irish ales are still popular and decent Irish food is served. It's a hit with sports fans because it has big screens on each level – and can show live football, cricket and rugby at the same time, by patron demand.

Fringe Club Bar

G/F & rooftop, 2 Lower Albert Road (2521 7251/ www.fringeclub.com). Central MTR (exit D1, D2)/ 12M, 13, 23A, 40M bus. **Open** noon-midnight Mon-Thur; noon-3am Sat; 9am-9pm Sun. **Credit** AmEx, MC, V. **Map** p328 C4 ⓫

There are actually two bars at this mini-art centre. The walls in the lower one provide gallery space for a rotation of two-dimensional art and a backdrop for live bands on weekend evenings (cover charge HK$80, including a standard drink). No prizes for guessing what's usually displayed in the Fotogalerie bar two flights up; you can drink alfresco on its astro-turfed rooftop terrace hemmed in by nearby towers. Arty and media types hang out in both bars and drink prices are reasonable (though happy hour applies only from Monday to Friday).

Le Jardin

1/F, 10 Wing Wah Lane, Lan Kwai Fong (2526 2717). Central MTR (exit D1, D2)/12M, 13, 23A, 40M bus. **Open** 4.30pm-late Mon-Sat. **Credit** MC, V. **Map** p328 C4 ⓬

A hidden-away hotspot in Lan Kwai Fong, Le Jardin has a huge outdoor terrace. It's up, up and away from the bustling streets below – you'll find the steps leading to it at the end of Wing Wah Lane, past the cluttered alfresco dining area. The jukebox has one of the best choices of sounds in town.

Lotus

37-43 Pottinger Street (2543 6290). Central MTR (exit D1, D2)/12M, 13, 23A, 40M bus. **Open** noon-2.30pm, 6pm-late Mon-Sat. **Credit** AmEx, DC, MC, V. **Map** p328 C3 ⓭

This new cocktail spot, on a quiet pedestrianised street, became hot the moment it opened in late 2006. All the drinks are made with premium spirits – such as 42 Below Zero and Grey Goose vodkas – and many are 'foamed', meaning they are topped with a layer of flavoured foam that doesn't disappear but blends in additional flavour. More taste-bud tickling is added by the fact that much of the fruit is first grilled (and thus caramelised). Walk through the open-fronted bar space to reach the small restaurant, where the menu features an Australian take on Thai food.

Lux

Upper G/F, California Tower, 30-32 D'Aguilar Street, Lan Kwai Fong (2868 9538). Central MTR (exit D1, D2)/12M, 13, 23A, 40M bus. **Open** noon-late daily. **Credit** AmEx, DC, MC, V. **Map** p328 C4 ⓮

The people-watching potential is great from this perch overlooking the busy main thoroughfare of LKF. The house cocktails really pack a punch and offer great twists on the classics, often throwing

Revolutionaries, this way: **Club 71**.

Join the hip set at **MO Bar**.

in an extra liqueur or two for good measure. The friendly mixed crowd includes serious party people on an after-dark mission along with the more genteel yuppified set.

MO Bar

G/F, Landmark Mandarin Oriental, 15 Queen's Road Central (2132 0188). Central MTR (exit C)/buses along Queen's Road Central. **Open** 11am-2am Mon-Thur, Sun; 11am-4am Fri, Sat. **Credit** AmEx, DC, MC, V. **Map** p329 D4 ⑮

One of the hottest hotel bars (*see p166* **A higher crawling**) among the well-heeled wannabe hip set. And to be fair, both interior vibe and drinks list are very impressive. Imaginative house cocktails that look and taste good are sipped as the sound system cranks up mid-evening and a DJ takes over. A small discreet 'VIP' zone can be booked in advance. Posy, pricey and definitely fun.

Post 97

Upper G/F, 9 Lan Kwai Fong (2810 9333/www. ninetysevengroup.com). Central MTR (exit D1, D2)/12M, 13, 23A, 40M bus. **Open** 9.30am-1am Mon-Thur; 9.30am-3am Fri, Sat; 9.30pm-midnight Sun. **Credit** AmEx, DC, MC, V. **Map** p328 C4 ⑯

One of the city's most relaxed venues for extended meals, Post 97 has also been the choice late-night hangout of stars and the Hong Kong 'it' crowd for more than a decade. Excellent food, a good selection of wine by the glass and surroundings you can flop in make it the perfect chill-out drinking zone on any night of the week. It's a popular weekend brunch setting too, and offers good buffet lunches on weekdays.

Red

Level 4, Podium, IFC Mall, 8 Finance Street (8129 8882). Central MTR (exit A). **Open** 11.30am-midnight Mon-Wed; 11.30am-3am Thur-Sat; 11.30am-10pm Sun. **Credit** AmEx, DC, MC, V. **Map** p329 D3 ⑰

Overlooking the Outlying Island and Star Ferry piers from the breezy rooftop of the IFC Mall, this popular bar pulls a buzzing crowd every night for its fairly pricey cocktails, wine and beers. Plenty of suits from nearby Exchange Square end up staying till the wee hours. The chilled-out space here (and at next-door Isobar) makes for a laid-back alternative to LKF and SoHo. **Photo** *p165*.

Staunton's

10-12 Staunton Street, SoHo (2973 6611). Mid-Levels Escalator/12M, 13, 23A, 26, 40M bus. **Open** 10am-2am daily. **Credit** AmEx, DC, MC, V. **Map** p328 C3 ⑱

Located right next to the Mid-Levels Escalator, Staunton's is heaving seven nights a week. Its glass windows make it a perfect spot for people-watching, and it's understandably popular with trendy twenty- and thirty-somethings. Food is pricey here, so many use it solely as a watering hole.

Tuscany by H

G/F, corner of 58-62 D'Aguilar Street & 15-16 Lan Kwai Fong (2522 9798/www.tuscany-by-h.com). Central MTR (exit D1, D2)/12M, 13, 23A, 40M bus. **Open** noon-2.30pm, 6.30-11pm Mon-Sat; 6.30-11pm Sun. **Credit** AmEx, DC, MC, V. **Map** p328 C4 ⑲

The bar at the entrance of this pricey new Italian restaurant, though limited to three tables and a small bar counter, arguably serves up some of the finest wines by the glass (all Italian) anywhere. Non alcohol-drinkers are also catered for with fresh concoctions that are either listed or suggested by the affable and immaculately turned-out serving team. You may not know it but those drinkers at the nearby table are probably pretty big cheeses locally – the clientele includes many a tycoon. Slightly tinted windows and dim lighting along the bar mean you're visible as you overlook a prime piece of LKF but don't feel like you're in a goldfish bowl.

Wan Chai, Causeway Bay & Happy Valley

The Bridge
107 Lockhart Road, Wan Chai (2865 5586). Wan Chai MTR (exit A1, C)/buses along Hennessy Road. **Open** 24hrs daily. **Credit** DC, MC, V. **Map** p330 B3 ⑳
Ever since the famed Old China Hand (a bar that has been around since the era of Suzie Wong) opted for a makeover and decided to open a mere 21 hours a day, those who want to keep drinking between 5am and 8am come to the Bridge. It's a decent enough watering hole with a good range of beers and spirits.

Brown
18A Sing Woo Road, Happy Valley (2891 8558). Bus 5A/trams to Happy Valley. **Open** 10am-2am daily. **Credit** AmEx, MC, V. **Map** off p331 E5 ㉑
A sophisticated bar in Happy Valley, Brown is owned by an architect – the clean lines and dark wood interior are a bit of a giveaway. Divided into three small areas, including a terrace out the back, it's an ideal place to sample top-shelf spirits and good wine, and it also offers a good menu of modern but inexpensive fusion cuisine.

Delaney's
G-1/F, One Capital Place, 18 Luard Street, Wan Chai (2804 2880/www.delaneys.com.hk). Wan Chai MTR (exit A1, C)/buses along Gloucester Road & Hennessy Road. **Open** noon-2am Mon-Thur, Sun; noon-3am Fri, Sat. **Credit** AmEx, DC, MC, V. **Map** p330 B3 ㉒
The prices would make a Dubliner wince (HK$60-plus for a pint of Guinness or Kilkenny), but Delaney's is a Hong Kong Irish pub institution. Much better value is its excellent pub grub – the daily lunch carvery is among the best in town and starts at a reasonable HK$68. Downstairs is a great setting to sip your beer, while upstairs is more action-packed, with a big-screen TV showing football and rugby.
Other locations: Basement, Mary Building, 71-7 Peking Road, Tsim Sha Tsui, Kowloon (2301 3980).

1/5
Starcrest, 9 Star Street, Wan Chai (2520 2515). Bus 5, 5A, 10. **Open** 6pm-late Mon-Fri; 8pm-late Sat. **Credit** AmEx, DC, MC, V. **Map** p330 A4 ㉓
One of the instigators of the fashionable Star Street bar scene, this large loft-type bar – pronounced One Fifth – in a once quiet part of Wan Chai attracts an exclusive crowd; at weekends it's glamour galore,

along with plenty of off-duty suits. With high ceilings and dark wood, the place has a classy feel, but although it is spacious, it can get uncomfortably crowded unless you grab a booth. Fun comes at a premium with drink prices here.

Typhoon
37-39 Lockhart Road, Wan Chai (2527 2077/www.igors.com). Wan Chai MTR (exit A1, C)/buses along Hennessy Road. **Open** 4pm-2am Mon-Thur; 4pm-4am Fri-Sun. **Credit** AmEx, MC, V. **Map** p330 A3 ㉔
This no-nonsense newbie, in pole position on Wan Chai's main drag, is always up for a serious drinking session. For HK$500 anyone can ring the Typhoon bell, which treats the whole gaff to a round of standard drinks. This is a popular and very late-night drinking den.

The Peak

Café Deco (*see p144*) and **Peak Lookout** (*see p145*) are highly recommended for a meal or just a drink or two.

South & east coasts

Beaches
92B Stanley Main Street, Stanley (2813 7313). Bus 6, 260, 973. **Open** 9am-midnight Mon-Fri; 9am-1am Sat, Sun. **Credit** AmEx, DC, MC, V. **Map** p93 ㉕

Laid-back late nights at **Red**. *See p164.*

A higher crawling

Start: The Four Seasons, Central.
Finish: The Peninsula, Tsim Sha Tsui.
The Central and Tsim Sha Tsui districts have long been home to the best clusters of swish hotel bars in which to savour a refined tipple while taking in a colourful crowd cocktail that blends equal measures of locals and visitors. As these two neighbourhoods lie immediately opposite each other across Victoria Harbour – on the central northern fringe of Hong Kong Island and the southern tip of the Kowloon Peninsula respectively – the views from these bars are often impressive. If you're up to it, both legs of this bar crawl can easily be linked by hopping on and off the Star Ferry or the MTR.

CENTRAL
Sundown across Victoria Harbour often throws a magical orange reflection around the buildings that line it. Few places are better equipped to take this in than the clean-lined, high-ceilinged environment of the **Blue Bar** (❶ see p162) at the **Four Seasons** – which adjoins the IFC Mall on Finance Street

and overlooks Central's ferry piers. So, kick off your crawl during the early evening Blue Hour (5.30-7.30pm), when complimentary bar snacks make the deluxe cocktails and fine wine list even more appealing. There is a real buzz at this time, when plenty of brokers from the nearby stock exchange flock here to quaff while reflecting on the day's markets action.

Seen the sunset? Then exit the hotel's main entrance and turn left at the elevated walkway that follows Connaught Road; take the first right turn where the walkway crosses over Connaught Road in front of Exchange Square. This sets you down on Pottinger Street; carry on up this street and take the first left, on to Des Voeux Road. At the second major junction, follow Chater Road, passing the Legislative Council Building (on your right), where a final decision was made in 2006 to turn the majority of indoor bars non-smoking as of 1 January 2007 (nightclubs and certain bars have a couple of years' grace, though). Next on the right you'll see Chater Gardens, where many a glass of Pimm's would have been drunk in the days when it was home to the Hong Kong Cricket Club. Opposite this, head for the serene colonial drawing-room appeal of the **Chater Lounge** bar (❷ open until 1am, 2am Fri & Sat) on the first floor of the **Ritz-Carlton** (see p56), where you can warm up with hot toddies in the cooler months. There is no need to strain your vocal cords to make conversation in this cosy environment overlooking some of Central's most prominent buildings.

Get ready to strain those vocal cords, though, and head to one of Hong Kong's cocktail spots *du jour*. From the Ritz, cross Chater Road and head west to the end of the gardens, take the first left down narrow Jackson Road, then the first right at its end; walk along Des Voeux Road – after the junction with Ice House Street you will see the Landmark shopping mall across the street. Head inside and follow the signs to the **Landmark Mandarin Oriental**, where you will find the chic **MO Bar** in the lobby (❸ see p164). While sipping a fresh fruit martini or another

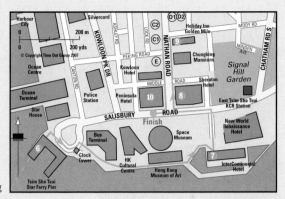

concoction from the long, creative cocktail list, witness the beautiful, well-heeled types get animated, especially once the music cranks up at around 9pm.

Time for a classy nightcap or two or a snifter before crossing the harbour. Exit the hotel through the mall again; turn right and cross Des Voeux Road at its junction with Ice House Street, following the latter – so named as it was once home to Hong Kong's limited supply of ice in the pre-refrigeration 19th century – to the flagship **Mandarin Oriental** hotel at the junction with Chater Road. Immerse yourself in the genteel but unstuffy gents' club-like **Chinnery Bar** (④ see p162 and p155 **Superior pub grub**). Although a variety of beers – in silver tankards – wine and other drinks are on offer, it's for premium Scotch that this wood-panelled bar is best known – there more than 200 single malts.

From here, you can either call it a night or head for the Star Ferry for the Tsim Sha Tsui crawl below (note that the last ferry in either direction is 11.30pm; the less scenic MTR runs till around 1am). To reach the ferry pier, take the pedestrian subway at the right of the hotel's entrance and cross under Connaught Road; upon resurfacing, turn first right into Connaught Place, passing the General Post Office, then right again at its end, down Man Yiu Street, which leads to the Star Ferry pier (⑤).

TSIM SHA TSUI

From the Tsim Sha Tsui Star Ferry terminal (⑥), stroll along the waterfront promenade – which runs parallel to Salisbury Road – past the built-in 'Avenue of Stars' display. Just beyond the Space Museum, veer towards the road from the promenade to reach the entrance of the **InterContinental** at number 18 (see p62), whose **Lobby Lounge** (⑦ open until 1am) is big on glitz factor. Signature drinks include the Nine Dragon cocktail series, which can be enjoyed while watching arguably the best view of the Symphony of Lights display across Victoria Harbour at 8pm nightly, through the impossibly tall windows. Or indulge in premium whisky and brandy while enjoying the laid-back band that performs nightly.

Take the pedestrian subway outside the InterCon to cross beneath Salisbury Road; after a short dodge left and right you can ascend to Nathan Road, where the stripped-down style of the **Sky Lounge** (⑧ 2369 1111, ext 4, open until 1am, 2am Fri & Sat) on the 18th floor of the **Sheraton** (20 Nathan Road) doesn't try to compete with the perfect harbour view. Some 30 wines by the glass complement a menu that offers tapas-sized portions of Asian and Western fare.

Back on the ground, turn right and walk less than five minutes further up Nathan Road to number 50 on the same side of the street, for a drink at utterly unpretentious **Hari's** (⑨ 2369 3111, ext 1345, open until 2am) at the **Holiday Inn Golden Mile** (see p63). Although standard cocktails are available, overly imaginative concoctions are not a feature here. Some drinkers huddle at the wood-panelled bar, which feels like a relaxed upmarket pub, and cover bands play every evening.

Cross over Nathan Road and walk due south again to its end to get to **The Peninsula**. Two distinct drinking areas are built into the Philippe Starck-designed **Felix** (⑩ see p146 and p168) at the top of the hotel's tower extension. The Long Table laps up the most atmosphere; enjoy superbly mixed cocktails here, while watching the harbour and Hong Kong Island glow.

Stanley Main Street is packed each weekend with an odd assortment of expat families, young Chinese couples and Hell's Angels (OK, they're actually off-duty accountants and office manager-types with a fetish for Harleys and leather). Beaches is one of the more relaxed venues along the waterfront, and in addition to booze it serves simple pastas and pub grub at cheap prices.

Boathouse

86-8 Stanley Main Street, Stanley (2813 4467/ www.igors.com). Bus 6, 260, 973. **Open** 11.30am-10.30pm Mon-Thur; 11.30am-11.30pm Fri-Sun. **Credit** DC, MC, V. **Map** p93 ㉖

One of the fancier bar restaurants along the strip, the Boathouse attracts an expat crowd and is particularly busy in the months leading up to the June Dragon Boat Races (*see p204*) as thirsty crews seek refreshment after a few hours' practice on the sea. After dark it serves good dinners, with plenty of fish and seafood on the menu. On weekends the crowds spill on to tables outside.

Kowloon

Tsim Sha Tsui

For a tour of high-class (and high-in-the-sky) hotel bars, *see p166* **A higher crawling**.

Aqua Spirit

29/F, 1 Peking Road (3427 2288). Tsim Sha Tsui MTR (exit E)/buses to Tsim Sha Tsui Ferry Pier & along Salisbury Road/Tsim Sha Tsui Star Ferry Pier. **Open** 6pm-2am daily. **Credit** AmEx, DC, MC, V. **Map** p333 B6 ㉗

Dramatic pooled lighting and wraparound views of Victoria Harbour, Hong Kong Island and much of Kowloon creates an instant wow-factor here that is nearly matched by some stunning cocktails – and prices. The place has few equals in Hong Kong for a drinks experience; both visitors and locals agree.

Bahama Mama's

4-5 Knutsford Terrace (2368 2121/www.mhihk. com). Tsim Sha Tsui MTR (exit B2)/buses along Nathan Road & Chatham Road South. **Open** 3.30pm-3am Mon-Thur; 3.30pm-4am Fri, Sat; 4pm-2am Sun. **Credit** AmEx, DC, MC, V. **Map** p333 C5 ㉘

In existence for over a decade (almost a miracle in fickle Hong Kong), this tropical theme bar was one of the first on the now-thriving scene of Knutsford Terrace. It's an odd place – a mix of faux foliage, table football and dance music – but with a terrace out front it keeps pulling in the punters.

Felix

28/F, Peninsula Hotel, Salisbury Road (2366 6251/ 2315 3188/www.hongkong.peninsula.com). Tsim Sha Tsui MTR (exit E)/buses to Tsim Sha Tsui Star Ferry Pier & along Salisbury Road/Tsim Sha Tsui Star Ferry Pier. **Open** 6pm-2am daily. **Credit** AmEx, DC, MC, V. **Map** p333 B6/C6 ㉙

This place is rated by some as the city's finest bar, and it certainly boasts the best view – a magnificent panorama of the Hong Kong skyline. Perched at the top of the Peninsula hotel (*see p62*), it attracts a chic crowd and has a feel of exclusivity to rival anywhere in the world. The Philippe Starck-designed interior is a visual treat, with a cool island bar and cocooned private rooms. The bars here – there are two – sometimes get less attention than the gents' loos, whose urinals look out over Kowloon. A shame as the Long Table bar is one of Hong Kong's best cocktail spots. *See also p146.* **Photo** *p169.*

Hard Rock Café

G-1/F, Silvercord Centre, 30-33 Canton Road (2375 1323/www.hardrockcafe.com.hk). Tsim Sha Tsui MTR (exit A1). **Open** 11am-1am Mon-Thur, Sun; 11am-3am Fri, Sat. **Credit** AmEx, DC, MC, V. **Map** p333 B6 ㉚

If you want corporate American familiarity, this branch of the worldwide chain serves Bud, burgers and fries in a roomy environment. The usual rock 'n' roll mementoes adorn the walls and service is good.

Mes Amis

15 Ashley Road (2730 3038/www.mesamis.com.hk). Tsim Sha Tsui MTR (exit A1, C1). **Open** noon-2am Mon-Thur, Sun; noon-3am Fri, Sat. **Credit** AmEx, DC, MC, V. **Map** p333 B6 ㉛

Part of the Mes Amis chain of bars, this place adds some Central style to Tsim Sha Tsui's rough and ragged drinking scene. This is the pick of the crop on Ashley Road, although there are plenty of other options in the cul-de-sac. Attention has been paid to the decor, and the atmosphere is friendly, lively and sophisticated. Food platters and an extensive choice of wines by the glass are further draws.

Other locations: 83 Lockhart Road, Wan Chai, HK Island (2527 6680); 13/F, Langham Place, 8 Argyle Street, Mong Kok, Kowloon (3428 3699).

The New Territories

East New Territories

Cheers Sports Bar & Restaurant

28 Yi Chun Street, Sai Kung (2791 6789). Choi Hung MTR (exit C) then minibus 1A. **Open** 11.30am-late daily. **Credit** MC, V.

Sai Kung has a large expat population, so the pubs in the area tend to get quite lively in the evening, especially when football and rugby are shown on the big screens. Many bars around here stay open until the wee small hours and Cheers is no exception. In terms of clientele, there's a good mix of local Chinese and expats, who are drawn by the friendly vibe. Above-average pub grub is served in the restaurant upstairs.

Steamers

G/F, Kam Wah Building, 18-32 Chan Man Street, Sai Kung (2792 6991). Choi Hung MTR (exit C) then minibus 1A. **Open** 9am-1am daily. **Credit** AmEx, DC, MC, V.

Chic and exclusive **Felix**. *See p168.*

This is another bright and cheery Sai Kung bar with a strong emphasis on sports. There's a decent choice of beer and wine, and the menu offers some good meat and seafood dishes alongside standard pub fare. It's an ideal place to drop in on after a browse around town or a walk through the surrounding country park.

The Outlying Islands

Lamma

Deli Lamma
36 Main Street, Yung Shue Wan (2982 1583). Yung Shue Wan Ferry Pier. **Open** 9am-late daily. **Credit** AmEx, MC, V.
A young, hip crowd packs the Deli in the evenings, partaking of its on-tap cider and Stella. The food is your basic pub fare – pizzas, curries, Sunday roasts – and the terrace backs right on to the harbour.

Diesel Sports Bar
51 Main Street, Yung Shue Wan (2982 4116). Yung Shue Wan Ferry Pier. **Open** 6pm-late Mon-Fri, Sun; noon-late Sat. **No credit cards**.
Like most pubs on Lamma, this one is a hangout for the sizeable expat community. It's rammed on Saturday nights, when live football and rugby are played on the big screen, but since it's tiny inside, punters tend to spill on to the pavement.

Island Bar
6 Main Street, Yung Shue Wan (2982 1376). Yung Shue Wan Ferry Pier. **Open** 5pm-2am Mon-Fri; noon-2am Sat, Sun. **No credit cards**.
Lamma is no longer the hippie hangout it was before 1997 – nowadays it's home to young families and Terence Conran-loving couples. A rather middle-of-the-road watering hole for the new yuppie class.

Lantau

China Bear
Mui Wo Centre, Mui Wo (2984 9720). Mui Wo Ferry Pier. **Open** 10am-3am daily. **No credit cards**.
This glass-fronted pub with outdoor seating is an ideal place to unwind before catching the ferry back to the city. There's a good range of beers, including local microbrews, and the British pub food isn't bad.

Cheung Chau

Cheung Chau Windsurfing Centre & Outdoor Café
1 Hak Pai Road, Kwan Yam Wan (2981 8316/9735 0049/www.ccwindc.com.hk). Cheung Chau Ferry Pier. **Open** 10am-7pm Tue-Sun. **Credit** MC, V.
This is a great spot for a drink as the sun goes down. Many people drop in because of its celebrity connection – windsurfer Lee Lai-Shan, Hong Kong's only Olympic gold medallist, trained here.

Eat, Drink, Shop

Shops & Services

A decade after the Handover, Hong Kong is still a temple to consumerism – prepare to shop till you drop.

Shanghai Tang. *See p185.*

Hong Kong easily lives up to its reputation as a shopper's paradise. The city is virtually one giant shopping mall, catering to all budgets and tastes. No matter where you turn, there is a dizzying abundance of shops, outlets, markets and malls, ready to offer you a heavy dose of retail therapy.

Shopping is the national pastime in Hong Kong – and it won't be going out of fashion any time soon. The entire population, from teenagers to the elderly, participates in active consumerism, while at the same time escaping the confines of their (usually small) flat.

Most shoppers beat the heat or torrential spring rains by heading to a comfortable, air-conditioned mall. Some of the giant malls (such as Langham Place in Mong Kok and Festival Walk in Kowloon Tong) are seemingly designed to be confusing, making you walk around for longer before finding the way out. Also, most malls do not have benches, so if you want to rest your feet, you'll have to spend cash in a restaurant or café to sit down.

For bargain shoppers, street markets (*see p190* **To market, to market**) dotted around the city are the places to find deals on everything from pashmina shawls and Chinese art to knock-off watches and cheap trainers. Many of the clothing stalls cater to local body types – meaning petite sizes – but if you look around, chances are you'll find a vendor carrying Western sizes.

What makes shopping in Hong Kong a breeze is the clustering of similar types of shops in one area or on a single street. The main clusters – and where the level of spoken English is highest – are in the areas edging both sides of Victoria Harbour: Central and Causeway Bay on Hong Kong Island, and Tsim Sha Tsui in Kowloon. Mong Kong, further north, is equally frenetic but you may be more likely to need your phrasebook. However, if communication is proving difficult, you can always use body language and type numbers into a calculator to agree upon a price.

AREA BREAKDOWN

At the tip of Kowloon peninsula, **Tsim Sha Tsui** (also known as TST) is a massive shopping hub for anything and everything. Located next to the Star Ferry Pier, Hong Kong's largest mall, **Harbour City** (*see p178*) has a labyrinth of 700 shops divided into four malls. Outside, the opulent shops at **One Peking Road** (think Cartier, Dior and Escada) are for those with serious cash to burn.

Moving into the side streets (**Hankow Road**, **Kimberly Road** and **Granville Road**), you'll find small independent shops selling local fashions, Chinese souvenirs, bespoke suits and excess factory stock at unbelievable prices – you could find a Banana Republic top for as little as HK$50.

Three MTR stops north is another major shopping district, **Mong Kok**, excellent for local fashions, street markets, computers and electronic goods (*see p178* **Tech savvy**) and the modern **Langham Place** (*see p179*) mall. As it's one of the most densely populated places on earth, hordes of shoppers flock here from morning till late at night.

Savvy computer shoppers can continue north to **Sham Shui Po**, a haven for hundreds of computer and electronic shops, either at the outdoor street market on **Ap Liu Street** or in the **Golden Computer Shopping Centre** (*see p178* **Tech savvy**).

Across the harbour, **Central** has so many luxury, designer fashion houses concentrated into a few blocks (mainly on **Des Voeux Road** and **Chater Road**), it would be hard not to bump into them with your Birken bag.

However, for all the ultra-posh stores in Central, there is great, inexpensive shopping to be had in the buzzing street market called **The Lanes**. It's spread over three narrow alleyways

(Douglas Lane, Li Yuen Street East and Li Yuen Street West), which run parallel to one another between Queen's Road Central and Des Voeux Road. Here you'll find a cornucopia of souvenirs, silk Chinese pyjamas, cheap copy watches, inexpensive fashions, fabrics, luggage and shoes. Try out your bargaining skills and you may get a few dollars knocked off the price.

Walking up from here, **Hollywood Road** (above Lan Kwai Fong) is your ticket to China's past. The road is lined with more than a hundred antique stores selling everything from an exquisite Ching dynasty porcelain vase to a hand-embroidered Imperial court robe and terracotta animals. Unfortunately, there are a number of fakes on the market, so beware. Look for a certificate of authenticity when buying expensive antiques (however, forged certificates are known to exist).

Continuing up from Hollywood Road (off the Mid-Levels Escalator) is the trendy **SoHo** neighbourhood, mainly on **Staunton Street** and **Elgin Street**. You'll find a mix of urban-cool locals and expats drinking at one of the many open-fronted bars and restaurants, or popping into fashionable cutting-edge shops (*see p193* **SoHo shopping**) to fill their chic wardrobes. Many stores in the neighbourhood carry cult brands from the US and Europe or clothes made by top local designers.

One MTR stop east of Central is **Admiralty**, home to one of Hong Kong's most popular malls, **Pacific Place** (*see p180*), which has the perfect combination of mid- to high-range retailers. A short jaunt away is the **Wan Chai Computer Centre** (*see p178* **Tech savvy**) where techno junkies can get their fix of the latest computer goods.

Next to Wan Chai is Hong Kong Island's busiest shopping district, **Causeway Bay**. Year round (except for one or two days during Chinese New Year), the streets are flooded with busy shoppers – all day, every day. Whatever your shopping-heart desires, you can find it at climate-controlled places such as the good-value Japanese department store **Sogo** (*see p177*) or the mammoth 13-storey shopping centre **Times Square** (*see p180*), which are both directly connected to Causeway Bay MTR. Or take to the streets (**Paterson Street** and **Lee Garden Road**) and discover an overwhelming choice of electronics, cosmetics, factory over-stock and local clothing retailers around every corner, on the ground and above.

SEASONAL SALES, OPENING TIMES

Expect to find some bargains during the sales, which are generally held in July and August to offload summer merchandise. Chinese New Year is the one time of the year

Picture This. *See p173.*

that most shops in the malls close (usually for two days); shops in other areas may close for up to five days over this period.

IT'S A RIP-OFF

Like many big cities in the world, Hong Kong is both consumer heaven and tourist trap. In order to avoid tourists being scammed, the Hong Kong Tourism Board (HKTB) has introduced the Quality Tourism Services (QTS) scheme as a means of identifying those shops and restaurants that have proven to offer excellent service. Look for the QTS sticker.

Antiques

Altfield Gallery

Shop 248-249, 2/F, Prince's Building, 10 Chater Road, Central, HK Island (2537 6370). Central MTR (exit K)/buses & trams through Central. **Open** 10am-7pm Mon-Sat; 11am-5pm Sun. **Credit** AmEx, MC, V. **Map** p329 E4.

Altfield has two different outlets – Altfield Gallery and, for furnishings, Altfield Interiors (*see p195*). While this shop deals in antique Chinese furniture, it also has a penchant for ancient prints and fantastic Asian maps. These date back as far as the 1500s, and, not surprisingly, come at a steep price.

Arch Angel Antiques

53-5 Hollywood Road, Central, HK Island (2851 6828). Central MTR (exit D1, D2, G)/Mid-Levels Escalator/12M, 13, 23A, 26, 40M, 43 bus. **Open** 9.30am-6.30pm daily. **Credit** AmEx, DC, MC, V. **Map** p328 C3.

This established fixture on Hollywood Road stocks a good range of quality Chinese antiques, and also does repairs and restorations.

Artemis

46 Wyndham Street, Central, HK Island (2530 2320). Central MTR (exit D1, D2, G)/13, 26, 43 bus. **Open** 10am-6pm Mon-Sat. **Credit** AmEx, MC, V. **Map** p328 C4.

This well set-out shop offers room to move, so you can work your way around the wealth of merchandise. And while it's not exactly cheap, it has stock that you'd be hard pushed to find elsewhere.

Gallery One

G/F, 31-3 Hollywood Road, Central, HK Island (2545 6436). Central MTR (exit D1, D2, G)/Mid-Levels Escalator/12M, 13, 23A, 26, 40M, 43 bus. **Open** 10am-6pm Mon-Sat. **Credit** AmEx, DC, MC, V. **Map** p328 C3.

If you're looking for antique jewellery, Gallery One is the shop for you. It sells a wonderful selection of necklaces, bracelets and rings, as well as Buddhist walnut carvings – you'll just have to sift through the mess to find your perfect purchase.

Gorgeous Arts & Crafts

Shop A, UG/F, Alaqmar House, 30 Hollywood Road, Central, HK Island (2973 0034). Central MTR (exit D1, D2, G)/Mid-Levels Escalator/12M, 13, 23A, 26, 40M, 43 bus. **Open** 10.30am-7pm Mon-Sat; 1-7pm Sun. **Credit** AmEx, MC, V. **Map** p328 C3.

Located close to the Mid-Levels Escalator, this place can be difficult to find – although you can see its window, stacked high with stock, above Gallery One (*see above*) on Hollywood Road. This shop has a wonderful selection of Chinese antiques at reasonable prices and staff are friendly.

Honeychurch Antiques

29 Hollywood Road, Central, HK Island (2543 2433). Central MTR (exit D1, D2, G)/Mid-Levels Escalator/12M, 13, 23A, 26, 40M, 43 bus.

Open 10am-6pm Mon-Sat. **Credit** AmEx, DC, MC, V. **Map** p328 C3.
Conspicuously located opposite Central Police Station, Honeychurch prides itself on reliability, honesty and courteous salesmanship. If you're not sure of what you're buying, you can trust the staff to explain the ins and outs of whatever's caught your eye. For the serious patron, it also handles English and Chinese silverware, a superb range of jewellery and a heady collection of Asian antiques.

Martin Fung Antiques & Furniture Company
Shop A, G/F, China Hong Kong Tower, 8-12 Hennessy Road, Wan Chai (2524 3306). Admiralty MTR (exit C1)/buses & trams through Central. **Open** 10am-7pm Mon-Fri; noon-7pm Sat, Sun. **Credit** AmEx, DC, MC, V. **Map** p329 F5.
A five-minute walk from Pacific Place, this shop has no specific bent, meaning there's a good mix of merchandise: paintings, sculptures, furniture and porcelain are all on offer, at very decent prices.

Picture This
Suite 603B, 6/F, Office Tower, 9 Queen's Road, Central, HK Island (2525 2820/www.picturethiscollection.com). Central MTR (exit D1, G)/buses & trams through Central/Central Ferry Pier. **Open** 11am-6pm Tue-Sat. **Credit** MC, V. **Map** p329 D4.
If you're looking for an authentic Bruce Lee movie poster, check out Christopher Bailey's art gallery. He also stocks a vast assortment (some pricey), of vintage posters, postcards and antique photographs of Hong Kong and China. **Photos** *above.*
Other locations: Shop 212, 2/F, Prince's Building, 10 Chater Road, Central, HK Island (2525 2803).

Wonder Dragon
30 Hollywood Road, Central, HK Island (2526 8863). Central MTR (exit D1, D2, G)/Mid-Levels Escalator/12M, 13, 23A, 26, 40M, 43 bus. **Open** 10.30am-7pm Mon-Sat; 1.30-6pm Sun. **Credit** AmEx, DC, MC, V. **Map** p328 C3.
Wonder Dragon was established in the 1970s and is still going strong. The interior is awkward and cramped but not only does it contain a fantastic variety of Chinese antiques, but it also has old upright phones, gramophones and typewriters. Sadly, service can be curt and somewhat haughty.

Zee Stone Gallery
G/F, Yu Yet Lai Building, 43-55 Wyndham Street, Central, HK Island (2810 5895/www.zeestone.com). Central MTR (exit D1, G)/13, 26, 43 bus. **Open** 10am-7pm Mon-Sat; 1-6pm Sun. **Credit** AmEx, DC, MC, V. **Map** p328 C4.
This gallery deals in a sophisticated selection of Chinese works of art, as well as antique furniture and Tibetan rugs. Staff are friendly and helpful.

Art supplies & stationery

The Artland Company
3/F, Lockhart Centre, 301-307 Lockhart Road, Wan Chai, HK Island (2511 4845). Buses along Hennessy Road. **Open** 9am-7pm Mon-Fri; 9am-5pm Sat. **Credit** MC, V. **Map** p330 C3.
An adequate assortment of art supplies is sold here, including the usual necessities like felt-tip pens, paints, crayons, paper, and inks and paint brushes. Prices are fair.

PaperArt
Shop 104-106, 1/F, Tung Ming Building, 40-42 Des Voeux Road, Central, HK Island (2545 8985/www.hkpaperart.com). Central MTR (exit C)/trams through Central/5, 5B, 10 bus. **Open** 10.30am-7pm Mon-Sat. **Credit** AmEx, MC, V. **Map** p328 C3.

Eat, Drink, Shop

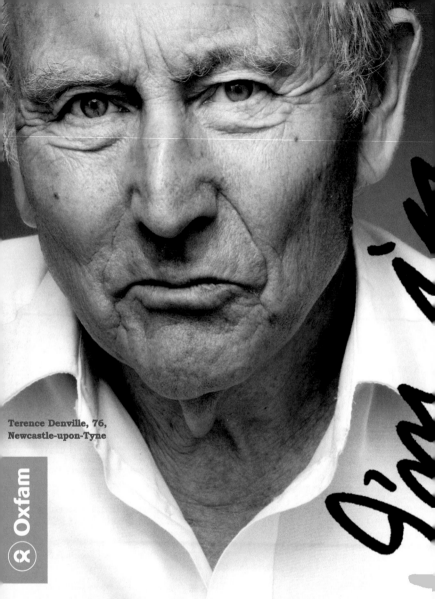

Terence Denville, 76,
Newcastle-upon-Tyne

Oxfam

Hundreds of thousands of people have said *I'm in* to fight the injustice of poverty. And this kind of pressure has already made a huge difference. In Ghana, for example, most of the country's debt has been wiped out. But there's so much more to do: every day, extreme poverty kills 30,000 children. That's unacceptable. Text 'TIMEOUT' and your name to 87099. We'll let you know how to help. We can do this. We *can* end poverty. Are you in?

I give my support to help end poverty. and you know what? things actually get done

Let's end poverty together. Text 'TIMEOUT' and your name to 87099.

Standard text rates apply. Registered charity No.202918

More a gift shop than a stationer's, PaperArt stocks rubber stamps from the US, handmade paper and artsy greeting cards, all at fairly high prices.

Prints

Shop 230, 2/F, Prince's Building, 10 Chater Road, Central, HK Island (2523 9811/www.prints-international.com). Central MTR (exit K)/buses & trams through Central/Central Ferry Pier. **Open** 10am-7.30pm Mon-Sat; noon-6.30pm Sun. **Credit** AmEx, MC, V. **Map** p329 E4.

Stationery and card shop that produces all its own greeting cards, wrapping paper, photo albums, notebooks and paper in sleek, contemporary designs and vibrant patterns.

Other locations: Shop C7, Queensway Plaza, 93 Queensway, Admiralty, HK Island (2527 1198).

Books & magazines

Bookazine

Shop 309-13, Prince's Building, 10 Chater Road, Central, HK Island (2522 1785/www.bookazine.hk). Central MTR (exit J1, J2, J3)/buses & trams through Central/Central Ferry Pier. **Open** 9.30am-7.30pm Mon-Sat; 10.30am-6.30pm Sun. **Credit** AmEx, MC, V. **Map** p329 E4.

These stores stock a good selection of fiction, non-fiction and imported magazines.

Other locations: throughout the city.

Commercial Press (HK) Limited

9-15 Yee Wo Street, Causeway Bay, HK Island (2890 8028/www.commercialpress.com.hk). Causeway Bay MTR (exit E)/buses along Hennessy Road. **Open** 11am-9.30pm daily. **Credit** AmEx, MC, V. **Map** p331 E3.

This large bookshop stocks both Chinese and English literature, with a focus on paperbacks and plenty of stationery.

Other locations: 608 Nathan Road, Mong Kok, Kowloon (2384 8228).

Dymocks

Shop 2007-2011, Level 2, IFC Mall, 8 Finance Street, Central, HK Island (2117 0360/www.dymocks.com.hk). Central MTR (exit A)/buses to Central Ferry Pier. **Open** 9.30am-9.30pm daily. **Credit** AmEx, DC, MC, V. **Map** p329 D2.

There are various Dymocks outlets all over Hong Kong. Much like its rival Bookazine, Dymocks stocks a good choice of US and UK magazines, along with children's, fiction and non-fiction books. Coffeetable books are a strong point.

Other locations: throughout the city.

Government Publications Centre/Information Services

Room 402, 4/F, Murray Building, Garden Road, Central, HK Island (2537 1910/www.bookstore.gov.hk). Admiralty MTR (exit B)/40M bus/buses along Garden Road. **Open** 9am-6pm Mon-Fri. **No credit cards. Map** p329 E5.

Located beside the main entrance of Pacific Place, this shop has the unappealing feel of a schoolroom-

Flow. *See p176.*

cum-dole office. It stocks everything relating to the inner and outer workings of the region, like the annual budget and exam reference books for schools, as well as, on a more useful level, excellent maps of Hong Kong.

Kelly & Walsh

Shop 236, Level 2, Pacific Place, 88 Queensway, Admiralty, HK Island (2522 7893/www.kellyandwalsh.com). Admiralty MTR (exit C1)/buses & trams through Central. **Open** 9.30am-8pm Mon-Sat; 11am-8pm Sun. **Credit** AmEx, MC, V. **Map** p329 F5.

The inside of Kelly & Walsh looks more like a stationer's than a bookshop, but it does stock a fantastic mix of local and imported magazines, as well as certain overseas newspapers that can be hard to come by in Hong Kong. It's somewhat cluttered, somewhat pricey but always busy with a mix of locals and tourists.

Page One

9/F, Times Square, 1 Matheson Street, Causeway Bay, HK Island (2506 0381/www.pageonegroup.com). Causeway Bay MTR (exit A)/63, 108, 117, 170, N170 bus. **Open** 10.30am-10pm Mon-Thur; 10.30am-11pm Fri-Sun. **Credit** AmEx, DC, MC, V. **Map** p331 D3.

Page One carries a comprehensive collection of fiction and non-fiction in both Chinese and English.

Other locations: Festival Walk, 80 Tat Chee Avenue, Kowloon Tong, Kowloon (2778 2808); 2/F, Century Square, 1-13 D'Aguilar Street, Central (2536 0111).

Swindon Book Company

13-15 Lock Road, Tsim Sha Tsui, Kowloon (2366 8001/www.swindonbooks.com). Tsim Sha Tsui MTR (exit C1, E)/buses along Nathan Road/Tsim Sha Tsui Star Ferry Pier. **Open** 9am-6.30pm Mon-Thur; 9am-7.30pm Fri, Sat; 12.30-6.30pm Sun. **Credit** AmEx, MC, V. **Map** p333 B6.

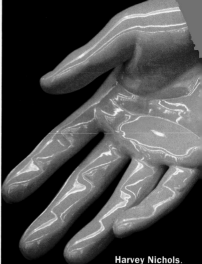

Harvey Nichols.

This is the bigger of the two Swindon Book Company outlets. It stocks a wide range of English-language titles stretching across two floors. Pricing is reasonable considering that most of the stock is imported, and the American paperbacks here tend to be the cheapest in town.

Other locations: Shop 310-18, Ocean Centre, Harbour City, 5 Canton Road, Tsim Sha Tsui, Kowloon (2735 9881).

The Travellers' Home Bookshop

2/F, 55 Hankow Road, Tsim Sha Tsui, Kowloon (2380 8380). Tsim Sha Tsui MTR (exit A1)/buses along Nathan Road. **Open** noon-8pm Mon-Sat; 1-7pm Sun. **No credit cards. Map** p333 B6.

Located in a grimy building, this bookshop's floor, sofas, tables and shelves are loaded with guidebooks and posters, as well as travel-related fiction and non-fiction in both English and Chinese. They also hold talks and art exhibitions.

Antiquarian/second-hand

Flow

1-2/F, 40 Lyndhurst Terrace, Central, HK Island (2964 9483). Central MTR (exit D1, D2, G)/Mid-Levels Escalator/12M, 13, 23A, 40M, 43 bus. **Open** noon-7pm daily. **No credit cards. Map** p328 C3.

This second-hand bookshop will exchange your old books, CDs and videos for cash. **Photo** *p175*.

Department stores & malls

Department stores

Harvey Nichols

Shop HL011, G/F, The Landmark, 15 Queen's Road, Central, HK Island (3695 3388/www.harvey nichols.com). Central MTR (exit D1, G)/buses & trams through Central/Central Ferry Pier.

Open 10am-9pm Mon-Sat; 10am-7pm Sun. **Credit** AmEx, D, MC, V. **Map** p329 D4.

While the staff outnumbering the customers may be off-putting, this British luxury store – complete with in-store restaurant Fourth Floor – has the Hong Kong exclusive for prestigious brands such as stationers Smythson, French luggage label Goyard, cult beauty line Dr Brandt, and womenswear from Carolina Herrera and J Mendel. **Photos** *above*.

Jusco

Kornhill Plaza 2, Kornhill Road, Quarry Bay, HK Island (2884 6888). Quarry Bay MTR. **Open** 9.30am-10.30pm daily. **Credit** AmEx, DC, MC, V.

Jusco, one of the largest department stores in Japan, set up its first Hong Kong outlet in Quarry Bay back in 1987. Although some branches are showing their age, they are all exceptionally large and well stocked with fashion, food and household items. Another bonus is that prices are quite low, making it a better choice than other Japanese megastores.

Other locations: throughout the city.

Lane Crawford

Pacific Place, 88 Queensway, Admiralty, HK Island (2118 3668/www.lanecrawford.com). Admiralty MTR (exit C1)/buses & trams through Central. **Open** 10am-9pm daily. **Credit** AmEx, DC, MC, V. **Map** p329 F5.

One of the city's largest and oldest department stores, Lane Crawford is Hong Kong's answer to Harrods. Set over several floors, it's home to quality ranges such as Aveda, plus excellent household, shoe and handbag sections. The Causeway Bay location is pitched towards the younger market, while the other outlets cater to a more mature clientele.

Other locations: Podium 3, IFC Mall, 8 Finance Street, Central, HK Island (2118 3388); G-1/F, Times Square, 1 Matheson Street, Causeway Bay, HK Island (2118 3638); Shop 100, Ocean Terminal, Harbour City, 5 Canton Road, Tsim Sha Tsui, Kowloon (2118 3428).

Marks & Spencer

B-1/F, Central Tower, 28 Queen's Road, Central, HK Island (2921 8082/www.marksandspencer.com). Central MTR (exit D1, D2, G). **Open** 10.30am-8.30pm Mon-Fri; 10.30am-8pm Sat, Sun. **Credit** DC, MC, V. **Map** p329 D4.

This is the most accessible of Hong Kong's M&S stores, and it also has the best grocery section. While the stock mirrors that of the UK outlets, the prices are considerably higher. There's a good choice of clothing, and small but adequate food and cosmetics sections.

Other locations: 6/F, Times Square, Russell Street, Causeway Bay, HK Island (2923 7970); Shop 254, Ocean Centre, Harbour City, 5 Canton Road, Tsim Sha Tsui, Kowloon (2926 3346); Shop 428, New Town Plaza 1, Sha Tin, New Territories (2929 4332).

Seibu

Pacific Place, 88 Queensway, Admiralty, HK Island (2971 3888). Admiralty MTR (exit C1)/buses & trams through Central. **Open** 10.30am-8pm Mon-Wed, Sun; 10.30am-9pm Thur-Sat. **Credit** DC, MC, V. **Map** p329 F5.

Although it has a Japanese name, the Hong Kong Seibu stores are actually owned by Dickson 'Harvey Nichols' Poon and are decidedly cosmopolitan. The chic four-floor store in Pacific Place houses the food hall – the city's answer to Dean & Deluca – in the basement, while the other floors brim with a mix of desirable cosmetics, gifts, household items, kitchenware, accessories, shoes and clothes – from brands such as French Connection to Vivienne Westwood, as well as various Japanese labels. Both branches have a different feel – the one in Causeway Bay is geared towards young street fashion.

Sogo

555 Hennessy Road, Causeway Bay, HK Island (2833 8338/www.sogo.com.hk). Causeway Bay MTR (exit B, D2)/buses along Hennessy Road. **Open** 10am-10pm daily. **Credit** AmEx, DC, MC, V. **Map** p331 D3.

This Japanese store has a little bit of everything, and is very popular among the local well-heeled Chinese. However, it's not quite as flush – or as well set out – as its rival, Seibu (*see above*). But it does have a good assortment of household accessories such as glasses, plates and vases, not to mention necessities like irons, kettles, teapots and electrical merchandise. Much of the stock is Japanese and well-priced.

Other locations: B/F, 12 Salisbury Road, Tsim Sha Tsui, Kowloon (3556 1212).

Wing On

Wing On Centre, 211 Des Voeux Road Central, Sheung Wan, HK Island (2852 1888/www.wingonet. com). Sheung Wan MTR (exit E3)/buses & trams through Central. **Open** 10am-7.30pm daily. **Credit** AmEx, DC, MC, V. **Map** p328 C2.

It may be one of the oldest department stores in the city – it was founded in 1907 – but Wing On has been constantly upgraded. Its motto is 'value for money', and it stays true to its word. Prices are very reasonable, and the choice is fantastic and aimed mainly at the Chinese market. Merchandise includes cosmetics, clothing and housewares.

Other locations: throughout the city.

Malls

Fashion Walk

Kingston Street, Causeway Bay, HK Island. Causeway Bay MTR (exit E)/A11, 103, 170, N170 bus. **Open** 11am-11pm daily. **Credit** varies. **Map** p331 E2.

This sheltered pedestrianised street is lined with restaurants with outdoor tables as well as trendy boutiques, many of them featuring local designs.

Festival Walk

80 Tat Chee Avenue, Kowloon Tong, Kowloon. Kowloon Tong MTR. **Open** 10.30am-8pm daily. **Credit** varies.

Tech savvy

Many visitors come to Hong Kong with the intention of buying the latest laptop computer or electronic gadgetry at a steal. However, if you compare prices at reputable electronic chain stores here with those back home, you are likely to find only a marginal price difference, and some products may even be cheaper in your home country, depending on exchange rates.

In Hong Kong, the advantage of buying electronic goods is the unbeatable selection of computers, cameras, PDAs, hardware and software, some of which are sold up to six months before being released in Europe or North America. You can find stores specialising in one brand (such as Fujitsu laptop computers) or just amplifiers, with the shop carrying a full range of models (whereas overseas your choice will likely be limited to only a few).

Savvy tech shoppers looking for a deal will need to do some legwork. The best shopping areas are spread out in computer malls located in Wan Chai, Mong Kok and Sham Shui Po. Prices can vary slightly between districts, with the highest price competition within malls. Beware of Tsim Sha Tsui, where the streets (Nathan Road in particular) are packed with electronics and camera shops; it's notorious for ripping off customers.

If you aren't clued up on the latest products, head to one of the no-nonsense big chain stores – **Fortress** (see p180) or **Broadway** (see p179), where the staff will happily explain the features of each product. If you are nervous about being cheated, buy your goods from one of these stores, which both have excellent customer service.

If you have any problems, bring the item back to the shop within a week and (unlike many other electronics stores) they'll exchange it for a new one.

Once you know the specific product (with model number) you want, you can start hunting for the best price. Consider yourself lucky if you can get about a 30 per cent discount compared with overseas prices.

If you feel confident you won't be cheated, **Sham Shui Po** in Kowloon is the electronic mecca for hardcore technophiles looking for computer goods (both the legitimate and, more famously, the pirated). The streets around Apliu Street are lined with hundreds of computer and electronic shops. Here you can find the huge **Golden Computer Shopping Centre** (146-152 Fuk Wa Street, Sham Shui Po, Kowloon, 2729 2101), the grand-daddy of all computer malls. The **Mong Kok Computer Centre** (8-8A Nelson Street, Mong Kok, Kowloon, 2302 0858) is another crowded mall crammed with fast-talking salespeople and customers looking for the latest electronic gear.

On Hong Kong Island, the pirate CD, DVD, VCD and software market is alive and kicking at a crazy warren of stores packed into three floors at **298 Hennessy Road** (ten minutes' walk from Wan Chai MTR; take exit A3 and turn left) in Wan Chai. As this is illegal, the extremely low prices do not guarantee quality, which can be shoddy.

Another popular hunting ground for local shoppers and tourists is the multi-level **Wan Chai Computer Centre** (130 Hennessy Road, Wan Chai, HK Island). Shopping here can be more enjoyable since the standard of English

---

Although Festival Walk resembles Pacific Place in appearance, its target clientele is more midmarket. The mall also has an ice rink, an AMC cinemaplex and some decent restaurants.

Harbour City

5 Canton Road, Tsim Sha Tsui, Kowloon (2118 8666/www.harbourcity.com.hk). Tsim Sha Tsui MTR (exit E)/buses to Tsim Sha Tsui Star Ferry Pier & along Salisbury Road/Tsim Sha Tsui Star Ferry Pier. **Open** 10.30am-8pm daily. **Credit** varies. **Map** p333 B5/6.

A short walk from the Star Ferry terminal, Harbour City is divided into four interconnected shopping arcades, including the massive Ocean Terminal – the oldest mall in Hong Kong – and Ocean Centre. This gigantic mall is undoubtedly the largest

shopping emporium in Tsim Sha Tsui and it's easy to get lost (pick up a guide on your way into the mall). A street-fashion concept store, LCX, on Level 3, has a mix of clothing and accessories as well as international restaurants with harbour views.

IFC Mall

8 Finance Street, Central, HK Island (2295 3308/ www.ifc.com.hk). Central MTR (exit A)/buses to Central Ferry Pier. **Open** daily (time varies). **Credit** varies. **Map** p329 E2.

At the bottom of Hong Kong's tallest building, this mall is quickly becoming one of city's most popular shopping destinations, with 200 mainly international and luxury stores, including Zara, Mango, Burberry and Georg Jenson. If you need a shopping break, there's the Palace IFC cinema, Pure Fitness

is better and it's more centrally located. Prices are similar to other malls, provided that your bargaining skills are up to scratch.

Get price quotations from a bunch of different shops within a computer mall (or concentrated shopping area) for your specific model, but the key is to grab a business card in each shop and write the price on the back with the model number. With this card in hand, go to the next shop, first asking for the price without showing the card. If the price is higher than your lowest quotation, take out that business card. Like magic, you'll immediately see the price drop. When stores start quoting the same low price, you've hit rock bottom.

The best time to shop is off-peak hours (outside lunchtime or before people finish work). Staff members are friendlier and have the time to explain products. If a shop doesn't have what you're looking for, they won't try to sell you something completely different. Compare prices and shop around, that's the best strategy for finding a bargain.

Coxell Digital Camera

Shop 256, 2/F, Southern Centre, 130 Hennessy Road, Wan Chai, HK Island (2832 9781). Wan Chai MTR (exit A4). **Open** 11am-9pm Mon-Sat; noon-8pm Sun. **Credit** AmEx, MC, V. **Map** p330 B3.
Friendly and knowledgeable staff, and a full range of cameras, digital cameras, camcorders and accessories.
Other locations: Shop 23, G/F, Golden Building, 146-152 Fuk Wah Street, Sham Shui Po, Kowloon (2626 0970).

Designer Group

Shop 1118-21, 11/F, Windsor House, 311 Gloucester Road, Causeway Bay, HK Island (2504 4122). Causeway Bay MTR (exit E)/buses & trams through Causeway Bay. **Open** 11.30am-8.30pm Mon-Sat; noon-6pm Sun. **Credit** AmEx, DC, MC, V. **Map** p331 E3.
Opened in 1994, this well laid-out shop was the first appointed Apple Centre in Asia. It covers all your Mac needs, with books, software, computers and iPod accessories.
Other locations: Shop 2012, Podium Level 2, IFC Mall, 8 Finance Street, Central, HK Island (2295 4488); Shop 903C, 9/F, Times Square, 1 Matheson Street, Causeway Bay, HK Island (2506 1338).

Sunny Computer Technology Company

Shop 140-149, 1/F, Wan Chai Computer Centre, 130 Hennessy Road, Wan Chai, HK Island (2147 0430). Wan Chai MTR (exit A4). **Open** 11.30am-8.30pm; 1-8pm Sun. **Credit** AmEx, DC, MC, V. **Map** p330 B3.
Competitive prices for computer components, with staff willing to assist with queries before and after a sale.

Computer Mall at Windsor House

10-11/F, 311 Gloucester Road, Causeway Bay, HK Island (2895 6796). Causeway Bay MTR (exit E)/buses & trams through Causeway Bay. **Open** 11.30am-8.30pm. **Credit** varies. **Map** p331 E3.
More upmarket than Wan Chai and Mong Kok computer malls, this plaza has two floors of shops dedicated to Mac and PC wares.

gym, upmarket food shop City Super and some of the city's best restaurants, with drop-dead views.

The Landmark

16 Des Voeux Road, Central, HK Island. Central MTR (exit G)/buses & trams through Central/Central Ferry Pier. **Open** 10am-7.30pm daily. **Credit** varies. **Map** p329 D4.
The Landmark may be one of the older malls in Hong Kong, but it has managed to maintain its prestigious status and elegant appearance. Inside, there's a huge central atrium and a wide range of shops, which are worth checking out for their flash window displays, even if you're not in a buying mood. All the boutiques here are from higher-end brand names, among them Tod's, Christian Dior, Louis Vuitton and Gucci.

Langham Place

8 Argyle Street, Mong Kok, Kowloon (2148 2160/ www.langhamplace.com.hk). Mong Kok MTR (exit C3). **Open** daily (times vary). **Credit** varies. **Map** p332 B2.
Shooting out of Mong Kok's shopping madness is this modern 15-storey mall, with 300-plus stores catering to a young, hip crowd. You'll also find a cinema, a bunch of reasonably priced restaurants and a five-star hotel by the same name (*see p64*).

Lee Gardens

33 Hysan Avenue, Causeway Bay, HK Island. Causeway Bay MTR (exit F). **Open** 10.30am-8pm daily. **Credit** varies. **Map** p331 E3.
Lee Gardens provides a relaxed environment in which the most prestigious (and expensive) brands

Eat, Drink, Shop

congregate. Hermès, Louis Vuitton, Chanel, Cartier and Dior are just a few examples. You can also find a gourmet supermarket in the basement, aptly named Gourmet.

Pacific Place

88 Queensway, Admiralty, HK Island (2844 8988). Admiralty MTR (exit C1)/buses & trams through Central. **Open** 10.30am-8pm daily. **Credit** varies. **Map** p329 F5.

Pacific Place's exit from the MTR station is sleek and chic – just like the four-storey mall itself. Well designed and easily accessible, its outlets (particularly the landmark department stores Lane Crawford (*see p176*) and Seibu (*see p177*) cater for a wide range of clientele.

Rise Commercial Building

5-11 Granville Circuit (off Granville Road), Tsim Sha Tsui, Kowloon. Tsim Sha Tsui MTR (exit B1, B2)/ buses along Nathan Road/Tsim Sha Tsui Star Ferry Pier. **Open** daily (times vary). **Credit** varies. **Map** p333 C5.

Despite its rather rundown appearance, this arcade is the current fashion hotspot. Tucked away from view near the factory outlets in Granville Road, the four floors draw a younger crowd, attracted by the lesser-known designers, henna tattoo parlour, homeware shops and other quirky stores.

Times Square

Russell Street, Causeway Bay, HK Island. Causeway Bay MTR (exit A)/buses along Hennessy Road. **Open** 10.30am-9pm daily. **Credit** varies. **Map** p331 D3.

This Causeway Bay landmark building caters to a wide range of shoppers. On the ground floor and at The Lobby on 2/F are Gucci, Ferragamo and the like, whereas floors 3-9 are allocated for themes such as Suit & Dress, Casual Living, Electronics World and Kids. The 10th-14th floors house the Food Forum, a hub of restaurants, while the basement has the Marketplace, for fast food and supermarkets. There's also a Lane Crawford on the first floor.

Dry cleaners

Goodwins of London

Basement, Great Food Hall, Seibu Department Store, Pacific Place, 88 Queensway, Admiralty, HK Island (2525 0605/www.goodwinsoflondon.com). Admiralty MTR (exit C1, C2). **Open** 10am-10pm daily. **Credit** MC, V. **Map** p329 F5.

An all-English, extra-refined dry cleaners that provides a reliable, careful service for cleaning clothes. **Other locations**: Shop A, 2/F, Dairy Farm Complex, 35 Beach Road, Repulse Bay, HK Island (2812 2400).

Jeeves

Shop 108A, The Galleria, 19 Queen's Road, Central, HK Island (2973 0101/www.jeeves.com.hk). Central MTR (exit H)/buses & trams through Central/Central Ferry Pier. **Open** 10am-7pm Mon-Sat. **Credit** AmEx, DC, MC, V. **Map** p329 D4.

One of the city's older dry-cleaning establishments, this is an upmarket place for the upwardly mobile. In other words, prices are steep.

Electronics

You can find electronic stores throughout Hong Kong, but computer malls are the best places to find a large selection in a concentrated (and competitive) space. For further ideas, *see p178* **Tech savvy**.

Broadway

Shops 704 & 714, Times Square, 1 Matheson Street, Causeway Bay, HK Island (2506 1330/2506 0228/ www.broadway.com.hk). Causeway Bay MTR (exit A). **Open** 11am-10pm daily. **Credit** DC, MC, V. **Map** p331 D3.

Like its rival Fortress (*see below*), Broadway also has branches scattered all over the territory. Smart shoppers will visit them both to compare prices before going ahead and making a purchase.
Other locations: throughout the city.

Citicall

G/F, Hung Kei Mansion, 5-8 Queen Victoria Street, Central, HK Island (2391 4366/www.citicall.com.hk). Central MTR (exit B)/buses & trams through Central. **Open** 9.30am-8.30pm daily. **Credit** MC, V. **Map** p328 C3.

From its humble beginnings as a small camera shop in Mong Kok, Citicall has blossomed into a chain of electronics and audio-visual shops that rivals corporation-backed Fortress and Broadway. Prices are considerably cheaper as the owner has the connections that allow him to cut out the middleman. Don't be put off by the chaos inside the stores – the staff are usually friendly and willing to give a good price.
Other locations: throughout the city.

Fortress

Shop 3320, Level 3, Harbour City, 5 Canton Road, Tsim Sha Tsui, Kowloon (2116 1022/www.fortress. com.hk). Tsim Sha Tsui MTR (exit C1, E)/buses to Tsim Sha Tsui Star Ferry Pier/Tsim Sha Tsui Star Ferry Pier. **Open** 11am-9pm daily. **Credit** AmEx, DC, MC, V. **Map** p333 B5/6.

If you're after a TV, camera, stereo, CD player, plug or hairdryer, one of the many Fortress outlets around town will no doubt stock it. They also have a small collection of CDs, DVDs and VCDs. These, like the rest of the store's stock, are reliable and the prices always low. The friendly, helpful staff are another pull.
Other locations: throughout the city.

Fortress Zoom/Fortress Digital

59 Russell Street, Causeway Bay, HK Island (2504 4525). Causeway Bay MTR (exit A). **Open** noon-10pm daily. **Credit** AmEx, DC, MC, V. **Map** p331 D3.

Part of the Fortress group, these Zoom/Digital branches around town specialise in personal electronic products including audio-visual, photographic and portable computing products.

Fashion

For high-end shopping, head for Central or Admiralty; for streetwear, go to Causeway Bay; and for factory outlets, try Tsim Sha Tsui. The more adventurous can trek further up the Kowloon peninsula to **Temple Street Night Market** (*see p190* **To market, to market**) and Mong Kok for local bargains.

Accessories

For a wide range of accessories and knick-knacks, try the street stalls on **Jardine's Crescent** in Causeway Bay, HK Island.

Bally Leather

90B Nathan Road, Tsim Sha Tsui, Kowloon (2366 2588). Tsim Sha Tsui MTR (exit B1)/buses along Nathan Road. **Open** 9.30am-11pm daily. **Credit** AmEx, DC, MC, V. **Map** p333 C6.
Leather accessories including handbags, briefcases and shoes. Prices aren't too hard on the wallet, and service comes with a smile.

Mandarina Duck

Shop B54, The Landmark, 16 Des Voeux Road, Central, HK Island (2845 4898/www.mandarina duck.com). Central MTR (exit G)/buses & trams through Central/Central Ferry Pier. **Open** 10am-7pm daily. **Credit** AmEx, DC, MC, V. **Map** p329 D4.
Every self-respecting dapper local has probably owned a Mandarina Duck bag at some stage. The neat, compact designs, often made from hardened man-made fabric, have an almost sci-fi appearance. OK, they're pricey, but they wear well.

Renommé

Flat B, 13/F, North Point Mansions, 702 King's Road, North Point, HK Island (2522 6435). Quarry Bay MTR (exit B4)/buses along King's Road. **Open** 10am-6pm Mon-Fri; by appointment Sat. **No credit cards.**
This shop is run by a group of Filipinos who design superb hats for every occasion. You can bring your own materials and fabric if you choose.

Samsonite

Shop X, Level 2, Windsor House, 311 Gloucester Road, Causeway Bay, HK Island (2736 1936/www. samsonite.com). Causeway Bay MTR (exit F)/23B bus. **Open** 10am-10pm daily. **Credit** AmEx, MC, V. **Map** p331 E3.
If you're in need of an extra case (or two) to carry home your Hong Kong purchases, Samsonite is the place to go for its famously robust cases and travel bags.
Other locations: throughout the city.

Style

35B Granville Road, Tsim Sha Tsui, Kowloon (2721 0110). Tsim Sha Tsui MTR (exit B2)/buses along Chatham Road South. **Open** noon-11am daily. **Credit** MC, V. **Map** p333 C5.12-11
This trinket store stocks all manner of cheap accessories, from hairclips to wigs and feathered masks.

Budget

Bossini

G/F, On Lok Yuen Building, 27A Des Voeux Road, Central, HK Island (2524 9313/www.bossini.com). Central MTR (exit A). **Open** 10am-8pm daily. **Credit** AmEx, DC, MC, V. **Map** p329 D3.
Luckily for budget shoppers, there's a Bossini outlet on almost every street in Hong Kong. Aside from its well-made basics, the store's seasonal collections tend to put many high-street labels to shame.
Other locations: throughout the city.

Giordano Ladies

Shop 4, G/F, China Building, 29 Queen's Road, Central, HK Island (2921 2028). Central MTR (exit D1, D2, G)/buses along Queen's Road Central. **Open** 10am-8.30pm Mon-Sat; 11am-8pm Sun. **Credit** AmEx, MC, V. **Map** p329 D4.
Like Bossini, Giordano is pretty much everywhere in town and offers a good selection of basics, from accessories through to jeans and T-shirts. As for the pricing: it's so low it's a sin. In recent years, however, the label has established an upmarket – and pricier – line, Giordano Ladies, which features high-quality fabrics and cuttings (confusingly, for both men and women). Note that not all branches sell this newer range.
Other locations: throughout the city.

Children

Crocodile for Kids

Shop 15-16, Park Lane Shopping Boulevard, 111-181 Nathan Road, Kowloon (2730 1190). Tsim Sha Tsui MTR (exit C1, C2)/buses along Nathan Road. **Open** 10.30am-9pm daily. **Credit** AmEx, DC, MC, V. **Map** p333 B6.
The various branches of the Chinese Crocodile label sell the Western look (trainers, T-shirts, jeans and more) at exceptionally low prices, but this outlet near Kowloon Park carries one of the biggest children's departments.
Other locations: throughout the city.

Kingkow

Shop OT, G46-47, Ocean Terminal, Harbour City, 5 Canton Road, Tsim Sha Tsui, Kowloon (2317 4088/www.kingkow.com.hk). Tsim Sha Tsui MTR (exit C1, E)/buses along Chatham Road South. **Open** 10am-8pm daily. **Credit** AmEx, DC, MC, V. **Map** p333 B6.
Kingkow stocks inexpensive clothes for kids (under the age of 16 years) to suit any occasion.

Designer: international

Birkin

Shop G001-002, G/F, World Trade Centre, 280 Gloucester Road, Causeway Bay, Hong Kong Island (2970 2231). Causeway Bay MTR (exit D3)/A11, 103, 170, N170 bus. **Open** noon-10pm daily. **Credit** AmEx, DC, MC, V. **Map** p331 E2.

Eat, Drink, Shop

Come to Birkin for the latest pieces from big names such as Prada, Miu Miu and Gucci, all at lower prices than at the official outlets.
Other locations: Basement, Sun Arcade, 28 Canton Road, Tsim Sha Tsui, Kowloon (2377 2880).

Extravaganza

Shop 104, 1/F, Causeway Bay Plaza 1, 489 Hennessy Road, Causeway Bay, HK Island (2915 0051). Causeway Bay MTR (exit B)/trams & buses along Hennessy Road. **Open** noon-10pm Mon-Thur, Sun; noon-10.30pm Sat. **Credit** AmEx, DC, MC, V. **Map** p331 E3.

Like Birkin (*see p181*), Extravaganza offers the latest designer brands at prices lower than at the official outlets.
Other locations: 1/F, Miramar Shopping Centre, 1-23 Kimberley Road, Tsim Sha Tsui, Kowloon (2730 0500).

Giorgio Armani

G/F, Chater House, 11 Chater Road, Central, HK Island (2532 7700/www.giorgioarmani.com). Central MTR (exit B)/buses along Des Voeux Road Central. **Open** 10am-7.30pm daily. **Credit** AmEx, DC, MC, V. **Map** p329 D3.

With 2,000sq m (21,500sq ft) of retail space, this Armani superstore has everything you could possibly want from the legendary Italian design house. When all the browsing has worn you out, nourishment can be had at the cool Armani Bar.

Gucci

G1, The Landmark, 16 Des Voeux Road, Central, HK Island (2524 4492/www.gucci.com). Central MTR (exit G)/buses & trams through Central/Central Ferry Pier. **Open** 10.30am-7.30pm Mon-Sat; 11am-7pm Sun. **Credit** AmEx, DC, MC, V. **Map** p329 D4.

If you've got cash in your pocket and/or credit on your card, Gucci's temple of extravagance is a favourite place to head.
Other locations: Shop 368, Pacific Place, 88 Queensway, Admiralty, HK Island (2524 2721).

IT

G/F, Sino Plaza, 255-7 Gloucester Road, Causeway Bay, HK Island (2834 4393/www.ithk.com). Causeway Bay MTR (exit C)/buses along Gloucester Road. **Open** noon-10pm daily. **Credit** AmEx, MC, V. **Map** p331 D2.

The IT chain stocks favourite brands like Paul Smith, Helmut Lang, Vivienne Westwood and Comme des Garçons, as well as desirable furniture and selected homewares. This two-storey outlet is decked out like an early '80s disco, with smoked glass, mirror balls and dark furnishings, which doesn't exactly make for a comfortable shopping experience. If the prices are beyond your budget, try their discount branch across the harbour (Shop 72-119, Silvercord, 30 Canton Road, Tsim Sha Tsui, 2377 9466).
Other locations: Shop 120, Level 1, Pacific Place, 88 Queensway, Admiralty, HK Island (2167 8287); Shop 215, 2/F, Ocean Centre, Harbour City, 5 Canton Road, Tsim Sha Tsui, Kowloon (2114 0268).

Joyce

106 Canton Road, Tsim Sha Tsui, Kowloon (2367 8128). Tsim Sha Tsui MTR (exit C1, E)/buses along Nathan Road/Tsim Sha Tsui Star Ferry Pier. **Open** noon-10.30pm Mon-Sat; noon-7pm Sun. **Credit** DC, MC, V. **Map** p333 B6.

Named after its founder, Joyce Ma, this store is a bit of an institution in Hong Kong. Several outlets around the city stock designer names such as Comme des Garçons, Dolce & Gabbana, Anna Sui and Ghost, alongside top-brand shoes, accessories and cosmetics. The Tsim Sha Tsui outlet is the mainstream venue (and has a Prada concession); the Central store is reserved for more upmarket brands; and the Admiralty branch is geared to the young and trendy.

The Joyce empire also controls individual boutiques for Dries Van Noten (The Landmark; *see p179*), Dolce & Gabbana (Alexandra House, 16-20 Chater Road, Central, 2877 5558), Jil Sander (30 Queen's Road, Central, 2869 9121), Y's by Yohji Yamamoto (Lee Gardens; *see p179*) and Boss (Pacific Place; *see p180*).
Other locations: New World Tower, 16 Queen's Road, Central, HK Island (2810 1120); Shop 334, Pacific Place, 88 Queensway, Admiralty, HK Island (2523 5944).

Joyce Warehouse

21/F, Horizon Plaza, 2 Lee Wing Street, Ap Lei Chau, HK Island (2814 8313). Bus 90B, 590. **Open** 10am-7pm Tue-Sat; noon-6pm Sun. **Credit** DC, MC, V.

Joyce Warehouse may be hard to get to, but keen shoppers will be rewarded by the range and prices – womenswear is often vastly reduced.

Louis Vuitton

Shop 7-17, G/F, The Landmark, 16 Des Voeux Road, Central, HK Island (2736 6100/www.louisvuitton. com). Central MTR (exit D1, G)/buses through Central/Central Ferry Pier. **Open** 10am-8pm Mon-Sat, 11am-7pm Sun. **Credit** AmEx, DC, MC, V. **Map** p329 D4.

This massive Louis Vuitton store with three floors takes up a prime corner spot in Central. For top customers (or celebrities), who want some privacy before splashing out thousands on an LV bag, there's a VIP room with private loo. **Photo** *p183*.
Other locations: throughout the city.

Prada

Shops G4 & 102, G/F-1/F, Alexander House, 18 Chater Road, Central, HK Island (2522 2989/ www.prada.com). Central MTR (exit G)/buses & trams through Central/Central Ferry Pier. **Open** 10am-8pm Mon-Sat; 11am-7pm Sun. **Credit** AmEx, DC, MC, V. **Map** p329 D4.

This two-storey flagship store carries everything you would expect from the Italian fashion powerhouse, and some things you wouldn't, like a checkers board game and deck of cards.
Other locations: Shop G28, Sogo, 555 Hennessy Road, Causeway Bay, HK Island (2836 5686).

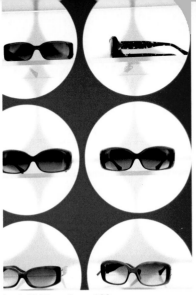

Louis Vuitton. *See p182.*

The Swank Shop

Shop 202, 2/F, Alexander House, 18 Chater Road, Central, HK Island (2810 0769/2868 3804). Central MTR (exit G)/buses & trams through Central/Central Ferry Pier. **Open** 10.30am-7.30pm daily. **Credit** AmEx, DC, MC, V. **Map** p329 D4.

Don't be put off by the naff name – the Swank Shop is one of the city's oldest fashion stores. It sells an odd but extensive assortment of designer labels, such as Gianfranco Ferre and Roberto Cavalli, for both men and women. Even if these names aren't for you, there's a slick collection of accessories on offer as well.
Other locations: Shop 230, Level 2, Pacific Place, 88 Queensway, Admiralty, HK Island (2845 4929); Level 2, Ocean Centre, Harbour City, 5 Canton Road, Tsim Sha Tsui, Kowloon (2735 0842).

Versace

Shop 2053, Podium Level, IFC Tower 2, 8 Finance Street, Central, HK Island (2912 1000). Central MTR (exit E1, A2)/63, 108, 117, 170, N170 bus. **Open** 11am-8.30pm daily. **Credit** AmEx, DC, MC, V. **Map** p329 E2.

The Versace label has a large following in Hong Kong and, therefore, plenty of outlets. All are cold and crisp, topped off by service with a (thin) smile.
Other locations: Pacific Place in Admiralty, Ocean Centre and Peninsula Hotel in Tsim Sha Tsui, Kowloon.

Vivienne Tam

Shop 302, Times Square, 1 Matheson Street, Causeway Bay, HK Island (2506 0098/www. viviennetam.com). Causeway Bay MTR (exit A)/63, 108, 117, 170, N170 bus. **Open** 11am-8pm Mon-Thur, Sun; 11am-9pm Fri, Sat. **Credit** AmEx, DC, MC, V. **Map** p331 D3.

Sometimes you'll wander into a store selling the New York-based Chinese designer Vivienne Tam's latest collection and be wowed by her exquisite sexy silk dresses covered in intricate Chinese embroidery. Other times, you'll be appalled by the downmarket nylon fabrics and cheap-looking T-shirts. Still, as one of the territory's greatest design exports, Tam is something of a local treasure.
Other locations: Shop 209, Pacific Place, 88 Queensway, Admiralty, HK Island (2918 0551)

Designer: local

Cloud 9

1/F, 7 Lan Kwai Fong, Central, HK Island (2847 3339/www.cloud9asia.com). Central MTR (exit D1, G)/13, 26, 43 bus/buses along Queen's Road Central. **Open** 11am-7.30pm Mon-Sat. **Credit** MC, V. **Map** p329 C4.

Not everyone has a petite Asian body, so Ilse Kerling set up a women's clothing shop catering to sizes 8 to 18. Designing her own label of Western and Asian-inspired clothes, there are taffeta silk dresses, reversible tops and hand-embroidered jackets at reasonable prices. Free alterations. **Photo** *p185.*

G2000

Shop 276, Park Lane Shoppers Boulevard, 111-181 Nathan Road, Tsim Sha Tsui, Kowloon (2730 9975/www.g2000.com.hk). Tsim Sha Tsui MTR (exit A1). **Open** 11am-11.30pm daily. **Credit** MC, V. **Map** p333 B5.

G2000 is a very popular local brand for suits and classic sportswear. Most of its suits are made from European fabrics, and workmanship is very good. Prices are extremely reasonable for what you get.
Other locations: throughout the city.

Eat, Drink, Shop

Cloud 9. *See p183.*

Gay Giano

Shop 2315-2316, Gateway Arcade, Harbour City,
5 Canton Road, Tsim Sha Tsui (2956 3784/www.
gaygiano.com). Tsim Sha Tsui MTR (exit A1)/Tsim
Sha Tsui Star Ferry Pier. **Open** 11.30am-8.30pm
daily. **Credit** AmEx, DC, MC, V. **Map** p333 B5/6.
Gay Giano could easily be mistaken for an Italian
brand – indeed, many Hong Kongers don't know it's
actually a local label. All items are well designed and
of very high quality and only a fraction of the price
you'd pay for something genuinely Italian.
Other locations: Shop 525, 5/F, Times Square,
1 Matheson Street, Causeway Bay (2506 2082); Shop
36, G/F, Fashion Island, 19 Great George Street,
Causeway Bay, HK Island (2576 8187).

http://www.izzue.com

Basement, Island Beverly, 1 Great George Street,
Causeway Bay, HK Island (2890 3560/www.izzue.
com). Causeway Bay MTR (exit E). **Open** noon-11pm
daily. **Credit** AmEx, DC, MC, V. **Map** p331 E3.
Founded just a few years ago, this local fashion company has already captured the hearts of local young-
sters with its hip hop and street styles. The only
downside is that most stock seems to be geared to
Asian (ie petite) people. Some branches also have
cafés and gadget showcases.
Other locations: throughout the city.

Shanghai Tang

G/F, Pedder Building, 12 Pedder Street, Central, HK
Island (2525 7333/www.shanghaitang.com). Central
MTR (exit D1, G)/buses & trams through Central/
Central Ferry Pier. **Open** 10am-8pm Mon-Fri;
noon-6pm Sat, Sun. **Credit** AmEx, DC, MC, V.
Map p329 D4.
The money-making brainchild of local entrepreneur
David Tang, Shanghai Tang is a favourite shopping spot for many. Trad China with a kitsch twist,
the shop sells everything from silk-covered diaries
to Mao clocks, and leather coats to cheongsams. The
store also has its own troupe of tailors, some of
whom can still create a real cheongsam – those
worn by Maggie Cheung in *In The Mood For Love*
were made here. *Photo p170.*

Other locations: Shop ML2-3, Peninsula Hotel,
Salisbury Road, Tsim Sha Tsui, Kowloon (2537 2888).

'SPY' by Henry Lau

11 Sharp Street East, Causeway Bay, HK Island
(2893 7799/www.spyhenrylau.com). Causeway Bay
MTR (exit A). **Open** 1-11pm daily. **Credit** AmEx,
DC, MC, V. **Map** p331 D3.
With shops in Japan, Taiwan, Canada and Macau,
Lau is one of the few local designers to enjoy an
international profile. His flamboyant designs mix
street chic with splashes of the theatrical.
Other locations: Shop 406-7, Rise Commercial
Building, 5-11 Granville Circuit, Tsim Sha Tsui,
Kowloon (2366 5899).

U2

Shops B225 & 530, Basement 2 & 5/F,
Times Square, 1 Matheson Street, Causeway
Bay, HK Island (women 2576 6745/men 2506
2821/www.u2.com.hk). Causeway Bay MTR
(exit A). **Open** noon-10pm Mon-Fri; 11.30am-
10pm Sat, Sun. **Credit** AmEx, DC, MC, V.
Map p331 D3.
Occupying a number of locations around town, U2
is the popular sportswear line of G2000 (*see p183*)
and sells good-quality casualwear, in both classic
and trendy styles, for women (in the basement) and
men (on level five). On the whole, prices are incred-
ibly reasonable.
Other locations: throughout the city.

Factory outlets

Esprit Outlet

G/F & Basement, 4-6 Hankow Road, Tsim Sha Tsui,
Kowloon (2721 3318). Tsim Sha Tsui MTR (exit
E)/buses along Nathan Road. **Open** 10am-11pm
Mon-Thur; 10am-midnight Fri-Sun. **Credit** AmEx,
DC, MC, V. **Map** p333 B6.
A large Esprit outlet, well stocked with bargain-
priced women's and menswear, shoes, bags, bed
clothes, baby clothes and make-up line Red Earth.
Other locations: Shop A, B/F, Hollywood Plaza,
610 Nathan Road, Mong Kok, Kowloon (2388 0064).

Second-hand luxury

Hong Kong's female population has made shopping an art form. It's all about looking good and flaunting it. Office ladies, *tai-tais* (the Cantonese word for rich housewives) and socialites are not modest in showing off their latest purchase, especially when it comes to designer brands that are considered the ultimate luxury. 'If you can afford it, then buy it,' is the motto here.

But what happens when you want a fashion fix and don't have HK$20,000 to shell out on a Fendi bag? The answer: head to one of the city's many luxury second-hand boutiques where you can find members of the designers' club – Prada, Chanel, Louis Vuitton, Tod's and Dior – for a steal.

For people who don't want to spend a mini-fortune, the second-hand market that has taken off in the last few years has much to offer. One of the most popular resellers is **Milan Station**, which opened in 2000 and now has multiple branches for women aspiring to own an authentic designer item.

As closet space is limited in many flats, *tai-tais* are all too happy to offload last season's goods, replacing them with newer, flashier models. Thus retailers have no shortage of supply, and discounts can vary from 30 to 50 per cent off the original price – which still means that you could part with a few hundred (or thousand) HK dollars for a mere purse.

Each store (and outlets within a chain) carries a different range of recycled goods, but the main bulk of merchandise is handbags. These are easier to sell since any size bag fits its potential owner.

It's best to go to the original boutique and check out the latest styles and prices. This way you can work out how much to pay at a second-hand shop. Thoroughly check items for details. For clothes, look at the seams and zippers; for handbags, look at the condition of base and shape, and for any scratches. Be aware that each brand has a signature trademark (for example, LV has a serial number in different locations) to indicate its authenticity.

France Station

G/F, A60 Russell Street, Causeway Bay, HK Island (2895 5700). Causeway Bay MTR (exit A)/63, 108, 117, 170, N170 bus. **Open** noon-10pm daily. **Credit** AmEx, DC, MC, V. **Map** p331 D3.

Similar to Milan Station (*see below*), this customer-friendly shop features a ton of LV bags and luggage, plus Hermès, Birken, Prada and Gucci lines. For second-hand snobs, there are brand-new, current-season items (marked with a red tag) – you might get lucky and find a Chloé handbag for HK$8,800 (original price HK$12,800).

Granville Road & Kimberley Road

Tsim Sha Tsui, Kowloon. Tsim Sha Tsui MTR (exit B1, B2)/buses along Nathan Road. **Map** p333 C5.
Two parallel streets where lots of factory outlets sell competitively priced clothes.

Sun Outlet

G/F, 6 Li Yuen Street East, Central, HK Island (2377 1188). Central MTR (exit D1, D2, G)/buses along Queen's Road Central. **Open** 10am-8pm daily. **Credit** MC, V. **Map** p329 D3.
Nestled in The Lanes street market, this shop is worth seeking out for its great stock of heavily discounted designer T-shirts, tops, coats and skirts by the likes of Max Mara, Betsey Johnson, Marc Jacobs and Issey Miyake.

Second-hand

See also above **Second-hand luxury**.

Beatniks

Shop 1, Rise Commercial Building, 5-11 Granville Circuit, Tsim Sha Tsui, Kowloon (2739 8494). Tsim Sha Tsui MTR (exit B1, B2)/buses along Chatham Road South. **Open** 3-11pm daily. **Credit** AmEx, DC, MC, V. **Map** p333 C5.
A well-known name among second-hand clothing fans, Beatniks has many vintage fashion items targeted at the grunge type. But don't think that means things are cheap here – it costs big bucks to dress down in Hong Kong.
Other locations: G/F Hyde Building, 221-226 Gloucester Road, Causeway Bay, HK Island (2881 7153).

Salvation Army Thrift Store

G/F, 1A Cliff Road, Yau Ma Tei, Kowloon (2332 4448). Yau Ma Tei MTR (exit C). **Open** 10.30am-7pm Mon-Sat. **No credit cards**. **Map** p332 B3.
The Salvation Army runs the city's most established line of thrift stores and, even better, it's all for charity. But don't think that thrift stores sell only rubbish: many of the items on offer here are well-known labels, and if you dig in you might even come across a Donna Karan or Gaultier.
Other locations: throughout the city.

Ladyplace

Unit A, 1/F, World Trust Tower, 50 Stanley Street, Central, HK Island (2854 2321/ www.ladyplace.com). Central MTR (exit D1, D2, G)/buses along Queen's Road Central. **Open** 10am-7pm Mon-Fri; 10am-1pm Sat. **Credit** MC, V. **Map** p329 C3.

If you don't mind sifting through jam-packed racks of clothes kept in clear plastic bags, this is a 1,200-square-foot treasure trove of second-hand designer clothes, expensive watches (Tiffany and Cartier), and shoes and bags by the likes of Cacharel, Vivienne Westwood, Miu Miu and Gucci at bargain prices. You can also order online – there's a door-to-door delivery service available.

Milan Station

Shop F-H, G/F, 81 Chatham Rd, Tsim Sha Tsui, Kowloon (2730 2528). Tsim Sha Tsui MTR (exit A1, B2)/buses along Nathan Road/Tsim Sha Tsui Star Ferry Pier. **Open** noon-10pm daily. **Credit** AmEx, DC, MC, V. **Map** p333 B6.

With six branches, Milan Station is the most popular second-hand designer shop in the territory. Each shop is a different size and the stock available at each vastly differs. The branch in Central primarily carries a variety of handbags by the likes of Chloé, Chanel, Burberry and Gucci. At the Tsim Sha

Tsui outlet, you'll find a selection of clothing, sunglasses and wallets, and a ton of Fendi and Louis Vuitton handbags.
Other locations: throughout the city.

Pedder Building

12 Pedder Street, Central, HK Island. Central MTR (exit D1, D2)/buses & trams through Central/Central Ferry Pier. **Open** daily (times vary). **Credit** varies. **Map** p329 D3.

Built in 1924, the building houses a concise selection of factory outlets and discount stores (and chic Chinese atelier Shanghai Tang), plus a good range of cashmere and silk. Best way to navigate through the shops is to take the lift to the top floor, then walk down floor by floor.

The 3rd Avenue

Shop 304B, Pedder Building, 12 Pedder Street, Central, HK Island (2537 9168/www. 3rd-ave.com.hk). Central MTR (exit D1, G)/ buses & trams through Central/Central Ferry Pier. **Open** 10am-7pm Mon-Sat; noon-6pm Sun. **Credit** AmEx, MC, V. **Map** p329 D3.

Crammed full of second-hand designer leather goods, clothes and shoes, this shop is one of the highlights of the Pedder Building (*see above*). They accept trade-ins and offer cash for new, used and vintage products, notably Hermès, Louis Vuitton and Chanel.

Shoes

Millie's

Shop 13, G/F, Central Building, 1 Pedder Street, Central, HK Island (2523 8001/www.millies.com.hk). Central MTR (exit D1, G)/buses & trams through Central/Central Ferry Pier. **Open** 10am-8pm Mon-Sat; 10am-7pm Sun. **Credit** AmEx, DC, MC, V. **Map** p329 D4.

This long-established shop stocks a decent collection of Italian shoes and handbags. Prices are fair and the designs flatter any modern man or woman.

Ming Kee

30 Bowring Street, Jordan, Kowloon (2730 4815). Jordan MTR (exit C1, C2)/buses along Nathan Road. **Open** 11am-9pm Mon-Sat. **No credit cards. Map** p333 B4.

This is where local pop and movie stars have their glitzy shoes made. Orders normally take two weeks, but a rush job can be done in ten days, or you could get in touch in advance of your visit. Bring a sketch or picture of the shoe you want copied. Expect to pay upwards of HK$650.

Nine West

Shop 11-12, Central Building, 1 Pedder Street, Central, HK Island (2921 2628). Central MTR (exit D1, G)/buses & trams through Central/Central Ferry Pier. **Open** 9.30am-7.30pm daily. **Credit** AmEx, DC, MC, V. **Map** p329 D4.

Having conquered the US and UK markets, Nine West has become every gal's favourite shoe store. If you're lucky enough to be around during the sales, prices are slashed by more than half.
Other locations: throughout the city.

Streetwear/clubwear

Bape

G/F, 10 Queen's Road, Central, HK Island (2868 9448/www.bape.com). Central MTR (exit D1, G)/buses & trams through Central/Central Ferry Pier. **Open** 11am-8pm daily. **Credit** AmEx, DC, MC, V. **Map** p329 D4.

With neon graffiti-like window displays, local clubbers and people looking for street cred go bananas for the Japanese clothing label. The gorilla logo and its signature camouflage print are plastered on caps

Bape. *See p187.*

and T-shirts, while its popular multicoloured sneakers rotate under a trippy glass-floor conveyor belt. **Photo** *above.*

D-Mop

G/F, 11-15 On Lan Street, Central, HK Island (2840 0822/www.d-mop.com). Central MTR (exit D1, G)/ 13, 26, 43 bus/buses along Queen's Road Central. **Open** 11am-8pm Mon-Sat; noon-7pm Sun. **Credit** AmEx, DC, MC, V. **Map** p329 D4.

D-Mop is one of the trendier shops in Hong Kong, selling stuff that no self-respecting, fashion-conscious guru would be without. Patrick Cox and Komodo woollies, clothes by Martine Sitbon, and a great selection of jeans, including good old ever-fashionable Levi's, are all stocked.

Other locations: 8 Kingston Street, Causeway Bay, HK Island (2203 4130).

Tailors

Jantzen Tailor

Shop 256, 2/F, Worldwide House, 19 Des Voeux Road, Central, HK Island (2570 5901/www. jantzentailor.com). Central MTR (exit B, C)/buses & trams through Central/Central Ferry Pier. **Open** 11am-8pm Mon-Sat; noon-5pm Sun. **Credit** AmEx, MC, V. **Map** p329 D4.

A tiny shop which seems even smaller with its non-stop flow of loyal customers ordering well-made, custom shirts (about HK$300) and suits, starting from HK$3,200.

Linva Tailor

38 Cochrane Street, Central, HK Island (2544 2456). Mid-Levels Escalator/buses along Queen's Road Central. **Open** 9.30am-6pm Mon-Sat. **Credit** AmEx, DC, MC, V. **Map** p328 C3.

A friendly, reliable tailor that can make almost any woman look good in a traditional fitted Chinese dress (cheongsam), at a reasonable price, and also does alterations.

Raja Fashions

G/F, 34C Cameron Road, Tsim Sha Tsui, Kowloon (2366 7624/www.raja-fashions.com). Tsim Sha Tsui
MTR (exit B1, B2)/buses along Nathan Road/Tsim Sha Tsui Star Ferry Pier. **Open** 9am-9pm Mon-Sat; 11am-3pm Sun. **Credit** AmEx, MC, V. **Map** p333 C5.

Since setting up shop in 1957, the family-run business has had such a following they take their tailors on tour each year to the US, UK and Ireland, then send the finished clothes from Hong Kong.

Sam's Tailor

G/F, Burlington Arcade, 94 Nathan Road, Tsim Sha Tsui, Kowloon (2367 9423/www.samstailor.com). Tsim Sha Tsui MTR (exit B1)/buses along Nathan Road. **Open** 10am-7.30pm Mon-Sat; 10am-midnight Sun. **Credit** AmEx, DC, MC, V. **Map** p333 C6.

Despite its location, in a rundown arcade on Nathan Road, this tiny shop caters to the stars, as you can tell by the photos and letters that adorn the walls and counter. From Bill Clinton to Princess Diana, there's only one place celebrities go – Sam the tailor. The nice thing about Sam is that you don't have to be rich to see him – he's a very easy-going bloke and is willing to cater to different budgets.

Underwear

Jilian

31C-D Wyndham Street, Central, HK Island (2826 9295). Central MTR (exit D2). **Open** 11am-8pm Mon-Sat; 11am-6pm Sun. **Credit** V. **Map** p328 C4.

Buying good lingerie can take time, and that is exactly the concept behind this shop. The staff pamper you – even the fitting room is softened by a fluffy rug. The brand names carried here are mostly European (Argentovivo, Aubade), and cover everything from push-up bras to corsets.

Lily Co

17 Li Yuen Street East, Central, HK Island (2810 7178). Central MTR (exit C)/buses & trams through Central. **Open** 9.30am-7pm daily. **Credit** MC, V. **Map** p329 D3.

Concealed by the chaotic market stalls of Li Yuen Street East, Lily Co has possibly the best selection of knickers a girl could wish for – at good prices. Jockey and Sloggi sit among other well-known labels, but more obscure brands also feature.

Watches

City Chain

Shop 120, 1/F, Man Yee Building, 60-68 Queen's Road, Central, HK Island (2259 9020/www.citychain. com.hk). Central MTR (exit D1, D2, G)/buses along Queen's Road Central. **Open** 10am-8pm daily. **Credit** AmEx, DC, MC, V. **Map** p329 D3.

It can seem like there is a City Chain watch outlet on virtually every street corner in Hong Kong, selling the best-known brands of watches such as Seiko, Adidas, Cat and Esprit. Don't expect anything too impressive from the service and you won't be disappointed.

Other locations: throughout the city.

Eldorado Watch Co Ltd

Peter Building, 60 Queen's Road, Central, HK Island (2522 7155). Central MTR (exit D1, D2, G)/buses along Queen's Road Central. **Open** 10.30am-7pm daily. **Credit** AmEx, DC, MC, V. **Map** p329 D3.

This gigantic store oozes elegance and sells chic, sleek watches. As well as being the official agent for Omega in Hong Kong, it also has a range of Cartier and Rolex timepieces.

Masterpiece (by King Fook)

Shop 216-7, Level 2, Pacific Place, 88 Queensway, Admiralty, HK Island (2845 6766). Admiralty MTR (exit C1)/buses & trams through Central. **Open** 10.30am-8pm Mon-Sat; 11.30am-8pm Sun. **Credit** AmEx, DC, MC, V. **Map** p329 F5.

If you're after a major brand of watch, you'll find most brands on display at Masterpiece's two stores in Central.

Other locations: Shop G-21, Central Building, 1-3 Pedder Street, Central, HK Island (2526 6733).

Florists

The Leighton Centre branch of home store **GOD** (*see p198*) also has an in-house florist.

Anglo-Chinese Florist

G/F, 50 Wellington Street, Central, HK Island (2921 2986/www.anglochinese.com). Central MTR (exit D1, G)/12M, 13, 23A, 40M, 43 bus. **Open** 8am-10pm daily. **Credit** AmEx, MC, V. **Map** p328 C4.

Established in 1946, this small yet slightly pricey florist sells a wonderful selection of flowers for any event, and plants for the home. You can also order flowers from their website and delivery is available.

Other locations: Shop 9, LG1, Great, Pacific Place, 88 Queensway, Admiralty, HK Island (2918 1718); G/F, 22 Stanley Street, Central, HK Island (2526 3511); B/F, Gourmet, Lee Gardens 1, 33 Hysan Avenue, Causeway Bay, HK Island (6330 1596).

Sim's Flower Workshop

Shop 9, 1 Lyndhurst Terrace, Central, HK Island (2542 4544). Central MTR (exit D1, D2, G)/ Mid-Levels Escalator/12M, 13, 23A, 40M, 43 bus. **Open** 9am-6.30pm Mon-Sat. **Credit** AmEx, MC, V. **Map** p328 C3.

Sim's Flower Workshop is a long, lean shop, filled with sweet-smelling flora that can be made up into bouquets. Service is polite.

Food & drink

Bakeries & confectioners

Cova Pasticceria & Confetteria

Shop G-10, G/F, Lee Gardens, 33 Hysan Avenue, Causeway Bay, HK Island (2907 3060/www.cova. com.hk) Causeway Bay MTR (exit F). **Open** 10am-9pm daily. **Credit** AmEx, DC, MC, V. **Map** p331 E3.

This Milan-based company, which was founded nearly two centuries ago, is home to some of the best Italian chocolates and freshly baked cakes in town.

Other locations: throughout the city.

Godiva

Shop 309-10, Lee Gardens, 33 Hysan Avenue, Causeway Bay, HK Island (2907 4818). Causeway Bay MTR (exit F). **Open** 10.30am-8pm Mon-Sat; noon-7pm Sun. **Credit** AmEx, MC, V. **Map** p331 E3.

Belgian chocolatier Godiva dishes up the crème de la crème of chocolates in Hong Kong. The assortment of sweet stuff is heady, as are the prices.

Coffee & tea

For a quality brew in refined surroundings, *see p151* **A fancy cuppa**.

Fook Ming Tong Tea Shop

Shop 3006, Level 3, IFC Mall, 8 Finance Street, Central, HK Island (2521 0337/2595 0368/www. fookmingtong.com). Central MTR (exit B1)/buses & trams through Central/Central Ferry Pier. **Open** 10am-7.30pm Mon-Sat; 11am-6pm Sun. **Credit** AmEx, DC, MC, V. **Map** p329 D4.

The people at Fook Ming Tong are accommodating and ready to help you with your every tea whim. They'll not only grant on-the-spot tastings, but they stock the most remarkable array of tea-leaves.

Other locations: Shop 3225, Harbour City, 5 Canton Road, Tsim Sha Tsui, Kowloon (2735 1077); B2, Sogo, 555 Hennessy Road, Causeway Bay, HK Island (2834 9978).

MingCha

7 Star Street, Wan Chai, HK Island (2520 2116/ www.mingcha.com.hk). Admiralty MTR (exit F). **Open** noon-9pm Wed-Mon; noon-7pm Sun. **Credit** MC, V. **Map** p330 A4.

This sophisticated, contemporary teahouse specialising in oolong teas (along with puer, red, black and white teas) may have the trendiest packaging, but there's also a mini tea museum, tea bar and lounge area upstairs. For tea connoisseurs who want to try the tea before buying, ask if it's a free tasting or you may be charged a whopping HK$95 for a cuppa.

Other locations: B/F, Gourmet, Lee Gardens 1, 33 Hysan Avenue, Causeway Bay, HK Island (3693 4101); Shop 9, LG1, Great, Seibu, Pacific Place, 88 Queensway, Admiralty, HK Island (2918 9986).

To market, to market

A visit to a Hong Kong market is an experience, whether you're up for a full-on haggling session or just want to immerse yourself in the atmosphere. Here's our pick of the best.

Apliu Street

Sham Shui Po, Kowloon. Sham Shui Po MTR (exit A2, C2)/2, 2C, 6, 6A, 12 bus. **Open** noon-10pm daily.

Apliu Street is a haven for gadgets and second-hand electronic goods. The former are available from the shops on both sides of the street, while the latter are displayed on the street-side stalls or even just on the roadside on top of a tablecloth. Old coins, 'antique' clocks and watches and even 'vintage' clothes are sold from these vendors, although the antiquity of these goods is questionable. Perhaps the most enjoyable part of a visit here is the chance to sample indigenous foods from the snack stalls.

Bird Market

Bird Park, off Flower Market Road, Mong Kok, Kowloon. Prince Edward MTR (exit B1). **Open** 7am-8pm daily. **Map** p332 C1.

The Bird Market is surprisingly clean and pristine. Much-prized songbirds kept in cages fill the air with cacophonous sounds. Also on sale are wonderfully carved wood and bamboo birdcages, which are ornaments in themselves and reasonably priced. If you're an animal lover of any sort, however, give the place a miss.

Jade Market

Kansu & Shanghai Streets, Yau Ma Tei, Kowloon. Yau Ma Tei MTR (exit C) or Jordan MTR (exit A, B1). **Open** 10am-3.30pm daily. **Map** p333 B4.

The earlier you arrive at the Jade Market the more likely you are to bag a bargain but recognising such a deal may not be so easy. Jade is priced according to a complicated system that merits the consistency of its colour, the thickness, translucency and purity of the material. Unless you really know what you're doing, stick to cheap trinkets or the freshwater pearls sold alongside the jade.

Lai Chi Kok Market

Lai Chi Kok, Kowloon. Lai Chi Kok MTR. **Open** times vary (late morning to early afternoon).

If you fancy a meander through industrial Hong Kong, trek out to Lai Chi Kok Market. Located in an area of clothing factories and wholesalers (behind the MTR station close to Wing Hong Street), this remarkably busy market sells stuff (including clothes) that might well have walked out of the back door of nearby factories. This is the kind of place you'll find real bargains.

Tsit Wing

G/F, Capitol Plaza, 2-10 Lyndhurst Terrace (2544 2237/www.twcoffee.com). Central MTR (exit A, B, C)/12M, 13, 23A, 40M, 43 bus. **Open** 10am-7pm Mon-Sat. **Credit** AmEx, DC, MC, V. **Map** p328 C3.

Founded in 1932 as a grocery store, Tsit Wing was the first company to popularise coffee- and tea-drinking among the Chinese in Hong Kong. The shop is mainly a café now, and still serves up some of the best coffee that you will find in Hong Kong.

Speciality food stores

Others options include **Castello del Vino** (*see p192*), **CitySuper** (*see below*) and **Great Food Hall** (*see p191*).

Health Gate

8/F, Hung Tak Building, 106-108 Des Voeux Road, Central, HK Island (2545 2286/www.health-gate.com). Sheung Wan MTR (exit E1, E2, E3)/ buses & trams along Des Voeux Road. **Open** 9.30am-6.30pm Mon-Fri; 9.30am-5.30pm Sat. **Credit** MC, V. **Map** p328 C2.

Everything from dietary supplements and gluten-free chocolate biscuits to natural green tea toothpaste and handmade skin care products from Carol Priest. There's also a good selection of health-related books and green music CDs.

Oliver's Delicatessen

Shop 233, 2/F, Prince's Building, 10 Chater Road, Central, HK Island (2905 1122/2810 7710). Central MTR (exit J1, J2, J3)/buses & trams through Central/Central Ferry Pier. **Open** 8.30am-8pm daily. **Credit** MC, V. **Map** p329 E4.

If you're after some good old European tucker, Oliver's is the place for you – the shelves here are stocked with items that are difficult to find elsewhere. Further draws come in the form of tempting meat, fish, cheese, salad and pâtisserie counters.

Supermarkets

CitySuper

Basement One, Times Square, 1 Matheson Street, Causeway Bay, HK Island (2506 2888/www.city

selling herbs, spices, wicker items and some damn cheap and good tropical-print shirts and trunks. Be sure to don sensible footwear as the path is constantly wet, slippery and covered in fruit peels.

Stanley Market

Stanley, HK Island. Buses 6, 6A, 6X, 61, 66, 260, 262 to Stanley. **Open** *11am-6pm daily.* **Map** *p93.*
At one time Stanley Market was known for its rock-bottom prices, but, as tourists discovered the market, they've gradually risen. However, you can still uncover some decent souvenirs, factory seconds, fake goods, trinkets and arts and crafts. The bus ride from Central is a pleasure in itself.

Temple Street Night Market

Jordan, Temple Street, Kowloon. Jordan MTR (exit A, C2). **Open** *2-10pm daily.* **Map** *p333 B4.*
After 6pm, Temple Street comes alive with stalls, entertainers and buzzing crowds. It's a good place to give your bargaining skills a go, especially if you're after copy CDs, watches or bags. At the far end are fortune-tellers and small street shows performing Chinese opera, aimed more at the locals than tourists. Not far away, north of Yau Ma Tei MTR, on Tung Choi Street, are the Ladies' Market and Goldfish Market (for both, *see p102*).

Spring Garden Lane Market

Spring Garden Lane, Wan Chai, HK Island. Wan Chai MTR (exit A3)/trams through Wan Chai/23, 23A, 23B, 25, 25 bus. **Open** *9am-10pm daily.* **Map** *p330 B4.*
Very few places on Hong Kong Island retain their local heritage as well as this street in Wan Chai. It is where some of the oldest buildings in the city still stand, especially at the intersection with Johnston Road across from Southorn Playground. Here you also find a line-up of factory outlets – places that sell brand-new designer sportswear items from the last season at cut-throat prices. The surrounding wet market is a mix of fresh-produce stalls and Asian grocery stores

super.com). Causeway Bay MTR (exit A). **Open** 10am-10pm Mon-Thur, Sun; 10.30am-11pm Fri, Sat. **Credit** AmEx, DC, MC, V. **Map** p331 D3.
CitySuper is the biggest upscale supermarket in town, and it stocks an extensive selection of gourmet grocery items from around the world, including fine cheeses and wines.

Great Food Hall

Shop 9, LG1, Pacific Place, 88 Queensway, Admiralty, HK Island (2918 9986/www.greatfood hall.com). Admiralty MTR (exit C1)/buses & trams through Central. **Open** 10am-10pm daily. **Credit** AmEx, DC, MC, V. **Map** p329 F5.
Like CitySuper, Great Food Hall is also a heaven for gourmets. It carries well-known brands including Harrods, Harvey Nichols and Fortnum & Mason.

Park 'n' Shop

Shop 1029-1043, 1/F, United Centre, 95 Queensway, Admiralty, HK Island (2861 0850/www.parknshop. com). Admiralty MTR (exit D)/buses & trams through Central. **Open** 7.30am-10pm daily. **Credit** AmEx, MC, V. **Map** p329 F5.

The biggest problem with Hong Kong's supermarkets is the selection of food, which inevitably lies somewhere between Chinese and American. But if you fancy turning out a proper stir-fry or sampling some microwave dim sum, then this is the place. Don't expect much in the way of service, though. **Other locations:** throughout the city.

Shing Fat Coconut & Spices

G/F, 18 Spring Garden Lane, Wan Chai, HK Island (2572 7725). Wan Chai MTR (exit A3)/buses along Queen's Road East. **Open** 8am-7pm daily. **No credit cards.** **Map** p330 B4.
This shop has the most extensive assortment of spices in town, from Malaysia, Indonesia, Thailand and, of course, India. There is also a full range of other goodies to make the perfect curry.

Wellcome

G/F, 25-9 Great George Street, Causeway Bay, HK Island (2577 4958/3215/www.wellcome.com.hk). Causeway Bay MTR (exit B, D2)/buses through Causeway Bay. **Open** 24hrs daily. **Credit** AmEx, MC, V. **Map** p331 E3.

Eat, Drink, Shop

Wellcome sells a mix of foods catering for local tastes, but its 'superstores', such as this one, offer more international foods, fresh grocery counters and delicatessens. Many, but not all, are open 24 hours. **Other locations**: throughout the city.

Wine, beers & spirits

Castello del Vino
G/F, 12 Anton Street, Wan Chai, HK Island (2866 0587). Admiralty MTR (exit F)/trams along Johnston Road. **Open** 10.30am-6.30pm daily. **Credit** AmEx, MC, V. **Map** p330 A3.
This small shop with lovely service specialises in Italian wines and fine foods.
Other locations: Shop 23, Basement, Luk Hoi Tong Building, 31 Queen's Road, Central, HK Island (2866 0577).

Ponti Wine Cellars
Shop G10, G/F, Hotel Miramar Shopping Arcade, 118-130 Nathan Road, Tsim Sha Tsui, Kowloon (2730 1889). Tsim Sha Tsui MTR (exit B1, B2)/buses along Nathan Road. **Open** 11am-9pm. **Credit** AmEx, MC, V. **Map** p333 C5.
It may seem slightly sterile with its white decor and bright lights, but this cellar stocks a good selection of New and Old World wines, particularly Australian and Bordeaux. Plus there's a heap of wine glasses, corkscrews, decanters and accessories.
Other locations: Shop B2, B-1/F, Alexandra House, 18 Chater Road, Central, HK Island (2810 1000); G/F, 3 Yuen Yuen Street, Happy Valley, HK Island (2972 2283).

Watson's Wine Cellar
31 Queen's Road, Central, HK Island (2147 3641/www.watsonswine.com). Central MTR (exit D1, D2, G)/buses along Queen's Road Central. **Open** 8am-9pm daily. **Credit** AmEx, MC, V. **Map** p329 D3.
Your best bet for a good international selection of wines, plus beers, spirits and liqueurs.
Other locations: throughout the city.

Gifts & souvenirs

Chinese Arts & Crafts
Star House, 3 Salisbury Road, Tsim Sha Tsui, Kowloon (2735 4061/www.crcretail.com). Tsim Sha Tsui MTR (exit E)/buses to Tsim Sha Tsui Star Ferry Pier & along Salisbury Road/Tsim Sha Tsui Star Ferry Pier. **Open** 10am-9.30pm daily. **Credit** AmEx, DC, MC, V. **Map** p333 B6.
If you're looking for Chinese gifts to take home (antiques, linens, clothes, bags, embroidered goods) this is a great one-stop destination. The jewellery section is one of the best in town, with an extensive collection of pearls, jade, precious and semi-precious stones, all at very reasonable prices.
Other locations: Asia Standard Tower, 59 Queen's Road, Central, HK Island (2901 0328); Shop 220, 2/F, The Mall, Pacific Place, 88 Queensway, Admiralty, HK Island (2523 3933); China Resources Building, 26 Harbour Road, Wan Chai, HK Island (2827 6667).

Just Gold
27A Nathan Road, Tsim Sha Tsui, Kowloon (2312 1120/www.justgold.cc). Tsim Sha Tsui MTR (exit E)/buses along Nathan Road/Tsim Sha Tsui Star Ferry Pier. **Open** 11am-8pm Mon-Thur; 11am-8.30pm Fri-Sun. **Credit** AmEx, DC, MC, V. **Map** p333 C6.
Just Gold produces everything from earrings to gifts in gold, at reasonable prices.
Other locations: throughout the city.

King & Country
Shop 362, Level 3, Pacific Place, 88 Queensway, Admiralty, HK Island (2525 8603/www.kingandcountry.com). Admiralty MTR (exit C1)/buses & trams through Central. **Open** 10.30am-8.30pm Mon-Sat; 11am-7pm Sun. **Credit** AmEx, DC, MC, V. **Map** p329 F5.
Beautifully wrought Victorian-style model soldiers and scenes – heaven for boys of all ages.

Mountain Folkcraft
12 Wo On Lane, Central, HK Island (2525 3199). Central MTR (exit D1)/12M, 13, 23A, 40M, 43 bus. **Open** 9.30am-6.30pm Mon-Sat. **Credit** AmEx, DC, MC, V. **Map** p328 C4.
This tiny but popular Aladdin's cave of a store has knick-knacks from all over Asia.

My House
67A Yung Shue Wan Main Street, Lamma (8105 0044). Yung Shue Wan Ferry Pier. **Open** 11am-6pm Mon-Sat (note: closes on any one of Tue, Wed or Thur each week); 11am-6.30pm Sun. **Credit** (over HK$200) MC, V.
As well as kiddies' toys and accessories, My House also offers girlie bits and bobs such as mirrors and ornaments. The staff are friendly, the prices are decent and the stock is cute.

Oriental Crafts
Shop B, G/F, 53-5 Hollywood Road, Central, HK Island (2541 8840). Central MTR (exit D1, D2, G)/Mid-Levels Escalator/12M, 13, 23A, 26, 40M, 43 bus. **Open** 10am-7pm daily. **Credit** AmEx, MC, V. **Map** p328 C3.
For a gift with a difference, stop by this tiny, jumbled shop, which deals (allegedly) in mammoth – as in the extinct animal – carvings. All kinds of sizes and shapes are on offer, from minute ornaments to gigantic carved boats with a crew of skeletons.

Yue Hwa
301-309 Nathan Road, Jordan, Kowloon (2384 0084). Jordan MTR (exit A)/buses along Nathan Road. **Open** 10am-10pm daily. **Credit** AmEx, DC, MC, V. **Map** p333 B4.
This main branch in Jordan is an emporium for everything Chinese, from the sort of rosewood furniture that is now hugely popular in the West to cheongsams and other items of traditional clothing. This shop may be a decade old but it now sells many fashion items that can rival Shanghai Tang's, but at a fraction of the cost.
Other locations: throughout the city.

Eat, Drink, Shop

SoHo shopping

More than a decade ago the area from Elgin Street down to Queen's Road Central was a mish-mash of Chinese herbal shops, grocery stores, laundromats and *dai pai dongs* (cheap fast-fooderies). Since then, the area has changed into an über-chic neighbourhood named **SoHo** (**So**uth of **Ho**llywood Road, which may be slightly disorienting since the area is uphill from Hollywood). It caters to a cool moneyed crowd from this high-density residential area and nearby Mid-Levels.

Known for its edgy street vibe, SoHo mainly consists of **Staunton Street** and **Elgin Street**, which initially became trendy with a few quaint cafés and open-fronted restaurants. Nowadays, it buzzes with a recent influx of boutique clothing stores, independent jewellers, local fashion designers and homeware shops. Rents in the area are not cheap, so don't expect too many bargains.

Take the Mid-Levels Escalator from its starting point in Central to Staunton Street, then kick back at loft-like **King's Cross@Soho** (M/F, 5 Staunton Street, 2988 8592), complete with big leather sofa. It carries discounted men's and ladies' designer street wear and jeans. Another hip choice is local designer store **'SPY' by Henry Lau** (G/F, 21 Staunton Street, 2530 3128), with racks of flamboyant clothes for men and women.

There's no shortage of designer denim on the street. **Indigo** (32 Staunton Street, 2147 3000) has jeans, jeans and more jeans, importing celebrity-favourite brands from the US such as Dream of Virtue, hand-finished Habitual jeans and Kasil for women. Men needn't feel left out – **Jeanious** (51 Staunton Street, 2189 7148) is a so-called premium denim bar stocking brands for men only.

Another stylish spot for men is **Dialogue** (49 Staunton Street, 2540 3101). The entire clothing line is designed by owner Casey Chung, who lines the racks with non-conservative corporate wear. He obviously spends a lot of time in the shop: check out the open-view shower and toilet at the back.

For women looking to turn heads, SoHo is dotted with trendy clothing boutiques (some the size of a walk-in closet). Glamorous, up-market retailer **Pretty Woman** (36A Staunton Street, 2152 1933) will surely make you look pretty with elegant eveningwear, sexy crop jackets and whimsical dresses from Italy and France. **Tiare** (53 Staunton Street, 2540 3380, www.tiareboutique.com) is a little slice of LA in SoHo, offering the California-girl look by LA brands such as Velvet and Vince.

One of Hong Kong's best designers is Ranee Kok, who opened a shop after interning at Donna Karan. **Ranee_K** (47K Staunton Street, 2108 4068, www.raneek. com) is a fanciful boudoir of Asian-inspired show-stopping dresses and tops, which don't come cheap. Many of the unique, feminine designs can be custom-made.

For knick-knacks and quirky finds, **Morn Creations** (Shop C, G/F, 34B Staunton Street, 2869 7021, www.morn.com.hk) is a little shop crammed with pig-shaped lighters, panda-faced handbags and retro clocks. Suitably kooky, **Chocolate Rain** (Shop A, 18 Elgin Street, corner of Staunton Street (2975 8318, 2155 1313, www.chocolaterain.com) sells funky, youthful handmade accessories and jewellery using non-conventional trinkets and semi-precious stones. The shop also holds jewellery-making classes.

Top-quality leather-goods shop **Lianca** (B/F, 27 Staunton Street, 2139 2989, www.lianca. com.hk) is worth a peek. Despite its south-western atmosphere, the shop carries a full range of locally designed items – everything from oversized weekend bags and cute clutches to stationery and wine-bottle carriers made from soft Italian leather. Another good bet is reasonably priced **Liberation** (16 Elgin Street, 2973 6933), a girly leather-bag shop with mainly its own designs, but which also carries a limited selection of discounted designer wallets and handbags from labels such as Marc Jacobs and Che Che New York.

For stylish goods for the home, **Lalang** (40 Staunton Street, 2914 4221, www.lalang. com.hk, closed Mon) won't disappoint. The majority of the sleek wood, lacquer and copper/aluminum products are imported from Bali, but it also stocks a range of South African silverware and gorgeous French-designed jewellery.

The old family-run shops are disappearing, but **Tung Shan Porcelain** (Shop 2, G/F, Ying Pont Building, 69-71 Peel Street, 2857 3665) has stood the test of time. The small shop packs in a huge selection of bargain-priced blue and white porcelain tableware, Chinese propaganda figurines, gleaming kitsch Buddhas and something you shouldn't leave without – a waist-high Mao statue.

Eat, Drink, Shop

Savings made in China

Once known as the city of copy bags and other pirated goods, **Shenzhen** is now touted as China's most 'cosmopolitan Chinese' city. Everywhere you walk you'll hear dialects from every part of the country and see architecture that is simply cutting-edge.

These days, tourists and Hong Kong locals alike rush in to take advantage of all the city has to offer: on the one hand significantly lower prices for quality goods and services and on the other a plethora of tourist attractions that clearly convey you've entered a very different place from Hong Kong. For shoppers, the big draw is **Lowu Commercial City**, a huge mall with around 1,500 small shops located at the exit of the Chinese customs office. The mall is just 40 minutes from the centre of Hong Kong (not counting time waiting in Customs) and offers more variety per square foot than anywhere else. Shoppers can find a tailor, fabric and get a suit or any other garment custom-tailored at short notice by heading to the Fabric Mall on the fifth floor. Expect to pay upwards of (the equivalent of) US$110 for a man's custom-made suit, and US$40 for a woman's.

Handbag, shoe and ready-to-wear shops are found on every floor of the centre. The styles are current, often heavily inspired by international designer brands and the prices are low by any standard. Even so, bargaining is de rigueur, and you can often negotiate the price down at least 50 per cent, if you persist long enough.

The jewellery markets, one on the second floor, the other on the third, have stalls selling pearls, semi-precious stones, jade and all kinds of beads with shopkeepers willing to tailor-make any bauble at your request. Touters pester you mercilessly and the haggling frenzy is enough to drive you to the massage centre, which in fact, is a wonderful way to end the day.

But Shenzhen is much more than Lowu Commercial City. With its new and attractive underground Metro transit system, whole parts of the city are easy to reach, including Windows of the World and its two satellite theme parks. **Dongmen**, the locals' favourite shopping haunt is a few minutes away as is **Hua Qiang Bei Lu**, the computer and electronics street where the maxim 'if it sounds too good to be true, it probably is' has never been more true. Nearby, world-class golf courses (Mission Hills Golf Club), Safari Park, Sea World, a gorgeous botanical garden and top-notch hotels have sprouted up along with sophisticated high-end malls (such as **The MixC**), all of which reflect the growing prosperity of the local middle class.

PRACTICALITIES

Foreign passport holders travelling to Shenzhen need to get a separate visa. Most travellers (but not US passport holders) can get a single-entry, five-day visa at the checkpoint starting from HK$150. Brits pay a premium for their quickie visa at the Shenzhen border: HK$450 for one visit. However, there is no need to get a special visa for Shenzhen if you already have one for China. For more details, call the Chinese Visa Office (852 3413 2424) or their agent, China Travel (852 2315 7188/www.ctshk. com). Getting to Shenzhen is an easy 10- to 40-minute ride on the MTR/KCR urban train depending on where you get on. Shopping trips are organised by the YWCA (3476 1340/www.esmdywca.org.hk), which takes care of all transportation.

You can buy Chinese *renminbi* (RMB) at any Hong Kong bank but if you only plan to go to Lowu Commercial City, Hong Kong dollars are all you need. Finally, pickpockets are rampant so dress down, hide your valuables and keep a close watch on your handbag.

Ellen McNally is the author of Shop in Shenzhen – An Insider's Guide *(HK$95), sold at bookstores around town and on her website, www.shopinshenzhen.com*

Health & beauty

Spas of all levels are in high demand in Hong Kong, so reservations are essential. For hotel-based spas, *see p196* **A good day's rest**.

The Body Shop

Shop 308, Pacific Place, 88 Queensway, Admiralty, HK Island (2537 7072/ *www.bodyshop.com). Admiralty MTR (exit C1)/ buses & trams through Central.* **Open** 10.30am-9.30pm Mon-Sat; 11am-7pm Sun. **Credit** AmEx, DC, MC, V. **Map** p329 F5.

The Body Shop franchise first appeared in Hong Kong in the late 1980s and now has more than a dozen branches scattered throughout the territory, selling its familiar ranges of eco-friendly toiletries. **Other locations**: throughout the city.

Charlie's Acupressure & Massage Centre of the Blind

Room 903, 9/F, Canton House, 54-6 Queen's Road, Central, HK Island (2877 9999). Central MTR (exit D)/buses along Queen's Road Central. **Open** 9am-9pm daily. **No credit cards. Map** p329 D3.

Blind people are said to have a greater sense of touch than sighted. Massages here are a bargain, at around HK$240 per hour. It's usually by appointment but it's worth stopping by on the off chance.

Elemis Day Spa

9/F, Century Square, 1 D'Aguilar Street, Central, HK Island (2521 6660/www.elemisdayspa.com.hk). Central MTR (exit D1, D2)/23A, 40M bus. **Open** 10am-10pm Mon-Fri; 9am-8pm Sat; 10am-8pm Sun. **Credit** AmEx, DC, MC, V. **Map** p328 C4.

The ambience of relaxation and indulgence is felt as soon as you step out of the lift at this spa, one of the most luxurious in Hong Kong. Specialities include the temple room for two people, and the 'Hawaiian wave' four-hands massage. A standard facial costs around HK$800-$900 and a body massage HK$800.

Frederique

4/F, Wilson House, 19-27 Wyndham Street, Central, HK Island (2522 3054/www.frederiquespa.com.hk). Central MTR (exit D1, D2)/13, 26, 43 bus. **Open** 9am-9pm Mon-Fri; 9am-7pm Sat. **Credit** AmEx, DC, MC, V. **Map** p328 C4.

Another top-notch retreat, with an enormous menu of treatments. Frederique's Darphin facial (HK$880) includes two different masks plus a head, neck and shoulder massage. Expect to shell out HK$600 or more for a standard massage.

Professional Hair Products

49A Wellington Street, Central, HK Island (2536 0603). Central MTR (exit D1, D2, G). **Open** 10am-8pm Mon-Sat. **No credit cards. Map** p328 C3.

On offer here is a fantastic collection of haircare goods for stylists and ordinary punters alike.

Pure Beauty

Shop B212A-B214A, Basement 2, Times Square, 1 Matheson Street, Causeway Bay, HK Island (2506 1521). Causeway Bay MTR (exit A). **Open** 10am-10pm daily. **Credit** AmEx, MC, V. **Map** p331 D3.

As part of Watson's (see p199), Pure Beauty is a dedicated cosmetics store with professional brands such as Korres from Greece, organic skin care Lavera from Germany, Dermatologica, Philosophy and Boots products.

Sasa Cosmetic Company

62 Queen's Road, Central, HK Island (2521 2928). Central MTR (exit D1, D2, G)/buses along Queen's Road Central. **Open** 9.30am-8.30pm daily. **Credit** AmEx, DC, MC, V. **Map** p328 C3.

Sasa is quickly taking over Hong Kong's cosmetics market – the number of outlets is staggering. Though some of the lines may be limited or out of stock, all is forgiven when you see the low prices. **Other locations**: throughout the city.

Shu Uemura Beauty Boutique

Shop 204, Ocean Centre, Harbour City, 5 Canton Road, Tsim Sha Tsui, Kowloon (2735 1767). Tsim Sha Tsui MTR (exit C1, E)/buses along Canton Road/Tsim Sha Tsui Star Ferry Pier. **Open** 10.30am-7.30pm Mon-Sat; 12.30-6pm Sun. **Credit** AmEx, DC, MC, V. **Map** p333 B6.

Shu Uemura's range of brushes and make-up is every girl's dream. This place is like a paint box dedicated to beautifying oneself, but the prices will strain the average wallet.

Other locations: 1/F, Harvey Nichols, The Landmark, 15 Queen's Road, Central, HK Island (3695 3117); Shop 128, Pacific Place, 88 Queensway, Admiralty, HK Island (2918 1233).

Sunny Paradise Sauna

341 Lockhart Road, Wan Chai, HK Island (2831 0123). Causeway Bay MTR (exit B)/buses along Hennessy Road. **Open** noon-6am daily. **Credit** AmEx, DC, MC, V. **Map** p331 D3.

Admittedly the name sounds a bit dodgy, and admittedly it's in Wan Chai, but no, there are no 'extras' at this budget spa… or at least not of that kind. Refreshments run to Chinese tea and fish balls, and entertainment is a Cantonese TV channel, but you can spend as long as you like enjoying the steam room, sauna and an hour's massage, all for around HK$250.

Interiors, furniture & fabrics

There are a number of fabric shops in Kowloon – in particular on Bowring Street and just off Nathan Road.

Altfield Interiors

Shop 223-225, Prince's Building, 10 Chater Road, Central, HK Island (2524 7526). Central MTR (exit H)/buses & trams through Central. **Open** 10am-7pm Mon-Sat; 11am-5pm Sun. **Credit** AmEx, MC, V. **Map** p329 E4.

Dedicated to soft furnishings, with a wide range of lamps and lights, elegant cushions and repro furniture, Altfield promises to make your home into a cosy comfort zone. The nearby fabric department at Shop 605, 9 Queen's Road, Central (2525 2738, 2524 3318), deals with upholstery orders. For the Altfield Gallery, see p172.

Aluminium

Basement, 19-21 Lyndhurst Terrace, Central, HK Island (2546 5904/www.hk-aluminium.com). Central MTR (exit D1, D2, G)/Mid-Levels Escalator/12M, 13, 23A, 40M, 43 bus. **Open** 4-8pm Mon-Fri; 1-6pm Sat. **Credit** AmEx, MC, V. **Map** p328 C3.

Aluminium stocks some of the coolest European furniture and PC accessories that you'll find in Hong Kong. The emphasis is on colourful, space-age, 1970s-style pieces, so if you happen to be looking for a bubble chair or a JVC Videosphere TV, this is where you'll find it.

Eat, Drink, Shop

A good day's rest

Most decent Hong Kong hotels have beauty treatment facilities – and a spa splurge is one way to live it up without blowing your budget on a glitzy room – but check first that they're available to non-residents. Reservations are always advisable. For more spas, see p194.

Chuan Spa

Langham Place, 555 Shanghai Street, Mong Kok, Kowloon (3552 3510/www.chuanspa. com). Mongkok MTR (exit C). **Open** 10am-10.45pm daily. **Credit** AmEx, DC, MC, V. **Map** p332 B2.

The contemporary Chinese vibe is as relaxing as it is immediate here. Many signature treatments match your physical and mental state to one of the spa's unique aromatherapy blends, rooted in the principles of traditional Chinese medicine. The pièce de résistance is the two-hour Indoceane (HK$1,650): a sea salt and citrus body scrub, followed by an Egyptian milk bath, Indian Ayurvedic massage and moisturising Chinese-ingredient body wrap. Other treatments incorporate Thalgo French wellness products, which draw on algae and marine ingredients. Rooms feature latticed dark-stained wood, warm spotlighting and the odd flash of colour, and many have striking city views.

I-Spa at the InterContinental Hong Kong

InterContinental Hotel, 18 Salisbury Road, Tsim Sha Tsui, Kowloon (2721 1211/2313 2306/www.hongkong-ic.intercontinental.com). Tsim Sha Tsui MTR (exit E)/buses along Salisbury Road/Tsim Sha Tsui Star Ferry Pier. **Open** 8am-10pm daily. **Credit** AmEx, DC, MC, V. **Map** p333 C6.

A real treat of a spa, designed in accordance with feng shui principles. There's an outdoor pool and several spa pools, and private spa rooms for one or two people. Treatment options include jetlag relief and Oriental healing alongside various packages. As an example of prices, a body polish costs around HK$400, while massages start at HK$790 for an hour.

Mandarin Oriental Spa

24/F, 5 Connaught Road, Central, HK Island (2825 4888/2522 0111/www.mandarin oriental.com). Central MTR (exit F, H)/buses to Central Ferry Pier/Central Ferry Pier. **Open** 10am-11pm daily. **Credit** AmEx, DC, MC, V. **Map** p329 E3.

The renovated Mandarin Hotel's spa offers a long list of treatments to soothe and pamper. There is Ritual Time to restore body balance and harmony for HK$1,650 for 2 hours (HK$2,250 for 3 hours), and programmes for cleansing and rejuvenating for HK$300-$4,000. The likes of Body Harmony, Aqua Experiences and Body Scrub are in the HK$320-$2,530 range. Traditional Chinese medicine and Ayurvedic consultation are also offered (HK$700-$1,500). **Photo** above.

The Peninsula Spa by Espa

*7/F, Peninsula Hotel, Salisbury Road,
Tsim Sha Tsui, Kowloon (2315 3322).
Tsim Sha Tsui MTR (exit E)/buses to
Tsim Sha Tsui Ferry Pier & along Salisbury
Road/Tsim Sha Tsui Star Ferry Pier.*
Open 8am-11pm daily. **Credit** AmEx, DC,
MC, V. **Map** p333 B6/C6.
You'd expect the best hotel in Hong Kong
to have a top spa – and it does. Decor is
effortlessly stylish, combining traditional
Chinese elements such as rosewood and
bamboo with Italian marble and a soothing
Japanese water feature. Visit the steam
room, sauna and ice fountain, then slip under
a thick bedspread in the relaxation room
overlooking the harbour. Highly skilled
therapists provide facials, massages and
body treatments (check the website for
the full list) using Espa's gorgeous products.
A holistic body massage starts at HK$940
for 50 minutes.

The Plateau

*Grand Hyatt, 1 Harbour Road, Wan Chai, HK
Island (2584 7688/www.plateau.com.hk).
Wan Chai MTR (exit A1/C)/A12, 18, 88
bus/Wan Chai Star Ferry Pier.* **Open** 9am-
10pm daily. **Credit** AmEx, DC, MC, V.
Map p330 B2
If you've seen *Lost in Translation*, you'll
recognise The Plateau's similar tranquil
design (by the same architect as Tokyo's
Park Hyatt). The 7,400-square-metre (80,000-
square-feet) spa, which is dead quiet and
shut off from the outside world, encompasses
minimalist-style treatment rooms, hotel
rooms, a swimming pool and peaceful garden
terrace. Luxury like this starts at HK$1,100
for a facial, and a one-hour Swedish massage
costs HK$860.

The Spa at the Four Seasons

*Four Seasons Hotel Hong Kong, 8 Finance
Street, Central (3196 8888/www.fours
easons.com/hongkong) Central MTR
(exit E) & buses to Exchange Square.* **Open**
daily 8am-11pm. **Credit** AmEx, DC, MC, V.
Map p329 D2.
The deluxe Four Seasons hotel is home
to an equally deluxe spa. Clad in pale orange
marble, it offers beautiful relaxation areas
with mosaic-tiled pool, sauna, steam room
and rasul (mud) chamber, as well as 16
treatment rooms, including two stunning spa

suites with vitality pool, TV and bar. Facials,
massages, body treatments, manicures
and pedicures fuse Oriental and European
elements, and have evocative names such
as Luxurious Silk Facial (HK$1,400 for 90
minutes) and Aromatic Caress (HK$2,000 for
two hours). If you're on a budget, try the Four
Seasons Polish (HK$600 for 45 minutes)
or Executive Escape (HK$780 for 45-minute
massage, facial or manicure and pedicure,
plus a healthy poolside lunch).

The Oriental Spa

*The Landmark Mandarin Oriental,
15 Queen's Road, Central, HK Island
(2132 0011/www.mandarinoriental.com).
Central MTR (exit D1, G)/buses & trams
through Central/Central Ferry Pier.* **Open**
10am-9pm daily. **Credit** AmEx, DC, MC, V.
Map p329 D4.
This Mandarin Oriental spa is as beautiful as
the boutique hotel itself. In addition to a high-
tech fitness centre, there's a Turkish bath
'hamam' for men, and rasul mud treatment
for women. As at any top hotel spa, you can
expect the usual menu of body massages,
facials and a few unique treatments thrown in
(try the 20-minute honey, sesame and green
tea body scrub for HK$450), but here the
main attraction is the heat and water facilities
– a vitality pool, laconium sauna, amethyst-
crystal steam room, heated lounge chairs and
experience showers (which spray refreshing
scents). These facilities are complimentary
when you book a one-hour or longer treatment
(starting at HK$850).

Victorian Spa

*Level 1, Disneyland Hotel, Hong Kong
Disneyland Resort, Lantau Island (3510
6388/www.victorianspa.com.hk). Disneyland
Resort MTR.* **Open** 9am-10pm daily. **Credit**
AmEx, MC, V. **Map** p324.
If you need to escape Mickey Mouse and
his goofy friends, the Victorian Spa is just a
short walk away. Inside this old-world spa,
you can unwind in one of ten treatment rooms
(two with stand-alone Victorian baths), an
indoor and outdoor pool, relaxation room,
whirlpool and sauna. The signature Victorian
Clubhouse Classic massage will set you back
HK$1,600 for 105 minutes, while the Elemis
30-minute foot massage is HK$450. There
are even treatments for the kids, such as
face painting for HK$250.

Eat, Drink, Shop

Other locations: Shop D, G/F, 8 Kingston Street, Causeway Bay, HK Island (2577 4766); Shop F, G/F, Queen's Centre, 58-64 Queen's Road East, Wan Chai, HK Island (2577 4066).

GOD

Leighton Centre, 77 Leighton Road (entrance on Sharp East Street), Causeway Bay, HK Island (2890 5555/www.god.com.hk). Causeway Bay MTR (exit A). **Open** noon-10pm daily. **Credit** AmEx, MC, V. **Map** p331 D3.

Not to be mistaken for a pious outlet, GOD stands for Goods of Desire, a popular home and lifestyle store that is a cross between an upmarket IKEA and kitsch Chinese paraphernalia, stocking everything from Chinese-style candles and Chinese newsprint bed linens to chic furniture and stationery.

Other locations: 3/F, Hong Kong Hotel, Harbour City, 5 Canton Road, Tsim Sha Tsui, Kowloon (2784 5555); 48 Hollywood Road, Central, HK Island (2805 1876).

Graham 32

32 Graham Street, Central, HK Island (2815 5188). Mid-Levels Escalator/26 bus. **Open** 11am-8pm Mon-Fri; 11am-7.30pm Sat; noon-6pm Sun. **Credit** AmEx, MC, V. **Map** p328 C3.

Promoted as a 'style concept' store, Graham 32 is home to a range of hip homeware as well as a small line of casual clothes.

Ito Futon

G/F, 64-6 Wellington Street, Central, HK Island (2845 1138/www.itofuton.com). Central MTR (exit D1, D2, G)/12M, 13, 23A, 40M, 43 bus. **Open** 10am-7pm Mon-Sat. **Credit** AmEx, MC, V. **Map** p328 C3.

No matter what size, style, status or colour you desire in a futon, Ito Futon will have one to suit you. It also does a funky range of bed covers and Japanese lights.

Kinari

Shop 306, 43-55 Wyndham Street, Central, HK Island (2869 6827). Central MTR (exit D1). Mid-Levels Escalator/12M, 13, 23A, 40M bus. **Open** 10am-7.30pm Mon-Sat. **Credit** AmEx, MC, V. **Map** p328 C4.

Kinari is a treasure trove of products from Thailand and Burma. Ornate carved wooden pieces, big beds, silver Buddhas and lacquered boxes cover the shop's floor, although, not surprisingly, such riches come with high pricetags.

Tequila Kola

Horizon Plaza, South Horizon, 2 Lee Wing Street, Ap Lei Chau, HK Island (2877 3295/www.tequilakola.com). **Open** 10am-7pm Mon-Fri; 10am-6pm Sat; noon-5pm Sun. **Credit** AmEx, DC, MC, V.

Since Tequila Kola opened in the early 1990s, it has acquired a dedicated cluster of rich clients, who are seduced by its extensive (and expensive) mix of furniture, including teak tables, wrought-iron beds and big mirrors.

Music

HMV

1/F, Central Building, 1 Pedder Street, Central, HK Island (2739 0268/www.hmv.com.hk). Central MTR (exit D1, G)/buses & trams through Central/Central Ferry Pier. **Open** 9am-10pm daily. **Credit** AmEx, DC, MC, V. **Map** p329 D4.

This mega music store sells everything and anything for watching and listening to. Prices of CDs are comparable with those in the US, while magazines are almost half the price of those on sale in bookshops and at newsstands. The Tsim Sha Tsui branch is the largest.

Other locations: 1/F, Style House, The Park Lane, Causeway Bay, HK Island (2504 3669); G-1/F, HK Pacific Centre, 28 Hankow Road, Tsim Sha Tsui, Kowloon (2302 0122); Shop K3, 1/F, Queensway Plaza, 93 Queensway, Admiralty, HK Island (3692 4178).

Shun Cheong Record Showroom

Shop 801, Bank Centre, 636 Nathan Road, Mong Kok, Kowloon (2332 2397/www.shuncheongrec.com). Mong Kok MTR (exit E2). **Open** 11am-7pm Mon-Sat. **Credit** MC, V. **Map** p332 B2.

A haven for classical music lovers, Shun Cheong has been around for more than 30 years. Its selection includes many albums that you just can't find at mainstream record stores. Along with classical, expect to find jazz and New Age.

Other locations: 3/F, Chung Nam House, 59 Des Voeux Road, Central, HK Island (2189 7363).

Tom Lee Music

G/F, 1-9 Cameron Lane, Tsim Sha Tsui, Kowloon (2723 9932/www.tomleemusic.com). Tsim Sha Tsui MTR (exit B2). **Open** 10am-8pm Mon-Thur, Sun; 10am-9pm Fri, Sat. **Credit** MC, V. **Map** p333 C5.

The Tom Lee Music chain stocks instruments, accessories, written music and instructional videos. The company is also a music promoter, selling tickets for major concerts.

Other locations: throughout the city.

Opticians & eyewear

Lens Crafters

G/F, China Building, 29 Queen's Road, Central, HK Island (2810 6022). Central MTR (exit D1, D2, G)/buses along Queen's Road Central. **Open** 9am-7.30pm Mon-Sat; 10am-7pm Sun. **Credit** AmEx, DC, MC, V. **Map** p329 D4.

Formerly known as the Optical Shop, this company has rebranded as the US chain Lens Crafters and given its 50-odd shops a makeover. They will happily test your eyes and equip you with a funky pair of bifocals or comfy contacts. And if Hong Kong is too bright for you, it's also got a choice collection of sunglasses – DKNY, Calvin Klein, Gucci, Ray-Ban and so on.

Other locations: Shop 111, Pacific Place, 88 Queensway, Admiralty, HK Island (2845 9442).

Optical 88

*17 Cameron Road, Tsim Sha Tsui, Kowloon
(2367 3200/www.optical88.com). Tsim Sha
Tsui MTR (exit A1)/buses along Canton Road/
Tsim Sha Tsui Star Ferry Pier.* **Open** 10.30am-
9.30pm daily. **Credit** AmEx, DC, MC, V.
Map p333 C5.
This big, bright shop has opticians to test your eyes,
and assistants to see to all your eyewear needs.
Other locations: Shop 105, Man Yee Arcade, 50-58
Des Voeux Road, Central, HK Island (2259 5188).

Senses Optik

*1/F, 28 Wellington Street, Central, HK Island (2869
5111/www.sensesoptik.com.hk). Central MTR (exit
D1, D2, G)/12M, 13, 23A, 40M, 43 bus.* **Open**
10am-8.30pm Mon-Sat; 11am-6pm Sun. **Credit**
AmEx, DC, MC, V. **Map** p328 C3.
The Senses Optik assistants will test your eyes and
kit you out with a classy pair of specs. A good range
sunglasses is also sold, from standard to designer.

Pharmacies

Watson's

*G/F, Melbourne Plaza, 33 Queen's Road, Central,
HK Island (2523 0666/www.watsons.com.hk).
Central MTR (exit D1, D2, G)/buses along Queen's
Road Central.* **Open** 9.30am-8pm daily. **Credit**
AmEx, DC, MC, V. **Map** p329 D3.
Watson's is a megastore of a chemist, with lots of
outlets throughout the region. It sells a wide range
of hair products and designer make-up, and has a
useful drug counter with helpful staff.
Other locations: throughout the city.

Photography & film processing

Fotomax

*G/F, Far East Mansion, 5-6 Middle Road, Tsim
Sha Tsui, Kowloon (2722 0639/www.fotomax.com).
Tsim Sha Tsui MTR (exit E).* **Open** 8.30am-8pm
Mon-Sat; 10.30am-8pm Sun. **Credit** AmEx, DC,
MC, V. **Map** p333 B6.
One of the most established names in photo pro-
cessing, Fotomax has stores all over town. Staff can
help you with anything from simple developing to
complicated jobs involving image enhancement.
Other locations: throughout the city.

Hing Lee Camera Company

*25 Lyndhurst Terrace, Central, HK Island
(2544 7593). Central MTR (exit D1, D2, G)/Mid-
Levels Escalator/12M, 13, 23A, 40M, 43 bus.*
Open 9.30am-7pm Mon-Sat; 11.30am-6pm Sun.
No credit cards. Map p328 C3.
Hing Lee sells guaranteed stock, including famous
brands like Nikon, Kodak and Olympus, at a good
price. Staff are laid-back, honest and helpful, which
adds to the attraction. **Photo** *p200.*

Robert Lam Color

*1/F, Glory Industrial Building, 22 Lee Chung Street,
Chai Wan, HK Island (2898 8418). Chai Wan MTR
(exit C).* **Open** 8.30am-7pm Mon-Fri; 8.30am-4pm
Sat. **Credit** AmEx, DC, MC, V.
Professional photographers have been coming to
Robert Lam Color for years to get their photos
processed. And if you're looking for a specific kind
of slide film or photo paper, the able staff will be
happy to assist you.

Union Photo Supplies

*Shop 1008, 10/F, South China Building, 1 Wyndham
Street, Central, HK Island (2526 6281). Central
MTR (exit D2)/buses & trams through Central.*
Open 9.30am-5.30pm Mon-Fri; 9.30pm-2pm Sat.
Credit MC, V. **Map** p328 C3.
Union Photo Supplies is a pristine store that oozes
professionalism. It boasts an extensive and well-
priced stock of cameras, lenses, filters, films, photo
paper and other accessories and friendly, knowl-
edgeable staff.

Sport

Giga Sports

*Shop 124, Pacific Place, 88 Queensway, Admiralty,
HK Island (2918 9088/www.gigasports.com).
Admiralty MTR (exit C1)/buses & trams through
Central.* **Open** 10.30am-9.30pm daily. **Credit** AmEx,
DC, MC, V. **Map** p329 F5.
Make just one stop to Giga Sports and you can find
everything you need for your next sporting adven-
ture or gym workout.
Other locations: throughout the city.

The Golf House

*Shop 601, Times Square, 1 Matheson Street,
Causeway Bay, HK Island (2506 2522). Causeway
Bay MTR (exit A).* **Open** 11am-10pm daily. **Credit**
AmEx, DC, MC, V. **Map** p331 D3.
The Golf House is stuffed with a comprehensive
selection of golfing gear, from clubs and bags to
balls and tees.

Marathon Sports

*Shop 144, L1, Pacific Place, 88 Queensway,
Admiralty, HK Island (2524 6992/www.imarathon.
com). Admiralty MTR (exit C1)/buses & trams
through Central.* **Open** 10am-9pm daily. **Credit**
AmEx, DC, MC, V. **Map** p329 F5.
There are almost 30 Marathon Sports outlets across
Hong Kong and the New Territories. The Pacific
Place shop is one of the longest established and spe-
cialises in trainers. Brands such as Puma, Adidas,
Converse and Diesel all feature, alongside a small
line of sports clothing and accessories.
Other locations: throughout the city.

Running Bare/Rush

*Shop 1, G/F, Wyndham Mansion, 32 Wyndham
Street, Central, HK Island (2526 0620). Central
MTR (exit D1, G)/13, 26, 43 bus.* **Open** 11am-7pm
Mon-Sat. **Credit** AmEx, DC, MC, V. **Map** p328 C4.

Eat, Drink, Shop

Hing Lee. *See p199.*

Having already built up a string of clients selling sportswear from her flat, Lynn Fong Boseley has now opened this tiny store in Central. Running Bare sells her own label, plus Wahini bikinis and the Rival range.

Other locations: throughout the city

X Game
Shop A1, L/G, Wilson House, 19-27 Wyndham Street, Central, HK Island (2366 9293/www. xgamehk.com). Central MTR (exit D2). **Open** 10am-8pm Mon-Fri; 10am-7pm Sat. **Credit** AmEx, DC, MC, V. **Map** p328 C4.

X Game is almost a little club for the surfer dudes and dudettes in town. Experienced players can find the flashy and high-performance gear that suits their status, while novices come to get tips from the helpful staff and to sign up for the courses. Stock covers all the latest surfer fashions.

Other locations: 1/F, 11 Pak Sha Road, Causeway Bay, HK Island (2881 8960); China Minmetals Tower, 79 Chatham Road South, Tsim Sha Tsui, Kowloon (2375 0225).

Tobacconists

Cohiba Cigar Divan
Lobby, Mandarin Oriental Hotel, 5 Connaught Road, Central, HK Island (2825 4074). Central MTR (exit F, H)/buses to Central Ferry Pier/Central Ferry Pier. **Open** 10am-9pm Mon-Sat; noon-6pm Sun. **Credit** AmEx, DC, MC, V. **Map** p329 E3.

This sleek, sweet-smelling cigar shop is the place to pick up a choice Cohiba or two. Service is appropriately charming.

Davidoff
Lobby, Peninsula Hotel, Salisbury Road, Tsim Sha Tsui, Kowloon (2368 5774/www.davidoff.com). Tsim Sha Tsui MTR (exit E)/buses to Tsim Sha Tsui Star Ferry Pier & along Salisbury Road/Tsim Sha Tsui Star Ferry Pier. **Open** 10am-8pm daily. **Credit** AmEx, DC, MC, V. **Map** p333 B6.

Davidoff sells all sorts of cigars, and staff are happy to help you make an informed choice. But be warned, none of them are cheap.

Red Chamber Cigar Divan
Shop M1, Pedder Building, 12 Pedder Street, Central, HK Island (2537 0977). Central MTR (exit D1, G)/buses & trams through Central/Central Ferry Pier. **Open** 11am-9pm Mon-Sat. **Credit** AmEx, DC, MC, V. **Map** p329 D3.

The man behind Shanghai Tang (*see p185*), David Tang raises the bar with his imperial-red cigar shop named after a Chinese folk tale which resembles an opium house with glam-retro decor.

Toys & games

Bumps to Babes
Shop 501, 5/F, Pedder Building, 12 Pedder Street, Central, HK Island (2522 7112/www.bumpstobabes. com). Central MTR (exit D1, D2)/buses & trams to Central/Central Ferry Pier. **Open** 10am-7pm Mon-Sat; 11am-6pm Sun. **Credit** MC, V. **Map** p329 D4.

A must for mums-to-be, this superstore stocks everything you would need for newborns and kids, from baby-friendly detergents and organic baby food to maternity wear, toys and push chairs.

Other locations: Unit 14-18, 21/F, Horizon Plaza, 2 Lee Wing Street, Ap Lei Chau, HK Island (2552 5000).

Toys 'R' Us
Shop 32, B/F, Ocean Terminal, Harbour City, 5 Canton Road, Tsim Sha Tsui, Kowloon (2730 9462/ www.toysrus.com.hk). Tsim Sha Tsui MTR (exit C1, E)/buses along Chatham Road South. **Open** 10am-9pm daily. **Credit** AmEx, MC, V. **Map** p333 B6.

This huge international toy emporium is every kid's dream (and some parents' nightmare). Along its aisles are clothes, toys, games and sporting goods.

Other locations: 3/F, Windsor House, 311 Gloucester Road, Causeway Bay, HK Island (2881 1728); Shop 4, G/F, Man Yee Building, 68 Des Voeux Road, Queen's Road, Central, HK Island (2259 9166).

Arts & Entertainment

Features

Mid-Autumn Festival. *See p204.*

Festivals & Events

Chinese culture is evident – often spectacularly so – in Hong Kong's biggest and best celebrations.

Like Hong Kong itself, the territory's calendar of festivals and events is densely crowded, cross-cultural and brimming with contrasts and surprises. At the core of the celebrations are half a dozen important traditional festivals linked to the lunar calendar and mirroring the rhythms of the seasons. Often expressing renewal and ancestral worship, rich and poetic festivals such as the **Mid-Autumn Festival**, **Hungry Ghost Festival** and the exciting **Dragon Boat Festival** draw upon ancient rural folklore and the rituals of Taoist, Buddhist and Confucian traditions.

Acknowledging its colonial history and its multicultural institutions, Hong Kong also celebrates major Western holidays. While most of the Chinese community do not attach religious importance to Christmas or Easter, these are still public holidays. Hong Kong's romantics celebrate Valentine's Day with fervour, and, on Halloween, a local fascination with ghost stories and the supernatural mixes with US-style trick-or-treating.

The local calendar is also dotted with annual artistic, cultural and sporting events. The **Hong Kong International Literary Festival**, **Hong Kong Arts Festival** and **Hong Kong International Film Festival** form an impressive cultural season at the start of the year, while annual running, golf, and horse racing events bring things to an exciting close.

TICKETS AND INFORMATION

The Hong Kong Tourism Board website (www.discoverhongkong.com) is the first place to look for details about annual and seasonal events, though the local press is a useful source of information about individual events. It's always wise to check the dates/times of a particular event nearer the time. Tickets to events are available directly from venues and many can also be purchased from **URBTIX** (2734 9009, www.urbtix.cityline.com.hk; *see also p241*) and **HK Ticketing** (3128 8288, www.hkticketing.com; *see also p241*).

Spring

Hong Kong International Literary Festival

2511 4211/www.festival.org.hk. **Date** Mar.
This ten-day festival focuses on world literature written in English and includes readings, writing workshops and debates. Local poets, screenwriters and publishers are featured alongside international literary stars. Past festivals have included readings by Nobel laureates Seamus Heaney and JM Coetzee and Booker Prize winners Thomas Keneally and John Banville. Events are held at venues across town, and tickets (around HK$100, with some free events) are available from HK Ticketing and the Fringe Club.

Art Walk

www.hongkongartwalk.com. **Date** early Mar.
This annual fund-raising evening is essentially an unguided tour of more than 30 art galleries in the Wan Chai, Central, Soho and Sheung Wan neighbourhoods. After buying a programme that gives gallery names, addresses and maps, you can stroll from one to another, enjoying the art, and free food and drink provided by sponsor restaurants. Some galleries feature music and other entertainment, and the evening ends with a party. All proceeds go to local charities. Tickets cost HK$400 and are available directly from participating galleries.

Arts & Entertainment

Top five Festivals

Cheung Chau Bun Festival
A festival based on buns? See p203.

Chinese New Year
The biggest event of the year is mainly for locals, but the fireworks and lantern displays can be enjoyed by all. See p205.

Christmas
Witness as Hong Kong's skyscrapers are transformed into towers of tacky tinsel. See p205.

Dragon Boat (Tuen Ng) Festival
Watch the beautiful boats compete in this fast and furious race, which dates back two centuries. See p204.

Hong Kong International Film Festival
This major player among the world's biggest cinematic events is a must-see. See p203.

One of a kind: the **Cheung Chau Bun Festival**.

Hong Kong Rugby Sevens

Hong Kong Stadium, 55 Eastern Hospital Road,
So Kon Po, Causeway Bay, HK Island (2504 8311/
www.hksevens.com.hk). Bus 5B. **Date** late Mar.
Map p331 E4/F4.

First played in 1976, the three-day Hong Kong Sevens rugby tournament is the most prestigious leg of the International Rugby Board's World Sevens Series. See some of the world's finest players in action, and some wild partying from the very partisan fans. *See also p258.*

Hong Kong International Film Festival

Enquiries 2970 3300/Urbtix 2734 9009/
www.hkiff.org.hk. **Date** Mar-Apr.

Asia's oldest film festival showcases the best of Eastern and Western filmmaking over the course of two weeks. Films are shown in venues around the city and many screenings feature Q&A sessions with directors. Each year the programme includes a major retrospective of works by an international name and a tribute to a local star or film-maker. Tickets are easy to obtain and it is often possible to pick up tickets for about HK$50 a few nights before a screening. Postal bookings can be made about a month before the festival begins and all remaining seats are then sold on a first-come, first-served basis through URBTIX.

Le French May Festival of Arts

Urbtix 2734 9009/HK Ticketing 3128 8288/
www.frenchmay.com. **Date** late Apr-early June.

This annual month-long celebration of all things Gallic is the biggest French festival in Asia. Expect an eclectic range of shows, exhibitions, films and concerts at venues across the territory. Tickets are sold through URBTIX and Hong Kong Ticketing outlets.

Birthday of Tin Hau

Date Apr/May (23rd day of the 3rd lunar month).

Tin Hau, the goddess of the sea, occupies a special place in the heart of the Harbour City. To celebrate her birthday, fishermen decorate their boats and head to temples dedicated to the goddess to pray for good catches during the coming year. It makes for a colourful and very local holiday. Traditional birthday rites can be seen at the Tin Hau Temple in Joss House Bay (in the eastern New Territories) and in the 40 or so other temples to Tin Hau around the territory. A birthday parade with colourful floats and lion dances also takes place in Yuen Long in the western New Territories, while Lamma Island hosts a week-long Cantonese opera extravaganza at this time. *See also p39.*

Cheung Chau Bun Festival

Pak Tai Temple, Cheung Chau. Cheung Chau Ferry
Pier. **Date** 1 week in Apr/May/June.

What is surely the world's one-and-only bun festival takes place on the island of Cheung Chau. This week-long village fiesta is dedicated to peace, renewal, harmony and, well, buns. The dates of the festival are divined by Taoist priests (although cynics note that the most colourful celebrations often coincide with a weekend, thus enabling more visitors to attend). During the festival, three 20-metre (66-foot) bamboo towers (representing heaven, earth and man) are studded with sweet buns and raised in

---

▶ For a list of public holidays, *see p311.*
▶ For more film festivals, *see p221.*
▶ For gay-oriented festivals, *see p228.*
▶ For performing arts events, *see p248.*
▶ For other sports events, *see pp249-258.*

The colourful **Mid-Autumn Festival**.

front of the Pak Tai Temple. The buns are stamped with auspicious pink symbols and are intended, some say, as offerings to the ghosts of pirates.

After a 25-year ban resulting from an accident in which several people were injured, young men are once again allowed to scramble up the towers in a mad race to collect the highest buns. Today's bun fighters, however, must wear safety equipment and undergo pre-race training in the finer nuances of tower scrambling. After the dash, buns are handed out to patiently queuing crowds. Another highlight of the festival is a large procession that features 'floating' children who are (almost invisibly) carried on supporting poles hidden beneath their elaborate costumes. Expect huge crowds on the day.

Summer

Dragon Boat (Tuen Ng) Festival

Date June (5th day of the 5th lunar month).
The 2,000-year-old Dragon Boat ('Tuen Ng') Festival is surely one of Hong Kong's most exciting annual events. It features elaborately decorated ten-metre (33-foot) dragon boats with crews of 20 paddlers racing to the sounds of pounding drums and the screams of spectators. Now an international event (and unofficial start of the rainy season), the festival commemorates the death of the popular Chinese national hero Qu Yuan, who, in the third century BC, drowned himself as a protest against the corrupt government. Legend has it that as the hero threw himself into the river, the townspeople raced to rescue him, beating their drums to scare away fish and throwing dumplings into the sea to keep them from eating the martyr's body. Today the eating of rice and meat dumplings commemorates this part of the story, while the dragon boat races symbolise the attempt to rescue Qu Yuan. Dragon boats can be seen at Aberdeen, Chai Wan, Sha Tin, Tai Po, Mui Wo and Stanley (which has the rowdiest crowds), with the action starting at around 8.30am and lasting throughout the day.

Hungry Ghost Festival (Yue Laan)

Date mid-late Aug (for 1 lunar month).
According to local lore, this is the time of the year when the mouth of hell opens and renegade spirits come looking for a place to stay. To keep spirits out of their houses, people leave offerings of food on the street and burn paper money and gold. The festival is celebrated all over the SAR, but older and more traditional neighbourhoods like Sheung Wan, Wan Chai and Cheung Chau village are the most fascinating places to experience the event.

Autumn

For the **Macau Grand Prix**, held in November, *see p273*.

Mid-Autumn Festival

Date late Sept/early Oct.
As the northwest monsoon begins to cool Hong Kong, families and friends gather in the evening to watch the full moon rise and to eat traditional lotus-paste 'moon cakes' with salted egg-yolk centres. This lovely ritual commemorates a 14th-century uprising against the Mongols, when Chinese rebels are said to have slipped pieces of paper into the cakes, which were smuggled to their compatriots. The festival is a peaceful affair and Hong Kong's streets glow with lanterns in all shapes, sizes and colours. Local children stay up late, public transport runs all night and the celebration is followed by a public holiday. The most popular spots to light lanterns and feast on cakes are Victoria Park, Repulse Bay, Cheung Chau's beaches and the Peak.

China National Day

Date 1 Oct.
Every year, to celebrate the founding of the People's Republic, Hong Kong puts on a dazzling night-time fireworks display in the harbour. The best viewing spot is the Tsim Sha Tsui esplanade, although the square in front of City Hall on Hong Kong Island is much less crowded. Throughout the National Day

holiday week in mainland China there is very heavy traffic at the border crossings between Hong Kong and Shenzhen and between Macau and Zhuhai.

Marco Polo German Bierfest

6/F, Concourse, Marco Polo Hong Kong Hotel, Harbour City, Tsim Sha Tsui, Kowloon (2113 0088/ www.gbfhk.com). Buses along Canton Road/Tsim Sha Tsui Star Ferry Pier. **Date** Mid Oct-early Nov. **Map** p333 B6.

Swill steins of beer, table dance to oompah music, and tuck into a pork knuckle between 5.30pm and 11pm daily during these couple of festive weeks. With its sweeping views of the harbour and lederhosen-clad performers, the Hong Kong Bierfest is one of the year's most improbable but zany events. Tickets (HK$85-$150) can be bought at the hotel.

Rockit Hong Kong Music Festival

Victoria Park, Causeway Bay, HK Island (www.rockit-hk.com). Causeway Bay MTR (exit E)/ trams & buses along Causeway Road. **Date** Mid Oct. **Map** p331 E2/F2.

Started in 2003, this annual weekend outdoor rock festival brings together overseas and local indie performers. The combination of alternative music, autumn sunshine and cold beer makes for a great weekend, and with each successive festival, the crowds and line-ups at this Victoria Park event have grown in size and energy.

Trailwalker

www.oxfamtrailwalker.org.hk. **Date** Nov.

This popular and tough charity walk takes place along the 100-kilometre (62-mile) MacLehose Trail in the New Territories (*see p115* **Walks on the wild side**). Pre-registered, sponsored walkers have to finish the course (which takes in 20 hills and mountains, including Tai Mo Shan, Hong Kong's tallest) within 48 hours, which means continuing through the night. Trailwalker unofficially marks the start of the Hong Kong hiking season.

Winter

Winter Solstice Festival (Dong Zhi)

Date 22 Dec.

If you're walking the streets of Hong Kong on this day, you'll probably notice the late-afternoon stampede of office workers dashing off to gather round a table with their families. It's been said that to understand Chinese culture, one needs to appreciate rituals associated with family and food. This holiday, marked by a shared meal, rather than organised public festivities, affords an opportunity to observe both. If you can, try to go to a Chinese restaurant to experience the warmth and rites that bond familial relationships across generations.

Christmas

Date run-up to 25 Dec.

Taking a boat trip across the harbour or a stroll along the Tsim Sha Tsui East esplanade are both exhilarating experiences the week before Christmas. Hong Kong welcomes the season with an amazing display of lights and decorations. Shopping centres are draped in baubles and tinsel, Statue Square in Central becomes a faux-winterland marketplace, and entire skyscrapers are turned into giant neon Yuletide scenes. A recent favourite was that of a gigantic neon Santa pedalling a bicycle above the Bank of China's soaring geometric entrance. In their efforts to outdo one another, Hong Kong's most impressive buildings radiate with light and colour. Many of the Christmas lights are cleverly reconfigured a few weeks later for Chinese New Year, when Santa might miraculously morph into the Chinese god of prosperity. Hong Kong's churches are well attended over Christmas and the New Year (and also at Easter). Catholic and Protestant services are delivered in English, and when the territory's large community of Filipino domestic helpers (who worship every Sunday) are joined by sporadic expat churchgoers at Christmas, churches are filled to capacity. **Photo** *p206*.

Chinese New Year

Date late Jan/early Feb.

Chinese (or Lunar) New Year is the biggest festival of the calendar, and the three-day public holiday involves great preparation and ritual. Businesses (including many restaurants) close, families travel across the border to be reunited, and this is the only time of the year when street vendors shut up shop and take a well-earned rest. On the eve of the holiday, throngs of smiling people promenade the streets. Victoria Park becomes a giant outdoor market, and the flower markets in Mong Kok are packed with families buying unblossomed peach trees and kumquat-laden trees, narcissus and pussy willow, which signify new beginnings, prosperity and good luck. Children and unmarried young adults receive *lai see* (gifts of freshly minted notes in red envelopes) and the greeting of '*kung hei fat choi*' (prosperous wishes) can be heard as people visit relatives and friends.

Although the holiday is seen mainly as a family celebration (and tourists who don't have friends here can feel a bit left out of the proceedings), there are still things for visitors to enjoy, including fantastic lighting displays, beautiful lantern decorations outside the Cultural Centre in Tsim Sha Tsui, a parade of floats through the streets of Central on the first day of the New Year, and lion or dragon dances in the following days. A visit to Wong Tai Sing Temple in Kowloon makes for a most auspicious beginning to the year, and the fireworks above Victoria Harbour (on the evening of the second day of New Year) are consistently spectacular.

Carlsberg Cup/Chinese New Year Football Tournament

Hong Kong Stadium, 55 Eastern Hospital Road, So Kon Po, Causeway Bay, HK Island (2895 7895/ 2504 8311/tickets 2712 9122). Bus 5B. **Date** late Jan/early Feb. **Map** p331 E4/F4.

Central sparkles at **Christmas**. See p205.

Soccer is hugely popular in Hong Kong, even if the SAR's team remains no more than a minnow within the football world. To coincide with the Chinese New Year holidays, three international football teams compete for the Carlsberg Cup, Hong Kong's most popular annual soccer tournament. In recent years Brazil, South Korea, Sweden, the Czech Republic and Mexico have battled on the pitch. Expect to pay around HK$140-$380 for tickets.

Hong Kong Arts Festival

2824 3555/programme enquiry hotline 2824 2430/ www.hk.artsfestival.org. **Date** early Feb-early **Mar**.
One of the world's premier arts festivals, this month-long feast of classical music, ballet, opera, theatre and popular performances attracts first-rank names such as Yo-Yo Ma, Mikhail Baryshnikov, the Royal Shakespeare Company and the Hamburg Ballet. The festival follows a tried-and-tested formula that guarantees at least one major visiting orchestra, several classical recitals and chamber concerts, a splashy imported opera event, a range of dance and theatre productions, a world music concert, and a performance by an international jazz legend. Venues include the Hong Kong Arts Centre, Hong Kong Cultural Centre, City Hall and the Hong Kong Academy for Performing Arts.

Festival programmes are available in early November from the Cultural Centre, City Hall and Hong Kong Tourism Board centres. Preferential tickets can be ordered on the internet or by fax on

2802 8160 until 1 December, then remaining seats go on sale through URBTIX box offices.

Hong Kong Marathon

2577 0800/www.hkmarathon.com. **Date** early Feb.
Attracting world-class competitors, this day of races also features a half-marathon and a 10K race. All three races start at Nathan Road in Tsim Sha Tsui and finish at the Convention & Exhibition Centre in Wan Chai. Runners can enter as individuals or as a team (write to the Marathon Secretariat, PO Box 98843, Tsim Sha Tsui, Kowloon; fees are from HK$270 before November, HK$320 before January).

One-off events

Hong Kong will host the equestrian events of the Beijing **Olympic Games** in 2008. Some 300 horses and 1,150 athletes will compete over the course of three days, joined by 30,000 staff, spectators and members of the media. A total of six sets of medals will be awarded for three disciplines: dressage, show jumping and cross-country. For dates and details about all of the Olympic events, see www.Beijing2008.com

Hong Kong will be back in the sporting spotlight the following year when it hosts the 2009 **East Asian Games**. One of Asia's showpiece athletic gatherings, it will feature top-class athletes from around the region. For details see www.2009eastasiangames.hk.

Children

Beyond its magical skyline, Hong Kong offers all manner of curious sights and outdoorsy attractions to keep kids of all ages enthralled.

For most kids, Hong Kong is an exotic treat, its streets filled with lots of noise and sights they probably won't have seen at home – weird food, creaking trams, old men taking caged birds for walks. The constant bustle should stir even the moodiest teenager, as will the array of shops selling an array of goods for everyone from young fashion victims to electronics geeks.

The excitement begins while you're still in the air: as your plane circles over Hong Kong's archipelago of 235 islands, the view is an exhilarating one of ships and sparkling water. Once through the airport – itself an architectural wonder (*see p37*) the visual journey continues. First there are the majestic bridges connecting the islands to Kowloon, then comes the view of Victoria Harbour, with the Peak towering over the rows of high-rise buildings guarding the shoreline; when the sun is shining their glass and steel glitters, while on a grey day clouds cling to the tallest towers, making them loom out of the mist. For a child it's sheer magic.

The best Kids' stuff

Hong Kong Island
Marvel at the traditional shops with dried sea horses and snakes in jars in **Sheung Wan**. See p209.

Kowloon
Explore the old streets and sounds in the **Hong Kong Museum of History**. See p210.

The New Territories
Climb in and out of the coaches and operate the signals at the **Hong Kong Railway Museum**. See p211.

The Outlying Islands
Spend the day on **Lantau** island and ride the Ngong Ping 360 to see the world's tallest outdoor seated Buddha. See p213.

On the water
Join **Dolphinwatch** to visit the 'pink' dolphins. See p214.

Hong Kong may not have as many world-class museums as some cities but the SAR nonetheless offers a wealth of things to see and do. And thanks to its efficient and good-value public transport system, a lot can be packed into one day. With careful planning, you can easily spend at least a day in each of a handful of areas in the territory. Thankfully, with all manner of restaurants and fast-food chains, you'll never be far from refreshments.

Hong Kong Island

Central

Chances are that jetlag will have got you and you'll be awake in the early hours. If so, grab the opportunity to watch people practising the graceful martial art of t'ai chi. Groups gather in most parks in Hong Kong around 7am; if you head to **Chater Garden** (*see p75*) or the **Zoological & Botanical Gardens** (*see p77*; photo *p211*) you won't be disappointed. (There are also free t'ai chi classes across the harbour; *see p253*.) In the Botanical Gardens, t'ai chi is performed around the fountain (opposite the Government House entrance). Nearby, the caged orang-utans will be enjoying their breakfast. If you have food in mind yourself, leave by the Government House exit, walk down Garden Road to Queen's Road Central and beside the HSBC building you'll find **Mix** (Standard & Chartered Bank Building, 3 Queen's Road Central, 2523 7396), a restaurant serving delicious breakfast wraps and smoothies.

Reinvigorated, take a trip around the **HSBC** HQ itself (*see p76*). Enter under the portcullis, ride the escalator up into the mouth of the banking hall, circle around the atrium and then go back down in one of the inside-out lifts. A visit to the 47th-floor viewing gallery of the **Bank of China Tower** (*see p76*), a hundred metres or so east along the road, is an obvious next step, if heights don't scare you or the little ones.

Continuing eastwards, kids can explore the huge linked malls of **Queensway Plaza** and **Pacific Place** (*see p79* and *p180*) in air-conditioned comfort. There are three shops in Pacific Place that might specifically interest young shoppers. **King & Country** (*see p192*),

A typical reaction to an action man's inaction at **Madame Tussaud's**. *See p209.*

on Level 3, sells detailed military and civilian cast-metal models, including ones of Hong Kong street life at the turn of the 19th century: look out for the rickshaw man and the street dentist. On Level 2 is the **Kelly & Walsh** bookshop (*see p175*) and, on Level 1, **Wise-Kids Educational Toys**. There are also plenty of food options here, from **Dan Ryan's** (Level 1, 2845 4600), for the hamburger addict, to **Starbucks** and the Asian food hall on Level 1, and Eastern and Western food in the **Great Food Hall** on the Lower Ground Floor (*see p191*). For further eating and shopping ideas, pick up a shopping directory at one of the information boards throughout the complex.

From Pacific Place take the lift to the Island Shangri-La hotel and exit through the lobby – or ride the steep escalator above the Seibu department store. Either route will lead you to the eastern end of **Hong Kong Park** (*see p78*). A water-curtain fountain at the entrance is a good place to splash feet, arms and faces. A bit further in you'll find the large shady terrace of **L16** (2522 6333), a pleasant restaurant serving Thai and Italian food. For a respite from the heat, relax with traditional Chinese tea and snacks at the cool and quiet **Chinese teahouse** opposite. At weekends this area of the park often hosts craft stalls or children's events, and behind the Flagstaff House Tea Museum is an area paved with small acupressure cobbles where old folks and kids alike can test the strength of their feet – and their pain tolerance levels.

At the heart of the park is a waterfall that cascades into a pool inhabited by cygnets, fish and turtles. Above it, a conservatory houses cacti and tropical plants. Just a little further west

is the huge, excellent **Edward Youde Aviary** (*see p78*) – actually a chunk of re-created forest through which you can descend on a wooden walkway, past an impressively exotic collection of brightly coloured birdlife.

An equally arresting spectacle at weekends is the sight of the massed brides, like living dolls in rented, frilly white dresses, being photographed with their grooms near the Garden Road Registry Office.

If you leave the park at the western end, you can follow the signs to the **Peak Tram** (*see p89* and *below*), and climb aboard for a breathtaking and fun ride up the Peak.

If you're in Central a little later in the day, head for Li Yuen Street and Chiu Lung Street (the market lanes between Queen's Road West and Des Voeux Road) for cheap knick-knacks. Then take a short ride on the Mid-Levels Escalator to Hollywood Road, walk west to visit **Man Mo Temple** and finally stroll along **Cat Street** (real name: Upper Lascar Row) to pick up unusual trinkets or second-hand Mao and Bruce Lee memorabilia.

The Peak

Don't rush your trip to the Peak. You can easily base several hours around this area, especially if you decide to eat a leisurely lunch, take a stroll to look down over the island or hike back down to Central. It's self-consciously touristy, of course, but that's not necessarily a bad thing. The number-one way to get there is to take the almost-vertical ride on the **Peak Tram**, a trip that's bound to provoke nervous giggles and shrieks as the skyscrapers tilt around you as you ascend. Once at the top you'll find yourself inside the **Peak Tower** (www.thepeak.com.hk) where there are knick-knack shops and cafés aplenty, as well as the waxwork 'celebrities' at **Madame Tussaud's** (*see p90*; **photo** *p208*) – and, best of all, a new 360^{0} rooftop viewing terrace for breathtaking wrap-around views of the city – weather (and smog) permitting.

Across the road is the **Peak Galleria** (*see p90*), where kids can stock up on the nastier end of the souvenir spectrum: Mao caps, pigtailed Chinese hats and so on. Amid the shopping frenzy, don't overlook the fact that there are amazing views from the rooftop terrace of this mall as well. The Galleria has several eating spots kids are sure to like: **Delifrance** on the ground floor serves pastries and other savoury and sweet snacks; **Uncle Gene's**, just above, specialises in sticky doughnuts; and **Café Deco** (*see p144*) has great home-style cakes and sundaes. If you fancy a more alfresco experience, head for the garden patios of **The Peak Lookout** (*see p145*) across from the Peak Tower, before setting off on a stroll around the leafy circular path that swings westwards around Victoria Peak. The path runs along Harlech and Lugard roads (*see also p88* **Peak around**) and is a friendly hike for short legs that offers outstanding views of the city and harbour. There's a nature trail to follow here, and toilets, snacks and drinks are available near the playground halfway round, at the junction of Harlech and Hatton roads. You can also climb to the top of the Peak (don't be misled into thinking that the Peak Tram terminus is at the Peak itself), a rewarding climb through a series of ascending parks and sculpted trails. If uphill does not appeal, try walking down to Central via Old Peak Road: turn left out of Peak Tower and take the narrow path that zigzags downhill through thick tropical vegetation and past some fine old colonial houses; a lovely walk in spring. The path eventually gives way to what must be one of the world's steepest residential streets – this route is not for those with dodgy knees. An alternative scenic way to descend is to take the hair-raising ride on the number 15 double-decker back to Admiralty or Central.

Trams to Causeway Bay

Trams have been an essential part of Hong Kong life since 1904 and they haven't changed much over the years. The distinctive non air-conditioned wood and metal double-decker vehicles rattle along the north side of Hong Kong Island from Kennedy Town through Central to Causeway Bay and on to the eastern end of the island, and they're great for kids –

you enter at the back, clamber up to the top and enjoy a bird's-eye view of life on the street. Tickets are just HK$1 for kids under 12 and HK$2 for adults. You can get off anywhere you want, have a look around and then jump straight on to the next tram.

If you get on in Kennedy Town, the tram will drive along Des Voeux Road West past endless rows of pungent dried-seafood shops. Your first stop should be an exploration of **Sheung Wan** (*see p79*), where you can wander along Herbal Medicine (Ko Shing) Street and Bird's Nest (Wing Lok) Street. Watch as a cocktail of strange ingredients is weighed and wrapped, walk on to **Western Market** (*see p79*), then hop back on the tram. (The ultimate destination is marked on the front of the tram, so if you want to go to Causeway Bay don't get on one marked Happy Valley but take either North Point or Shau Kei Wan). Hop off by **Sogo**, the Japanese department store (*see p177*), for the children's and toy sections on the 6th floor.

If you're travelling with teenagers, head along East Point Road and trawl the floors of trendy boutiques in the **Island Beverly Centre** and then continue on to the **World Trade Centre** where the Level P5 video games in the non-seedy Namco Wonder Park will keep the over-16s amused for hours. If you have any energy left, head back to **Times Square** (*see p180*), a huge complex of shops of all types; pop on the **Genki Sushi** restaurant (2506 9366) in the basement for the ultimate sushi conveyor-belt experience.

East Hong Kong Island

From Times Square, hop on the Causeway Bay MTR and go to Shau Kei Wan on the Island line. Leave by exit B2 and walk uphill for about five minutes (or take a cab) to reach the **Hong Kong Museum of Coastal Defence** (*see p87*). This restored fortress was originally built as a defence against the numerous pirates that plied the waters around Hong Kong from the 16th century onwards. The fortress is also situated at the point where the Japanese landed on Hong Kong Island during World War II. Kids, especially boys, will love exploring the ramparts and batteries overlooking the eastern harbour, as well as the indoor displays of weapons and uniforms.

For less militaristic options in the same area, jump on a number 9 bus from the Shau Kei Wan MTR (exit A3) for a twisting coastal ride to **Shek O** village (*see p93*) where you can relax on the sandy beach and end the day with some satisfying food. Or take the children to the **Law Uk Folk Museum** (*see p210*), a few minutes' walk from Chai Wan MTR.

Arts & Entertainment

Law Uk Folk Museum

14 Kut Shing Street, Chai Wan, HK Island (2896 7006/www.lcsd.gov.hk/CE/Museum/History/lawuk/ english). Chai Wan MTR (exit B2) then 5mins walk. **Open** 10am-1pm, 2-6pm Mon-Wed, Fri, Sat; 1-6pm Sun. **Admission** free.

This 200-year-old ethnic Hakka family home may be dwarfed by the neighbouring 30-storey blocks but it's nonetheless a charming place, which has been converted into a folk museum. The rooms are laid out and furnished as they would have been two centuries ago – a huge steamer and wok stand in the kitchen, a waxwork model of a Hakka lady sifting rice sits in the traditionally decorated living room. The house is surrounded by a well-planted little park tended by Hakka women who wear distinctive hats with a black gauze frill that sways (to keep the flies off) as they sweep the paths.

South coast

Ocean Park (*see p212* **Variations on a theme**) may not be the biggest theme park your kids have been to, but there's definitely enough here to keep them amused for most of the day. The rides are fun, the location is clean and leafy, the surrounding land- and seascape beautiful, and the cable-car, atoll reef and panda habitat are worth a look in themselves.

Further south-east, the fishing village of **Stanley** (*see p92*) is an excellent place to spend a whole day with children. Take a number 6 or 66 bus from Central and sit on the upper deck if you want a stomach-churning rollercoaster of a ride over the top of the island – or for a calmer experience, catch the 260 express service. Stanley's narrow market streets are lined with stalls selling factory seconds and Chinese trinkets. Along the waterfront area there are new playgrounds, and a large canopied open space for picnicking. **Murray House** (*see p93*), an old colonial building transplanted brick by brick from Central, has historical displays, a **Maritime Museum** (2813 2322, www. hkmaritimemuseum.org) and you can take a well-earned break in one of its restaurants, which include a family-friendly branch of the **Wildfire** chain (*see p146*).

While you're here you can introduce the kids to a Chinese temple – just down from Murray House is the **Tin Hau Temple** (*see p93*), dedicated to the goddess of the sea. It was built in 1767 to protect the Stanley fishing community. Inside, huge yellow incense coils and sculptures of unfamiliar deities are fascinating. Also here is **Stanley Main Beach** (*see p93*), so don't forget to pack the swimming cossies. For the bus ride back, pick up a packet of 'sour plums' from a vendor. These dark red, prune-like dried fruits are the local equivalent of fruit gums, and most children love them.

Kowloon

The **Star Ferry** ride between Central and Tsim Sha Tsui costs mere pennies, making it one of the best value attractions in Hong Kong. The Tsim Sha Tsui Ferry Pier abuts the lengthy **waterfront promenade** in front of the Hong Kong Cultural Centre, which itself offers stunning views across the harbour towards Hong Kong Island. Here, you'll find martial arts action heroes and other celebrities immortalised in the **Avenue of Stars** (*see p96*); most mornings you can try the gentler art of t'ai chi with free classes (8am Mon, Wed-Fri). Nearby, the domed **Hong Kong Space Museum**'s Omnimax theatre (*see p97*), has 3-D films on geographical themes (rainforests, glaciers, Everest) and differing levels of adrenaline rush.

Keep going along the waterfront and you'll eventually reach the **Hong Kong Science Museum** (*see p99*) on Chatham Road, where kids can spend hours pushing buttons and learning about everything from household appliances to computers. It's very well-designed, hands-on, child-orientated stuff.

To give everyone a real feeling of Hong Kong's history, visit the **Hong Kong Museum of History** (*see p99*). Don't be put off by the unattractive modern building: inside, a thematic exhibition, 'The Hong Kong Story', traces life from some 400 million years ago to Hong Kong's return to Chinese sovereignty in 1997. It is not the early galleries that will capture the kids' imagination, but rather the street scenes and tableaux from the 19th and 20th centuries, all of which are beautifully presented.

Riding north on the MTR from Tsim Sha Tsui will bring you to the heart of Kowloon. You can exit at Prince Edward MTR to explore the **Flower Market** on Flower Market Road, at the end of which is the astonishing **Bird Market** (*see p190* **To market, to market**). There's lots to fascinate little people here, with a huge variety of South China's most colourful birds on display. Exquisite bamboo cages with blue and white water pots adorn the stalls, and all manner of bird food is on sale, including live grasshoppers by the thousand, in their own tiny cages.

Along the edge of the market sit groups of men reading newspapers or chatting, while on nearby tree branches hang their birdcages. The chirping of the tiny songbirds within is thought to improve by being in contact with its fellow birds. When it's time to go home, a cotton cloth is placed over the cage and off man and bird go.

The nearby **Goldfish Market** (*see p102*) is also worth a visit – with goldfish of every shape and size – and there's also the **Ladies'**

Zoological & Botanical Gardens. *See p207.*

Market (*see p102*), with acres of stalls filled with bargain finds that are not only for girls.

If more retail therapy is needed, head back to the MTR and catch the train to Kowloon Tong to reach **Festival Walk** (*see p177*). It's not just about the shopping here – an ice rink and cinema are also on the site. When everyone gets hungry there are options from McDonalds to upmarket Japanese, all perfectly child-friendly.

From Festival Walk, you can descend to the Kowloon Tong KCR station and take the train north into the New Territories.

The New Territories

Get off the KCR train at Sha Tin station for the excellent **Hong Kong Heritage Museum** and the **Ten Thousand Buddhas Monastery** (for both, *see p107*), which should each appeal to children. The museum is a well-designed space, with an exciting Children's Discovery Gallery and Cantonese Opera Heritage Hall. Of all the Buddhist temples in Hong Kong, the Ten Thousand Buddhas is the most likely to seize a child's imagination, if only because it is quite outlandish. (Beware: it's a long climb, up some 500 steps.) As the name implies, there are indeed 10,000 statues of Buddha on this landscaped hilltop. To add to the fascination, one of its temples contains the embalmed and gilded body of the monastery's founder.

Before you leave ShaTin, those of you with little Snoopy fans may want to head back to New Town Plaza and visit **Snoopy's World**

(Level 3, Podium Phase 1), an outdoor playground with a *Peanuts* theme.

Train enthusiasts can take the KCR to Tai Wo, and then a short taxi ride to the **Hong Kong Railway Museum** (*see p110*), housed in the quaint former Tai Po Market Station. This is a small, hands-on place where kids can clamber in and out of railway carriages and push buttons to make engines run. From here there is a great view up the Tolo channel, which, in the Song Dynasty, was the fishing ground for the Chinese Emperor's most prized pearls. If railways are not your thing, take a taxi from Tai Wo KCR station to see the **Wishing Tree** in Lam Tsuen Village. This famous banyan recently lost some branches under the weight of all the wishes directed at it, but it's still a favourite pilgrimage place at Chinese New Year. From Tai Wo you can also take a taxi to the **Kadoorie Farm & Botanic Garden** (*see p113*), which nestles on the side of Kwun Yum Shan ('Goddess of Mercy Mountain'). This is a beautifully terraced farm that's involved in the conservation of Hong Kong's diverse wildlife. It boasts stunning walks, flowers and lots of animals – plus organised events on the first Sunday of each month. It's not to be missed, but be sure to call for an appointment if you want a guided tour.

If the weather is cool enough, and the kids are energetic enough, there are any number of short hikes to be found all over the New Territories. **Sai Kung** (*see p118*) has wonderful

Arts & Entertainment

Variations on a theme

After years of construction, plenty of localised controversy and an above-average number of teething problems, **Hong Kong Disneyland** (*pictured above*) opened in September 2005. It wasn't a great start: the first day coincided with some of Hong Kong's worst recorded air pollution, and it was almost impossible to see the fireworks for atmospheric gunk.

Disneyland was controversial in Hong Kong long before construction even began. Agreement to build the theme park was reached by the Hong Kong Government and Disney as part of an attempt during the post-Asian crisis recession years to boost investor confidence. Unfortunately, these negotiations failed to secure the rights for the Hong Kong park to be the only one in China, and it seems likely that a second Disneyland will be built in the environs of Shanghai within the next decade.

For visitors to Hong Kong with children, a trip here will fill at least half a day. But compared with Disney theme parks elsewhere in the world, Hong Kong Disneyland is small: some visitors have claimed that a visit for a few hours is enough time to see it all (though this is a bit of an exaggeration). Lengthy queues – in fairness, a feature at other theme parks – may also prove a disincentive if the weather is particularly hot, humid and polluted, and you have a few young children to keep happy.

As with the other Disney parks around the world, Hong Kong Disneyland is home to themed areas such as Adventureland, Fantasyland, Tomorrowland and Main Street USA. All have numerous outlets serving a great variety of food (both Chinese and Western cuisines). Visitor opinion seems to be that for food and refreshments, Disneyland offers reasonable value and plenty of choice. And for afters there's the 'Disney in the Stars' fireworks show, which starts at 7pm every evening.

The park is home to two new hotels, the Victorian-styled Hong Kong Disneyland Hotel (room rates start at HK$1,900 a night) and Disney's Hollywood Hotel (HK$1,100 and up). If you're planning on marrying off your children, check out the Disneyland hotels' variety of wedding packages. According to the promotional literature, 'Couples will receive a special Fairy Tale Wedding certificate to remember their wonderful day.'

Hong Kong Disneyland even has its own MTR station (and MTR line!), complete with

beaches and a remote feel. The **Shing Mun** reservoir (take the MTR to Tsuen Wan and jump in a cab) is ringed by a fairly flat walking path and is home to large groups of macaques. Or go to the **Lion Rock Country Park** (best approached from Tai Wai KCR station). To climb to **Amah Rock** (*see p107*) is tough but pays off with great views, and from there it is relatively easy to keep climbing up to the Lion Rock itself. For any of these slightly out-of-the-way destinations it is wise to get your hotel to write the names in Chinese characters.

The Outlying Islands

Walking in wild countryside is one of the great attractions of the SAR's numerous islands. One of the easiest to reach is **Lamma** (*see p120*), a 40-minute ferry ride from Central's Outlying Islands Ferry Pier. Start early, breakfast in one of the cafés in **Yung Shue Wan**'s main, narrow street, and then set off on the gentle hike (allow a couple of hours) that takes you past two beaches and over the hill to **Sok Kwu Wan**. Just outside the village are the

Mouse-eared windows. To get there, take the Tung Chung Line from Hong Kong Station in Central to Sunny Bay station, and cross the platform to board a Disneyland Line train.

At least in part to ensure that it will be able to compete with Disneyland, **Ocean Park** (*pictured below*), has been treated to a major makeover. The three-decade-old, perennially popular theme park on Hong Kong Island's south side gets four million visitors each year, which makes it one of Hong Kong's most popular attractions. A large proportion of these visitors are from within Hong Kong.

For many visitors, a prime attraction is the 1.5-kilometre-long (about a mile) cable-car, which gives stunning views out across Middle Island and Deep Water Bay on those increasingly rare clear-visibility days. Other exciting rides include the Dragon, Eagle, Crazy Galleon, Ferris Wheel, Flying Swing, Raging River and the Abyss Turbo Drop, which features a free fall from a height of 62 metres (200 feet). Not for the fainthearted!

As you might expect, aquariums are a major Ocean Park feature. These include the Atoll Reef Aquarium, Shark Aquarium, and the newly opened (and more impressive than it sounds) Sea Jelly Spectacular. There are also animal shows featuring various parrots, cockatoos and macaws – though the birds can't compete with the dolphins and sea lions. Other animal 'must-sees' are Ocean Park's pair of pandas, An An and Jia Jia; these seem much happier than the pandas commonly on display in zoos elsewhere in China.

Two new restaurants (2814 9198) have opened at Ocean Park: the Terrace Café and the Bayview Restaurant both offer a range of international menu items and are open on weekends and public holidays.

Hong Kong Disneyland

Sunny Bay, Lantau Island (3550 3388/www. hongkong.disneyland.com). MTR Disneyland Resort line/R11, R21, R22, R32, R44 bus (service 9am-9.45pm). **Open** 10am-7pm daily. **Admission** HK$295; HK$210 under-12s; free under-3s. **Credit** AmEx, MC, V. **Map** p324.

Ocean Park

Aberdeen (2552 0291/www.oceanpark. com.hk). Bus 6, 70, 75, 90, 97, 260/ Admiralty MTR then Ocean Park Citybus/ Central Ferry Pier then Ocean Park Citybus. **Open** 10am-6pm daily. **Admission** HK$185; HK$93 under-12s; free under-3s. **Credit** AmEx, DC, MC, V. **Map** p325.

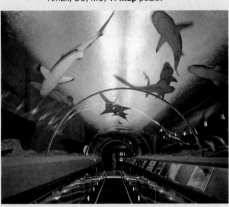

Kamikaze Caves (said to have been used to hide small Japanese boats during World War II; *see p122*), and in Sok Kwu Wan you can also grab a bite (great seafood; *see p156*) before catching a boat back to Central or Aberdeen.

For an excursion lasting a whole day, head to **Lantau**. For the slower, more old-fashioned experience take a ferry from the pier in Central to Silvermine Bay (Chinese name: Mui Wo; *see p124*). From there, if the weather's nice, you can catch a bus or taxi to either **Pui O** or **Cheung Sha** beaches, have a swim, chase

some hermit crabs, and clamber over the rocks. Or just go straight to the **Po Lin Monastery** (*see p125*), home to a giant Buddha statue, which sits atop a hill surveying a stunning mountainscape. For a faster, more commercial (but stunningly spectacular) route to the Big Buddha, take the MTR to Tung Chung and ride the **Ngong Ping 360** cable car over expanses of sea and mountains to the Ngong Ping tourist village next to the monastery. The views are breathtaking and the ride is a treat that kids won't want to miss. At Ngong

Arts & Entertainment

Ping village there are two attractions worth seeing: the **Monkey's Tale Theatre**, showing an animated version of the Buddhist Jataka stories, and **Walking with Buddha**, about the life and enlightenment of Siddhartha. If you're in need of refreshments, Ngong Ping village is full of cafés and snack shops or you can have good traditional vegetarian food at the monastery itself.

Not to be missed is **Tai O** (*see p126*), the little fishing village on the western end of the island. The village straddles two islands and was once only connected by a flat-bottomed boat pulled across by a rope. Now a small pedestrian bridge allows you to wander through the narrow lanes between small village houses – some of which are built on stilts over the water. In the village you can buy old-fashioned snacks and dried fruit or fish, which hang outside to dry half wrapped in pink paper. For a fun half-hour spotting egrets, mudskippers – and, if you're lucky, a dolphin – take a trip in a small open boat around the watery lanes between the village houses and out into the deeper waters. A bus will take you back to Silvermine Bay and the ferry.

Although it won't give you much of a sense of island life, the new **Disneyland Hong Kong** (*see p212* Variations on a theme) will likely appeal to kids of a certain age.

Hong Kong by sea & air

No visit to Hong Kong is complete without a trip on the water and the Tourism Board runs a number of different **harbour tours** through the day and evening which the kids are bound to love, including free afternoon tours on the authentic red-sailed Chinese junk, *Duk Ling*, or morning cruises around the harbour to watch the firing of the **Noon Day Gun** (*see p86*). Perhaps the most exciting trip on the water, though, is dolphin observation; Hong Kong boasts a colony of pink dolphins that live just off the island of Lantau. To arrange a dolphin-watching tour, contact **Dolphinwatch** (2984 1414, www.hkdolphinwatch.com), which runs half-day excursions on Wednesday, Friday and Sunday mornings, with pick-ups in both Central and Kowloon (HK$360, HK$180 under-12s). This trip is both fun and eco-friendly: Dolphinwatch follows a strict code of conduct to protect the creatures.

Finally, those with cash to splash (and who aren't worried about their carbon output) can take a tour of Hong Kong by helicopter. There are lots of packages on offer – both **Helitours** (2108 9899, www.helihongkong. com) and **Heliservices Ltd** (2802 0200, www.heliservices.com.hk) offer a huge variety.

Festivals & events

Hong Kong offers a variety of annual events that should interest children. Many are based on the lunar calendar, so you'll need to check actual dates with the Hong Kong Tourism Board. **Chinese New Year** (late January/early February; *see p205*) is, at heart, a home-based family celebration, but visitors can always enjoy the big fireworks display (on the second day of the holiday) over Victoria Harbour. Avoid watching it from the overly packed Tsim Sha Tsui waterfront if you have young kids in tow. Later in the year, the **Mid-Autumn Festival** (late September/early October; *see p204*) is celebrated in the streets and parks with lanterns, candles and mooncakes. Go out after dark and you'll see families strolling with younger children thrilled to be up so late to greet the full moon with their lanterns – a touch of real beauty. Victoria Park (*see p86*) is a good place to see the lights and buy battery-operated cartoon lanterns of your own. On the same evening, in nearby Tai Hang, the wild and smoky **Fire Dragon parade** takes place with a dancing dragon of straw and incense sticks. The **Dragon Boat (Tuen Ng) Festival** (June; *see p204*) is also a great spectacle. The shambolic races at Stanley feature a lot of expat participation and a great deal of alcohol consumption, but it's reasonably clean fun. More serious international competition can be seen at the Shing Mun River in Sha Tin or you can head to Cheung Chau for a more relaxed local day out that can be topped off with good seafood.

The **Cheung Chau Bun Festival** held every spring (April/May/June; *see p203*) brings alive this little island off the coast of Lantau. Although the crowds may put you off, kids love the rush of music, lion dances and especially the children's parade, featuring Cheung Chau's younger residents riding on floats and stilt-walking over the crowds.

Resources

For general queries about any aspect of visiting Hong Kong with children, get in touch with the **Community Advice Bureau** (2815 5444, www.cab.org.hk) or the **Hong Kong Tourism Board** (HKTB; *see p310*).

Child-minding

The majority of four- and five-star hotels offer a babysitting service. Private services are not common here, but **Rent-a-Mum** (2523 4868) specialises in finding well-referenced nannies, babysitters and short-term childcare.

Film

Experiencing a spot of déjà vu? Chances are you've seen more of Hong Kong on screen than you realised.

Film buffs head to the **Broadway Cinematheque** for art-house flicks and more. *See p221.*

Hong Kong's cityscape is spectacularly filmic – there are times when a late-night taxi ride along a flyover threading its way between outrageous skyscrapers and crumbling tenements will transport you straight into *Blade Runner*. It is also a city obsessed with film. Whenever you visit you're likely to be faced with a wide-ranging choice of local and world film treats – with the latter ranging from blockbusters to silent classics, indie shorts and animation. Keep your eyes peeled for special film events.

Although there is much debate among local cinephiles about when and by whom the first films were shown and shot in Hong Kong – the earliest known film screenings are currently pinned down to the 1890s, the first truly local silent production was shot in 1913 and the first movie with sound in 1933 – it wasn't until the 1950s and '60s that the city's movie production really came into its own. For two decades its two largest studios, Shaw and Cathay, engaged in intense moviemaking rivalry, each churning out over a hundred films a year, covering a diverse range of genres, including martial arts, Chinese opera, melodrama and comedy. In 1957, after the death of Cathay's head, **Lo Ke Wan**, Shaw became the undisputed leader of the Chinese film industry and built an empire of cinemas across Southeast Asia. Charismatic mogul **Run Run Shaw** – one of the original Shaw founders – ruled with an iron fist, reputedly pushing actors and crew to their physical and creative limits. With no guild to negotiate between studios and performers, some actors and stuntmen turned to triads for 'representation', creating ties between organised crime and showbiz, which, according to some industry insiders, still exist today.

In the 1970s Shaw's assistant, **Raymond Chow**, left to form Golden Harvest Films, whose roster of talent was to include **Bruce Lee** and **Jackie Chan**. Based largely on their work, Hong Kong action flicks began to find a worldwide audience. The local cinema scene reached new heights in the 1980s when **Tsui Hark**, a prolific director widely respected among fans of period martial-arts films, split from Golden Harvest to form Film Workshop, a production company that went on to hire the likes of director **John Woo** and actor **Chow Yun-fat**. During the late 1980s and early '90s, Hong Kong films consistently topped the local box office. But the success came to an abrupt end later that decade, as Hollywood blockbusters stole a large share of the audience and local films were increasingly pirated.

Indeed, over the last few years the number of films made in Hong Kong has dwindled and box office figures for local films have fallen significantly. However, tougher piracy laws and Shaw Studios' development of a new state-of-the-art production and post-production centre in the territory have given the industry some hope. Further optimism comes from a number of government-backed measures, such as the establishment of a film development fund, a commitment to selling Hong Kong as a location, and **FILMART** (www.hkfilmart.com), a film and television trade fair set up by the Hong Kong Trade Development Council.

Extra cash has also been injected into Hong Kong's film industry by Hollywood studios hot for remakes and distribution rights for local films – **Andrew Lau** and **Alan Mak**'s *Infernal Affairs* was distributed by Miramax and then remade by Martin Scorsese as *The Departed* (2006), for example. But this move has met with mixed response from film fans – many of whom are also dismayed by Hollywood's heavy-handed dubbing and reworking of original local movies – and has also led to some disasters, notably **Stephen Chow**'s *Shaolin Soccer* (2001), which was snapped up by Miramax, who promptly cut and dubbed it, added a disco soundtrack and then delayed distribution.

Recent years have also seen increased co-operation between international production companies, filmmakers and artists, not only within Asia, but also between Asia and the West. In 2003 Hong Kong and Taiwanese talent collaborated on Warner Brothers' first Chinese-language film, *Turn Left, Turn Right*, a romance starring Japanese-Taiwanese heartthrob **Takeshi Kaneshiro**. Other co-productions include *Hero* (Hong Kong, China, Taiwan), *Crouching Tiger, Hidden Dragon* (Hong Kong, China, Taiwan, USA) and *Three* (Hong Kong, South Korea, Thailand). Whether Hong Kong film will be able to maintain its separate and distinct identity despite these trends remains to be seen, but there are still a handful of directors forging their own paths.

ALL THE RIGHT MOVES

The defining characteristic of mainstream Hong Kong cinema is not subtlety, but irrepressible energy, non-stop action, slapstick humour and an almost fetishistic obsession with comic-book violence. Genres are mixed and blended, and current trends and issues tackled in an irreverent way. In a typical season, most cinemas will show a selection of cop and gangster movies, a smattering of love stories, a Jackie Chan blockbuster, a comedy or two and the inevitable prequels and sequels… all vehicles for big local names such as **Andy Lau**, **Tony Leung Chiu-Wai** and various other handsome heartthrobs and starlets, some of whom have made their mark on the international circuit (*see p219* **Hong Kong's screen idols**).

They've also made their mark – quite literally – in Kowloon. If you're looking for a touch of Hollywood Boulevard-style film glitz, head to the **Avenue of Stars** on the Tsim Sha Tsui waterfront of an evening and hunt for the handprints of local cinema icons. Built in 2004 to honour Hong Kong's film professionals, the walkway is also a good place to shop for Jackie Chan souvenirs, view the Hong Kong skyline and take in a busker or two as well.

LOCAL ART-HOUSE

Over the years Hong Kong has produced a number of widely respected art-house directors, who have addressed themes such as cultural identity, local traditions, ties to the mainland and homosexuality. Many of these films have been well received both abroad and locally.

Hong Kong's most established auteur, **Wong Kar-wai** is an influential director who has developed a loyal fan base since his 1988 directorial debut with *As Tears Go By*. His long-term collaborations with Australian cinematographer **Christopher Doyle** and designer/editor **William Chang** have created a distinct visual style that extends through *Chungking Express* and *In the Mood for Love*, culminating in the seductive, if baffling, *2046*, released in 2004.

Fruit Chan (if his first name seems amusing, *see p45* **Moniker mayhem**), known internationally for his uncompromising take on social realism, had his independent breakthrough in 1997 with *Made in Hong Kong* – famously shot in just two months using non-professional actors. The film won international acclaim both for Chan and for its lead, **Sam Lee Chan-sam** (*Beast Cops, Gen-Y Cops*), and provides a critical and compassionate look at the film industry's glamorisation of recruitment to triad life and the breakdown of traditional moral codes.

Arts & Entertainment

Don't miss | Hong Kong films

A Better Tomorrow
(John Woo, 1986)
A stock gangster tale taken to a new level, thanks to Woo's verve and a superb performance from Chow Yun-fat. 'The *Citizen Kane* of Hong Kong cinema,' is how one critic enthusiastically described it.

A Chinese Ghost Story
(Ching Siu-tung, 1987)
A fantastic tale featuring an ancient tree demon with a life-sapping tongue. Combines tradition with Hong Kong energy.

Chungking Express
(Wong Kar-wai, 1994)
This beautiful, open-hearted romantic comedy paints an unforgettable picture of Hong Kong in the 1990s. An art-house gem.

Election
(Johnnie To, 2005)
A tough and stylish account of the power struggles surrounding the election of a new triad boss, with echoes of *The Godfather* and excellent performances by Tony Leung Kar-fai and Simon Yam.

Going Home
(Peter Chan, 2002)
The last short in the pan-Asian collection *Three*, this subtle and almost dream-like ghost story features stunning cinematography by Christopher Doyle.

Infernal Affairs
(Andrew Lau and Alan Mak, 2002)
This box-office hit, which led to sequels as well as international remakes, stars Tony Leung Chiu-wai and Andy Lau in a taut tale about an undercover cop and a triad spook.

In the Mood for Love
(Wong Kar-wai, 2000)
A sensuously shot story of unrequited love; full of tension and unspoken passion.

Made in Hong Kong
(Fruit Chan, 1997)
An unglamorised look at the process of triad recruitment, public-housing estates and a potential hitman.

My Life as McDull
(Toe Yuen, 2001)
This charming animation features the comic pig McDull and his offbeat observations of life in the city.

Peking Opera Blues
(Tsui Hark, 1986)
The female actors shine in this rip-roaring romantic action-comedy. Great stunts too.

Rouge
(Stanley Kwan, 1987)
Conjuring up Hong Kong's past, this clever, warm and funny melodrama has much to say about the city's changing culture.

Shaolin Soccer
(Stephen Chow, 2001)
The second highest-grossing local film – pushed out of first place only by Chow's later film *Kung Fu Hustle* (2004) – this deadpan mix of kung fu and soccer shows Hong Kong film at its wackiest and Stephen Chow looking uncannily like Bruce Lee.

Ann Hui, one of Asia's top female directors, came to prominence in 1979 with *The Secret*. Her work tackles issues such as identity, local traditions, and the impact of history and urban development, and encompasses a range of genres from social realism (*Ordinary Heroes*) to martial arts (*The Romance of Book & Sword, Parts I and II*) and ghost stories (*Visible Secret*, a commercial genre-bending horror film).

Another festival favourite, **Stanley Kwan**, became an international name in 1987 with the release of *Rouge*, a supernatural romance starring **Leslie Cheung** and the late **Anita Mui**. In 1996 he came out as one of the few openly gay local directors with his film *Yang ± Yin: Gender in Chinese Cinema*. Several of his movies, such as *Centre Stage* (1992) and *Lan Yu* (2001), were prize-winners abroad.

With annual events such as the Independent Film & Video Awards (IFVA) **Short Film & Video Festival** and support from a number of local organisations, there is a growing number of fledgling independent directors that are likely to hit the international festival circuit and are definitely worth watching out for.

CINEMA-GOING

Hong Kong is home to a vast number of cinemas – ranging from modern multiplexes to a few remaining dusty one-house cinemas – screening anything from the latest Hollywood blockbusters to Middle Eastern art-house flicks.

While most venues have excellent facilities, be warned that you could still occasionally find yourself in an aggressively air-conditioned old hall, where the cleaner insists on starting work ten minutes before the credits start rolling. Even in the best of places mobile phones and pagers are likely to go off and conversations continue regardless.

Daily **listings** can be found in all of the local Chinese and English-language newspapers (the *South China Morning Post* provides reviews on Thursdays), as well as in *HK* and *BC* magazines – free 'what's on' guides that can be picked up around town (for both, *see p305*). Alternatively, go online to the www.cinema.com.hk or www.cityline.com websites.

Ticket **prices** vary from HK$50 to HK$75, according to which cinema you pick and the time you go, and it's often best to book in advance (add a HK$5-$9.50 booking fee for online/phone bookings made with credit cards). Tuesdays and matinées are generally cheaper – around HK$45 or less. All films are rated according to the following categories: **I** – suitable for all ages; **IIA** – not suitable for children; **IIB** – not suitable for young adults or children; and **III** – over-18s only.

Most films are shown in their original version, with the addition of English or Chinese subtitles. Children's films, animated films and, less commonly, Mandarin films, are often dubbed, and there are usually two versions – the original and dubbed – shown on different screens around town at the same time.

RESOURCES
For useful websites and suggested reading material about Hong Kong cinema, *see p313*.

Major commercial cinemas

AMC Festival Walk
Level UG, 88 Tat Chee Avenue, Kowloon Tong, Kowloon (2265 8933/www.amccinemas.com.hk). Kowloon Tong MTR/KCR (exit C1, C2). **Credit** MC, V.
Deep within one of Hong Kong's largest shopping centres, the AMC complex has 11 screens showing international and local films. It's easy to find from the MTR/KCR, and the seats are comfy.

AMC Pacific Place
Pacific Place, 88 Queensway, Admiralty, HK Island (2265 8933/www.amccinemas.com.hk). Admiralty MTR (exit C1). **Credit** AmEx, DC, MC, V. **Map** p329 F5.
This new cinema is a fine addition to Hong Kong's movie scene, with six modern theatres and a prime location in one of the island's most popular malls.

Palace IFC. *See p221.*

Hong Kong's screen idols

Jackie Chan

Chan began his career as a stunt man with Golden Harvest Films. His big break came in 1980, when he was given top billing in *The Young Master*, which broke box-office records in Hong Kong and Japan. With around 100 films under his belt, including smashes *Rush Hour* (1998) and *Rush Hour 2* (2001), Chan is one of the most bankable stars on earth.

Leslie Cheung

This big local star, who sadly took his own life in 2003, played Tony Leung Chiu-wai's petulant boyfriend in *Happy Together* (1997). He starred in Chen Kaige's *Farewell My Concubine* (1993), John Woo's *A Better Tomorrow* (1986), Stanley Kwan's *Rouge* (1987), and Wong Kar-wai's *Days of Being Wild* (1990) and *Ashes of Time* (1994).

Maggie Cheung

Winner of the Best Actress award at Cannes for *Clean* (2004), Cheung *(pictured)* first mesmerised the world in 2000 in Wong Kar-wai's *In the Mood for Love*. Before that she had starred in *The Soong Sisters* (1997) with Michelle Yeoh, and in the unusual French film *Irma Vep* (1996), written for her by director (and ex-husband) Olivier Assayas. Other notable appearances include Wong's *2046* (2004) and Zhang Yimou's *Hero* (2002).

Bruce Lee

The ultimate Hong Kong icon. He had it all: looks, charm and a seductive on-screen presence. Though he was actually born in San Francisco, Lee started his acting career as a young boy in Hong Kong. Films such as *The Way of the Dragon* (1972) and *Enter the Dragon* (1973) made him a household name. When he died in July 1973, aged just 33, film fans around the world mourned his passing.

Tony Leung Chiu-wai

This handsome local idol has an avid fan base throughout Asia and is increasingly recognised around the world. He played the romantic lead opposite Maggie Cheung in *Hero*, *2046* and *In the Mood for Love*, for which he also won Best Actor at Cannes. Leung also played lead roles in earlier Wong Kar-wai films, including *Happy Together* (1997) and *Chungking Express* (1994), and starred in Tran Anh Hung's *Cyclo* (1995) and John Woo's *Hard Boiled* (1991).

Tony Leung Kar-fai

Hong Kong-born heartthrob Tony Leung Kar-fai caught the eye of a wider audience in 1992 as the paramour in Jean-Jacques Annaud's *The Lover*. More recently he played a violent contender for the position of triad boss in *Election* (2005) and a philandering husband in Fruit Chan's *Dumplings* (2004).

Michelle Yeoh

Yeoh is famous for being the only female artist whom Jackie Chan allows to perform her own stunts. Born in Malaysia – but an honorary Hong Kong star – she gained international recognition for her performances in *Crouching Tiger, Hidden Dragon* (2000) and *Tomorrow Never Dies* (1997), as well as *Memoirs of a Geisha* (2005).

Chow Yun-fat

Born on Lamma Island, and Hong Kong's most debonair export, Chow first became known for his roles as an urbane gunman in works such as *The Killer* (1989) and *Hard Boiled* (1991). At the end of the '90s he won new fans with lead roles in *The Replacement Killers* (1998), *Anna and the King* and *The Corruptor* (both 1999), and as the noble warrior in Ang Lee's *Crouching Tiger, Hidden Dragon* (2000) and a pirate captain in *Pirates of the Carribbean: At World's End* (2007).

Mass appeal

Stephen Chow's films may not appeal to lovers of picture-perfect martial arts melodramas such as *Hero* and *The Banquet*, but whether you love him, loathe him or just don't get him, director and actor Stephen Chow (*pictured*) is seen by many Hong Kongers as the voice of a generation.

A master of pop culture, Chow spins slang, crude jokes and pastiche to create a high-energy style that is uniquely his own but nonetheless accessible to a mass local audience. The fast-forward speed with which he delivers verbal gags, cultural references and sheer craziness has made his movies – until recently at least – seem pretty much untranslatable for an international audience.

Although pastiche and recycling is nothing unusual for local movies, Chow's films always include an extra layer of crazy invention that makes them stand out. And yet, despite the fact that his films are wildly irreverent in tone, there is a just perceptible level of seriousness that shows a great understanding of, and respect for, the hybrid cultural world he grew up in: one of traditional Chinese values, martial arts comics, Bruce Lee, and films of all varieties.

Chow famously came to public attention in the '80s as the offbeat host of a children's TV programme alongside Tony Leung Chiu-wai. But his acting career truly came into its own in 1990 with *All for the Winner*, a Jeff Lau parody of *The God of Gamblers* (which starred Chow Yun-fat). In fact, it was Jeff Lau who encouraged Chow to try his hand at directorial work.

After directing, writing and starring in a run of comedy hits through the '90s, Chow was in danger of wearing out his formula for success and started to look for something different. The result was *Shaolin Soccer*, a spectacularly zany film that broke local box-office records and might have put him squarely on the world map if Miramax had had a clearer game plan for its distribution.

Thankfully, the success of the original version drew Sony to cooperate with the production of his next film, *Kung Fu Hustle*, which went on to top his previous box-office triumph.

With another movie on the way – rumours of *Kung Fu Hustle 2* or a film involving aliens in China – it looks likely that Chow will be pleasing even bigger audiences in the future.

Broadway Cinematheque

Prosperous Garden, 3 Public Square Street, Yau Ma Tei, Kowloon (2388 3188/www.cinema.com.hk). Yau Ma Tei MTR (exit C)/buses along Nathan Road. **Credit** MC, V. **Map** p332 B3.

Although the screens here are not the largest in town, the Cinematheque offers some of the most diverse listings around, including a great selection of Asian and art-house films, plus regular festivals and retrospectives. There's also a poster and DVD shop on site. Next door, the Kubrick Book Café has a film library and sells a respectable selection of film literature and international magazines, in addition to drinks and snacks. **Photo** *p215.*

Grand Ocean

3 Canton Road, Tsim Sha Tsui, Kowloon (2377 2100/www.goldenharvest.com). Tsim Sha Tsui MTR (exit C1, E)/buses to Tsim Sha Tsui Star Ferry Pier/Tsim Sha Tsui Star Ferry Pier. **No credit cards.** **Map** p333 B6.

Grand Ocean's greatest attraction is its enormous screen. For action-packed local productions and blockbuster hits, this is the place to come.

JP Cinema

JP Plaza, 22-36 Paterson Street, Causeway Bay, HK Island (2881 5005/www.mclcinema.com). Causeway Bay MTR (exit E)/2A, 8, 103, 170 bus. **Credit** MC, V. **Map** p331 E2.

Tucked in among the shopping malls of Causeway Bay, JP has two large screens and mainly shows the latest Hollywood releases. The cinema's steep incline allows uninterrupted viewing – something Hong Kong's older venues can't claim.

Palace IFC

Podium L1, IFC Mall, 8 Finance Street, Central, HK Island (2388 6268/www.cinema.com.hk). Hong Kong MTR (exit B1)/buses through Central/Central Ferry Pier. **Credit** MC, V. **Map** p329 D2.

Despite its small theatres, the Palace IFC has well-proportioned screens – and extremely comfy seats from which to view the mix of blockbusters and arthouse films. It also has a café, and a well-stocked shop selling DVDs and books. Be warned, though – due to its limited size and downtown location, screenings are often sold out, so be sure to book in advance. **Photo** *p218.*

UA Langham Place

8-11/F, Langham Place, 8 Argyle Street, Mong Kok, Kowloon (2111 5999/3514 9031/www.cityline.com). Mong Kok MTR (exit C3). **Credit** AmEx, DC, MC, V. **Map** p332 B2.

The new Langham Place looms like a postmodern beacon deep in the mêlée of Mong Kok's market streets – and inside this snazziest of new malls you'll find an ultra-comfy six-screen theatre complete with reclining seats. The screenings are mostly Asian blockbusters – though now and again arthouse features find their way here too – but there's no better place to go for weekend late-night zombie and horror flicks.

UA Windsor

Windsor House, 311 Gloucester Road, Causeway Bay, HK Island (2388 0002/2388 3188/www.cityline.com). Causeway Bay MTR (exit E)/2A, 8, 23 bus/buses along Gloucester Road. **Credit** MC, V. **Map** p331 D2.

The Windsor cinema plays host to a fair number of premières in addition to the latest, biggest local and international features. The two-seater benches in its back rows are part of its appeal.

Resources & other cinemas

Agnès b Cinema

Hong Kong Arts Centre, 2 Harbour Road, Wan Chai, HK Island (2582 0200/2734 9009/www.hkac.org.hk). Wan Chai MTR (exit A1)/18, 88 bus/buses along Gloucester Road. **Credit** V. **Map** p330 B3.

Once a regular venue for art-house festivals, the number of screenings in this cinema has sadly declined. However, it still hosts the IFVA Short Film & Video Festival in February/March *(see below)*, and regularly screens video and short-film productions by young directors. For details check the Arts Centre newsletter, *Artslink*, or the HKAC website.

Hong Kong Film Archive

50 Lei King Road, Sai Wan Ho, HK Island (2739 2139/www.filmarchive.gov.hk). Sai Wan Ho MTR (exit A)/2A, 8, 77, 110, 606 bus. **Open** 10am-8pm daily. *Resource centre* 10am-7pm Mon-Wed, Fri; 10am-5pm Sat; 1-5pm Sun. **Credit** MC, V.

The HKFA is home to an exhibition hall, film and information archives, and a comfy cinema. Stored in its vaults are over 4,300 films and 85,000 pieces of film heritage dating back to 1898. Materials cannot be taken away, but individual booths and a group viewing room are available for a nominal charge. It frequently screens Hong Kong classics from the 1950s and '60s, and holds regular retrospectives of major international filmmakers.

Festivals & events

The most exciting annual cinematic event is the **Hong Kong International Film Festival** (HKIFF; *see also p203*) in April, which features a wide range of international and local films. In February/March the IFVA's **Short Film & Video Festival** (www.ifva.com) features work by up-and-coming local talent. French cinema is showcased during May as part of **Le French May** arts festival *(see p203)*, while German cinema appears every month at the **Goethe Institut** and annually at the **MAX** festival in October. In June the **FILMART** international film and TV trade fair is held at the Hong Kong Cultural & Exhibition Centre.

To see what's on, look for flyers in lobbies of major venues or log on to www.cinema.com.hk, www.cityline.com.hk or the websites of the Arts Centre, HKIFF or Film Archive *(see above)*.

Arts & Entertainment

Galleries

Traditional Chinese roots and edgy, cosmopolitan highlights.

Many of the city's commercial galleries are located along Hollywood Road.

Despite the city's reputation as a hub of commercial consumerism, there is a really thriving and productive community of visual artists in Hong Kong – you just have to know where to find them.

If Chinese classical art is what you're interested in, the government-run museums are the places you should head to. The **Hong Kong Museum of Art** (*see p224*), especially, boasts a good range of calligraphy, an impressive ceramics and antiquities collection, a wealth of *shui mo* brush and ink paintings, as well as one space devoted to local contemporary art. The **Art Museum The Chinese University of Hong Kong** and the **University Museum & Art Gallery** at the University of Hong Kong (for both, *see p225*) also house substantial permanent collections of Chinese antiquities, as well as hosting temporary exhibitions, while the **Hong Kong Heritage Museum** (*see p224*) has displays of brush and ink paintings, ceramics and bronzes.

Hong Kong's contemporary art scene started to emerge in the 1960s, when Lui Shou-kwan's fusions of Chinese ink painting with Abstract Expressionism inspired the New Ink Painting Movement, which in turn led others such as

Wucious Wong to combine Eastern and Western influences, reflecting the city's hybrid nature as both Chinese and British.

In the 1980s and '90s, this approach was abandoned by a new generation of younger artists. Instead of attempting to compete with the rest of the world, they focused attention to themselves, shedding the ink and brush elements and adopting more Western media to explore the ambiguous identities of Hong Kong citizens. Not surprisingly, this emphasis on self-identity became pronounced in the lead-up to the 1997 Handover. Fears about the future of the territory and freedom of expression gave way to new art forms, while photography became especially popular with people wanting to record this unique period of history.

In 1998, a new era began with the development of the Oil Street Artist Village in North Point, Hong Kong Island, which sprang up after the high rents and commercial focus of established galleries led some local artists to take over abandoned government land to display their work. Just a year later, however, the artists were relocated to the rather out-of-the-way Ma Tau Kok Cattle Depot. Seven years on, despite its location, the **Cattle Depot**

Artist Village (*see below*) continues to thrive – and there are currently plans for another new artist village project to be developed in a disused factory building in Shek Kip Mei.

As Hong Kong's manufacturing industries began to close down, artists started to move their studios to former industrial areas such as Aberdeen, Chai Wan and Kwun Tong. In Fo Tan, a large and well-established community of artists holds studio open days twice a year (www.fotanart.com). Following their lead, a handful of commercial gallery owners have recently opened interesting warehouse spaces in these districts to complement their Central premises, notably **Osage Loft** (5/F, Kian Dai Industrial Building, 73-75 Hung To Road, 2793 4817, www.osagegallery.com) in Kwun Tong, Kowloon, and **10 Chancery Lane Warehouse Annex** (*see p225*), in Chai Wan, out east on Hong Kong Island. Check listings and opening times before heading out to these galleries as many of them are tricky to get to.

Understandably, spaces in the heart of the city attract bigger audiences. In an historic building overlooking the nightlife mecca of Lan Kwai Fong, the **Fringe Club** (*see p224*), with its tiny theatres and galleries, and annual CityFringe festival in January, has played a vital role in nurturing the arts scene since 1984. The **Hong Kong Arts Centre** in Wan Chai continues to host occasional events, although recent shifts towards arts education rather than promotion have caused a slight lull in activity at its **Pao Galleries** (*see p225*). In the same building, the Goethe Institut's excellent **Goethe Gallery** (*see p224*) has a steady programme of interesting events and exhibitions.

In 2006, the non-profit foundation **MOCA China Museums of Contemporary Art** (www.mocachina.org) was pushing for a centralised art space for exhibiting work by contemporary local and south China artists. While discussions with the government continue about a suitable location – at present the foundation is making a bid for the Central Market building – the group are putting together their collection. If the bid for space is successful, it would mean a huge sea change in the perceived value of contemporary art in the community.

Most of the city's commercial galleries are scattered around the restaurants and low-rise architecture of the SoHo district and along Hollywood Road. Enjoy them with a walking tour: the area is a quaint one to explore by foot. Should you be around in the first week of March, try to catch the **Art Walk** (www.hongkongartwalk.com; *see p202*), a charity gallery crawl organised by various local institutions. Many of these commercial galleries are dominated by Asian art of the decorative kind, although there are exceptions, such as the must-see **Hanart TZ Gallery** (*see p225*), which was responsible for introducing mainland, avant-garde art to the West in the 1980s.

Recent years have seen a number of small alternative gallery spaces appear around the city housed in cafes, bars and bookshops. Although the nature of the spaces often means that the artwork is not always displayed to best advantage, if you want to see examples of contemporary, local, non-commercial work it is definitely worth checking them out. Shopping malls and office blocks have perhaps unsurprisingly also emerged as exciting spaces for temporary exhibitions that offer a soothing break from stressful shopping or deal-making.

USEFUL INFORMATION

For gallery listings, check the *South China Morning Post* on Thursdays, the *Standard* on Saturdays, the weekly *HK Magazine* or pick up an *Art Map* brochure (www.artmap.com.hk). Ex-gallery-owner John Batten's website (www.johnbattengallery.com) has interesting articles about the local art scene.

The **Asia Art Archive** (Room 208, 2/F, 8 Wah Koon Building, 181-91 Hollywood Road, Sheung Wan, HK Island, 2815 1112, www.aaa.org.hk, closed Sun) is an invaluable source of information, with exhibition catalogues, artists' monographs, art books and audio and video recordings from Hong Kong, Macau, Taiwan and the mainland.

Museums & public spaces

Art Museum The Chinese University of Hong Kong

The Chinese University of Hong Kong, Sha Tin, New Territories (2609 7416/www.cuhk.edu.hk/ics/amm). University KCR then museum shuttle bus (2nd stop). **Open** 10am-4.45pm Mon-Sat; 12.30-5.30pm Sun. **Admission** free.

Despite its location, the Art Museum at the Chinese University is a great place to visit if you're looking for historical Chinese art. The museum has a collection of Chinese antiquities and fine art, research archives and a conservation annex, and also hosts several exhibitions of Chinese art a year.

Cattle Depot Artist Village

No 13, Block PB 567, Ma Tau Kok Cattle Depot, 63 Ma Tau Kok Road, To Kwa Wan, Kowloon (2529 0087/www.oneaspace.org.hk). Bus 101, 111/Kowloon City ferry from North Point. A former cattle depot isn't the sort of place you'd associate with high-quality art, but it's here you'll find some of Hong Kong's more creative individuals at work. As it's hard to find, check that there are exhibitions on before you set off, although the unusual architecture of this expansive low-rise space is worth the effort of seeking it out for its own sake.

In the central and largest barn is the Artist Commune (2104 3322, www.artist-commune.com), an exhibition space dedicated to mainland visual, performance and installation art. Videotage (2573 1869, www.videotage.org.hk) is a new-media art collective, whose sleek headquarters are in the barn to the left. The leading contemporary-art organisation 1aspace (2529 0087, www.oneaspace.org.hk), next door, hosts well-conceived, curated exhibitions.

Fringe Club

2 Lower Albert Road, Central, HK Island (2521 7251/www.hkfringe.com.hk). Central MTR (exit D1)/ 23A bus. **Open** from noon Mon-Sat. **Admission** free. **Map** p329 D4.

The Fringe Club has several spaces devoted to art. The Economist Gallery, in the foyer, is a key platform for local artists. Paintings, photography and mixed media works also line the walls of the bar on the ground floor. To the left of the main entrance is the newest addition: the Fotogalerie. Although most people use it as an access to the roof garden outside, the regular shows are always worth a look.

Goethe Gallery

14/F, Hong Kong Arts Centre, 2 Harbour Road, Wan Chai, HK Island (2802 0088/www.goethe.de/ hongkong). Wan Chai MTR (exit C)/18, 88 bus/ buses along Gloucester Road & Harbour Road. **Open** 10am-8pm Mon-Fri; 2-6pm Sat. **Admission** free. **Map** p330 B3.

The Goethe Institut's Goethe Gallery is an attractive space that often hosts shows promoting German arts and culture. It also puts on a number of exhibitions a year featuring high-quality local work.

Hong Kong Heritage Museum

1 Man Lam Road, Sha Tin, New Territories (2180 8188/www.heritagemuseum.gov.hk). Sha Tin or Tai Wai KCR then 15min walk/A41, E42, 72A, 80M, 86, 89, N271, 282 bus. **Open** 10am-6pm Mon, Wed-Sat; 10am-7pm Sun. **Admission** HK$10; HK$5 concessions. Free to all Wed. **No credit cards**.

This out-of-the-city museum of art, history and culture offers more of a grass-roots experience than the Museum of Art. The Chao Shao-an Gallery is devoted to a local ink brush painting master, while other galleries host visiting art shows. *See also p109.*

Hong Kong Museum of Art

10 Salisbury Road, Tsim Sha Tsui, Kowloon (2721 0116/www.hk.art.museum). Tsim Sha Tsui MTR (exit E)/buses to Tsim Sha Tsui Star Ferry Pier & along Salisbury Road/Tsim Sha Tsui Star Ferry Pier. **Open** 10am-6pm Mon-Wed, Fri-Sun. **Admission** HK$10; HK$5 concessions. Free to all Wed. **No credit cards**. **Map** p333 C6.

The Hong Kong Museum of Art is much maligned, but does host a number of major international exhibitions a year and is worth checking out. There is one gallery devoted to Hong Kong artists and several displaying Chinese fine art, a strong ceramics collection, diverse amount of calligraphy and ink brush paintings, and a jade and gold antiquities collection. *See also p98.*

Making their mark

Although most of the Hong Kong art world's attention is focused on work produced by local or mainland Chinese artists, other groups of visual artists are quietly establishing themselves in the city – and one of these groups comes from the Philippines.

Over the years a handful of local gallery owners have played a major part in bringing Filipino artists working in the Philippines to the attention of the Hong Kong market. But in spring 2006 a group of Filipino professionals, photographers, graphic artists and painters living in Hong Kong took it into their own hands to reconnect with the art scene back home, recognise their own achievements in Hong Kong and show Filipino art in the city.

In June 2006, after only six weeks preparation, the enthusiastic group pulled together the first Filipino arts festival in Hong Kong: **Unang Sulyup** (First Glimpse). With support from the Filipino Consulate

they held large exhibitions of painting and photography in a number of locations, as well as outdoor events in **Statue Square** – including a hugely popular drawing competition for domestic helpers. The festival showcased a diverse collection of quality work and attracted a large audience of locals and foreign residents alike.

Organisers are already planning the next fest for June 2007 (www.philartsfesthk.com) and are optimistic that the event will become an annual one – perhaps eventually growing into a fully fledged Filipino arts month. Catch it if you can.

Filipino visual art can be also seen regularly at SoHo's **Osage City Gallery** (G/F, 45 Caine Road, Central, HK Island, 2537 0688, www.osagegallery.com) and **Karin Weber Gallery** (G/F, 20 Aberdeen Street, Central, HK Island, 2544 5004, www.karinwebergallery.com).

Arts & Entertainment

Pao Galleries

*4-5/F, Hong Kong Arts Centre, 2 Harbour Road,
Wan Chai, HK Island (2582 0200/www.hkac.org.hk).
Wan Chai MTR (exit C)/18, 88 bus/buses along
Gloucester Road & Harbour Road.* **Open** usually
10am-8pm daily; phone to check. **Admission** free.
Map p330 B3.

Since the Hong Kong Arts Centre shifted its focus
from being an arts venue to being a place of education, the number of exhibitions at the Pao Galleries
has fallen. However, there are still fairly regular
exhibitions of local art, and occasionally some gems,
so check out their *ArtsLink* magazine or website.

Para/Site Art Space

*2 Po Yan Street, Sheung Wan, HK Island (2517
4620/www.para-site.org.hk). Sheung Wan MTR
(exit A2)/10, 26, 37A bus.* **Open** noon-7pm Wed-
Sun. **Admission** free. **Map** p328 A2.

Located on a side street across from the Hollywood
Road Park, this independent art space showcases
local work with an emphasis on group shows and
installations. The team of mostly local artists who
run the gallery also organises workshops.

University Museum & Art Gallery

*University of Hong Kong, 94 Bonham Road, Pok Fu
Lam, HK Island (2241 5500/www.hku.hk/hkumag).
Bus 3B, 23, 40, 40M, 103.* **Open** 9.30am-6pm Mon-
Sat; 1.30-5.30pm Sun. **Admission** free.

The oldest museum in Hong Kong, the University
Museum & Art Gallery has a Chinese antiquities collection and holds regular exhibitions of Chinese and
local art. The new wing attached to the old Fung
Ping Shan Museum throws occasional visual-art
exhibitions. *See also p82.*

Commercial galleries

Grotto Fine Art

*2/F, 31C-D Wyndham Street, Central, HK Island
(2121 2270/www.grottofineart.com). Central MTR
(exit D1, D2, G)/23A, 26, 40M bus.* **Open** 11am-
7pm Mon-Sat. **Map** p328 C4.

One of the few commercial galleries to deal exclu-
sively in contemporary Hong Kong art, Grotto Fine
Art's focus is on new and avant-garde work by local
Chinese artists. The gallery features photography,
paintings, ceramics and sculpture, and for those
interested in buying, prices are pretty affordable.

Hanart TZ Gallery

*2/F, Henley Building, 5 Queen's Road, Central,
HK Island (2526 9019/www.hanart.com). Central
MTR (exit H, K)/buses along Queen's Road Central.*
Open 10am-6.30pm Mon-Fri; 10am-6pm Sat.
Map p329 D4.

Despite its incongruous location – in an office block
in the financial heart of Central – this is one of the
city's most important art galleries. It was responsible for introducing Chinese avant-garde art to the
West during the 1980s and '90s, and the owners continue to show experimental art from Hong Kong,
Taiwan and the mainland.

Schoeni Art Gallery.

Reflections Contemporary Indian Art

*22/F, Onfem Tower, 29 Wyndham Street, Central,
HK Island (2525-5438). Central MTR (exit D1, D2,
G)/23A, 26, 40M bus.* **Open** 10.30am-6.30pm Mon-
Sat. **Map** p328 C4.

This sleek and modern gallery situated in the heart
of Central is the only one in Hong Kong dedicated
to contemporary Indian art, displaying vibrant,
high-quality pieces by a selection of both emerging
and established artists.

Schoeni Art Gallery

*G/F, 21-31 Old Bailey Street, Central, HK Island
(2869 8802/www.schoeni.com.hk). Mid-Levels
Escalator/buses along Hollywood Road & Caine Road.*
Open 10.30am-6.30pm Mon-Sat. **Map** p328 C4.

This enormous gallery (and its smaller branch down
the hill) exhibits a steady stream of oil paintings and
prints by contemporary artists from mainland China.
Other locations: G/F, 27 Hollywood Road, Central,
HK Island (2542 3143).

10 Chancery Lane Gallery

*G/F, 10 Chancery Lane (off Old Bailey Street),
Central, HK Island (2810 0065/www.10chancerylane
gallery.com). Central MTR (exit D1, D2)/23A, 40M
bus/buses along Caine Road.* **Open** 11am-7pm Mon-
Fri; 11.30am-6pm Sat. **Map** p328 C4.

This stylish gallery is hidden behind the back wall
of the Central Police Station. Owner Katie de Tilly
deals with a stellar bunch of international artists,
and has recently opened the loft-style Warehouse
Annex in Chai Wan (Warehouse Exhibition Space,
Chai Wan Industrial City Phase 1, Warehouse 614,
60 Wing Tai Road, noon-5pm Sat & Sun, weekdays
by appointment only).

Arts & Entertainment

Gay & Lesbian

Hong Kong's gay scene is small but growing in confidence and variety.

In the last few years Hong Kong's gay and lesbian communities have taken on a much more public profile: the city staged its first ever gay rights parade; a 20-year-old gay man launched a high court challenge to the territory's sodomy laws (which carry a life imprisonment sentence for men under 21 who engage in consensual sodomy); and two bilingual gay issues and lifestyle magazines have been launched.

While these developments signal a more proactive effort to take gay issues into the public arena, there's still a long way to go before homosexual communities are widely accepted. Although a network of bars, karaoke lounges, saunas and social groups has long catered to local gays and lesbians, the city's *tongzhi* (literally, 'comrades') have, in the past, generally kept to themselves and been reluctant to lobby for legislation that acknowledges and protects gay rights. Homosexuality remains a taboo in traditional Chinese society: sons and daughters are expected to marry and bear heirs, gay people are rarely 'out' in the workplace, and the confrontational nature of gay rights movements in the West is distinctly at odds with the Chinese value of social harmony. The government, which only decriminalised homosexuality in 1991, has refused to bring the age of consent for gay sex (now 21) in line with that for heterosexuals (16), and has suggested that including sexual orientation in newly drafted anti-discrimination laws might be overindulging gays' rights.

The gay scene focuses on a half-dozen bars and clubs in and around Central and Tsim Sha Tsui. Saturday night is the best time to hit the town, with punters following a well-worn party trail along Hollywood Road to three or four venues. Hong Kong's lesbian scene is not very visible, and the few karaoke bars and cafés that specifically cater to women are in Wan Chai.

Clubs & bars

Unless otherwise stated, the places listed below generally cater to men.

Club Bliss

1 Elgin Street, Central, HK Island (2147 2122/ www.club-bliss.com.hk). Central MTR (exit D1, D2)/ 12M, 13, 23A, 40M bus. **Open** 6pm-2am Tue-Sun. *Happy hour* 6-9pm. **Admission** free (except special events). **Credit** AmEx, MC, V. **Map** p328 B3.

A two-level SoHo venue – combining a friendly cocktail bar upstairs and a busy weekend basement dance club – Bliss is injecting some buzz into the scene with sponsored events such as fashion shows and tarot readings. 'Kitekat', a lesbian speed-dating event, takes place on the first Sunday of every month (7-11pm, HK$100 incl 1 drink).

Club 97

9 Lan Kwai Fong, Central, HK Island (2810 9333). Central MTR (exit D1, D2)/12M, 13, 23A, 40M bus. **Open** 9pm-1am daily. *Gay happy hour* 6-10pm Fri. **Admission** free. **Credit** AmEx, MC, V. **Map** p328 C4.

A groovy (mixed) lounge bar and a Hong Kong institution, Club 97 is still a hangout for many local celebrities. Every Friday evening, the boys in suits turn up for its pre-dinner 'Gay Happy Hour'. After 10pm, it reverts to a mixed venue.

Meilanfang Bar

14 On Wo Lane, Sheung Wan, HK Island (2152 2121). Sheung Wan MTR (exit A2)/buses along Queen's Road Central. **Open** 7pm-2am Sun-Fri; 7pm-3.30am Sat. **Credit** MC, V. **Map** p328 B3.

Also known as 'M Bar', this baroque cocktail bar is named after a legendary Beijing opera star, who was famous for portraying both male and female characters. On weekends a DJ spins big tunes and the small dance floor gets crowded. **Photo** *p230*.

New Wally Matt Lounge

G/F, 5A, Humphreys Avenue, Tsim Sha Tsui, Kowloon (2721 2568). Tsim Sha Tsui MTR (exit A2)/buses along Nathan Road. **Open** 5pm-4am daily. **Admission** free. **Credit** MC, V. **Map** p333 C5.

Decked out like an old British-style pub, with shields, battleaxes and some 1980s beefcake posters, this place attracts a clientele of middle-aged, burly *gweilo* guys and friendly younger locals. The ambience is pretty laid-back, if not subdued.

Propaganda

Lower G/F, 1 Hollywood Road, Central, HK Island (2868 1316). Central MTR (exit D1, D2)/Mid-Levels Escalator/12M, 13, 23A, 26, 40M bus. **Open** 9pm-4am Mon-Thur; 9pm-5am Fri & Sat. *Happy hour* 9-10.30pm. **Admission** free Mon-Thur; HK$120 Fri; HK$200 Sat. **Credit** AmEx, DC, MC, V. **Map** p328 C3.

Also known as 'PP', Propaganda is the oldest gay disco in town and it welcomes men and women. Given the hefty entry fees, the surliness of door staff and the often monotonous music served up by the resident DJs, the local crowd has a love/hate relationship with the place, but first-time visitors should be seduced by its fervour on a Saturday night.

Middle Bay Beach. *See p230.*

Moveable feasts

Like most things in Hong Kong, the gay scene is forever re-inventing itself. Venues come and go, and 'regular' events quickly blossom and wilt. Hong Kong's erratic hothouse energy, however, also results in a number of irregular but very enjoyable gay events. Here is a sampler of some of the best.

HX circuit parties

Each held in conjunction with a major public holiday, the **Decadence**, **Redemption** and **China Pride** parties cater to the muscle crowd, who like to jam the dancefloor in one sweaty pack. Parties usually climax in a live show with buffed boys and a local diva. Check www.hxproduction.com for details.

Fruits in Suits (FinS)

Held on the third Tuesday of each month (6.30-10.30pm), FinS is an informal professional networking event where gay guys and gals come to meet new people. It's held at **Veda** (1/F, 8 Arbuthnot Road, Central, HK Island, 2868 5885) and costs HK$50 (donated to a local charity), including canapés; all drinks HK$40. See www.fruits insuits.com.hk for a venue map.

Les Peches

There's a different theme every month at this regular lesbian night, held on the first Tuesday of each month (6.30-10pm). Women descend on the D'Apartment nightclub (B/F, 34-36 D'Aguilar Street, Lan Kwai Fong, Central, HK Island, 2523 2002) to socialise and have a go at karaoke. Tickets cost HK$50 (includes a drink and canapés).

Floatilla

If you'd like to combine a day on a junk with a floating pride party, join the annual flotilla that anchors at scenic Turtle Bay (off Lamma Island) for a day in May (*pictured*). Hundreds of party-goers jump from boat to boat and groove to the beats of a DJ, located on the 'Mothership'. Check www.fridae.com or *Dim Sum* or *G Magazine* for upcoming dates and details of how to join in.

Hong Kong Lesbian & Gay Film Festival

Held every autumn at the IFC cinemas in Central and the Broadway Cinematheque in Yau Ma Tei, this festival presents 40 to 50 local and international features, short films and documentaries. Filmmakers are often present for Q&A sessions, and a number of after-screening parties are held at venues around town. Movie tickets cost HK$60. See www.hklgff.hk for programme details.

Rainbow Pub

14/F, Pearl Oriental Tower, 225 Nathan Road (entrance on Bowring Street), Jordan, Kowloon (2735 6882/www.rbhk.com). Jordan MTR (exit C1)/buses along Nathan Road. **Open** 6pm-3am Mon-Thur, Sun; 6pm-5am Fri, Sat. **Admission** free Sun-Fri; HK$100 (incl 2 drinks) Sat. **Credit** (over HK$200) DC, MC, V. **Map** p333 B4.

Billed as Hong Kong's only 'official chubbies bar', Rainbow is a friendly karaoke bar that attracts larger men and their admirers. Saturday evenings can get raucous as the DJ and karaoke singers compete with each other. Try to grab a table in the corner for great views down Nathan Road and

across to Hong Kong Island. They also run a sauna in Yau Ma Tei (14/F, KK Centre, 46-54 Temple Street, 2385 6652).

Rice Bar

33 Jervois Street (corner of Mercer Street), Sheung Wan, HK Island (2851 4800/www.rice-bar.com). Sheung Wan MTR (exit A2)/buses along Queen's Road Central. **Open** 7pm-1am Sun-Thur; 7pm-2am Fri; 8pm-late Sat. **Admission** free. **Credit** MC, V. **Map** p328 B2.

Tucked away in the up-and-coming Mercer Street district of Sheung Wan, this intimate but classy bar features an interesting rice-themed retro interior. A good spot for a quiet midweek drink.

Tony's Bar

G/F, 7-9 Bristol Avenue, Tsim Sha Tsui, Kowloon (2723 2726). Tsim Sha Tsui MTR (exit D2)/buses along Nathan Road. **Open** 5pm-4am daily. *Happy hour* 5.30-9.30pm. **Admission** free. **Credit** MC, V. **Map** p333 C6.

Close to the hotel belt of Tsim Sha Tsui, Tony's is an unpretentious kind of place that attracts a local crowd but also provides a warm welcome to visitors. As well as a daily happy hour, the bar's draw cards are karaoke and internet access.

Works

1/F, 30-32 Wyndham Street, Central, HK Island (2868 6102). Central MTR (exit D1, D2)/13, 26, 40M bus. **Open** 7pm-2am daily. *Happy hour* 7-9pm. **Admission** free Sun-Thur; HK$120 Fri, Sat before 11.30pm; HK$60 Sat after 11.30pm. **Credit** AmEx, DC, MC, V. **Map** p328 C4.

Situated at the five-way junction near Lan Kwai Fong and the Fringe Club, Works is a pretty tired old venue that has housed a gay bar in various incarnations since the early '90s. The black interior barely masks the ageing labyrinthine premises, which attracts a mix of ages and nationalities. Busiest on Friday and Saturday nights at around 11pm.

Cafés & karaoke lounges

For an alternative to the Central bar scene, check out the little café belt that is emerging in the Mercer Street area of Sheung Wan. For the more adventurous – and those seeking a grass-roots experience – Hong Kong's karaoke bars make for an interesting night out. There's little to choose between them in terms of style and ambience: each usually features a small stage with a microphone for crooners, long tables with groups playing dice games, and occasional beer hostesses promoting cheap drinks.

Billy Boy Café & Bar

19 Mercer Street, Sheung Wan, HK Island (3107 9986). Sheung Wan MTR (exit A2)/buses along Queen's Road Central. **Open** 11am-10pm Mon-Thur; 11am-6am Fri & Sat. **Credit** MC, V. **Map** p328 B2.

A neighbourhood café whose friendly staff serve good food, hot drinks and alcohol to go with magazines and mellow music. Gets busy on weekends.

Boris & Matthew

G/F, 25 Jervois Street, Sheung Wan, HK Island (2854 2834/www.bnm.hk). Sheung Wan MTR (exit A2)/buses along Queen's Road Central. **Open** 10am-7pm Mon-Sat. **No credit cards. Map** p328 B2.

A daytime café that doubles as a florist, Boris & Matthew caters to a mix of ages and nationalities and serves sandwiches, salads, cakes, coffee and teas.

Space

4/F, King Dao Building, 14 Burrows Street, Wan Chai (2792 7979/www.hk-space.com). Wan Chai MTR (exit A3). **Open** 8pm-5am Mon-Sat; 9pm-3am Sun. **Admission** free. **Credit** MC, V. **Map** p330 C4.

A modern karaoke bar that attracts a young local crowd. After midnight on weekends, sentimental love songs give way to fast-track Canto-pop.

Virus

6/F, Allways Centre, 468 Jaffe Road, Causeway Bay, HK Island (6180 6255). Causeway Bay MTR (exit C)/buses & trams along Hennessy Road. **Open** 9pm-4am Mon-Sat. **Admission** free Mon-Fri; minimum spend HK$140 Sat. **No credit cards. Map** p331 D3.

This karaoke bar caters mainly for lesbians, but their gay male friends are also welcome. A young and mostly local crowd.

Saunas

For a place the size of Hong Kong, there are an impressive number of gay saunas. This is not all that surprising given that many local gay men live at home with their families – saunas provide a discreet venue for meeting up and relaxing, and end up functioning as de facto living rooms.

Finding many of these saunas can be an adventure in itself and will take you on a fascinating trail through high-rise office towers, residential buildings and dubious-looking but harmless stairwells in old buildings. For more venues, refer to the *Dim Sum* and *G Magazine* monthlies, or the gay websites listed on page 230. **AIDS Concern** (2898 4422, www.aidsconcern.org.hk) conducts free HIV tests at some of the saunas.

CE (Central Escalator)

2/F, Cheung Hing Commercial Building, 37-43 Cochrane Street (entrance on Gage Street), Central, HK Island (2581 9951/www.gayhk.com/ce). Central MTR (exit D1/D2)/Mid-Levels Escalator/buses along Queen's Road Central. **Open** 2-11pm daily. **Admission** HK$118. **Credit** AmEx, MC, V. **Map** p328 C3.

This tiny but popular sauna attracts a mix of local and overseas patrons. It has a sauna, steam room, dark room, tanning, massage, shower and jacuzzi.

Galaxy

5/F, Harilela Mansion, 81 Nathan Road, Tsim Sha Tsui, Kowloon (2366 0629). Tsim Sha Tsui MTR (exit A1)/buses along Nathan Road. **Open** noon-midnight daily. **Admission** HK$56. **No credit cards. Map** p333 B5.

Described by a resident wag as resembling a 'mainland hospital ward', Galaxy certainly doesn't win any points for decor. It is, however, spacious and well-located for those staying in Tsim Sha Tsui.

Game Boy

2/F, Fook Yee Building, 324-330A Lockhart Road, Wan Chai, HK Island (2574 3215). Buses & trams along Hennessy Road. **Open** 3pm-midnight daily. **Admission** HK$98. **No credit cards. Map** p330 C3.

Arts & Entertainment

A favourite spot for locals and visitors, this place has a sauna, steam room, a large video room with sofas and a cruisy but sociable central shower area.

Prince House

Postal address: Shop B, G/F, 9 Old Bailey Street, Central, HK Island (2810 0144/http://quickly.to/ prince). **Open** 4pm-midnight Sun-Thur; 4pm-3am Fri; 4pm-late Sat. **Admission** HK$65. **No credit cards**. **Map** p328 C3/4.

A tiny Japanese-style 'cruising den' devoted to rippling muscles and bulges, Prince attracts the weekend party crowd on their way to or coming from the clubs on Hollywood Road. To get there, disregard the postal address and instead go to Staunton Street via the Central Escalator, turn left at the Escalator, then turn left down the little alley just near the Eurotreat grocery store.

Beaches & swimming pools

The territory has some excellent gay beaches. The official one is **Middle Bay Beach** (*see p92; photo p227*) on South Bay Road. To get here, catch the 6, 6A, 6X or 260 bus, or a minibus at Tang Lung Street, Causeway Bay, to Repulse Bay Beach, then walk a short distance along South Bay Road to a long flight of narrow steps down to the beach.

South Bay (*see p92*), the next beach along from Middle Bay (and a ten-minute walk along South Bay Road) is mixed but very gay-friendly. It's a nicer beach than Middle Bay, with more shelter and better swimming. On Sunday evenings in summer the beach's rooftop bar mixes cocktails and music to become Hong Kong's very own Café del Mar.

On Lantau there's **Cheung Sha** beach (*see p124*), a lovely, relatively secluded sandy beach on the southern coast of the island. The gay section is located between the netted areas of Upper and Lower Cheung Sha. To get there, take bus 1S, 2, 2S or N1 from the Mui Wo Ferry Pier, get off at the Upper Cheung Sha beach bus stop, and then walk back along the beach a couple of hundred metres toward Mui Wo.

Several of Hong Kong's pools attract a gay crowd. These include **Kowloon Park Public Pool** (*see p256*), **Victoria Park Public Pool** (*see p256*) and **Morrison Hill Public Pool** (Oi Kwan Road, Wan Chai, HK Island). Pools are generally open 6.30am-noon, 1-5pm and 6-10pm every day. Most also close for some time during winter for maintenance. Admission is normally around HK$20.

Magazines & websites

Two free bilingual monthly gay magazines, *Dim Sum* (www.dimsum-hk.com) and *G Magazine* (www.gmagazinehk.com), combine listings for the month with features on visual arts, fashion, music and film. Both mags also feature shots of pretty guys in brand name clothing or swimwear, and a good splash of gossip. The pocket-sized *Dim Sum Q* booklet (also available online at www.dimsum-hk.com/qguide) includes a handy map siting venues. Both publications can be picked up at the bars and saunas listed above.

Hong Kong's gay community frequently logs on to several excellent sites, in particular **GLB Hong Kong** (http://sqzm14.ust.hk/ hkgay), a veritable goldmine of community information, and **www.gayhk.com**, a guide to gay bars and saunas. The regional site **www.fridae.com** and international gay sites **Gaydar** (www.gaydar.co.uk) and **Gay.com** (www.gay.com) also have local chat rooms and personals sections. For **AIDS Concern**, *see p229*.

Meilanfang Bar. *See p226.*

Nightlife

The live music scene may have a way to go still, but if you want to dance till dawn you've come to the right place.

C Club. See p233.

Clubs

Lounge bars-cum-clubs have been leading the direction of Hong Kong's nightlife for a few years now. That's not to say that there are no alternatives. Both biggish nightclubs and small bar-clubs can be relied upon to spin music at volume levels that no sane person would put up with were they not there to shake their booty.

Top international DJs still regularly stop off here, and the trend for smaller clubs and DJ bars has created a more sophisticated scene that's less trend-driven and drug-fuelled. Hong Kong does, however, remain a place where you can party till you drop: a few clubs keep the music blasting full-throttle till 10am.

Canny promoters have opted for smaller, less-pricey parties (HK$200-$400) in recent years, after crowds voted with their wallets, snubbing bigger, more expensive dance events that they'd been prepared to shell out for in the late '90s. Top spin doctors – such as Sasha, Paul Oakenfold, Goldie, Grandmaster Flash and Jazzy B – have played to sell-out crowds in a far more accessible environment, and a crop of talented local DJs has also emerged (*see p232* **Turning the tables**). Instead of just trance, the nightlife scene offers plenty of variety: hip-hop nights have proved successful and house has undergone a renaissance, especially with the sexy deep grooves suited to the city's swanky smaller clubs.

For the discerning clubber, these small clubs are by far the best bet. Places such as **Drop**, **C Club** and **Dragon-i** (for all, *see p233*) in Central aren't cheap for drinks but they are well designed, have good sound systems and often bring in international DJs to complement the residents. And there's always a good mix of locals, expats and overseas Chinese. By far the best nights to go out are Thursdays, Fridays and Saturdays.

Niche nights – with everything from reggae, drum 'n' bass and indie music to dress-up parties on offer – are held in small bars and clubs around town and are usually inexpensive and fun. Big parties are very occasionally still held at **HITEC** (a warehouse-style exhibition centre in Kowloon Bay) if someone like Fatboy Slim comes to town, but these days most parties

Turning the tables

Hong Kong has no shortage of home-grown and adopted DJ talent. Not only have many of the top mixmasters on the local scene played alongside big-name visitors, but some have even guested at top clubs in Europe, America and around Asia. Most famous of all the spin doctors is the pioneering **Joel Lai**, a former Club 97 resident who now co-runs Drop (for both, *see p233*) in Central, where he regularly spins his funky house, and has released CDs of his own mixes. **Steve Yau**, purveyor of dirty house, who spent many years in UK clubland, is another regular Drop spinner.

Young French-born **DJ Eric Byron** also has cut CDs and plays uplifting sets in venues around town, among them Drop and Red (*see p164*). Other DJs worth checking out include **Abby Lai**, **Tommy**, **Galaxy**, **Ladystar**, **Frankie Lam**, **Prawn**, **Roy Malig** and **Yeodie**, as well as breakbeat champion **Bodhi** and his deck partner **AXN**. Also try to catch **Steve Bruce**, who can often be found playing alternative sounds – from mod to lounge – around the city. One of the best venues in town to spot talented turntablists scratching their stuff is Yumla (*see p235*) in Central; look out for Frankie Lam and Prawn.

In terms of age, the granddaddy of them all is **DJ Kulu**. In his mid-sixties and with a wispy white beard, he looks more like the stereotypical wise old Chinese man than a top DJ, but he's undoubtedly the oldest swinger in town, playing acid jazz and funky sets right through till dawn at several clubs.

But without doubt the greatest inspiration to all Hong Kong DJs is **Lee Burridge**. Ranked for years in the top 30 of *Mixmag*'s top-100 DJs, and receiving plenty more accolades, Burridge emerged from the fledgling club scene in Hong Kong in the early 1990s. He fine-tuned his sets during 12-hour marathon spinning sessions at Wan Chai's hedonistic and seemingly never-ending club nights, which ran until noon on Sundays at the Big Apple and Neptunes (now both closed). Those days are long gone, but not before Burridge played support to Sasha and Craig Richards at a rave. The pair were wowed by Burridge's mixing and ability to work the crowd, so they encouraged him to up decks back to his native Britain, where they jointly set up the Tyrant club night and brand.

Burridge attributes much of his success to those heady nights in Hong Kong. His 'local boy made good' story reveals the city to be anything but a clubbing backwater, so dive into the local clubs and listen for yourself.

take place in existing clubs such as **The Edge** in Central (*see p238*) or in spacious bars and restaurants converted to clubs for the evening.

High-profile drug busts still flare up now and then but much less frequently than a few years ago, when various narcotics (notably ecstasy and the horse tranquilliser ketamine) seemed to fuel nightlife in the 'cooler' joints on both sides of Victoria Harbour. Such raids now mostly occur in parts of Kowloon that are not usually investigated by the average tourist. In any event, going on an all-night bender could hardly be safer in Hong Kong – expect none of the 'What you lookin' at, pal?' insanity of Europe and the US; violence is generally restricted to occasional feuding triad gangs and hardly ever witnessed by anyone else.

WHERE TO GO

These days **Central** is still the party hot spot. **Tsim Sha Tsui** and **Causeway Bay** have some huge clubs, but they are rarely frequented by Westerners and, while most folk are friendly, be sure to mind your manners; you don't want to upset any possible gang members.

Wan Chai has many clubs, including La Bamba, which open past dawn every day of the week. But consider yourself warned: many bars in the area have their own house bands playing Bontempi organs over records and are so high on the cringe factor that they go way beyond humorous. If you want a real club experience, you'd do best to avoid them.

And if you come to Hong Kong looking for Suzie Wong – the Wan Chai prostitute immortalised in Richard Mason's novel of the same name, you won't find her here. She and thousands like her are long gone. The district she once inhabited has changed dramatically in the past 40 years, and while pockets of sleaze still linger in the area, these girlie bars struggle to make a living (except when US navy warships make port calls in Victoria Harbour).

The fleshpots are hard to miss. Walk along Lockhart Road near the junction with Luard Road and you'll see young 'dancers' and their *mamasans* (Chinese women who act as pimps) standing under flashing neon, cajoling men inside. By all means go in and take a look – but beware: while the bars are no more risqué than those in any Asian city, naïve foreigners often start off buying a pole dancer a drink, only to be confronted four hours later with a bill for HK$1,000. Remember, these aren't exactly places where you can haggle.

USEFUL INFORMATION

Details of events can be found in flyers around bars and clubs, in free local entertainment guides *HK Magazine* and *BC Magazine*, the *South China Morning Post*'s listings section or online. The two best local clubber's websites – hkclubbing.com and www.absolute.com.hk – are both invaluable resources, featuring details on international and local parties. Also take a look at the informative website of the city's now-defunct DJ training centre: www.hkdjs.com.

Armani Bar

2/F, 11 Chater Road, Central, HK Island (2805 0028). Central MTR (exit E, F)/buses along Queen's Road. **Open** 11am-midnight Mon-Sat; 11am-7pm Sun. **Credit** AmEx, DC, MC, V. **Map** p329 D3.
What would you expect of the restaurant/bar/club in the Georgio Armani flagship store, other than über chicness? Chilled out sounds emanate from the sound system until around 10pm, when a live DJ takes control. Monday evenings are Latin jazz and mambo themed. Look out for special sets from visiting DJs – Soul II Soul's founder Jazzy B played in late 2006.

C Club

Basement, California Tower, 30-32 D'Aguilar Street, Central, HK Island (2526 1139/www.lankwaifong. com). Central MTR (exit D1, D2)/12M, 13, 23A, 40M bus. **Open** 6pm-2am Mon-Thur; 6pm-late Fri; 9pm-4.30am Sat. **Admission** free. **Credit** AmEx, DC, MC, V. **Map** p328 C4.
Undoubtedly the best club in the heaving Lan Kwai Fong entertainment district, C Club is sexy in both decor and sounds. The red velvet sofas are sumptuous to sink into and the dance floor often allows plenty of elbow room. The crowd is dominated by after-work suits during the week and can be a bit posey – fellas, note the no trainers or sandals rule – but the music is good and things tend to loosen up with a more fun crowd after 11pm. Drink prices aren't cheap, but if you want a livelier night than those on offer in the surrounding bars, you'll find it's worth paying the extra. **Photo** *p231*.

Club 97

UG/F, 9 Lan Kwai Fong, Central, HK Island (2810 9333/www.ninetysevengroup.com). Central MTR (exit D1, D2)/12M, 13, 23A, 40M bus. **Open** 9pm-1am daily. **Admission** free. **Credit** AmEx, DC, MC, V. **Map** p328 C4.
Club 97 was the first bar-club of its type in Central. After two decades it underwent a dramatic transformation, opening its front wall to the street and replacing the dance floor with an 'island bar' surrounded by saddle-shaped stools and illuminated with candles. Leather and velvet sofas complete the

transformation from club to lounge, although there is still room to dance to the jazzy house or Latin grooves from the resident DJ – or reggae tunes on Sunday evenings. The clientele is not as exclusive as in the '90s – when its door staff were famously tough – but Club 97 still attracts a chic crowd. For the gay happy 'hour' (6-10pm) on Friday nights, *see p226*.

Dragon-i

UG/F, The Centrium, 60 Wyndham Street, Central, HK Island (3110 1222/www.dragon-i.com.hk). Central MTR (exit D1, D2)/12M, 13, 23A, 40M bus. **Open** noon-2.30pm, 6pm-2am Mon-Thur; 6pm-late Fri, Sat. **Admission** free. **Credit** AmEx, DC, MC, V. **Map** p328 C4.
This celebrity hangout, a restaurant/bar/nightclub, counts film stars Jackie Chan, Zhang Ziyi and Michelle Yeoh among its customers, as well as the city's wealthiest hipsters. Add to the roster various visitors from overseas, from David Beckham to Naomi Campbell, who all drop in to use its private rooms, and you get the picture. It's the kind of place where you sip champagne through a straw before dancing in your Manolos. The brainchild of bleached-blond party impresario Gilbert Yeung – who also spins on the decks a few nights a week – Dragon-i shows the touches of chic international designer India Mahdavi, and features giant birdcages on the terrace in keeping with its Chinese theme. Food is Japanese and old-school Chinese. Expensive but worth it if hanging out with 'the beautiful set' is your favourite pastime.

Drop

Basement, On Lok Mansion, 39-43 Hollywood Road, Central, HK Island (2543 8856/www.drophk.com). Central MTR (exit D1, D2)/Mid-Levels Escalator/12M, 13, 23A, 26, 40M bus. **Open** 7pm-late Tue-Sun. **Admission** free unless there's an event (Fri, Sat mostly members only). **Credit** AmEx, MC, V. **Map** p328 C3.
This tucked-away club has established a loyal clientele in the past few years, and for good reason – it's cool, funky and fun. The watermelon Martinis are fab and, together with the uplifting music policy and swish decor, have kept the club cognoscenti purring with delight. The atmosphere is friendly and there's a good crowd most nights of the week, plus regular visits by DJs from London and New York, who lay down laid-back and sexy grooves.

Hei Hei Club

Basement, 2-3, Lan Kwai Fong, Central, HK Island (2899 2068/www.heiheiclub.com). Central MTR (exit D1, D2, G)/Mid-Levels Escalator/12M, 13, 23A, 26, 40M bus. **Open** 11am-2pm, 6pm-5am Mon-Fri; 6pm-5am Sat. **Credit** AmEx, MC, V. **Map** p328 C4.
Swish but relaxed clubbing is the main draw here for a well-turned-out yuppie set, many of whom are overseas-educated Chinese. A large dance floor is regularly carved up by crowds paying homage to one of the club's three resident DJs – especially DJ Dim Sum (*see p232* **Turning the tables**). On the sizeable terrace you'll find a plunge pool and a

Arts & Entertainment

petal-strewn jacuzzi, both of which occasionally lure the odd punter – usually females who have thought to bring a bikini with them.

Home

2/F, 23 Hollywood Road, Central, HK Island (2545 0023). Central MTR (exit D1, D2, G)/Mid-Levels Escalator/12M, 13, 23A, 26, 40M bus. **Open** 10pm-3am Tue-Thur; 10pm-9am Fri, Sat. **Admission** free (except HK$100 for men after 4am Fri & Sat). **Credit** AmEx, MC, V. **Map** p328 C3.

Just as everywhere else in Central is closing its doors, this place is filling up. Running until at least 9am on weekends, Home is the place for those with no home to go to – or who simply wish to keep the night going. It's popular with gay clubbers, so the vibe is energetic – even more so considering most of the people here have been partying all night. The music is soulful (there's no trance), while the large chill-out area at the back features giant leather beds for clubbers to sprawl over.

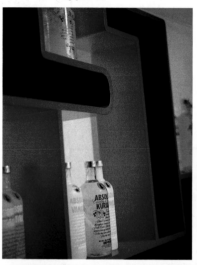

Tribeca. *See p235.*

The Sin Bar

G/F, Tonnochy Towers, 250-274 Jaffe Road, Wan Chai, HK Island (2877 4688/www.thesinbar.com). Wan Chai MTR (exit B1)/buses along Hennessy Road. **Open** Thur-Sat (times vary). **Admission** free. **Credit** AmEx, MC, V. **Map** p330 C3.

DJs take to the decks at this contemporary and rather swish bar-club from Thursday to Saturday nights, spinning a mix of dance genres, including hip hop and whatever's topping the pop charts. The lively crowd is made up of mostly local professionals, many getting down still in their work attire. The cosy open-fronted layout and friendly atmosphere are both conducive to chatting to other club-goers.

Tribeca

4/F, Convention Plaza, 1 Harbour Road, Wan Chai, HK Island (2836 3690). Wan Chai MTR (exit A1, C)/buses along Gloucester Road. **Open** Thur-Sat. **Admission** HK$120 (incl 1 drink) for men, free (incl free standard drinks) for women Thur; HK$160 for men, HK$140 for women (open bar all night for standard drinks for all) Fri; HK$220 for men, HK$140 (incl 1 drink) for women Sat. **Credit** AmEx, MC, V. **Map** p330 B2.

A top NYC club consultant was brought in to style this sprawling many-roomed club – hence its name – that now stands where popular Club Ing once was. The dance floors are mostly trodden by a fun-loving twentysomething crowd, though a few 'old' types in their thirties can be spotted. Musically, it runs the gamut from pop to house, via parties with visiting DJs and hip-hop nights – James Lavelle and Wu Tang Clan played here in 2006. Its bar zones are good for chilling and chatting while absorbing cocktails. Or you can eye the action from elevated booth tables around the main dancefloor. Women take note – it's a free night out on Thursdays. **Photo** *p234.*

Volar

38-44 D'Aguilar Street, Central, HK Island (2810 1272/www.volar.com.hk). Central MTR (exit D1, G)/12M, 13, 23A, 26, 40M bus. **Open** 6pm-late Mon-Sat. **Admission** free. **Credit** AmEx, MC, V. **Map** p328 C4.

It's only been open since December 2004, but snazzy-looking two-floored Volar wasted no time snagging international DJs such as Derrick Carter and West Bam, among others, to play here. Resident spinners include several of Hong Kong's best, including DJs Thierry and Yeodie. Music spans all club genres, and the LED lighting effects change the mood in sync with the tunes. The vibe is friendly inside, despite the judgemental reputation of this club's door wardens; supposedly a members-only club, this policy seems open to interpretation by these charming charges.

Yumla

Lower Basement, Harilela House, 79 Wyndham Street, Central, HK Island (2147 2383/www.yumla.com). Central MTR (exit D1, D2)/12M, 13, 23A, 26, 40M bus. **Open** 5pm-2am Mon-Thur; 7pm-4am Fri-Sat; **Admission** free. **Credit** AmEx, MC, V. **Map** p328 C3.

This great bar-club (which means 'drinking' in Chinese) is tucked away on the right a few steps down cobbled Pottinger Street from Wyndham Street, bearing a New York-style graffiti art mural on its façade. It's small but offers great music and a friendly vibe. Local DJs play here most nights of the week, with regular breakbeat and other genre-specific parties. Expect a good mixed crowd of local and expat clubbers aged 20 to 35 or so.

Live music

It may currently tout the tag of 'Asia's World City' but Hong Kong has long been a non-event when it comes to international music action, especially compared with Japan or even Singapore. It was so far off the map that the annual visit of Air Supply was one of the highlights. Thankfully, things have changed for the better in recent times. From edgy acts like the Chemical Brothers and Primal Scream to superbands like the Rolling Stones, and relative newcomer Norah Jones, the city is now proving a popular stop-off en route to Australia, Japan or, increasingly, China.

The downside is that available venues are not really up to scratch, with poor acoustics, insufficient facilities and inexperienced security staff. Ticket prices are also high, often reaching HK$1,000-plus for a seat close to the stage. But having the option is better than no choice at all.

Sadly, following a litany of cock-ups, the city also has a laughable reputation among music promoters and rock stars. Concerts are banned at the 40,000-seater Hong Kong Stadium because noise levels would be too high for nearby residents – at one gig, audience members were given cotton gloves to soften the sound of their clapping. But October 2003 was a watershed month. A four-week festival backed by HK$100 million of government money brought acts such as Westlife, Santana, José Carreras, the Rolling Stones, Prince and Neil Young to a temporary stage at the Harbourfront Tamar Site in Admiralty. The event was marred by controversy over alleged inept organisation, overpricing and ticket fiascos, plus a host of other problems, so there hasn't been a repeat – but local promoters hope that the tide has turned and that rock concerts may get support in the future. Also that October the two-day **Rockit** festival (*see p205*) debuted, attracting some 8,000 people to Victoria Park to hear more than 20 local and international acts. The fourth festival (in 2006) played to a couple of thousand more as Ian Brown headlined.

Months can go by, however, without a decent touring international act (unless you want some often sugary Canto-pop) but a local indie scene does exist – just about. Guitarist singer Paul

Club cultured

Sure, going out and getting hammered is as much a pastime in Hong Kong as it is in any other sensitively developed city. And so is forsaking conversation to the thud of a nightclub sound system. But in recent years a bizarre notion seems to have taken seed: stimulating the mind (while simultaneously maybe destroying a few brain cells with a bevvy or two). Art 'jams' were one of the first alternative events to capture the thinking person's attention; then poets outed themselves and wine-tastings began mushrooming. Here are a few suggestions for a fulfilling night out.

PAINTING THE TOWN VERMILLION

A colourful Hong Kong artistic experience can be found at the **Meli-Melo** studio, which several nights a week throws 'Art Jams' that have become very successful with well-paid professionals. Here you get to don an apron, choose from a buffet of acrylic paints and attack a canvas. These popular all-night get-togethers attract a cross-section of urban dwellers, although the steep admission prices (fees from HK$350 including a canvas) might keep genuine starving artists away. Session times are fairly flexible, lasting till 11pm from Tuesday to Friday (if six or more participants are in the house) and till 2am Saturdays (last check-in is around 10pm). Private parties can be arranged, and though there's complimentary water, juice and tea, you can bring your own food and booze to fuel your artistic drive.

Meli-Melo has spawned a few other 'jammer operations that open and close with irregularity, including **Dirty Dip**, a newish art studio that offers sessions from one to eight hours (HK$80-$520; bring your own food and drink). Check *HK Magazine* for news of other art jamming events.

SAY IT LOUD

On the first Thursday of each month, the **Fringe Club** (2521 7251, 8-11pm; *see p239*) hosts poetry readings in the form of Out Loud meetings, in which people read their works

Wong, formerly of pop rock band Beyond, leads the pack. Others to watch out for are the Pancakes – an innovative female solo act that has landed a record deal in, for some reason, Spain – as well as electronic duo Slow Tech Riddim, angsty indie-rock quintet Synfia and grunge rockers Qui Hong. There are also plenty of student bands and quite a few expat rockers, who play local music bars like **The Wanch** (*see p239*) and **Carnegie's** (*see p238*).

Besides Canto-pop, locals tend to be heavily into J-Pop from Japan, K-Pop from Korea and Mando-pop from mainland China. Hong Kong's international charts are packed with Western boy and girl band pap – which is also played in heavy rotation on Asia's two satellite music channels, MTV and Channel [V].

Jazz buffs saw reasonable-sized venues close some years ago. However, a few restaurants and bars continue to support the few local performers. While touring international jazz acts are fewer, some big names, such as Herbie Hancock and Pat Metheny, have played City Hall as part of the government-sponsored Jazz Up series that runs throughout the year. There is also a plethora of local talent here worth seeing: watch out for gigs by singer and guitarist Eugene Pao, local chanteuse Elaine Liu, trumpeter Mark Henderson – who plays music in the style of the classic 1950s and '60s Blue Note sound – along with guitarists Guy Le Claire and William Tang, and pianist Allen Youngblood. Folk fans can look forward to an annual festival late in the year.

and have a chat about all the texts that were recited. A week later (every second Thursday of the month), the **V13 Vodka Bar** holds its Vodka Slam – as opposed to the ongoing slamming of drinks every night. A poetry 'slam', for those unaware of the US-born phenomenon, is an open-mic knockout poetry bout. Contestants read their works and remain in the game for as long as the crowd cheer their spoken words; not much clapping and whooping means they're eliminated. The last person speaking is proclaimed 'winner'. For a weekly word fix, head to Wednesday's poetry night at the bizarrely named **Joyce Is Not Here** bar/café (*pictured*). This arty hangout also hosts a music jam night every Thursday and live music performances on Fridays. Sunday evenings are movie nights – projected on to a 72-inch screen.

WINE GOGGLES

If you fancy learning a thing or two about wine, short courses crop up from time to time – check the listings of local lifestyle publications (*see p305*). Alternatively, contact **Concord Wines**, which runs appreciation classes in small groups, covering certain grape varieties or growing regions. These short courses change frequently; some are informal while others lead to certification.

Concord Wines

4/F, B2B Centre, 35-36 Connaught Road West, Sheung Wan, HK Island (2111 3009/ fax 2111 0253/www.concordwines.com.hk). Sheung Wan MTR (exit C)/buses & trams

along Des Voeux Road. **Open** (courses) 6-10pm Mon-Fri. **Fees** varies. **Credit** MC, V. **Map** p328 A1.

Dirty Dip

2/F, 19 Sharp Street, Causeway Bay, HK Island (2882 1969/www.dirty-dip.com). Causeway Bay MTR (exit A)/buses along Leighton Road/trams to Percival Street. **Open** noon-10pm Mon-Thur; noon-1am Fri, Sat. **Admission** HK$80-$520 (plus HK$30-$85 for a canvas). **Credit** AmEx, MC, V. **Map** p331 D3.

Joyce Is Not Here

38-44 Peel Street, SoHo, Central, HK Island (2851 2999/www.joycebakerdesign.com). Central MTR (exit D2)/Mid-Levels Escalator/ buses along Queen's Road. **Open** 8pm-late Tue-Sun. **Admission** free. **Credit** MC, V. **Map** p328 B3/C3.

Meli-Melo

G/F, 123 Wellington Street, Central, HK Island (2541 8816/www.artjamming.com). Sheung Wan MTR (exit B2)/buses along Queen's Road. **Open** 2-6pm, 7-11pm Tue-Fri for groups of six or more (7-9pm for fewer than six people); 7pm-2am Sat; 1-6pm Sun. **Admission** HK$350 and up (incl canvas). **Credit** AmEx, MC, V. **Map** p328 C2.

V13 Vodka Bar

13 Old Bailey Street, SoHo, Central, HK Island (9803 6650/www.vodkabar. com.hk). Central MTR (exit D2)/Mid-Levels Escalator. **Open** 8-10.30pm. **Credit** AmEx, MC, V. **Map** p328 C3/C4.

Hotel bands may not sound like much of an option, but some are very talented and provide an entertaining night out. Check out **Talk of the Town** (or ToTT's) at the Excelsior and the **Lobster Bar** at the Island Shangri-La (for both, *see p240*). Visiting bands from the Caribbean and South America have been known to have even the most supine onlookers up and dancing.

Good bands can also be found at **The Edge** in Central (*see p238*). More down-at-heel, but offering straight-up fun, are the cover bands who ply some of the packed music bars around town, such as **Insomnia** (*see p239*) and **Dusk Till Dawn** (*see p238*), which keep rocking till after 5pm. They're not the classiest places, but if it's good old-fashioned fun and if it's a boogie you want, you'll find it here.

Major venues

For the following venues, tickets are available through either **URBTIX** (2734 9009, www.lcsd. gov.hk/urbtix) or **HK Ticketing** (3128 8288, www.hkticketing.com).

AsiaWorld-Arena

Level 1, AsiaWorld-Expo, Chek Lap Kok, Lantau (3606 8828/www.asiaworld-expo.com). AsiaWorld-Expo Airport Express Station. **Box office** bookings through HK Ticketing. **Open** 10am-6pm Mon-Sat. **Admission** ticket prices vary. **Credit** AmEx, MC, V. **Map** p324.

This new convention centre, two minutes from the airport, has specially-built auditoria (unlike the HKCEC; *see p238*). Oasis was one of the first acts to christen the stage, in 2006; Il Divo and Eric Clapton

Arts & Entertainment

were booked for 2007. It's a bit of a schlep from downtown but the MTR has thoughtfully offered heavily discounted fares if you use an Octopus card (*see p296*), though that's not much consolation when you're paying double what you would elsewhere to see a live act.

Hong Kong Coliseum
Stadia Office, 9 Cheong Wan Road, Hung Hom, Kowloon (2355 7234/www.lcsd.gov.hk/urbtix). Kowloon KCR/101, 104, 110 bus. **Box office** bookings through URBTIX. **Admission** ticket prices vary. **Credit** AmEx, MC, V. **Map** p333 D5.
The glory days of the Coliseum are long over. This 12,500-seat venue is a bit dilapidated, which is a shame as it's still a good place to see major acts – unless you're stuck up in the gods. Canto-pop stars still perform long runs here, but international acts are laid on mostly at the more accessible Convention & Exhibition Centre (*see below*). Still, Bob Dylan, Deep Purple and Santana have all played the Coliseum. A further bonus is that you can even get out of your seat and dance if you want, which is not the case everywhere in HK.

Hong Kong Convention & Exhibition Centre
1 Expo Drive, Wan Chai, HK Island (2582 8888/ www.hkcec.com). Wan Chai MTR (exit A1)/buses along Gloucester Road/Wan Chai Star Ferry Pier. **Box office** bookings through HK Ticketing. **Admission** ticket prices vary. **Credit** MC, V. **Map** p330 B2.
The largest hall of the Hong Kong Convention & Exhibition Centre (HKCEC; *see also p83*) was the most popular venue for laying on big acts before AsiaWorld-Expo opened its concert hall (*see p237*); it had hosted everyone from Oasis to Ibrahim Ferrer. Unfortunately, that doesn't mean it's a good place for a rock concert. It has been plagued by problems, most notably poor acoustics and crowd chaos. People don't know whether to sit or stand – and security often has little control. Instead of fixed seating, there are portable plastic chairs and, as these are mostly laid out on the same level, it is difficult to see the stage in the premium seats a few rows back. The owners have long said they were sorting out the problems but didn't – thus AWE took up the mantle. Ticket prices for concerts here are high; the advantage is that it's easy to get to.

Ko Shan Theatre
Ko Shan Park, 77 Ko Shan Road, Hung Hom, Kowloon (2740 9222/2734 9009/www.lcsd.gov.hk/ urbtix). Bus 111, 101, 107, 116. **Box office** bookings through URBTIX. **Admission** ticket prices vary. **Credit** AmEx, MC, V. **Map** p332 E3.
This 1,000-seat theatre has proved popular with indie bands who can't fill a bigger venue – though such acts have not been dropping in much in the mid-noughties. Decent acoustics, sound and lighting mean good shows can be put on here. Like the Coliseum, though, it's a bit out of the way.

Queen Elizabeth Stadium
18 Oi Kwan Road, Wan Chai, HK Island (2591 1346/www.lcsd.gov.hk/qes). Causeway Bay MTR (exit A)/5A, 10 bus/buses along Hennessy Road. **Box office** 9am-1pm, 2-5.45pm Mon-Fri. Bookings also through URBTIX. **Admission** ticket prices vary. **Credit** AmEx, MC, V. **Map** p330 C4.
British popsters Suede like this venue so much they played it three times, but such acts are few and far between. With 3,500 seats, it's good for bands who have sizeable, rather than huge, followings. There's no mosh pit and over-zealous security staff often shine torches in the face of anyone who dares to stand up and dance.

Other rock venues

All Night Long
9 Knutsford Terrace, Tsim Sha Tsui, Kowloon (2367 9487). Tsim Sha Tsui MTR (exit B2)/buses along Nathan Road & Chatham Road South. **Open** 3pm-6am daily. **Admission** free. **Credit** AmEx, DC, MC, V. **Map** p333 C5.
This old-fashioned get-down-and-boogie joint hosts cover bands – mostly from the Philippines – who play old and new hits by mainstream acts. The musical style depends on what band you get; some are surprisingly good, but all become better as the night grows old and more ale has been sunk. Bands rotate between All Night Long, Dusk Till Dawn (*see below*) and Insomnia (*see p239*), ensuring that all three venues have live sounds every night of the week. On the downside, they are all rowdy and have reputations for being meat markets.

Carnegie's
53-5 Lockhart Road, Wan Chai, HK Island (2866 6289/www.carnegies.net). Wan Chai MTR (exit A1, C)/buses along Hennessy Road. **Open** 11am-very late daily. **Credit** AmEx, MC, V. **Map** p330 B3.
Twelve years is a long time in the HK nightlife scene and yet Carnegie's shows no sign of slowing down. A small stage and cramped space don't stop this place rocking most nights. If there's no band, a DJ cranks things up and revellers take to dancing on the bar. Sadly, the second-floor loft – a good vantage point from which to watch the madness – had to be removed in 2003 by order of killjoy officials.

Dusk Till Dawn
76 Jaffe Road, Wan Chai, HK Island (2528 4689). Wan Chai MTR (exit A1, C)/buses along Gloucester Road or Hennessy Road. **Open** noon-around 6am Mon-Fri; 3pm-6am Sat, Sun. **Admission** free. **Credit** AmEx, DC, MC, V. **Map** p330 B3.
Cover bands begin to play at 10pm nightly. For more details, *see above* **All Night Long**.

The Edge
G/F, The Centrium, 60 Wyndham Street, Central, HK Island (2523 6690). Central MTR (exit D1, D2)/ 23A, 26, 40M bus. **Open** 6pm-late Thur-Sat. **Admission** HK$160 (incl 1 drink). **Credit** AmEx, MC, V. **Map** p328 C4.

This upmarket live-music venue may be a relative newcomer, but it always hosts a fun-loving crowd. Its interior glows with red lighting and furnishings, while the dance floor moves to the beat of a talented house band, which plays both covers and original material. DJs fill in the breaks between sets, and special parties are occasionally laid on. Ever since Prince played an after party here, the Edge has moved towards the centre of the live scene – Jocelyn Brown has also graced the stage.

Fringe Club

2 Lower Albert Road, Central, HK Island (2521 7485/www.hkfringeclub.com). Central MTR (exit D1)/23A bus. **Open** noon-midnight Mon-Thur; noon-2am Fri, Sat. **Admission** usually free. **Credit** AmEx, MC, V. **Map** p328 C4.

Fringe's Nokia Gallery is a reliable space that has long served aspiring home-grown musical talent. The venue helped launch the career of successful local chanteuse Susie Wilkins, and hosts everything from rock bands to the Saturday Night Jazz Orchestra, a local collective of Japanese businessmen who play swing pretty well. The beer is cheap, and the venue provides a real pub-gig atmosphere that is otherwise hard to find in Hong Kong. There is normally live music on Friday and Saturday nights, but it's wise to phone ahead to check what's on. *See also p138 and p243.*

Insomnia

LG/F, 38-44 D'Aguilar Street, Central, HK Island (2525 0957/www.lankwaifong.com). Central MTR (exit D1, D2, G)/12M, 13, 23A, 40M bus. **Open** 9am-6am daily. **Admission** free. **Credit** AmEx, DC, MC, V. **Map** p328 C4.

Happy hour 5-9pm; live bands from 10.30pm every night. *See also p238* **All Night Long**.

Pit Stop

Harbour Plaza Hotel, 20 Tak Fung Street, Hung Hom, Kowloon (2621 3188/2996 8455/www.harbour-plaza.com/hphk). Kowloon KCR/101, 104, 110 bus/6 green minibus. **Open** noon-1am Mon-Thur, Sun; noon-2am Fri, Sat. **Admission** free. **Credit** AmEx, DC, MC, V. **Map** off p333 E5.

A better-than-average hotel live-music joint, the Pit Stop offers a good selection of bands who like to perform their own songs as well as the usual covers. Car-racing buffs will dig the chrome-tinged decor, which is themed around the world of motorsports.

Venue/Bar Amazonia

G/F, 15-19 Luard Road, Wan Chai, HK Island (3105 8990/www.venue.com.hk). Wan Chai MTR (exit A1, C)/buses along Gloucester & Hennessy Road. **Open** noon-4am Mon-Thur; 5pm-5am Fri, Sat. **Admission** free. **Credit** AmEx, MC, V. **Map** p330 B3.

A flash-looking bar with a small stage, this venue purports to offer an upmarket spot to hear cover bands and sip cocktails or beers. For all the bright lights and chrome fittings, in reality the place has much in common with Wan Chai's more down-at-heel

music venues, but the atmosphere is a little more sophisticated – you won't find people dancing on the bar here. Monday night is jam night, with a great musical collective – if you would like to join in, let staff know when you arrive.

The Wanch

54 Jaffe Road, Wan Chai, HK Island (2861 1621). Wan Chai MTR (exit A1, C)/buses along Gloucester Road & Hennessy Road. **Open** 11am-2am Mon-Sat; noon-2am Sun. **Admission** free. **Credit** DC, MC, V. **Map** p330 B3.

Hong Kong's very own Tardis. The Wanch doesn't look much bigger than a phone kiosk, but it manages to squeeze in a band and plenty of punters most nights. Perhaps the city's most famous pub-gig venue, it has hosted the debuts of many indie and folk bands who went on to become local fixtures. And it's still going strong. Wednesday is jam night here; Sunday is 'sing-along' music; resident and drop-in bands perform on other nights.

Jazz & blues bars

See also above **Fringe Club**.

Blue Door

5/F, 37 Cochrane Street, Central, HK Island (2858 6555/www.bluedoor.com.hk). Central MTR (exit D2). **Open** 10.30pm-2am Fri, Sat. **Admission** HK$100 (incl 1 drink). **Credit** AmEx, MC, V. **No credit cards**. **Map** p328 C3.

A real jazz and blues den tucked away inside a commercial building, the Blue Door plays host to local and, occasionally, visiting musicians. It provides aficionados with the only weekend hangout to offer a wide range of jazz (10.30pm-12.30am). All the best local musicians perform here, perhaps because it's such an intimate space.

Ned Kelly's Last Stand

11A Ashley Road, Tsim Sha Tsui, Kowloon (2376 0562). Tsim Sha Tsui MTR (exit A1, C1)/Tsim Sha Tsui Star Ferry Pier. **Open** 11.30am-2am daily. **Admission** free. **Credit** MC, V. **Map** p333 B6.

Kelly's Gang brings the sound of Dixieland to Hong Kong every night of the week. The decor may be yellowed with age, but it's a friendly pub. And, despite its name, it pulls in an international mix of expats and younger Chinese as well as Aussies; the crowd is mostly over 30, though.

Pizza Express

21 Lyndhurst Terrace, Central, HK Island (2850 7898/www.pizzaexpress.com.hk). Central MTR (exit D1)/Mid-Levels Escalator/23A bus. **Open** noon-11.30pm daily. **Credit** AmEx, DC, MC, V. **Map** p328 C3.

Every Thursday evening, the saxophonist Oliver Smith takes to the small stage here for a few sets along with an ever-changing accompaniment of jazz musicians. It's one of the most intimate gig venues in town, and very popular – reservations are recommended. *See also p139.*

Arts & Entertainment

Hotel lounge bars

Captain's Bar

Lobby, Mandarin Oriental Hotel, 5 Connaught Road, Central, HK Island (2522 0111/www.mandarin oriental.com). Central MTR (exit F, H)/buses to Central Ferry Pier/Central Ferry Pier. **Open** 11am-2am Mon-Sat; 11am-1am Sun. **Admission** free. **Credit** AmEx, DC, MC, V. **Map** p329 E3.

The Mandarin Oriental's lobby bar is a great place to relax before or after dinner in comfortable yet opulent surroundings. The floor gets taken over for hip shaking later on (9pm until just before closing), when the resident band runs through jazz standards, or ups the tempo with pop and R&B.

Eyes

1/F, Miramar Hotel, 118-130 Nathan Road, Tsim Sha Tsui, Kowloon (2315 5888). Tsim Sha Tsui MTR (exit B)/buses along Nathan Road. **Open** 5pm-2am daily. **Admission** free. **Credit** AmEx, DC, MC, V. **Map** p333 C5.

Eyes is great if you want to take a peek at the Chinese letting their hair down. Here, expats mingle with locals and visiting business folk from Taiwan and the mainland in a lively setting. There's always entertainment, but if you're here when cabaret act Danny Diaz is in town you're in for a treat of musical impersonations and interpretations, plus plenty of Bob Hope-style comic banter.

Lobby Lounge

Kowloon Shangri-La Hotel, 64 Mody Road, Tsim Sha Tsui (2721 2111). Tsim Sha Tsui MTR (exit C1)/203, 973 bus/buses along Chatham Road South & Salisbury Road. **Open** 7am-midnight daily. **Admission** free. **Credit** AmEx, DC, MC, V. **Map** p333 C6.

The lobby lounge at the Kowloon Shangri-La Hotel provides another sumptuous setting for a night out, with a decent resident singer to provide background entertainment while you drink or eat.

Lobster Bar

Lobby Level, Island Shangri-La Hotel, Pacific Place, 88 Queensway, Admiralty, HK Island (2820 8560). Admiralty MTR (exit C1)/buses along Queensway. **Open** noon-1am Mon-Thur, Sun; 5pm-2am Fri, Sat. **Admission** free. **Credit** AmEx, DC, MC, V. **Map** p329 F5.

Swish cosiness, fantastic wine and cocktails, plus a decent (albeit pricey) menu make a perfect backdrop for an increasingly impressive stream of overseas band residencies here that stretch to three months each. Class acts of the stage and lounge-bar scene have recently included blues and soul-tinged outfits. Sets start at 8pm nightly.

ToTT's Asian Grill & Bar

Excelsior Hotel, 281 Gloucester Road, Causeway Bay (2894 8888/www.mandarin-oriental.com/excelsior). Causeway Bay MTR (exit D1)/buses along Gloucester Road. **Open** 6.30-11.30pm Mon-Thur; 6.30pm-1.30am Fri, Sat. **Admission** free. **Credit** AmEx, DC, MC, V. **Map** p331 E2.

This restaurant/bar/nightclub offers great views, fusion food and fancy cocktails, plus music from an always exuberant house band or DJ, who manage to get the dance floor heaving most nights. It's popular with a mix of local and expat residents.

ToTT's: because lounge bars aren't just for lounging about.

Performing Arts

Although overshadowed by Hong Kong's towering commercial presence, the cultural scene offers a rich mix of Chinese and Western traditions.

Hong Kong's culturally diverse arts scene may be under-appreciated – Western sophisticates have long lampooned the cultural crassness of the city's tycoons, and Beijing's intelligentsia delights in deriding the territory's cultural diet of horseracing and Canto-pop – but it offers plenty of surprises.

At first glance, however, these stereotypes about its cultural vapidity seem to have some credence. Hong Kong is better known for exporting action-film stars than writers, dancers or orchestras; and while lion-dance troupes and Cantonese operas are admired for their colour and zest, most visitors would cite the territory's shopping or dining, rather than its performing arts, as its chief tourist attraction.

Hong Kong's performance spaces also fail to suggest a dynamic cultural landscape. Increasingly dated and self-conscious, these venues are no more than functional at best, and far from captivating. Banks, rather than concert halls or theatres, are the city's architectural showpieces, and until the much-debated **West Kowloon Cultural District** materialises there remains no arts centre or civic building with the cultural promise of Sydney's Opera House or New York's Lincoln Center.

However, like most things in Hong Kong, appearances can be deceptive. Perhaps overwhelmed by the consumer madness and garish physical density of the city, short-term foreign visitors sometimes fail to grasp the rich and complex cultural ambiguities that lie at the heart of the city. As in Venice or Istanbul – other places where East meets West – Hong Kong has always been an exciting junction of cultures. Resident composers, writers, musicians and dancers have long drawn inspiration from this hybrid state to create original and unique local compositions. In addition, a number of well-funded local performing arts companies – including the **Hong Kong Philharmonic Orchestra**, the **Hong Kong Chinese Orchestra** and the **Hong Kong Ballet** – testify to the city's eclectic cultural tastes.

TICKETS AND INFORMATION

Tickets for most performances around town can be obtained from **URBTIX**, a ticket agency run by the Hong Kong Government Leisure & Cultural Services Department. For general information on performances and reservations call 2734 9009 (10am-8pm daily); online, you can log on to www.urbtix.hk for information about upcoming events, and www.lcsd.gov.hk/urbtix for tickets. You can buy tickets over the counter at an URBTIX outlet, or make advanced telephone bookings by providing an ID or passport number (no credit card required). URBTIX has outlets at the Hong Kong Cultural Centre (*see p243*), Hong Kong City Hall (*see p242*), the Hong Kong Academy for Performing Arts (*see below*) and at the New Territories venues listed on page 243.

HK Ticketing (3128 8288/www.hkticketing.com) also runs several ticket outlets around Hong Kong, including booths in the Hong Kong Arts Centre, branches of Tom Lee Music (*see p199*), and the Fringe Club (*see p243*). The last of these is also a good place for information about the city's fringe theatre, folk music, cabaret and poetry performance scenes.

Weekly *HK Magazine* (www.asia-city.com.hk) and fortnightly *BC Magazine* (http://hk.bcmagazine.net) also provide listings of performances, concerts and cultural events. The Performing Arts page of the Hong Kong Government Leisure & Cultural Services Department website (www.lcsd.gov.hk) is another useful source of information. Bilingual classical radio station Radio 4 (97.6-98.9 FM) previews arts events on its Thursday evening *Artbeat* programme (7-8pm).

Major venues

Hong Kong Academy for Performing Arts (HKAPA)

1 Gloucester Road, Wan Chai, HK Island (2584 8500/www.hkapa.edu). Wan Chai MTR (exit A1, C)/buses along Gloucester Road. **Open** *Box office* noon-6pm Mon-Sat. **Credit** AmEx, DC, MC, V. **Map** p330 A3.

Unique within Asia, the Hong Kong Academy for Performing Arts brings together schools of dance, drama, music, television and film under one roof. Many HKAPA students have gone on to achieve major success at prestigious international competitions, and worked as soloists and choreographers. The building houses Hong Kong's second major arts venue, incorporating the Lyric Theatre, intimate Drama Theatre, a studio theatre, a small concert

Hong Kong Academy for Performing Arts. *See p241.*

hall, and a recital hall. HKAPA presents student productions (including free weekly evening performances) and professional performances by local and visiting companies. Check out the website for programme details.

Hong Kong Arts Centre

2 Harbour Road, Wan Chai, HK Island (2582 0200/ www.hkac.org.hk). Wan Chai MTR (exit A1)/buses along Gloucester Road/Wan Chai Star Ferry Pier. **Open** *Box office* 10am-6pm daily. **Credit** MC, V. **Map** p330 B3.

Located across the road from the Hong Kong Academy for Performing Arts, the Hong Kong Arts Centre stages mainly avant-garde theatre and community productions in English and Cantonese in its Shouson Theatre and McAuley Studio.

Hong Kong City Hall

5 Edinburgh Place, Central, HK Island (2921 2840/ www.cityhall.gov.hk). Central MTR (exit J3)/buses to Central Ferry Pier & along Connaught Road Central/ Central Ferry Pier. **Open** *Box office* 10am-9.30pm daily. **Credit** AmEx, DC, MC, V. **Map** p329 E3.

Located across the road from Statue Square, and recently given a much-needed facelift, the City Hall hosts regular concerts and recitals by local and international artists in its concert hall.

Hong Kong Convention & Exhibition Centre

1 Harbour Road, Wan Chai, HK Island (2582 8888/ www.hkcec.com.hk). Wan Chai MTR (exit A1)/buses along Gloucester Road/Wan Chai Star Ferry Pier. **Credit** V. **Map** p330 B2.

The main stage at this venue was the site of the ceremony marking the 1997 Handover. Nowadays the centre tends to be used for less culturally charged events such as Robbie Williams concerts – despite dubious acoustics. For full programme and ticket details, check with HK Ticketing (*see p241*).

Hong Kong Cultural Centre

10 Salisbury Road, Tsim Sha Tsui, Kowloon (2734 2009/www.hkculturalcentre.gov.hk). Tsim Sha Tsui MTR (exit E)/buses to Tsim Sha Tsui Star Ferry Pier & along Salisbury Road/Tsim Sha Tsui Star Ferry Pier. **Open** *Box office* 10am-9.30pm daily. **Credit** AmEx, DC, MC, V. **Map** p333 B6.

A buttressed slab of cement and tiles that wildly ignores its magnificent location, the Cultural Centre has been likened to a crushed carton of cigarettes and a giant urinal. This is the territory's premier arts venue and its Concert Theatre is home to both the Hong Kong Philharmonic Orchestra and the Hong Kong Chinese Orchestra. Most of the city's Western opera and ballet is performed in its 2,100-seat Grand Theatre. The complex includes a smaller concert hall, a studio theatre and an arts library. Free performances often take place in the foyer and forecourt.

Other venues

Fringe Club

2 Lower Albert Road, Central, HK Island (2521 7251/box office 3128 8288/www.hkfringeclub.com). Central MTR (exit D1, G)/23A bus. **Open** *Box office* noon-10pm Mon-Sat. **Credit** MC, V. **Map** p328 C4.

The Fringe Club is the place to see alternative performances in Hong Kong. Housed in a colonial-era former dairy, it's run by a non-profit organisation that supports aspiring artists. The site includes two intimate theatres, a ground-floor bar (which is also a live-music venue) and a couple of exhibition galleries. The rooftop bar is one of the best-kept secrets in Hong Kong and occasionally hosts music performances and outdoor film screenings. The Fringe's ground-floor gallery also hosts art and photography exhibitions.

Kwai Tsing Theatre

12 Hing Ning Road, Kwai Chung, New Territories (2408 0128). Kwai Fong MTR (exit C)/30, A31, E32, 42, 47X, 91, 93 bus. **Open** *Box office* 10am-9.30pm daily. **Credit** AmEx, DC, MC, V.

Located in the heart of a New Territories housing estate, this comfortable and well-appointed venue is one of the best in Hong Kong. In the last couple of years it has hosted outstanding performances by local and international talent, including Philip Glass, the Royal Shakespeare Company and Cubanismo. Chinese opera is regularly performed here.

Ma Tau Kok Cattle Depot

63 Ma Tau Kok Road, To Kwa Wan, Kowloon (2529 0087/www.onespace.org.hk). Bus 101, 111/Kowloon City ferry from North Point. **Open** 2-8pm. **Admission** free.

Formerly a livestock depot and slaughterhouse, this intriguing 95-year-old complex has been turned into an artists' village (*see p222*) housing workshops, offices for design, multimedia and theatre companies, and two spaces for community theatre performances and multimedia art exhibitions.

St John's Cathedral

4-8 Garden Road, Central, HK Island (2523 4157/ www.stjohnscathedral.org). Central MTR (exit K)/ buses along Garden Road. **Open** 7am-6pm daily. **Admission** free. **Map** p329 E4.

This Anglican cathedral frequently stages free lunchtime (1.15-1.45pm Wed) and evening concerts by a variety of local and visiting vocal ensembles; Christmas and Easter programmes are particularly good. The cathedral also sponsors a series of moderately priced professional choral concerts during festive holidays.

Venues in the New Territories

To arouse wider public interest in the arts and to cater to the demographic heart of the SAR, Hong Kong's Leisure & Cultural Services Department (*see p248*) organises a rich selection of musical and dramatic performances at venues around the New Territories. In addition to the **Kwai Tsing Theatre** (*see above*), these include **Tsuen Wan Town Hall** (72 Tai Ho Road, Tsuen Wan, 2493 7463); **Tuen Mun Town Hall** (3 Tuen Hi Road, Tuen Mun, 2450 1105); **Sha Tin Town Hall** (1 Yuen Wo Road, Sha Tin, 2694 2542); **Tai Po Civic Centre** (12 On Ping Road, Tai Po, 2665 4477); and **Yuen Long Theatre** (9 Yuen Long Tai Yuk Road, Yuen Long, 2476 1029).

Western classical music & opera

The Western classical music scene in Hong Kong is proudly anachronistic and rich with complex cultural contradictions. In a city driven by free-wheeling capitalism, the main musical bodies enjoy generous government funding and are administrated by civil servants and society patrons. Hong Kong is known for its collective impatience, yet performances by local orchestras are broadcast in their entirety on RTHK Radio 4. Although concerts are often marred by late audience arrivals and the occasional ringing mobile phone, classical music audiences are well educated and appreciative, and many of the SAR's music lovers are amateur musicians or choristers. Classical music programmes reflect Hong Kong's eclectic tastes and sentiments: in the same week and same venue, it's possible to

Arts & Entertainment

enjoy a sensitive performance of an Elgar concerto and a contemporary ode to Chinese nationalism.

Orchestras

Hong Kong Philharmonic Orchestra (HKPO)
2721 2030/www.hkpo.com
The Hong Kong Phil is the territory's first and only full-time, professional Western classical music ensemble. The 93-piece orchestra comprises musicians from a range of Asian and Western countries and is under the baton of Edo de Waart. During its September to June season, the HKPO performs from a wide repertoire and is frequently joined by world-class soloists. The company is committed to performing works by emerging local composers and has toured extensively in North America, Asia and Europe. The orchestra's website gives information on the season's concert programmes. **Photo *p247*.**

Hong Kong Sinfonietta
2836 3336/www.hksinfonietta.org
The medium-sized Hong Kong Sinfonietta was formed by local musicians in 1990. Many in the ensemble were trained at the Hong Kong Academy for Performing Arts, and the Sinfonietta has become a bridge of sorts between the HKAPA and the HKPO. As such, it is evolving into Hong Kong's second professional (Western music) orchestra and, like the HKPO, regularly performs works by local composers, both at home and abroad, and teams up with visiting artists.

Composers

A growing stable of local composers, who combine Western forms with Chinese themes, is receiving international recognition. Names worth noting include orchestral composer **Victor Chan Wai-kwong**; film and theatre composer **Law Wing-fai**; Macanese **Doming Lam**, a celebrated composer of liturgical music; Scottish-born composer, academic and conductor **David Gwilt**; and **Clarence Mak Wai-chu**, whose work includes chamber music, electronic music, and music for local contemporary Chinese theatre productions.

Choirs

Hong Kong Bach Choir
www.bachchoir.org.hk
Established three decades ago for a single performance of a Bach cantata, the Hong Kong Bach Choir now performs from a wide repertoire, ranging from Palestrina to Elgar. The choir numbers more than 80 singers and welcomes new members. They also hire themselves out for performances at corporate events, balls and charity functions.

Hong Kong Oratorio Society
www.oratorio.org.hk
This is the oldest, largest and most active choir in Hong Kong. Since it was founded in 1956, the Society has performed more than 80 oratorios, and places strong programming emphasis on works from the baroque and classical canons. On average, the choir gives six performances a year.

Hong Kong Welsh Male Voice Choir
www.hkwmvc.com
Formed in 1978, the choir was the brainchild of a young Welsh engineer who gathered together a small but enthusiastic group of singing fellow countrymen. Since then, the group has grown to 70 members and expanded its geographical base to include singers from around the world. Still, about half the current members are from Wales or have Welsh connections, and the choir's repertoire of songs includes Welsh hymns and folk songs. For membership and programme details (and a robust sampler of their singing), visit their website.

Kassia Women's Choir
www.katterwall.com
Named after a Byzantine composer of chants and hymns, Kassia caters to the women of Hong Kong who love to sing. Its 70 members come from all walks of life. The group welcomes all; sings from a repertoire of pop, world music and gospel, and performs three or four charity concerts a year at various venues around town. For details on concerts and auditions, see their website.

Western opera

Although there is no full-time resident Western opera company in Hong Kong, it is possible to see four or five opera performances a year. A major event in the **Hong Kong Arts Festival** (*see p206*) is the production of a grand opera by a visiting company. In past years the Bolshoi Opera, Berlin's Komische Oper, the Welsh National Opera and the Los Angeles Opera companies have all appeared.

Innovative and smaller-scale productions of lesser-known operas by composers such as Piazzolla and Janacek have also featured. The **Opera Society of Hong Kong** (www.opera.org.hk) stages an annual full-scale production in the Hong Kong Cultural Centre.

Dance

The dance scene in Hong Kong is surprisingly rich, and much of the interest in – and audience for – classical and contemporary dance performances comes from the region's large number of dance students themselves. The **Hong Kong Dance Alliance** (2584 8753, www.hkdanceall.org) is a federation of dance

Cantonese opera.
See p246.

Chinese performing arts

Hong Kong's distinctive cultural flavour is shaped by many forces: it is a high-tech postmodern port; a Manhattan-style financial hub; and a place where you can hear a Britten song cycle, see a Pina Bausch dance performance or weep at a Puccini opera. Yet, despite the seemingly pervasive Western cultural influences, much of the city's soul remains forever Chinese, with a performing arts circuit that reflects this bedrock.

Accessing this scene is a rewarding adventure, and with a bit of background knowledge, most operatic, dance and musical performances can be appreciated by non-Chinese-speaking audiences. You can get acquainted with the rituals of traditional Chinese performance at the Folk Culture in Hong Kong exhibit at the **Hong Kong Museum of History** in Tsim Sha Tsui (see p98), which includes a short film of performers in action.

Cantonese opera (Xiqu)

The most immediate image of Chinese performance arts is probably the brightly made-up faces and vibrant embroidered silk costumes of Chinese opera. Actors go about their age-old scripts with exaggerated movements, stylised high-pitched vocals and clashing percussion, which is compelling for some and an acquired taste for others. Dating back to the 13th century, choreographies are built around the Confucian principles of courage, honesty and piety, with liberal splashes of scandal, doomed romance, sword fighting and acrobatics.

Unlike its Western counterpart, Cantonese opera derives most of its dramatic power from costumes and gestures. Costumes, headdresses and make-up are colour-coded to convey a character's qualities: a black face denotes honesty, a yellow face belongs to a celestial being, and a white nose is a sure sign of villainy. Even an actor's beard (there are 18 varieties) helps to establish dramatic nuance. Most storylines are based on Chinese legends the audience has heard many times over, so it is the quality of stylised gesture, rather than plot development that engrosses the viewers. Symbolism also helps to propel the storyline – a red cloth draped over an actor's face means that he's just died. If you'd like a bit more information before attending a Chinese opera, visit the Cantonese Opera permanent exhibition in the **Hong Kong Heritage Museum** (see p109).

Local and touring mainland opera troupes give a full calendar of performances in Hong Kong, so check with venues for details or ask in the Hong Kong Tourism Board offices. Since many performances take place in theatres in Kowloon or the New Territories, a night at the opera usually includes the cultural experience of discovering parts of Hong Kong less frequented by tourists. Two of the most easily accessible venues are the **Sunbeam Theatre** (423 King's Road, North Point, HK Island, 2856 0161) and the **Kwai Tsing Theatre** (see p243). As little English is spoken at either, ask hotel staff to make inquiries for you.

Informal opera performances take place before certain festivals in temporary open-air theatres. Productions are not for the faint-hearted: they can last up to five hours, with people casually coming and going and having a chat during intermissions. Chiu Chow communities erect such theatres annually during the **Hungry Ghost Festival** (see p204) – notably in large playgrounds in Kowloon City (opposite the old airport site at Kai Tak) and in Hung Hom (off Chatham Road). Enclosures also go up during the festivities surrounding the **Birthday of Tin Hau** (see p203) – one of the largest is in Yung Shue Wan on Lamma, which regularly attracts some of Hong Kong's biggest operatic stars.

Other venues for both Cantonese opera and Chinese music performances include: **Ko Shan Theatre** (77 Ko Shan Road, Hung Hom, Kowloon, 2740 9222); **Sheung Wan Civic Centre** (5/F, Sheung Wan Complex, 345 Queen's Road Central, Sheung Wan, HK Island, 2853 2678) and **Tai Po Civic Centre** (12 On Pong Road, Tai Po, New Territories, 2665 4477).

There are also some regular outdoor amateur opera performance spots around town. The best known is the area near **Public Square Street** on the right side of Nathan Road as you're walking south from exit C of Yau Ma Tei MTR station.

Opera clubs

Cantonese opera clubs are a fascinating but dying part of Hong Kong's cultural scene. The half-dozen or so that survive cater to older folk in the working-class areas of Kowloon. Not unlike an old-fashioned cabaret, these clubs feature singers who perform from a repertoire of favourites without the dramatic assistance of make-up and costumes. Clubs charge a modest entrance of about HK$30 and 'opera' shows (sometimes incongruously accompanied by a go-go dancer or a transvestite) usually take place between 8pm and midnight. Simply go in, take a seat and wait for a waiter to bring you tea and ask for the fee. Many singers have been crooning for a living for years and appreciate a tip.

Opera clubs in the Yau Ma Tei neighbourhood include **Foon Lok** (47 Temple Street, next to Public Square Street); **Kam Fung Wong** (directly opposite the Foon Lok) and **Koh Sing Club** (on the eighth floor of the same building as Kam Fung Wong). All opera clubs have pictures of female and male singers in gowns on show next to their red doorways. For all three, take the MTR to Yau Ma Tei (exit C).

Chinese folk dance

Dance troupes from all over China regularly visit Hong Kong, offering fascinating ancient ritualistic performances – some animalistic, others extremely graceful. The long flowing gown of the Yunnanese female dancer is in marked contrast to the brief jungle-warrior attire of her male counterpart. With its deep Muslim traditions, the dancers of Xinjiang province move to an Arabic musical accompaniment and look every bit the desert nomad. Provincial folk orchestras rarely play in events that do not include dance segments. Check the Leisure & Cultural Services Department's website (*see p241*) and venues such as the **Kwai Tsing Theatre** (*see p243*) for details.

The best time to see a lion dance, accompanied by costumed drummers, is during the Chinese New Year festivities (*see p205*). If you're in Hong Kong during the **Mid-Autumn Festival** (*see p204*), you may be lucky enough to see the dance of the Tai Hang fire dragon, a 70-metre-long (230-foot) 'dragon' made of straw and giant incense sticks that parades along Tai Hang Road.

Free dance and music events are also held on weekends in the amphitheatre of **Hong Kong Park** (*see p78*), in **Kowloon Park** (*see p99*) and in front of the **Hong Kong Cultural Centre** (*see p243*).

Hong Kong Chinese Orchestra (HKCO)

One of the largest Chinese orchestras in the world, the 58-piece HKCO consists of four sections of instruments: bowed strings, plucked strings, wind and percussion. It is designed to promote traditional and contemporary Chinese music, and to experiment with techniques and styles. Its repertoire includes traditional folk music and contemporary works. For more information, see www.hkco.org/index_eng.htm.

Arts & Entertainment

Hong Kong Philharmonic Orchestra.
See p244.

companies, teachers and student groups committed to promoting dance. It publishes the bilingual *Dance Journal HK* and is a good source of information on dance performances. It is also the official Hong Kong organisation of the World Dance Alliance.

City Contemporary Dance Company (CCDC)

2326 8597/www.ccdc.com.hk

Hong Kong's longest established dance company, the CCDC is dedicated to the development and performance of modern dance. Under its founder and artistic director Willy Tsao, the CCDC mostly performs from a repertoire created by local choreographers, and frequently collaborates with artists from other media.

Hong Kong Ballet

2573 7398/www.hkballet.com

The territory's only ballet company, the Hong Kong Ballet performs regularly throughout the year at venues such as the Hong Kong Cultural Centre's Grand Theatre. Its repertoire includes classics such as *The Nutcracker* and *Lady of the Camellias*, as well as original works created by local choreographers. Like the Philharmonic Orchestra, the ballet maintains close ties with the Hong Kong Academy for Performing Arts, and many of the company's principal dancers choreograph and prepare productions at their alma mater. Australian John Meehan is the current artistic director.

Hong Kong Dance Company (HKDC)

3103 1888/www.hkdance.com

Devoted to promoting Chinese dance, the HKDC has a growing repertoire that includes traditional and folk dances, as well as original dance dramas based on Chinese and Hong Kong themes. It regularly gives free performances and provides an audience-building programme, with visits to schools and community centres.

English-language theatre

More than a few of Hong Kong's English-speaking expatriates have complained – without a hint of irony – that the local theatre circuit is limited, impoverished and just doesn't compare with what's happening in London or New York. They're absolutely right. However, it's amazing that such a comparison is made, given that more than 90 per cent of the city speaks Cantonese as its first language. While it's never going to compete with the West End or Broadway – and tends to cater to a well-heeled, middle-aged, expat audience – a reasonably interesting English-language theatre scene does exist here.

Most local productions of English-language theatre are performed by community companies such as the **Hong Kong Players**, and the **Hong Kong Singers**. There are also performances by visiting companies, including the UK's Young Vic and National Theatre, Melbourne's Playbox Theatre, and Canadian Robert LePage's company. Musicals are also popular: excellent imported productions of *Chicago, The Phantom of the Opera* and *Mamma Mia!* have had successful runs.

Hong Kong Players

www.hongkongplayers.com

This is the city's foremost English-language community theatre group. The semi-professional Players are successors to the Garrison Players (a company that was established in colonial days) and the Hong Kong Stage Club. The group mounts three or four productions a year, performing from a repertoire that includes works by Shakespeare, Noël Coward and Samuel Beckett. It also stages an annual Christmas pantomime at the Hong Kong Arts Centre's Shouson Theatre. For information on productions and auditions, visit their website.

Hong Kong Singers

www.hksingers.com

This semi-professional musical performance group has been singing and dancing for Hong Kong audiences since 1931. It originally presented classical concerts and performed Haydn's *Creation* for the troops at Stanley Fort just before the territory fell to the Japanese in 1941. Nowadays it presents works of less historical gravitas, staging popular musicals such as *Fiddler on the Roof, South Pacific* and *La Cage aux Folles*. The group performs at the Hong Kong Academy for Performing Arts, Hong Kong City Hall and the Fringe Club.

Zuni Icosahedron

2893 8704/www.zuni.org.hk

This independent cultural collective is committed to original productions of alternative theatre, multimedia performance, sound experimentation and installation arts. Performances focus on exploring a range of themes across cultures, media and art forms. The collective has formed artistic partnerships with arts groups from Beijing, Tokyo, Taipei, New York, London and Berlin.

Festivals & events

Held every even year in November, the **New Vision Arts Festival** is a superb and eclectic dance, music and drama festival, which focuses on performers from across the Asia-Pacific region. Contact the Hong Kong Government Leisure & Cultural Services Department on 2370 1044 or visit www.newvisionfestival. gov.hk. For the complete range of permanent arts festivals in Hong Kong, *see pp202-206.*

Sport & Fitness

Let off a little steam amid the skyscrapers or get active in the territory's impressive countryside.

Learn how to move your hips at **Herman Lam**'s dance classes. *See p251.*

Horse racing is the most intensely followed sport in Hong Kong, and the last-minute decision for the SAR to co-host the equestrian events for the 2008 Olympics (*see p206*) put the spotlight on the Hong Kong Jockey Club's superb riding facilities.

That there was enough green space for a 5.7-kilometre (3.5-mile) cross-country course did not surprise locals, who know that almost 70 per cent of the SAR comprises country parks and rural land – within 20 minutes of almost anywhere in the city you can be out in the countryside. Despite the ever-worsening air quality, residents are opting to spend more time hiking, running, biking and making the most of the territory's 733 kilometres (455 miles) of coastline.

Back among the urban skyscrapers, office workers are filling up the gyms and yoga studios, and basketball courts are bustling. Government sports and leisure facilities are widespread and inexpensive, but nothing is more 'Hong Kong' than the sight of people practicing t'ai chi; if you're up early enough, join in with (or simply enjoy the sight of)

locals practising along the harbourfront or in many of the city's larger parks.

If you're in need of some inspiration, get in touch with the **South China Athletic Association** (SCAA, 2577 6932, www.scaa. org.hk) or the YMCA of Hong Kong (*see p250*). Both offer information on a wide range of sports, and at very reasonable prices.

For all games halls run by the Leisure and Cultural Services Department, go online to www.lcsd.gov.hk/en/home.php, where you will also find general information on beaches, pools, parks, zoos and gardens, and activities such as water sports and golf. It also has a customer helpline: 2414 5555.

Alternatively, get hold of a copy of *HK Magazine* or *BC Magazine*, which list the main sports events, or *Fit! HK* magazine (www.fithk.com), which has extensive listings for all manner of sports- and fitness-related events. For a real urban escape, **Kayak and Hike** (9300 5197, www.kayak-and-hike.com) organises active half- and full-day trips to remote and rarely visited areas of Hong Kong's countryside.

Participatory sports & fitness

Archery

Hong Kong Archery Club

1204 Koon Fook Centre, 9 Knutsford Terrace, Tsim Sha Tsui, Kowloon (2739 8969/www.hk-archery centre.com). Tsim Sha Tsui MTR (exit B2). **Open** 3.30-7.30pm Mon-Fri. **Credit** MC, V. **Map** p333 C5.
Contact the Hong Kong Archery Club to help kick-start your arrow action. Courses for beginners cost HK$250 per hour; group packages work out a bit cheaper (phone for details).

Athletics

Jogging tracks and athletic clubs abound in Hong Kong, and marathons take place throughout the year. For details of how to get involved, plus a complete calendar of events, club listings and track venues, contact the **Hong Kong Amateur Athletics Association** (2504 8215, www.hkaaa.com). Triathlons are also becoming increasingly popular. The **Hong Kong International Tri** takes place towards the end of the year, with sprint and Olympic distance races, and is a great place to do your first tri. For more information, check out www.triathlon.com.hk.

Badminton

Prices at the public facilities listed here are HK$59 per hour. Courts are heavily booked in the evenings, so advance booking is advisable.

Harbour Road Indoor Games Hall

27 Harbour Road, Wan Chai, HK Island (2827 9684). Wan Chai MTR (exit A1)/18, 25A, 104, 720, 961 bus. **Open** 7am-11pm daily. **No credit cards.** **Map** p330 C3.

Hong Kong Park Government Indoor Games Hall

29 Cotton Tree Drive, Central, HK Island (enquiries 2521 5072/booking 2927 8080). Buses (12, 12A, 15C, 23, 40, 103) along Cotton Tree Drive. **Open** 7am-11pm daily. **No credit cards.** **Map** p329 E5.

Sheung Wan Sports Centre

12/F, Sheung Wan Complex, 345 Queen's Road, Central, HK Island (2853 2574). Sheung Wan MTR (exit A2). **Open** 7am-11pm daily. **No credit cards.** **Map** p328 B2.

Basketball

Concrete courts are dotted around town and you can often find locals having a casual game. It's more comfortable to play inside during summer, though,

unless you want to sweat like crazy. The **Harbour Road Indoor Games Hall** and **Hong Kong Park Government Indoor Games Hall** (for both, *see above*) have indoor courts, for HK$236 per hour.

Bowling Olympian City Super Fun Bowl

Shop 148, Olympian City 2, Kowloon (2273 4773). Olympic MTR (exit D). **Open** 10am-1am Mon-Fri, Sun; 10am-2am Sat. **Fees** (per game) HK$35 before 6pm Mon-Fri; HK$42 after 6pm Mon-Fri; HK$46 Sat, Sun. *Shoe rental* $10. **Credit** (over HK$200) MC, V.

Climbing

One of the best days out in Hong Kong is to take the old ferry/fishing boat to **Tung Lung** island, walk over the hill to the 'Technical Wall' and enjoy a day's climbing while the waves crash around you. The sport is increasingly popular and there are many other superb climbs across the territory: **Shek O** (granite; good for beginners and fans of bouldering), **Lion Rock** (granite) and **Kowloon Peak** (volcanic rock).

King's Park YMCA

Centenary Centre, 22 Gascoigne Road, Yau Ma Tei, Kowloon (2782 6682/www.ymcahk.org.hk). Jordan MTR (exit B2)/buses along Nathan Road. **Open** 8.30am-10pm daily. **Fees** HK$70 before 5.30pm; HK$90 after 5.30pm. **No credit cards.** **Map** p333 C4.
With 18m (59ft) of wall, this is the best venue in the city for wall climbing, but you need to take an assessment before you climb.

YMCA of Hong Kong

2/F, 41 Salisbury Road, Tsim Sha Tsui, Kowloon (2268 7000/climbing wall 2268 7099/www.ymcahk. org.hk/fw). Tsim Sha Tsui MTR (exit E)/buses to Tsim Sha Tsui Star Ferry Pier & along Salisbury Road/Tsim Sha Tsui Star Ferry Pier. **Open** noon-10pm Mon-Fri; 10am-10pm Sat, Sun. **Fees** HK$80. **No credit cards.** **Map** 313 B6.
You'll have to do a half-day assessment (HK$170, 6.45-9.45pm Mon, 2.30-5.30pm Sat only) to get a per-mit to climb at this 7m (23ft) wall, but after that you are allowed to climb here whenever you like.

Dance

Franky Wong

Fringe Club, 2 Lower Albert Road, Central, HK Island (2521 7251/9410 8652/www.fun4u.com.hk). Central MTR (exit D1, D2). **Credit** AmEx, MC, V. **Map** p328 C4.
Hong Kong Cultural Centre, 10 Salisbury Road, Tsim Sha Tsui, Kowloon (2734 2009). Tsim Sha Tsui MTR (exit E)/1, 1A, 6, 7, 8, 110 bus. **No credit cards.** **Map** p333 B6.
Franky teaches salsa at the Fringe on Thursdays (improvers 7-8pm; show moves 8-9pm; beginners 9-10pm) and at the Cultural Centre on Tuesdays

(7-10pm). Eight lessons cost HK$800. Between 9pm and 10pm, one lesson is HK$150.

Herman Lam

1/F, Kai Kwong House, 13 Wyndham Street, Central, HK Island (2320 3605/www.hermanlam dance.com). Central MTR (exit D1, D2). **No credit cards**. **Map** p328 C4.

If you book a package, you can try out all of Herman Lam's classes (ballroom, jazz, rock 'n' roll, hip-hop, tango, rumba…). It costs HK$150 for a drop-in fee, or HK$1,000 for ten lessons. Check out the website for times. **Photo** *p249*.

Golf

If you have a spare million, then go ahead and join one of the private country clubs for the best golf in Hong Kong. However, if you're only here for a holiday you can play at the following public courses; unlike the private clubs they cost less than the price of a house on the Peak. Note that handicap requirements in Hong Kong are around 36.4 for men and 40.4 for women, though this varies from course to course. China is less strict, and most clubs organise various day or weekend packages there.

The **Hong Kong Golf Association** (2504 8659, www.hkga.com) has details of courses, driving ranges, handicaps and upcoming tournaments.

Discovery Bay Golf Club

Discovery Valley Road, Discovery Bay, Lantau (enquiries 2987 7273/booking 2987 2112/www. discoverybay.com.hk). Ferry (from Central pier number 3) to Discovery Bay. **Tee times** *18 holes* every 15 minutes from 10am-1.42pm daily. *9 holes* from 4pm daily. **Fees** HK$1,400. **Credit** AmEx, MC, V. **Map** p326.

Non-members can play on Mondays, Tuesdays and Fridays only, and need to book two days in advance.

Jockey Club Kau Sai Chau

Kau Sai Chau, Sai Kung, New Territories (2791 3390/3344/www.kscgolf.com). Buses to Sai Kung. **Tee times** *18 holes* 7.30am-1 or 2pm daily. *9 holes* 7.30am-3 or 4pm daily. **Fees** (Mon-Fri) HK$460 HK ID-card holder; HK$660 overseas player. (Sat, Sun) HK$$620 HK ID-card holder; HK$980 overseas player. **Credit** MC, V. **Map** p325.

This is the only golf course in the area that's open to the public at the weekend. Last tee times vary, so phone to check first. Advance booking from one to seven days.

Royal Hong Kong Golf Club

Fanling Lot No.1, New Territories (2670 1211/ hkgolfclub.org). Sheung Shui KCR. **Open** 7am-6pm daily. **Fees** HK$1,200-$1,400. **Credit** AmEx, MC, V. **Map** p325.

Non-members can play on weekdays only (but not on public holidays); one-day advance booking is permitted from 3pm.

Tuen Mun Golf Centre

Tuen Mun Recreation & Sports Centre, Lung Mun Road, New Territories (2466 2600/www.lcsd.gov.hk/ tmrsc/en/golf.php). Bus 962. **Open** 8am-10pm daily. **Fees** (per bay) HK$12/hr. **No credit cards**. **Map** p324.

A two-storey driving range with 91 bays.

Gyms & fitness centres

Most hotels have well-equipped gyms that are free for residents; some have personal trainers. For spas, *see p196* **A good day's rest**.

California Fitness

1 Wellington Street, Central, HK Island (2522 5229/www.calfitness.com.hk). Central MTR (exit D1, D2, G)/12M, 13, 23A, 40M, 43 bus. **Open**

Wacky races

'There are more races on offer now in Hong Kong, but there are also more people participating,' says Katie McGregor of *Fit! HK* magazine. 'Running on a treadmill in a gym is not enough any more, and quotas for races fill up within 24 hours of opening.'

Hong Kong's growing enthusiasm for fitness and the outdoors is confirmed when you see 40,000 athletes charging along Nathan Road on a winter Sunday morning. The event is the **Hong Kong Marathon** (www.hkmarathon.com; *see p255*), which has grown immensely from the 1,000 participants when it was first run in 1997. It's held annually in February or March, when the weather is cool, but poor air quality can be an issue.

Those in search of more rugged terrain opt for the **King of Hills** series of races, organised by Seyon Asia (www.seyonasia. com), that takes participants through some challenging elevation in the New Territories but compensates with fantastic views. Revolution Asia's **Splash 'n Dash Aquathon** races (www.revolution-asia.com), also draw runners into the countryside – and into and across some of Hong Kong's more attractive bays.

Other runners looking for fun sign up for the **Matilda Sedan Chair Charity Race** (www.sedanchairace.org), an enjoyable annual spectacle, when teams of eight, plus a passenger in a sedan chair, race around the Peak in weird and wacky costumes.

Arts & Entertainment

Repulse Bay.
See p256.

6am-midnight Mon-Sat; 8am-10pm Sun. **Fees**
Day pass HK$150. **Credit** AmEx, DC, MC, V.
Map p328 C4.
High-volume, American-style gym.
Other locations: throughout the city.

Fitness First
G/F, Cosco Tower, Grand Millennium Plaza, 181-3
Queen's Road, Central, HK Island (3106 3000/
www.fitnessfirst.com.hk). Sheung Wan MTR (exit
A2). **Open** 6.30am-11pm Mon-Fri; 7am-10pm Sat;
8am-10pm Sun. **Fees** *Day pass* HK$200. **Credit**
AmEx, DC, MC, V. **Map** p328 B2.
This is the biggest Fitness First branch, with all the
usual gym facilities on three floors, and steam rooms
and saunas adjacent to the changing rooms.
Other locations: throughout the city.

Pure Fitness
Mall Level 3, Two IFC, 8 Finance Street, Central,
HK Island (8129 8000/www.pure-fit.com). Central
MTR (exit A, E). **Open** 6am-midnight Mon-Sat;
8am-10pm Sun. **Fees** *Day pass* HK$250. *2-week pass*
HK$1,500. **Credit** AmEx, MC, V. **Map** p329 E2.
This vast state-of-the-art gym has dedicated studios
for weights, cycling, boxing, climbing and classes
such as 'bodypump', kick-boxing and yoga. Part of
the same group as Pure Yoga (*see p257*).

Hiking

There are myriad hiking trails on Hong Kong
Island and Kowloon, as well as on the outlying
islands. Some may be along well-trod paths, but
you'll still go through lovely countryside on
virtually all of them. Try the **Dragon's Back**
over to Shek O (*see p90* **Taming the dragon**),
or **Violet Hill** followed by **The Twins** (aka
the Thousand Steps) – if you're feeling super-
energetic – which will take you over to Stanley.
You can end a walk on Lantau at Cheung Sha
Beach and kick back at the **Stoep** restaurant
(*see p157*). Local bookshops sell plenty of
helpful books that explain how to get wherever
you want to go or check with Hong Kong
Tourism Board (2508 1234).
   Extreme hikers might want to join a team
for the annual **Trailwalker** event (*see p205*),
which takes place each November. It's a
gruelling 100-kilometre (62-mile) course, but
worth it as all money raised goes to Oxfam.
Kayak and Hike (*see p249*) takes groups
through the countryside's tiny villages on a
traditional hike, and also arranges helicopter
rides to Sai Kung Country Park so you can start
your day's hiking in (not green friendly) style.

Horse riding

If you've been to the races at **Happy Valley**
(*see p258*) or **Sha Tin** (*see p109*) and are dying
for a go yourself, you're in luck. Most horses at

schools here are retired racehorses – so it's
odds-on you'll have a good ride. The gorgeous
scenery is an added bonus.
   Most clubs cater to both experienced riders
and beginners, but may insist that you prove
you know what you're doing before letting you
go on a hack on the trails. Some offer reduced
rates for children.

Lo Wu Saddle Club
Ho Sheung Heung, Sheung Shui, New Territories
(2673 0066/www.lowusaddleclub.org). Sheung Shui
KCR then 51K minibus. **Open** 8am-noon, 2-6pm
Tue-Sun. **Fees** *Tue-Fri* HK$310/session. *Sat, Sun*
HK$350/group. **Credit** AmEx, MC, V. **Map** p325.

Pok Fu Lam Public Riding School
75 Pok Fu Lam Reservoir Road, Pok Fu Lam, HK
Island (2550 1359). Buses along Pok Fu Lam
Reservoir Road. **Open** 8am-noon, 2-6pm Tue-Sun.
Fees HK$360/hr. **Credit** MC, V. **Map** p325.
Riding level assessment costs HK$200. Book two
days ahead for weekends.

Tuen Mun Public Riding School
Lung Mun Road, Tuen Mun, New Territories (2461
3338/www.lcsd.gov.hk/tmrsc/en/rid.php). Bus 962.
Open 8am-7pm Tue-Fri; 8am-6pm Sat, Sun. **Fees**
from HK$360/hr. **Credit** MC, V. **Map** p324.

Ice skating

The Glacier
Festival Walk, 80 Tat Chee Avenue, Kowloon Tong,
Kowloon (2844 3588/www.glacier.com.hk). Kowloon
Tong MTR/KCR (exit C)/buses to Festival Walk.
Open 10.30am-10pm Mon-Thur (Tue until 8.30pm);
10.30am-3pm, 3.30-5.30pm, 6-10pm Fri, Sat; 1-3pm,
3.30-5.30pm Sun. **Fees** HK$50 Mon-Fri; HK$70 Sat,
Sun. **No credit cards.**

Kickboxing

'The One' Martial Gym
23/F, Asia Standard Tower, 59-65 Queen's Road,
Central, HK Island (2526 6648/www.fightinfit.
com.hk). Central MTR (exit D1, D2, G)/buses
along Queen's Road Central. **Open** 8am-9.30pm
Mon-Sat. **Fees** HK$ 800/mth. **Credit** MC, V.
Map p328 C3.
Formerly known as Fightin' Fit, 'The One' runs
martial arts classes, including muay thai and karate.

Martial arts

When in China, do as the Chinese do – and have
a go at a martial art, which here is culture,
history and exercise all rolled into one.
According to many Hong Kongers, **t'ai chi**
is the best way to start the day – even just
watching the smooth movers on the promenade
in Tsim Sha Tsui or in parks all over the city
will have you feeling calm and refreshed.

Arts & Entertainment

You can try t'ai chi for free on the waterfront promenade in Tsim Sha Tsui (8-9am Mon, Wed-Fri; call the Hong Kong Tourism Board on 2508 1234 for details). Otherwise, for karate, tae kwon do, judo, kung fu, t'ai chi or *wing chun* try the **YMCA of Hong Kong** (*see p250*), **'The One'** (*see p253*) or the **South China Athletic Association** (*see p249*).

Wan Kei Ho International Martial Arts Association

3/F, Yue's House, 304 Des Voeux Road Central, Sheung Wan, HK Island (2544 1368/www.kungfu wan.com). **Open** 6.30-7.30pm, 8-9pm Mon-Thur. **Fees** HK$250/class; HK$1,300 for 8 classes. **No credit cards. Map** p328 B2.

Private lessons can be arranged with *sifu* (master) William Wan, who teaches *choy li fut* kung fu, Northern Shaolin kung fu and elements of sun-style t'ai chi.

Mountain biking

Mountain biking offers a fantastic, high-adrenaline experience, and many of the biking trails lead through lovely countryside. Lamma Island has some quite technical routes. For more details on where to bike, check out the **Hong Kong Mountain Bike Association** (www.hkmba.org) for routes, maps and information. You will need a licence or permission to bike through country parks (see http://www.afcd.gov.hk/english/country/cou_vis/cou_vis_cou/cou_vis_cou.html).

The Bicycle World

G/F, 15 Wood Road, Wan Chai, HK Island (2892 2299). Wan Chai MTR (exit A2). **Open** 11am-8pm Mon-Fri; noon-8pm Sun. **Credit** MC, V. **Map** p330 C3.

Flying Ball Bicycle Company

G/F, 478 Castle Peak Road, Cheung Sha Wan (2381 3661/www.flyingball.com). Cheung Sha Wan MTR (exit C2)/buses along Nathan Road & Prince Edward Road. **Open** 10am-8pm Mon-Sat. **Credit** AmEx, DC, MC, V. **Map** p332 B1.

Friendly Bicycle Shop

Shop 12, Mui Wo Centre, Mui Wo, Lantau (2984 2279). Mui Wo Ferry Pier/Tung Chau MTR then bus/taxi. **Open** 10am-8pm daily. **No credit cards**. **Map** p324.

Bicycle rentals cost HK$50 for the whole day.

Paragliding

Hong Kong's gusty winds make it a playground for experienced flyers, who launch off from the **Dragon's Back** in the near Shek O or from **Sunset Peak** on Lantau at the weekends. But those same winds make it a difficult place for beginners. Anyone paragliding in Hong

Kong must do so under the advice of the **Hong Kong Paragliding Association** and a pilot's licence is necessary. The HKPA website (www.hkpa.net) has information about sites, weather and briefs for visiting pilots.

Pilates

Iso Fit

8/F, California Tower, 30-32 D'Aguilar Street, Central, HK Island (2869 8630/www.isofit.com.hk). Central MTR (exit D1, D2). **Open** 8am-8pm Mon-Fri, 9am-6pm Sat. **Fees** from HK$150/class; phone for details of packages. **Credit** AmEx, MC, V. **Map** p328 C4.

All newcomers to Iso Fit are given an hour's one-on-one consultation and then can choose between individual or group classes.

Rollerblading & skateboarding

Happy Valley Racecourse (*see p258*) has a track around the outside where you can blade; alternatively, join the joggers on **Bowen Road**.

King's Park YMCA Centenary Centre

22 Gascoigne Road, Yau Ma Tei, Kowloon (2782 6682/www.kpcc.ymcahk.org.hk). Jordan MTR (exit B2)/buses along Nathan Road. **Open** 7.30am-10.30pm daily (but may be closed for events or courses, so phone ahead). **Admission** *In-line skating rink* HK$50; HK$25 children. *Skate park* HK$15/session. **No credit cards. Map** p333 C4.

You must pass a test of competence and become a member (free of charge) to use the skate park and its tubes and obstacles; pads and skates can be hired. King's Park is also the home of Hong Kong's adult and youth in-line hockey leagues (see the website for schedules).

Running & jogging

The gentle three-kilometre (two-mile) loop on **Lugard Road** around the Peak (*see p88* **Peak around**) is great for a pre-Sunday brunch run. Otherwise, try **Bowen Road**, which stretches for four kilometres (two-and-a-half miles) from near Robinson Road to Magazine Gap Road. The views are well worth the effort. Or pretend you're a thoroughbred and gallop round the jogging track at **Happy Valley** (*see p258*). All are traffic-free.

Throughout the year there are organised races to suit all levels of abilities, such as the **Athletic Veterans of Hong Kong** (AVOHK) series of 5km races; 10km races like the Shatin Riverside 10km and the Clearwater Bay Annual Chase; and the 15km Mount Butler Race. Places fill up quickly so plan ahead by looking at the **Hong Kong Runners**' website (www.hkrunners.com), which has a substantial number of race listings. The biggest race of the year is the **Hong Kong Marathon** (www.hkmarathon.com), which takes place in March. (*See also p251* **Wacky races**.)

For a sociable time and a bit of running, find out what the **Hash House Harriers** are up to on their website (www.wanchaih3.com). They run most Sundays, starting at 4pm, for about an hour (HK$30 women, HK$60 men). Alternatively, try the **Little Sai Wan Hash House Harriers** (www.datadesignfactory. com/lsw), who run Wednesdays at 6.45pm (HK$20 for the run; drinks extra). Runs usually last an hour.

Sailing, paddling & kayaking

If you're around at the end of June, you might want to participate in the annual **Dragon Boat Festival** (*see p204*). Spurred on by drums and your fellow paddlers, you'll be taking part in a quintessentially Chinese sport at the same time as straining your back to the breaking point. The **Hong Kong Island Paddle Club** (www.hkipc.com) meets regularly to practise dragon boating and outrigger canoeing. **Kayak and Hike** (*see p249*) takes groups out for fun kayaking around the outlying islands offshore from Sai Kung.

There are few more pleasant ways of escaping the hectic bustle of the city than on board a yacht. If you don't have your own craft,

check out the boards outside the yacht clubs listed below, as owners often advertise for crew. Experienced crew is preferred but beginners can sometimes get lucky. Both clubs below also run courses. The **Hong Kong Sailing Federation** (www.sailing.org.hk) also has an extensive list of courses on its website.

Royal Hong Kong Yacht Club

Kellett Island, Causeway Bay, HK Island (2832 2817/www.rhkyc.org.hk). Causeway Bay MTR (exit C)/buses along Gloucester Road. **Open** *Phone enquiries* 8am-10pm daily. **Credit** AmEx, MC, V. **Map** p331 D2.

You might get a crew spot at the members-only RHKYC. Otherwise, Yachting Ventures, based here, runs a variety of courses (for details, call 9333 8084 or log on to www.yachtingventures.com).

St Stephen's Beach Water Sports Centre

Wong Ma Kok Path (near the police station), Stanley, HK Island (2813 5804/www.lcsd.gov.hk). Buses to Stanley. **Open** 8.30am-5pm Mon, Wed-Sun. **No credit cards. Map** p93.

Scuba diving

Hong Kong might not boast the clearest waters in the world, but it's better than you might imagine. The **Sai Kung** and **Clearwater Bay** peninsulas, **Shek O** and the **Po Toi** islands are just some of the many good dive sites, harbouring some 50 types of coral and 400

Take a dip: Hong Kong is swimming with decent pools. *See p256.*

Arts & Entertainment

varieties of sea life. The diving season falls roughly between March and October. Contact the following clubs for details of courses.

Mandarin Divers
G/F, Unit 2, Aberdeen Marina Tower, 8 Shum Wan Road, Aberdeen, HK Island (2554 7110/www. mandarin-divers.com). Buses to Aberdeen. **Open** 9.30am-7pm Mon-Sat. **Credit** AmEx, MC, V. **Map** p325.

Marine Divers
3E, Block 18, Dynasty View, 11 Ma Wo Road, Tai Po, New Territories (2656 9399/9194 0221/www. marinedivers.com). Buses to Tai Po. **Open** phone for details. **No credit cards. Map** p325.

Squash

The **Harbour Road Indoor Games Hall** and **Hong Kong Park Government Indoor Games Hall** (for both, *see p250*) each have squash courts costing HK$27 for half-an-hour, HK$54 for one hour.

Victoria Park
Hing Fat Street, Causeway Bay, HK Island (2570 6186/bookings 2927 8080). Tin Hau MTR (exit A1, A2)/10, 15B, 18, 102, 106, 110, 116 bus. **Open** 7am-11pm daily. **Fees** HK$27/30mins; HK$54/hr. **No credit cards. Map** p331 E2/F2.

Surfing

The minute the typhoon signal is hoisted, Hong Kong's little gang of surfers surge on to the **Big Wave Bay Beach** (*see p94*) near Shek O and get ready for the waves. Sadly, when there are no storm warnings, waves are usually no more than a foot high. The **Big Wave Bay Kiosk** (no telephone) is right on the beach and, along with renting boards (approx HK$100 per day), also sells food and drinks. Waves at **Long Wan Beach** at Sai Kung in the New Territories (*see p118*) are usually bigger and better shaped, but it's quite a trek to get there.

To learn how to surf, call Nelson Chan (6036 0360), whose company, **Surf 360**, holds courses throughout the summer at Big Wave Bay in Shek O. Three hours' tuition and equipment hire costs HK$400 per person; lessons are given on Saturday and Sunday (but call on Friday to book). For surfing gear, head to the **Island Wake Surf Shop** (20 Pak Sha Road, Causeway Bay, HK Island, 2895 0022, www.islandwake.com), which also runs courses.

Swimming

Beaches in Hong Kong are generally clean and have shops with beach mats, snacks and drinks. It's the water itself that leaves a little to be

desired, although some days – and some beaches – are better than others. **Tai Long Wan**, out in Sai Kung Country Park (*see p118*), is an effort to get to – a sampan from Sai Kung or a fairly demanding walk through the country park is involved – but it boasts the clearest water in Hong Kong. If you camp there you might be lucky enough to swim in phosphorescence if you venture out at night, but be careful of sharks. Otherwise, **Repulse Bay** (photo *p252*) and **Deep Water Bay** (for both, *see p92*) are the nearest beaches to Central. **Big Wave Bay** (*see p94*) near Shek O is good too. **Stanley** (*see p92*) is better for water sports than swimming.

If sand in your cossie isn't your thing, try a day at a swanky hotel pool, which usually costs upwards of HK$250 for non-guests, or go local and dive into an outside public pool; for a full list, see www.lcsd.gov.hk/beach/en/index.php

Kennedy Town Swimming Pool
12N Smithfield Road, Kennedy Town, HK Island (2817 7973). Bus 5B, 10, 101, 104, 904. **Open** *Apr-Nov* 6.30am-noon, 1-5pm, 6-10pm daily. Closed Dec-Mar. **Admission** HK$19; HK$9 concessions. **No credit cards. Map** p325.

Kowloon Park
Austin Road, Tsim Sha Tsui, Kowloon (2724 3577). Jordan MTR (exit C)/buses along Austin Road. **Open** *June-Mar* 6.30am-noon, 1-5pm, 6-10pm daily. Closed Apr & May. **Admission** HK$19; HK$9 children. **No credit cards. Map** p333 B5.

South China Athletic Association
Club House, 88 Caroline Hill Road, Causeway Bay, HK Island (2577 6932/www.scaa.org.hk). **Open** 7-11.45am, 1-6pm, 7.30-9.45pm daily. **Admission** HK$22; HK$10 under-12s. Closed mid Jan-Mar.
Indoor heated ten-lane 50-metre pool and 25 metre-training pool plus an outdoor diving pool.

Victoria Park
Hing Fat Street, Causeway Bay, HK Island (2570 8347). Tin Hau MTR (exit A2)/10, 15B, 18, 102, 106, 110, 116 bus. **Open** *Apr-Oct* 6.30am-noon, 1-5pm, 6-10pm daily. Closed Nov-Mar. **Admission** HK$19; HK$9 children. **No credit cards. Map** p331 F2.

Table tennis

The **Harbour Road Indoor Games Hall** (*see p250*) hires out table-tennis facilities at a cost of HK$21 an hour.

Tennis

Tennis courts are everywhere in Hong Kong, and they're relatively cheap. Below are some of the best.

Causeway Bay Sports Ground

Causeway Road, Causeway Bay, HK Island (2890 5127). Tin Hau MTR (exit B)/buses along Causeway Road. **Open** 7am-11pm daily. **Fees** HK$42/hr before 6pm; HK$57/hr after 6pm. **No credit cards.** **Map** p331 F3.
Six floodlit courts bookable up to 30 days in advance.

Hong Kong Tennis Centre

Wong Nai Chung Gap Road, Happy Valley, HK Island (2574 9122/bookings 2927 8080). Bus 6, 41A, 61, 63, 66, 76. **Open** 7am-10pm daily. **Fees** HK$42/hr before 6pm; HK$57/hr after 6pm. **No credit cards.** **Map** p331 D4.
There are 17 floodlit courts.

King's Park Sports Ground

15 King's Park Rise, Yau Ma Tei, Kowloon (2385 8985). Bus 2C, 103. **Open** 7am-10.30pm daily. **Fees** HK$40-$70/hr. **No credit cards.** **Map** p332 C3.
Six floodlit courts.

Victoria Park

Hing Fat Street, Causeway Bay, HK Island (2570 6186/www.lcsd.gov.hk). Tin Hau MTR (exit A2)/ buses along Hing Fat Street. **Open** 7am-11pm daily. **Fees** HK$42/hr before 6pm; HK$57/hr after 6pm. **No credit cards.** **Map** p331 E2/F2.
Fourteen floodlit courts, which can be booked online.

Volleyball

The **Harbour Road Indoor Games Hall** (*see p250*) hires out courts at an hourly rate of HK$236.

Wakeboarding, waterskiing & windsurfing

Not surprisingly, given the climate, water sports are very popular in Hong Kong, with wakeboarding being the trendiest at the moment. **Wakeboard.com.hk** (3120 4102, www.wakeboard.com.hk) runs three centres in beautiful locations: Tai Tam on Hong Kong Island, Shai Sha in Sai Kung in the New Territories, and Wakeland on the north coast of Lantau. Boats, boards and equipment are provided (HK$600 weekdays, HK$700 weekends; see website for details of packages). Book a day or two in advance.

Cheung Chau Windsurfing Centre

Hai Pak Road, Tung Wan Beach, Cheung Chau (2981 2772). Cheung Chau Ferry Pier. **Open** Mar-Oct 11am-6pm daily. *Nov-Feb* open on public holidays only. **Fees** HK$120/hr; HK$270 for 4 hours. *Beginners* HK$90/hr. **No credit cards.** **Map** p324.

Wave Star – The Windsurfing Spirit

Stanley Main Beach (2813 7561/www.28137561. com). Buses to Stanley. **Open** 9.30am-7pm Sat, Sun; phone for weekday hours. **No credit cards.** **Map** p93.

This beach shop has been open for nearly 30 years. Its main instructor is Olympic competitor Barry Ho, who charges HK$800 for two days of lessons (four hours each day). To book, call two days in advance.

Yoga

Yoga is extremely popular in Hong Kong. **Fitness First** (*see p252*) and **California Fitness** (*see p251*) also run classes in yoga. For more listings, see www.yogahongkong.com

Planet Yoga

20/F, Silver Fortune Plaza, 1 Wellington Street, Central, HK Island (2525 8288/www.planetyoga. com.hk). Central MTR (exit D2). **Open** 7am-11pm Mon-Fri; 7am-10pm Sat, Sun. **Fees** varies; phone for details. **Credit** AmEx, MC, V. **Map** p328 C4.
Most of the instructors at this dedicated studio above California Fitness (*see p251*) are from India.

Pure Yoga

16/F, The Centrium, 60 Wyndham Street, Central, HK Island (2971 0055/www.pure-yoga.com). Central MTR (exit D1, D2)/23A, 26, 40M bus. **Open** 6am-10.30pm Mon-Fri; 7.45am-8pm Sat; 9am-8pm Sun. **Fees** HK$200/class. **Credit** AmEx, MC, V. **Map** p328 C4.
Pure Yoga, an offshoot of Pure Fitness (*see p253*), runs classes in hatha, pregnancy and power yoga. **Other locations:** 25/F, Soundwill Plaza, 38 Russell Street, Causeway Bay, HK Island (2970 2299).

Spectator sports

Athletics

For the **Standard Chartered Hong Kong Marathon** in February, *see p206.*

Dragon boat racing

For some Asian-style action, come to Hong Kong in June and take in – or take part in – the frenzied **Dragon Boat Festival** (*see p204*).

Football

Although its own team may not be among the world's major players, soccer is extremely popular in Hong Kong, and international teams fly into town in January to compete in the annual **Carlsberg Cup** (*see p205*).

Golf

In Hong Kong itself there is only one major annual event, the **Hong Kong Open**, which is played at Fan Ling or Clearwater Bay in November. Slightly further afield there is also the **Macau Open** in December, and there are events throughout the year in Shenzhen.

Arts & Entertainment

Horse racing

Hong Kong loves to gamble – but gambling is illegal. The only way to have a flutter without attracting the attention of the police is to bet with the **Jockey Club** on horse-racing or football only. At the horse racing meetings at the **Happy Valley Racecourse**, it's a high-adrenalin, high-tech experience, with race-goers from every walk of life – from the blue-collar worker cheering in the stands to the *tai tais* peering out over glasses of champagne from the Jockey Club. Billions go through the books at each meeting, and a percentage of the profit goes to the Jockey Club's chosen charities.

For a whole day's racing, the modern **Sha Tin Racecourse** in the New Territories (www.shatinracetrack.com; *see p109*) holds events on Saturdays and Sundays. Among the major meetings held there are the **Hong Kong Derby** in March, the **Queen Elizabeth II Cup** in April and the **Hong Kong International Races** in December. For details, go to www.hkjockeyclub.com

Happy Valley Racecourse

2 Sports Road, Happy Valley, HK Island (2895 1523/Jockey Club Hotline 183 5888/www.happyvalley racecourse.com). Trams to Happy Valley. **Open** varies. Closed July & Aug. **Admission** HK$10. **No credit cards. Map** p331 D4/D5.
Racing in Hong Kong is followed as fanatically as a religion, and Happy Valley is the altar at which most people pray. The high-intensity floodlights, expectant atmosphere, booming loudspeakers, billions of dollars, streaming crowds and streaking horses make for one of the most exciting evenings out the city has to offer. The minimum bet is only HK$10,

so there's no excuse not to join in. For a bird's-eye view, climb up to the top of the stands – if your horse doesn't come in, tear your betting slip and throw it over the edge where it joins thousands of others in Happy Valley's version of snow. For close-up, hoof-thundering action, stand on the rails, beer in hand, and cheer your horse round. The season lasts from September to June and meetings are usually every Wednesday from 7.30pm (check first).

Rugby

Known throughout the world as one of the biggest rugby parties of the year, the annual **Hong Kong Rugby Sevens** (www.hk sevens.com) brings bedlam to the city at the end of March. Rugby teams warm up in front of the stands, run out for the short clash with their opponents and then, the serious stuff over, run round the stadium, playing to the hysterical crowds. In the days before the big weekend, look out for the **Women's Rugby Sevens & Asia Championship** and the **Hong Kong Tens** (www.hongkongtens.com), which focuses on the best teams from New Zealand, Australia and the UK.

Tennis

Three annual tournaments pull in current champions and crowd favourites from the past: the **Salem Open** and **Watson's Water Challenge**, both in Victoria Park, and the **Cathay Pacific Championships** at the Hong Kong Convention & Exhibition Centre. Check the website of the **Hong Kong Tennis Association**, at www.tennishk.org.

Happy Valley Racecourse.

Trips Out of Town

Wynn Macau. *See p276*.

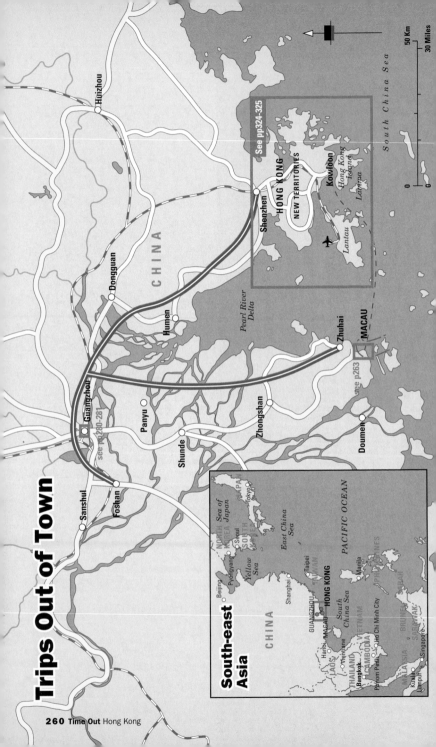

Trips Out of Town

See pp324-325

HONG KONG

NEW TERRITORIES

Kowloon

Hong Kong Island

Lamma

Lantau

South China Sea

Shenzhen

CHINA

Dongguan

Humen

Huizhou

Pearl River Delta

Zhuhai

MACAU

see p263

Zhongshan

Doumen

Guangzhou

see pp280-281

Panyu

Shunde

Sanshui

Foshan

50 Km

30 Miles

South-east Asia

CHINA

Beijing

NORTH KOREA

Pyongyang

Sea of Japan

Japan

Seoul

SOUTH KOREA

Tokyo

Yellow Sea

East China Sea

PACIFIC OCEAN

Shanghai

Taipei

TAIWAN

GUANGZHOU

MACAU

HONG KONG

South China Sea

PHILIPPINES

Manila

Haikou

VIETNAM

Vientiane

LAOS

THAILAND

CAMBODIA

Bangkok

Ho Chi Minh City

Phnom Penh

BRUNEI

SABAH

SARAWAK

MALAYSIA

Kuala Lumpur

Singapore

Macau

New casinos may have upped the ante, but this enclave's superbly preserved
architecture and great cuisine are still strong suits.

Macau Tower. *See p269.*

The mainland Chinese peninsula of Macau has
one *raison d'être* – gambling. From the gaming
tables and one-armed bandits in the casinos to
horse and greyhound racing, it's a flutter that
most people are here for. But there is much
more to Macau than this. Many Hong Kong
residents, especially expats, use it as a peaceful
and comparatively inexpensive getaway – it's
just 70 kilometres (45 miles) from the territory
and easily accessible by ferry (or, for those
who can afford it, helicopter). The city is home
to excellent restaurants, colonial buildings,
decent shopping, and plenty of interesting
sights and leisure facilities.

Macau is an example of East-meets-West
integration refined over more than four
centuries, since Portuguese explorers hived
it off as a colonial trading outpost. Buddhist
temples nestle cheek by jowl with baroque
Catholic churches, old coffee shops lie next
to traditional Chinese teahouses, and the
neon lights of the casinos flash a mere die's
throw from classical 19th-century European
buildings. Although Macau returned to
Chinese sovereignty in 1999, a heavy

Portuguese influence remains, which can be
seen everywhere from the fusion Macanese
food to the city's scooter-filled streets and its
'live-and-let-live' attitude.

Macau's main similarity to Hong Kong is
that it is an autonomous Special Administrative
Region (SAR) of China. Beijing has its hand on
the tiller, but local government is the skipper.
Both cities are also free ports (meaning no
taxes are imposed on goods imported from
other countries) and each is a full member of
the World Trade Organisation in its own right.

The similarities largely end there. Macau is
tiny, its 25 square kilometres (ten square miles)
represent just two per cent of Hong Kong's
total land area. It is densely populated, but its
440,000 inhabitants make up just six per cent
of Hong Kong's overall population. And while

> ▶ Green numbers '❶' given in this
> chapter correspond to the location of
> each hotel as marked on the street map
> on p263. Likewise, purple numbers '❶'
> indicate the location of restaurants.

Macau's GDP is high in Asian terms – it rocketed to fourth place thanks to the surge in gaming revenue – its currency is pegged to the Hong Kong dollar and it has no stock market.

EARLY HISTORY

The name Macau is a corruption of 'A-Ma Gau', meaning 'Bay of A-Ma'. Legend has it that A-Ma – the Goddess of Seafarers (known in Hong Kong as Tin Hau) – was a maiden who calmed a storm that threatened to engulf a boat. When the boat reached land, its passengers built a temple to her in the inner harbour, which still attracts worshippers today.

Macau was both the first area east of Malaysia to be settled by Europeans and the last to be released from colonialisation. The first recorded Portuguese navigator to visit China was Jorge Alvares, who made it as far as nearby Lintin, an island in the Pearl River estuary, in 1513. Even though he spent ten months on the island, he didn't establish a long-term base there, and it was nearly 40 years later, in 1557, that the Portuguese were given permission by the local magistrate at Heung Shan (in modern Zhuhai) to settle on the Macau peninsula – reportedly in return for helping drive away pirates.

Macau, therefore, became the Portuguese headquarters for trade in this part of Asia. As the Chinese had banned Japanese traders from entering their ports (which had been ravaged by Japanese pirates for centuries), the Portuguese became crucial intermediaries in the trading of copper and silver and raw silks. By the early 1600s it was a thriving city, home not only to traders but also Portuguese missionaries determined to convert the Asian communities to Catholicism.

However, Macau's golden era did not last long. In 1637 Japan entered a self-inflicted period of exclusion and trade, and with it the role of the Portuguese declined. By this time the Dutch were also threatening Portugal's domination of world trade. Macau's prosperity suffered and the city became a backwater.

The Portuguese remained, however, and since there were few European women around, the Portuguese men tended to marry Asians, resulting in the distinctive look of the Macanese people. In addition, a local patois developed, which combined Portuguese, Malay, Japanese and Cantonese elements. Sadly, the dialect is dying out – not many people under 70 speak it today. Other elements of the Macanese culture, such as dress, were also derived from Malacca and elsewhere, and until the early 20th century many elderly Macanese women still wore *sarong kebaya* (traditional Malay dress) and lived relatively secluded lives.

In 1887, although they had already been in Macau for over 300 years, the Portuguese finally formalised their presence in the city by securing a concession of sovereignty from the Chinese. By then Macau was being used as a base by many Europeans and Americans trading with Canton (as Guangzhou was known).

CONTEMPORARY MACAU

It was not until the mid 20th century that Macau found true prosperity again, through licensed gambling, which now accounts for 40 per cent of the government's revenue and forms the backbone of the economy. It also made Hong Kong-based businessman Stanley Ho a billionaire, as he was the sole gambling licensee until 2001, when his monopoly was revoked. Competition arrived in 2005 when two gambling moguls from Las Vegas opened their own casino and entertainment complexes (*see p275* **Cash Macau**), with much more to come, including some major Asian gambling outfits.

At times Portugal's rule of Macau has been reluctant. Following the Portuguese revolution of 1974, and in a fit of post-colonial guilt, the Portuguese tried to withdraw from Macau, yet, despite years of anti-colonial rhetoric, the Chinese asked them to stay. Portugal agreed to remain in name, but withdrew its troops and declared Macau a Chinese sovereign territory under Portuguese administration. The Sino-Portuguese Joint Declaration – signed in 1987 – finally provided for Macau's return to Chinese administration in 1999.

After the signing of the declaration, Macau experienced a few years of unsustained property boom, and massive land reclamation schemes were undertaken, completely changing the peninsula's appearance. Bridges were built connecting the mainland peninsula to the islands of Taipa and Colôane, and Macau International Airport was constructed. It has become a hub for low-cost carriers such as Tiger Air and Air Asia, with some very good deals to and from Singapore, Bangkok and Kuala Lumpur available.

Outbreaks of gang in-fighting in the late 1990s earned Macau the nickname the 'Wild East', as Chinese triads flexed their muscles and staked claims to various pieces of business linked to gambling. But the trouble has since calmed considerably and the transition of sovereignty went quite smoothly. Compared with Hong Kong and southern China, Macau was relatively unscathed by the SARS pandemic in 2003. The city authorities won praise for their handling of the isolated cases that did occur.

Trips Out of Town

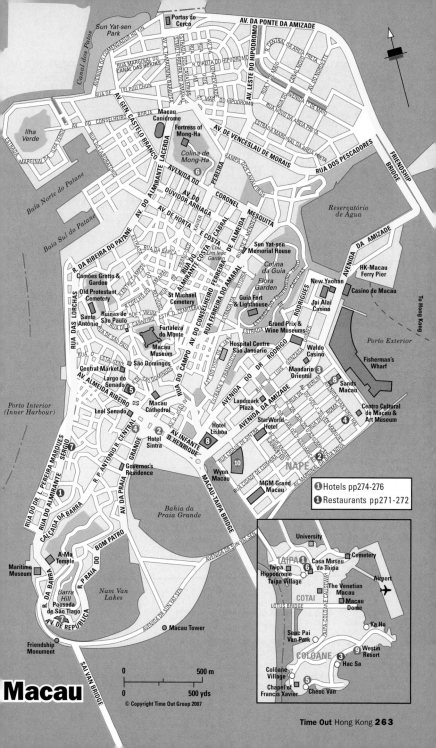

Macau

Cruising through the environs of the **Porto Interior** (Inner Harbour).

Now firmly established as a gambling and tourism destination, Macau has spent tens of millions of dollars on new attractions, such as the Macau Tower – the tenth tallest free-standing building in the world – and on restoring old buildings for use as entertainment venues or museums. There is talk of building a bridge to link Macau with Hong Kong and Zhuhai, though details are still to be agreed. In 2005 Macau hosted the East Asian games, which boosted its profile in the region as more than just a gambling centre.

But it's as a gambling centre that Macau has its hopes pinned on. The coming years will see a slew of new hotels and resorts open on the reclaimed land of the Cotai Strip, the focus of much of the US$20 billion of planned investment over the next few years to achieve the SAR's ambition to be known by the unimaginative moniker of 'Asia's Las Vegas'. It's also ironic, given that Macau's revenue from gambling surpassed that of the glitzy US city in 2006. Macau's position as the playground of the Pearl River Delta suggests that the financial gamble the government has taken on building for its future is likely to be a winner.

Sightseeing

Macau has plenty to see, from historic colonial architecture and baroque churches to ancient Chinese temples and ruined forts. The city is split into three areas: the peninsula joined to

mainland China, and the islands of **Taipa** and **Colôane** (although the area of reclaimed land known as **Cotai** filling up the sea between the two has effectively created one land mass). The heart of the city, with most of the sights and the action, is to be found in the mainland section, while the two islands – particularly the more distant Colôane – offer more peaceful respite, at least until the Vegas-style Cotai Strip shakes things up a bit.

Central Macau

Central Macau's famous waterfront avenue, the **Avenida da Praia Grande**, is an excellent place to start a tour of the city. The grand street once extended in a graceful banyan-lined crescent from the ramparts of São Francisco Battery & Gardens, along the coast to the fortress of Bom Patro, around the cliffs towards the fortress of Barra, eventually reaching the **Porto Interior** (Inner Harbour). Lined with magnificent buildings, the Praia Grande used to be one of Macau's renowned beauty spots. Sadly, extensive reclamation has diminished the beauty of the Praia Grande in recent years, though the southern end of Avenida de República, beyond the Governor's Residence, still gives a tangible echo of what it originally looked like.

Walking down Avenida da Praia Grande, one of the first significant sights is the **Jorge Alvares Monument**, which honours the

Portuguese explorer. Here he is remembered by a stone statue that depicts him as a stocky bearded figure in a medieval tunic and long cape, holding a sheathed sword, with the *padrão* (marker stone) he erected at Lintin standing behind him. *See also p13.*

Turn left off Avenida da Praia Grande on to Avenida Almeida Ribeiro and you will reach the buildings of the **Leal Senado** (Loyal Senate; *see p266*). Built in classic Portuguese Manueline style in 1784 (and extensively renovated several times since), it stands on the site of a much older, open-sided Chinese pavilion dating from the very first Portuguese settlement in Macau. It was here that the Red Guards gathered to express their anger during the riots of December 1966. Today the building houses the Municipal Council.

Opposite the Leal is the **Largo do Senado** (Senate Square), the symbolic heart of Macau. Many cultural events take place here, and it's worth visiting in the evening when it is often illuminated for a festival. The square is surrounded by a number of lovely colonial structures, including the **General Post Office** and the charitable foundation **Santa Casa da Misericordia**. Well-preserved Portuguese architecture abounds here – the **Edificio Ritz**, which now houses a branch of the tourist office, is a good example.

A short walk through the square to Rua de São Domingos, on its northern side, will bring you to the church of **São Domingos** (*see p268*), also known as Santa Rosa. Next to it is the **São Domingos Market**, or Central Market, which is one of the busiest, and the most splendidly restored, in Macau.

Just east of here, Rua de São Paulo leads to the Jesuit Collegiate Church of Madre de Deus, more commonly known as the **Ruinas de São Paulo** (or Ruins of St Paul; *see p268*). For many, this is quite simply *the* symbol of Macau – the elaborate stone façade has been featured on postcards since the 19th century. The original church was built by Japanese Christians who had fled from persecution in their homeland. Unfortunately, only the stone façade remains, the rest of the building having been destroyed by fire in 1835.

Perched on a hill directly above the Ruinas de São Paulo, the **Fortaleza do Monte** (*see p266*) provides the strongest connection between modern Macau and its colonial roots. Also built by the Jesuits from 1616 onwards, this was the first home of the Portuguese settlers. Dug into the hillside near the fortress is the **Museum of Macau** (*see p267*), which tells the history of the peninsula.

From the Ruinas de São Paulo, it's a short walk to the church of **Santo António**

(*see p268*). A place of worship has stood here since the mid 1500s, which makes the modern structure on the site today the oldest church in Macau. Churches here seem to be ill fated, having burned down on several occasions. Next to Santo António stand the tranquil **Camões Grotto & Garden** (*see p266*), where locals come to relax. On the eastern edge of the garden is the defunct **Old Protestant Cemetery** (*see p268*), which was established in 1821 to provide for the non-Roman Catholic foreign community. The cemetery was badly needed as tenets of Catholicism forbade the burial of non-believers in consecrated soil, which effectively meant there was no place to bury Protestants in Macau until it was created.

About 15 minutes' walk from the Old Protestant Cemetery, on Estrada do Cemitério, is the lovely **St Michael Cemetery**. This large Catholic cemetery is filled with statues of angels and features some beautiful, elaborate tombs. From the cemetery, walk north along Avenida do Conselheiro Ferreira de Almeida, lined with historic buildings, to the peaceful **Lou Lim Ieoc Garden** (*see p267*), with its ornate mansion and shady gardens. Early in the morning you'll see people here practising t'ai chi or strolling with their birds in cages. Just around the corner from the garden is the **Sun Yat-sen Memorial House** (*see p268*), which is only marginally connected to the rebel and founder of the Chinese Republic. Sun never actually lived in this house, but he did practise medicine in Macau before becoming a revolutionary.

From here it's a short walk along Avenida Sidónio Pais to the **Flora Garden**, the largest of Macau's gardens, and one of the most beautiful. Its grounds contain a miniature zoo, lovely landscaped gardens and a pond. This is also the place to catch the cable car (open 7.30am-6.30pm daily) up to Guia Hill, at the top of which you'll find the **Guia Fort & Lighthouse** (*see p266*), which have stood watch over Macau since 1638. Wander down Guia Hill and along Estrada de Cacilhas in the direction of the harbour if you wish to visit the **Grand Prix & Wine Museums** (*see p266*), both housed in the Macau Forum.

Further south, in among the waterfront developments of the reclaimed land known as Nape, stands the **Centro Cultural de Macau** (797 7215, 2870 0699, www.ccm.gov.mo; *see also p273*), which houses the **Art Museum** (*see p266*) and hosts an interesting programme of music, opera, dance, theatre and film, as well as the annual Macau Arts Festival (*see p273*). The surrounding area has been going through a development boom, with new casinos popping up and the opening of **Fisherman's Wharf** (**photo** *p273*), a rather bizarre pastiche of historical buildings and settings – from an ancient Roman coliseum to New Orleans' Bourbon Street – housing restaurants and shops, plus a regularly erupting faux volcano.

Art Museum
Centro Cultural de Macau, Avenida Xian Xing Hai (791 9814). **Open** 10am-7pm Tue-Sun. **Admission** MOP$5; MOP$3 concessions. Free to all Sun. **No credit cards**. **Map** p263.
This permanent collection is a showcase for art works that are related to Macau in some way, and includes such diverse styles as French abstraction and traditional Chinese art works.

Camões Grotto & Garden
Praca Luis de Camões (visitors hotline 2833 3000). **Open** daily. **Admission** free. **Map** p263.
The grotto and its gardens are dedicated to 16th-century Portuguese poet Luis Vaz de Camões, who is beloved in Macau, despite the fact that there is no hard evidence that he actually lived here. (Nonetheless, many Macau residents firmly believe that he did, and that he penned one of his most famous works, 'The Lusiads', here.)

Fortaleza do Monte
Praceta do Museu de Macau (visitors hotline 2833 3000). **Open** 10am-6pm daily. **Admission** free. **Map** p263.
The fort – reached by walking east from the Ruins of St Paul – was built in the early 17th century around the early settlement here, so its walls became those of the city. It wasn't long before the settlers found out how strong the walls of the fort were. In 1622 the Dutch attacked Macau, but were ultimately defeated by artillery fired from the fortress, as the settlers huddled inside. After the military was withdrawn in 1966, the grounds were opened to the public. On a clear day the view from Monte takes in much of Macau and as far north as Zhuhai.

Grand Prix & Wine Museums
Rua de Luis Gonzaga Gomes (798 4108). **Open** 10am-6pm daily. **Admission** *Grand Prix Museum* MOP$10. *Wine Museum* MOP$15. *Joint admission* MOP$20. **No credit cards**. **Map** p263.
The Grand Prix Museum is home to numerous interesting exhibits from the local Formula 3 Grand Prix, including several cars. There are simulators that test your driving skills and TV monitors that let you see what it's like to drive around the Macau race circuit. The Wine Museum, displaying (predominantly Portuguese) wines and wine-making tools, is impressive if you're into wine; tastings are also sometimes possible.

Guia Fort & Lighthouse
Estrada de Cacilhas (visitors hotline 2833 3000). **Open** 9am-5pm daily. **Admission** free. **Map** p263.
The fort was built in 1637 on the highest point of the peninsula, overlooking the border with China. In the mid 19th century, it started a third life as a lighthouse – making it the oldest on the China coast. If you want to enter the lighthouse, you need to get permission from the Marine Department, which has offices on site.

Leal Senado
Largo do Senado (visitors hotline 2833 3000). **Open** 9am-5.30pm daily. *Gallery* 9am-5.30pm Tue-Sun. **Admission** free. **Map** p263.

Lou Lim Ieoc Garden. See p267.

Future in the past

In 2004, after some years of effort, a number of sites in Macau achieved World Heritage status. These locations range from the obvious, such as the ruins of St Paul's Collegiate Church – which has been a symbol of Macau since postcards were invented – to more obscure temples, churches, gardens, fortifications and streetscapes.

Macau was originally considered as a possible World Heritage Site in the 1970s. But powerful vested interests within the local gambling industry swiftly put paid to any such suggestion. World Heritage listing would oblige the local government to gazette numerous buildings and entire precincts, and accept ongoing, non-trivial financial obligations for their maintenance. No one wanted the responsibility and, arguably, Macau could not have afforded the level of recurrent expense at that time.

Also, mass tourism then was not what it is now. Very few visitors came to Macau specifically for a cultural heritage experience. (Relatively few do now either, especially those from mainland China, but overall numbers are higher.) But Macau – unlike Hong Kong – has begun explicitly to recognise that to survive in today's tourist world it must add value to the visitor experience. The UNESCO listing also encourages a different type of visitor; one more likely to stay a few days, spend more in the town and less in the casino precincts – and return to Macau time and again.

Recognition of World Heritage status was a little problematic. For the last few decades of Portuguese rule it was politically expedient, for both Portugal and China, to regard Macau and its cultural heritage as a Sino-Chinese and Portuguese legacy. The significant role in Macau's evolution played by other places influenced by Portugal, such as Malacca, Timor, Japan, and Goa, was downplayed. This sidestepped the potentially controversial issue that, in a deeper sense, Macau over the centuries has belonged to many different peoples and places.

In general this mindset has now changed, largely as a result of China's increased openness to the world, and in recognition of the role Macau can play as an economic bridgehead to resource-rich Portuguese-speaking nations (in particular Brazil and the former Portuguese African territories of Angola and Mozambique).

Return visitors, especially those who knew Macau in the 1980s and '90s, will immediately note that much of the centre of Macau is now better maintained than it has ever been. As a tourist strategy, the UNESCO listing has led to more active preservation, conservation and documentation efforts.

There is a general recognition that while mass development can take place in certain peripheral areas, such as around the ferry terminal and along the Cotai Strip – the eponymous reclamation between the islands of Taipa and Coloane – the centre of town is subject to limitations.

More effective heritage preservation has led to needs for greater vigilance. As in Hong Kong, developers in Macau have been known to demolish quickly and quietly buildings that may have conservation value, reasoning (rightly, in their case) that an empty site is worth much more than a potentially troublesome building.

Chinese and Portuguese officials used to meet here to discuss trade and other issues relating to the Portuguese presence in Macau. The name came about as a result of the Macau Senate refusing to accept the so-called dual kingdom of Spain and Portugal. From 1580 until the countries were separated again in 1640 it was the Portuguese flag – not the Spanish one – that flew in Macau. As a result, in 1654 the city was rewarded with the title Cidade de Nome de Deus, Não Há Outra Mais Leal (City of the Name of God, There is None More Loyal).

It's worth popping in to admire the colonial architecture and gallery, which hosts regularly changing shows of local interest. Today the building is used by the Provisional Municipal Authority but there are interesting displays and a lovely courtyard.

Lou Lim Ieoc Garden

Estrada de Adolfo Loureiro (2833 7676). **Open** 6am-9pm daily. **Admission** MOP$1. Free on Fri. **No credit cards. Map** p263.

This garden, and the ornate house that stands in it (which is now a school), used to belong to a wealthy Chinese family. There are huge shady trees reminiscent of European gardens, but also twisting pathways and ornamental mountains as seen in traditional Chinese landscape paintings, as well as lotus ponds and bamboo groves. **Photo** *p266.*

Museum of Macau

112 Praceta do Museu do Macau (2835 7911/www. macaumuseum.gov.mo). **Open** 10am-6pm Tue-Sun. **Admission** MOP$15; MOP$8 concessions. **No credit cards. Map** p263.

Macau derives its name from A-Ma Gau, worshipped at the **A-Ma Temple**. *See p269.*

Getting to the Museum of Macau is actually more fun than looking around it, as it is reached by way of an outdoor escalator near the Ruinas de São Paulo. Its extensive, educational exhibits begin with the early colonial years and continue through to modern times, and feature multimedia displays and videos.

Old Protestant Cemetery

Camões Garden, Praca Luis de Camões (visitors hotline 2833 3000). **Open** 6am-11.30pm daily. **Admission** free. **Map** p263.
Many American and European Protestants lived in Macau in the early part of the 19th century, prior to the establishment of Hong Kong as a British colony. Among them was George Chinnery, the well-known China Coast painter, who is buried here; as is Dr Robert Morrison, the first Protestant missionary to China. The cemetery fell into disrepair after its closure to burials in the 1860s, when the new Protestant Cemetery at Mong Ha was established. However, it was gradually restored between the 1950s and '70s by the Vice-Chancellor of Hong Kong University, Sir Lindsay Ride, and his wife Lady May.

Ruinas de São Paulo

Rua de São Paulo (2835 3444). **Open** 7am-6pm daily. **Admission** free. **Map** p263.
The first Western theological college established in the Far East, São Paulo trained missionary priests before they headed off to work in mainland China and Japan. Constructed between 1602 and 1638 of wood with a stone façade, most of the stone carving was completed by Japanese Christians fleeing persecution in their homeland in the 1630s. All but the façade burned down in 1835.

Santo António

Rua de Santo António (2857 3732). **Open** 7am-5.30pm daily. **Admission** free. **Map** p263.
Numerous fires over the years have necessitated repeated reconstruction of this structure. Much of the church you see here today was built after the 1930s.

São Domingos

Largo do Domingos (visitors hotline 2833 3000). **Open** 10am-6pm daily. **Admission** free. **Map** p263.
This enormous place of worship was built in 1587 by the Spanish Dominicans, which accounts for its distinctively Spanish look. Not long after the church was completed, though, Portuguese friars took over from the previous Spanish incumbents. Upstairs is a small museum of ecclesiastical items, some centuries old and made in Macau.

Sun Yat-sen Memorial House

Avenida Sidónio Pais (2857 4064). **Open** 10am-5pm Mon, Wed-Sun. **Admission** free. **Map** p263.
This monument to Sun Yat-sen was once home to his first wife. The house contains a collection of flags, photos and other relics.

Southern Macau

Compared with the historic centre, the southern end of the peninsula holds decidedly less of interest to the visitor, having been recently developed as primarily an office zone. However, the **Macau Tower** (*see p269*) is a must-see attraction, despite its ugly concrete monolithic appearance, as the views can be spectacular if you visit on a clear day.

There are a few attractions to the west of the tower worth visiting. If, from the tower, you walk past the **Friendship Monument** and keep going around the coast you'll come across the **Pousada de São Tiago** hotel (*see p274*), which is built into the hillside in the ruins of a 17th-century fort. Further around, on the westernmost tip of Macau, there is the **Maritime Museum** and, opposite, the **A-Ma Temple** (for both, *see p269*). A motorised junk moored next to the museum takes tourists on rides around the harbour on weekends and Mondays.

If you turn back you can head up to Barra Hill and towards Avenida da Praia Grande. Walking towards Central Macau you will pass a stunning colonial building on your left, which used to be the famous Bela Vista Hotel, but is now home to the Portuguese consul in Macau. Continuing along this road, you will also pass the pink-painted **Santa Sancha**, the Chief Executive's official residence.

A-Ma Temple

Rua de São Tiago da Barra (visitors hotline 2833 3000). **Open** 9am-5pm daily. **Admission** free. **Map** p263.

This temple is dedicated to A-Ma, who came to be known by the Portuguese as A-Ma Gau, and thus gave her name to the colony. Although the temple has several Ming shrines, they are probably 'recent' additions thought to date from the 17th century. **Photo** *p268*.

Macau Tower

Largo da Torre de Macau (2893 3339/www.macau tower.com.mo). **Open** 10am-9pm daily. **Admission** MOP$70; MOP$35 concessions. **Credit** AmEx, MC, V. **Map** p263.

As high as the Eiffel Tower but more than a century newer, Macau Tower is the city's latest tourist attraction. The concrete column isn't much to look at, but once you've taken the glass elevator to the 223m-high (731ft) observation deck, there are spectacular views over the Chinese border as far as 55km (34 miles) away – although pollution often reduces the range dramatically. The viewing platform has glass floor panels, so it's not for those who suffer from vertigo, although the revolving 360° Café and the 180° Lounge both offer more relaxed ways of taking in the view. Unfortunately, there's no guide explaining what you can see, but the view is impressive nonetheless.

For thrill seekers, adventure holiday specialist AJ Hackett (988 8656) offers a range of activities; if you've got enough nerve, you can climb up the 90m (27ft) metal mast on the very top of the observation deck. For those who prefer to keep their feet closer to sea level, the tower grounds feature a carousel, an amusement arcade, a motion simulator and several bars and restaurants overlooking the water. The complex also has shops and a cinema. **Photo** *p261*.

Maritime Museum

Largo do Pagoda da Barra (2859 5481/www.museu maritimo.gov.mo). **Open** 10am-5.30pm Mon, Wed-Sun. **Admission** MOP$10. **No credit cards**. **Map** p263.

The Maritime Museum is home to a number of ships, including a flower boat, a tugboat, a Chinese fishing vessel and a dragon boat (still used for racing). It also has artefacts relating to Macau's seafaring past, and some interesting dioramas and maps.

Taipa

The highlight of this island is the village of **Taipa** on what was, until the recent reclamation, the southern tip. The north's hotel and casino developments are making it a bit of a bedroom community for mainland Macau, while it is also home to the horse-racing track and the airport. You can reach Taipa by one of three bridges: the original Macau-Taipa Bridge, the Amizade (Friendship) Bridge and the Sai Van Bridge.

The view across to **Taipa**.

In Taipa Village there is the picturesque **Casa Museu da Taipa** (*see below*), with its small collection of period furnishings. The area around it is great for a walk and often has musicians or dancing at weekends. Although it's surrounded by high-rise housing blocks, life is calm and traditional amid the two-storey colonial buildings that line the village's narrow lanes and alleys. A small and somewhat shoddy gifts and crafts market is held in the square on Sundays.

Casa Museu da Taipa

Avenida da Praia, Carmo Zone (2882 7527). **Open** 10am-6pm Tue-Sun. **Admission** MOP$5; MOP$2 concessions. Free to all on Sun. **Map** p263.
One of five colonial buildings on Avenida da Praia, this museum combines European and Oriental design. The rooms are filled with furniture, paintings, art and artefacts that reflect Macau's dual heritage.

Cotai

Just a few years ago, little more than a causeway connected Colôane and Taipa. But massive reclamation projects have created a swathe of land – named after the first letters of the islands' names – that is quickly filling in the gap, and which is just as swiftly being built upon by Western and Asian developers keen to cash in on the gambling boom. A wave of spectacular casino resorts were in the works at press time – notably the colossal Venetian Macau, the heart of the so-called Cotai Strip – adding endless hotel rooms, shopping, restaurants and entertainment.

Colôane

Further away from Macau than Taipa, Colôane offers the perfect antidote to the relative hustle and bustle of central Macau. Connected to Taipa via a causeway (now marooned in the ever expanding reclaimed lands of Cotai), the less developed island offers few sights but more in the way of natural beauty, with some reasonable beaches and verdant scenery. The best beaches are **Cheoc Van** and **Hac Sa** (meaning 'black sand') on the southern side of the island. Both have lifeguards on duty (during the summer months), boards for hire and public swimming pools that stay open late. Hac Sa is also home to the renowned restaurant **Fernando's** (*see p271*), while Cheoc Van beach has a giant swimming pool and a restaurant/bar. If you want to take a walk on the green side, then head for **Seac Pai Van Park** (*see below*) on the western side of the island, where there are good hiking trails and an aviary, as well as a botanical garden.

The village of **Colôane**, which has been subjected to less development than that of Taipa, is centred around a small, tiled square, at the end of which is the **Chapel of St Francis Xavier** (*see below*).

Chapel of St Francis Xavier

Rua do Meio (visitors hotline 2833 3000). **Map** p263.
Dedicated to Asia's most famous missionary, the chapel contains some of his bones. It was built in 1928 in classic Portuguese style, and is decorated with Chinese artworks.

Seac Pai Van Park

Estrada de Seac Pai Van (2887 0277/www.macautourism.gov.mo). **Open** 8am-6pm daily. **Admission** free. **Map** p263.
This large expanse of greenery on the western side of the island has a walk-through aviary, hillside hiking trails, Chinese-style pavilions, a small botanical garden, a popular children's playground and a picnic area.

The beach at **Hac Sa**.

Where to eat

Macau is a food-lover's paradise. It was serving fusion food decades before East-meets-West cuisine became a global fad. Indigenous Chinese and traditional Portuguese influences were melded here to create the unique Macanese style, which also incorporates African, South American and South-east Asian spices – with delicious results. The real value of Macau can be found in its many restaurants: big servings of hearty food at prices far cheaper than in Hong Kong. In terms of drink, there's plentiful Portuguese wine at reasonable prices, and excellent coffee in the many cafés here, where egg tarts (*pasties de nata* in Portuguese) are a delectable local speciality that should not be missed. In Taipa Village there are dozens of shops selling home-made nougat and cake.

The variety of food available in Macau increases every year – you can now get everything from French and Italian to Indian, Japanese, Mexican and Vietnamese – and shows no sign of stopping. The recent opening of Fisherman's Wharf has introduced restaurants as varied as its globe-hopping architecture and the new casino resorts promise to increase the range of fine-dining options.

In addition to the following places, the restaurant at the **Pousada de São Tiago** (*see p274*) is also highly recommended.

A Lorcha

289 Rua do Almirante Sérgio (2831 3193). **Open** 12.30-3pm, 6.30-11.30pm Mon, Wed-Sun. **Main courses** MOP$40-$80. **Credit** AmEx, DC, MC, V. **Map** p263 ➊

Wooden beams and arches provide a European setting for one of the best dining experiences in town. A Lorcha offers great value for money, with giant helpings of traditional Portuguese and Macanese food. It's busy most nights – locals love the place – so it's advisable to make a reservation.

Café Virginia

173 Alameda Dr Carlos D'Assumpção, Rua Gang Fai (2871 5383). **Main courses** MOP$35-$70. **No credit cards. Map** p263 ➋

The comfy booths inside this sleek wood-and-glass café are miles away from the rustic charm of most Macau restaurants. Nonetheless, the chef specialises in old-fashioned Portuguese favourites, such as baked *bacalhau* (salted cod) with mashed potato and cream. It also offers a no-MSG guarantee.

Fernando's

Hac Sa Beach, Colôane (2888 2531). **Open** noon-9.30pm daily. **Main courses** MOP$70-$200. **No credit cards. Map** p263 ➌

This popular stop-off for day-trippers is so successful you may have to wait for a table. It's a low-key sort of place, and the red brick barn-style back room

near the beach is always packed with large groups. The curried crab, prawns, clams and African chicken are all irresistible – especially when washed down with a glass of sangria. Transport to Fernando's can be a problem due to its remoteness, but there is a minibus to the Hotel Lisboa, which works out far cheaper than the MOP$100 taxi ride.

La Comédie Chez Vous

1/F, 'G' Edifício, Avenida Xian Xing Hai (2875 2021). **Open** *Restaurant* noon-2.30pm, 7-10.30pm Mon-Sat. *Café & bar* 11am-midnight Mon-Sat. **Main courses** MOP$80-$150. **Credit** AmEx, MC, V. **Map** p263 ➍

La Comédie is in the shadow of the Cultural Centre and sits above its sister café, which serves crêpes, omelettes, sandwiches, coffee and a huge range of teas. Upstairs, the refined Parisian ambiance continues with elegant red and pink decor and a menu offering such classics as foie gras and duck breast. The set menus (from MOP$120) are great value.

Long Kei

7B Largo do Senado (2857 3970). **Open** 11.30am-3pm, 6-11.30pm daily. **Main courses** MOP$25-$40. **Credit** AmEx, DC, MC, V. **Map** p263 ➎

Macau has plenty of Macanese and Portuguese restaurants, but Chinese food, unsurprisingly, gets a look-in too. Long Kei has a huge menu (with upwards of 350 dishes), including favourites such as dim sum, along with specialities like double-boiled chicken.

O Manel

90 Rua Fernão Mendes Pinto, Taipa Village, Taipa (2882 7571). **Open** noon-3.30pm, 6.30-10.30pm daily. **Main courses** MOP$40-$80. **Credit** MC, V. **Map** p263 ➏

Taipa Village has more than a dozen good eateries but this is definitely one of the best. Typical hearty Portuguese fare is served up in no-nonsense style by chef/owner Manel. The fish dishes are the must-tries, in particular the delicious imported Norwegian cod (*bacalhau*). Go for the baked apple if you have room for dessert.

Restaurante Litoral

261A Rua do Almirante Sérgio (2896 7878). **Open** noon-3pm, 6-10.30pm daily. **Main courses** MOP$70-$100. **Credit** AmEx, MC, V. **Map** p263 ➐

Macanese food at its best. The Litoral has a classic restaurant setting, friendly service and magnificent food. Owner Manuela Ferreira brought her home recipes and set up this restaurant to the delight of all who tasted her cooking. Try the charcoal-black stewed duck with herbs or the African chicken.

Robuchon a Galera

3/F, Hotel Lisboa, 2-4 Avenida de Lisboa (2857 7666). **Open** noon-2.30pm, 6.30-10.30pm daily. **Main courses** from MOP$300. **Credit** AmEx, DC, MC, V. **Map** p263 ➑

Run by French super-chef Joël Robuchon, this is Macau's best and most expensive restaurant, boasting a menu and wine list to rival anything in Asia,

Trips Out of Town

all for lower prices than in Hong Kong (though it's still not cheap). The gaudy Lisboa Hotel makes a strange home for this restaurant, but nonetheless it's done with taste.

Nightlife

Macau's nightlife is a mixed bag. While thriving restaurants, casinos, strip clubs and 'massage' parlours are two-a-penny, finding a good bar or club is a bit more difficult. They have always tended to be scattered around Macau, making it difficult to move between them and even if you know the name of place they can be difficult to find. Things eased a few years ago when the waterfront area, known as the Nape reclamation, sprang up between the the Hotel Lisboa and the Mandarin Oriental (*see p274*), which is home to the **Vasco Bar & Lounge** (open 11am-1am), where a pianist and saxophonist play from 9pm onwards.

About 20 bars can now be found on or close to Avenida Dr Sun Yat-sen. To find it by taxi, just say 'Lan Kwai Fong' to the driver (the name is taken from Hong Kong's best-known entertainment district). There are bars here to suit most tastes, but the area hasn't taken off as much as some had hoped. Many drinking dens are empty even on weekend nights – apart from the odd mainland Chinese tour group dropping in – and considering the low level of the bands and karaoke entertainment on offer, this is not surprising. Nonetheless, there are a few good hangouts – you just need to check out a few places first to see which vibe suits you best. The downside is that drinks here are closer to Hong Kong prices (MOP$30-$40 for standard drinks). How the nightlife in the new casino complexes measures up remains to be seen.

The area around the Macau Tower has outdoor restaurants and cafés where you can enjoy a beer, while most coffee shops serve a good range of spirits at half the price of the waterfront bar area. Many of the larger hotels also house above-average bars and clubs.

In general in Macau, the lingering Portuguese influence means the bars and clubs don't usually begin filling up until the evening is already quite old. People are friendly and you can mingle easily if you want to, but there have been problems in the past for anyone who fails to heed a few simple rules. Macau is a gambling town and gang wars have long been fought here – it is often dubbed the 'Wild East'. Triads tend to leave tourists alone, but it's unwise to get into a needless argument with anyone, especially in the clubs after midnight.

Shopping

Shopaholics will find plenty to keep them occupied here. With prices significantly cheaper than Hong Kong, Macau's biggest draw is its antiques – both the real thing and good-quality reproductions – furniture and curio shops. Bargains can be found, but as with anywhere, you have to be careful that what you're buying is authentic and worth the money. Is that Ming dynasty vase real? To the inexpert eye it's hard to tell, so be cautious of sellers' claims.

As in Hong Kong, some traders distinguish between antiques and reproductions. Factories over the border in Zhuhai churn out replica tables, chairs, wardrobes and ottomans, while others strip down and restore furniture thrown out as worthless on the mainland for a hefty mark-up to tourists. Yet many of these restored items are beautiful additions to any home, in particular the dark woods, florid engraving and colourful tiled mosaics.

Haggle successfully and you may well end up with a bargain. You can sometimes cut the cost in half or more if you're buying several items from the same shop. Don't worry about carrying them home – most shops can arrange delivery anywhere in the world. As a final word of warning: if you come from a cold climate, make sure the wood has been treated properly to withstand the temperature differences and the drying effects of central heating.

Many of these shops are found on the **Rua de São Paulo**, the popular tourist walkway leading to the ruined church. Try **Wa Fat Trade Company** at No.11 for Ming dynasty-style furniture; **Mobilias e Antiquidades Lu Va** at No.23 for beautiful but expensive antiquities; **Iok Ngai** at No.31 for classical Chinese furniture, and **Mobilias Soi Cheong Hong** at No.38 for leather and wooden boxes. In between are heaps more shops selling furniture and curios such as bamboo birdcages, carved walking sticks and jewellery boxes.

Another popular buy in Macau is knitwear, since manufacturing woollen and cotton garments is a major local industry. Many recognisable labels (usually overruns, discontinued lines and seconds) can be picked up for a snip. Rummage around the clothing shops and stalls in **Largo do Senado** and the market on **Rua de São Domingos** and you may well find something to suit you.

Other items to look out for in Macau include competitively priced electrical goods and gold jewellery (which you'll find in many of the shops lining **Avenida Almeida Ribeiro**), and – for their novelty value – unusual Chinese herbs and medicine.

Not even a Vegas-style casino can out-kitsch the new **Fisherman's Wharf**. *See p265.*

For more modern and established shops, head for the **New Yaohan** shopping centre next to the ferry terminal, which has all the usual department-store offerings, or **Central Plaza** and the **Landmark**, which both brim with trendy shops such as Esprit and Episode. Also near the ferry terminal, the new commercial centre of **Fisherman's Wharf** has shops tucked into an Aladdin's Fort and other architectural oddities. Many of the Western-style casinos opening up promise an influx of glitzy brand-name boutiques. The **Wynn Macau** (*see p276*) is already home to upscale names such as Prada and Tiffany, while the **Grand Canal Shoppes**, at the Venetian Macau, looks set to be as flashy a mall as its Las Vegas forebear, gondoliers included.

Foodies will find **Taipa Village** a fascinating stop-off. The nougat and biscuit shops lining the main street sell different flavours of nutty sweets, including an excellent peanut brittle. The Sunday market here offers a much bigger selection of foods to try.

Arts & entertainment

Macau may be small but it punches above its weight in many areas, the arts included. Along with its many museums, there is also a thriving cultural scene. Occupying pride of place in the waterfront redevelopment is the **Centro Cultural de Macau** (*see p265*), which hosts plays, classical music and arts exhibitions, both home-produced and by visiting performers, artists and musicians. Many internationally renowned artists who visit Hong Kong will stop off in Macau for at least one night, so it's always worth checking to see what's on. The influx of Vegas-style casinos look set to increase pickings – in the Cotai Strip

alone, there are plans for half a dozen new venues, including an 1,800-seat theatre for Cirque du Soleil shows (from spring 2008) and a 15,000-seat arena.

Festivals & events

Any time of year is good for a visit to Macau, but there are some festivals and special events that could make your trip more memorable if you time it right. Here are a few of the best:

New Year's Eve is celebrated in Macau with an impressive fireworks display over Nam Van Lakes at midnight, while thousands of people throng the illuminated main square, Largo do Senado.

Chinese New Year takes place on the first day of the first moon of the Chinese New Year. Besides the traditional lion and dragon dances, Macau has an edge over Hong Kong in that firecrackers and fireworks are legal for anyone to set off.

In March/April the **Macau Arts Festival** features outstanding dance, theatre, Chinese opera and art. What the shows may sometimes lack in production quality they make up for in colour. For details, visit www.icm.gov.mo

Macau also has a **jazz festival** every May, with concerts in the Cultural Centre; for information, call 596014 or 2870 0699.

The **International Fireworks Display Contest** in September/October is billed as the largest fireworks competition in the world, with pyrotechnic experts from different countries trying to outblast each other over Nam Van Lakes. Also in October is the **International Music Festival**, which brings in orchestras, choirs and musicians from around the world. Shows are staged around town, in baroque churches and gardens, as well as the Cultural

Trips Out of Town

Centre's auditoria, the largest of which hosts a Chinese opera that closes the festival.

The city's most famous event is the **Formula 3 Grand Prix** (7962 2268, www.macau.grand prix.gov.mo) weekend, held in November.

Where to stay

Whether you want a cheap bed for the night or to indulge in luxurious surroundings, Macau has a hotel to match your budget. The maxim that you get what you pay for holds true, but many of the lower-end hotels are comfortable, clean and have all the necessary facilities.

Many hotels, including those listed below, can be booked through travel agencies at the ferry terminal either in Hong Kong or Macau. Up until now, it has sometimes been difficult to get a room – and always a problem around the time of the Formula 3 Grand Prix in November – but the swathe of casino-resorts and hotels jumping on the bandwagon (Four Seasons, Raffles, Hilton and Shangri-La are just some of the big chains allocated land near the Venetian Macau) will more than double the number of hotel rooms over the next couple of years. Nonetheless, booking in advance is always a good idea and often gets you a better price. For details of which new properties have opened, contact the Macau tourist office (*see p276*).

Many hotels run free shuttle buses to and from the ferry terminal, airport and major casinos.

Grandview

142 Estrada Governador Albano de Oliveira, Taipa (2883 7788/www.grandview-hotel.com). **Rates** MOP$980 single/double; MOP$2,180-$6,280 suite. **Credit** AmEx, DC, MC, V. **Map** p263 ❶
This is a good bet if you want a modern hotel with decent facilities for a budget price. Rooms are compact but comfortable and some have a view of the racecourse. There's 24-hour room service, an internet bar and both Western and Chinese restaurants (although eating out is a much better option).

Hotel Sintra

Avenida de Dom João IV (2871 0111/www.hotel sintra.com). **Rates** MOP$860-$1,260 single/double. **Credit** AmEx, DC, MC, V. **Map** p263 ❷
The Sintra is located in the heart of Macau, a short walk from many of the top tourist sights and casinos. It's moderately priced and although it was built in 1975 it looks almost new, thanks to a mid 1990s renovation. Rooms are large and some have partial harbour views, but the real reason for staying here is to be in the middle of all the fun.

Mandarin Oriental Resort & Spa

956-1110 Avenida da Amizade (2856 7888/www. mandarinoriental.com/macau). **Rates** MOP$1,500-$1,900 single/double. **Credit** AmEx, DC, MC, V. **Map** p263 ❸

Probably the best deal in town for those who want to be pampered, the Mandarin Oriental is a destination in its own right. Cheaper than its Hong Kong counterpart, it nonetheless offers impeccable service, luxurious Portuguese-style surroundings and a giant pool. The restaurants and bars here are all good, especially the Vasco Bar & Lounge (*see p272*), Mezzaluna restaurant and NAAM Thai restaurant.

Metropole

493-501 Avenida da Praia Grande (2838 8166). **Rates** MOP$530-$700 single/double. **Credit** AmEx, MC, V. **Map** p263 ❹
A well-located hotel in the heart of Macau, the Metropole offers affordable rooms with basic but decent facilities, including laundry, a passable restaurant and a shuttle bus services. The hotel's main draw, though, is its proximity to many of the city's key attractions.

Pousada de Colôane Beach Hotel

Praia de Cheoc Van, Colôane (2888 2144/www. hotelpcoloane.com.mo). **Rates** MOP$750 single/ double. **Credit** MC, V. **Map** p263 ❺
If you want to stay out of town without paying a fortune, then this quiet 22-room hotel near the beach in Colôane could be just the place. It's peaceful, remote and has a (small) pool. Despite a recent refurbishment, the rooms remain a little shabby in places and it's cold in winter, but staff are always very welcoming and the sea-view terrace makes up for any shortcomings.

Pousada de Mong-Ha

Colina de Mong-Ha (2851 5222/www.ift.edu.mo). **Rates** MOP$500-$800 single/double; MOP$1,000 suite. **Credit** AmEx, MC, V. **Map** p263 ❻
A great find for the budget-conscious traveller, this hotel is run by students from the adjacent Institute for Tourism Studies. Service is excellent, but the real charm of this hotel is its beautiful rooms, with carved wooden furniture, large beds and tasteful Portuguese decorations. Each has a balcony and a big private bathroom with decent showers. With its quiet courtyards and proximity to the 19th-century Mong-Ha fort and gardens, this is an ideal place for a romantic getaway – provided you don't mind going without a pool or a gym. The restaurant also offers a great Sunday lunch buffet for MOP$110.

Pousada de São Tiago

Fortaleza de São Tiago de Barra, Avenida da República (2837 8111/2739 1216/www.saotiago. com.mo). **Rates** MOP$1,620-$1,960 single/double. **Credit** AmEx, DC, MC, V. **Map** p263 ❼
Built within the ruins of a 17th-century fort, this hotel will seduce even the most world-weary traveller with its beauty and charm. It's the closest you'll get to a boutique hotel around here. Rooms are small but beautifully decorated – in addition to imported Portuguese furniture and tiles, some incorporate the curved walls of the hillside into their design. The pool is tiny, but the excellent terrace restaurant offers good food and a laid-back ambience.

Cash Macau

The vast majority of people who come to Macau come here to gamble. Of course, where most punters lose, Macau gains – casino tax payments account for nearly 70 per cent of the government's annual budget revenue. It's no surprise then that Chief Executive Edmund Ho has pronounced gambling the key to the enclave's future economic development, and that the city has licensed an unprecedented expansion of the industry by allowing Las Vegas tycoons Steve Wynn and Sheldon Adelson to build casinos here. Macau is well on its way to becoming China's very own Sin City.

Until just a few years ago Macau was the personal playground of business mogul Dr Stanley Ho, whose Sociedade de Tourismo e Diversões de Macau (STDM) operated all the local casinos under a government franchise. But the 'God of Gamblers' now has some stiff competition, although it's a challenge he's happy to take on as more and more gamblers are being attracted to the city: estimates suggest the ten million or so (mainly Chinese) visitors a year will double within a decade.

Wynn Resorts and Adelson's Sands (to be joined by other Western players such as the MGM Grand) have promised to transform the rough and often seedy gambling centre into a world-class gaming destination. The change has already begun, with the smaller casinos set up by the American invaders to make a quick entrance into the trade being followed by ever grander visions over the next few years. Not everyone thinks the Chinese are ready for such a cultural shift, however – though new, the casinos opened by Hong Kong-based Galaxy have kept the focus firmly on the gaming tables. Ho himself has already fired an early response, opening the Pharaoh's Palace casino, complete with faux Egyptian symbols, on reclaimed land in the Nape area. It's not pretty but it adds to the kitsch casino architecture and is a sign of things to come – not least the dramatic extension arching above the Hotel Lisboa.

GAMBLING

By 2008 there will be two dozen casinos in Macau, ranging from the glitzy to the downright dodgy. There's no entry fee, but foreigners must be over 18 (locals over 21). There's also no real dress code, but don't wear sandals or carry food, and be prepared for bag searches.

Apart from the usual casino fare of baccarat, blackjack and roulette, you can try your luck at the Chinese games of *fantan* (played with a silver cup and porcelain buttons) and *dai siu* (a three-dice game). No photos can be taken inside any of the casinos, and the bets are usually set at a minimum of MOP$50. If you do get lucky, you're not obliged to tip the croupiers, but be warned: they normally skim ten per cent of your winnings as a matter of course. And for those expecting all of the casinos to be filled with Vegas-like smiles and free drinks, think again: Macau's traditional casinos give you action, but they also give you smoky rooms and a lot of pushing and shoving.

If you plan on visiting just one Macau casino, it has to be the **Hotel Lisboa** (2-4 Avenida de Lisboa, (2857 7666, 2837 7666, www. hotelisboa.com). Looking like a Gaudí-inspired spinning top, Stanley Ho's landmark 24-hour entertainment centre constitutes the busiest, smokiest and most anarchic casino in town. As well as casino betting, wagers can be placed on sports such as English Premiership football. The two-floor complex is huge, with over 1,000 guest rooms, plus 18 restaurants, a nightclub and coffee shops. Free shuttle buses run from the Macau Ferry Pier.

HORSE RACING

Betting on the nags comes second to casinos in Macau and the enclave's racing has long been seen as a poor relation of its Hong Kong equivalent. But the **Macau Jockey Club** at the Taipa Hippodrome (2882 1188, www.mjc.mo) has improved its facilities in recent years and upgraded the standard of its horses and riders. Free shuttle buses run to the racecourse from the Hotel Lisboa on race days (several times a week; call for details). Entry MOP$20.

GREYHOUND RACING

Macau's greyhound racing club is one of the largest and best in the world, occupying the former Macau national football stadium, the Macau (Yat Yuen) Canidrome, on Avenida General Castelo Branco (2822 1199, 2833 3399, www.macauyydog.com). Facilities are first class, with grandstands, private boxes, a VIP lounge and coffee shop. With 14 races on each card, the odds are you'll pick at least one winner. Races are held from 8pm on Tuesdays, Thursdays, Saturdays and Sundays. Admission is MOP$10, but an extra MOP$3 will get you into the members' stand.

Wynn Macau.

Sands Hotel Macau

Casino Sands, Avenida da Amizade (2888 3388/ www.sands.com.mo). **Rates** phone for details. **Credit** AmEx, MC, V. **Map** p263 ❽
Opened in 2004, the gold-mirror-glazed Sands was the first Western-style casino operation in Macau. The 51 suites available here range up to 745 square metres (8,000 square feet), with every facility imaginable – but for now are for 'VIP guests' only. Although there were no regular rooms available in this 'hotel' at the time of updating this guide, guestrooms are scheduled to be built in late 2007 and the concept is already creating a buzz.

Westin Resort

1918 Estrada de Hac Sa, Colôane (2887 1111/www. westin.com/macau). **Rates** MOP$2,100-$2,450 single/ double. **Credit** AmEx, DC, MC, V. **Map** p263 ❾
If you want to wallow in the lap of luxury, this resort has it all. Among the facilities are an indoor and two outdoor swimming pools, tennis courts, a health club and an 18-hole golf course. Every room has a big (although not very private) balcony, and many of them overlook Hac Sa beach. It's far from the centre of town, but the emphasis is on relaxation and once you're here, you'll never want to leave.

Wynn Macau

Rua Cidade de Sintra, Nape (2888 9966/www.wynn macau.com). **Rates** MOP$1,800 single/double; MOP$4,000-$5,000 suite. **Credit** AmEx, MC, V. **Map** p263 ❿
With 600 rooms and suites, the new Wynn Macau – modelled closely on the Wynn Las Vegas – has significantly raised the bar among Macau's high-end luxury hotels. And its six gourmet restaurants are a

fine addition to Macau's already interesting dining scene. A notable feature is the enormous spa and health club contained within the complex. Further expansion is planned in the coming years.

Resources

Hospital

Hospital Centre São Januario, Estrada do Visconde de São Januario (2831 3731/www.ssm.gov.mo). **Open** 24hrs daily (emergency services available). **Credit** AmEx, DC, MC, V.

Internet

Central Library of Macau *89A-B Avenida Conselheiro Ferreira de Almeida (2856 7576/2855 8049).* **Open** 2-4pm daily.
Cyber Cafe Varandah *1/F, Landmark, Avenida Amizade (795 6181).* **Open** 10am-10pm daily.
UNESCO Centre of Macau *Alameda Dr Carlos d'Assumpção, Nape (2872 7058).* **Open** noon-8pm Mon, Wed-Sun.

Police station

Avenida de Rodrigo Rodrigues (2857 3333).

Post office

CTT de Macau, 789 Avenida de Praia Grande, Largo do Senado (2832 9490/2857 4491/www.macaupost. gov.mo). **Open** 10am-7pm Mon-Sat.

Tourist information

Macau Government Tourist Office, PO Box 3006, 9 Largo do Senado (2831 5566/2851 3355/www. macautourism.gov.mo). **Open** 9am-6pm.
The MGTO also has information counters at the following locations: Guia Fort & Lighthouse (2856

9808, 9am-5.30pm daily); Ferry Terminal (2872 6416, 9am-10pm daily); International Airport (2886 1436, 9am-10pm daily); and Ruínas de São Paulo (2835 8444, 9am-6pm daily). Alternatively, you can always try calling the Tourist Assistance Helpline (2834 0390, 9am-6pm daily).

If you want information before you leave Hong Kong, visit the MGTO at Chek Lap Kok Airport (+852 2769 7970, 2382 7110) or at 336 Shun Tak Centre, 200 Connaught Road Central, Sheung Wan, Hong Kong Island (+852 2857 2287, 2559 0147).

Other useful information

Language

The official languages are Mandarin, Cantonese and Portuguese, but English is widely understood in hotels and at tourist attractions, though not by taxi drivers.

Money

Macau's official currency is the **pataca** (usually symbolised by MOP$), which is divided into 100 **avos**. It is indexed to the Hong Kong dollar, with a conversion rate of MOP$1.03 to HK$1, but translates as dollar for dollar in everyday use in shops and bars. If you pay in Hong Kong dollars you will often receive your change in patacas; don't take many back to Hong Kong, as businesses often won't accept them.

Foreign currency and travellers' cheques can easily be changed in hotels, banks and at authorised money-changers, which are located throughout Macau. Alternatively, you can withdraw money from one of the city's many ATMs. Credit cards are accepted in many hotels, shops and restaurants.

Telephones

Local calls are free from private phones, but cost MOP$1 from public phones. You can buy phone cards to the value of MOP$50, $100 and $150. Credit card phones are found in busier areas.

To call abroad from Macau, dial 00 + country code + local number (omitting the 0 of the area code if necessary). When calling Hong Kong, dial 01+ the eight-digit number. International calls from Macau are very expensive.

Dial 181 for directory enquiries in Macau; 101 for overseas enquiries. Macau's international code is 853.

Visas

All visitors must have a valid passport (except Hong Kong Permanent Identity Card holders). Citizens of the US, UK, Canada, Australia, South Africa, New Zealand and most European countries do not require a visa for a stay of 20 days or less. Visas are issued for 20 days on arrival, and cost MOP$100 for an individual (MOP$50 for under 12s); MOP$200 for a family visa that is valid for under 12s; and MOP$50 per member of groups of ten or more.

Getting around

However you arrive in Macau, you will probably either hop on to a hotel shuttle bus, bus or taxi to your final destination. Buses cover virtually

every corner of the city, are frequent and fares are low: there is a flat fare of MOP$2.50 on the Macau peninsula, rising to MOP$4-$5 to Colôane. Taxis are metered and are also inexpensive (minimum MOP$11). There are two kinds of taxis: the black with cream roof ones and the yellow ones. There is also a radio-taxi service (2893 9939, 2851 9519).

Alternatively, once you are in the centre of town, most places are within walking distance of one another. And if you do get tired, there are always two-seater pedi-cabs for hire, which cost around MOP$25 for a short trip, or MOP$100 for an hour if you want one to give you a guided tour of the sights – just make sure you negotiate the fare before you get on board.

Once you get out on to the islands of Taipa and Colôane, you might want to consider hiring bicycles, which cost about MOP$40 an hour, from near the Municipal Council Building in Taipa.

Getting there

By air

Most of the flights into Macau's airport on Taipa island are from China, Taiwan, Singapore and Korea. On arrival, there are free shuttle buses from the airport to all the leading hotels, as well as buses (MOP$3.30) travelling downtown to the ferry terminal and the border crossing. In addition, there are plenty of taxis.

There are at least 20 helicopter flights per day from Hong Kong, which land at Macau's international airport; the flight time is 16 minutes. The cost of a one-way flight is MOP$1,205 on weekdays, MOP$1,309 on weekends/holidays. For more information, visit www.helihongkong.com or phone +852 2108 9898.

By sea

A number of ferries operate more than 100 sailings daily between Hong Kong and Macau, with jetfoils operating round-the-clock services. The jetfoil also provides the quickest seaborne method of making the 60km (38-mile) journey, taking just 55 minutes. There are two ferry terminals in Hong Kong serving Macau: the Hong Kong China Ferry Terminal in Tsim Sha Tsui and the larger Hong Kong–Macau Ferry Terminal on the waterfront (opposite the Shun Tak Centre) in Sheung Wan on Hong Kong Island.

New World First Ferry (+852 2131 8181, www.nwff. com.hk) operates catamarans from the China Ferry Terminal to Macau; fares start at HK$137 during the week. Weekends and holidays (HK$152-$161) are busy, so book in advance through a travel agent or online. TurboJET (+852 3602 0220, www.turbojet.com.hk) offers similar deals from the Macau Ferry Terminal, and a pricier service (HK$180 and up, www.turbojetsea express.com.hk) from Hong Kong International Airport.

On arrival in Macau, there are free shuttle buses from the ferry terminal to all the leading hotels, otherwise check with the Tourist Information desk in the terminal for public transport facilities to your destination. If in doubt, take a taxi.

Guangzhou

Big and brash, this is the face of China's steamroller economy.

Pity poor Guangzhou – in fact, many travellers insist it is a low point to be avoided at all costs. Unfortunately, much of this reputation is well deserved, thanks to the fact that the global economy has externalised most of its unpleasant aspects of manufacturing to this corner of the globe. Becoming the 'workshop of the world' is having unpleasant side effects; SARS and 'bird flu' both resulted from the Dickensian living conditions that accompany the sweat shops that fuel economic development, and many visitors who stay for more than a few days come away with at least a 'Canton cold' as a souvenir. Even so, in the days of growing environmental awareness, visionaries such as cinematographer Ron Fricke (*Koyaanisqatsi*, *Baraka*) and photographer Ed Burtynsky (who has a series of works documenting the rapidly changing China, from recycling mountains to old industrial works) have shown that the adverse effects of rapid growth can be just as fascinating as ancient temples and dusty museums. While Guangzhou does have conventional tourist sights such as these, they generally are not of the standard found in other major destinations. Instead, take the time to venture away from

the main drag and you'll be rewarded with insights into a completely different way of life and standard of living.

EARLY HISTORY

Guangzhou (formerly Canton) was a thriving trading port as far back as the second century AD, when Indian and Roman merchants regularly visited. Officially it was part of the Celestial Empire, but because few of the inhabitants were Han Chinese (northerners who traditionally ruled over all the other ethnic minorities), it was difficult for Beijing to retain control, and rebellions and subsequent massacres were commonplace. Guangdong province was largely Chinese in name only and revolts by minority groups continued until the 12th century.

In an attempt to counter the rebellious nature of the region, large numbers of Han Chinese were relocated to the fertile Pearl River Delta, along with strong military support from the imperial armies, who mercilessly attempted to wipe out the indigenous Yi and Miao minorities. Eventually, so many Han migrated south to Guangdong, lack of space meant that many were forced to move again, inland this time to provinces such as Guangxi, Guizhou and Sichuan. These days the original minorities have all but disappeared, and the only reminder of them is the Cantonese language.

In the 1500s the Portuguese arrived but were haughtily rebuffed by the Chinese, so they eventually settled downriver in Macau. It wasn't until the late 17th century that the British came along, in an attempt to open up the city to trade. They made a few inroads but the mandarins refused to grant what they considered lowly barbarians diplomatic recognition and restricted the British to dealing with Chinese merchants (rather than civilians). The imbalance in trade – the Chinese offered silk, porcelain and tea but wanted only silver in return – led the British to start flogging opium, resulting, predictably, in a vast increase in

▶ Green numbers '❶' given in this chapter correspond to the location of each hotel as marked on the street map on pp280-281. Likewise, purple numbers '❶' indicate restaurants and pink numbers '❶' bars.

addiction. The government's belated attempts to crack down on this socially and economically devastating trade triggered the invasions and one-sided battles of the mid 19th century known as the Opium Wars (*see pp15-18*).

Guangzhou was also a hub for later political developments: Sun Yat-sen, leader of the Nationalist Party and one of the principals in the 1911 overthrow of the imperial government, was born nearby, and the city was briefly capital of the nascent Republic of China under his auspices.

CONTEMPORARY GUANGZHOU

But why the bad press today? It's easy to forget that tourism in China, both domestic and international, is a recent phenomenon. Indeed, it was only 50 years ago that the country was in the throes of a social revolution that left millions of Chinese dead. Until recently recreational travel was strictly controlled. Government-approved sightseeing was designed to show off the might of China rather than to make a profit or to indulge customer satisfaction. For many years Guangzhou's highlights included such communist relics as the Peasant Movement Institute, the Memorial to the Revolutionary Martyrs and the Huangpu Military Academy – suitably patriotic, but not exactly major crowd-pullers.

But things have changed. Ever since China began opening its doors to the rest of the world, Guangzhou has been trying to become a powerhouse of trade and commerce. These days it is growing in importance, and though it hasn't yet arrived, it's definitely on the way. Half-demolished and half-built, the city has one foot in the past and one in the future. Glistening glass office towers back on to truck stops that double as markets on waste grounds that only yesterday were shantytowns.

Economically, recent years have been tough on the city. After the 1997 Handover of Hong Kong, the former colony's economy plummeted and Guangzhou, only 120 or so kilometres (75 miles) upriver, faithfully hung on to its coat-tails into the slide. Only a decade ago Guangzhou was the number-one choice for Western multinationals wanting to get a foothold in the huge Chinese economy. Hong Kongers and Taiwanese were so active in the area that a number of infamous 'second wife villages' sprang up to cater to the 'needs' of businessmen who spent a lot of time in the city. The glory days of these areas are now long gone. The City of Five Rams is no longer the first choice of entry into the middle kingdom for global corporations, and this can easily be seen in the recent exodus of Hong Kongers, Taiwanese and other expats, many of whom have relocated to Shanghai. Even around notorious Taojin Lu ('Gold-digging Road'), where there were once five major discos and nightclubs, only one remains, and even this is a shadow of its former raucous self.

The Westerners have been quickly replaced and in some areas even eclipsed by a massive wave of entrepreneurs from the Middle East, Africa, Russia and the Indian subcontinent. This has quickly been reflected in the number of restaurants catering to these new foreigners. While the likes of the Hard Rock Café closed down many moons ago, there are now growing numbers of Indian eateries, plush Arab restaurants and exotic establishments from the various ex-Soviet 'stans.

Nonetheless, for a tourist wishing to experience the 'real' China, Guangzhou has an undeniable appeal, provided you bear certain things in mind. The road system is chaotic. The city is dirty. The pollution can be all but incapacitating – on bad days carbon monoxide hangs off the flyovers like an untucked bed sheet. The noise of construction sites, car horns, squealing brakes on buses, haggling street vendors and people shouting into mobile phones goes on and on… and, like this list, never stops.

Guangzhou also has something intangible that Hong Kong has lost. For a start, the locals have none of the (post-) colonial 'chippiness' of Hong Kongers. If they do have a chip on their shoulder about something, it's that they have had to struggle through a socialist-planned economy while their Hong Kong cousins have been free to take the capitalist road. Which is why they're now doing everything they can to catch up.

Sightseeing

The two natural landmarks of Guangzhou are the **Zhu Jiang** (Pearl River), which cuts through the city from west to east, and **Bai Yun Shan** (White Cloud Mountain; *see p286*), which dominates the city from the north. Its major streets are Huan Shi Lu, Zhong Shan Lu and Dongfeng Lu, all of which run east–west through the city. The area south of the river, Henan, offers little for tourists.

The city's traditional heart is in the western **Xiguan** and **Liwan** districts. These provide a glimpse of old Guangzhou, with hundreds of narrow streets and twisting alleys, though many of these are in the process of being demolished under the pressures of development (largely for development's – and profit's – sake).

The districts continue to be a magnet for Western tourists, who are drawn in particular to the notorious and atmospheric **Qing Ping Market**, just north of Liu'Ersan Lu, between

Guangzhou

Ⓨ Subway station
— Subway line

❶ Hotels pp289-290
❶ Restaurants pp286-288
❶ Bars pp288-289

Guangzhou Provincial
Bus Station

RENMIN BEILU

XILU

ZHAN QIANLU

Trade Fair
Hall

HUAN SHI

LIUHUA

DONGFENG

LIUHUA LU

Liuhua Lake Park

XIWAN LU

LIUHUA LU

XILU

NAN'AN GONGLU

LIWAN LU

Guang Xiao Si
(Bright Filial
Piety Temple)

BEILU

RENMIN ZHONGLU

GUANGFU

Ximenkou

Chenjiaci Ⓨ

Chenjia Si
(Chen Clan
Temple)

ZHONG SHAN QILU

ZHONG SH

PEARL RIVER
BRIDGE

ZHONG SHAN BALU

HUAGUI LU

LONGJIN
ZHONGLU

LONGJIN DONGLU

HUIFU XILU

RENMIN ZHONGLU

GUANGFU

Liwan
Lake

XILU

PENGYUAN LU

Liwan
Lake Park

❶

LONGJIN

Changshoulu Ⓨ

BAOHUA LU

Dai He Lu
Antiques Market

CHANGSHOU
DONGLU

Glasses
Market

HUANGSHA

DUOBAO

CHANGSHOU XILU

LU

Hualin Si
(Hualin Temple)

Jade
Market

Liwan Plaza

SHANG XIA JIU

DADE LU

ENNING LU

DISHIPU

ZHUJI LU

SHISANHANG LU

ZHUANG
YUAN
FONG

RENMIN NANLU

Zhu Jiang (Pearl River)

LIWAN

DATONG LU

DADAO

Huangsha

Qing Ping
Market

LIU'ERSAN LU

YID

SHIWEITANG

Shiweitang
Station

PEARL RIVER TUNNEL

Former
US Consulate

Guangzhou
Youth Hostel

SHAMIAN BEIJIE

❻

Shamian
Island

Monument to the
Martyrs in the
Shaji Massacre

NANHUA XILU

Haichua
Park

RENMIN BRIDGE

White Swan
Hotel

HONGDE LU

XILU

FANCUN DADAO

BAITER TAN BAR ST

FANGCUN

Fangcun Ⓨ

TONGFU

SHANCUN LU

To Huadiwan Market ↘

D

Guangzhou West Railway Station

To Bai Yun Shan (White Cloud Mountain) & Baiyun International Airport

E

F

Luhu Lake

LUHU LU

HENGFU LU

0   1 km

© Copyright Time Out Group 2007

0   0.5 mile

Guangzhou Art Museum

HENGFU LU

TAOJIN LU

6

1

Orchid Garden

HUAN SHI ZHONGLU

Yuexiu Gongyuan

Yuexiu Park

BEILU

TONGXIN LU

HENGFU LU

Mausoleum of the 72 Martyrs

LU

JIEFANG

Zhen Hai Tower (Guangzhou Municipal Museum)

BEILU

YUEXI

9

British Consulate

HUAN SHI DONGLU

Friendship Department Store

1

Hua Qiao Xing Cun Overseas Chinese Residential Quarter

Holiday Inn

3

2

2

omb of the nyue King

QIX

XIANLI

NANLU

3
8

Jiniantang

BEILU

JIEFANG

Sun Yat-sen Memorial Hall

LIANXIN LU

DONGFENG ZHONGLU

BEILU

DONGFENG

Lie Xi Ling Yuan (Memorial Garden to the Martyrs)

XIANLI DONGLU

To Tian He

ZHIXIN NANLU

Liu Rong Si Temple of the Six Banyans

JIEFANG

BEILU

LILU

Xin Da Xin Department Store

Nongjiangsuo

City Library

Peasant Movement Museum

ZHONG SHAN SILU

BEILU

YUEXIU ZHONGLU

ZHONG SHAN SANLU

Lieshi Lingyuan

10

China Plaza

ZHONG SHAN ERLU

Dongshankou

Dongshankou

3

Wu Xian an (Temple of the Five mortals)

ZHONG SHAN WULU

Gongyuanchuan

JIEFANG ZHONGLU

GUANGZHOU

Giordano

XIHU LU

Guang Bai Department Store

Tai Bai

Da Fo Si (Big Buddha Temple)

SILU

WENDE NANLU

WENMING LU

YUEXIU ZHONGLU

DONGHUA XILU

2

DONGHUA

DONGLU

5

XINHEPU LU

QIYI

DANAN LU

BEIJING LU

WANFU LU

YUEXIU NANLU

HEQUN YI MA LU

5

Dong Lake

Shishi Jiaotang (Sacred Heart Church)

JIEFANG NANLU

Haizhu Guangchang

TAIKANG LU

DIAGANG LU

Guangzhou Harbour Passenger Terminal

CHEBIAN LU

Dongshan Lake Park

4

HAIZHU SQUARE

4

YANJIANG ZHONGLU

DONGHU LU

HONGLU

1

Haizhu Wholesale Market

7

XILU

HAIZHU BRIDGE

JIEFANG

YANJIANG XILU

BINJIANG LU

Hai Yin Fabric Market

JIANGWAN BRIDGE

DASHATOU LU

HAIYIN BRIDGE

To Xing Hai Concert Hall & Guangdong Museum of Art

ER SHA DAO

BINJIANG XILU

NANHUA DONGLU

XIUE

JIU DAO

Zhu Jiang (Pearl River)

NANHUA ZHONGLU

JIANGNAN DADAO

SUSHE ZHILIE

BINJIANG DONGLU

TONGFU

TONGFU DONGLU

Shiergong

JIU DAO

QIANJIN LU

WANSHOU BEIJIE

HENAN

Jiangnanxi

D

E

F

Datong Lu and Zhuji Lu. This is China's most infamous live-animal market, and although it has been greatly sanitised in recent years, with many of the characteristic outdoor stalls moved into modern multi-storey housings, there is still plenty to see. Many masochistic tourists come to gawp at the tragic-looking dogs and cats in cramped cages. Much easier on the eye are the spice and dried-medicine stalls. Vendors sell scorpions by the bowl and snakes are everywhere. Souvenirs here are comparatively overpriced, and stall owners tend to be a bit grabby and overbearing (you may want to give an especially wide berth to the pushy antiques dealers).

Just across a number of small footbridges is **Shamian Island**, the former British concession area, which is home to the old British and American consulates (they have both since relocated). As recently as the 19th century the movements of foreign merchants were restricted to the small island; the bridges were closed at 10pm and traders lived under the threat of execution if they even began to study the Chinese language. This is also where the buildings of the great colonial trading houses such as Jardine Matheson and Butterfield & Swire are located. To the east is the old French concession. Historic sites worth a look in this area are the old French Consulate, Shamian Park (formerly the French Consul's Garden), Our Lady of Lourdes Catholic Church and the former French missionary residence.

Back across the river, going north, head up Datong Lu, then eastwards along Dishipu and Shang Xia Jiu (*see below*). Look for a large English sign on Changshou Xilu, just to the east of Liwan Plaza, to find the famed **Jade Market**. Real bargain-hunting is best left to the experts, but assorted knick-knacks can be picked up for a few renminbi. Inside, keep an eye out for the almost hidden **Hualin Temple** (Hualin Si; *see p285*).

Just north of here, look for **Dai He Lu**. It's often touted as an antiques market, but genuine antiques hunters might be a little disappointed that most of the so-called 'antiques' are mass produced in local factories. Everything from strings of old coins to huge pieces of Qing Dynasty furniture is on offer, though hardly any of it is genuine. Even so, there are still plenty of souvenir shopping opportunities, with ceramic bracelets and amber trinkets cheaper than anywhere else in China.

The area around **Shang Xia Jiu** is another part of the city that has been massively renovated. This is the old centre of town and is popular with tourists as it is within easy walking distance of Shamian Island (*see above*). Again, wholesale markets dot the surrounding area, including an aquarium market and the

haberdashers' street (Guang Fu Zhonglu). The largely pedestrianised **Shang Jiu Lu** is a great place to hang out and people-watch. The glasses market close by at 260 Renmin Nanlu is a wholesale market for spectacles. If you happen to have your prescription with you, this is the place to choose a new pair of frames and lenses for a fraction of the price back home.

Just south of here is a little alley known as **Zhuang Yuan Fong**. At one time this was home to many shops specialising in props and costumes for traditional Chinese Opera. These days, sadly, virtually all of them are gone, and the area has been transformed into the town's most fashionable (and most crowded) shopping street for teenagers.

East of Shamian Island, off Yanjiang Xilu (running alongside the Pearl River), **Haizhu Square** is where many visitors begin to understand what a truly enormous range of products are made in the Pearl River Delta. If it has a 'made in China' label on it, then it probably came from this region. Proof of this can be found near the square at the **Haizhu Wholesale Market**. Back in the 1900s this was a fruit and vegetable market, well outside the city limits, but is now where many factories that produce household goods have their wholesale outlets. There are hundreds of small stalls stocking everything from novelty lighters to full suits of armour, with plenty of items made using traditional silk, and beautiful 'paper cuts' (rice paper painted with brightly coloured inks, a craft that dates back nearly two centuries). The market is north-west of **Haizhu Bridge**, and sprawls east along Yide Zhonglu. The giant statue of the PLA soldier nearby was erected in October 1959 in commemoration of the tenth anniversary of the Guangzhou Liberation (when the communists under Mao successfully drove Chiang Kai-Shek out of the city and founded the People's Republic).

A few blocks east of Haizhu Square, **Beijing Lu** is the Oxford Street of Guangzhou. It was pedestrianised a few years ago, and is a great place to see what 21st-century China is all about. Here capitalism reigns supreme in a country that still refers to itself as communist. As always in China, bargain hunters should avoid the department stores, of which the two largest are Xin Da Xin (4 Zhong Shan Silu, 8332 2811) and Guang Bai (295 Beijing Lu, 832 2348), and aim for the smaller outlets. Admittedly, some of the bigger names do have bargains – the second and third floors of **Giordano** (305 Beijing Lu, 833 3208) are a good place to start – but it's in the one-man shows where the real surprises lie. **Tai Bai** (284 Beijing Lu, no phone) is a good choice for belts, bags and boots, as well as just about anything

Haizhu Bridge. See p282.

else fashioned out of fake leather. There is an excellent selection of clothes, jewellery, cosmetics and accessories to be found here as well, all at very reasonable prices.

For more Western-style shopping, try the **Friendship Department Store** (369 Huan Shi Donglu, 8333 6628), a couple of kilometres to the north-east. At one time these flagship department stores were the only places that sold imported goods. These days, so many items are made locally for export that Friendship outlets have become dinosaurs. They not only have the highest prices in town, but also seemingly the most staff, only a few of whom have any real concept of customer service, and most of whom just wander around aimlessly. If you really want to buy designer label items, save your money for Hong Kong.

Shoppers in the know generally prefer **China Plaza** (33 Zhong Shan Sanlu, 8373 9099, www.china-plaza.com). Right on top of the Lie Xi Ling Yuan subway station, it's the very latest of Guangzhou's mega malls and certainly the trendiest at the moment. Wander the eight floors to get a feel for modern Chinese commerce, and head to the basement for a mass of fashion boutiques, nail salons and fast food. For those wanting to see what China is going to look like in the decades to come, this is definitely the place to look.

South-east of here, near Hai Yin Bridge, the fanciful **Hai Yin Fabric Market** is a treasure trove of fantastic fabrics and a vivid respite from the drab browns and greys found in most of the city. Whether you are looking for

a custom-made *qipao* (traditional Chinese dress) or simply a new pair of curtains, this place has everything on its four levels. For the highest-quality Hangzhou and Shanghai silk, begin on the ground floor at A71, where even the most exquisite dragon and phoenix designs start at just RMB70 a metre. For more choice, head up to B22 and B107, but be prepared for more of a hard sell as these two stalls are more used to dealing with foreign customers. Try B82 for tailoring, and take a look at the multicoloured yarns in B97. The fourth floor is mainly gents' suits tailors, though if you're after a man's suit, Lowu Commercial City in Shenzhen is probably a better bet as staff there are much more familiar with the needs of foreigners.

South of the river in Fangcun District is **Huadiwan Market** (Huadiwan subway station). From the subway entrance this looks like just another furniture market, but venture further inside and some pleasant surprises await. Huadiwan consists of literally acres of furniture, plants, tropical fish and other assorted pets. Songbirds of every colour and description fill the bird market, and repro antique stores fill the spaces in between. Best of all is the bonsai section (the miniature trees are termed *penjing* in China, where they were first developed) and the mysterious 'viewing stones' (rocks with odd, naturally occurring shapes such as dragons).

For concerts and culture, head east to **Er Sha Dao** (Er Sha Island), a grassy island in the Pearl River that is home to the **Xing Hai Concert Hall** (33 Qing Bo Lu, 8735 222/312), where international classical stars often appear,

Trips Out of Town

Walk back in time

Right on the Pearl River is a corner of China seemingly little-touched by the passage of time: the former foreign settlement of **Shamian Island**. Sometimes rendered Shameen, which means 'sand face', this lovely, unlikely island in the heart of Guangzhou, formerly an undeveloped sandbank on the Pearl River, became a concession area following the Second Opium War (1857-60; see p17). Shamian was divided into British and French sections; each nationality had their own postal service and their own church.

Between the 1860s and the 1930s, Shamian evolved into one of the most attractive, well-ordered corners of an often chaotic city. As a foreign concession, residence on Shamian was restricted to foreigners and their servants, and smartly uniformed Sikh police guarded the '**English Bridge**' across the creek from the city.

Like other concession and treaty port areas elsewhere in China, Shamian was returned to Chinese administration by treaty agreement in 1943. After the Japanese occupation forces were ejected from the city in 1945, the island came under the control of the Guangzhou municipality.

Hong Kong film-makers often use Shamian as a set for scenes depicting 'old Hong Kong';

most corners of the island resemble what much of Hong Kong Island's urban areas looked like before the construction frenzy started in the 1950s. The **White Swan Hotel** (see p290), built on the waterfront in the early 1980s by Hong Kong investors, remains almost the only modern building.

For a while it seemed that the rest of old Shamian was doomed to slow decay and eventual demolition. Not before time, the entire island was gazetted as a national historic site in 1996, and restoration work on old buildings is periodically undertaken; many are in urgent need of structural repairs.

Shamian gets almost no vehicular traffic, which makes for a quiet, pleasant refuge from the rest of bustling, car-choked Guangzhou. On hot, humid summer evenings the air is heavy with the rich smell of camphor exuded by dozens of mature camphor trees.

SHAMIAN ISLAND TO THE BUND

Most of Shamian's old buildings bear plaques that indicate their use or ownership in the past. Some companies represented on Shamian, such as Hong Kong conglomerate Jardine, Matheson and Co, or Butterfield and Swire (now part of the Swire Group), are still household names in Hong Kong and elsewhere, while others have long-since

and the **Guangdong Museum of Art** (see p285), which now surpasses the **Guangzhou Art Museum** (see p285) in Luhu Park, a couple of kilometres to the north.

Tour groups still visit a selection of the city's temples, even though the examples remaining after the chaos of the Cultural Revolution are rather squalid compared with other Asian cities. The most famous include the **Temple of the Five Immortals** (Wu Xian Guan; see p286), the **Temple of the Six Banyans** (Liu Rong Si; see p286), the snappily named **Bright Filial Piety Temple** (Guang Xiao Si; see below) and the **Chen Clan Temple** (Chenjia Si; see p285).

Be warned, though: something depressing you may well encounter is the handicapped and disfigured beggars who surround almost every temple. Some of them are delivered to the temples every day by local entrepreneurs for whom they act as professional employees, taking advantage of sympathetic tourists.

If you're craving some decent greenery, head for **Yuexiu Park** (see p286), alongside Jiefang Beilu two kilometres (1.5 miles) north

of the river. The park is home to the city's emblematic **Sculpture of the Five Rams** and the dull **Guangzhou Municipal Museum**. A far more engaging place is the **Tomb of the Nanyue King** (see p286), across Jiefang Beilu from the park. This is the burial place of Zhao Mo, the second ruler of the Nanyue Kingdom.

Bright Filial Piety Temple (Guang Xiao Si)

109 Guangxiao Lu (8108 1961). **Open** 8am-5pm daily. **Admission** RMB4. **No credit cards**. **Map** p280 C3.

Founded in 397 BC, Guang Xiao Si is reputed to have been the first Buddhist temple in China; it's certainly the most unkempt temple in the country. Locals come here for good luck rather than to receive any kind of spiritual blessing. Discarded incense is everywhere, and the resident monks seem to spend most of their time trying to sell associated paraphernalia. The most interesting thing on the site is the row of small headless stone lions behind the main temple, all decapitated by Red Guards during the Cultural Revolution.

vanished into history. There are a number of bilingual maps scattered around Shamian; these make it difficult to get lost.

From the White Swan Hotel, it's an easy walk across the island and then along the Canton Bund, as the tree-lined waterfront between Shamian and the Haizhu Bridge, built in 1932, was known. A good place to start your explorations is the Anglican **Christ Church**, visible not far from the White Swan Hotel on the island's south-west corner. The church was built in 1863 and services are still held there today.

Walk one street back from the river to reach **Shamian Dajie**, Shamian's central thoroughfare. Head eastwards and you will soon see the attractive, tree-shaded old **Canton Club** premises. Not far from the Canton Club, the **Victory Hotel**, just across the English Bridge, originally opened its doors as the Victoria Hotel; at one time this was the only first-class European-style hotel in the city.

The eastern third of the island was the French cantonment, where you'll see the **French Church**; like Christ Church, it can be visited on Sundays when services are held. At the eastern end of Shamian you should see the prominent red-brick former **Chinese Maritime Customs** quarters; playwright Mary Hayley-Bell lived there in the 1920s when her father was Commissioner of Customs.

Cross the bridge over the creek to the main city, keep walking and you can see (but unfortunately not go inside) the **Customs House** building with its squat clock tower. A number of other commercial buildings from the 1920s and 1930s remain prominent landmarks. The impressive old **Post Office** along here has been opened as a museum.

Further east, the old Canton Bund stretches along the north bank of the Pearl River. Halfway along the Bund, the **Ai Qun Hotel** was the tallest building in the city when it opened in 1937. Canton's answer to Shanghai's famous Peace Hotel (formerly the Cathay) on the Bund, the Ai Qun is sadly rather dilapidated, but its art deco exterior remains a rare glimpse of earlier, more stylish times.

Keep walking along the waterfront promenade and you will end up at the Haizhu Bridge; there are plenty of open-air places along the way to stop and enjoy a drink.

HOW TO GET THERE

Catch the underground to Huangsha station, then walk across the bridge on to Shamian Island (the route is well signposted). Otherwise, take a taxi to the White Swan Hotel and then explore from there.

Chen Clan Temple (Chenjia Si)

34 Yin Long Li, off Zhong Shan Qilu (8181 9653). **Open** 9.30am-5pm daily. **Admission** RMB10. **No credit cards**. **Map** p280 B3.
Built in the late Qing Dynasty (1894) by the hugely powerful Chen family, this temple is also known as the Chen Classical Learning Academy because it served as both an altar for ancestor-worship and a school to prepare students for the national civil service examination. Decorations include numerous frescoes, carved stone pillars, brick mosaics and clay sculptures on the ridges of the roofs.

Guangdong Museum of Art

38 Yan Yu Lu, Er Sha Island (8735 1468). **Open** 9am-5pm Tue-Sun. **Admission** RMB15. **No credit cards**. **Map** off p281 F4.
This museum opened in 1997 and specialises in contemporary Chinese art (much of it abstract), and also has an interesting schedule of visiting national and overseas exhibitions.

Guangzhou Art Museum

13 Luhu Lu (8350 7904). **Open** 9am-5pm daily. **Admission** RMB30. **No credit cards**. **Map** p281 E1.

Opened in September 2000, this museum combines modern architecture with traditional Chinese design elements. There are nine galleries, various temporary exhibition halls, and a traditional Guangdong garden. The sheer number of fish in the garden pools is astounding and the feeding frenzy that ensues as they all push at once for tossed breadcrumbs is astonishing. There are also dedicated galleries for each of four famed artists from the Cantonese school of painting called Ling-Nan that emerged in the late 1800s. Expect to see exquisite scrolls complete with pastoral scenes, plum blossoms and bold calligraphy. One gallery is filled with impressive and rare Tibetan *tangkas* (religious paintings), which were donated by a Hong Kong art collector. **Photo** *p288*.

Hualin Temple (Hualin Si)

Hualin Xin Jie, off Changshou Xilu (no phone). **Open** 8am-5pm daily. **Admission** free. **Map** p280 B4.
Founded in AD 526, this temple was rebuilt after the chaos of the Cultural Revolution, and reopened again in 1988. It appears modest from the exterior, but inside you'll find an impressive collection of life-sized golden *arhats* (Buddhist saints).

Trips Out of Town

Temple of the Five Immortals (Wu Xian Guan)

Huifu Xilu (8333 6853). **Open** 9am-noon, 1.30pm-5pm daily. **Admission** RMB5. **No credit cards**. **Map** p281 D3.

This temple was originally built in 1377 during the Ming Dynasty in honour of the five immortals believed to be responsible for the quality of harvests. The temple has recently had a complete and rather unfortunate facelift – the central statue now looks suspiciously like moulded cement, although one of the many confusing description plaques dates it to 1113, during the Northern Song Dynasty. At the rear stands a 17-metre (55-foot) bronze bell tower dating from 1374 (similar to the East Gate Bell that was looted by British soldiers and placed in Nottingham Arboretum). Perhaps the most interesting feature is a 1907 map of Canton, stored away in a back room. This large reproduction gives an interesting perspective on the city, showing the mint, the imperial archery grounds and the fact that most of this sprawling city was at that time rice paddies.

Temple of the Six Banyans (Liu Rong Si)

87 Liu Rong Lu, off Jiefang Beilu (8339 2843). **Open** 8am-5pm daily. **Admission** *Grounds* RMB1. *Tower* RMB10. **No credit cards**. **Map** p281 D3.

The main structure in this mediocre Buddhist temple is an octagonal concrete tower that reaches up nine storeys. The staircase is steep and narrow, with a low ceiling that all but guarantees most people will thump their skull at least once. The top storey is closed, but there is no sign publicising this until you've climbed all the way up. Far more interesting are the religious shops surrounding the temple. Beware, though, of con men dressed as monks who offer jade bracelets along with Buddha's blessing and then ask for money.

Tomb of the Nanyue King

Jiefang Beilu (no phone). **Open** 9am-5pm daily. **Admission** RMB15. **No credit cards**. **Map** p281 D2.

For years Guangzhou suffered from a lack of ruins and historical artefacts. Chinese from the northern provinces scoffed at those in the south, referring to them as the 'southern barbarians'. But in 1983, while excavating a low hillside site for a downtown hotel, workers unearthed an ancient imperial tomb, built 2,200 years ago (the Western Han Dynasty) for the second king of the Nanyue Kingdom. The red sandstone tomb itself, along with five chambers, is intact. More than 1,000 articles, including three gold seals, which confirm the identity of King Zhaomo, have been found and are now on display. These include ceremonial jars, jade cups and pendants, and the remains of the emperor's jade burial suit.

White Cloud Mountain (Bai Yun Shan)

Fifteen kilometres (9 miles) north of the city (3722 6736). **Open** 9-11.45am, 1.30-4.45pm daily. **Admission** RMB5. *Cable car* RMB25. **No credit cards**. **Map** off p281 D1.

Despite the name, this is hardly a mountain, at only 384 metres (1,259 feet). Pagodas, monasteries and teahouses are dotted about the base, and when the weather is clear, and the pollution not too bad, views from the top are gorgeous. However, it can be hard to get away from other tourists. Some cramped cable cars ascend to the peak – known as the 'Ridge that Scrapes the Stars' (Moxing Ling) – but be aware that it is a good three-hour trek back down to the base. Recently, bungee jumping, grass skiing and tobogganing facilities have been added to the park, but it is locally famous as somewhere for couples to escape from prying relatives and get intimate in their cars. To get to the park it's best to take a taxi.

Yuexiu Park

Jiefang Beilu (no phone). **Open** 9am-5pm daily. **Admission** *Park* RMB5. *Attractions* prices vary. **No credit cards**. **Map** p281 D1/2.

This was China's largest urban park when it first opened more than 50 years ago. Most domestic tourists are herded to the Sculpture of the Five Rams, the symbol of Guangzhou. Otherwise, there is a dull museum in the park's Zhen Hai Tower (with much emphasis put on how it was occupied by the British and French imperialists during the Opium Wars), the disappointing Guangzhou Municipal Museum (which covers the period from the Nanyue kingdom during the first southern Chinese dynasty to the days of the foreign concessions on Shamian Island), a football stadium and some plastic pedal boats on the park's three man-made lakes. *See also p291* **Green respites**.

Where to eat & drink

Restaurants

In a survey on national dining habits, people here spent on average three times as much on eating out than did residents in second-ranked Shanghai and seven times as much as the national average. Even so, Cantonese food can no longer be ranked as one of the world's great cuisines. The Cultural Revolution destroyed the culture of food by ending the training of chefs and wiping out the audience for good cooking. Modern food reflects the nouveau-riche aspirations here, where flashy labels are everything. The status conveyed by the obscene prices of delicacies such as shark's fin, abalone, bird's nest, fish maw and bamboo webs is more important than whether the dish tastes like wallpaper paste.

Banxi

151 Longjin Xilu (8181 5718). **Open** 6.30am-11.30pm daily. **Main courses** from RMB100. **Dim sum** from RMB5. **Credit** AmEx, DC, MC, V. **Map** p280 B3 **❶**

The old (1949) Banxi Restaurant recently had a facelift and now comes complete with chandeliers and frosted-glass screens in many of its private

Haizhu Wholesale Market. *See p282.*

rooms. The staff's English is almost non-existent but that's hardly a factor when all you need to do is point at whatever you fancy from the dozens of dim sum trolleys. There are plenty of curious-looking dishes to choose from, at prices that that will please even the most budget-conscious traveller.

Dong Bei Ren – The Manchurian
65-67 He Qun Yi Ma Lu (8760 0688). **Open** 10.30am-10.30pm daily. **Main courses** RMB30-100. **Credit** AmEx, DC, MC, V. **Map** p280 C2 ❷

This colourful chain provides an excellent introduction to Manchurian cuisine. However, it's wise to try choosing from the trolleys before you succumb to the waitresses' efforts to recommend the most expensive dishes on the menu.

Other locations: 36 Garden Building, Tian He Nan Erlu (8750 1711); 2/F, 1 Taojin Beilu (8357 6277).

Gao Li Jiu Jia Korean Restaurant
4/F, 26 Song Bai Donglu (8657 3168). **Open** 11am-11pm daily. **Main courses** RMB20-100. **Credit** DC, MC, V. **Map** off p281 E1 ❸

A strong Korean expat community means cuisine from their home country is especially well represented in Guangzhou. This newly opened establishment is the best of four in the immediate vicinity and serves authentic fare without the noisy crowds of more established Korean places.

Hong Xing
9 Guangzhou Da Dao Nan (8429 7557). **Open** 11am-2pm, 6.30pm-3am daily. **Main courses** RMB78-300. **Credit** AmEx, DC, MC, V. **Map** p281 D4 ❹

This Cantonese seafood chain has locations all over the city, but this branch, just around the corner from the Landmark Hotel, is a good place to start. Let a *qipao*-clad hostess seat you at a table and pour you a cup of sweet flower tea, then head back down to the entrance to choose your dishes from the aquariums (don't bother with a menu, just point to what you like the look of). More adventurous diners might

like to try freshwater cockroaches (*nong shi*), although the range of shellfish is excellent too – from razor clams and sea urchins to horseshoe crabs.
Other locations: throughout the city.

Hui Ying Chang Fen Dian
94 Dong Chuan Lu (8386 1967). **Open** 6.15am-1.15am daily. **Main courses** RMB5-10. **No credit cards. Map** p281 F3 ❺

Just five minutes' walk from China Plaza along Dong Chuan Lu (on the left, just past the Provincial Cardiovascular Hospital and opposite the Songsha air-conditioner store), Hui Ying is perhaps the best place to sample the *chang fen*, a delicious kind of steamed rice-flour pasty served in soy sauce. Ask for *shah huh jee dan* and you'll get a tasty shrimp and egg dish that is typical of Guangzhou. Accompany it with *jok* and *yo tiao* thick rice broth with tasty fried bread sticks for dipping. Fantastic fare at ultra-low prices means it's massively popular with locals and busy at all times of the day and night.

My Home Hunan
2/F, 77 Ti Yue Xilu (8559 2101). **Open** 11am-10.30pm daily. **Main courses** RMB30-100. **No credit cards. Map** p281 F1 ❻

Come home to fiery dishes of the Hunanese variety, in a renovated space that reflects the high quality of the food served. If you prefer something slightly more casual, try the small associated noodle shop next door, where a huge bowl of noodles with mushrooms and green vegetables is only RMB8.
Other locations: 19 Taojin Beilu (8358 0544); 181-7 Tian He Donglu (3881 0808).

1920
183 Yanjiang Xilu (8333 6156). **Open** 11am-2pm daily. **Main courses** RMB30-100. **No credit cards. Map** p281 D4 ❼

This small restaurant has excellent set lunches with a distinctly German flavour – just the thing after a morning exploring Shamian Island.

Guangzhou Art Museum.
See p285.

Saint Germain

475 Huan Shi Donglu (8760 6465). **Open** 11am-
11pm daily. **Main courses** RMB50-250. **Credit**
DC, MC, V. **Map** off p281 F2 ❽
While this place is small enough to feel intimate
and cosy, the cuisine is surprisingly impressive
both in terms of its taste and presentation, thanks
to a returnee head chef who trained extensively in
Paris. This is where locals come to sample the
famed French cuisine that they have heard so much
about, and the transition from chopsticks to cutlery
is often hilarious to watch. In addition to the lengthy
à la carte menu, there's a helpful pick-and-mix selection for those more familiar with rice and noodles
than snails and crêpes. It's located amid a cluster
of restaurants serving everything from Ottoman
barbeques to Guizhou hotpots.

Shami House

*2/F, Zhaoqing Building, 304 Huan Shi Zhonglu
(8354 8023).* **Main
courses** RMB30-1,500. **Credit** DC, MC, V.
Map p281 E2 ❾
The Arab community has grown quickly here over
the last few years and the number of Middle Eastern
restaurants in town reflects this. The Shami House
specialises in Lebanese and Syrian cuisine with a
great selection of Turkish barbecue for kebab fans.

Zheng Gong Fu (Kung Fu)

7/F, China Plaza (8386 8999). **Open** 7am-11pm
daily. **Main courses** RMB20-40. **No credit cards.**
Map p281 F3 ❿
As Chinese authorities fall back on increasingly
nationalistic fervour to draw attention from economic disparities, the passion for McDonald's is
beginning to wane and some KFCs are even closing
down. Local fast-food joints – notably the Kung Fu
chain – have been quick to take up the slack. Relying

heavily on the Bruce Lee brand, the menu here may
consist of mediocre meat and rice dishes served with
chicken soup but it's filling convenience food that's
handy if you're whizzing about town.
Other locations: throughout the city.

Bars & nightlife

It is estimated that around 10,000 punters
regularly fill downtown Guangzhou's 500 bars,
so if you're heading out for the night, loneliness
is unlikely to be a problem. Nor will availability
of booze – beer prices are usually quoted by the
dozen, 12 bottles costing RMB160-360. If you
want to buy fewer, expect the price per bottle
to be quite a bit higher. Also be aware that
few places liven up before 10pm.
   Guangzhou nightlife has suffered greatly in
the last few years as the municipal authorities
constantly change their minds as to where the
centre of things should be, but the government
has attempted to set up an area similar to Hong
Kong's Lan Kwai Fong. It opened a mile-long
row of new bars and coffee shops along the
south bank of the river on Chang Ti Lu.
Unfortunately, the location is way off the beaten
track and the promenade of glowing neon has
few customers. If they're still open when you
arrive, try **D&D One** for its river views, or
Atlantic for its modern design.

Babyface

83 Chang Di Da Ma Lu (8335 5771). **Open** 8pm-
2am daily. **No credit cards.** **Map** p281 D4 ❶
This has been the trendiest spot in town for the
past few years (not that there's been much serious
competition), and is always packed to bursting
with fashion snobs and jet-set wannabes. Sadly, the

music has gone downhill, with a handful of lazy DJs letting mixed CDs do all the work, and you'll have to be prepared for lots of crushed feet, banging elbows and lecherous looks.

Sleeping Wood

1 Guangming Lu, Hua Qiao Xin Cun (3758 9257). **Open** 10am-2am daily. **No credit cards.** **Map** p281 F2 ❷
A quiet drinking den directly behind the Holiday Inn, favoured by long-term expats, especially the large French community. Good choice of food (both Cantonese and Western) and drinks as well as polite English-speaking staff.

Windflower

387 Huan Shi Donglu (8358 2446). **Open** 6pm-2am daily. **No credit cards.** **Map** p281 F2 ❸
This stylish bar in the heart of town used to be the 'in' place for Guangzhou's young and beautiful people, but has seen a number of ups and downs since its glory days. Still, the minimalist decor, excellent service and resident Western DJs will hopefully induce a come back by the time you read this.

Yes

2/F, Liu Hua Square, 132 Dong Feng Xilu (8136 6154). **Open** 8pm-2am daily. **No credit cards.** **Map** p280 C2 ❹
Completely remodelled and refurbished in 2005, this could well be the largest disco in China. Ascend the entrance escalators to be greeted by hostesses in formal gowns. Inside, the deafening throb of imported house and techno hypnotises a sea of locals on the cavernous dancefloor. Svelte beauties gyrate on raised podiums, while punters play *sik jong* ('liar dice') at their tables. Although Western musicians are generally barred from Chinese soil, the owners here regularly flex their *guanxi* ('connections') by importing big-name international DJs.

Where to stay

Whether you book through a Hong Kong travel agent, a website or directly with the hotel, you're bound to get a discount on published rates. The entire city is best avoided during the last two weeks of March and of October, when it hosts the country's largest trade fair. Hotel prices triple, fake currency abounds and tempers fray very quickly as hordes of businessmen descend en masse.

Garden Hotel

368 Huan Shi Donglu (8333 8989/fax 8335 0706/ www.gardenhotel-guangzhou.com). **Rates** RMB1,160-1,330 single/double; RMB3,740 suite. **Credit** AmEx, DC, MC, V. **Map** p281 F2 ❶
The Garden Hotel is the top business traveller's choice in town, due to its convenient central location, excellent executive floor and the largest convention hall in Asia. Even so, it is beginning to look a little frayed around the edges.

Globelink Hotel (Quan Qiu Tong Da Jiudian)

208 Yuexiu Nanlu (8389 8138/fax 8389 8899/ globalh@public.guangzhou.gd.cn). **Rates** RMB480 double; RMB580-680 suite. . **Credit** AmEx, DC, MC, V. **Map** p281 E3 ❷
Another excellent choice that is ignored by most guide books, even though it boasts the largest rooms in the city. The location is very central, with easy access to the subway as well as large shopping areas such as Beijing Lu and China Plaza. The staff is friendly, helpful and a few even speak English. Best of all, the discounted prices for this four-star are a great deal.

Grand Palace Hotel

148 Linhe Zhong (3884 0968/fax 3884 0960/www. grandpalace-hotel.com). **Rates** RMB580-800 double; RMB1,080 suite. . **Credit** AmEx, DC, MC, V. **Map** off p281 F2 ❸
Located right by the new railway station, this hotel remains a well-kept secret among the more budget-conscious of Hong Kong's business community. That's not surprising given its decent eating and drinking facilities, with both Chinese and Western restaurants, a comfortable bar and a coffee shop.

Guangzhou Youth Hostel

Shamian Island (8188 4298/fax 8188 4979). **Rates** RMB50-210 single/double. **No credit cards.** **Map** p280 B5 ❹
This is one of the best places in town to meet up with backpackers, if that's your thing. Unfortunately, along with being the cheapest place in town, it also has a sometimes surly staff and a steady lack of vacancies. Despite the name, it is not recognised by the World Youth Hostel Federation.

Hequn Dasha

43 Hequn Yi Ma Lu, Dongshan Kou (8716 1858/ fax 8776 3818). **Rates** RMB380-480 double; RMB880-1080 suite. **Credit** AmEx, DC, MC, V. **Map** off p281 F3 ❺
This bizarrely named hotel (it roughly translates as the PLA Kindergarten Teachers' Hotel) has large, well-appointed rooms and yet retains a number of uniquely Chinese amenities, such as steel thermoses of boiling water. As it's located on the edge of the sprawling military district, its clients are predominantly trainee teachers or army officers, with the occasional foreign tour group. Watch out for all the army-licensed SUVs charging around nearby; immune to the law, the drivers don't seem to worry about pedestrians.

Shamian Hotel

Shamian Island (8121 2288/fax 8121 8628/www. gdshamianhotel.com). **Rates** RMB238 double; RMB288-360 suite. **Credit** AmEx, DC, MC, V. **Map** p280 B5 ❻
This is a reasonable choice if you'd rather not mix with the shoestring travellers at the nearby youth hostel, although be prepared that not all rooms have private baths.

Trips Out of Town

White Swan Hotel

Shamian Island (8188 6968/fax 8186 1188/ www.white-swan-hotel.com). **Rates** RMB700-900 double; RMB2,290-2,576 suite. **Credit** AmEx, DC, MC, V. **Map** p280 B5 **7**

Dubbed the 'White Stork Hotel' because of its popularity with American couples coming to adopt Chinese orphans, this place is right next to the former US consulate on Shamian Island. All 843 rooms have white marble bathrooms and gold-trimmed fixtures. It is still the number-one choice for visiting foreign dignitaries; in 2006 every single guest was kicked out with just one night's notice when North Korean dictator Kim Jong-Il paid a flying visit.

Resources

Hospital

Can-Am International Medical Center, 5/F, Garden Tower, Garden Hotel (8386 6988).

Internet

Net bars abound, but are usually small smoky dens full of raucous, swearing teenagers. Big hotels are the best choice if you want to check your email as their computers are more likely to have English-language versions of Windows. A more reasonably priced alternative is the city library, **Guangzhou Tu Xu Guan**, on Zhong Shan Silu (9am-5pm, closed Wed), where there are almost a hundred clean PCs available on the second floor for just RMB2 per hour.

Police

Taojin Lu, between Häagen-Dazs & KFC (8359 7560).

Post offices

Smaller post offices don't have English-speaking staff, but some of the bigger hotels have their own postal services. These include the **White Swan Hotel** (*see p290*) and the **Garden Hotel** (*see p289*).

Tourist information

The days of the national tourist agency **CITS** (China International Travel Service) are numbered. Once the only bureau for foreign travellers, it stopped being efficient long ago. You're much better off dropping in to the nearest Western-style hotel where an in-house agency will meet your needs in English and with a smile. Commissions are negligible and ticket prices competitive. The international hotels all run English-language tours of Guangzhou – if getting on a bus with the blue rinses is your idea of a good time. For air or train tickets, head to a local hotel for help.

A locally run agency used to dealing with the needs of foreigners is **Xpat Travel Planners** (Flat E, 20/F, Regent House, 50 Taojin Lu, 8358 6961, xpats@public.guangzhou.gd.cn).

Other useful information

Addresses

Throughout this chapter, and on the map on pages 280-281, we have used the full names of major roads, including prefixes that indicate their location

(*bei* means north, *nan* means south, *xi* is west and *dong* is east.) For example, Renmin Beilu is the northern part of Renmin Street.

Language

Cantonese is the lingua franca of the city. Most natives also speak Mandarin, while English is spoken at all major hotels and Western bars. Watch out for young locals wanting to practise their English. Some can be helpful and will happily act as a tour guide just for the chance to speak with you, others are a nuisance and a few are just touts in disguise.

Media

There are various forms of local English-language media. The official *Guangzhou Morning Post* (no relation to the *South China Morning Post*) offers anodyne business news and the odd tidbit of cultural information. *That's Guangzhou* (www.thatsguangzhou.com) and *City Talk* are both free monthly city mags available at some international bars and hotels but, at that price, do not expect very much.

Money

The basic unit of Chinese currency goes by two names: the **yuan** and the **renminbi** (RMB is used for both; the symbol for yen – ¥ – is also sometimes used to denote yuan), which is the international name and the one we have used throughout this chapter. (Locals also use the term *kwai*, and, just to confuse matters, often translate yuan/renminbi/kwai as 'dollar', which should not be taken to mean US dollar.) One Hong Kong dollar is roughly equivalent to one renminbi. Although some places in Guangzhou accept Hong Kong dollars, you'll certainly need to change some cash into renminbi. Tourist hotels, branches of the Bank of China and major entry points all have such facilities; rates vary little. Bank of China **ATMs** accept international cards as do the small number of foreign financial institutions such as Citibank and HSBC, although most other Chinese banks do not. You shouldn't have any problems changing renminbi back to HK dollars in Hong Kong.

Telephones

To dial abroad from Guangzhou, dial 00 (not 001 as in Hong Kong), followed by the country code and local number (omitting the 0 of the area code if there is one). It is easiest to find phones that accept IDD calls in the big international hotels, but you'll pay heavily for the privilege. Calls from Guangzhou to Hong Kong are considered international, but are cheap. The international code for China is 86, while the area code for Guangzhou is 20.

Visas & consulates

Don't be tempted by so-called 'budget travel agencies' in and around Tsim Sha Tsui in Hong Kong offering visas for China at hugely inflated prices. Legitimate agencies can do it quickly (sometimes on the spot or overnight) for a fairly reasonable price. The cost varies according to how quickly you want the visa, and for how many trips/months. To get around, you should be prepared to pay upwards of HK$500. *See also p301.*

Try the alarmingly named but reputable **Grand Profit International Travel Agency** (705AA,

7/F, New East Ocean Centre, 9 Science Museum Road, Tsim Sha Tsui, Kowloon, 2723 3288) or one of the branches of **China Travel Service** (*see p295*).

Guangzhou is home to US, UK and Australian consulates, among others. Overseas consulates in China usually have a well-deserved reputation for being officious, overly bureaucratic and dismissive.

This is perhaps not surprising considering the number of bogus applications they receive.
Australia *Guangdong International Hotel (8335 0909/5911).*
UK *Guangdong International Hotel (8335 1354/ 8333 6520).*
US *Nan Jie, Shamian (8188 8911/8121 8418).*

Green respites

While Guangzhou is perhaps the best-known shopfront for China's breakneck economic transformation, the city's attractive public gardens provide a refreshing antidote to the crowds. For centuries 'old Canton' was known for its numerous corners of scenic beauty, and the gardens were always popular. The willow-pattern images of China, popularised from the 18th century onwards, were patterned from the gardens of Canton.

Guangzhou's residents greatly enjoy their city's green spaces, and as a result there are always quite a few people around. To best appreciate the parks and gardens, you need to time your visits. Late afternoons see the gardens fill up with children, usually accompanied by doting grandparents. Weekends and public holidays are always crowded, though gardens that charge admission, such as the Orchid Garden, are quieter. Entrance fees to Guangzhou's gardens vary, though none charges more than a few renminbi for the entire day.

South China Botanical Gardens

723 Xingke Lu, Tianhe District.
Established in 1954 as a much larger extension of a botanical institute first set up in 1929, this impressive horticultural gem in the north-east of the city is one of the foremost botanical gardens in China. Enormous ferneries, ornamental lakes, and extensive palm and orchid sections all provide hours of relaxation. The gardens are so big that golf-cart-like vehicles are often used to transport visitors.

Liwan Lake Park

Longjin Xilu. Map p280 A3/B3.
Located a short taxi ride from Shamian Island, the historic former foreign settlement on the riverfront (*see p282*), this spread of gardens and ornamental lakes dates from the early 19th century. This area was home to the enormously wealthy *compradors* who amassed their fortunes as middlemen between European and Chinese trade. Their families lived in expansive mansions dotted

around the area; some still exist, and one, near the entrance to the gardens, has been opened as a museum and can be visited.

Liuhua Lake Park

Dongfeng Xilu. **Map** p280 C2.
Right in the centre of Guangzhou, Liuhua Lake Park is another sprawling lake-and-gardens complex, with numerous secluded corners, humpback bridges, pavilions and trees. The tower-blocks of modern Guangzhou are all around, yet this place somehow remains a serene reminder of a fast-vanishing 'old China', even though the gardens were only developed in 1952. Along with nearby Yuexiu Park, Liuhua is probably best enjoyed early in the morning or at the start of the evening.

Yuexiu Park

Jiefang Beilu. **Map** p281 D1/2.
Yuexiu Park, the scenic hillside north of the Sun Yat-sen Memorial Hall, provides another pleasant respite from the crowds and noise. The largest park in Guangzhou, Yuexiu contains seven hills, which give sweeping views out over the downtown area, especially from the Five-Storey Pagoda. Occupied by Anglo-French forces in 1858-1860, the pagoda contains an interesting exhibition about this period. *See also p286.*

Orchid Garden

Jiefang Beilu. **Map** p281 D1.
Guangzhou Orchid Garden – known locally as Lanpu – is a delightful retreat. Surrounded by high walls, and filled with palms, exotic cacti and other interesting botanical specimens, as well as the advertised orchids, this green oasis has a delightful tea pavilion, which overlooks a pond filled with gently circling, vividly coloured *koi*. Excellent varieties of Chinese tea and light snacks make this a delightful corner to relax for a while before heading out into the noise and bustle of the city. The entrance fee includes a pot of tea, and ranges from RMB8 to RMB20 depending on the type of tea you select.

Trips Out of Town

Getting around

By bike

Bicycles can be rented at a small number of hotels around Guangzhou. But given the traffic and pollution, this is an option best reserved for kamikaze diehards. And be warned: although China has only two per cent of the world's automobiles, it accounts for nearly 20 per cent of the world's traffic accidents.

By bus

Buses are not geared for tourists, partly because most only have Chinese characters saying where they are heading, but more importantly because locals usually jam themselves in like sardines. Emergency exits do not exist here, and neither does queuing or any other form of communal politeness. Many of the buses themselves should have been retired years ago and few seem to have any dashboard dials that still work. Pickpockets are rife, especially around Chinese New Year, and most other locals will actively avoid sitting next to foreigners.

By subway

Now that the second and third subway lines have opened up, getting around the city is much easier. The **yellow line** goes from north to south, with stops at the old train station and Haizhu Square, before veering off to the south-eastern suburbs. The **red line** goes largely from west to east, where it terminates at the Guangzhou East railway station, which is also the terminus for the north–south **blue line** serving the Tien He district. Facilities are much like Hong Kong's MTR. Recorded announcements and signs are in English (or a version thereof) and Chinese. You can get change from an attendant and go to a machine to get a ticket (RMB2-5).

By taxi

Air-conditioned taxis with uniformed drivers and clean vehicles cost RMB2.60 per kilometre, with a minimum of RMB7 (plus a recent RMB1 for oil price rises). If you don't speak Cantonese, you need to have your destination written for you in Chinese script to show the driver, unless they're taking you from a major hotel, in which case the doorman will tell the driver where to take you.

By train

Guangzhou has two train stations, which can be confusing for first-time visitors. The newer station, in the east of the city (Tian He district), serves mainly Hong Kong and is known locally as 'Dong Zhan'. It is new and modern (for China, that is). The old station ('Lao Zhan') is a chaotic, nerve-wracking place on the west side of the city. The old station serves the hinterland and travellers going to popular inland tourist destinations such as Guilin (for Yangshuo) and Kunming (for Dali and Lijiang).

Getting there

By air

Flights from Hong Kong land in Guangzhou almost as soon as they've taken off. It's a 20-minute hop, hardly worth the effort of getting out to the airport – which takes twice as long as the flight itself – and through customs, especially when the train is more environmentally friendly and almost as quick.

The new **Guangzhou International Airport** is located well outside of the city, in a distant suburb almost 30 kilometres (19 miles) to the north. Although it resembles a flash international airport, service levels remain at mainland standards and finding an English speaker can often be difficult.

As with all airports, taxi drivers will happily fleece the ignorant so do not be surprised if you are quoted RMB500 for the short trip downtown. A more realistic fare would be RMB100-150. Fortunately, there are plenty of shuttle buses that serve most city locations for RMB16-36. Of the seven main bus routes, the most useful are route one, which goes to the old station, and number two, through Tian He and past the big hotels on Huan Shi Lu. Further details are available from the **Baiyunport Bus Service** (3129 8077). The section of the blue metro line connecting the airport with the city had been due to open in late 2006 but latest reports say 2009.

By bus

Bus is second-choice to train when making the journey between Guangzhou and Hong Kong, mainly because the time spent at the border makes the trip a hassle. Going by bus is cheaper, however, with a return journey costing HK$80. Around 20 buses make the journey each way every day, from various hotels around town, including the **White Swan Hotel** (*see p290*) and the **Garden Hotel** (*see p289*). Buses leaving from the Garden Hotel on the way to Hong Kong stop at either Hung Hom, Chek Lap Kok or Prince Edward MTR.

For those on a budget, upmarket coaches leave for Shenzhen from Guangzhou's **Guang Yuan Lu bus station** every few minutes, costing RMB60. At the terminus, simply cross the border on foot and jump on a KCR (Kowloon–Canton Railway) train headed to Hung Hom or the metro interchange at Mong Kok for another HK$32. Obviously this works equally well in reverse.

If you are really stuck, in a mad rush or have some friends to share the cost with, there are always Guangzhou taxis in Shenzhen looking for a fare back to the city. You can get them down to around RMB400 one way.

By train

As demand continues to grow, so does the frequency of express trains from Hong Kong to Guangzhou, roughly once an hour. Prices range from HK$180 to HK$230 for a one-way ticket. The 8.25am commuter train, operated by the Hong Kong company **KCR** (www.kcrc.com), is cleaner and more efficient than those run by China Railways, though expresses run by either company take under two hours.

For the return journey to Hong Kong, first check your luggage in on the second floor; then check yourself in on the fourth floor (with your passport and ticket). All formalities including customs are taken care of here.

Directory

Bus in Kowloon.

Directory

Getting Around

By air

The largest covered space in the world, **Hong Kong International Airport** (2508 1234, www.hongkongairport. com) is situated on the levelled island of Chek Lap Kok, just north of Lantau. Designed by British architect Sir Norman Foster, it opened in 1998.

Transport to Kowloon, Hong Kong Island, the New Territories and Lantau, as well as to Macau and China, is available from the four-level Ground Transportation Centre.

The **Airport Express** train service operated by the Mass Transit Railway (2881 8888, press 3 for English, www.mtr.com.hk) is the quickest link, but is also pretty expensive. You can be in Kowloon in under 20 minutes, while the journey to Central (to a dedicated station, which is connected by a subway to Central MTR) takes 23 minutes. Trains run every ten minutes from 5.50am to 1.15am daily. A one-way adult fare to Kowloon is HK$90 (HK$160 return); to Central it's HK$100 (HK$180). Return tickets are valid for one month. Credit cards are accepted; Octopus cards (*see p296*) can also be used. From Kowloon and Central stations, you can catch up a free shuttle-bus (every 30 minutes, 6.20am-11pm) to major hotels, as well as Hung Hom KCR Station and the China Ferry Terminal.

Alternatively, a more leisurely journey is offered by the **Citybus** express service (www.citybus.com.hk) to

different parts of Hong Kong Island (A10, A11, A12, HK$40-$45 single), Kowloon (A21, A22, HK$33-$39 single) and the New Territories (A31, A33, A35, A41, A41P, A43, HK$17-$28 single). Services operate 6am to midnight and continue with night buses (HK$20-$30). The N11 goes to HK Island, N21 to Kowloon, N21D to Disneyland and N29, N31, N35, N42, N42A to the New Territories. DB02R is a 24-hour service to Discovery Bay (HK$28).

You can buy tickets in the Meeters and Greeters Hall of the Arrivals Hall or you can pay on board with the exact fare. Buses take approximately 35 minutes to reach Kowloon and, given the cross-harbour tunnel and the stops the buses have to make, up to 95 minutes to Hong Kong Island.

Before returning to the airport aboard the Airport Express or the express bus, you can check in your luggage (from one day before up to 90 minutes prior to take-off with some airlines – but check as each airline has its own procedure) at the check-in halls in Kowloon and Central, though due to security restrictions this is not allowed for flights by US airlines or on airlines with US destinations; it's worth verifying even with other airlines as the situation is liable to change.

Taxis are the most expensive way to travel to and from the airport (not least because of the various road tolls, both ways, which are included in the fare). Taxis are located on the left-hand ramp as you leave the arrivals hall. Expect to pay anything from

HK$300 to HK$400, depending on your destination and traffic conditions. Red taxis serve HK Island and Kowloon, green taxis the New Territories, and blue ones Lantau.

New World First Ferry (2131 8181, www.nwff.com.hk) has a fast **ferry** service from Tung Chung to Tuen Mun in the New Territories. It leaves every 20 to 40 minutes (6am-11pm daily), takes nine minutes and costs HK$15 one way. Two buses, the S56 and the S64P, run from Tung Chung MTR station and Tung Chung New Development Ferry Pier to the passenger terminal at the airport.

Car parks (2286 0163, 2949 1083) have pick-up and drop-off zones and offer complimentary 30-minute parking for departing or arriving passengers in car parks 1 and 4. Parking spaces in lots 1, 2, 3 and 4 are closest to the terminal and have ramps and wheelchair access for the disabled (the cost is HK$16 per hour in the open car park and HK$20 in the covered one). The SkyCity long-term car park costs HK$200 for a minimum of three days, then HK$70 per day.

In the Meeters and Greeters Hall are service counters for hotel reservations and pick-ups, private limo services, the Macau Government Tourist Office (*see p276*), China Travel Service (*see p295*) and ferry and train reservations.

If you intend to travel directly on to **Macau** or to mainland **China** (for visas, *see p295* and *p301*), you can buy coach tickets at the Meeters and Greeters Hall between 7am and 11pm from a variety of companies, including **Eternal**

East Border Coach (2261 0176, www.eebus.com) in Arrival Hall 8 and **Gogobus** (2261 0886, www.gogotil.com) in Arrival Hall 809 (7.50am-8.50pm). **Trans-Island Limousine Service** is in (2261 2636) Arrival Hall 801.

You can also travel to Macau, Shenzhen and other mainland destinations by ferry from the airport with either **Cross Boundary Ferry Transfer Service** (2858 3876, www.cksp.com.hk, 9am-9pm) on level 5, transfer areas E1 and E2, or **Turbojet** (2859 3333, www.turbojetseaexpress.com.hk, 8am-8pm) via the shuttle from SkyPier.

AIRPORT FACILITIES

A free porter service is available in the baggage reclaim hall (and at all Airport Express city stations). There is also a left-luggage counter (2261 0110, open 6am-1am daily) located in the Meeters and Greeters Hall.

Banks with ATMs and foreign exchange outlets can be found in both the arrivals and departures areas.

The Hong Kong Tourist Board (*see p310*) can be found in the buffer halls and transfer area T2. Public payphones, card vending machines, courtesy phones and 24-hour help phones are located throughout the terminal.

In-terminal electric vehicles are available in the East Hall, and an automated people-mover in the basement of the passenger terminal travels between the East and West Halls every three minutes between 6am and midnight.

Befitting a modern airport, Hong Kong's is wired for the 21st century. Multimedia lounges provide 24-hour free broadband access to email and the net, and visitors with PCs and LAN cards can also access the internet from almost anywhere in the terminal, with charges being based on

time online. In addition, the **CyberMall Cyber Break Café** (2928 6421), with 16 iMac terminals, and **Cyberzone**, near gates 21, 22 and 61, provide unlimited free internet access. Powerphone connections are available at the Ground Transportation Centre and passenger terminal.

In the Level 7 check-in hall you'll find wireless high-speed internet service at **PCCW** (2888 0088, www.pccw.com), plus items such as mobile phones and phone cards. Also on this level is a branch of **Fortress**, the one-stop electronics shop (2186 6627, open 7am-11pm; *see also p180*).

Facilities for the physically, visually and hearing impaired are provided in the form of toilets, telephone access, escalators, elevators, car parks, drinking fountains, tactile guide paths and wheelchairs and a people-mover (*see above*).

Other facilities at the airport include a police station in the check-in hall (2183 1334, open 24 hours daily), and a medical centre (2261 2626, open 7am-midnight) and a lost & found room (2182 2018, open 8am-11pm) on Level 6. Nursing rooms with changing and feeding facilities and children's play areas are on the central concourse, and there are prayer rooms (2182 2024) in the check-in hall. In addition, there are 12 highly comfortable air-conditioned smoking lounges; all are open 24 hours and located in the arrival and departure halls.

Visas for mainland China are available at the airport through a number of agencies, including **Gogobus** (*see above*) and **China Travel Service** (www.ctshk.com), which has a counter at Arrivals AO4, AO5, BO8 (2261 2472, open 7am-8pm) and a larger office in the Arrival Central Concourse near Gate 27 (2261 2062, open 8.45am-9pm).

By rail

Trains from mainland China arrive at Hung Hom station in Kowloon. Taxis line up outside and directions to bus services are well marked. The Hung Hom ferry pier is a ten-minute walk away.

If you wish to travel by train to China (for which you'll need a visa; *see above* and *p301*), tickets can be purchased at Hung Hom Station or in advance from either of the China Travel Service branches listed below or directly from the Kowloon–Canton Railway Corporation (2947 7888, www.throughtrain.kcrc.com).

China Travel Service

1/F, Alpha House, 27 Nathan Road, Tsim Sha Tsui, Kowloon (2315 7188, www.ctshk.com). Tsim Sha Tsui MTR (exit C1, E)/buses along Nathan Road/ Tsim Sha Tsui Star Ferry Pier. **Open** 9am-7pm Mon-Fri; 1-6pm Sat; 9am-12.30pm, 2-5pm Sun. **Map** p333 C2.

G/F, CTS House, 78-83 Connaught Road, Central, HK Island (2853 3888). Sheung Wan MTR (exit E4)/buses along Connaught Road Central. **Open** 9am-5pm Mon-Sat. **Map** p328 C2.

By sea

Ferry services to and from Macau (*see also p277*) dock either at the Hong Kong–Macau Ferry Terminal in the Shun Tak Centre, Sheung Wan, HK Island (**map** p328 B1) or the China Ferry Terminal, China HK City, Canton Road, Tsim Sha Tsui (**map** p333 B6). The latter is also the arrival point for ferries from China.

At the Hong Kong–Macau Ferry Terminal, taxis are available at exit level, while buses are at street level. Sheung Wan MTR station is connected to the terminal; follow the signs and you will find it a short walk away.

At the China Ferry Terminal, taxis and buses are available

Directory

at street level, while both the Star Ferry and MTR are 15 minutes away on foot.

Tickets for the ferries can be purchased at the terminals. Fares vary according to the type of vessel and class. If you wish to travel on a weekend or public holiday, it's advisable to book in advance – and consider buying a return fare.

By road

The only way to arrive in Hong Kong by road is from mainland China by a coach service from Guangzhou (see p292) or the Citybus routes linking the Shenzhen economic zone (see p194 **Savings made in China**) and Hong Kong.

Public transport

Public transport in Hong Kong is reliable, affordable, clean and safe. Because of the SAR's compact nature, you can reach most parts within an hour using public transport. That is, as long as you don't get caught in rush-hour traffic (8-10am and 5-7pm) or delayed by an accident or road works.

Three companies operate tha bus routes covering the territory; the green and yellow minibuses are privately owned. The railways, both underground (MTR) and above (KCR and Light Rail), are connected to housing estates and main shopping and business areas.

All buses, minibuses, taxis and long-haul ferries are air-conditioned.

Transport Complaints
2889 9999/www.td.gov.hk
Transport Department Enquiries
2804 2600/fax 2248 0433.

Fares & tickets

Visitors who are planning to use public transport fairly frequently over a week or more can buy an **Octopus card** (a stored-value smart

card). Available from MTR stations, it can be used on all public transport systems except for green and some yellow minibuses, and most ferries. You pay a deposit of HK$50 for the card, which is refunded upon its return, and then add the value to the card you expect to need – you can add more at the machines located in MTR stations or at supermarkets and 7-Eleven stores all over Hong Kong.

Place the Octopus card on the machine displayed in the buses, minibuses, trams and ferries to log in the fare. If you reach your destination before the end of the route, place the card on the machine again when alighting to retrieve the rest of the fare. Some routes take a flat fare with no refunds. Octopus fares work out cheaper than normal fares by a few dollars and the card can also be used in convenience stores, parking meters and various fast-food outlets.

A three-day **Hong Kong Transport Pass** is also available for HK$220. It can be used for one Airport Express single journey between the airport and most destinations in Central, Causeway Bay and Kowloon, and three days of unlimited rides on the MTR. For an extra HK$20, it can be used on other transport modes. There is also a one-day MTR pass for HK$50, giving unlimited rides. These passes are available at Airport Express and MTR stations.

On many types of tickets, discounts are available for children, students and the elderly – ask when booking.

Buses

Buses run regularly and frequently, particularly during rush hour. Bus stops display the bus numbers and routes they serve, as well as the fares. If you don't have an Octopus card, make sure you have the

exact fare ready, (HK$2-$15 depending on your destination and the type of bus.

For more information call:
Citybus *2873 0818/www.citybus.com.hk*
Kowloon Motor Bus *2745 4466/www.kmb.com.hk*
New World First Bus *2136 8888/www.nwfb.com.hk*
New Lantau Bus Company *2984 9848/www.newlantaobus.com*

Minibuses

Yellow minibuses with red stripes do not always ply fixed routes, and passengers can get on or off anywhere (except in restricted zones). Fares can be much higher than on buses, as they are dictated by the whim of the driver, and range from HK$2 to HK$20. Yellow minibuses with green stripes are called maxi-cabs and travel to residential areas with fixed fares. They, too, can be flagged down anywhere and called to a halt near your destination. A quick shout (of 'lee doe') should be enough to alert the driver that you wish to get off.

Ferries

Ferries sail between Hong Kong Island and Kowloon, and to the Outlying Islands, Macau and mainland China. The New World First Ferry Service, better known as **Star Ferry**, provides services to Central, Wan Chai and North Point on HK Island, as well as to Tsim Sha Tsui and Hung Hom on Kowloon and Discovery Bay on Lantau. The new Central Ferry Pier is situated along the Outlying Islands Ferry Pier promenade, where you'll find services to Lamma, Cheung Chau, Peng Chau and Lantau. Fares for fast ferries are higher, but the journey time can be almost half.

In addition, there are inter-island ferries for island hopping that have fixed fares, as well as a number of small owner-operated sampan ferries plying

Directory

their trade between Aberdeen (on the south side of Hong Kong Island) and the Outlying Islands. Be sure to bargain the fare down for the latter.

For more information contact:

New World First Ferry
2131 8181/www.nwff.com.hk
Star Ferry
2367 7065/www.starferry.com.hk
HK Kowloon Ferry
2815 6063/www.hkkf.com.hk
Discovery Bay Transport
2987 6128/www.hkri.com
HK & Macau Hydrofoil & Turbocat Services
2859 3333/www.turbojet.com.hk
Chun Kee Ferry (Aberdeen to Sok Kwu Wan on Lamma)
2375 7883/www.ferry.com.hk

MTR (underground)

The **Mass Transit Railway** or **MTR** (2881 8888, www.mtr.com.hk) is clean, fast and efficient. It runs along the north coast of Hong Kong Island, and travels beneath the harbour to Kowloon, the New Territories and Lantau. Trains run from 6am to 1am daily, and the maximum fare is HK$13 for a single journey (except to Tung Chung on Lantau, which is HK$23, or HK$20 with an Octopus card). The network is made up of five interconnected lines: the **blue** line runs along the harbour on Hong Kong Island from Sheung Wan in the west to Chai Wan in the east; the **red** line runs from Central, Hong Kong Island, under the harbour to Tsuen Wan in the New Territories; the **green** line starts at Yau Ma Tei, Kowloon, looping around to the east to Tiu Keng Leng. The **purple** line starts at North Point and crosses the harbour to terminate at Po Lam in the New Territories. The **yellow** line runs from Central to Tung Chung on Lantau and links to the **pink** Disneyland line.

All MTR stations have been refurbished, with new coaches, safety doors, and shops selling food, clothes and electronics, plus banks and other services. Charts show the network of train lines, fares to destinations and the types of travelcard available. Free internet service is being set up in iCentres in some stations. Throughout this guide, we give the nearest exit for each destination, but there's a map on the wall in each station if you need to check.

Rail services

Aside from the Airport Express, Hong Kong has several rail systems that fall under the control of the **Kowloon–Canton Railway** or **KCR** (2929 3399, www.kcrc.com), although talks of a merger with the MTR were ongoing as this guide went to press. The north–south **East Rail** runs from East Tsim Sha Tsui station (linked to Tsim Sha Tsui MTR by a subway) northwards to the boundary with mainland China at Lo Wu, stopping on the way at various towns in the New Territories. These trains run every three to ten minutes from 5.30am until 12.30am. The maximum single fare is HK$36.50 (HK$34.80 if you use an Octopus card), double for first class. A new spur line, **Ma On Shan Rail**, branches off at Tai Wai and veers northeast to Wu Kai Sha.

West Rail links Nam Cheong to Tuen Muen in the western New Territories and runs from 5.45am to 12.45am, every three to 12 minutes. Fares start at around HK$4.

The **Light Rail** (or **LR**) connects the New Territories towns of Tuen Mun and Yuen Long. It runs from 5.30am to 12.30am daily, with fares between HK$4 and HK$5.80.

Further developments to Hong Kong's rail system are ongoing, with an extension of the West Rail south to East Tsim Sha Tsui scheduled to open in 2009 and other lines planned for future years.

Trams

Double-decker trams run by **Hong Kong Tramways** (2548 7102, www.hktramways.com) travel along the north side of Hong Kong Island from Kennedy Town to Chai Wan, with a flat fare of HK$2 (HK$1 children). You enter the tram at the rear and exit at the front, paying the fare before alighting. Tram stops are in the middle of the main road, splitting the two-way traffic.

On a clear day, the **Peak Tram** (2522 0922, www.thepeak.com.hk; *see also p35* and *p89*) affords panoramic views over Hong Kong on its thrilling ascent to the Peak up a very steep slope from Garden Road in Central. Fares are HK$22 (HK$8 under-12s) one way, HK$33 (HK$15) return. All trams run 7am-midnight daily every 10-15 minutes.

Octopus cards can be used for fares on all trams and trains.

Taxis

Taxis are plentiful in major areas and fares are reasonable. You will find red taxis on Hong Kong Island and Kowloon, green in the New Territories and blue on Lantau. All of them will go to the airport. Taxis can only stop at hotels or on the road if there are no single or double yellow lines. Although many taxi drivers do speak some English, it is advisable to have your destination written down in Chinese to avoid confusion. Remember to put on your seat belt – the law requires it.

Fares vary according to the colour of the taxi: the flag fall for red cabs is HK$15 (HK$1.40 for each additional 200 metres); for green it is HK$12.50 and for blue HK$12 (both add HK$1.20 for each additional 200 metres). There are extra charges for telephone hiring, tunnel tolls, the driver's return toll, and luggage placed in the boot

(HK$4-$5 – carry your bags with you if you want to avoid this). Tipping HK$5-$10 is optional but appreciated. Avoid trying to pay with larger bills of HK$500 or HK$1,000 as sometimes drivers don't have change.

If you want to book a taxi call 2861 1008 or 2529 8822.

Cycling

Don't even think about cycling in the car- and bus-dominated canyons of Central or Tsim Sha Tsui. In contrast, cycling on the islands and in the New Territories can be immensely enjoyable. For information, contact the **Hong Kong Cycling Association** (2573 3861) or the HKTB (see p310). For cycling permits and rules, go to www.cycling.org.hk.

Bicycle hire

Bikes can be hired in Tai Wai near Sha Tin in the New Territories and on Cheung Chau and Lantau islands. Rates are roughly HK$30-$50, depending on the type of bike you choose, and a deposit of about HK$100 is often required. See also p254.

Driving

Due to the cheap and efficient public transport system and hefty parking charges, driving is an option that many visitors pass over. If you do, however, choose to drive, the following information will be of use:
● vehicles drive on the left-hand side.
● traffic signs and street names are in both Chinese and English.
● stopping on a double or single yellow line is illegal except in side lanes, bays or at designated areas and times.
● use of seat belts in cars and taxis is mandatory.
● unless otherwise indicated, the speed limit is 80kmph (50mph).
● drinking and driving is not tolerated, and heavy penalties are

in place for those caught over the legal limit of 50 milligrams of alcohol per 100ml of blood.
● mobile phones may not be used while driving.
● an international driving licence is not required by most visitors as they can drive up to 12 months on their home country's valid and current licence (if recognised by Hong Kong Transport Authority), but must carry their passport with the visa stamped in it while driving.

Transport Department
3/F, United Centre, 95 Queensway, Admiralty, HK Island (enquiry hotline 1823/www.td.gov.hk).

Breakdown services

HK Automobile Association

2304 4911/insurance 2739 5273/ www.hkaa.com

Fuel stations

Esso/Mobil Oil

1 Lockhart Road, Wan Chai, HK Island (2865 3563). **Open** 24hrs. **Credit** AmEx, DC, MC, V. **Map** p330 A3.

Insurance

Third-party insurance is compulsory by law.

Parking

Parking is available on some streets payable at Octopus card-operated meters for short-term parking (HK$2 for 15 minutes, 30 minutes in less busy areas). Meters operate from 8am to midnight.

Parking is expensive in malls and office buildings, but some restaurants and hotels offer complimentary valet parking. There are several public car parks in the city, including, on Hong Kong Island, City Hall, International Finance Centre, Pacific Place and in the basement of department stores such as Sogo and Seibu in Causeway Bay; and in Tsim Sha Tsui at Ocean Terminal and Middle

Road (behind the Sheraton Hotel). Charges are HK$20-$30 per hour, with a minimum charge of two hours.

Vehicle hire

Try the *Yellow Pages* (see p309) for further ideas.

Avis

Head office: G/F, Park Lane Hotel Carpark, 310 Gloucester Road, Causeway Bay, HK Island (international rentals in Hong Kong 2882 2927/Kowloon 2890 6988/www.avis.com.hk). **Credit** AmEx, MC, V. **Map** p331 E3.

Toplink

Head office: Flat F, 20/F, 23 Greig Crescent, Quarry Bay, HK Island (2880 0616/fax 2880 0269/ www.ringabenz.biz.com.hk). **No credit cards**.

Walking

In spite of jostling crowds and fumes from vehicle emissions, irregular sidewalks and steep steps, walking is the way to go in Hong Kong, so a good pair of lungs and stout footwear are recommended. In contrast, walking in the New Territories and on the Outlying Islands is often a joy – and a popular recreational activity with both visitors and residents.

Suggested itineraries in this guide include walks around the Peak (see p88 **Peak around**) and the **Dragon's Back** (see p90), as well as longer routes across the territory (see p115 **Walks on the wild side**).

Bookstore chains such as **Dymocks** and **Bookazine**, as well as the **Government Publications Centre** (for all, see p175), sell a range of maps and hiking and walking books. The *Hong Kong Guidebook* and *Hong Kong Directory* are both highly recommended. In addition, the HKTB offices (see p310) at Causeway Bay MTR (exit F) and the Star Ferry terminal in Kowloon sell good maps as well as offering free, detailed street maps.

Resources A-Z

Addresses

Addresses in Hong Kong are written: name, apartment number (if applicable) and floor/house number, name of building, road/street and area. There is no post/zip code. Taxi drivers know most addresses, but you'd be wise to get hotels to write them in Chinese.

You'll find the relevant floor of the building an intrinsic part of most Hong Kong addresses. G/F (ground floor) is the floor at street level; 1/F (first floor) is the next one up, etc. You might see variations such as G-29, which will be room 29 on the ground floor, and 702 (flat number 2 on the seventh floor).

Age

The minimum legal age for drinking, driving, sex and smoking is 18.

Attitude & etiquette

Hong Kong is a cosmopolitan city, but Chinese etiquette prevails. Respect for local customs and beliefs – such as the importance of family – is evident. Surnames are written first. Elders and men are traditionally introduced first. If you want to give a gift, fruit, chocolates and money are suitable, but not clocks or watches as they are considered bad luck (the word 'clock' sounds like 'death' in Chinese).

Hong Kong Chinese are used to having foreigners around and are non-intrusive. They are sometimes perceived as being abrupt and rude, but it is only a manner, nothing personal. As in China, keeping face is of paramount concern – to such a degree that it can sometimes seem quite traumatic for a Hong Kong person to admit common errors to a foreigner. If you cause someone to lose face, you too will be perceived negatively. Losing your temper in front of others is seen as loss of face for both you and them. For more on local culture and customs, *see pp38-45.*

Business

Business cards are usually written in English on one side, Chinese on the other. Many hotels can print them within 24 hours. They should be presented with both hands, and received similarly; you should take care to read them. Business meetings and entertainment engagements require suits. Wait for the host to initiate drinking any beverage on offer. Note that no business is conducted during Chinese New Year (*see p205*).

Business centres & office hire

There are many business centres offering space and communication facilities – the fancier and larger the offices the higher the costs. Terms and conditions differ, so it is worthwhile to phone around two or three to check the rates and services available.

Harbour International Business Centre

Room 2802, Tower 1, Admiralty Centre, 18 Harcourt Road, Central, HK Island (2529 0356/ www.hibc.com). Admiralty MTR (exit A1)/buses along Harcourt Road. **Map** *p329 F4.*
Contact for secretarial help and office rentals.

Regus Business Centre

35/F, Central Plaza, 18 Harbour Road, Wan Chai, HK Island (2593 1111/www.regus.com.hk). Wan Chai MTR (exit A1)/buses along Gloucester Road & Harbour Road. **Map** *p330 B3.*

Provides 35 fully serviced executive office suites and a full range of secretarial services.

Conventions & conferences

International conventions, conferences and exhibitions are held throughout the year at the Hong Kong Convention & Exhibition Centre.

Hong Kong Convention & Exhibition Centre

1 Expo Drive, Wan Chai, HK Island (2582 8888/2582 1818/ www.hkcec.com). Wan Chai MTR (exit A1)/25A, 25C, 961 bus. **Map** *p330 B2.*

Couriers & shippers

DHL

Head office: 11/F, Trade Square, 681 Cheung Sha Wan Road, Kowloon (24hr hotline 2400 3388/www.dhl.com.hk).
Drop-off booths are located in the following MTR stations: Causeway Bay (exit F); Admiralty (exit E); Central (exit F); Tsim Sha Tsui (exit D1, D2); Mong Kok (exit B).

Federal Express

Shop 43, 1/F, Shopping Arcade, Admiralty Centre, Queensway, HK Island (2730 3333/www.fedex. com.hk). Admiralty MTR (exit C1)/ buses through Central. **Open** 9am-7.30pm Mon-Fri; 9am-6pm Sat. **Map** *p329 F4.*
Also in the Houston Centre, 63 Mody Road, Tsim Sha Tsui.

Translators & interpreters

Language Line

Flat 1B, 163 Hennessy Road, Wan Chai, HK Island (2511 2677/www.languageventure.com). Wan Chai MTR (exit A2, A4)/ buses along Hennessy Road. **Open** 9am-6pm Mon-Fri; 9am-1pm Sat. **Map** *p330 B3.*
Can provide European/Asian translation, copywriting, editing and proofreading services.

Directory

Polyglot

Flat 14B, Times Centre, 53 Hollywood Road, Central, HK Island (2851 7232/www.polyglot. com.hk). Central MTR (exit D1, D2)/Mid-Levels Escalator/12M, 13, 23A, 26, 40M, 43 bus. **Open** 9.30am-6pm Mon-Fri; 9.30am-1pm Sat. **Map** p328 C3.

Offers translation and typing services and equipment rentals.

Useful organisations

Chambers of commerce have useful information (including directories) related to doing business in Hong Kong, China and other Asian cities. They also run events such as seminars and workshops. They are also up to date on government business policies and laws. Fees are charged for some services.

American Chamber of Commerce

Room 1904, Bank of America Tower, 12 Harcourt Road, Central, HK Island (2526 0165/www. amcham.org.hk). **Map** p329 F4.

Australian Chamber of Commerce

4/F, Lucky Building, 39 Wellington Street, Central, HK Island (2522 5054/www.austcham.com.hk). **Map** p328 C3.

British Chamber of Commerce

Room 1201, Emperor Group Centre, 288 Hennessy Road, Wan Chai, HK Island (2824 2211/www. britcham.com). **Map** p330 C3.

Canadian Chamber of Commerce

Suite 1003, 1301 Kinwick Centre, 32 Hollywood Road, Central, HK Island (2110 8700/www.cancham. org). **Map** p328 C3.

Chinese General Chamber of Commerce

4/F, 24-5 Connaught Road, Central, HK Island (2525 6385/ www.cgcc.org.hk). **Map** p329 D3.

HK General Chamber of Commerce

22/F, United Centre, 95 Queensway, Admiralty, HK Island (2529 9229/www.chamber.org.hk). **Map** p329 F5.

Hong Kong Stock Exchange

12/F, One International Finance Centre, 1 Harbour View Road, Central, HK Island (2522 1122/ www.hkex.com.hk). **Map** p329 D3.

Hong Kong Trade Development Council

G/F, New Convention Centre, 1 Exposition Drive, Wan Chai, HKIsland. (1830 668/2584 4333/ www.tdc.org.hk). **Map** p330 B2. *Postal address: 36/F, Office Tower, Convention Plaza, 1 Harbour Road, Wan Chai, Hong Kong.*

Japanese Chamber of Commerce

38/F, West Wing, Hennessy Centre, 500 Hennessy Road, Causeway Bay, HK Island (2577 6129/ www.hkjcci.com.hk). **Map** p331 D3.

US Commercial Service

21/F, St John's Building, 33 Garden Road, Central (2521 1467/www.buyusa.gov/hongkong). *Buses along Garden Road.* **Open** 8.30am-12.30pm, 1.30-5.30pm Mon-Fri. **Map** p329 E5.

Consumer

The **Consumer Council** in Hong Kong is an independent organisation that protects consumers' rights and interests, tests products in the market to establish the claims made by manufacturers and retailers, and publishes the journal *Choice*, which details the results of its findings. Visitors and residents can call its hotline below for help with problems about products and services or visit their centres:

Central & Western Consumer Advice Centre

G/F, Harbour Building, 38 Pier Road, Central, HK Island (hotline 2929 2222/fax 2856 3113/www. consumer.org.hk). Sheung Wan MTR (exit E4)/buses along Connaught Road Central. **Open** 9am-5pm Mon-Fri. **Map** p328 C2.

Consumer Council

22/F, K Wah Centre, 191 Java Road, North Point, HK Island (2929 2222, press 2 for English). North Point MTR (exit A2, A4)/ buses & trams along King's Road. **Phone enquiries** 9am-5pm Mon-Fri; 9am-noon Sat.

Tsim Sha Tsui Consumer Advice Centre

G/F, 3 Ashley Road, Tsim Sha Tsui, Kowloon (2926 2222). Tsim Sha Tsui MTR (exit E). **Open** 9am-5pm Mon-Fri; 9am-noon Sat. **Map** p333 B6.

Customs

At the time of going to press, visitors were allowed to bring the following items into Hong Kong duty free:
● 200 cigarettes or 50 cigars or 250 grams of tobacco.
● one litre bottle of wine or spirits.
   A doctor's prescription will be required if large amounts of medication for personal use are brought into the country.

The following may not be brought into Hong Kong:
● animals, plants or soil.
● firearms/weapons (which must be declared and handed into custody until departure).
● narcotics.

The following must be declared and duty paid:
● commercial merchandise for trade or import.
● alcohol, cigarettes, tobacco or cigars in excess of duty-free allowances.
● cars.

For more information, go to www.customs.gov.hk or call 8100 3553.

Disabled

Space being precious, every inch is utilised, so shops, offices, restaurants, theatres and malls are located on every level of a building accessible by elevator, escalator or stairs.

   The Hong Kong Government is taking measures to provide facilities in public places and on transport systems to improve accessibility for people with mobility and sensory disabilities. Facilities such as braille on tickets and card-processing machines, and LED displays of upcoming stations, are installed in public transport. Priority seats with reachable bells are installed on trams and buses. Taxis can pick up and set down disabled people at restricted roadsides (but they need to get in touch with the Hong Kong Council of Social Services on 2864 2929 for a special certificate). Public transport staff are trained to assist people with disabilities when requested; generally, bus and taxi drivers are helpful.

The **Hong Kong Society for Rehabilitation** provides a transport network, Rehabus, with a scheduled route service, feeder bus service and dial-a-ride service (call 2817 8154 or fax 2855 7106). You can also contact the **Transport Department** (2804 2600).

If you feel you are being denied access anywhere, complain to the **Equal Opportunities Commission** (19/F, Cityplaza 3, 14 Tai Koo Wan Road, Tai Koo Shing, HK Island, 2511 8211, fax 2511 8142, www.eoc.org.hk).

Drugs

Drugs such as heroin and ecstasy are a big problem among young people in Hong Kong, as teens are vulnerable to triad pushers. As a result, the police patrol areas where there are big parties and conduct random drugs testing. Foreign nationals caught with drugs could face imprisonment and deportation.

Anti-Drug Abuse Line
2366 8822 (press 2 for English). **Phone enquiries** times vary. Run by the Narcotics Division of the Security Bureau.

Police Narcotics Bureau
2860 2888. **Phone enquiries** 24hrs daily.

Electricity

The voltage in Hong Kong is 220 volts, 50 cycles. Most hotels provide adaptors, or you can buy one from an electrical shop for around HK$20.

Embassies & consulates

Australian Consulate
21-24/F, Harbour Centre, 25 Harbour Road, Wan Chai, HK Island (2827 8881/fax 2585 4457/ Immigration 2585 4139/www.
australia.org.hk). Wan Chai MTR (exit A1)/buses along Gloucester Road. **Open** 8.45am-5pm Mon-Fri. Immigration 9.30am-1.30pm Mon-Fri. **Map** p330 B3.

British Consulate
1 Supreme Court Road, Central, HK Island (2901 3000/fax 2901 3066/www.britishconsulate.org.hk). Admiralty MTR (exit C1)/buses along Queensway. **Open** 8.45am-noon, 2-4.30pm Mon-Fri. **Map** p329 F5.

Canadian Consulate
Visa Section: GPO 1142 HK, 11-14/F, One Exchange Square, 8 Connaught Place, Central, HK Island (2847 7555/fax 2847 7493/www.hongkong.gc.ca). Central MTR (exit A)/buses along Connaught Road Central. **Open** 8.30am-5pm Mon-Fri. Immigration 8-11.30am Tue, Thur, Fri. **Map** p329 D3.

Irish Consulate
8/F, Princes Building, 10 Chater Road, Central, HK Island (2527 4897/fax 2810 0702/www. embassyofireland.cn). Wan Chai MTR (exit K)/buses along Hennessy Road. **Open** 10am-noon, 2-4.30pm Mon-Fri. **Map** p330 A3.

New Zealand Consulate
Room 6501, Central Plaza, 18 Harbour Road, Wan Chai, HK Island (2525 5044/fax 2845 2915/www.nzembassy.com/ hongkong). Wan Chai MTR (exit A1)/buses along Gloucester Road/Wan Chai Star Ferry Pier. **Open** 8am-1pm, 2-5pm Mon-Fri. Immigration 9am-1pm, 1.30-3pm Mon-Fri. **Map** p330 B3.

US Consulate General
26 Garden Road, Central, HK Island (2523 9011/2841 2219/ 2323/fax 2845 1598/www. usconsulate.org.hk). Admiralty MTR (exit C1) or Central MTR (exit K) then 10min walk/buses along Garden Road. **Open** 8.30am-12.30pm, 1.30-5.30pm Mon-Fri. **Map** p329 E5.

Visas for China

To obtain visas at the airport, *see p295.*
Visa Office of the People's Republic of China
Office of the Commissioner of the Ministry of Foreign Affairs, 7/F, Lower Block, China Resources Building, 26 Harbour Road, Wan Chai, HK Island (3413 2300/3413
2424/fax 3413 2312/www. chinavisa.com.hk). Wan Chai MTR (exit A5). **Open** 9am-noon, 2-5pm Mon-Fri. **Map** p330 C3. You can apply in person for a visa for mainland China at this office. It normally takes up to three working days but staff can issue one-day visas for a higher fee. Visas cost upwards of HK$400, but it can be cheaper (and quicker) to get one from a travel agent in Hong Kong.

The **HYFCO** travel agency (www.hkf.com) has branches all over Hong Kong, including Room 611, Hang Lung Centre, 2-20 Paterson Street, Causeway Bay, HK Island (2882 8193) and Room 704, Prestige Tower, 23-25, Nathan Road, Tsim Sha Tsui, Kowloon (2730 8608). Open 10am-7pm Mon-Sat.

Japan Travel Agency, Room 507, East Ocean Centre, 98 Granville Road, Tsim Sha Tsui East, Kowloon (2368 9151, fax 2724 4551, www.jta. biz-chinavisa), can get you a six-month/multi-entry visa for China for HK$400 in one day if you apply right at opening time (9am-6pm Mon-Fri).

Emergencies

See also p302 Accident & emergency.

Ambulance/police/fire
999.

Complaints against the police
2866 7700/fax 2240 4460.

Lost credit cards
American Express *emergency card replacement 2811 6122/ 24hr hotline 2277 1010.*
Diners Club *2860 1888.*
HSBC *2748 4848.*
MasterCard *Hong Kong 2810 8033/global 800 966 677.*
Visa *Hong Kong 2810 8033/ global 800 900 782.*

Lost passports
Contact your consulate (*see above*) after notifying the police on 2860 2000.

24-hour crime hotline
2527 7177 (press 3 for English).

Directory

Police stations

Peak & Central *2522 8882.*
Wan Chai & Happy Valley
2519 0076.
North Point & Chai Wan
2563 6487.
Citizens' Easy Link *1823.*

Gay & lesbian

For gay-related websites and
other media, *see p230.*

Freemen

*PO Box 2443, Hong Kong (9106
4983/http://freemenhk.tripod.com).*
This gay male social group offers
counselling and social activities.

Horizons

2815 9268/www.horizons.org.hk.
Phone enquiries 7.30-10.30pm
Tue, Thur.
Provides counselling and organises
social activities such as hiking
trips, concerts and movie nights.

Health

Ensure that you have adequate
personal medical insurance
prior to travelling to Hong
Kong. Vaccinations against
typhoid, flu, hepatitis A and B
are precautionary. Routine
polio, tetanus, mumps, measles
and diphtheria updates are
recommended. Check with
your doctor about immunisation
prior to travelling. For further
information, go to the website
www.healthinasia.com

In 2003, Hong Kong suffered
1,755 (including 386 health
workers and medical students)
cases of SARS (Severe Acute
Respiratory Syndrome), with
a disturbingly high death rate
among the elderly and health-
care workers. In June 2003 the
disease was finally contained
and Hong Kong was declared
safe by the WHO. For more
information check out www.
info.gov.hk/info/sars. More
recent outbreaks of the H5N1
virus ('bird flu') in China and
South-East Asia have raised
awareness levels in Hong
Kong, which has a website
(www.info.gov.hk/info/flu/eng)
for alerts and further details.

Accident & emergency

The **Hospital Authority
One-Stop Enquiry Service**
has two 24-hour hotlines
(2882 4866 and 2300 6555)
giving information on accident
and emergency services,
hospital fees, help with
complaints, hospital phone
numbers, locations and
transport information.

A full range of A&E
services are provided 24 hours
a day at the places listed
below. If an ambulance is
required, dial 999 (*see also
p301* **Emergencies**).

Caritas Medical Centre

*111 Wing Hong Street, Sham
Shui Po, Kowloon (3408 7911/
www.ha.org.hk). Cheung Sha Wan
MTR (exit A3) then 45M minibus.*

Matilda Hospital

*41 Mount Kellett Road, The Peak,
HK Island (2849 0123/www.
matilda.org). Minibus 1 from
Queen's Pier or hospital shuttle
(every 20mins from City Hall).*

Prince of Wales Hospital

*30-32 Ngan Shing Street, Sha
Tin, New Territories (2632 2211/
www.ha.org.hk). Bus A41, 73A,
80K, 85A.*

Queen Mary Hospital

*102 Pok Fu Lam Road, Pok Fu
Lam, HK Island (2855 3838/
www.ha.org.hk). Minibus 54, 55
from Worldwide House, Central/
bus 7, 71, 91, 94 from Central
Ferry Pier.*

Complementary medicine

The *Natural Life Directory*,
published by **Heartbeat**
(www.heartbeat.com.hk) lists
local complementary medicinal
services and products.

Integrated Medicine Institute HK Limited

*7/F, Baskerville House, 13 Duddell
Street, Central, HK Island (2523
7121/www.imi.com.hk). Central
MTR (exit D1, D2, G)/buses along
Queen's Road Central.* **Open** 9am-
6.30pm Mon-Fri; 9am-1pm Sat.
Map p328 C3.

Optimum Health Centre Alexander Yuan

*2/F, Prosperous Commercial
Building, 54 Jardine's Bazaar,
Causeway Bay, HK Island (2577
3798/www.naturalhealing.com.hk).
Causeway Bay MTR (exit F)/
buses along Hennessy Road.*
Open 9am-8pm Mon-Fri; 9am-
4pm Sat. **Map** p331 D3.

Contraception & abortion

For advice, call the **Family
Planning Association** (2711
9656 in Kowloon, 2575 4477
in Wan Chai, www.famplan.
org.hk, open 9am-8pm Mon-
Fri, 9am-5pm Sat).

Dentists

Foreign qualified and English-
speaking doctors and dentists
are the norm in Hong Kong.
They offer excellent services
in private practice and are
situated in main commercial
and business areas, but tend
to be expensive, so make sure
you have insurance coverage.
A typical consultation costs
HK$350-$500. The following
two clinics are recommended:

Dr Eric Carter

*Room 1103, Century Square,
1-13 D'Aguilar Street, Central,
HK Island (2525 4285). Central
MTR (exit D1, G)/buses 12M,
13, 23A, 40M, 43.* **Open** 8am-
4.30pm Mon-Fri; 8am-12.30pm
Sat. **Map** p328 C4.

Dr James Woo & Associates

*9/F, Lane Crawford House,
70 Queen's Road, Central, HK
Island (2869 6986). Central MTR
(exit D2)/buses along Queen's
Road Central.* **Open** 9.30am-1pm,
2-6pm Mon-Fri; 9am-1pm Sat.
Map p329 D3.

Doctors

The following clinics are both
recommended. There are also
travel clinics at the Matilda
Hospital (*see above*) and the
Adventist Hospital (*see p303*).

Dr Nicholson & Associates

Room 402B, New World Tower 1, 18 Queen's Road, Central, HK Island (2525 1251). Central MTR (exit D1, D2, G)/buses along Queen's Road Central. **Open** 9am-1pm, 2-6pm Mon-Fri; 9am-1pm Sat. **Map** p329 D4.

Raffles Medical Group

Room B, 24/F, 9 Queen's Road, Central, HK Island (2525 1730/ www.rafflesmedical.com).Central MTR (exit K)/buses to Central Ferry Pier/Central Ferry Pier. **Open** 8.30am-6pm Mon-Fri; 8.30am-1pm Sat. **Map** p329 F4.

Hospitals

For hospitals with 24-hour accident and emergency wards, *see p302*. Decent medical care is widely available in Hong Kong thanks to a large number of foreign-qualified local and expatriate practitioners. The private hospitals listed below have English-speaking staff and all operate outpatient departments at the following (approximate) times: 8.30am-4pm Mon-Fri, 8.30am-12.30pm Sat.

For emergency numbers, *see p301*.

Adventist Hospital

40 Stubbs Road, Mid-Levels, HK Island (2835 0566/2574 6211/outpatient appointments 3651 8888/www.hkah.org.hk). Bus 6, 15, 15B, 61, 66, 76. **Map** p328 C3.

Baptist Hospital

222 Waterloo Road, Kowloon (2339 8888/www.hkbh.org.hk). Kowloon Tong KCR/MTR (exit A2)/buses along Waterloo Road & Cornwall Street.

Canossa Hospital

1 Old Peak Road, Mid-Levels, HK Island (2522 2181/www.canossa hospital.org.hk). Bus 3B, 12, 12M, 23, 23A, 40/hospital shuttlebus every 20mins from Shanghai Commercial Bank, 12 Queen's Road, Central. **Map** p328 C5.

Opticians

See p198.

Pharmacies

Over-the-counter medicines for colds, headaches, fevers and minor ailments are available in pharmacies, such as Mannings and Watson's (*see p199*), in malls and most shopping areas. Most open 9am-6pm daily.

Doctors' clinics are licensed to sell prescription drugs, but if you do go to a pharmacy, be aware that only prescriptions from Hong Kong-based doctors will be accepted. Shops with dispensaries will display a red-cross sign.

The Adventist (*see above*) and Queen Mary (*see p302*) hospitals have pharmacies that are open 24 hours a day; those in other hospitals are usually open 10am-6pm daily. Hospital pharmacies accept prescriptions from the doctors registered in their hospitals only.

STDs, HIV & AIDS

AIDS Concern

2898 4422/www.aidsconcern. org.hk. **Phone enquiries** 7-10pm Thur, Sat.
This community-based AIDS organisation provides support, advocacy and prevention programmes.

AIDS Counselling Service

2780 2211 (press 2 for English). **Phone enquiries** 24hrs daily.

St John's Cathedral HIV Education Centre

4-8 Garden Road, Central, HK Island (2523 0531/2501 0653/ education centre & counselling 2525 7207/www.sjhivctr.com). Central MTR (exit J2)/buses along Garden Road. **Phone enquiries** 9am-5pm Mon-Fri. **Map** p329 E5. St John's run an HIV education centre and free counselling service.

Women's health

There are well-woman clinics located within the Adventist (*see above*) and Matilda hospitals (*see p302*).

Helplines

These helplines are all manned by English-speaking operators:

Alcoholics Anonymous

2522 5665. **Phone enquiries** 6-7pm daily.

Community Advice Bureau

2815 5444/www.cab.org.hk. **Phone enquiries** 10am-4pm daily.

Kely Support Group

2521 6890/www.kely.org. **Phone enquiries** 9am-6pm daily.

Rape Crisis/Shelter

2572 2733 (press 3 for English).

The Samaritans

2896 0000/www.samaritans.org.hk. **Phone enquiries** 24hrs daily.

SARDA (Society for Aid & Rehabilitation of Drug Abusers)

2527 7723/English hotline 2574 3300. **Phone enquiries** 9am-11pm daily.

St John's Ambulance

HK Island 2576 6555/Kowloon 2713 5555/ New Territories 2639 2555. **Phone enquiries** 24hrs daily.

ID

Visitors and residents are officially 'advised' to carry their passport or other photo ID with them at all times while in Hong Kong. The police do random street checks and if you are found without any identification you are liable for a fine. Some bars and clubs ask for ID if they suspect you are under age for entry – these tend to be managed or owned by foreigners.

Insurance

Make sure you have adequate travel and health insurance prior to arrival in Hong Kong, as the territory does not have reciprocal arrangements with other countries.

Directory

Internet

Hong Kong has a considerable number of cyber-cafés (though there aren't as many as might be expected in a city that has embraced technology – in the form of mobile telephony – so avidly); terminals can also be found in cafés and even hairdressers. The HKTB (*see p310*) offers free internet access at the airport and at its info centres. Many hotels provide wireless or broadband access in their business centres and in the guest rooms (*see p55*).

Mix

G/F, Amber Lodge, 23 Hollywood Road, Central (2851 6038/www. mix-world.com). Central MTR (exit D1). **Open** *7.30am-1am Mon-Wed; 7.30am-2am Thur-Sat; 7.30am-midnight Sun.* **Map** *p328 C3.*
This healthy café chain has branches throughout the city. You can get internet access for 20-30 minutes along with your smoothie.

Pacific Coffee Company

Shop 1022, Level 1, Southern Retail Podium, International Finance Centre, Harbour View Street, (2868 5100/www.pacific coffee.com). Central MTR (exit A)/buses through Central. **Open** *7am-10pm daily.* **Map** *p329 D3.*
This coffee shop chain offers access in all of its branches, free of charge (with drink purchase).

Language

English and Chinese are the official languages (*see p312*), but away from business and main shopping areas, English is rarely spoken or understood; communicating in restaurants and shops can be a challenge. If you expect to go beyond the main shopping and business areas, ask your hotel concierge to write out the name and destination in Chinese, as well as return directions.

Cantonese, Mandarin and English-language institutes are plentiful in Hong Kong, though for some you have to be a full-time student to enrol in their Chinese language courses. *See also p308.*

Left luggage

There are no left-luggage facilities in any of the public transport terminals – except at the Airport Express stations of Central (2868 3190) and Kowloon (2736 0162), and at Arrivals Hall B (2261 0110) at the airport. The service is open 6am-1am daily and charges HK$35 per piece for up to three hours, or HK$50 per piece for 24 hours, HK$80 per subsequent day.

Legal help

For help in finding a lawyer and basic information on Hong Kong law, call 2521 3333 or 2522 8018. For embassies and consulates, *see p301.*

Libraries

The Leisure and Cultural Services Department (customer service 2414 5555, Citizen's Easy Link 1823, www.lcsd.gov.hk) runs a network of libraries with a wide selection of books, newspapers, magazines, videos, cassettes, records, slides and microfilm. For non-residents, a passport, proof of address and a resident guarantor's identity card is required for a three-month temporary library card.

Alliance Française

123 Hennessy Road, Wan Chai, HK Island (2527 7825/www. alliancefrancaise.com.hk). Wan Chai MTR (exit B1)/buses along Hennessy Road. **Open** *9am-9pm Mon-Fri.* **Map** *p330 B3.*

British Council Library

1 Supreme Court Road, Central, HK Island (2913 5100/fax 2913 5102/www.britishcouncil.org/ hongkong). Admiralty MTR (exit C1)/buses along Queensway. **Open** *noon-8pm Mon-Fri; 10.30am-5.30pm Sat.* **Map** *p329 F5.*

Central Library

66 Causeway Road (3150 1234/ www.hkpl.gov.hk). Causeway Bay MTR (exit F)/8A, 15B, 19, 25, 63, 77, A11 bus. **Open** *10am-9pm Mon, Tue, Thur-Sat; 1-9pm Wed; 10am-7pm Sun.* **Map** *p331 E3.*

Goethe Institut Library

14/F, Hong Kong Arts Centre, 2 Harbour Road, Wan Chai, HK Island (2802 0088/www.goethe.de/ hongkong). Wan Chai MTR (exit A1)/buses along Gloucester Road. **Open** *5.30-8.30pm Mon-Fri; 2-6pm Sat.* **Map** *p330 B2.*

Urban Council Library

2-6/F & 8-11/F, City Hall High Block, Central (2921 2555/www. hkpl.gov.hk). **Open** *10am-7pm Mon-Thur; 10am-9pm Fri; 10am-5pm Sat, Sun.* **Map** *p329 E3.*

Lost property

Call **2860 2000** if you lose anything in the city and you'll be told which police station to contact. The following are all lost property numbers:

Airport

Level 6 (2182 2018). **Open** *8am-11pm. See p295.*

Buses

Citybus *2873 0818.*
Kowloon Motor Bus (KMB) *2745 4466.*
New World First Bus *2136 8888.*

Ferries

Discovery Bay Ferries *2987 7351.*
New World First Ferry Service *2131 8181.*
Star Ferry *2366 2576.*
Hong Kong Kowloon Ferry *2815 6063.*

Taxis

Lost property hotline *187 2920.*
HK Island taxis *2574 7311.*
Kowloon taxis *2760 0411.*

Trains

MTR (at Admiralty) *2881 8888.*
KCR *2602 7799.*
LR *2468 7788.*

Trams

HK Tramways *2548 7102.*
Peak Tramways *2522 0922.*
Public Lightbus *2804 2600.*

Media

Newspapers

Since the Handover, Hong Kong's freedom of speech has been closely monitored – and most agree that it generally hasn't suffered as badly as many people thought it might. However, self-censorship is increasingly and worryingly widespread as the owners of some publications tread carefully to protect their Chinese interests. Of the main English-speaking newspapers, the *South China Morning Post* (www.scmp.com) boasts the biggest circulation and wields the heaviest clout, but its reporting has lost some of its punch. The *Standard* is primarily a business rag.

Of the Chinese language newspapers, the most popular are *Apple Daily, Oriental Daily News, Ming Pao* and *Sing Tao Daily*. The first two tend to go a step further in their efforts to shock Hong Kongers awake with sensational pictures full of blood and guts spread across the front page. If there is any sex and violence to be had, the Chinese paparazzi are on the scene snapping away before the blood has dried on the pavement.

Magazines

As you'd expect from the financial hub of Asia, there are piles of locally based magazines reporting on business and finance, including *Time Asia* and the *Asian Wall Street Journal*. Society magazines *Hong Kong Tatler* (www.hong kongtatler.com) and *Talkies* (www.talkieshk.com) are full of pictures of fashionable *tai-tais* attending glossy launches of international haute-couture fashion collections, as well as reports on the latest local and international gossip. *Home Journal* takes a peek at the

multi-million-dollar residences on the Peak. There are Chinese versions of *Marie Claire, Elle, Cosmopolitan* and other UK and US publications, with Chinese models and articles on beauty and fashion.

HK Magazine (www.asia-city.com), which comes out on Fridays, has its finger on the weekly pulse of the Hong Kong world of clubbing, film, art, bars and restaurants, as well as illuminating and confrontational articles on life in the region. *BC Magazine* (www.bcmagazine.net) is a bi-monthly, available on the second and third Thursdays of the month, loaded with information about what's on in the entertainment world and what's happening around town, without the 'in your face' style of *HK Magazine* but more shoddily written. Both can be picked up for free in venues around town.

Of course, major international magazines are available, too, albeit at a huge mark-up.

Radio

Radio Television Hong Kong (RTHK) is publicly funded and editorially independent. It frequently criticises the Chinese Government and airs public opinions without restraint on its talkback programmes. **RTHK3** (567AM, 1584AM) is the main provider of English news, finance and current affairs. **RTHK4** (97.6-98.9FM) plays Western and Chinese classical music. **RTHK6** (675AM) broadcasts the BBC World Service. **Metro Plus** (1044AM) is a local station with news and music.

TV

Two locally based English-language channels air good documentaries, not-so-good American sitcoms, sports, cooking shows, and local and

international news. **Star TV**, Hong Kong's satellite TV station, and **Cable TV** provide a wider choice of international news coverage and programmes, including movie channels. Hotels rooms often feature a package of cable and/or satellite channels.

Money

Hong Kong is an expensive place to live due to high rents and the cost of imported merchandise. But some things are cheaper than in many other cities, in particular public transport (especially taxis), locally made clothes and other goods, and local food. Visitors from Western countries with strong currencies often find Hong Kong relatively cheap.

The Hong Kong dollar is pegged to the US dollar at HK$7.80, though this may fluctuate slightly. Other rates at press time include AUS$1= HK$6.10, GBP£1= HK$15.30, 1 Euro (€) = HK$10.08. Hong Kong dollar notes come in denominations of 1,000 (orange), 500 (brown), 100 (red), 50 (mauve/green), 20 (blue) and 10 (green/purple). Coins come in denominations of 10 dollars (two-tone, gold circled by silver), 5, 2 and 1 dollar in silver colour, and brass-coloured 50, 20 and 10 cent pieces.

There is no central mint; bank notes are issued by various banks and the Hong Kong Monetary Authority, and are interchangeable.

Exchange bureaux and banks charge a fee for changing money and cashing travellers' cheques – unless you take the latter to the issuing bank or to American Express (*see p306*).

ATMs

There are ATMs on virtually every street corner in Hong Kong, as well as at Star Ferry terminals and MTR stations.

Banks

Bank of America

Bank of America Tower, 12 Harcourt Road, Admiralty, HK Island (2843 8988/fax 2843 8989/www.bankofamerica. com.hk). Admiralty MTR (exit B). **Open** 9am-5pm Mon-Fri; 9am-1pm Sat. **Map** p329 F4.

Bank of China

1 Garden Road, Central, HK Island (2826 6888/fax 2810 5963/www.bochk.com). Admiralty MTR (exit B)/buses along Garden Road. **Open** 9am-5pm Mon-Fri; 9am-1pm Sat. **Map** p329 E4.

Citibank

3 Garden Road, Central, HK Island (2868 8888/www.citibank. com.hk). Admiralty MTR (exit B)/buses along Garden Road. **Open** 9am-4.30pm Mon-Fri; 9am-12.30pm Sat. **Map** p329 E4.

HSBC

1 Queen's Road, Central, HK Island (customer hotline 2748 8222/2822 1111/fax 2288 2401/www.hsbc.com.hk). Central MTR (exit K)/buses along Queen's Road Central. **Open** 9am-4.30pm Mon-Fri; 9am-12.30pm Sat. **Map** p329 E4.

Standard Chartered Bank

4 Des Voeux Road, Central, HK Island (2820 3333/fax 2856 9129/www.standardchartered.com .hk).Central MTR (exit K). **Open** 9.30am-4.30pm Mon-Fri; 9.30am-12.30pm Sat. **Map** p329 E4.

Bureaux de change

These are plentiful, though banks usually offer better exchange rates.

American Express

1/F, Henley Building, 5 Queen's Road, Central, HK Island (3192 7788/2277 1888/www.american express.com.hk). Central MTR (exit K, G)/buses along Queen's Road Central. **Open** 9-5pm Mon-Fri. **Map** p329 D4.

1/F, China Insurance Building, 48 Cameron Road, Tsim Sha Tsui, Kowloon (3191 3838/2315 9188). Tsim Sha Tsui MTR (exit B). **Open** 9am-5pm Mon-Fri. **Map** p333 C5.

Travelex

8/F, Man Yee Building, 68 Des Voeux Road, Central, HK Island (3196 5388/www.travelex.com.hk). Central MTR (exit C)/buses & trams along Des Voeux Road. **Map** p329 D3.

Rooms 910-912, 9/F, Hong Kong Pacific Centre, 28 Hankow Road, Tsim Sha Tsui, Kowloon (2723 8212). Tsim Sha Tsui MTR (exit A). **Open** 9am-5.30pm Mon-Fri; 9am-1pm Sat. **Map** p333 C6.

There are also branches in the Peak Tower and Peak Galleria (open 10am-10pm daily).

Credit cards

Credit cards are widely accepted in the city (though hardly at all in rural areas). The majority of large shops, department stores, restaurants, travel agents and hotels take most of the major cards.

For lost credit cards, *see p301* **Emergencies**.

Natural hazards

Hong Kong's subtropical climate is at its most oppressive during the summer (*see p310*). July to September is typhoon season. During the approach of a typhoon, a system of numbers tracks its progress and defines its severity and the precautions to be taken by schools and workplaces. Warnings and weather information are given out on TV and radio channels, or you can call 187 8066.

An **amber** rainstorm warning means that more than 30 millimetres (1.2 inches) of rain an hour is expected; a **red** warning is for 50 millimetres (1.9 inches) and over of rain; while a **black** rain signal warns of rainfall in excess of 70 millimetres (2.8 inches) in an hour. If the last comes into effect, you can expect roads to become flooded, landslides to take place and public facilities to be closed down.

Typhoon Signal 1 indicates that a tropical cyclone is within 800 kilometres (500 miles) of the city; **Typhoon Signal 3** means that winds of up to 62 kilometres (39 miles) per hour are expected across Hong Kong; **Typhoon Signal 8** is when the typhoon is close and possibly on the path for a hit with storm-force winds of up to 117 kilometres (73 miles) per hour and gusts of up to 180 kilometres (112 miles) per hour; **Typhoon Signal 10** is as bad as it gets – a 'direct hit' is expected with winds higher than 117 kilometres (73 miles) per hour and gusts up to 220 kilometres (137 miles) per hour. From Signal 8 upwards, you should stay indoors – most of Hong Kong's buildings can withstand such winds, but there's a danger of being hit by flying debris. However, only about 12 maximum severity typhoons have hit the city in the last 50 years.

There are not many flies in Hong Kong but mosquitoes during the summer months can leave you scratching in parks and green areas. As a deterrent, repellents are recommended, but if you do get bitten, try locally made medicated White Flower Oil (available in drugstores) to calm the itching. For suggested vaccinations and health precautions, *see p302*.

Air pollution can be a problem for asthma sufferers, particularly in drier months.

Opening hours

Generally, office hours are 9am to 6pm Monday to Friday (with lunch usually from 1pm to 2pm) and 9am to 1pm on Saturday. Major banks are open 9am to 4.30pm Monday to Friday and 9am to 12.30pm Saturday. Most government offices are open from 9.30am to 5pm Monday to Friday; some (such as police and immigration) are also open 9.30am to noon on Saturday.

Most shops open 10.30am to 6.30pm every day. However, in major shopping areas like Causeway Bay and Nathan Road, Kowloon, shopping goes on until 9pm or later at the weekends. During Chinese New Year (*see p205*) the city shuts down for three days.

Police

The Hong Kong Police (www.info.gov.hk/police) is still largely run and staffed as it was under the British. It is proud of its reputation as one of Asia's best forces. Officers wear grey-green uniform in summer and dark blue in winter. English-speaking policemen wear a red strip under their shoulder badge.

Police stations

Hong Kong Island

Central Division, 1 Arsenal Street, Admiralty, HK Island (Head Office 2860 2000/Central Division 2522 8882). Admiralty MTR (exit E1, E2) buses along Hennessy Road. **Map** p330 A2.

Kowloon

190 Argyle Street, Mong Kok, Kowloon (2761 2228). Mong Kok MTR/buses along Nathan Road & Argyle Street. **Map** p332 B2.

213 Nathan Road, near Kowloon Park (2721 0137). Tsim Sha Tsui MTR (exit A1). **Map** p333 B5.

Postal services

The Hong Kong postal service (www.hongkongpost.com) is generally reliable and efficient. Airmail letters and postcards to Zone 1 countries (all parts of Asia except Japan) cost HK$2.40 for 20 grams (0.7oz) or less – delivery time is three to five days; to Zone 2 (all other countries) costs HK$3 for 20 grams (0.7oz) or less – delivery time is five to seven days. Local mail costs HK$1.40 and takes one to two days. International (Speedpost) and local courier

services are also available. For Federal Express and DHL *see p299* **Couriers & shippers**.

Post offices

General Post Office

2 Connaught Place, Central, HK Island (2921 2222). Central MTR (exit A)/buses along Connaught Road Central/Central Ferry Pier. **Open** 9am-6pm Mon-Sat; 9am-2pm Sun. **Credit** (over HK$300) AmEx, DC, MC, V. **Map** p329 E3.

Post office

10 Middle Road, Tsim Sha Tsui, Kowloon (2366 4111). Tsim Sha Tsui MTR (exit E)/buses along Nathan Road/Tsim Sha Tsui Star Ferry Pier. **Open** 8am-6pm Mon-Sat; 9am-2pm Sun. **Credit** (over HK$300) AmEx, DC, MC, V. **Map** p333 B6.

Poste restante

The poste restante service operates out of the General Post Office (*see above*) near the Central Ferry Pier. You can collect poste restante mail from 8am until 6pm Monday to Saturday; don't forget to take your passport with you.

Religion

Buddhism, Confucianism and Taoism have a wide following in Hong Kong and the city is home to many temples. Other religions have facilities and are practised freely.

Anglican

St John's Cathedral, 4-8 Garden Road, Central, HK Island (2523 4157/www.stjohnscathedral.org.hk). Central MTR (exit K)/buses along Garden Road. **Services** 7am, 6pm daily. **Map** p329 E4.

Baptist

Kowloon English Baptist Church, 300 Junction Road, Kowloon (2337 2555/www.hkkibc.org). Kowloon Tong KCR/MTR (exit A2)/Lok Fu MTR/buses along Junction Road. **Services** 7.30pm Wed; 8.20am, 11am, 6pm Sun.

Catholic

St Joseph's, 37 Garden Road, Central, HK Island (2522 3992).

Central MTR (exit K)/buses along Garden Road. **Services** 7.45am, 6pm Mon-Fri; 6pm Sat; from 7am (& every hr thereafter) Sun. **Map** p329 E5.

Hindu

Hindu Temple, 1B Wong Nai Chung Road, Happy Valley, HK Island (2572 5284). Bus 5A/trams to Happy Valley. **Services** 8am Mon-Sat; 7.30pm daily (bhajan); 11am Sun.

Interdenominational

Union Church Interdenominational, 22A Kennedy Road, Mid-Levels, HK Island (2522 1515/www.unionchurchhk.org). Admiralty MTR then 12A bus or 28 minibus from in front of Alexandra House. **Services** 9.30am, 11am, 6pm Sun. **Map** p328 B3.

Islamic

Kowloon Mosque & Islamic Centre, Junction of Nathan Road & Cameron Road, Tsim Sha Tsui, Kowloon (2724 0095). Tsim Sha Tsui MTR (exit A1)/buses along Nathan Road. **Open** 9am-10pm daily. **Services** phone for details. **Map** p333 B5.

Jewish

Ohel Leah Synagogue, 70 Robinson Road, Mid-Levels, HK Island (2549 0981/2801 5440/www.jcc.org.hk). Bus 3B, 12M, 13, 23, 23B, 40. **Services** 6.55am Mon, Thur; 7.05am Tue, Wed, Fri; 8.30am Sun. *Rosh Chodesh* 6.45am. *Shabbat* 9am, 6.30pm. **Map** p328 B4.

Lutheran

Church of All Nations, 8 South Bay Close, Repulse Bay, HK Island (2812 0375). Bus 6, 66, 6A, 6X, 260. **Services** 10.15am Sun.

Methodist

English Methodist Church, 271 Queen's Road East, Wan Chai, HK Island (2575 7817). Wan Chai MTR (exit A3)/buses along Queen's Road East. **Services** 7.45am Wed; 8.15am, 11am Sun. **Map** p330 B4.

Mormon

Church of Latter Day Saints, 118 Gloucester Road, Wan Chai, HK Island. (2910 2910). Wan Chai MTR (exit A1)/buses along Gloucester Road. **Services** phone for details. **Map** p330 C3.

Sikh

Sikh Temple, 371 Queen's Road East, Wan Chai, HK Island (2572 4459). Bus 10. **Services** 6am, 6.30pm daily. **Map** p330 B4.

Directory

Average climate

Month	Avg High (°C/°F)	Avg Low (°C/°F)	Rainfall (mm/inches)
Jan	18.6/65.5	13.6/56.5	23.4/0.9
Feb	18.6/65.5	13.9/57.0	48.0/1.9
Mar	21.3/70.3	16.5/61.7	66.9/2.6
Apr	24.9/76.8	20.2/68.4	161.5/6.4
May	28.7/83.7	23.9/75.0	316.7/12.5
June	30.3/86.5	25.9/78.6	376.0/14.8
July	31.5/88.7	26.6/79.9	323.5/12.7
Aug	31.3/88.3	26.3/79.3	391.4/15.4
Sept	30.3/86.5	25.5/77.9	299.7/11.8
Oct	27.9/82.2	23.1/73.6	144.8/5.7
Nov	24.2/75.6	19.2/66.6	35.1/1.4
Dec	20.5/68.9	15.4/59.7	27.3/1.1

Safety & security

For a city of its size, Hong Kong is remarkably safe – even at night. Violent crime is very rare, and almost entirely confined to triad disputes and domestic incidents. A common petty crime to watch out for is pickpocketing, and even that is not widespread. However, all the normal city precautions apply (particularly in the main tourist areas): don't flash large wads of cash around; don't leave bags where you can't see them (hanging from the back of seats, etc); keep cash and wallets in front pockets, and don't put anything valuable in your backpack.

Although you will come across touts anxious to lure you into their shops in some tourist areas, they are rarely very persistent.

Sexual harassment is rare; many well-travelled female residents claim that this is the safest city they've ever lived in.

Smoking & spitting

Smoking is considered anti-social in Hong Kong. As of 1 January 2007, all offices, shops, restaurants, bathing beaches, entertainment venues and bars are non-smoking, as is public transport. Hawking and spitting in the street is common in the rest of China, but less so here. Spitting is, in fact, strictly forbidden in public areas and a hefty fine is imposed on defaulters.

Study

Language colleges in Hong Kong spring up and close frequently. *HK Magazine* (*see p305*) is the most reliable source of information.

Hong Kong has eight universities offering degree programmes in a wide variety of subjects, both academic and vocational. Student unions are visible and active. All of Hong Kong's universities also offer continuing education programmes. Details of their degree, sub-degree and further education programmes can be found on the websites below.

Smaller institutions run informal courses on everything from jewellery beading to photography. These include the **YMCA of Hong Kong** on Salisbury Road in Tsim Sha Tsui (2268 7000, www.ymca. org.hk) and the **YWCA** (3476 1340, www.esmdywca.org.hk) on MacDonnell Road in Mid-

Levels. For Chinese-language courses (in Cantonese and Mandarin) contact the **British Council** (www.britishcouncil. org.hk), the **Chinese University of Hong Kong** (*see below*) or one of a number of private language centres, such as the **HK Institute of Languages** (2877 6160, www.hklanguages.com).

Check the classifieds of *HK Magazine* for full listings.

Universities

Chinese University of Hong Kong
Sha Tin, New Territories (2609 6000/fax 2603 5544/www.cuhk.edu.hk).

City University
83 Tat Chee Avenue, Kowloon Tong, Kowloon (2788 7654/fax 2778 1167/www.cityu.edu.hk).

Hong Kong Baptist University
224 Waterloo Road, Kowloon Tong, Kowloon (3411 7400/fax 2338 7644/www.hkbu.edu.hk).

Hong Kong Polytechnic University
Yuk Choi Road, Hung Hom, Kowloon (2766 5111/fax 2764 3374/www.polyu.edu.hk).

Hong Kong University
Pok Fu Lam Road, HK Island (2859 2111/fax 2858 2549/ www.hku.hk).

Lingnan University
Tuen Mun, New Territories (2616 8888/fax 2463 8363/ www.ln.edu.hk).

Open University of Hong Kong
30 Good Shepherd Road, Ho Man Tin, Kowloon (2711 2100/fax 2761 3935/www.ouhk.edu.hk).

University of Science & Technology
Clearwater Bay, Kowloon (2358 6000/fax 2358 0769/www.ust.hk).

Tax

Hong Kong is a duty-free port; import duty is only payable on alcohol, tobacco and cars (*see p300*). No tax is levied on purchased merchandise or in restaurants, but hotels charge a ten per cent service tax and three per cent government tax

Directory

(check when you book if it's included in the rate quoted). There is an airport departure tax for adults of HK$120 (included in the ticket price); the tax for leaving Hong Kong by boat or ferry (HK$15-$20) is also included in the ticket price.

Telephones

Dialling & codes

The international code for Hong Kong is **852**, so to call the city from abroad, dial the international access code (00 in the UK, New Zealand and Ireland, 011 in the USA and Canada, 0011 in Australia), then 852 and the eight-digit local number. There are no area codes within Hong Kong. For Macau codes, *see p277*; for Guangzhou, *see p290*.

To call abroad from Hong Kong, dial the international access code 001, then 44 for the UK, 1 for the USA and Canada, 61 for Australia, 64 for New Zealand and 353 for Ireland, then the local area code (omit the initial 0 if necessary) and the local number. Long-distance IDD calls are the cheapest in Asia, but only if you are calling from a public payphone – hotels tend to levy excessive surcharges.

Local calls from public coin phone boxes cost HK$1 for five minutes. Local calls from private homes, restaurants, offices and shops are free, but most hotels charge for local calls. If you want to call abroad from a public phone, you'll need to purchase a phone card from one of the HKTB centres (*see p310*), the Star Ferry piers, convenience stores such as 7-Eleven and Circle K, Wellcome (*see p191*) and Mannings supermarkets, or PCCW shops (*see below*). These cards come in denominations of 50, 100, 200 and 300 dollars. Some public phones accept credit cards and Octopus cards (*see p296*).

Operator services

Directory assistance *1081.*
International inquiries *10013.*
Reverse-charge/collect calls from any private or public phone *10010.*
The **Home Direct** system allows direct access to an operator in the country being called, making collect calls cheaper or allowing you to charge the call to your phone card. The Home Direct access numbers from Hong Kong are:
Australia *800 96 0161.*
Canada *800 96 1100.*
UK *800 96 0044.*
USA *800 96 1111 for AT&T; 800 96 1121 for MCI; 800 96 1877 for Sprint.*

Telephone directories

Directories are provided in most hotel rooms and by some public phones. There are *Yellow Pages* (which has business listings by category; also available online at www.yp.com.hk) and *White Pages* (with both business and residential numbers listed alphabetically).

Mobile phones

Hong Kong residents love their mobile phones. In fact, the SAR boasts the world's highest per capita usage of pagers and mobiles. Most dual-band phones work here.

If you want to hire a phone while in Hong Kong, you'll find rental packages (one week minimum) on offer from one of the many **PCCW** shops (www.pccw.com). These include G/F, 161-3 Des Voeux Road, Central, HK Island (2543 0603) and 168-76 Sai Yeung Choi Street, Mong Kok, Kowloon (2394 8131). It may be cheaper to swap the SIM card in your own phone for one purchased here. SIM cards and top-ups are available at PCCW, Sunday, Smartone, Vodaphone, Fortress and Peoples, and convenience stores such as 7-Eleven.

Faxes

Most hotels are willing to accept incoming faxes for their guests. Faxes can either be sent from hotels or (generally, more cheaply) from photocopy shops. The charge is about HK$10 (local) or HK$80 (international) per page.

Xerox

New Henry House, 10 Ice House Street, Central (2524 9799). Central MTR (exit H)/buses & trams through Central. **Open** 9am-6pm Mon-Sat. **Credit** (over HK$300) AmEx, DC, MC, V. **Map** p329 D4.

Time

Hong Kong does not have Daylight Saving Time. Time differences between Hong Kong and major cities are:

Chicago	-14hrs (-13hrs during DST)
London	-8hrs (-7hrs)
Los Angeles	16hrs (-15hrs)
New York	-13hrs (-12hrs)
Sydney	+2hrs (+3hrs)

Tipping

Tipping isn't a part of Chinese culture, but Westerners have been in Hong Kong so long that it is now widely expected. A standard ten per cent service charge is added to the bill at most restaurants and hotels. Where there is no service charge, tipping is at your discretion, but ten per cent is the usual amount given. Small tips of HK$3-$20 may be given to taxi drivers, bellboys, doormen and washroom attendants.

Toilets

Toilets in parks, malls, hotels, restaurants, bars, cafés and department stores are usually clean and well maintained. Toilets in some parks/beaches have no toilet paper. In the more Chinese areas, you had better be prepared to squat.

Directory

Tourist information

The official visitors and general city information organisation, the **Hong Kong Tourism Board** (HKTB; www.discoverhongkong.com), produces excellent maps (including hiking maps) and brochures on eating, shopping and sightseeing, which you can pick up for free at its service centres located on both sides of the harbour (*see below*). A Quality Tourism Services (QTS) sticker in the windows of shops and restaurants denotes that the establishment meets HKTB standards and is deemed reliable.

HKTB branches are located in: Causeway Bay MTR (exit F) and Tsim Sha Tsui Star Ferry Concourse. Both are open 8am-6pm daily. Here you can get advice, pick up brochures, maps, events schedules, and find out about trips and tours.

The HKTB multilingual hotline (2508 1234) is the general line to call for any information on Hong Kong, including directions to a place, or queries about events, addresses or phone numbers.

I-Cyberlink is the HKTB's internet access to information about Hong Kong. These information points can be found at the airport on arrival as you leave the terminal and at the HKTB visitors' centres.

Visas & immigration

All foreigners entering Hong Kong for education, training employment or business purposes (as well as their dependants) require a visa. The only exceptions are those born in Hong Kong or holding a permanent identity card, HKSAR or BNO passport.

For visitors, a visa is valid for a month, though it can be extended, but no employment of any kind is permitted during stays. Visitors are not allowed to change their visitor status to working status after they've arrived in Hong Kong, except in exceptional cases.

Entry permits/visas can be obtained from a Chinese consulate in your country. Visitors must hold a passport that is valid for at least a month after their planned departure from Hong Kong. For visas to mainland China, *see p301.*

In addition, nationals of the UK and British Commonwealth dependent/protected countries do not require a visa for a visit of fewer than three months; neither do US and South African visitors coming for less than a month, and other nationalities for a stay of less than eight days; but it's best to check to make sure. For frequent visitors, a pass or multiple-entry visa can be obtained.

HK Immigration Department

7 Gloucester Road, Wan Chai, HK Island (2824 6111/fax 2877 7711/www.immd.gov.hk). Wan Chai MTR (exit A1)/buses along Gloucester Road. **Open** 8.45am-4.30pm Mon-Fri; 9-11.30am Sat. **Map** p330 B3.

Water

Tap water in Hong Kong is considered safe to drink. But residents tend to filter or boil their water before drinking it, not quite trusting the condition of the pipes in their buildings. If in doubt, you can purchase a variety of local and imported bottled water in supermarkets and convenience stores.

Beaches are given a daily pollution rating, as many are below WHO standards, and ocean pollution is a serious problem. Check the reports in local newspapers before setting out to a beach.

Weights & measures

Hong Kong uses the metric system, although you will sometimes see pounds and ounces in use in supermarkets, as well as a Chinese measurement of weight, the 'catty' (600 grams/21 ounces).

1 kilometre = 0.621 miles
1 metre = 1.093 yards
1 centimetre = 0.3937 inches
1 kilogram = 2.2046 pounds
1 gram = 0.0352 ounces
1 litre = 0.2642 imperial gallon
0 degrees Celsius = 32 degrees Fahrenheit

What to take

Everything you're likely to need can be bought in Hong Kong, although some items may be more expensive than they are back home. It's wise to bring all essentials with you – important medication may not be available here, and foreign prescriptions will not be accepted at pharmacies unless endorsed by a local, certified practitioner.

When to go

Hong Kong has a subtropical climate and there are times of the year when its high humidity can be seriously debilitating, making a visit to the city uncomfortable. A summary of what to expect during the year follows, but bear in mind that the weather can be very unpredictable.

Spring (March to mid May) is often pleasant, but humidity can be high and some of the heaviest rainfall is recorded during this time. Bring a light jacket or sweater for the evenings, which can be cool.

Summer (late May to mid September) is hot and stiflingly humid. Ironically, you'll probably still need to bring an extra layer for when you're indoors, as shops, restaurants, bars and hotels tend to crank up the air-conditioning to icy levels. This is also typhoon season (*see p306* **Natural hazards**) and rainfall is at its highest.

Autumn (late September to early December) is usually the best time to visit; temperatures are comfortably warm, and humidity drops to a bearable level. Sunny days and clear skies are relatively common.

Winter (mid December to February) can be a good time to come, with temperatures of 13°C to 20°C (55-68°F) and humidity of around 72 per cent. It can get chilly, windy and cloudy, though, so you'll need to bring extra layers.

For daily weather forecasts, contact the **Hong Kong Observatory** (2926 8200) or **Dial-a-Weather** (8200). Also, the websites www.hko.gov.hk and www.underground.org.hk feature detailed information about local conditions.

Public holidays

Many holidays in Hong Kong are Chinese festival days that are subject to the lunar calendar, so the dates tend to change from year to year. **New Year's Day** (1 January); **Chinese Lunar New Year** (three days in January/February); **Good Friday** and **Easter Monday** (March/April); **Ching Ming Festival** (March/April); **Buddha's Birthday** (April/May); **Labour Day** (1 May); **Tuen Ng Dragon Boat Festival** (June); **HKSAR Establishment Day** (1 July); **Day after Mid-Autumn Festival** (September); **China National Day** (1 October) ; **Chung Yeung** (October) ; **Christmas Day** (25 December); **Boxing Day** (26 December).

Women in Hong Kong are active and visible, holding high-profile jobs in private and government sectors as well as the legislative council. There are over 50 women's groups in Hong Kong, ranging from business and professional organisations for networking and socialising to charitable ones for community services. For helplines, *see p303*.

Organisations & resources

American Women's Association

C7, Monticello, 48 Kennedy Road, Mid-Levels, HK Island (2527 2961/fax 2865 7737/ www.awa.org.hk).

Association of Business & Professional Women

GPO Box 1526, Central, Hong Kong (2535 9198/fax 2904 0788/www.hkabpw.org).

The Helena May

1 Garden Road (2522 6766/ www.helenamay.com). Admiralty MTR/12S, 15C bus. **Open** 9am-5pm Mon-Fri; 9am-12.30pm Sat. **Map** p329 E4.

Hong Kong Women in Publishing Society

GPO Box 7314, Central, Hong Kong (www.hkwips.org).

Women's Corona Society

GPO Box 8151, Central, Hong Kong (2243 1486/2547 7100/ www.coronahk.org).

Working in Hong Kong

Prior to 1997 British citizens didn't need work visas to get a job in Hong Kong but since the Handover there are stricter procedures for all foreigners who want to work in the territory. To qualify for a work visa, visitors must prove they have skills that can't be found among local residents. In addition, the recent economic downturn had led to a record levels of unemployment, with the result that jobs have been hard to come by, even for locals.

Work permits

To work in Hong Kong, you have to have a sponsor or employer apply for a work visa for you. This application is then reviewed by immigration for its validity before a work visa is issued. Be warned that work visas can take up to a year to process.

Dependents are allowed to take up jobs on dependent visas. Permanent residents can sponsor family members provided they meet certain criteria. For more information, log on to www.immd.gov.hk or www.esdlife.com.

Travel advice

For current information on travel to a specific country – including the latest news on health issues, safety and security, local laws and customs – contact your home country's government department of foreign affairs. Most have websites with useful advice for would-be travellers.

Australia
www.smartraveller.gov.au

Canada
www.voyage.gc.ca

New Zealand
www.safetravel.govt.nz

Republic of Ireland
http://foreignaffairs.gov.ie

UK
www.fco.gov.uk/travel

USA
http://travel.state.gov

The Language

Cantonese, English and Mandarin are the official languages of Hong Kong.

Cantonese is the dialect of the southern Chinese province of Guangdong, from where most Hong Kongers originate and is, therefore, the SAR's lingua franca, being spoken in 89 per cent of households. Three decades ago it was considered rather low-brow and many Western sinologists predicted that it would fade away after the Handover, as Mandarin came to dominate, but it looks set to stay for good.

Cantonese is very difficult for foreigners to learn because of the seven tones involved, each of which can change the meaning of a word. For example, the word 'gai', when said in different ways, can mean either chicken, street or prostitute. Even for the Chinese, the various tones only avoid confusion up to a certain point: complete understanding is gained from the context.

As it is very difficult to master, many foreigners never bother to learn more than a few essential words of Cantonese, however long they live in Hong Kong. They do get by without it, but with a fair degree of frustration, because – despite the fact that it is an official language – many locals do not speak English.

Mandarin, as the Beijing dialect is known in the West, is not widely spoken in Hong Kong. However, a standardised form of it, **Putonghua**, is promoted by the Chinese government as the national language and is, therefore, spoken by 70 per cent of those living on the mainland.

Mandarin was the dialect used by government officials (or mandarins, hence its name) to communicate with one another in days gone by. Putonghua translates as 'the language that can be used everywhere', because it is common to so many of the mainland Chinese. The same – or at least a very similar – language is called Guoyu (national language) in Taiwan and Huayu (Chinese people's language) in Singapore.

The differences between these languages are minor, and can be compared with the distinctions between the English language spoken in Britain and that of the US.

What all Chinese dialects have in common is an ingeniously flexible system of non-phonetic writing. In other words, Chinese characters can be read by all Chinese people, whichever dialect they speak.

Hanyu pinyin, the official romanisation of Chinese characters, is used in major Chinese cities on street signs (alongside Chinese characters). This is useful for foreigners who can't read the characters, as it indicates the Chinese pronunciation, but is also confusing because it does not give the tones that must also be used.

Any attempt by foreigners to talk Chinese using pinyin is therefore likely to be unintelligible to the locals. If you are really keen to impress, the only way is to pick up a Chinese dictionary (be it Mandarin or Cantonese), because it also indicates the correct tones of characters.

Having said all that, here are some words and phrases, with approximations on how they should be pronounced: even if your attempt at communication is unintelligible, you will at least be applauded for trying.

Phrases

how are you?	nei ho ma?
fine, thank you	gay ho nei yau sum
good morning	jo sahn
good night	jo tau
goodbye	joy gen
hello! (on phone)	wai!
how much does it cost?	gaydo cheena?
too expensive	tei gway
I'm sorry (excuse me)	m'ho yi si
yes	hai
no	mm hai
please & thank you (for a service)	m'goy
please (invitation)	cheng
thank you (for a gift)	doh jeh
you're welcome	m'sai m'goy

Restaurant & bar phrases

beer	beh jau
water	soi
English tea	lai tcha
bill	my dan
telephone	deen wah

Taxi directions

street/road	gai/do
turn right	chin yau
turn left	chin jo
straight on	yat jik hui
hurry	fai dee
stop	teng
here	nee dow
wait here	tang hai

Geographical features

beach	wan
mountain	shan
harbour	o
headland	tau/kok
island	chau
village	tsuen
rock	shek

Numbers

one	yat
two	yih
three	sahm
four	sei
five	ung
six	lok
seven	chat
eight	baht
nine	gau
ten	sahp
zero	ling

Further Reference

Books

Non-fiction

Magnus & Kasyan Bartlett
Over Hong Kong
A pictorial record of Hong Kong.

Martin Booth *Gweilo*
An expat child's memoir of growing up in Hong Kong in the 1950s.

Mary Chan Ma-lai
Egg Woman's Daughter
Memoir of Tanka boat dweller.

Austin Coates *Myself a Mandarin*
A fascinating, often funny, insight into life in Hong Kong in the 1950s, when Coates was a Special Magistrate in Kowloon and the New Territories.

Maurice Collis *Foreign Mud*
An account of the shameful history of the Opium Wars in the 1800s.

Fredric Dannen & Barry Long
Hong Kong Babylon
Superb insight into the world of Hong Kong movies, with interviews, plot summaries and film ratings.

Jonathan Dimbleby
The Last Governor
The author, a close friend of Chris Patten, provides a compelling account of the government side of the final chapter in the city's colonial history.

Jonathan Fenby
Dealing with the Dragon
A year (1999) in the life of Hong Kong and the author, then editor of the *South China Morning Post*.

Patricia Lim *Discovering Hong Kong's Cultural Heritage*
Half of this book is dedicated to the cultural heritage of Hong Kong; the other half is more like a guide book.

Wendy Mctavish *Expat*
Memoir that looks back at 35 years of living in Hong Kong.

Jan Morris
Epilogue to an Empire: Hong Kong
An insightful study of Hong Kong.

James O'Reilly, Larry Habeggar & Sean O'Reilly (editors)
Travellers' Tales of Hong Kong
Fifty tales by travel writers, including Bruce Chatwin and Jan Morris.

Christopher Patten *East and West*
The last governor gives his side of the story of the final years of the colony.

Russell Spurr *Excellency (The Governors of Hong Kong)*
A riveting look at the 28 British governors and two Japanese generals who ruled Hong Kong for 150 years.

Han Suyin
A Many Splendoured Thing
This book describes Han Suyin's love affair with Ian Morrison, a foreign correspondent for *The Times*.

Frank Welsh
A History of Hong Kong
A comprehensive history of the city.

Jason Wordie *Streets*
An explanation of Hong Kong's streets, their names and the shops on them.

Fiction

John Le Carré
The Honourable Schoolboy
Exciting Cold War novel set in Hong Kong.

James Clavell *Noble House*
Rival *taipans* seek revenge for ancient blood feuds with the CIA, the KGB and China.

James Clavell *Taipan*
Set in the 19th century in Hong Kong. Pretty dull, but a popular read.

Cecilia Gamst-Berg *Blonde Lotus*
Humorous, often raunchy, account of a Norwegian female's two decades in Hong Kong and China.

Richard Mason
The World of Suzie Wong
This 1950s novel paints an unusually frank picture of the lives of Wan Chai's bar girls.

Paul Theroux *Kowloon Tong*
The worries of expats on the brink of the Handover.

Macau

Charles Ralph (CR) Boxer is an authority on Macanese history and has written a number of books on the subject (most are out of print, though).

Luiz Vaz de Camões (translated by William C Atkinson) *The Lusiads*
The story of Vasco da Gama's voyage via southern Africa to India.

Austin Coates
City of Broken Promises
Historical novel based on the true story of a love affair between a Chinese orphan and the son of the British founder of Lloyd's.

Austin Coates & Cesar Guillen-Nunez *A Macau Narrative*
A concise history of the former Portuguese colony.

Leila Hadley *Give Me the World*
Tells of the author's riotous years of travelling in Asia in the 1950s.

Jill McGivering *Macau Remembers*
Interviews with 30 different people in Macau upon its handover to China.

Lindsay & May Ride
(abridged, with additional material by Jason Wordie)
The Voices of Macau Stones
This book documents the importance of the stones, statues and memorials dotted all over Macau.

China

David Bonavia *The Chinese*
An excellent introduction to the people of China.

Jonathan Spence
The Search for Modern China
The definitive work on modern China.

Tiziano Terzani
Behind the Forbidden Door
A fascinating account by an Italian journalist of life in communist China.

Film

See p216 **Don't miss** Hong Kong films.

Websites

Note that Chinese characters will appear as question marks if you do not have Chinese fonts on your computer, though most of the following have a link to an English-language version of their site:

BC Magazine
www.bcmagazine.net
Detailed listings and articles.

Funhongkong.com
www.funhongkong.com
Listings of activities in the city.

Health in Asia
www.healthinasia.com
Medical information for Asia.

Government of the Hong Kong SAR of the People's Republic of China
www.info.gov.hk
Facts and figures on the SAR.

HK Magazine
www.asia-city.com
Events listings and features.

Hong Kong Tourism Board
www.discoverhongkong.com
Award-winning information site.

Macau Government Tourist Office
www.macautourism.gov.mo
Macau's tourist board website.

No.1 Expat Site in Asia
www.hongkong.asiaxpat.com
Loads of useful information.

South China Morning Post
www.scmp.com
Online version of Hong Kong's English-language newspaper.

The Standard
www.thestandard.com.hk
Online edition of the English-language tabloid newspaper.

That's Guangzhou
www.thatsguangzhou.com
A comprehensive guide to Guangzhou for expat residents and visitors.

Directory

Index

DISCOVER MORE CITIES

Tell us what you think and you could win £100-worth of City Guides

Your opinions are important to us and we'd like to know what you like and what you don't like about the Time Out City Guides

For your chance to win, simply fill in our short survey at
timeout.com/guidesfeedback

Every month a reader will win £100 to spend on the Time Out City Guides of their choice – a great start to discovering new cities and you'll have extra cash to enjoy your trip!

Place of interest and/or entertainment	....	▢
Railway or bus station	....	▢
Park	....	▢
Hospital/university	....	▢
Area	....	CENTRAL
Tram Route	....	—
Elevated Walkway	....	=
Post Office	....	✉
MTR Station	....	Ⓜ
MTR Station Exit	....	Ⓔ③
Hotel	....	⓱
Restaurant	....	⓽③
Bar	....	⓺⓪

Maps

Hong Kong

Pearl River Delta

Shenzhen Bay

Shenzhen

Window of the World
Xintang
Dalinqxia
Honey Lake Resort
Shanbu
Chiwei
Ma Tso Long
Shen Zhen University
Baishizhou
Changxingwei
Xiangnen Beitou
Xineun
Chegongmao
Shatou
Jiushixia
Lok Ma Chau
Nwu Tung
Nanyuan
Houhai
Wanxia
Zucun
San Tin
Hang Tai Po
Dahuzai
Shalwantou
Song Ho Park
Shekou
Nam Sha Po
Mai Po
Shek Wu Wai
Ngau Tam Mei
Lin Tong Mei
Chiwan
The Seaworld
Lau Fau Shan
Fairview Park
Kei Kung Leng
572
Lam Tsuen Country Park
Moda Tseng Wai
Mai Po Marshes
Ponds
565
Tai To Ya
Sha Kong Tsuen
Wang Chau
Sha Po
Ngau Hom Sha
Ha Tsuen
Yuen Long
Kat Hing Wai
Ping Shan
Kam Tin
Hung Shui Kiu
Fui Sha Wai
Shui Tsiu San Tsuen
Walled Village
Pat Heung
Shek Kong
Tai Shui Hang
Nim Wan
Pak Sha Tsuen
Yuen Kong
Lin Fa Tei
Kai Lun Wai
Miu Fat Buddhist Monastery
Lam Tei
Ma On Kong
Tai Wo
Ching Chung Koon Temple
Chung Wong Toi
Pei Tu Temple
Tai Lam Country Park
NEW TER
Lung Kwu Tan
583 Castle Peak
Tuen Mun
Tai Lam Chung Reservoir
Tin Fu Tsai
Chuen Lung
Lung Kwu Chau
Ching Shan Monastery
So Kwun Wat
Yeun Monastery
Chuk Lam Shir
Siu Lang Shui
Shek Kek Tsui
Gordon Hard
Tai Lam Chung
Sham Tseng
Airport Core Programme Exhibition Centre
Yuen Yuen Institute
Sam Tung
Pillar Point
Castle Peak Bay
Siu Lam
So Kwun Tan
Ting Kau
Uk Museum
Sam Tung
Tsuen Wan
Pearl Island
Gen Mun Rd
Tsing Lung Tau
Ma Wan
Tsing Ma Bridge
Tsing Yi Town
Sha Chau
Brothers Point
Tsing Chau Tsai
Tang Lung Chau
Shek Wan
Nam Wan
Tsing Yi
Mo To Chau (The Brothers)
Siu Mo To
Mong Tung Hang
Penny's Bay
Hong Kong Disneyland
Tai Mo To
AsiaWorld-Expo
Sam Pak
Hong Kong International Airport
Yi Pak
Discovery Bay
Discovery Bay
Peng Chau
Siu Kau Yi Chau
Kau Yi Chau
Green Island
Chek Lap Kok
Pak Mong
Ngau Kwu Long
Nim Shue Wan Tsuen
Tin Hau Temple
Sha Lo Wan
San Tau
Tung Chung Wan
Ma Wan Chung
Hung Fa Ngan
Trappist Monastery
Tai Shui Hang
Chau Kung To (Sunshine Island)
Sham Shek Tsuen
Tung Chung Fort
Pak Ngan Heung
Mui Wo
Tung Chung
Lantau North Country Park
Luk Tei Tong
Silvermine Bay
Hei Ling Chau
Sai Pok Liu Hoi Ha (West Lamma Channel)
Po Lin Monastery & Big Buddha
Ngong Ping
869
Lantau
Chi Ma Wan
Boulder Point
Tai O
Ying Hing Monastery
934 Lantau Peak
Sunset Peak
Pui O
Chung Hau
Yung Shu
Keung Shan
South Lantau Country Park
Cheung Sha
Chi Ma Wan Peninsula
Tin Hau Temple
Man Cheung Po
Shek Pik Reservoir
Tong Fuk
Ha Keng
Power Station
Shek Pik
Tong Fuk Miu Wan
Cha Kwo Chau
Lammo
Fan Lau
Tai Long Wan
Shuihau
Shek Kwu Chau
Pak Tai Temple
Tung Wan Beach
Cheung Chau
Cheung Chau
Kau Ling Chung
Siu A Chau
Tin Hau Temple
Ha Mei Tsui
Soko Islands
Tai A Chau

To Macau

0   5 miles
0   5 km

324 Time Out Hong Kong

© Copyright Time Out Group 2007

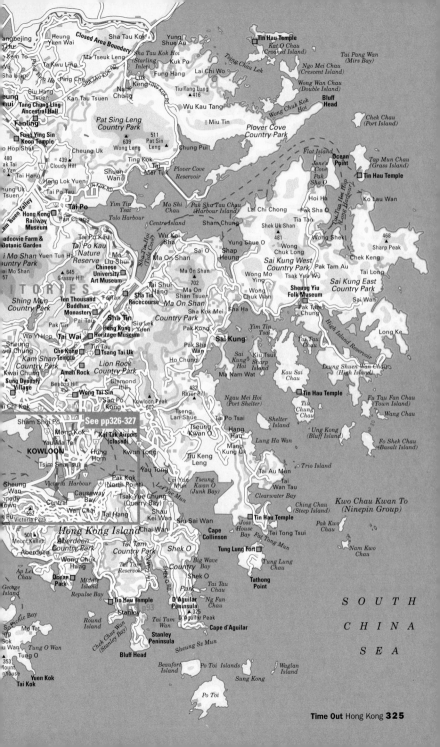

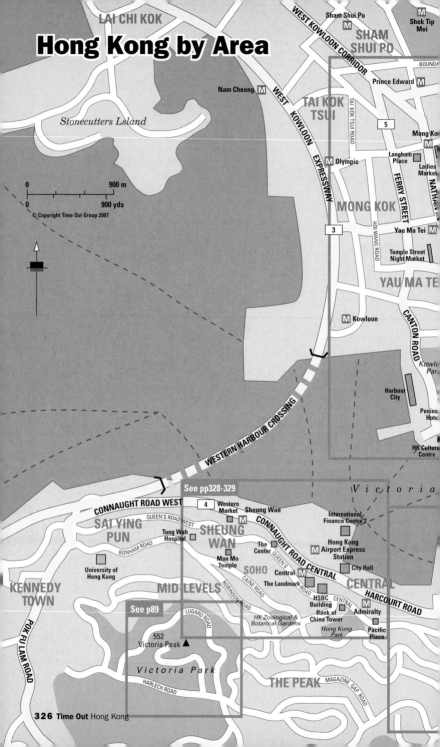

Hong Kong by Area

LAI CHI KOK

Sham Shui Po

WEST KOWLOON CORRIDOR

Shek Tip Mei

SHAM SHUI PO

BOUNDA

Prince Edward

Nam Cheong

WEST KOWLOON EXPRESSWAY

TAI KOK TSUI

TAI KOK TSUI ROAD

5

Mong Ko

Stonecutters Lsland

Olympic

Langham Place

Ladies Market

FERRY STREET

NATHAN

0   900 m
0   900 yds

© Copyright Time Out Group 2007

MONG KOK

HOI WANG ROAD

3

Yau Ma Tei

Temple Street Night Market

YAU MA TE

Kowloon

CANTON ROAD

Kowlo Par

Harbour City

Penins Hote

WESTERN HARBOUR CROSSING

HK Cultura Centre

See pp328-329

Victoria

CONNAUGHT ROAD WEST

QUEEN'S ROAD WEST

4 Western Market

Sheung Wan

International Finance Centre 2

SAI YING PUN

Tung Wah Hospital

SHEUNG WAN

CONNAUGHT ROAD CENTRAL

Hong Kong Airport Express Station

BONHAM ROAD

The Center

QUEEN'S

University of Hong Kong

Man Mo Temple

SOHO

CAINE ROAD

Central

City Hall

KENNEDY TOWN

MID-LEVELS

ROBINSON ROAD

The Landmark

CENTRAL

POK FU LAM ROAD

See p89

LUGARD ROAD

HSBC Building

CENTRAL

HARCOURT ROAD

Bank of China Tower

Admiralty

552 Victoria Peak ▲

HK Zoological & Botanical Gardens

Hong Kong Park

Pacific Place

Victoria Park

HARLECH ROAD

THE PEAK

MAGAZINE GAP ROAD

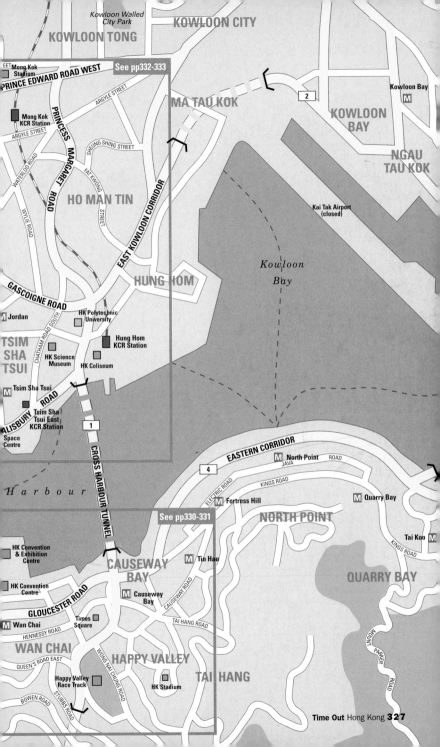

Kowloon Walled
City Park

KOWLOON CITY

KOWLOON TONG

EET ■ Mong Kok
Stadium

PRINCE EDWARD ROAD WEST

See pp332-333

ARGYLE STREET

MA TAU KOK

■ Kowloon Bay
Ⓜ

2

**KOWLOON
BAY**

■ Mong Kok
KCR Station

ARGYLE STREET

SHEUNG SHING STREET

**NGAU
TAU KOK**

WATERLOO ROAD

PRINCESS MARGARET ROAD

PAT KWONG STREET

EAST KOWLOON CORRIDOR

HO MAN TIN

Kai Tak Airport
(closed)

WYLIE ROAD

*Kowloon
Bay*

GASCOIGNE ROAD

HUNG HOM

CHATHAM ROAD SOUTH

Ⓜ Jordan

■ HK Polytechnic
University

**TSIM
SHA
TSUI**

□ HK Science
Museum

■ Hung Hom
KCR Station

□ HK Coliseum

Ⓜ Tsim Sha Tsui

ROAD

ALISBURY

■ Tsim Sha
Tsui East
KCR Station

1

□ Space
Centre

CROSS HARBOUR TUNNEL

EASTERN CORRIDOR

Ⓜ North Point
ROAD
JAVA

H a r b o u r

4

ELECTRIC ROAD

KINGS ROAD

Ⓜ Quarry Bay

Ⓜ Fortress Hill

NORTH POINT

Tai Koo

KINGS ROAD

See pp330-331

□ HK Convention
& Exhibition
Centre

QUARRY BAY

□ HK Convention
Centre

Ⓜ Tin Hau

**CAUSEWAY
BAY**

CAUSEWAY ROAD

GLOUCESTER ROAD

Ⓜ Causeway
Bay

Ⓜ Wan Chai

□ Times
Square

TAI HANG ROAD

WONG NAI CHUNG ROAD

HENNESSY ROAD

MOUNT PARKER ROAD

WAN CHAI

Queen's ROAD EAST

HAPPY VALLEY

TAI HANG

Happy Valley
Race Track

□ HK Stadium

BOWEN ROAD

STUBBS ROAD

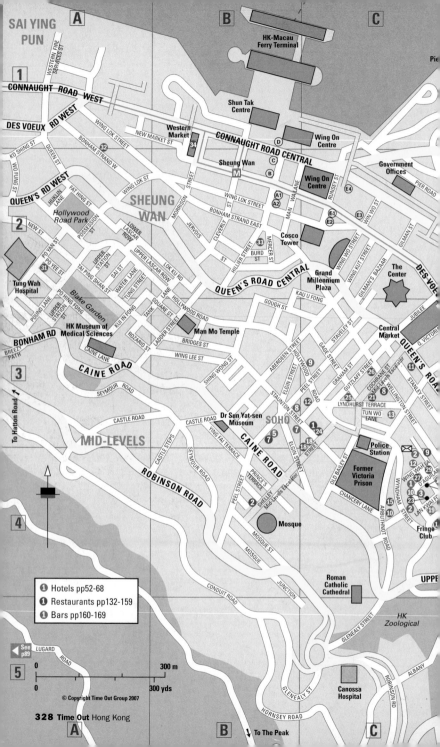

SAI YING PUN

A

B

C

HK-Macau
Ferry Terminal

Pie

1

CONNAUGHT ROAD WEST

Shun Tak
Centre

Wing On
Centre

DES VOEUX RD WEST

Western
Market

New Market St

Wing Lok Street

CONNAUGHT ROAD CENTRAL

D

Sheung Wan
M

C

B

Government
Offices

Pier Road

QUEEN'S RD WEST

Fat Hing St

Wing Lok St

Wing Lok Street

A1
A2

SHEUNG
WAN

Bonham Strand East

Cleverly St

Hillier Street

Mercer St

Burd St

E4

E1
E2

E3

Cosco
Tower

Wing Wo Street

Wing Kut Street

Gilman's Bazaar

The
Center

DES VO

2

NEW ST

Po Yan St

Po Yee St

Hollywood
Road Park

Lower
Lascar
Row

Upper Lascar Row

Lok Ku Rd

QUEEN'S ROAD CENTRAL

Grand
Millennium
Plaza

Kau U Fong

Jubilee

Tung Wah
Hospital

Blake Garden

Tai Ping Shan St

Sai St

Water Lane

Tung Street

Square Street

Tank Lane

Hollywood Road

Gough St

Staveley St

Gage Street

Central
Market

Q. VICTORIA

QUEEN'S ROA

BONHAM RD

HK Museum of
Medical Sciences

Caine Lane

Man Mo Temple

Bridges St

Wing Lee St

Shing Wong St

Aberdeen Street

Elgin Street

Peel Street

Hollywood Road

Graham St

Gutzlaff Street

Cochrane St

9

26

Wellington Street

Stanley Street

Mid-Levels Escalator

11

3

CAINE ROAD

SEYMOUR ROAD

Castle Road

MID-LEVELS

Castle Steps

Seymour Road

Castle Road

Ying Fai Terrace

Dr Sun Yat-sen
Museum

SOHO

CAINE ROAD

Staunton Street

Elgin Street

8

12

5

7

7

8

Lyndhurst Terrace

Tun Wo
Lane

21

8

13

25

1

24

18

18

Police
Station

Chancery Lane

Old Bailey St

Wyndham Street

Arbuthnot Road

Glenealy Street

18

1

9

12

27

21

2

3

23

15

19

1

1

29

D'AGUILAR

LAN KWAI FO

Fringe
Club

To Hatton Road

ROBINSON ROAD

Peel Street

Prince's
Terrace

Shelley St

Mid-Levels Escalator

2

4

Mosque

Mosque St

Mosque

10

15

Roman
Catholic
Cathedral

UPPE

Glenealy St

Robinson RD

HK
Zoological

❶ Hotels pp52-68

❶ Restaurants pp132-159

❶ Bars pp160-169

Conduit Road

5

See
p89

LUGARD
ROAD

0   300 m

0   300 yds

© Copyright Time Out Group 2007

Canossa
Hospital

Albany

Glenealy St

Hornsey Road

328 Time Out Hong Kong

A

B

↓ To The Peak

C

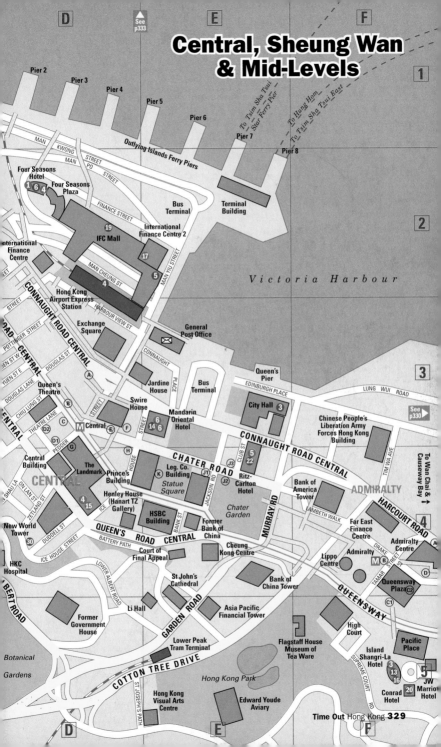

Central, Sheung Wan & Mid-Levels

D   E   F

See p333

1

Pier 2
Pier 3
Pier 4
Pier 5
Pier 6
Pier 7
Pier 8

To Tsim Sha Tsui, Star Ferry Pier
To Hung Hom
To Tsim Sha Tsui East

Outlying Islands Ferry Piers

MAN
KWONG
MAN
PO
STREET
STREET

Four Seasons Hotel
Four Seasons Plaza

FINANCE STREET

Bus Terminal

Terminal Building

19
IFC Mall

International Finance Centre 2

17

International Finance Centre

MAN CHEUNG ST
5
4

MAN YU STREET

Victoria Harbour

2

Hong Kong Airport Express Station

HARBOUR VIEW ST

Exchange Square

General Post Office

CONNAUGHT

CONNAUGHT ROAD CENTRAL

Queen's Pier

EDINBURGH PLACE

LUNG WUI ROAD

3

A

Queen's Theatre

Jardine House

Bus Terminal

City Hall
3

Chinese People's Liberation Army Forces Hong Kong Building

See p330

B

Swire House

Mandarin Oriental Hotel

6
14 6

CONNAUGHT ROAD CENTRAL

TIM WA AVE

To Wan Chai & → Causeway Bay

C

M Central
E F

CHATER ROAD

CLUB ST

5
22

Ritz-Carlton Hotel

Bank of America Tower

ADMIRALTY

HARCOURT ROAD

4

D2
D1
G
H

Central Building

The Landmark

Prince's Building

Leg. Co. Building

Statue Square

J3
K
J1
J2

JACKSON RD

BANK ST

Chater Garden

LAMBETH WALK

Far East Finance Centre

A

CENTRAL

4
15

Henley House (Hanart TZ Gallery)

HSBC Building

Former Bank of China

MURRAY RD

Admiralty Centre

B

New World Tower

30

QUEEN'S
ROAD
CENTRAL

DUDDELL ST

Court of Final Appeal

Cheung Kong Centre

Lippo Centre

Admiralty

M

DRAKE STREET

Queensway Plaza

C2

D

HKC Hospital

ICE HOUSE STREET

BATTERY PATH

St John's Cathedral

Bank of China Tower

TAMAR STREET

QUEENSWAY

C1

ALBERT ROAD

LOWER ALBERT ROAD

Li Hall

GARDEN ROAD

Asia Pacific Financial Tower

High Court

Pacific Place

Former Government House

Lower Peak Tram Terminal

Flagstaff House Museum of Tea Ware

SUPREME COURT RD

Island Shangri-La Hotel

3
13
16

5

JW Marriott Hotel

Botanical Gardens

COTTON TREE DRIVE

ST JOSEPH'S PATH

Hong Kong Visual Arts Centre

Edward Youde Aviary

Hong Kong Park

Conrad Hotel

20

D   E   F

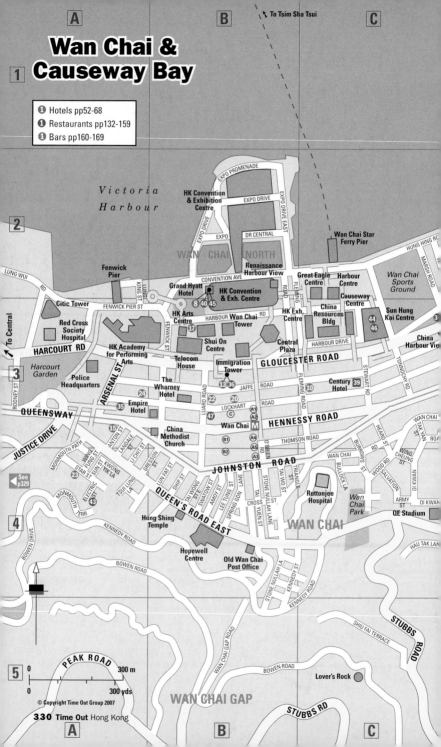

Wan Chai & Causeway Bay

- ❶ Hotels pp52-68
- ❶ Restaurants pp132-159
- ❶ Bars pp160-169

To Tsim Sha Tsui

Victoria Harbour

HK Convention & Exhibition Centre

EXPO PROMENADE
EXPO DRIVE
EXPO DRIVE EAST
EXPO DRIVE
EXPO
DR CENTRAL

Wan Chai Star Ferry Pier

HUNG HING RD

WAN CHAI NORTH

MARSH RD

Wan Chai Sports Ground

Fenwick Pier

LUNG WUI RD

KING ST
LUNG KING ST
CONVENTION AVE

Grand Hyatt Hotel

Renaissance Harbour View

Great Eagle Centre

Harbour Centre

Causeway Centre

Sun Hung Kai Centre

Citic Tower

FENWICK PIER ST

HK Convention & Exh. Centre

8 40 45

FLEMING RD

China Resources Bldg

Red Cross Society Hospital

HK Arts Centre

17

HARBOUR RD
Wan Chai Tower

HK Exh. Centre

44
46

China Harbour Vie

Harcourt Garden

HARCOURT RD

FENWICK ST

Shui On Centre

Central Plaza

HARBOUR DRIVE

STEWART RD

TONNOCHY RD

To Central

HK Academy for Performing Arts

ARSENAL ST

Telecom House

GLOUCESTER ROAD

RODNEY ST

Police Headquarters

Immigration Tower

FLEMING ROAD

Century Hotel **39**

QUEENSWAY

The Wharney Hotel

24

13 36
JAFFE

22
LOCKHART
C
47

10

ROAD

ROAD

WAN CHAI
TAK YAN

Empire Hotel

35

China Methodist Church

Wan Chai **M**

A1
A2

HENNESSY ROAD

HEARD ST

JUSTICE DRIVE

15
ANTON ST
LANDALE ST
LI CHIT ST

LUEN FAT ST

A4
A5
A3

O'BRIEN ROAD

WAN CHAI

BURROWS ST

WING CHEUNG ST

OI KWAN

MONMOUTH PATH
KWONG FUNG TERR
23
STAR ST
SUN ST
KWONG YIK LA

GRESSON ST
SHIP ST
TAI WONG ST E
SWATOW ST
AMOY ST
LEE TUNG ST
SPRING GDN LANE

B1

JOHNSTON ROAD

B2

TAI WO ST
STONE NULLAH LANE

THOMSON ROAD

TRIANGLE

BULLOCK LA

ARMY ST

OI KWAN

MONMOUTH TERR
ELECTRIC ST
43

TSUI LUNG LA

QUEEN'S ROAD EAST

CROSS ST
TAI YUEN ST

Ruttonjee Hospital

Wan Chai Park

SALVATION
WOOD RD

QE Stadium

See p329

Hung Shing Temple

Hopewell Centre

Old Wan Chai Post Office

STONE NULLAH LA

KENNEDY ST

WAN CHAI

HAU TAK LAN

BOWEN DRIVE

KENNEDY ROAD

KENNEDY ROAD

STUBBS ROAD

BOWEN ROAD

SHIU FAI TERRACE

WAN CHAI GAP ROAD

BOWEN ROAD

PEAK ROAD

| 0 | 300 m |
| 0 | 300 yds |

© Copyright Time Out Group 2007

Lover's Rock

STUBBS RD

WAN CHAI GAP

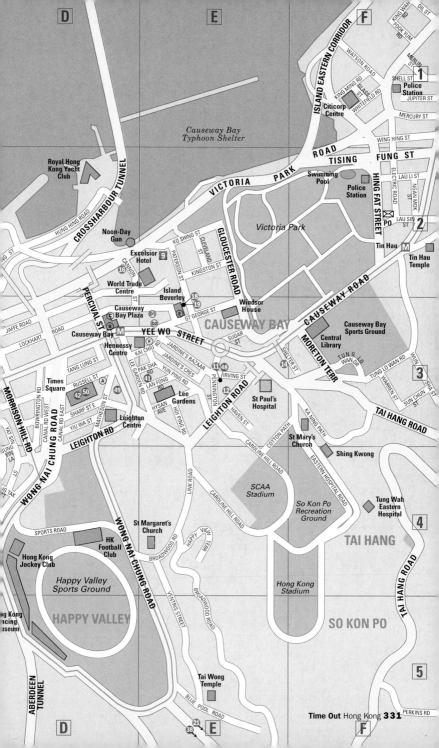

Kowloon

STREET

WUHU STREET

HUNG HOM ROAD

BAKER STREET

BULKELEY STREET

STATION LANE

WHAMPOA AVE

GILLIES AVE

WALKER ST

LUNG HANG ST

WINSLOW ST

BAKER ST

HUNG HOM

STREET

HUNG HOM BYPASS

WYLIE ROAD

CHATHAM ROAD

GASCOIGNE ROAD

ROAD

KOWLOON CRICKET CLUB

CHEUNG WAN ROAD

CHATHAM ROAD SOUTH

ON WAN RD

CHEUNG WAN RD

Hung Hom KCR Station

Hong Kong Coliseum

CROSS HARBOUR TUNNEL

To Central

Victoria Harbour

© Copyright Time Out Group 2007

500 m

500 yds

New East Ocean Centre

SCIENCE MUSEUM ROAD

Hong Kong Science Museum

Stanford Hillview Hotel

Rosary Church

Observatory

AUSTIN ROAD

AUSTIN AVE

HILLWOOD RD

St Andrew's Church

OBSERVATORY RD

KNUTSFORD RD

KIMBERLEY RD

KIMBERLEY STREET

GRANVILLE ROAD

CARNARVON ROAD

CAMERON ROAD

PRAT AVE

HART AVE

MINDEN AVE

HANOI RD

CHATHAM ROAD SOUTH

Royal Garden Hotel

Hong Kong Museum of Science

TSIM SHA TSUI EAST

SALISBURY ROAD

MODY RD

Kowloon Shangri-La Hotel

Wing On Plaza

East Tsim Sha Tsui KCR Station

New World Renaissance Hotel

InterContinental Hotel

Hong Kong Museum of Art

HK Cultural Centre

Signal Hill Garden

Sheraton Hotel

Space Museum

MODY RD

Hydrofoil Pier

To Central

Holiday Inn Golden Mile

Chungking Mansions

Tsim Sha Tsui

Peninsula Hotel

NATHAN ROAD

HUMPHREYS AVE

PEKING RD

LOCK RD

HAIPHONG RD

ASHLEY RD

Kowloon Hotel

Hong Kong Heritage Discovery Centre

Jamia Masjid Islamic Centre

Kowloon Park

KOWLOON PARK DR

CANTON ROAD

PARK DR

Silvercord

Police Station

Salisbury YMCA

SALISBURY RD

Clock Tower

Bus Terminal

To Wan Chai

China Ferry Terminal

Harbour City

Ocean Centre

Star House

Tsim Sha Tsui Star Ferry Pier

To Central

Ocean Terminal

CHATHAM ROAD

Eaton Hotel

CHI WO ST

TAK HING ST

NATHAN ROAD

PILKEM ST

PARKES ST

JORDAN ROAD

JORDAN ROAD

Jordan

TEMPLE ST

BOWRING ST

MIN ST

AUSTIN ROAD

PARKES ST

WYLIE ROAD

Kwong Wah Hospital

Temple Street Night Market

SHANGHAI ST

TEMPLE STREET

WOOSUNG STREET

KANSU ST

RECLAMATION ST

NANKING ST

SAIGON ST

BATTERY ST

CANTON RD

FERRY STREET

CHEUNG ST

MAN YING ST

WAI CHING ST

CANTON ROAD

PAK HOI ST

Bus Terminal

Government Offices

WUI CHEUNG ROAD

JORDAN ROAD

AUSTIN ROAD

NGA CHEUNG ROAD

Kowloon

Kowloon

① Hotels pp52-68
① Restaurants pp132-159
① Bars pp160-169

Hung Hom Ferry Pier

Street Index

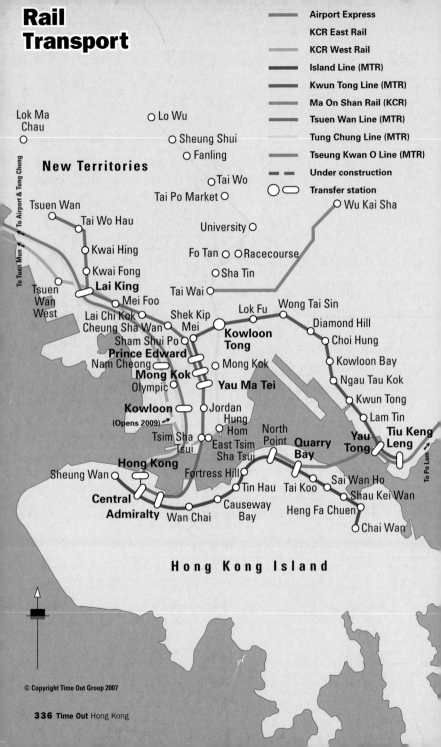

Rail Transport

Airport Express
KCR East Rail
KCR West Rail
Island Line (MTR)
Kwun Tong Line (MTR)
Ma On Shan Rail (KCR)
Tsuen Wan Line (MTR)
Tung Chung Line (MTR)
Tseung Kwan O Line (MTR)
Under construction
Transfer station

New Territories

Lok Ma Chau

Lo Wu

Sheung Shui

Fanling

Tai Wo

Tai Po Market

Wu Kai Sha

To Airport & Tung Chung

Tsuen Wan

Tai Wo Hau

Kwai Hing

Kwai Fong

University

Lai King

Fo Tan   Racecourse

To Tsuen Mun

Tsuen Wan West

Mei Foo

Sha Tin

Tai Wai

Lok Fu   Wong Tai Sin

Lai Chi Kok

Shek Kip Mei

Diamond Hill

Cheung Sha Wan

Sham Shui Po

Kowloon Tong

Choi Hung

Prince Edward

Kowloon Bay

Nam Cheong

Mong Kok

Ngau Tau Kok

Mong Kok

Yau Ma Tei

Kwun Tong

Olympic

Lam Tin

Kowloon
(Opens 2009)

Jordan

Yau Tong

Tiu Keng Leng

Hung Hom

Tsim Sha Tsui

North Point

Quarry Bay

East Tsim Sha Tsui

To Po Lam

Hong Kong

Fortress Hill

Sai Wan Ho

Sheung Wan

Tin Hau   Tai Koo

Shau Kei Wan

Central

Wan Chai

Causeway Bay

Heng Fa Chuen

Admiralty

Chai Wan

Hong Kong Island